Introduction to
INTERCOLLEGIATE ATHLETICS

Introduction to
INTERCOLLEGIATE
ATHLETICS

Edited by
EDDIE COMEAUX

Johns Hopkins University Press ▪ Baltimore

© 2015 Johns Hopkins University Press
All rights reserved. Published 2015
Printed in the United States of America on acid-free paper
9 8 7 6 5 4 3 2 1

Johns Hopkins University Press
2715 North Charles Street
Baltimore, Maryland 21218-4363
www.press.jhu.edu

Library of Congress Cataloging-in-Publication Data

Introduction to Intercollegiate Athletics / edited by Eddie Comeaux.
      pages cm
  Includes bibliographical references and index.
   ISBN 978-1-4214-1661-8 (Hardcover : acid-free paper) — ISBN 1-4214-1661-1 (Hardcover :
acid-free paper) — ISBN 978-1-4214-1662-5 (Paperback : acid-free paper) — ISBN 1-4214-1662-X
(Paperback : acid-free paper) — ISBN 978-1-4214-1663-2 (Electronic) — ISBN 1-4214-1663-8
(Electronic)   1. College sports—United States.   2. College sports—United States—
Management.   I. Comeaux, Eddie, 1973–
   GV351.I67 2015
   796.04'3—dc23   2014029353

A catalog record for this book is available from the British Library.

*Special discounts are available for bulk purchases of this book. For more information, please contact
Special Sales at 410-516-6936 or specialsales@press.jhu.edu.*

Johns Hopkins University Press uses environmentally friendly book materials, including recycled
text paper that is composed of at least 30 percent post-consumer waste, whenever possible.

CONTENTS

PREFACE

Intercollegiate athletics have received growing attention from the higher education research community. In 2005 the Research Focus on Education and Sport Special Interest Group of the American Educational Research Association was established to provide a forum for the presentation, discussion, and encouragement of research and critical thought on the interface of athletics and American higher education. Since then, a body of work has emerged and an increasing number of respected higher education scholars have been engaged in empirical research to examine crosscutting issues in this area. At the same time a growing number of students have enrolled in undergraduate and graduate programs in athletic administration, higher education or student affairs, sport management, sport studies, and sport leadership, and quite frequently these programs offer relevant courses in the area of intercollegiate athletics.

Surprisingly, there has been no foundational textbook for the study of intercollegiate athletics in higher education. Thus, instructors have had to rely on course packets, which can be quite cumbersome to compile, and books that offer an incomplete understanding of this topical area. Both the heightened enthusiasm for the study of intercollegiate athletics in American higher education and the absence of a comprehensive and prevailing teaching tool to consolidate baseline knowledge in this area have created the need for this edited volume.

Introduction to Intercollegiate Athletics is practical and particularly suitable for those who seek to enhance their understanding of the intercollegiate athletics landscape. This textbook is intended for upper-level undergraduate and graduate students, though scholars, teachers, practitioners, athletic administrators, and advocates of intercollegiate athletics will also find it essential. The book is arranged into 28 chapters that cover a wide range of topics. It is not exhaustive, but the editor believes that current concerns, challenges, and themes of relevance to higher education researchers and practitioners are certainly well addressed.

The text is organized into eight parts that describe the foundations and overarching structures and conditions that shape athletics and higher education (Historical Analysis, Governance and Leadership, and Ethics; Theoretical Perspectives on Higher Education and Athletics; The Business Enterprise of College Athletics), the ways that college athletes experience life on campus (The College Athlete Experience; The Significance of Race and Ethnicity Issues; Gender Equity and Compliance Issues), and the current and future policy context of intercollegiate athletics (NCAA and Member Institution Policy Concerns; The Academic Reform Movement). Each of the 28 chapters includes special features such as a list of key terms, reflections from an athletics stakeholder, a relevant case study, and questions for discussion. These special features are ideal for use as the basis of further conversation in the classroom setting.

Adopters of this textbook will find that the content takes the form of distinctive expert voices in the field. As more scholars and practitioners turn their attention to this important topic, we gain an even greater understanding of how central this topic is to the future of postsecondary education. The chapters that follow delve into some complex issues, shedding new light as well as presenting unique opportunities for the future study of intercollegiate athletics in American higher education.

I owe a tremendous debt to many people for their contributions to the design of this volume. Without their assistance, I would not have completed this project—or even started it. I wish to acknowledge the works of pioneering scholars who paved the way for empirical scholarship on the interplay of athletics and American higher education. I also sincerely thank the authors who agreed to participate in this volume and for their thoughtful and painstaking contributions. It has been a pleasure to work with all of you. As well, I am blessed with an amazing editorial team at Johns Hopkins University Press, and I thank the press for its support and encouragement throughout the development and production of this text. Finally, I continue to learn and be inspired my family, friends, students, and colleagues and thank them for helping to shape this volume.

PART ONE

Historical Analysis, Governance and Leadership, and Ethics

This first section of the book sets the stage for examining the interplay of intercollegiate athletics and American higher education. In chapter 1, John Thelin offers a brief historical account of college sports coverage in the national media to demonstrate its influence in American higher education. In particular, he highlights the coverage of major championship games in the revenue-generating sports of football and men's basketball, the episodic press coverage of problems associated with the commercialization and finances of athletic programs, and publicized scandals involving improprieties of stakeholders, including college athletes, coaches, and administrators. James Satterfield covers the NCAA's organizational and governance structure in chapter 2. He summarizes the organizational structure, role, and function of the NCAA, including the rule-making process and principles of conduct, and offers an overview of the NCAA divisional governance structure. Then, in chapter 3, Molly Ott and Evan Bates discuss stakeholder groups' often-competing interests and priorities with regard to intercollegiate athletics and describe the implications of leadership—by president, athletic director, faculty, and coach—for the well-being of college athletes. In chapter 4, the final chapter in part one, Angela Lumpkin examines ethical issues in intercollegiate athletics, with particular attention to the NCAA's amateurism ideals. She explores its mandated use of the label *student-athlete*, the clash between the educational model and business model in intercollegiate athletics, and the potential financial exploitation of football and men's basketball players. Lumpkin concludes with 10 recommendations to reconnect intercollegiate athletes to the NCAA's espoused values. Taken together, these chapters provide important context for the sections that follow. ■

FROM SPORTS PAGE to FRONT PAGE

*Intercollegiate Athletics
and American Higher Education*

John R. Thelin

KEY TERMS

intercollegiate athletics ◄

athlete ◄

college coaches ◄

National Collegiate ◄
Athletic Association
(NCAA)

Football Bowl ◄
Subdivision (FBS)

Knight Commission on ◄
Intercollegiate Athletics

While a source of immediate daily news, intercollegiate athletics is also a source of history in our own time. This dual character and contribution to American society can be illustrated by considering a core sample of college sports coverage in the national media from 2013. During the first two weeks of January, four distinct but related events made headline news nationwide. First, on January 7 every newspaper gave front-page coverage to the University of Alabama's triumph over Notre Dame for the national college football championship (Bishop, 2013). Then came a succession of other stories, also prominent, but less obvious and not at all predictable. Moody's reported that more colleges and universities in the United States suffered lowered bond ratings because their financial condition was continuing to deteriorate (Martin, 2013). Next, the Delta Cost Project at American Institutes for Research in Washington, D.C., released a national report with the dramatic news that campus spending per athlete was far more than spending per "regular" student—as much as six times more in some conferences, such as the Southeastern Conference (Desrochers, 2013; Lewin, 2013; Wolverton, 2013a). Finally, National Collegiate Athletic Association (NCAA) officials announced at their annual conference in Dallas on January 12 that they were ending sponsorship and funding of their scholarly colloquium and journal dealing with the study of college sports (Wolverton, 2013b).

These four events compressed within a few days illustrate how today intercollegiate athletics can quickly jump from the sports page to the front page. Even though these current events are volatile and newsworthy, they are not new. The net result is a rich core sample of intercollegiate athletics and the media attention it commands. An important implication for this anthology is that those who work with and study intercollegiate athletics are heirs to a distinctive tradition in the United States in which our information and images about higher education are shaped in large measure by college sports. The underlying thesis of this chapter is that there is a long American heritage, stretching back into the late nineteenth century, that has frequently and repeatedly catapulted varsity athletic programs and characters from the sports page to the front page.

SPORTS PAGES AND THE TRANSFORMATION OF MEDIA COVERAGE

We tend to take for granted pervasive media coverage of college sports. In fact, it was not an inevitable development but one that had two requirements: first, what historian Daniel Boorstin has called a "graphics revolution" in which the new technology of the late nineteenth century allowed for fast, large-volume publication of high-quality newspapers that included photographs (Boorstin, 1961, pp. 181–238); and, second, mass circulation and a readership composed of knowledgeable followers. On closer inspection one finds that it has been an acquired skill and habit. William Oriard's (1993) classic work, *Reading Football*, documents in detail how innovations in printing and distributing newspapers in the 1880s combined with expanding literacy among Americans to produce a new, enthusiastic reading audience: knowledgeable, loyal sports fans. It was, according to historian and literary analyst Oriard, no less than the story of "How the Popular Press Created an American Spectacle" (Oriard, 1993). Even though creation of the daily "sports page" was a successful innovation in American journalism, the most remarkable development was that publishers and editors were opportunistic and frequently moved coverage of a big college football rivalry to the front page, often for several days prior to a game—a strategy intended to sell newspapers and tickets. And, it worked, to the delight of athletic directors, coaches, and college presidents.

All this changed—or, at least, was interrupted—on October 24, 1929, when once again college sports made the front page of every daily newspaper. The difference was that the headlines did not proclaim about football scores such as that Michigan had defeated Illinois or that Yale triumphed over Princeton. Rather, the big news was that the Carnegie Foundation for the Advancement of Teaching (CFAT) had released its comprehensive, detailed study of the organization and control of college sports, which concluded that college and university presidents needed to provide the leadership to restore integrity to varsity sports programs that had become mired in professionalism and commercialism. Shortly thereafter, presidents at several prominent universities fumed and blustered that the CFAT report author, Howard J. Savage, had misrepresented *their* university, had misquoted figures, or misrepresented documents and data about *their* particular, beloved athletic program. Author Howard Savage calmly responded with documentation on every disputed claim.

He stood by every finding he had reported, and no one (including complaining university presidents) successfully refuted or derailed his data or discussion (Savage, 1929; Thelin, 1994, pp. 13–37).

The Carnegie Foundation report set into motion a succession of publicized critical analyses by foundations and educational groups that persist to this day. They make for good reading. And, important for this book, they manage to make the front page. The corollary is that they merely punctuate the avalanche of front-page and sports-page news about championships and victories. On the one hand, many of the reports deal with scandals and abuses, involving such topics as transcripts, grades, courses, and academic eligibility. On the other hand, in the past 30 years several have raised questions about broad policy issues, such as the efficacy and propriety of the financial model embraced by most varsity sports programs.

ROOTS OF THE NCAA

One interesting consequence of the sustained efforts at regulation and reform is that the NCAA is the organization that college sports fans love to hate. A recent prominent example is Joe Nocera's (2012) column claiming that charges of racial bias are yet another "blow to the NCAA's integrity." Add to this the criticisms that the NCAA has been "arrogant," "arbitrary," and "autocratic" in its penalties levied against some athletic programs. Its commercial success has led to its characterization as a "cartel" and "monopoly" that is "hypocritical" in its conduct of college sports. Given all this outrage, one wonders, How did the NCAA get this way? The answer is that this happened sixty years ago when college sports were mired in scandals that dominated newspaper headlines and even befuddled the United States Congress. By accident and luck, the NCAA was selected to be the regulator of intercollegiate athletics.

The NCAA was an unlikely candidate for this role. In 1951 it was a small organization housed in a single suite of a Chicago office building. Its main work was to promote selected sports. Its premier event—the NCAA college basketball championships—had to share prestige and publicity with the National Invitational Tournament. In 1948 the director of the NCAA persuaded college presidents and athletic directors to adopt a code of conduct for athletes and financial aid, but the ensuing resistance to and ridicule of the regulations prompted the NCAA to retreat from developing—or enforcing—national standards (Lawrence, 1987).

College sports literally were out of control after World War II. Zealous alumni and booster clubs made payments to recruit outstanding high school athletes. Conference commissioners had neither the power nor the desire to curb the most flagrant abuses of commercialism and recruiting. The Commissioner of the Pacific Coast Conference was unusual because he was vigilant in documenting "slush funds" and placed four programs on probation, making them ineligible for the famous (and lucrative) Rose Bowl. For a job well done he was fired, and the conference was dissolved. Many university presidents turned a deaf ear to reform as they encouraged

The Ivy League

The Ivy League was founded as an intercollegiate athletic conference in 1954 by the presidents of eight historic institutions—Harvard, Yale, Princeton, Brown, Columbia, Cornell, Dartmouth, and Pennsylvania. The impetus for this organizational innovation was a collective commitment among these academically prestigious institutions to create a conference that encouraged intercollegiate athletics excellence within the boundaries of educational priorities. Specifically, this meant that these institutions would not award athletic scholarships or allow football teams to compete in postseason bowl competition. In addition to these constraints, the conference—officially known as The Ivy Group—maintained commitments to having sports remain integral to campus life. Member institutions were required to have a football team. And Ivy League institutions demonstrated a commitment to a broad array of varsity sports—offering competition and championships in 33 sports each year.

The Ivy League started conference competition in 1956. Although the conference celebrated its fiftieth anniversary seven years ago, sportswriters and the general public often mistakenly think the conference is much older. The explanation is that the term "Ivy League" was used informally as long as a century ago. And, its member institutions that banded together in 1954 were, indeed, the nationally dominant athletic programs in the late nineteenth and early twentieth centuries. A group of student editors called for creation of an "Ivy League" in 1937, although this did not reach fruition.

An important historical reminder is that the creation of the Ivy League in 1954 was a direct counter to the unprecedented excesses and abuses of college sports in the years immediately following World War II. One institution that sought inclusion in the proposed Ivy League—the University of Pennsylvania—was a case in point as it invoked its historic academic roots from the colonial era while at the same time relying on an alumni slush fund, aggressive recruiting tactics, generous athletic scholarships, and the waiving of traditional admissions requirements to field a football squad that competed against (and often triumphed over) such large state universities as Michigan and Oklahoma in the late 1940s and early 1950s. The other seven university presidents of the proposed Ivy League warned the president of the University of Pennsylvania that it would not be invited to join the conference unless it ended its practices and policies of overemphasis on recruiting and promoting football and other sports. The literal and figurative result was that Penn did penance—and was allowed to join the Ivy League.

During its initial years of conference play the Ivy League often was the object of ridicule by sportswriters and by fans and alumni at nationally dominant football and basketball programs. From 1985 to 2010, under the leadership of Executive Director Jeffrey Orleans, the Ivy League demonstrated repeatedly that excellence in athletics and academics for men and women was compatible not only within an institution but also within the same individual—the genuine athlete. ■

their ambitious coaches to build a winning team that attracted large crowds and statewide adulation (Thelin, 1994, pp. 98–127).

The abuses in college sports were so alarming that the United States Congress was asked to create a federal regulatory agency. Because Congress was reluctant to intervene into higher education on any issue, it first sought to have academic leaders oversee the reform of college sports. Congress urged colleges to lead the way through the national organization of presidents, the American Council on Education (ACE). Over the course of a two-year debate in the early 1950s, ACE deliberations stalled, as some presidents squabbled with athletic directors and coaches over what the place of intercollegiate athletics should be. When no agreements within the ranks of university presidents could be reached about the balance of academics and athletics, discussions reached a stalemate.

Desperate to end the impasse, Congress gave up on the ACE and asked the NCAA to be the regulatory body. Even though football was the dominant spectator sport, it was men's basketball that provided the crucial test case for the NCAA's new watchdog mandate. The University of Kentucky was at center court along with the City College of New York, Bradley University, and Long Island University because of charges that some players were involved in the point shaving scandal at tournaments held in Madison Square Garden in New York City. The NCAA prohibited any member institution from playing against Kentucky, prompting the school to cancel its 1952–1953 varsity schedule. This sent a message nationwide to athletic directors, coaches, and presidents that the NCAA had the necessary strength to make (or break) high-profile programs. When it comes to the broad powers enjoyed by the NCAA today, it is important to note that without the University of Kentucky there would be no NCAA.

Beyond regulations and penalties, there was another overlooked part of the NCAA's eventual stature: it was able to become a commercial success because its member institutions granted it control over televising college games. Colleges had readily turned over television authority to the NCAA in 1948 in hopes that the NCAA's restrictions on live broadcast would erase the threat that potential ticket buyers would stay away from football stadiums in favor of watching games on TV. That transfer of power from the individual colleges and conferences to the NCAA was done willingly and not seen as controversial or conflicted in 1950. By 1960, however, when college football enjoyed both record-setting ticket sales and television broadcast revenues, the NCAA had consolidated both its authority and profitability—along with its exclusive regulatory power over institutional conduct of sports.

What is hard to imagine today is that as late as 1980 the NCAA had the authority to restrict televising college football to a total of eight games per weekend, further confined to a formula of two games in each of four regions. It could do this because the NCAA is an unusual organization that had acquired the power to *both* punish and promote programs. The conflicting priorities of commercialism and amateurism in college sports were joined. But an important reminder is that the NCAA is a *voluntary* association. A college does have the right to leave and form new cooperative alliances in tune with its own academic and athletic values.

Secession from the NCAA, however, is unlikely because many (perhaps most) gain a great deal from NCAA membership despite complaints and grumbling from some presidents from time to time. What had fallen into place was a discernible pattern of a prolonged period of front-page headlines about championship college teams interspersed periodically—about every decade—with an equally bold headline about corruption. The result was a melodrama in which sustained public cheers were interspersed with public outrage—and then with a resumption of cheers. Reform initiatives attracted a flurry of attention, but on balance Americans—and most college presidents—really did like big-time sports and were fickle in attempts to address problems in any genuine manner.

FROM REFORMS TO REGULATIONS

One irony of NCAA regulation is the source of many complaints. A recurrent anecdote depicts a president or coach or legislator at a press conference holding up a copy of the NCAA handbook and regulations. Usually the implication is that it is large and unwieldy and often deals with some arcane rule interpretation. A distinct and important criticism is that an investigation's result—for example, an athlete is forbidden to receive money for airfare home to a funeral or some other significant family event—is unreasonable and petty. What these statements of public outrage often omit, however, is that such detailed regulations and restrictions have come about less from serious concern by academic leaders and faculty and more from anger and jealousy of other coaches who fear that a renegade coach has gained an advantage. The result has been an athletics arms race.

Given this pattern and environment, a landmark event was the 1991 report by the Knight Commission on the Future of Athletics (Knight Commission on Intercollegiate Athletics, 1991). Led by Creed Black, former publisher of the *Lexington (Ky.) Herald Leader* who had gained fame and infamy for sponsoring a Pulitzer Prize–winning series about the excesses of the basketball program in his hometown at the University of Kentucky, the Knight Report put a spotlight on the call for nationwide reform. On one level its emphasis was on students—specifically, restoring a commitment to athletes as students. On another level, it was about presidents—urging presidents of colleges and universities to claim their rightful role as leaders and educators who did not necessarily defer to charismatic coaches, powerful athletic directors, and alumni boosters and donors. It resembled a resurrection of the 1929 Carnegie Foundation report, with added attention on suggestions for solutions and strategies. To maintain influence, pressure, and public visibility, the Knight Foundation Commission established an informative website, while continuing to release well-documented reports from time to time. Its 2010 report, for example, showed the alarming finding from both survey and budget data that most college and university presidents conceded that presidents had lost control of spending on college sports (Knight Commission on Intercollegiate Athletics, 2010; Oriard, 2009).

THE MIXED BLESSINGS OF COLLEGE SPORTS PUBLICITY

One recurrent justification for big-time, winning college sports is that it brings publicity to the entire university. This is true, although sometimes with an unexpected twist. In 2006 Auburn University was featured in a front-page story of the *New York Times*—unusual given that the preponderance of Auburn's press and media coverage is statewide and regional. This national story did, indeed, bring together academics and athletics, which might suggest a best-case scenario for college sports' halo effect and multiplier effect to enhance institutional prestige. Unfortunately the news was not good: according to the reporter, each year more than 60 Auburn students (most of them varsity athletes, especially football players) had enrolled in an independent-study course sponsored by one professor in the sociology department (Thamel, 2006). Variations on this theme appearing in smaller national syndicated articles included stories about UCLA football players who received parking permits allowing them to park in "disabled only" parking and the University of Georgia basketball coach who taught a credit course on Principles and Theories of Coaching, a course whose enrollees included some of his own varsity players.

Many of these garden-variety articles are tantamount to petty larcenies whose reports show up on the local police blotter. In contrast, there are landmark stories that stand out and endure when college sports have implications for the larger fabric, the governance of higher education. One example would include the news coverage at Pennsylvania State University from 2011 through 2013, emanating from charges (and convictions) of child abuse involving a coach. Beyond such specifics, this story raised fundamental concerns about the role of big-time sports in university governance and the responsibilities of its president and trustees. It provided an alert to all university presidents and boards. Long after headline stories on the front page returned to the sports pages, columnists such as Joe Nocera of the *New York Times* have devoted sustained attention to questions about the NCAA and big-time sports, suggesting that the fundamental legal and policy questions raised initially can be a continuing story in columns and op-ed pieces.

How do researchers and scholarly analysts best make sense of these historical patterns with their spikes, vacillations, and fluctuations? First, dramatic and substantive reports have power to elicit strong response at the moment, but this is not a reliable or certain source of reform because the concerns dissipate, and the path to reform is not clear. The NCAA is the likely source of reform because it is the major body of regulation, but this possibility is often trumped by the NCAA's additional role as the promoter of college sports.

Another mitigating factor is that the NCAA tends not to intrude into the internal operations and decisions of a member institution, such as its spending on college sports as part of total institution policies and practices. The NCAA may require as a condition of Division IA membership that an institution offer a large number of sports for men and women and that its football team show certain attainments in attendance. But these are categorical and thematic requirements and not really connected to an institution's appropriations and allocations. The NCAA requires a Division IA program to be self-supporting, and here one might expect this to be a standard of self-sufficiency from, for example, educational and general funds of a university. The salient detail is that an institution can demonstrate that it has a self-supporting athletic program through various revenue streams, including mandatory student fees or transfers from the financial aid office to the athletic department. An athletic department may be required to provide substantial academic support services for athletes, but there is no NCAA restriction on having the necessary funding coming from the provost's office, which may have drawn these resources from tuition revenues of the general student body.

These allowances—and deference to institutional autonomy and internal allocations—will be crucial in the twenty-first century because the cumulative pattern for many decades has been that only a few major athletic programs show that they can operate year after year in the black. One might expect that a rational organizational response would be to reduce or even eliminate those programs or subprograms that lose money. That is unlikely to happen.

Why are these financial trends and subsidies worthy of "front page" coverage? It is a residual of the persistent national (and front-page) attention given to rising college costs—and, from the point of view of students as consumers, rising college

---

Amos Alonzo Stagg

Amos Alonzo Stagg is prominent among pioneering college football coaches and players. He was elected to the college football hall of fame primarily on the basis of his contributions for having coached at the University of Chicago from 1892 to 1932—with 242 victories, 112 losses, and 27 ties. This included sellout crowds and seven Big Ten championships, the last coming in 1924. Stagg retired from the University of Chicago in 1932 and went on to coach in California at the College of the Pacific for 14 years. Since his death in 1965 at the age of 102 he has been revered. He made innovations in how football was played. Stagg has been credited with introducing the tackling dummy, the reverse, man in motion plays, the lateral pass, the posting of numbers on uniforms, and the end-of-season practice of awarding varsity letters to players.

Stagg's record as a winning football coach has ironically tended to overshadow his legacy for making the college coach and athletic director a dominant—and often domineering—role in American higher education. Beyond his playing and coaching on the field, he remains influential today for his innovations in the organization, promotion, commercialization, and funding of college sports. He combined football coach and director of the Department of Physical Culture. This was a concentration of power in which he literally "reported to himself." By our standards today, it constitutes both a conflict of interest and an overemphasis on sports at the expense of academics. Another achievement, perhaps insulting to academic values, was that along with his role as a celebrity coach he gained a faculty appointment with tenure. The president of the university allowed him to bypass conventional budgeting procedures required of other university departments. Stagg reported directly to the Board of Trustees and pioneered fundraising from the Chicago business community. As director of athletics he devised numerous sources of raising money and gaining publicity for his teams. He had the University of Chicago host Illinois state championship tournaments in track and field and other sports. Within the university community, he kept a close eye on facilities and funding—he even raised revenues by charging faculty and staff if they wished to play on university tennis courts. Such license provided opportunities for spending and recruiting without the distractions of interference or oversight. He was an organizational genius who set the precedent and created the mold for the powerful, autonomous intercollegiate athletic program within a university campus. For better and worse, higher education still lives with his legacy even into the twenty-first century. ■

price (Thelin, 2013). There seems to be a disconnect or avoidance that at many universities the general student—or student body—is facing an increase in tuition and fees in part because each year a growing dollar amount (and growing percentage) is transferred away from educational programs and toward athletic programs. This was one implication of both the Delta Cost Project of 2013 and the earlier 2009–2010 report published by the Knight Commission. The tone of caution and concern was affirmed by Jeff Orleans, executive director emeritus of the Ivy Group, in his keynote address at the NCAA colloquium in January 2013 (Orleans, 2013).

THE CONFLUENCE OF ACADEMIC LEADERS AND ATHLETICS ISSUES

Are academic leaders listening? Despite the preponderance of sobering data, some university boards and presidents persist in the pursuit of big-time football excellence as a source of institutional leverage. An incredible coincidence with the Delta Cost Project Report was the December 29, 2012, *New York Times* feature article on the University of Massachusetts, Amherst and its decision to enhance the program for Football Bowl Subdivision (FBS) eligibility and participation (Pennington, 2012). The new chancellor, according to the *New York Times* reporter, supported the decision to pursue FBS status as a "reasonable calculated risk." He elaborated, "If managed properly, we will come out better for it . . . There are risks to academic investments, too. When we build a new research center, it is with the hope of attracting more research grants. So that is a risk. It is important to keep in mind that the total athletics budget is 4 percent of our expenditures."

This public explanation and justification by the chancellor of the University of Massachusetts raises several questions for policy and practice. First, big-time college sports have a dubious record in demonstrating that they can be "managed properly." Second, to explain away the sports investment because it is "only 4 percent of the total university budget" is flawed. That is a large percentage and a lot of dollars. If a university has an annual budget of $1.5 billion, then its athletic department would have an operating budget of about $60 million per academic year. Its relatively large size becomes more evident if, for example, it is compared to the expenses of major academic units on campus, such as a College of Engineering or a College of Arts and Sciences.

Consider the actual numbers for the case of the University of Kentucky—a flagship state university with a total enrollment of about 25,000 students. It is a research university known as "R1," signifying a commitment to Ph.D. programs and sponsored federal research grants. It also has a medical center and teaching hospital. Its total annual operating budget was about $2.1 billion in 2011–2012. The intercollegiate athletics budget was about $80 million—slightly below the 4% standard. In contrast, the College of Arts and Sciences (the academic unit with the largest enrollment) has an annual budget of about $68 million; the College of Business, $32 million; the

College of Agriculture, including its statewide extension programs and institutes, $149 million; and the College of Engineering, $37 million.

In sum, this budgetary analysis shows that a big-time athletics budget tends to surpass the budget of most of the individual major academic units that offer courses and degree programs. Spending on academic programs was increasing at a rate lower than that for athletic programs. Furthermore, the early twenty-first century is not a very good time for aspiring institutions to attempt to ratchet up their spending on research institutes; these tend to be ill-fated, money losing ventures for those universities not members of the Association of American Universities. Finally, a decision by the board of trustees to allocate resources to an academic unit is markedly different from a commitment to athletics for the basic reason that academic programs are central to the institutional mission while the athletic department is not.

CONCLUSION

Even in the select circle of universities with lucrative intercollegiate sports programs, one may find in the early twenty-first century that the proverbial golden goose may lay an egg. Specifically, the move by big conferences (such as The Big Ten and the Southeast Conference and some institutions (notably the University of Texas) to create their own television networks and packages often is hailed as a new model for college sports financing. But this immediate source of revenue may be draining and dysfunctional over the long haul. Note that already in the greater Los Angeles area market, cable television providers require subscribers to pay for a sports package as part of their bundle, whether they want it or not. At some point, there will be saturation in viewers and advertisers for college sports. Already one finds in December that many of the college football bowl games year after year suffer low attendance with vast sections of empty seats and low TV ratings. Only the biggest games, usually played and broadcast in January, are an exception to this general rule.

The residual inference is that intercollegiate athletics in the twenty-first century calls out for reforms that are no less than a "New Deal" in both the conduct and the financing of this distinctively American enterprise. The historic move from the sports page to the front page increasingly will add sobering news to the headlines announcing the celebration of championship teams.

QUESTIONS FOR DISCUSSION

1. Has there ever been a golden age of college sports in which academic and athletics values were in appropriate balance? If so, when and where do you think this has taken place?

2. In contrast to the first question, is there an era in intercollegiate athletics when excesses and abuses of commercialism and overemphasis were most rampant?

3. What is the appropriate place and role of the athletic director in the organizational chart, governance, and culture of a college or university campus? Give examples where you think this balance is fulfilled reasonably well, and provide examples where it is seriously off course.

References

Bishop, G. (2013, January 8). All Alabama in title game: Alabama 42, Notre Dame 14. *New York Times*, p. A1.

Boorstin, D. (1961). *The image: A guide to pseudo events in America.* New York: Harper and Row.

Desrochers, D. M. (2013). *Academic spending versus athletic spending: Who wins?* Washington, DC: Delta Cost Project of the Association of Institutes for Research.

Knight Commission on Intercollegiate Athletics. (1991). *Keeping faith with the student-athlete.* Charlotte, NC: Knight Foundation.

———. (2010). *Restoring the balance: Dollars, values and the future of college sports.* Miami, FL: Knight Foundation.

Lawrence, P. R. (1987). *Unsportsmanlike conduct: The National Collegiate Athletic Association and the business of college football.* New York: Praeger.

Lester, R. (1995). *Stagg's University: The rise, decline, and fall of big-time football at Chicago.* Urbana: University of Illinois Press.

Lewin, T. (2013, January 16). At many top public universities, intercollegiate sports comes at an academic price. *New York Times*, p. A1.

Martin, A. (2013, January 16). Moody's gives colleges a negative grade. *New York Times*, p. A1.

Nocera, J. (2012, November 19). Race and the NCAA. *New York Times*, p. A25.

Oriard, M. (1993). *Reading football: How the popular press created an American spectacle.* Chapel Hill: University of North Carolina Press.

———. (2009). *Bowled over: Big-time college football from the sixties to the BCS era.* Chapel Hill: University of North Carolina Press.

Orleans, J. (2013, January 16). *The effects of the economic model of college sport on athlete educational experience.* Paper presented at the National Collegiate Athletic Association Scholarly Colloquium, Grapevine, Texas.

Pennington, B. (2012, December 29). Big dream, rude awakening. *New York Times*, p. B1.

Savage. H. J. (1929). *American college athletics.* New York: Carnegie Foundation for the Advancement of Teaching, Bulletin Number Twenty-Three.

Thamel, P. (2006, July 14). Top grades and no class time for Auburn players. *New York Times*, p. A1.

Thelin, J. R. (1994). *Games colleges play: Scandal and reform in intercollegiate athletics.* Baltimore: Johns Hopkins University Press.

———. (2013). *The rising costs of higher education.* Santa Barbara: ABC CLIO.

Wolverton, B. (2013a, January 16). Report describes big gaps in athletic vs. academic spending. *Chronicle of Higher Education*, p. A1.

Wolverton, B. (2013b, January 16). NCAA withdraws financial support for its scholarly colloquium. *Chronicle of Higher Education*, p. A1.

ORGANIZATION and GOVERNANCE of the NCAA

James Satterfield

The organization we know today as the National Collegiate Athletic Association (NCAA) is the policy arm for a wide range of sports, schools, and organizations throughout North America. Yet the NCAA as it exists today is the offspring of the early chaotic and homicidal organization with which football began (Crowley, 2006). As the United States was taking shape in the early post–Civil War era, America was also experiencing a growing interest in the game of football. In 1873 the Intercollegiate Football Association (IFA) was created, and it was the organization's rule changes to the early game that began the transition from a sport resembling soccer to one being played more like rugby, a rougher, more physical sport (Crowley, 2006). The first-ever championship football game was held in New York City in 1876 (Morris, 2004). Its popularity reached new heights by 1878 when a total of 4,000 people came to watch the Yale-Princeton game (Lindquist, 2006). Although the function of the IFA appeared to be strong initially, schools began dropping football, which weakened the organization, rendering it obsolete by the 1890s (Crowley, 2006; Morris, 2004). The IFA was followed by the brief existence of the American Football Rules Committee (AFRC). Despite further rule changes, the game was still brutal, and the complexity associated with controlling the game grew, as did its fan base and the institutional desire to win.

These early associations were largely controlled by students and did very little to curb the violence and brutality that had come to be associated with the game. The deaths caused by football caught the attention of President Theodore Roosevelt. Roosevelt had a true respect for football, as he believed in the virtue of the game and the values he believed it taught (Watterson, 2000). By 1905, the violence had now reached a point where turning a blind eye would have been irresponsible. President Roosevelt hosted a meeting at the White House with representatives from major football programs to discuss the rules of the game.

Although President Roosevelt's proposed changes were met with much resistance from some college presidents, he convinced the AFRC and the newly formed rules committee within the National Football Conference of Universities and Colleges to form a joint committee. As a result, a new executive committee was eventually formed to develop a constitution and bylaws to help standardize football across the country. Ultimately, this led to the first organized convention, held in December of 1906, and adoption of the name The Intercollegiate Athletic Association, which was changed to the National Collegiate Athletic Association (NCAA) in 1910 (Crowley, 2006; Smith, 2000).

ROLE AND FUNCTION OF THE NCAA

After the establishment of what we know today as the NCAA, it still took years for the organization to gain the power to reshape the culture within the administration of collegiate athletics. The original constitution outlined that activities "shall be maintained on an ethical plane in keeping with the dignity and high purpose of education" (NCAA.org). The idea of the NCAA acting as a central authority over all athletic programs was discussed during the association's infancy; however, the notion was rejected, and the responsibility of enforcing standards was left to the institutions through what was called home rule (Pierce, 1909). It took nearly 50 years for the NCAA to develop a different perspective on rule enforcement.

The NCAA's operation is very different from its original inception. Not only are there are more colleges and universities in North America today, but they also are more expensive to operate and attend and offer more opportunities for sport participation. There are also laws governing the equitable implementation of sports on college campuses for men and women. As such, the *NCAA Division I Manual* (2012a) has nine fundamental purposes that help it govern, outlined as follows:

- To initiate, stimulate and improve intercollegiate athletics programs for student-athletes and to promote and develop education leadership, physical fitness, athletics excellence and athletics participation as recreational pursuit

- To uphold the principle of institutional control of, and responsibility for, all intercollegiate sports in conformity with the constitution and bylaws of this Association

- To encourage its members to adopt eligibility rules to comply with satisfactory standards of scholarship, sportsmanship and amateurism

■ To formulate, copyright, and publish rules of play governing intercollegiate athletics

■ To preserve intercollegiate athletic records

■ To supervise the conduct of, and to establish eligibility standards for, regional and national athletic events under the auspices of this Association

■ To cooperate with other amateur athletics organizations in promoting and conducting national and international athletic events

■ To legislate, through bylaws or by resolution of a Convention, upon any subject of general concern to the members related to the administration of intercollegiate athletics

■ To study in general all phases of competitive intercollegiate athletics and establish standards whereby the colleges and universities of the United States can maintain their athletics programs on a high level (p. 1)

These specific purposes are rooted in what the NCAA calls a fundamental policy. The NCAA policy states, "The competitive athletics programs of member institutions are designed to be a vital part of the educational system. A basic purpose of this Association is to maintain intercollegiate athletics as an integral part of the educational program and the athlete as an integral part of the study body and, by so doing, retain a clear line of demarcation between intercollegiate athletics and professional sports" (p. 1). Together, these nine purposes and the fundamental policy of the NCAA establish an operating standard. It is the result of these two guiding principles from which all other regulatory aspects are derived and thus help to form the basis of the NCAA principles of conduct.

NCAA PRINCIPLES FOR CONDUCT OF INTERCOLLEGIATE ATHLETICS

The NCAA established 16 Principles of Conduct. The premise of these principles is to help to guide member institutions in the governance and administration of intercollegiate athletics. The first is the *Principle of Institutional Control and Responsibility*. Within this principle, there are two subprinciples: Responsibility of Control and Scope of Responsibility. The Responsibility of Control is rooted in the original idea of home rule, but not from the perspective of athletic programs establishing their own rules. This rule establishes control and responsibility within the member institution to comply with all of the rules and regulations of the NCAA. Through the Scope of Responsibility principle, the NCAA establishes accountability at the member level for the conduct of its athletic personnel.

The *Principle of Student-Athlete Well-Being* is in place to help protect the welfare of student athletes both educationally and physically. This principle is made up of six subprinciples: (a) Overall Educational Experience; (b) Cultural Diversity and Gender Equity; (c) Health and Safety; (d) Student-Athlete and Coach Relationship; (e) Fairness, Openness, and Honesty; and (f) Student-Athlete Involvement. This principle is vital to the overall prosperity of the athlete and the environment in which he or she participates.

The *Principle of Gender Equity* is the third principle and is rooted in the law Title IX passed in 1972. Its subprinciples—Compliance with Federal and State Legislation, NCAA Legislation, and Gender Bias—help ground this principle within the workings of the NCAA. Since most Division I institutions receive some form of federal aid, it is up to the institution to maintain compliance with the federal and state laws pertaining to gender equity. However, it is equally important for the NCAA not to embrace legislation that would hinder the ability of the institutions to comply with gender equity laws (NCAA Division I, 2012a).

Today, dishonesty and unethical conduct in intercollegiate athletics seem to occur more frequently. While the NCAA cannot control individual behavior, it can certainly make a statement on its position and have done so through the *Principle of Sportsmanship and Ethical Conduct*. The basic tenet of this principle is making sure that athletic programs maintain policies in sportsmanship and ethical conduct that are consistent with the educational mission and goals of the institution (NCAA Division I, 2012a).

Over the years, academic standards for athletes have changed to help ensure a clear and consistent path toward graduation for student athletes. The *Principle of Sound Academic Standards* helps safeguard that the admission, academic standing, and academic progress are consistent with the overall policies in the nonathlete general population. College athletes are required to enroll as full-time students and must complete 40% of their degree requirements by the end of their second year of athletic eligibility, 60% by the end of their third year of athletic eligibility, and 80% by the end of their athletic eligibility (Satterfield, Croft, Godfrey, & Flint, 2010).

Most organizations have a nondiscrimination policy, and the NCAA is no different. The *Principle of Nondiscrimination* is in place to ensure the "respect for and sensitivity to the dignity of every person" (NCAA Division I, 2012a, p. 4). However, it is the responsibility of the member institution to develop and maintain policies regarding nondiscrimination. Nevertheless, having policies in place does not mean the NCAA or member institutions are immune to lawsuits. In fact, a gender equity lawsuit filed in 2009 by members of the Quinnipiac University women's volleyball team argued that it was being discriminated against because the athletic department was eliminating women's volleyball in favor of competitive cheerleading. In 2010 the U.S. District Court issued an injunction against Quinnipiac University, ruling that cheerleading did not meet the standard of a sport as it pertained to Title IX. The lawsuit was ultimately settled in 2013 with Quinnipiac University agreeing to keep all of its current women's teams, to add scholarships, and to improve facilities for its female athletes (*Biediger v. Quinnipiac University*, 2009).

The NCAA also has a standard related diversity policy called the *Principle of Diversity within Governance Structures*, which works to address issues of gender and

Mountain View University: A Case of Gender Equity

Mountain View University is a new provisionally accepted Canadian university that has entered the NCAA under the 10-year pilot program. In preparation for entering the NCAA, Mountain View added competitive men's fencing but did not add any new women's sports programs. This angered a lot of women, and during a men's basketball game several women protested the athletic department's refusal to immediately add women's sports, citing the NCAA's commitment to Title IX. When approached by a local television station, Mountain View's athletic director, Brent Tanner, said, "Mountain View supports all its competitive and club sport athletes, and even though our men's sports outnumber our women's sports, we already have a gender equity policy in place that gets at the spirit of Title IX so we don't need to concern ourselves with the American idea of men and women competitive sport proportionality." This response did not go over well with American universities scheduled to play Mountain View and sparked some protest by American women's groups at some athletic events. Tanner responded again by publicizing a capital campaign to raise money to update some athletics facilities and commissioned a self-study to explore the possibility of adding new women's sports programs. However, the damage was already done. Three months later Brent Tanner was fired, and a new athletic director was hired, but no new women's sports were immediately added. ◾

ethnic diversity within the various NCAA divisional structures. To help move toward a more inclusive and representative NCAA, the Minority Opportunities and Interests Committee and the Committee on Women's Athletics specifically address issues related to diversity within its structure. The NCAA also has an Inclusion Oversight Committee that comprised members of the Minority Opportunities Committee and the Committee on Women's Athletics that help to maintain a checks-and-balance system (NCAA Division I, 2012a).

NCAA rules infractions committed by institutions or athletes themselves have received considerable public attention. Many people are familiar with the very public display of the Penn State University football scandal or the colloquial term "death penalty" imposed on the Southern Methodist University football in the mid-1980s. The *Principle of Rules Compliance* is a key element of the work associated with the operations of the NCAA. Within this principle, there are three subprinciples: Responsibility of the Institution, Responsibility of the Association, and Penalty for Noncompliance. The NCAA holds each member institution responsible for any noncompliance related matter and expects each member institution to be forthright in reporting potential noncompliance issues to the NCAA. The NCAA also assists each member institution in reaching full compliance (NCAA Division I, 2012a). The issues of noncompliance can vary from small infractions like an accidental phone call to a high school sophomore or a major infraction like paying athletes. It is considered advantageous for an athletic department to report an alleged violation to the NCAA in order to correct situations before they develop into a major infraction.

There has been a tremendous amount of discussion over the years regarding amateurism in sports. Some believe the amount of money generated by football bowl games and the NCAA Division I Basketball Championship coupled with the NCAA's perspective on amateurism is cartel-like behavior (Kahn, 2007). Nevertheless, the NCAA's *Principle of Amateurism* is clear. It views athlete participation as an avocation and thus should be insulated from professional trappings. The idea of this specific principle can be traced back to the early beginnings of football when many football programs used "ringers" like James Hogan, a football player at Yale in the early twentieth century. Hogan not only had his tuition paid but was also given all of the profits from game-day program sales and a commission from the American Tobacco Company on every pack of cigarettes sold in the city of New Haven (Crowley, 2006). Issues with professionalism such as this give credence to the NCAA's stance on amateurism in intercollegiate sports. The James Hogan situation at Yale also helps shed light on the NCAA's *Principle of Competitive Equity.*

The recruitment process of some athletes in some regard has taken on a life of its own, particularly in the revenue sports of football and men's basketball. For some recruits it has become customary to announce their college decision in front of the national media. Although the recruiting process has become high stakes, the *Principle Governing Recruiting* is based on the idea that the educational interest of the athletes and the institution match. This principle is also in place to help institutions

A Dream Not Yet Realized

Gary Morris is a former standout football player at Norfolk State University in Norfolk, Virginia, where he played wide receiver from 1987 to 1990. Like a lot of college football players, Gary wanted to carry his passion for the game of football into coaching. After playing for a couple of years in the Canadian Football League (CFL), Gary came back to Virginia and began teaching high school. He helped out the local high school football team but that proved not to be enough. Gary longed for the big lights of college football.

A chance encounter led him to become a part of the process of establishing a football program at George Mason University. While George Mason had no team, the institutional desire was there. Gary once told me "the fact that I am a part of something totally new and will help take it from club football to NCAA Division I football is better than winning the CFL Grey Cup." George Mason started playing club football in 1993. Gary coached a few years but learned quickly it takes more than desire for a school to transition from club to NCAA Division I football. George Mason eventually decided not to pursue the process of establishing an NCAA Division I football program, but it has participated in the Seaboard Conference, winning championships in 2000, 2001, 2003, 2004, and 2005.

Gary is now a public school administrator at a local high school. I recently spoke with him and asked whether he misses coaching and is disappointed that George Mason did not follow through with its plans. He has no regrets. Looking back on his time there, he just wishes he understood the NCAA process better so he could have helped the school make the transition sooner. ■

remember to protect students from internal and external pressures that could infringe upon their academic and athletic endeavors (NCAA Division I, 2012a).

In a similar vein, the idea of protecting athletes from internal and external pressures is the *Principle Governing Eligibility*. Simply put, this principle is constructed to assure that athletes maintain an academic standard that will move them toward graduation.

Over time, the cost to attend college has increased exponentially. The system of financial aid awarded to college athletes has been around in some fashion since players like Walter Camp and James Hogan of Yale in the early twentieth century. However, paying players or providing other types of financial perks blurs the line between professional and amateur sports. What the NCAA's *Principle Governing Financial Aid* seeks to do is allow athletes to receive some financial assistance paid out by the institution while adhering to the association's perspective on amateurism.

One might think the idea of playing a college sport as romantic, reaped with glory, and endless benefits; however, it is important not to disregard the time commitment and effort to balance the dual roles of student and athlete. The *Principle of Governing Playing and Practice Seasons* indemnifies athletes in a way that reduces interference that may hinder the quality of their educational experience (NCAA Division I, 2012a).

Intercollegiate sports have some of the most watched events and championships in American sports today. Every year, colleges and universities compete for championships that can bring their institutions financial windfalls and instant name recognition. Many of these championships are sponsored by organizations outside the realm of colleges and universities. To help athletic departments govern this level of play, the NCAA has the *Principle Governing Postseason Competition and Contests Sponsored by Non-collegiate Organizations*. The core of this principle is to ensure fairness among institutional competitors and to maintain the appropriate level of protection from athlete exploitation.

Finally, the *Principle Governing the Economy of Athletics Program Operation* holds athletic programs accountable for their fiscal management and health. The NCAA expects athletic programs to operate in a judicious manner that allows for appropriate and suitable competition. The NCAA holds this principle, as well as all of its principles, in earnestness because it values the opportunity of athletic competition and educational experiences.

MEMBERSHIP AND DIVISIONS

The NCAA has three specific divisions aptly classified Division I, Division II, and Division III and three membership categories: active, conference, and affiliated (Table 2.1). In Division I there are 347 member institutions and 167,089 athletes, while Division II includes 315 programs and 107,941 athletes, and Division III com-

TABLE 2.1

NCAA Memberships and Divisions

DIVISION I		
Active Members	**Conference Members**	**Affiliated Members**
Have the right to compete in the NCAA championships, to vote on legislation and other issues, and enjoy other privileges of membership designated in the constitution and bylaws of the association (p. 7).	A group of colleges and/or universities that conducts competition among its members and determines a conference champion in one or more sports (p. 7).	A coaches or sports association whose function and purpose are directly related to one or more sports in which the NCAA conducts championships, an emerging sport for women, or that has a direct connection to either the NCAA or its member institutions (p. 7).

DIVISION II	
Distinction: Two-year colleges may participate and the membership categories now include a provisional member and provisional conference member status.	
Provisional Member	**Provisional Conference Member**
A provisional member is a four-year college or university or a two-year upper-level collegiate institution that is accredited by the appropriate regional accrediting agency and that has applied for active membership in the association. Provisional membership is a prerequisite for active membership in the association (p. 7).	Conference provisional membership a prerequisite to conference membership. A provisional conference must have a minimum of six four-year colleges or universities or two-year colleges to be considered for provisional conference status (p. 7).

DIVISION III	
Distinction: Adds a probationary status and a restricted status to the classification.	
Probation	**Restricted**
The probation status serves as a warning that certain conditions and obligations of membership have not been satisfied and failure to correct such deficiencies shall result in the institution's reclassification to the category of restricted membership (p. 7).	The restricted status is assigned to an institution that fails to comply with the minimum requirements of its division (e.g., sports sponsorship) and has failed during its period of probation to rectify such deficiencies (p. 7).

Source: NCAA Division I, 2012a; NCAA Division II, 2012a; NCAA Division III, 2012a.

prises 446 programs and 178,441 athletes (NCAA Division I, 2012b; NCAA Division II, 2012b; NCAA Division III, 2012b).

The NCAA Division I membership level receives the most public attention. This membership level consists of four-year regionally accredited institutions. To maintain the Division I membership status an institution must meet and maintain all of the membership requirements or face division reclassification (NCAA Division I, 2012b).

Within the ranks of Division II athletic programs, there are some slight variations in membership as compared to other divisional classifications. While the membership levels active, conference, and affiliated, as well as the athletics consortium, are the same for all divisions, the major distinctions at the Division II level are that two-year colleges may participate and the membership categories now include a provisional member and provisional conference member status. Likewise, at the Division II level the NCAA has developed a 10-year pilot program to include Canadian institutions. Although provisional members receive all the documentation and publications that active members receive, the provisional status is a prerequisite for active member status. Conference provisional membership is similar in that it is a prerequisite to conference membership; however, a provisional conference must have a minimum of six four-year or two-year institutions to be considered for provisional conference status.

Division III athletic programs are a major part of the intercollegiate athletic representation (Athletic Scholarships, 2013). Even though Division III athletic programs do not award athletic scholarships in the way of tuition and fees, room, board, and required course-related books, institutions can provide academic scholarships. Despite the inability to provide athletic scholarships, Division III athletic programs have the largest number of member schools (NCAA Division III, 2012b).

Division III NCAA membership has the same membership categories as Division II but offers distinction by adding a probationary status and a restricted status to the classification. While the conference membership is the same, Division III conference members must have a minimum of seven colleges or universities and determine a conference champion in at least one sport.

NCAA ORGANIZATIONAL STRUCTURE AND DIVISION I STRUCTURE

There are two structures that help organize intercollegiate athletics within the NCAA: the NCAA divisional structure that governs athletics in Division I, II, and III, and the NCAA governance structure itself. The Division I structure is divided into five levels. At the first level is the Board of Directors. With its 18 members, the Board of Directors is central to the organizational structure and feeds out to structure and flows to the Committee on Infractions, Infractions Appeals Committee, Presidential Advisory Group, and the Committee on Academic Performance. The second level is the Leadership Council and Legislative Council. This level has a direct line of report to the Board of Directors. The third level consists of the committees that flow from the Leadership and Legislative Council. From both the Leadership Council and the Legislative Council the committees are: (a) Minority Opportunities and Interest Committee, (b) Committee on Sportsmanship and Ethical Conduct, (c) Student-Athlete Advisory Committee, and (d) Committee on Women's Athletics. However, the (a) Legislative Review/Interpretations Committee, (b) Subcommittee on Athletics Certification, and (c) Committee on Student Athlete Reinstatement flow only from the Legislative Council. The fourth level is the cabinet level. At this level the Leadership Council handles all policy issues and the Legislative Council handles all legislative issues. The last level is the specific cabinets: (a) Championships/Sports Management Cabinet, (b) Administrative Cabinet, (c) Academic Cabinet, (d) Awards Benefits, Expenses, and Financial Aid Cabinet, (e) Amateurism Cabinet, and (f) the Recruiting and Athletics Personnel Issues Cabinet; with the exception of the Awards Benefits, Expenses, and Financial Aid Cabinet and the Recruiting and Athletics Personnel Issues Cabinet, each cabinet has specific committees reporting to the cabinet.

The governance structure of the NCAA is broken down into different committees and councils with each having its own membership and responsibilities. The first level is Association Wide Committees and the Executive Committee. Extending down from the Executive Committee are the Division I Board of Directors, and the Division II and III President's Council. At the Division I level the Board of Directors also extends down to the Division I Leadership and Legislative Councils; however, at the Division II and III levels they extend down to Management Councils (see Appendixes 2.A, 2.B, 2.C, and 2.D for organizational charts).

NCAA POWER FIVE STRUCTURE

In the summer of 2014, the NCAA adopted the Power Five, a new policy that gives the 65 schools in the ACC, Big Ten, Big 12, SEC, and Pac-12 the ability to create some of their own rules that are associated with the legislation and voting rights for athletes. The NCAA believes conferences and the schools in these conferences are able to provide greater resources to athletes, such as stipends, expanded medical coverage, and some benefits to families to attend games.

The new structure does, however, impact the Division I board configuration at the Division I level. There are now 10 presidents in the football bowl subdivision and five presidents in the football championship subdivision, one athletic director, one senior women's athletic director, one faculty athletics representative, and one athlete. The new structure also gives weighted voting in conferences and is broken down as such: 37.5% for the Power 5 conferences; 18.8% to the five presidents in the Football Bowl Subdivision; 37.5% for the Football Champion Subdivision Division I non football conferences; 3.1% for college athletes; and 3.1% for faculty athletics representatives (Hosick, 2014). One of the most important aspects of this new policy is for the first time athletes will have a vote in what affects their lives.

NCAA ORGANIZATIONAL STRUCTURE
AND DIVISION II AND III STRUCTURES

The organizational complexities between Division I and II are simply not the same. There are primarily two levels in the Division II organizational structure, which actually flows upward to present more of a grassroots leadership style. The bottom level contains nine committees: (a) Division II Academic Requirements Committee, (b) Division II Championship Committee, (c) Division II Committee on Infractions, (d) Division II Committee for Legislative Relief, (e) Division II Committee on Student-Athlete Reinstatement, (f) Division II Legislation Committee, (g) Division II Membership Committee, (h) Division II Nomination Committee, and (i) the Division II Student-Athlete Advisory Committee. They flow upward to the Division II Administrative Committee, a Division II Management Council, and a Division II Planning and Finance Committee with the President's Council at the top. The Division III structure is almost the same as Division II; however, at the bottom it has an extra committee called the Division III Strategic Planning and Finance Committee and these committees only flow upward to a Division III Management Council, an Administrative Committee, and a Division III President's Council on top (see Appendixes 2.E, 2.F, 2.G, and 2.H for organizational charts).

CONCLUSION

From the first death penalty sanction, imposed on the Southern Methodist University football team in the 1980s, to the sweeping scholarship cancellations, vacated wins, and fiscal obliteration of Pennsylvania State University football, justly or unjustly, the NCAA has taken a fair amount of scrutiny over time. One thing is certain, America's and the world's interests in intercollegiate sports are certainly here to stay. As time goes on, the NCAA will have to become a greater voice in the discussion of athletic reforms and perhaps loosen its strong hold on amateurism to adjust to a more market-driven college athlete.

Appendix 2.A. NCAA Division II Legislative Process

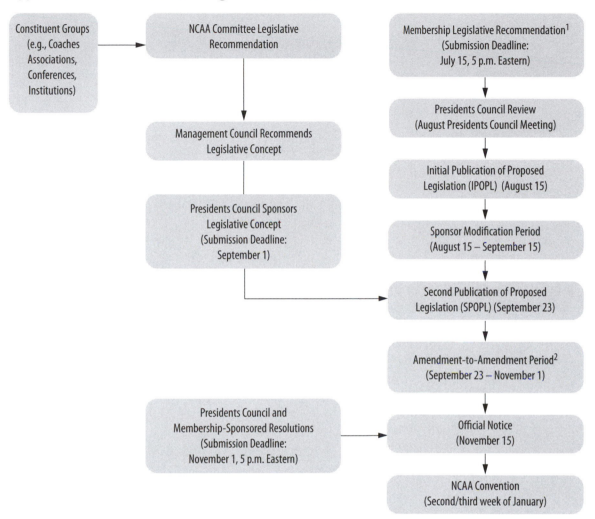

1 Per NCAA Constitution 5.3.4.1, legislative recommendations from the membership may be sponsored by 15 or more active member institutions with voting privileges or at least two voting member conferences on behalf of 15 or more active member institutions.

2 Per Constitution 5.3.4.2, an amendment-to-amendment may be sponsored by the Presidents Council, eight or more active member institutions with voting privileges, or at least one voting member conference on behalf of eight or more active member institutions.

Source: NCAA Division II, 2012a, p. 46.

Appendix 2.B. NCAA Division III Legislative Process

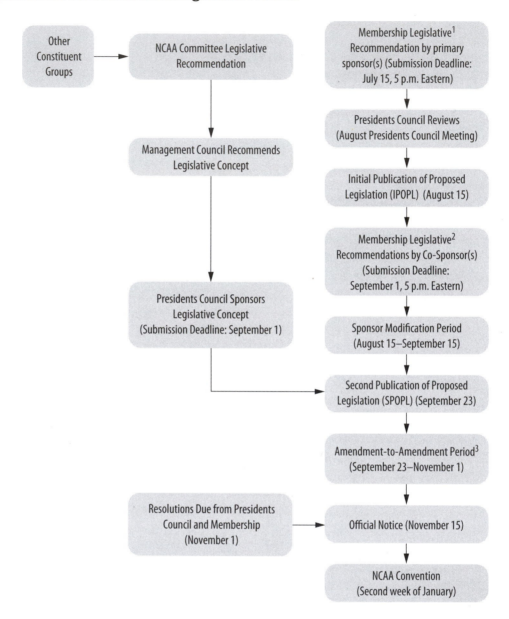

1 Per NCAA Constitution 5.3.4.1-(b) and -(c), legislative recommendations from the membership may be sponsored by 20 or more active member institutions with voting privileges or two or more voting member conferences. Per Constitution 5.3.5.3.1.1, at least one of the sponsors of a conference-sponsored amendment or at least 10 of the 20 individual institution sponsors must meet the deadline of 5 p.m. Eastern time July 15.

2 Per Constitution 5.3.5.3.1.1, the second co-sponsor of a conference-sponsored amendment or the additional 10 individual institutions must meet the deadline of 5 p.m. Eastern time September 1 or the amendment will be automatically withdrawn.

3 Per Constitution 5.3.4.2, an amendment to an amendment may be sponsored by the Management Council, Presidents Council, 20 or more active member institutions with voting privileges, or two or more voting member conferences.

Source: NCAA Division III, 2012a, p. 40.

Appendix 2.C. NCAA Division I Organizational Structure

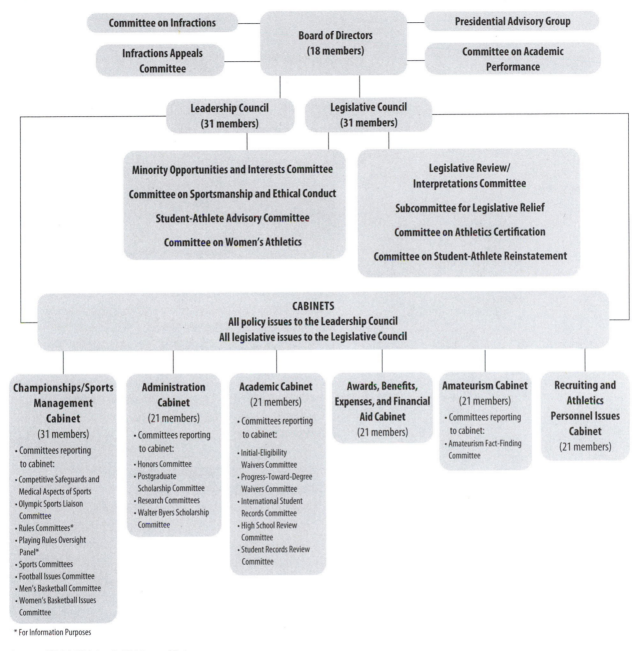

* For Information Purposes

Source: NCAA Division I, 2012a, p. 25.

Appendix 2.D. NCAA Division I Governance Structure

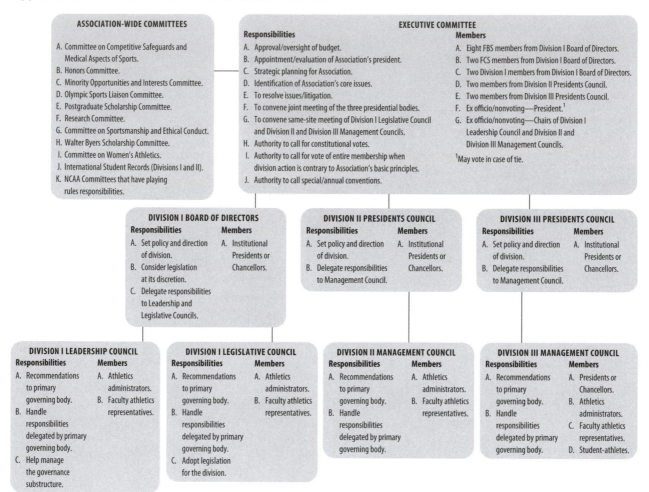

Source: NCAA Division I, 2012a, p. 26.

Appendix 2.E. NCAA Division II Organizational Structure

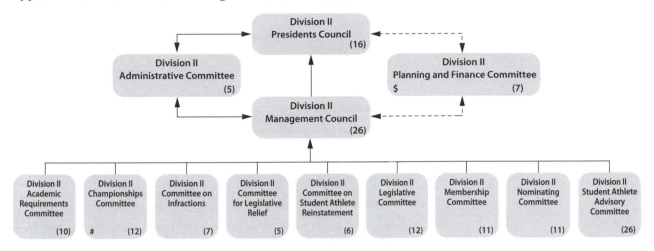

( ) The number in parentheses represents the number of individuals serving on the council or committee.

\# Division II sports committees report and make recommendations directly to the Division II Championships Committee. Such Division II sports committees include the following: Baseball; Men's Basketball; Women's Basketball; Field Hockey; Football; Men's Golf; Women's Golf; Men's Lacrosse; Women's Lacrosse; Women's Rowing; Men's Soccer; Women's Soccer; Softball; Swimming and Diving; Tennis; Track and Field; Women's Volleyball; and Wrestling.

$ The Division II Planning and Finance Committee is a group that advises the Division II Presidents Council and Management Council regarding the division's financial affairs and strategic plan.

Source: NCAA Division II, 2012a, p. 30.

Appendix 2.F. NCAA Division II Governance Structure

ASSOCIATION-WIDE COMMITTEES

A. Committee on Competitive Safeguards and Medical Aspects of Sports.
B. Honors Committee.
C. Minority Opportunities and Interests Committee.
D. Olympic Sports Liaison Committee.
E. Postgraduate Scholarship Committee.
F. Research Committee.
G. Committee on Sportsmanship and Ethical Conduct.
H. Walter Byers Scholarship Committee.
I. Committee on Women's Athletics.
J. International Student Records Committee (Divisions I and II).
K. High School Review Committee.
L. Student Records Review Committee.
M. NCAA Committees that have playing rules responsibilities.

EXECUTIVE COMMITTEE

Responsibilities
A. Approval/oversight of budget.
B. Appointment/evaluation of Association's president.
C. Strategic planning for Association.
D. Identification of Association's core issues.
E. Adopt/implement policy.
F. To resolve issues/litigation.
G. To convene joint meeting of the three presidential bodies.
H. To convene same-site meeting of groups within Division I Legislative Council and Division II and Division III Management Councils.
I. Authority to call for constitutional votes.
J. Authority to call for vote of entire membership when division action is contrary to Association's basic principles.
K. Authority to call special/annual conventions.
L. Review/coordinate catastrophic injury and professional career insuance.
M. Compile names of individuals in athletics who died in the preceding year.

Members
A. Eight Football Bowl Subdivision members from Division I Board of Directors.
B. Two Football Championship Subdivision members from Division I Board of Directors.
C. Two members from institutions that do not sponsor football from Division I Board of Directors.
D. Two members from Division II Presidents Council.
E. Two members from Division III Presidents Council.
F. Ex officio/nonvoting—NCAA President.[1]
G. Ex officio/nonvoting—Chairs of Division I Leadership Council and Division II and Division III Management Councils.

[1]May vote in case of tie.

DIVISION I BOARD OF DIRECTORS

Responsibilities
A. Set policy and direction of the division.
B. Adopt legislation for the division.
C. Delegate responsibilities to the Leadership and Legislative Councils.

Members
A. Institutional Presidents or Chancellors.

DIVISION II PRESIDENTS COUNCIL

Responsibilities
A. Set policy and direction of division.
B. Delegate responsibilities to Management Council.

Members
A. Institutional Presidents or Chancellors.

DIVISION III PRESIDENTS COUNCIL

Responsibilities
A. Set policy and direction of division.
B. Delegate responsibilities to Management Council.

Members
A. Institutional Presidents or Chancellors.

DIVISION I LEADERSHIP COUNCIL

Responsibilities
A. Recommendations to primary governing body.
B. Handle responsibilities delegated by primary governing body.

Members
A. Athletics administrators.
B. Faculty athletics representatives.

DIVISION I LEGISLATIVE COUNCIL

Responsibilities
A. Recommendations to primary governing body.
B. Handle responsibilities delegated by primary governing body.
C. Adopt legislation for the division.

Members
A. Athletics administrators.
B. Faculty athletics representatives.

DIVISION II MANAGEMENT COUNCIL

Responsibilities
A. Recommendations to primary governing body.
B. Handle responsibilities delegated by primary governing body.

Members
A. Athletics administrators.
B. Faculty athletics representatives.

DIVISION III MANAGEMENT COUNCIL

Responsibilities
A. Recommendations to primary governing body.
B. Handle responsibilities delegated by primary governing body.

Members
A. Institutional Presidents or Chancellors.
B. Athletics administrators.
C. Faculty athletics representatives.
D. Student-athletes.
E. Athletics direct reports.

Source: NCAA Division II, 2012a, p. 31.

Appendix 2.G. NCAA Division III Organizational Structure

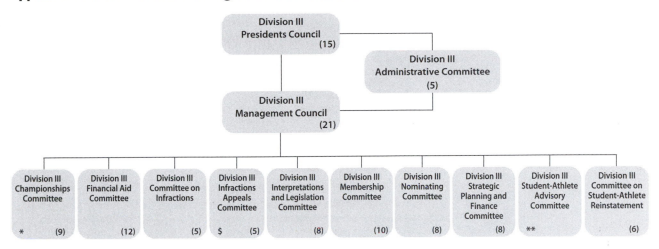

( ) The number in parentheses represents the number of individuals who will serve on the council or committee.

* All Division III sports committees report to the Division III Championships Committee. The following are common committees with playing
   rules and championships administration responsibilities: Women's Bowling, Men's and Women's Rifle, Men's and Women's Skiing, Men's
   and Women's Swimming and Diving, Men's and Women's Track and Field, Men's and Women's Water Polo and Wrestling.

** The size of the committee depends on the number of Division III conferences (see Bylaw 21.9.5.10).

$ The Division III Infractions Appeals Committee shall hear and act on an institution's appeal of the findings of major violations by the Division III Committee on Infractions.

Source: NCAA Division III, 2012a, p. 24.

Appendix 2.H. NCAA Division III Governance Structure

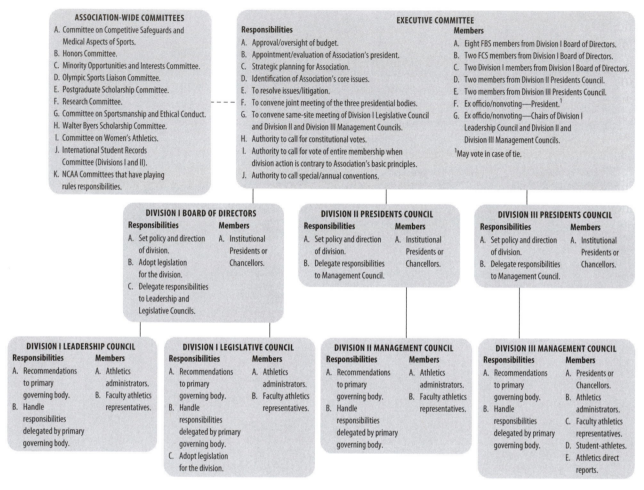

Source: NCAA Division III, 2012a, p. 25.

QUESTIONS FOR DISCUSSION

1. With Division III having the largest number of schools participating in sports programs, would it be advantageous for the NCAA to encourage Division III member institutions to move into Division II competition?

2. What might be the implications of allowing individual institutions themselves to determine the NCAA eligibility of their athletes?

3. In what ways do you believe institutions have moved away from the NCAA's idea of recruiting athletes with educational interest that match that of the institution?

References

Athletic Scholarships. (2013). *National letter of intent*. Retrieved from http://www.ncaa.org/wps/wcm /connect/nli/nli/document+library/athletic +scholarship

Biediger v. Quinnipiac University, 3 C.V. 621 (Conn. Dist. Ct. 2009).

Crowley, J. N. (2006). The NCAA's first century: In the arena. *NCAA Publications*. Indianapolis, IN: National Collegiate Athletic Association.

Hosick, M. (2014). Student-athletes will vote at every governance level. Retrieved from http://www.ncaa .org/about/resources/media-center/news/board -adopts-new-division-i-structure

Kahn, L. M. (2007). Cartel behavior and amateurism in college sports. *Journal of Economic Perspectives, 21*(1), 209–226.

Lindquist, D. C. (2006). "Locating" the nation: Football game day and American dreams in central Ohio. *Journal of American Folklore, 119*, 444–488.

Morris, P. S. (2004, November). Football in the USA: American culture and the world's game. Retrieved from http://homepage.smc.edu/morris_pete /resources/Papers-and-Presentations/football intheusa.pdf

NCAA Division I. (2012a). *2012–13 NCAA Division I manual*. Indianapolis, IN: National Collegiate Athletic Association.

———. (2012b). NCAA Division I Membership Report. Indianapolis, IN: NCAA Publications.

———. (2013). Facts & Figures. Retrieved from http:// www.ncaa.org/wps/wcm/connect/public/ncaa /divisioni/di+facts+and+figures

NCAA Division II. (2012a). *2012–13 NCAA Division II manual*. Indianapolis, IN: NCAA Publications.

———. (2012b). NCAA Division II Membership Report. Indianapolis, IN: NCAA Publications.

NCAA Division III. (2012a). *2012–13 NCAA Division III manual*. Indianapolis, IN: NCAA Publications.

———. (2012b). NCAA Division III Membership Report. Indianapolis, IN: NCAA Publications.

Pierce, P. E. (1909, January 2). Proceedings from *The Third Annual Convention of the Intercollegiate Athletic Association of the United States (IAAUS)*. New York.

Satterfield, J. W., Croft, C., Godfrey, M., & Flint, A. (2010). Academic progress reports: Leadership implications for college basketball coaches. *Academic Leadership Journal, 8*(2), 1.

Smith, R. K. (2000). A brief history of the National Collegiate Athletic Association's role in regulating intercollegiate athletics. *Marquette Sports Law Review, 9*(1), Article 5.

Watterson, J. S. (2000). *College football: History, spectacle, controversy*. Baltimore: Johns Hopkins University Press.

LEADERSHIP in INTERCOLLEGIATE ATHLETICS

Molly Ott and Evan Bates

Management literature defines a stakeholder as "any group or individual who can affect or is affected by the achievement of the firm's objectives" (Freeman, 2010, p. 25).

The stakeholder concept is a useful way to describe and understand leadership in intercollegiate athletics, because no single group claims full responsibility for the policies and practices of individual programs (Smith, 1988). Instead, a host of factions jockeys to affect (and, at times, deny accountability for) the activities and outcomes of college sports.

This chapter offers an overview of key stakeholder groups that take part in the leadership of intercollegiate athletics. Our focus is primarily at the campus level and considers the roles of presidents, athletic directors, faculty, and coaches. For each group, we begin by discussing its specific roles, interests, and priorities related to their institution's athletic programs. A central tenet of stakeholder theory is that group interests often conflict (Freeman, 2010). Coaches and faculty, for instance, may emphasize different values when making leadership decisions. Moreover, group interests can be internally heterogeneous (Wolfe & Putler, 2002). Perhaps Olympic sport coaches have distinctive priorities from those leading revenue-generating teams. For stakeholders, understanding one another's interests helps to craft strategies for working together (Freeman, 2010). For higher education practitioners, scholars, and observers of intercollegiate athletics, understanding the extent to which leaders' interests converge and diverge offers insight into the "peculiar institution" of college sports (Thelin, 1994).

Stakeholder theory also suggests that the roles of key stakeholder groups connect with how an organization operates and achieves its desired goals. A primary purpose of intercollegiate athletic departments is to support the academic, social, and physical development of athletes (Ward & Hux, 2011), and in the words of Covell and Barr (2001), "It is the idea of the student-athlete that is central to the entire intercollegiate athletic enterprise" (p. 417). Therefore, we end our discussion of each stakeholder group by considering the implications of its leadership for college athlete well-being. We conclude the chapter with a brief summary of the competing and often contradictory stakes confronting these athletic leaders (Estler & Nelson, 2005).

PRESIDENTS

Roles, Interests, and Priorities

Historically, college presidents approached intercollegiate athletics with "a strategy of avoidance and accommodation" (Thelin, 1994, p. 9), delegating program leadership and decision making to athletic directors and coaches. Yet in the 1980s, a series of gambling, drug use, point-shaving, and player payment scandals, coupled with ongoing concerns about academic integrity and finances, precipitated national efforts to make the leadership role of presidents more explicit (Smith, 2003). The Knight Foundation's Commission on Intercollegiate Athletics' "One-Plus-Three Plan" called for presidents to assume authority at the campus and national levels, especially pertaining to academic integrity, financial integrity, and the independent certification of athletic programs (Knight Commission on Intercollegiate Athletics, 1991). The Knight Commission proposal ushered in a more uniform model of presidential leadership. Today, most conferences are headed by an executive body comprised of their member institutions' presidents (Quarterman, 1998); presidential committees lead the NCAA, NAIA, and NJCAA; and the NCAA's Bylaw 2.1.1 assigns the president ultimate responsibility for intercollegiate athletics on his or her campus.

Leading a college or university is a complex undertaking, and, in reality, presidents are largely uninvolved in day-to-day athletics decisions (Duderstadt, 2003). Their contracts rarely mention responsibilities pertaining to oversight of athletics (Wolverton & Wells, 2012). Not even the contract of Rodney Erikson, who assumed the presidency of Penn State after Graham Spanier was terminated following a sex-abuse scandal centered in the football program, stated expectations explicitly pertaining to athletic leadership. Yet, as the Penn State–Spanier example illustrates, a sports scandal can take down a presidency and have major reputational and economic repercussions for the entire institution (Jones, 2013). Studies show that presidents at all levels, from the Football Bowl Subdivision (FBS)[1] to two-year colleges, are concerned about the ethics of their campus athletic programs (Bailey & Littleton, 1991; Williams & Pennington, 2008). Avoiding scandal and maintaining integrity, on the playing field as well as in the classroom, are major priorities for all college presidents.

While athletic scandals might damage an institution's standing, presidents also believe that a well-run program garners positive attention and offers reputational benefits that can be used strategically to meet broader objectives (Duderstadt, 2003). James Danko, who became Butler University's president in 2011, told an interviewer that Butler's men's basketball team success contributed to his interest in the position: "I'm a brand-builder, looking for a place that's ready to burst on the national scene. Basketball gave Butler a component that was very helpful in making that decision for me" (Schoenfeld, 2013, para. 41). As already noted, presidential contracts typically do not state responsibilities specific to athletics, although they emphasize fiscal management and fundraising more generally (Wolverton & Wells, 2012). Athletics is a primary means for presidents to maintain alumni relations and solicit donations (Hesel & Perko, 2010).

Presidents believe athletics can encourage donations, but they are also concerned about financing the enterprise in its entirety (Oriard, 2009). A 2009 study conducted by the Knight Commission indicated that most FBS presidents express pessimism about their own abilities to control costs (e.g., coaches' salaries, facilities, number of personnel employed in the athletic department), as well as ambivalence about the long-term sustainability of their programs (Hesel & Perko, 2010). More than 80% agreed there should be more transparency around operating and capital expenditures.

Implications of Presidential Leadership

Presidents attend sporting events and athletics receptions, but they rarely develop relationships with individual athletes (Duderstadt, 2003). Instead, presidents impact the athlete experience indirectly, through their work with the athletic director (AD), trustees, and other top administrators to shape the program's structure, culture, and direction. A president hoping to strengthen athletes' academic experiences might, for instance, direct the AD to design coaches' contracts to more heavily reward team classroom performance relative to win-loss records (Comeaux, 2013). At most schools, the athletic director reports directly to the president, and according to former University of Michigan president James Duderstadt (2003), "the selection and support of a strong athletic director [is] one of a president's most important tasks" (p. 61). The president and athletic director should share an understanding of the athletic program values and openly communicate about major decisions. However, on campuses where the president takes a more laissez-faire approach to athletics oversight, this leadership void will be filled by the athletic director. If the president does not clearly communicate his or her priorities, those of the athletic director will take precedence (Duderstadt, 2003).

ATHLETIC DIRECTORS

Roles, Interests, and Priorities

The AD is the top executive or manager directly responsible for the day-to-day operations of an intercollegiate program. Historically, most ADs were current or former head coaches. However, the escalating legal and financial stakes of college sports has been accompanied by a shift in AD backgrounds and skill sets. Coaching experience remains common, but universities are increasingly prioritizing business leadership and management expertise gained from academic as well as for-profit settings (Tracy & Woody, 2011).

Regardless of whether a program is a member of NCAA Division I, II, or III or another association, the range of tasks associated with being a contemporary college AD is extensive. ADs oversee program finances, often negotiating contracts with corporate sponsors or media, managing capital projects, supervising ticket sales, handling licensing deals and merchandise distribution, and cultivating alumni and booster donations. ADs typically hire coaches in consultation with the president or board of trustees; for football and men's basketball at big-time programs, this decision is especially high-stakes since hundreds of millions of dollars are associated with the performance of these teams (Belzer, 2013). In addition to the coaches, ADs supervise a staff that can number in the hundreds. Beyond their department, ADs are a key liaison to the campus community, including students, parents, faculty, and alumni, as well as with external stakeholders, including other ADs, their conference, and their association (Burton & Hagan, 2007). They also monitor program compliance with institutional, conference, and association requirements as well as state and federal laws.

Of these responsibilities, most scholars agree that the highest priority for Division I athletic directors today is to generate revenues (Duderstadt, 2003; Gerdy, 1997). One athletic administrator at a major program told Hoffman (2011), "ADs do two things. They raise money and manage people" (p. 18). ADs have a personal stake in their program's financial success, as their contracts and compensation are typically associated with program revenues (Marburger, in press). It follows that ADs will focus on sports that have the potential to generate revenue. In a study of FBS AD compensation in 2010–2011, Marburger (in press) found that earned bonuses were correlated with the football team's on-field performance but not with any other sport or with athletes' academic achievements. He concluded that "an AD has a vested incentive to devote more time and money toward building a successful football program than other alternative endeavor" (p. 11). This often leads ADs to place more emphasis on athletic success for revenue generating sports compared to nonrevenue Olympic sports (Cooper & Weight, 2011).

Athletic directors whose programs are outside of the FBS are more likely to stress educational rather than commercially oriented values. When asked by Cooper and Weight (2012) to characterize their organization's priorities, Division III ADs

Binghamton University

Binghamton University (BU), part of the State University of New York system, is consistently ranked among the top 50 public universities nationwide and known for its selectivity. BU also has a large intercollegiate athletic program. In 1995 BU's Intercollegiate Athletics Board proposed the university move from Division III to Division I. The Faculty Senate, concerned about financial costs as well as the university's academic reputation, voted against the proposal. BU president Lois DeFleur decided in favor of the transition despite the faculty opposition. To join Division I, BU provided the NCAA with a self-study report explaining its admissions process, which assigned decisions to Admissions Office professionals in consultation with the Faculty Athletic Representative and provost, assuring that only athletes likely to graduate would be admitted (Kaye, 2010).

BU became a full member of Division I in 2001–2002 and took several actions to bolster its men's basketball team. The university opened a $33.1 million arena in 2004. Three years later, the president and athletic director (AD) removed the head coach, whose seven-year record was 92-108 despite graduating 79% of his players. Soon after his replacement, Kevin Broadus, was hired, the *New York Times* published a critical article about Broadus's recruiting practices as an assistant at Georgetown University, targeting students with failing grades at unaccredited preparatory schools. Nonetheless, the president and AD expressed strong support for Coach Broadus (Kaye, 2010).

In his first year, Coach Broadus targeted recruits with weak academic records and past behavioral misconduct. BU's Admissions Office objected, but the basketball staff and AD Thirer intervened (contrary to the admissions process outlined in the self-study), noting that the recruits met the NCAA's minimum standards for admission. The FAR, who was appointed by President DeFleur on the AD's recommendation when Coach Broadus arrived at BU, also supported admitting the students (Kaye, 2010).

The next season, the *New York Times* published another article, detailing the diminished admissions standards and alleging that athletic administrators pressured faculty to modify their attendance policies and raise grades for players (Thamel, 2009). Off-court incidents involving fights, drugs/alcohol, and theft were also part of the *Times* story. Nonetheless, the team won the 2009 America East Conference (AEC) championship and qualified for the NCAA tournament. The president and AD communicated to other coaches that they expected more AEC championships from all BU teams, and discussions ensued about more flexibility to recruit talented athletes.

From the start of Coach Broadus's tenure, ADs and presidents of other AEC member schools were concerned that the BU program was having a deleterious effect on the conference's culture and reputation. In meetings with these colleagues and the conference commissioner, BU's president and AD vehemently defended their coach and his players (Kaye, 2010).

In September 2009, two basketball team members were found in possession of marijuana in separate incidents. Days later, four players used a stolen debit card to purchase merchandise. The next week, a player was arrested for selling cocaine, an incident characterized by BU insiders as the "tipping point" (Kaye, 2010). AD Thirer instructed Coach Broadus to remove the five players involved from the team.

The SUNY chancellor's office immediately ordered an independent investigation, and the fallout was substantial. President DeFleur forced AD Thirer's resignation. Coach Broadus was suspended, and his contract was bought out. The FAR was removed from her position. President DeFleur, who held her position since 1990, retired. Although the NCAA did not identify any major violations associated with the incidents, the men's basketball team struggled and, over the next four seasons, finished with records of 13-18, 8-23, 2-29, and 3-27 (Thamel, 2012). ■

identified as most essential ensuring that athletes have a valuable college experience both on and off the field. Also highly valued were academic excellence in the classroom, ensuring health and safety of athletic stakeholders, and developing a culture that contributes to the campus's broader educational mission. That is not to say that budgets or winning lack priority—fiscal responsibility ranked sixth of eleven values, and athletic excellence ranked seventh—but they are relatively less important compared to big-time programs.

Implications of Athletic Director Leadership

Several studies indicate that an AD's leadership affects how the athletic department as an organization functions (Branch, 1990; Kihl, Leberman, & Schull, 2010; Scott, 1999). In an examination of the changes in a Division I athletic department that occurred when a new AD was hired, Peachey and Burton (2012) concluded:

> When Mark, the new athletic director, arrived, he instilled a culture based on trust, accountability, communication and relationships. He also instituted a new core philosophy that focused on putting the athlete first, calling on all staff to make decisions based upon what was in the best interests of the athlete. Mark felt that while winning was important, it was secondary to creating a positive student-athlete experience. This was a conceptual shift from the prior regime, and from the dominant logic in the field of Division I intercollegiate athletics, which advocates for the importance of winning as a metric. (p. 174)

The AD shapes the culture and climate of his or her department (Schroeder, 2010) and has considerable discretion over policies and practices that can support athletes' physical, mental, and social development, such as academic support services and life-skill programs (Kamusoko & Pemberton, 2011).

FACULTY

Roles, Interests, and Priorities

Most colleges and universities operate under a model of decision making referred to as "shared governance," such that presidents and administrators work in consultation with faculty to set policies, define strategies, and allocate resources. A central governance responsibility of faculty is to uphold academic standards and values across every area of their institution, including intercollegiate athletics. Nonetheless, athletics is just one of many governance issues vying for professors' attention. A 2007 survey of faculty at 23 FBS universities indicated that most believed athletics was a relatively low priority for their campus governance groups (Lawrence, Hendricks, & Ott, 2007). Among the 11 areas identified as more pressing concerns were resources for research, graduate and undergraduate programs;

faculty salaries, benefits, and personnel policies; the financial health of their institutions; and racial/gender equity. These findings do not necessarily suggest that faculty lack interest in athletics (Lawrence & Ott, 2013), but certainly they have a myriad of issues confronting them.

Though a low overall priority, research shows that most faculty members are concerned about the academic integrity of their campus athletic programs. They also emphasize the importance of athlete academic experiences, social-moral citizenship development, and physical well-being (Trail & Chelladurai, 2000). The average professor does not assign much importance to athletic program goals that are farther removed from his or her institution's academic mission, such as team win-loss records, winning championships, athletics as a source of entertainment, or using intercollegiate programs as a means for the United States to develop its Olympic sports and compete on a global level (Trail & Chelladurai, 2000; Wolfe & Putler, 2002).

Professors serve in several formal leadership roles related to the governance of their campus intercollegiate programs. All NCAA, NAIA, and NJCAA members are required to appoint a faculty athletics representative (FAR) (Ridpath & Abney, 2012).

STAKEHOLDER PERSPECTIVE

Faculty Leadership

We asked a former Big 10 faculty athletics representative to reflect on what faculty leadership can accomplish with respect to intercollegiate athletics.

We have almost zero influence on money issues. Intercollegiate athletics is a huge financial juggernaut. I fought the twelfth football game and I tried to talk everybody, including [the university president] into voting against it. There are a dozen reasons why we shouldn't have a twelfth football game. I lost that big time, and it was for financial reasons. A football weekend here is $4 million, and the university needed the $4 million. There wasn't an easy alternate way of getting that money. Football funds our other programs here. So that was it.

Anything bearing directly on academics, like missed class time and admissions, should clearly be set by faculty, period. Those two things strike at the core of the integrity of athletics—the kids are in class, and they've got real students at that institution. Faculty should have huge influence on the number of presidential admits and the guidelines that are used for admitting athletes. At a lot of institutions that's behind the scenes, and nobody knows exactly how it happens.

Getting information to faculty on crucial issues like admissions is a tough nut to crack. Another place for sunshine that's important is athlete majors. On most campuses, faculty have no idea where the athletes are, whether they're majoring in, as

faculty think, basket weaving. I lobbied [my AD] for the transparency on majors. He didn't want to do it. The reason was not that he was afraid of the data, but he was afraid of the press. One of the greatest worries of any AD is that the media will take hold of a little nugget of information and twist it and end up getting negative headlines for a week. I said, don't worry about it; we need to have it out there. There's more to gain by sun shining on this than to have faculty spreading rumors about where we're putting our athletes. I've been reporting to the faculty senate on athlete majors for six years now, and it's gone fine. Transparency over academics is a big issue that's important to faculty. ■

The full range of FAR responsibilities varies from campus to campus, but NCAA FARs report that the largest proportion of their time is spent on academic issues, including monitoring and certifying athlete eligibility as set by association, conference, and institutional requirements, as well as providing counsel when athletes experience academic problems (Fulks, 2008). FARs also assist with compliance activities, such as investigating rules violations, conducting coaches' certifications, and executing waivers and appeals.

The most prominent faculty leadership position is the FAR, but other professors are also involved in athletics governance. Though not required by the NCAA, most institutions have a campus athletics board comprising faculty, administrators, students, and alumni that advise the athletic director or president. The NCAA (2012) mandates that if an athletics board exists, most of its members must be academic administrators and faculty. Some boards are a standing committee of the institution's faculty senate, while other campuses have a separate subcommittee of their faculty senate dedicated to athletics (Gerdy, 1997). Campus athletic boards and faculty senates often monitor data related to athlete admissions, academic progress, and graduation and review institutional policies pertaining to the athlete experience such as practice and travel schedules (Nichols, Corrigan, & Hardin, 2011).

The role of faculty leadership in athletics is primarily advisory rather than in a direct decision-making capacity (Clotfelter, 2011; Duderstadt, 2003). A 2010 survey by the Coalition on Intercollegiate Athletics found that when major athletics decisions are made (e.g., hiring of key personnel, changes in sports, initiation of capital projects), faculty senate leaders are consulted at only 19% of FBS universities (Nichols et al., 2011). Approximately half of the schools include campus athletics boards in such conversations, while 68% confer with the FAR. And while research suggests that FARs generally feel satisfied with their ability to ensure academic integrity and support athletes on their campuses (Fulks, 2008), some faculty in campus leadership positions have been criticized for being overly permissive to the demands of athletic administrators and coaches who have little regard for academics (Lawrence et al., 2007).

Implications of Faculty Leadership

Little research exists examining college athlete relationships with faculty in the formal governance roles just described (i.e., FARs, athletics boards, senate committees), but realistically, each program has only one or sometimes two FARs but often hundreds of athletes. For most athletes, their most frequent contact with professors comes through their courses. While some perceive that their instructors unfairly stereotype them on their status as athletes (Simons, Bosworth, Fujita, & Jensen, 2007), several studies demonstrate that most are satisfied with their interactions with faculty (Kamusoko & Pemberton, 2011; Williams, Colles, & Allen, 2010). College athletes typically identify their coaches and professional academic advisors as the strongest influences on their academic experiences (Bell, 2009), but they also credit faculty for encouraging their academic aspirations and offering career advice (Martin, Harrison, & Bukstein, 2010). These relationships may translate directly into academic success. Research by Harrison, Comeaux, and Plecha (2006), Comeaux and Harrison (2006), and Comeaux and Harrison (2007) demonstrates that athletes whose professors challenged them intellectually, encouraged graduate school, and supported their professional goals have higher GPAs during college compared to athletes whose interactions with faculty are minimal.

COACHES

Roles, Interests, and Priorities

Most observers and scholars agree that college coaches' top priority is to win games (Gerdy, 1997). Coaches are more likely to be dismissed when their teams lose (Holmes, 2011; Mixon & Trevino, 2004), and the terms set out in their contracts most heavily reward teams' on-field performance relative to other criteria, such as academic performance, athlete behavior, recruit quality, revenue performance, or athlete satisfaction (Cunningham & Dixon, 2003; Putler & Wolfe, 1999; Wilson & Burke, 2013). For example, Wilson and Burke (2013) observed that 42 out of 45 Division I men's basketball coaches had incentive clauses for athletic performance, while only 28 had academic-related incentive clauses. College athletes are often aware of this reward structure and its likely effect on their coaches' priorities. An athlete from the University of California, Berkeley told Martin, Harrison, and Bukstein (2010), Let's be real. These coaches are here to win football games. They get handshakes for making sure that we graduate, but get paid millions of dollars for having winning seasons. It's all about the money" (p. 288). Even outside of revenue generating sports at major programs, coaches are pressured to succeed on the playing field. In a case study of a private Division II school's values, Nite (2012) quotes the head women's basketball coach, "I mean, it comes down to it (wins and losses) and you know, that is my job. Our job is to win games" (p. 9).

Yet to succeed on the playing field, college coaches must also encourage athletes' academic success. Competitive associations establish baseline levels of the team members' progress toward their degrees, and when goals are not met, penalties may include reduced practice hours, competition penalties, coaching suspensions, financial aid reductions, or other membership restrictions. Individual athletes who do not meet minimum grade point average or course passage rates may be declared ineligible to play. Such sanctions could easily impair a team's on-field performance, so to ensure their teams make adequate academic progress, coaches may monitor class attendance and study halls, request progress reports from faculty, and advise athletes on academic major and course choices (Adler & Adler, 1991). Studies show that coaches also use academics strategically as a recruiting tool that especially appeals to parents (Bell, 2009; Martin et al., 2010; Ridpath, 2006).

Many coaches recognize the value of earning a college degree for their athletes' longer-term success. In response to a Knight Commission poll, 93% of NCAA Division I coaches said "making sure student-athletes get an education" should be the primary goal of a big-time athletic program (Lou Harris & Associates, 1990). This message resonates with the majority of athletes. The NCAA's 2010 SCORE survey indicated that 69% of athletes believed their coaches identified graduation as a high priority (Brown, 2011). A study of Division I football players' academic experiences by Bell (2009) indicated that coaches were very honest with athletes about their chances of playing professionally and emphasized the importance of degree completion in preparing most for a post-college career.

Implications of Coaches' Leadership

College athletes assign a high priority to having sound relationships with their coaches (Wang, Chen, & Ji, 2004). According to the NCAA's 2010 GOALS survey of almost 20,000 athletes, more than half chose to attend their institution primarily because of the head coach for their sport (Petr, Paskus, & Miranda, 2011). Coaches continue to be an immense presence throughout the college experience; NCAA Division I, II, and III athletes report spending between 29 to 43 hours per week on athletic activities in-season (Petr et al., 2011). For many athletes, this dedication results in the development of meaningful relationships with their coaches. Research shows that coaches' leadership is associated with athletes' satisfaction with their experiences in their sport (Aoyagi, Cox & McGuire, 2008). Moreover, athletes who characterize their coaches in positive terms report having higher levels of academic success (Menon, Loya, & Rankin, 2012).

Not all coaches have a positive impact on their athletes' well-being. In the 2010 NCAA GOALS survey, athletes were asked to name the one thing that they would most like to change about their collegiate experience, and 11% of respondents identified some aspect related to coaching (Petr et al., 2011). College athletes describe poor coaches in terms of sport-related knowledge, that is, an inability to impart mental, tactical, or technical skills, as well as broader failures to provide emotional support, effectively impart "life lessons," and role-model strong character (Gearity, 2011, 2012). In response, athletes feel that their cognitive skills are inhibited (e.g., they are distracted, have self-doubts, lack motivation), and team dynamics may suffer (Gearity & Murray, 2011). Also, when coaches are overly critical or place intense pressure on their teams to perform, athletes have a higher likelihood of burning out (Gould & Whitley, 2009).

Even for those athletes who report a positive relationship with their coaches, some observers express concern that coaches' roles can become outsized. In their four-year study of a Division I men's basketball team, Adler and Adler (1991) described how coaches not only controlled players' development as athletes but also exerted a strong influence over their academic and social activities, priorities, and relationships, ultimately narrowing their college experience to be primarily athletic-focused.

Moreover, in the NCAA Divisions I and II, where scholarships are awarded for athletic ability, coaches decide on an annual basis to renew or revoke their athletes' aid. Some critics opine this gives coaches too much power, compelling athletes to participate in "optional" off-season workouts or team-related tasks (Sperber, 2000). Gerdy (2006) advises that while coaches are naturally an influential presence in their college experience, athletes should be encouraged to seek additional counsel outside the athletic department from family, friends, and faculty.

CONCLUSION

Leading an intercollegiate athletic program involves multiple stakeholder groups with sometimes competing interests. Presidents are primarily interested in how athletics can contribute to institutional objectives, namely its potential to enhance the school's overall reputation and cultivate donors. Yet presidents also are concerned that a poorly run athletic program can be reputationally and financially costly. Athletic directors, especially those managing major programs, are focused on generating revenues to support the enterprise. At smaller institutions, ADs place relatively stronger emphasis on educational values and the athlete experience. The top priority for coaches at all levels is to achieve success on the playing field, though most also support their players' academic success and stress the importance of graduation. Faculty members are interested chiefly in ensuring the academic integrity of their institutions and supporting students' educational experiences. While there are many instances where the leadership of presidents, athletic directors, coaches, and faculty has enhanced athletes' well-being, this is not always the case. College sports today face many challenges, not the least of which is how to negotiate the diverging priorities and interests of campus leadership groups.

QUESTIONS FOR DISCUSSION

1. In the case of intercollegiate athletics, should each of the leadership stakeholders discussed in this chapter have equal consideration, or are there instances where certain groups should have more authority or importance than others?

2. Research suggests that the reward system for intercollegiate athletic leaders has a bearing on their priorities. How might the current structure be modified to more strongly emphasize college athlete well-being?

3. *New York Times* columnist Joe Nocera (2013) argues that "big-time college sports is a serious business that has to be managed by business executives who have an expertise in sports management" (p. A23). Do you agree with this assertion?

Note

1. Football Bowl Subdivision (FBS) is a designation that applies to Division I (DI) schools with varsity intercollegiate football programs competing nationally for an opportunity to participate in a series of postseason bowl games. FBS schools must meet specific NCAA regulations regarding athlete scholarships and home football game attendance (NCAA, 2012).

References

Adler, P., & Adler, P. (1991). *Backboards and blackboard: Colleges and role engulfment*. New York: Columbia University Press.

Aoyagi, M., Cox, R., & McGuire, R. (2008). Organizational citizenship behavior in sport: Relationships with leadership, team cohesion, and athlete satisfaction. *Journal of Applied Sport Psychology, 20*(1), 25–41.

Bailey, W., & Littleton, T. (1991). *Athletics and academe: An anatomy of abuses and a prescription for reform*. New York: ACE.

Bell, L. (2009). Examining academic role-set influence on the student-athlete experience. *Journal of Issues in Intercollegiate Athletics*, Special Issue, 9(4), 19–41.

Belzer, J. (2013, April 30). College athletics leadership and the rigor to succeed. *Forbes*. Retrieved from http://www.forbes.com/sites/jasonbelzer/2013/04/30/college-athletics-leadership-and-the-rigor-to-succeed-2/

Branch, D. D. (1990). Athletic director leader behavior as a predictor of intercollegiate athletic organizational effectiveness. *Journal of Sport Management, 4*(2), 161–173.

Brown, G. (2011, January 13). Second GOALS study emphasizes coach influence. *NCAA News*. Retrieved from http://www.ncaa.org/wps/wcm/connect/public/NCAA/Resources/Latest+News/2011/January/Second+GOALS+study+emphasizes+coach+influence

Burton, L., & Hagan, E. (2007). Examination of job descriptions in intercollegiate athletic administration: Application of gender typing of managerial subroles. *SMART Journal, 5*(1), 84–95.

Clotfelter, C. (2011). *Big-time sports in American universities*. New York: Cambridge University Press.

Comeaux, E. (2013). Rethinking academic reform and encouraging organizational innovation: Implications for stakeholder management in college sports. *Innovative Higher Education, 38*, 281–293.

Comeaux, E., & Harrison, C. (2006). Gender, sport, and higher education: The impact of student-faculty interactions on academic achievement. *Academic Athletic Journal, 19*(1), 38–55.

———. (2007). Faculty and male student-athletes in American higher education: Racial differences in the environmental predictors of academic achievement. *Race, Ethnicity, and Education, 10*, 199–214.

Cooper, C., & Weight, E. (2011). Investigating NCAA administrator values in NCAA division I athletic departments. *Journal of Issues in Intercollegiate Athletics, 4*, 74–89.

———. (2012). Maximizing organizational effectiveness: NCAA division III administrator core values and departmental culturization. *Journal of Issues in Intercollegiate Athletics, 5*, 339–353.

Covell, D., & Barr, C. (2001). The ties that bind: Presidential involvement with the development of NCAA division I initial eligibility legislation. *Journal of Higher Education, 72*, 414–452.

Cunningham, G., & Dixon, M. (2003). New perspectives concerning performance appraisals of intercollegiate coaches. *Quest, 55*, 177–192.

Duderstadt, J. (2003). *Intercollegiate athletics and the American university: A university president's perspective*. Ann Arbor: University of Michigan Press.

Estler, S., & Nelson, L. (2005). Who calls the shots? Sports and university leadership, culture, and decision making. *ASHE Higher Education Report, 30*(5). Hoboken, NJ: John Wiley & Sons.

Freeman, R. (2010). *Strategic management: A stakeholder approach*. New York: Cambridge University Press.

Fulks, D. (2008). *The faculty athletics representative: A survey of the membership*. Retrieved from www.farawebsite.org/files/FARA2008SurveyReport.pdf

Gearity, B. (2011). Poor teaching by the coach: A phenomenological description from athletes' experiences of poor coaching. *Physical Education & Sport Pedagogy, 17*(1), 79–96.

———. (2012). Coach as unfair and uncaring: A phenomenological study of ethics in the coach-athlete dyad. *Journal for the Study of Sports and Athletes in Education, 6*(2), 173–200.

Gearity, B., & Murray, M. (2011). Athletes' experiences of the psychological effects of poor coaching. *Psychology of Sport and Exercise, 12*(3), 213–221.

Gerdy, J. (1997). *The successful college athletic program: The new standard.* Phoenix, AZ: Oryx Press.

———. (2006). *Air ball: American education's failed experiment with elite athletics.* Jackson: University Press of Mississippi.

Gould, D., & Whitley, M. (2009). Sources and consequences of athletic burnout among college athletes. *Journal of Intercollegiate Sports, 2,* 16–30.

Harrison, C. K., Comeaux, E., & Plecha, M. (2006). Faculty and male football and basketball players on university campuses: An empirical investigation of the "intellectual" as mentor to the student athlete. *Research Quarterly for Exercise and Sport, 77*(2), 277–284.

Hesel, R., & Perko, A. (2010). A sustainable model? University presidents assess the costs and financing of intercollegiate athletics. *Journal of Intercollegiate Sport, 3,* 32–50.

Hoffman, J. (2011). The old boys network. *Journal for the Study of Sports and Athletes in Education, 5*(1), 9–28.

Holmes, P. (2011). Win or go home: Why college football coaches get fired. *Journal of Sports Economics, 12*(2), 157–178.

Jones, W. (2013). Does athletic scandal influence university operational health? A quantitative case study of Baylor University. *Journal of Issues in Intercollegiate Athletics*, Special Issue, 41–57.

Kamusoko, S., & Pemberton, C. (2011). Student-athlete well-being and higher education persistence. *Journal of Issues in Intercollegiate Athletics, 4,* 207–235.

Kaye, J. (2010, February 11). Report to the board of trustees of the State University of New York. Retrieved from www.suny.edu/Files/sunynewsFiles/Pdf/KayeReport.PDF

Kihl, L., Leberman, S., & Schull, V. (2010). Stakeholder constructions of leadership in intercollegiate athletics. *European Sport Management Quarterly, 10*(2), 241–275.

Knight Commission on Intercollegiate Athletics. (1991). *Keeping faith with the student-athlete: A new model for intercollegiate athletics.* Miami, FL: John L. & James S. Knight Foundation.

Lawrence, J., Hendricks, L., & Ott, M. (2007). *Faculty perceptions of intercollegiate athletics: A national study of faculty at NCAA Division I football bowl subdivision institutions.* Ann Arbor: University of Michigan Center for the Study of Higher & Postsecondary Education.

Lawrence, J., & Ott, M. (2013). Faculty perceptions of organizational politics. *Review of Higher Education, 36*(2), 145–178.

Lou Harris & Associates. (1990). *Survey conducted for the Knight Foundation Commission on Intercollegiate Athletics.* New York: Lou Harris & Associates.

Marburger, D. (in press). How are athletic directors rewarded in the NCAA football bowl subdivision? *Journal of Sports Economics.*

Martin, B., Harrison, C., & Bukstein, S. (2010). "It takes a village" for African American male scholar-athletes. *Journal for the Study of Sports and Athletes in Education, 4,* 277–296.

Menon, I., Loya, K., & Rankin, S. (2012). *The influence of climate and athletic personnel on the academic success of student-athletes in high profile sports.* Paper presented at the annual meeting of the American Educational Research Association, ancouver, BC.

Mixon, F., & Trevino, L. (2004). How race affects dismissals of college football coaches. *Journal of Labor Research, 25,* 645–656.

National Collegiate Athletic Association. (2012). *2012–13 NCAA Division I manual.* Indianapolis, IN: National Collegiate Athletic Association.

Nichols, J., Corrigan, T., & Hardin, M. (2011). Integration of athletics and academics: Survey of best practices at FBS schools. *Journal of Intercollegiate Sport, 4,* 107–120.

Nite, C. (2012). Challenges for supporting students-athlete development: Perspectives from an NCAA division II athletic department. *Journal of Issues in Intercollegiate Athletics, 5,* 1–14.

Nocera, J. (2013, June 6). The way to run college sports. *New York Times*, p. A23. Retrieved from http://www.nytimes.com/2013/06/06/opinion/nocera-the-way-to-run-college-sports.html?_r=1&

Oriard, M. (2009). *Bowled over: Big-time college football from the sixties to the BCS era.* Chapel Hill: University of North Carolina Press.

Peachey, J., & Burton, L. (2012). Transactional or transformational leaders in intercollegiate athletics? Examining the influence of leader gender and subordinate gender on evaluation of leaders during organizational culture change. *International Journal of Sport Management, 13*(2), 115–142.

Petr, T., Paskus, T., & Miranda, M. (2011, January 13). *Examining the student-athlete experience through the*

NCAA GOALS and SCORE studies. Paper presented at the NCAA Convention, San Antonio, Texas.

Putler, D., & Wolfe, R. (1999). Perceptions of intercollegiate athletic programs: Priorities and tradeoffs. *Sociology of Sport Journal, 16*, 301–325.

Quarterman, J. (1998). An assessment of the perception of management and leadership skills by intercollegiate athletics conference commissioners. *Journal of Sport Management, 12*, 146–164.

Ridpath, B. (2006). College athletes' perceptions of the emphasis their coaches place on academic progress and graduation. *SMART Journal, 3*(1), 14–40.

Ridpath, B., & Abney, R. (2012). Governance of intercollegiate athletics and recreation. In G. McClellan, C. King, & D. Rockey (Eds.), *The handbook of college athletics and recreation administration* (pp. 127–152). Hoboken, NJ: John Wiley & Sons.

Schoenfeld, B. (2013, March 28). The Butler way: Can the bulldogs maintain their soul? Retrieved from http://www.roopstigo.com/reader/the-butler -way-can-the-bulldogs-maintain-their-soul/

Schroeder, P. J. (2010). Changing team culture: The perspectives of ten successful head coaches. *Journal of Sport Behavior, 33*(1), 63–88.

Scott, D. (1997). Managing organizational culture in intercollegiate athletic organizations. *Quest, 49*, 403–415.

Simons, H., Bosworth, C., Fujita, S., & Jensen, M. (2007). The athlete stigma in higher education. *College Student Journal, 41*(2), 251–273.

Smith, R. (1988). Reforming intercollegiate athletics: A critique of the Presidents Commission's role in the NCAA's sixth special convention. *North Dakota Law Review, 64*, 423–427.

———. (2003). Increasing presidential accountability in big-time intercollegiate athletics. *Moorad Sports Law Journal, 10*(2), 3. Retrieved from http://digital commons.law.villanova.edu/mslj/vol10/iss2/3

Sperber, M. (2000). *Beer and circus: How big-time college sports is crippling undergraduate education*. New York: Henry Holt.

Thamel, P. (2009, February 21). At Binghamton, division I move brings recognition and regret. *New York Times*. Retrieved from http://www.nytimes.com/2009/02/22 /sports/ncaabasketball/22binghamton.html ?pagewanted=all&_r=0

———. (2012, February 29). After a costly scandal, Binghamton begins rebuilding. *New York Times*. Retrieved from http://www.nytimes.com /2012/03/01/sports/ncaabasketball/after-a -costly-scandal-binghamton-begins-rebuilding .html?pagewanted=all&_r=0

Thelin, J. (1994). *Games colleges play: Scandal and reform in intercollegiate athletics*. Baltimore: Johns Hopkins University Press.

Tracy, M., & Woody, K. (2011, June 15). Are colleges seeking athletic directors with business backgrounds? Retrieved from http://collegesports businessnews.com/issue/june-2011/article/are -colleges-seeking-athletic-directors-with -business-backgrounds

Trail, G., & Chelladurai, P. (2000). Perceptions of goals and processes of intercollegiate athletics: A case study. *Journal of Sport Management, 14*, 154–178.

Wang, J., Chen, L., & Ji, J. (2004). Athletes' perceptions on coaches' behaviors and competitive situations at collegiate level. *International Sports Journal, 8*(2), 1–14.

Ward, R., & Hux, R. (2011). Intercollegiate athletic purposes expressed in mission statements: A content analysis. *Journal for the Study of Sports and Athletes in Education, 5*(2), 177–200.

Williams, J., Colles, C., & Allen, K. (2010). Division III athletes: Perceptions of faculty interactions and academic support services. *Journal of Issues in Intercollegiate Athletics, 3*, 211–233.

Williams, M. R., Byrd, L., & Pennington, K. (2008). Intercollegiate athletics at the community college. *Community College Journal of Research and Practice, 32*(4–6), 453–461.

Wilson, M., & Burke, K. (2013). NCAA division I men's basketball coaching contracts: A comparative analysis of incentives for athletic and academic team performance between 2009 and 2012. *Journal of Issues in Intercollegiate Athletics, 6*, 81–95.

Wolfe, R., & Putler, D. (2002). How tight are the ties that bind stakeholder groups? *Organization Science, 13*(1), 64–80.

Wolverton, B., & Wells, A. (2012, September 3). Who's in charge of sports? Maybe not the president. Retrieved from http://chronicle.com/article/Whos-in-Charge -of-Sports-/134046/

ETHICAL ISSUES in INTERCOLLEGIATE ATHLETICS

Purpose Achieved or Challenged?

Angela Lumpkin

The National Collegiate Athletic Association's (NCAA) purpose is "to maintain intercollegiate athletics as an integral part of the educational program and the athlete as an integral part of the student body and, by so doing, retain a clear line of demarcation between intercollegiate athletics and professional sports" (NCAA, 2012–2013, p. 1). Among its essential principles have been institutional control and responsibility, student-athlete welfare, sportsmanship and ethical conduct, sound academic standards, rules compliance, amateurism, eligibility, and financial aid (NCAA, 2012–2013). This chapter focuses on ethical issues associated with and potentially threatening these principles.

Unlike in other countries, higher education in the United States sponsors intercollegiate sports teams, contending that athletic competitions enhanced students' educational experiences. Self-discipline, teamwork, responsibility, commitment, learning how to lead and follow, character development, and learning life lessons are values benefiting college athletes touted by NCAA representatives, college presidents, athletic administrators, and coaches. However, while most people believe athletes' collegiate experiences are enriched through sports competitions, others question whether ethical misconduct and misplaced priorities threatened positive outcomes.

Numerous justifications have been advanced for why colleges should sponsor competitive sports teams. Toma (1999) states that high-profile intercollegiate athletics serve as effective tools for external relations by helping shape favorable institutional identities and status. Marquee football and men's basketball teams, he suggests, garner support from major donors and annual fund contributors, gain increased legislative appropriations, and attract prospective students. Increased state appropriations, claim Alexander and Kern (2010), accrue primarily to institutions with winning football or men's basketball teams competing at the highest competitive level.

Martinez, Stinson, Kang, and Jubenville (2010) in their meta-analysis of 30 years of empirical studies about intercollegiate athletics report a small, but significant, influence on institutional fundraising, especially relative to success in football in institutions competing at the highest level. Alexander and Kern (2010) agree with Martinez et al. (2010) that success in big-time college sports increases public awareness, affords priceless advertising, and enhances institutional prestige while providing opportunities for gaining financial support from donors and politicians. Intercollegiate athletics, Desrochers (2013) adds, "provide nonfinancial benefits that are important to institutions, such as campus spirit, name recognition, and reputation" (p. 2). But, she cautions, the benefits associated with applications, enrollments, or fundraising are modest and often short-lived bonuses linked with championship seasons. Frank (2004) emphasizes that his examination of empirical literature revealed little, if any, systematic impact on academic quality of freshmen; and, if alumni giving and success in big-time college athletics were related, this occurred in only a few institutions with small and transitory effects. Countering these positives of whatever magnitude, numerous unethical actions associated with college sports threaten their popularity and status.

University presidents question whether intercollegiate athletics distort the ideal of sports for sports' sake and warp the values of the academy (NCAA, 2006). Numerous ethical concerns and NCAA rule violations citing lack of institutional control in recent years, such as at the University of Southern California, University of Miami, Ohio State University, University of North Carolina, Rutgers University, Pennsylvania State University, and Oklahoma State University, have elicited public ire and implicated governing boards and presidents for not exercising responsible fiduciary and operational oversight of intercollegiate athletic programs.

Reports in 2009 and 2012 issued by the Association of Governing Boards of Universities and Colleges (AGB) call for establishment and maintenance of higher standards of integrity, trust, and accountability. Specifically the AGB insists on athletic department congruence with each institution's academic mission and values, academic achievement of athletes, and compliance with national, conference, and institutional policies and rules. Green, Jaschik, and Lederman (2012) surveyed college presidents and reported their agreement or disagreement with several key statements dealing with intercollegiate athletics. Across all three NCAA divisions, 75% agreed or strongly agreed with this statement: "Colleges and universities spend way too much money on intercollegiate athletic programs." More than two-thirds (67.8%) agreed/strongly agreed with "The athletic scandals of the past year have hurt the reputation of all higher education, not just the institutions involved." Nearly half (48.2%) agreed/strongly agreed with this statement: "Scandals are inevitable in big-time college athletics." Possibly most disconcerting was only 13.1% agreed or strongly agreed with "The presidents of big-time athletic programs are in control of their programs" (p. 15).

Calls for greater institutional control and integrity suggest all is not well with intercollegiate athletics. Espoused values in too many cases have been replaced by ethical misconduct driven by incessant quests for victories and revenues. For this chapter's examination of ethical issues in intercollegiate athletics, I selected four provocative areas for investigation. First, and possibly most controversial, is whether the NCAA's staunch adherence to amateurism is essential to the enterprise of college sports? Second, inextricably linked with amateurism has been the NCAA's insistence upon referring to players as *student-athletes*, even though this label seems especially inane and archaic given the number of hours dedicated by athletes to their sports. Third, even though learning and academic success remain higher education's mission, intercollegiate athletics may have supplanted an educational model with a business model leading to ethical misconduct and erosion in academic achievement. Fourth, increased commercialization due to the millions of dollars associated with college sports, along with possible financial exploitation of football and men's basketball players, may characterize an unsustainable arms race and winning-at-any-cost ethos destructive to the values of everyone involved. Ten recommendations are provided in the final section of this chapter to offer hope for eliminating most of the unethical conduct currently negatively affecting the moral values potentially associated with intercollegiate athletics.

HYPOCRISY OF AMATEURISM?

The NCAA's bedrock principle of amateurism was founded on the British upper-class belief that amateurs who played sports for enjoyment should not compete against lower-class opponents who were paid to play. This nineteenth-century perspective held inviolate that receiving monetary compensation tainted sports. Reflecting this British amateur ideal, the NCAA's first definition of amateurism in 1916 described an amateur as "one who participates in competitive physical sports only for the pleasure, and the physical, mental, moral and social benefits derived therefrom" (Zimbalist & Sack, 2013, p. 3). In describing amateur sports, Davis (1994) claims college athletes are admired for exhibiting values like selflessness, devotion, sacrifice, and purity similar to how upper-class British males were viewed. Yet, given the money associated with college sports played at the highest competitive level, Davis concludes amateurism is outdated and vacuous. Adding to this, Branch (2011), in his riveting exposé of the myth of amateurism in college sports, emphasizes that "it's that two of the noble principles on which the NCAA justifies its existence — 'amateurism' and the 'student-athlete' — are cynical hoaxes, legalistic confections propagated by the universities so they can exploit the skills and fame of young athletes" (p. 82). Yet, the NCAA's principle of amateurism remains unequivocal:

Building Relationships with the Parents of College Football and Men's Basketball Players

Sometimes during the telecast of college football or men's basketball games the camera shows parents cheering for their sons. Most other parents, however, are not present even though many would like to be but simply could not afford it. While the NCAA allows players to receive four tickets (actually names on a list since players in the past have sold their tickets, which violated NCAA rules) to home games, it precludes colleges from paying the travel expenses of parents to watch their sons play. This case study describes a creative, yet indirect, way to reward football and men's basketball players by suggesting how athletic departments could be allowed to provide all-expenses-paid trips for parents (or two adult relatives of his choice) for every football and men's basketball player to one regular season home and one regular season away game.

Parents of college football and men's basketball players may not have attended college or played college sports, which means they do not fully understand or appreciate the experiences of their sons. This includes the time commitments for practices, travel, and competitions, academic expectations, and physical toll of being a college athlete. Spending a day on campus, attending a home game, traveling to an away game, and spending time with sons and their teammates could help bridge this gap. Additionally, having opportunities to attend two of their sons' games would help remunerate athletes without violating the NCAA's principle of amateurism.

Every football and men's basketball player would be allowed to invite his parents to choose one home and one away game to attend and provide these dates to his director of football or basketball operations. For home games, parents would be provided transportation to and from their homes to the airport, hotel, or campus, invited to pregame and postgame team meals, and provided a team jersey with his or her son's number and name. On the field or court prior to home games, parents would have photographs taken with their sons, which would be framed and given to them. For away games, parents would be invited to campus to travel on the bus or airplane with the team, ride to and from locations with the team, be housed at the team hotel, eat meals with sons and their teammates, and have tickets to the game. ■

Student-athletes shall be amateurs in an intercollegiate sport, and their participation should be motivated primarily by education and by the physical, mental and social benefits to be derived. Student participation in intercollegiate athletics is an avocation, and student-athletes should be protected from exploitation by professional and commercial enterprises. (NCAA, 2012–2013, p. 4)

Not so, claims Zimbalist and Sack (2013), who conclude that the NCAA maintains an "idiosyncratic, changing, frequently arbitrary, and often illogical definition of amateurism" (p. 7). Emphatically, Branch (2011) questions the claim made by many fans that paying athletes would destroy the "integrity and appeal of college sports" (p. 83). Amateurism, Davis (1995) contends, "perpetuates a false model which fails to comport with the present day social, economic and legal realities of intercollegiate athletics" (p. 621).

Unable to eliminate payments to athletes, the NCAA in 1956 approved awarding four-year grants-in-aid based on athletic ability to try to limit payments to only tuition, fees, room, and board (Oriard, 2009). Simultaneously, the NCAA proclaimed grants-in-aid did not constitute "pay for play." Also, to shelter institutions from potential workers' compensation claims, the NCAA mandated four-year grants-in-aid that could not be reduced or canceled on the basis of an athlete's contribution to team success, injury, or decision not to participate (Zimbalist & Sack, 2013). These caveats disappeared at the 1973 NCAA convention, when member institutions effectively cast aside this model of amateurism by replacing four-year with one-year grants-in-aid, a de facto change from *student-athlete* to *athlete-student*.

The issue became not whether athletes should be paid because they were already receiving pay through grants-in-aid, albeit within the constraints imposed by the NCAA. Rather, the issue was how much athletes should be compensated for their athletic performances. Limitations of what athletes received based on their athletic talents treated them differently than students who were musicians, artists, or photographers who could profit from their talents. Persistently, though, the NCAA adhered to arguably a self-serving definition of amateurism and even added a public relations masterpiece.

MYTH OF THE STUDENT-ATHLETE?

When the NCAA initially permitted awarding grants-in-aid, Executive Director Walter Byers invented the label *student-athlete* and firmly planted it in the English lexicon through the media's extensive use of this label at his insistence. "We crafted the term student-athlete, and soon it was embedded in all NCAA rules and interpretations as a mandated substitute for such words as players and athletes" (Byers, 1995, p. 69). Staurowsky and Sack (2005) expose this calculated ploy for what it was:

> The term student-athlete did not emerge because it was somehow judged to be more precise than the phrase college athlete or because athletes themselves preferred the term . . . When viewed in its historical context, the term student-athlete discloses a great deal about the politics of the NCAA and raises important questions about the uncritical use of ideologically biased terms. (p. 105)

Instead of being student-athletes, Staurowsky and Sack (2005) illustrate how they are athletes first and foremost: the one-year grant-in-aid limitation, which renders athletes mostly powerless and voiceless; coaches' expectations that athletes who want playing time would engage in workouts exceeding NCAA's maximums in number of hours spent in coach-directed activities (i.e., 4 hours per day and 20 hours per week with one day off per week during the season; maximum of 8 hours per week in the off-season); requirements to repeatedly miss classes for practices, competitions, and associated travel; and limited likelihood of graduating. The twin pillars of amateurism and the label student-athlete have undergirded the tenuous foundation upon which the NCAA-governed intercollegiate athletes have operated for more than a century. In the midst of media exposés about unethical conduct smearing the integrity of higher education, reformers like Branch (2011) have called for elimination of the hypocrisy of these two hoaxes.

In addition to the ethical issues associated with amateurism and the public relations label of student-athlete, other questionably ethical practices have included admission of many high profile athletes who subsequently failed to graduate and clustering of athletes into majors and courses used to keep them eligible.

ACADEMIC INTEGRITY OR ACADEMIC EXPLOITATION?

The potential for exploitation began early when prospective athletes who did not meet minimum academic requirements became special admits, thus potentially setting them up to fail academically. Once admitted, many of these athletes were enrolled in courses taught by athlete-friendly instructors and clustered in less demanding majors (Donnor, 2005). In response to criticisms about the absence of academic standards, the NCAA over the years passed several academic minima as admission requirements for prospective athletes. Additionally, to try to keep athletes and academic support personnel from focusing on eligibility, the NCAA required athletes

Faculty Athletics Representative's Perspective

Dr. Susan M. Stagg-Williams, a professor of chemical and petroleum engineering, serves as faculty athletics representative (FAR) for the University of Kansas (KU). Her primary responsibilities focus on promoting athlete well-being, fostering academic integrity, and working to ensure institutional control of intercollegiate athletics. Serving as FAR also includes representative and legislative duties to the Big 12 Conference and NCAA and open collaboration and communication with the chancellor, athletic director, and athletic department staff.

Dr. Stagg-Williams believes the time demands placed on athletes are the biggest challenges facing intercollegiate athletics. These young adults must adroitly balance practices, team meetings, strength and conditioning workouts, competitions, and travel with their academic requirements. Rather than seasonal, these time demands have become year-round and are further exacerbated because of the geographic broadening of conference realignments.

Because of its mission or core values based on a commitment to athletes' well-being and their academic success, the KU athletic department operates Student-Athlete Support Services that offers academic counseling and tutoring services to help athletes manage time and balance academic and athletic performance demands. As FAR, Stagg-Williams works with a faculty, staff, and student committee in monitoring the academic progress rates of each team as well as the graduation success rates of all KU athletes.

Dr. Stagg-Williams works with compliance staff members in the athletic department to ensure the number of hours athletes spend in countable athletically related activities comply with NCAA bylaws. The time each athlete voluntarily spends on athletically related activities is not tracked. KU athletics policy limits the number of days per semester an athlete can be absent from school for travel and competition to 10 days exclusive of conference or NCAA championships. The athletic director after consultation with FAR can make exceptions to this policy. ■

to declare majors prior to the beginning of their third years of enrollment and annually make satisfactory progress toward their degrees.

Begun in 2004, the Academic Progress Rate (APR) requires teams in Division I to score at or above a minimum score or face increasingly onerous penalties when athletes fail to graduate or leave college because of poor academic performances. Because graduation rates published by the federal government include athletes who transfer to other institutions or drop out of college, in 2004 the NCAA developed the Graduate Success Rate (GSR).

The APR and GSR, however, have raised ethical concerns. While institutions with fewer financial resources struggle to comply with APR requirements, athletic departments benefiting from the largesse of television rights fees have used creative strategies to manage their teams' APRs to avoid penalties and negative publicity, according to Gurney and Southall (2012). For example, they claim departments pay hundreds of thousands of dollars to class checkers, tutors, and academic advisors to help keep athletes eligible, and often athletes use selectively identified summer courses to raise their GPAs. Gurney and Southall (2012) also argue that the NCAA, rather than use graduation rates published by the federal government, tout the higher graduation percentages of the GSR while disregarding double digit negative graduation gaps between football and men's basketball players in Division I and the institutional student population, as well as the failure of many African American athletes on these teams to graduate.

In the NCAA's Growth, Opportunities, Aspirations, and Learning of Students in College (GOALS) study, athletes across all three divisions reported that the average number of hours spent per week in-season on athletics in 2010 far exceeded the maximum allowed in coach-directed activities (Brown, 2011). The most hours spent engaged in athletic-related activities in Division I occurred in these sports: Football Bowl Subdivision (FBS) football (43.3); baseball (42.1); Football Championship Subdivision (FCS) football (41.6); men's basketball (39.2); and women's basketball (37.6) (para. 23). Athletes competing in Divisions II and III spent fewer hours than these but still exceeded the NCAA maximum of 20 hours. Most football, men's basketball, and baseball athletes in Divisions I and II stated they spent as much or more time on athletics during the off-season. Data from this GOALS study also revealed Division I women's basketball, men's basketball, and baseball players missed an average of 2.5 classes per week for athletics (NCAA, 2011, para. 21).

These examples signal potentially egregious ethical issues pervading intercollegiate athletics and bombarding academic integrity. Inevitably, the driving forces for unethical actions are financial rewards associated with winning.

EXCESSIVE COMMERCIALISM?

Callahan (2004) states, "The yawning gap between winners and losers is also having a lethal effect on personal integrity. In a society where winners win bigger than ever before and losers are punished more harshly . . . more and more people will do *anything* to be a winner" (p. 69). Nowhere is this truer than when describing intercollegiate athletics. Bedford (2007) identifies commercialization, university involvement in providing entertainment, damage to the integrity of higher education, exploitation of athletes, and harm to nonathletes as problems associated with intercollegiate athletics. Examples of increasing commercialism, Bedford emphasized,

> can be found everywhere from the advertising plastered over sports venues' institutional images to the licensing and logo deals universities sign with apparel companies and producers of various sports trinkets to the predatory behavior of sports agents, to the hype and sensationalism generated by sports agents, to the bestowal of celebrity status upon select college athletes and coaches, to the pressure to schedule events every night of the week to fill the schedules for the increasing number of sports networks. (p. 9)

As profit maximization becomes almost all-consuming, unethical actions skyrocket.

Desrochers (2013) identifies striking differences between spending among Division I institutions on athletes and academic spending per student as another major ethical issue. In institutions competing in the FBS, median academic spending per full-time equivalent (FTE) student was $13,628, while the median athletic expenditure per athlete was $91,936. In the FCS, the median expenditures were $11,769 per FTE student and $36,665 per athlete; in Division I without football these differences were $11,861 per FTE student and $39,201 per athlete. Desrochers concludes such financial disparities should lead public institutions to reexamine their spending priorities. Presidents of institutions competing in the FBS questioned the sustainability and fairness of subsidizing programs benefiting only athletes through student fees and increased institutional resources (Knight Commission on Intercollegiate Athletics, 2009).

Kahn (2007) claims the NCAA operates as a cartel by limiting payments to athletes and restricting their output, including collusive restrictions on payments to athletes, roster size, player mobility (e.g., transfer rules), recruiting expenses, and output (number of games). Donnor (2005) and Kahn (2007) suggest a discriminatory inequity because most revenue-producing athletes were African Americans, while the revenues they produce mostly benefit middle- and upper-class white students through grants-in-aid they received and financing of nonrevenue producing teams such as crew and swimming.

CONCLUSION

A winner-take-all system permeates college sports and threatens their ethical foundations. Lofty values have been replaced by gamesmanship to circumvent the rules, trash talking and taunting have escalated, athletes have bracketed their morality using game reasoning while ignoring moral values, moral callousness, or the absence of concern for others' welfare, and rationalizations have attempted to make unethical actions seem defensible. Winning-at-any-costs justifies use of these ploys. To help address these unethical actions, 10 recommendations for change are suggested:

1. End the myth and hypocrisy of amateurism by acknowledging "pay for play" has existed for decades as well as eliminate the disingenuous use of the label student-athlete.

2. Require one-year residency for athletic eligibility for freshmen and transfer students so academic eligibility is based on an athlete's collegiate academic performance, thereby eliminating special admissions for recruited athletes who did not meet institutional admission requirements.

3. Award four-year grants-in-aid, which cover the full cost of attendance, to reduce the control coaches have over athletes and lessen pressure on them.

4. Eliminate academic courses and majors used by athletes primarily to maintain eligibility and provide academic support services to all students under the auspices of the office of academic affairs, not programs solely for athletes administered by athletic departments.

5. Limit sports seasons to one academic term, reduce the number of competitions, and allow athletes to miss no more than one class per week and eight classes per academic term for athletic competition and associated travel, while forbidding the scheduling of athletic competitions and associated travel, including for conference, regional, and national tournaments and championships, during final exams.

6. Require a minimum 50% graduation rate of all players before each team can qualify for a conference championship and other postseason competition and withhold for a period of five years one grant-in-aid for each athlete who does not graduate within six years.

7. Allow athletes to transfer and compete immediately.

8. Seek a partial antitrust exemption to permit setting a ceiling on salaries of head coaches and assistant coaches in football and men's basketball as well as athletic directors' salaries and ban coaches from receiving income from corporate sponsors and other third parties for activities associated with their coaching positions.

9. Reclaim from commercial interests control over when (location and time) games are played.

10. Eliminate corporate signage and advertising from facilities and sports equipment used in intercollegiate athletics and prohibit athletes from wearing corporate trademarks and logos on team uniforms and other athletic-issued clothing.

QUESTIONS FOR DISCUSSION

1. What are the desired outcomes that justify why institutions of higher education should sponsor intercollegiate athletic programs, and from an ethical perspective, why are these outcomes being or not being accomplished?

2. How and why are amateurism and the associated claim that athletes are students first essential or not essential to the existing governance structure of the NCAA and operation of intercollegiate athletics?

3. How are admission requirements, academic eligibility, progress toward earning degrees, class attendance, time commitments to athletics, and graduation expectations for college athletes, especially football and men's basketball players, violated, and how would you recommend eliminating any exploitation associated with each of these?

References

Alexander, D. L., & Kern, W. (2010). Does athletic success generate legislative largess from sports-crazed representatives? The impact of athletic success on state appropriations to colleges and universities. *International Journal of Sport Finance, 5*, 253–267.

Association of Governing Boards of Universities and Colleges. (2009). AGB statement on board responsibilities for intercollegiate athletics general oversight responsibilities. Retrieved from http://agb.org/sites/agb.org/files/u1525/AGBStatement_Athletics_final.pdf

———. (2012). Trust, accountability, and integrity: Board responsibilities for intercollegiate athletics. Retrieved from http://agb.org/sites/agb.org/files/KnightReport.pdf

Bedford, R. D. (2007). The college sports reform movement: Reframing the "edutainment" industry. *Sociological Quarterly, 48*, 1–28.

Branch, T. (2011). The shame of college sports. *Atlantic Monthly, 308*(3), 80–110.

Brown, G. (2011). Second GOALS study emphasizes coach influence. Retrieved from http://www.ncaa.org/wps/wcm/connect/public/NCAA/Resources/Latest+News/2011/January/Second+GOALS+study+emphasizes+coach+influence

Byers, W., with C. Hammer. (1995). *Unsportsmanlike conduct: Exploiting college athletes*. Ann Arbor: University of Michigan Press.

Callahan, D. (2004). *The cheating culture: Why more Americans are doing wrong to get ahead*. Orlando, FL: Harcourt.

Davis, T. (1994). Intercollegiate athletics: Competing models and conflicting realities. *Rutgers Law Journal, 25*, 269–327.

———. (1995). The myth of the superspade: The persistence of racism in college athletics. *Fordham Urban Law Journal, 22*, 615–698.

Desrochers, D. M. (2013). Academic spending versus athletic spending. Washington, DC: American Institutes for Research. Retrieved from http://chronicle.com/blogs/players/files/2013/01/deltacost.pdf

Donnor, J. K. (2005). Towards an interest-convergence in the education of African American football student-athletes in major college sports. *Race, Ethnicity and Education, 8*(1), 45–67.

Frank, R. H. (2004). Challenging the myth: A review of the links among college athletic success, student quality, and donations. Retrieved from http://www.readthehook.com/files/old/blog/wp-content/uploads/2009/03/2004_kcia_frank_report.pdf

Green, K. C., Jaschik, S., & Lederman, D. (2012). The *Inside Higher Ed* survey of college and university presidents. Retrieved from http://www.google.com/url?sa=t&rct=j&q=&esrc=s&frm=1&source=web&cd=1&ved=0CCwQFjAA&url=http%3A%2F%2Fwww

.insidehighered.com%2Fdownload%2F%3Ffile%3D2
012IHEpresidentssurvey.pdf&ei=FUM3Uvv3LKXT2
QXftIGYBg&usg=AFQjCNHxgFd0BDdTQLhzy2_JtZ
XkX2zdIw&sig2=l1kMhahyanTio5VT9ZoWZA&bvm
=bv.52164340,d.b2I

Gurney, G. S., & Southall, R. M. (2012). College sports'
bait and switch. Retrieved from http://m.espn.go
.com/general/story?storyId=8248046

Kahn, L. M. (2007). Cartel behavior and amateurism in
college sports. *Journal of Economic Perspectives,
21*(1), 209–226.

Knight Commission on Intercollegiate Athletics.
(2009). *Quantitative and qualitative research with
football bowl subdivision university presidents on
the costs and financing of intercollegiate athletics.*
Retrieved from http://www.knightcommission.org
/index.php?option=com_contentandview=article
andid=71andItemid=36

Martinez, J. M., Stinson, J. L., Kang, M., & Jubenville,
C. B. (2010). Intercollegiate athletics and institu-
tional fundraising: A meta-analysis. *Sport Marketing
Quarterly, 19*, 36–47.

National Collegiate Athletic Association. (2006). The
second-century imperatives Presidential leadership—Institutional accountability. Retrieved from
http://www.ncaapublications.com/product
downloads/PTF092.pdf

——. (2011). Summary of findings from the 2010
GOALS and SCORE studies of the student-athlete
experience. Retrieved from http://www.ncaa.org
/wps/wcm/connect/public/ncaa/pdfs/2011/summary
+of+findings+from+the+2010+goals+and+score
+studies+of+the+student+athlete+experience

——. (2012–2013). *2012–13 NCAA Division I manual.*
Indianapolis, IN: National Collegiate Athletic
Association.

Oriard, M. (2009). *Bowled over: Big-time college football
from the sixties to the BCS era.* Chapel Hill: University of North Carolina Press.

Sack, A. L., & Staurowsky, E. J. (1998). *College athletes
for hire: The evolution and legacy of the NCAA's
amateur myth.* Westport, CT: Praeger.

Staurowsky, E. J., & Sack, A. L. (2005). Reconsidering
the use of the term student-athlete in academic
research. *Journal of Sport Management, 19*, 103–116.

Toma, J. D. (1999). The collegiate ideal and the tools of
external relations: The uses of high-profile intercollegiate athletics. *New Directions for Higher Education, 105*(1), 81–90.

Zimbalist, A., & Sack, A. (2013). Thoughts on amateurism, the O'Bannon case and the viability of college
sport. Retrieved from http://thedrakegroup
.org/2013/04/10/drake-group-report-obannon
-amateurism-and-the-viability-of-college-sport/

PART TWO

Theoretical Perspectives on Higher Education and Athletics

The study of intercollegiate athletics takes place in various contexts, and it is conducted within a diversity of frameworks. In chapter 5, Leticia Oseguera and Allison Goldstein explore a variety of theoretical perspectives and discuss why they are useful for the study of higher education and intercollegiate athletics. They summarize different classes of theory used to study and understand college students, with a special focus on student development theories and how they have been applied to college athletes. Oseguera and Goldstein also discuss college impact models, critical theory, organizational theory, and a campus climate framework. This part demonstrates that the theoretical perspectives we choose to employ for the study of intercollegiate athletics generally influence our approaches to analysis, including the kinds of questions we ask and the focus of our exploration. ∎

THEORETICAL TENETS of HIGHER EDUCATION and COLLEGE ATHLETES

Leticia Oseguera and Allison Goldstein

Having theoretical lenses to understand the college athlete experience and the general athletic enterprise is useful to ensure healthy developmental processes of athletes and to understand athletics as an organization and athletes within a given organization. This chapter offers a rationale for the study of theory, assumptions guiding theory, and how theory can be applied to athletes in higher education. Parker (1977) wrote nearly 40 years ago that "the dilemma we have described requires that we choose between abstract, simplified models of reality which are researchable and the concrete, complex reality in which we act" (p. 421). A theory is a way of understanding a particular phenomenon. Formal theories are generated to describe the interrelationships of constructs. While formal theory is meant to help explain the phenomenon under investigation, we also use informal theory in everyday life. Informal theory has been defined by Parker (1977) as "the body of common knowledge that allows us to make implicit connections among events and persons in our environment and upon which we act in everyday life" (p. 420). Unfortunately, there is no way to know if our perceptions are accurate. They can be based on formal training but are likely the result of personal interactions, experiences, and values amassed over time. Theory can also be understood as cognitive maps or mental representations of how to help students make sense of and explain their experiences and social interactions with the environment that help guide professional action. Theory helps student and academic affairs professionals who work with athletes better understand the multiple aspects of development that occur.

Formal, validated theory allows us to approach our work more reflectively. We can more systematically gauge and assess the phenomenon

KEY TERMS

college athletes ◄

student development ◄
theory

campus climate ◄

critical theory ◄

campus environments ◄

we are experiencing. Another way to understand theory is to consider a paradigm. Guba (1990) defines a paradigm as an "interpretive framework, a basic set of beliefs that guides action" (p. 17). Paradigms guide theory and research, yet Guba and Lincoln (1994) remind us that paradigms are beliefs and they are subject to human error. As constructions of our reality, paradigms can never be proved, but they are useful in understanding and making sense of lived realities. Using this definition, we establish that theory is useful to guide our work and interactions on college campuses, but individual experiences may not always "fit" with a validated theoretical framework.

Depending on the theory, there are selected assumptions that guide understandings of lived realities. Reality assumptions are on a continuum. For example, positivism assumes an objective reality that is time and context free. Critical theory assumes there is a reality, but it is influenced by social, political, economic, ethnic, and gender-related factors. Critical theorists attempt to raise consciousness or correct injustices about the way theories have been formulated. Additionally, social constructivists/interactionalists view reality as relative—there is no single reality or truth; reality is based on specific experiences, and perceptions can change over time. Because of the personal nature of social constructions, they can be identified only through interactions between the researcher and participant, which suggests the investigators and research are linked (Evans, Forney, Guido, Patton, & Renn, 2010, pp. 18–19). As we apply the forthcoming theories to athletes, we do so with sensitivity to and an awareness of the researcher's perspective, as it may have implications for the design or interpretation of the phenomenon under investigation.

INTERCOLLEGIATE ATHLETES: RATIONALE FOR STUDENT DEVELOPMENT FOCUS

Collegiate athletes are required to successfully manage multiple roles within higher education. Tantamount to the priority placed on athletic success, students' academic achievement has received considerable scholarly attention (e.g., Comeaux & Harrison, 2011; Gaston-Gayles & Hu, 2009). With the support of coaches, faculty, peers, and administration, athletes must find ways to strike a balance between their sport's demands, adjustment to college life, and academic obligations. If unsuccessful, many institutions have repercussions in place that could hinder students' athletic participation and, potentially, affiliation with the institution. Given the overwhelming reality of an athlete's role as a "student," we focus heavily on student development issues to enable higher education institutions to create more conducive learning experiences for athletes guided by the current literature.

In order to better understand the experiences of athletes, we must focus on their student involvement, their affiliation with athletic organizations, and the broader campus environment. We open broadly with theory as it applies to traditionally aged college populations and theories designed explicitly with an athlete focus. We aim to outline the larger groupings of theory, focusing primarily on student development and college impact models. Next, we introduce critical theory, outlining specific theories under this general category. We then offer an overview of a campus climate model developed with college athletes in mind, followed by a brief discussion of organizational theory as it applies to athletics as an organization on a college campus.

STUDENT DEVELOPMENT THEORY AND STUDENT EXPERIENCES

We chose to situate the student experience in two widely used and comprehensive higher education texts. Evans et al.'s *Student Development in College* (2010) organizes major theoretical approaches to understanding college student development, while Pascarella and Terenzini's *How College Affect Students* (2005) produces a literature synthesis detailing how college impacts student experiences and outcomes. Both groups present a range of theoretical approaches, and we adapt portions of their organization for this chapter.

Development can be defined as a set of theories that guides the work of student affairs professionals, describing how students change and grow during college, and what activities or experiences best influence that growth (Evans et al., 2010, pp. 6–7). We primarily follow Evans et al.'s schema, which organizes classes of student development theory into foundational theories, integrative theories, and social identity theories. Because of space limitations, we offer a broad organization of selected theories and may omit discussion on some theories relevant to athletes.

Foundational Student Development Theories

We begin with seminal student development theories. Most of what is reviewed in this section is based on the early works of these theorists. Scholars for many decades since have built upon and refined these now foundational theories in their work with college students. We describe the basic tenets of each theory and include research as it applies to college athletes.

Psychosocial Theory

Psychosocial theories examine how individuals accomplish specific developmental tasks. They examine important issues of people's lives, such as how they age and mature. These theories help professionals understand how students make sense of defining themselves as individuals, determine what they want to accomplish in life, and interact and relate to others. Scholars most often identified with psychosocial theories include Erikson (1968) and Chickering and Reisser (1993). Erikson contributed the epigenetic principle describing sequential and age-related biological and psychological development and also how an individual's environment helps to shape these changes. Erikson differentiated individuals by phases based on their ages, important events, and outcomes. He categorized adolescence (12 to 18 years of age) as a time where teenagers begin to develop their own personal identities, followed shortly thereafter by young adulthood, where the outcome of developing strong relationships is achieved. Identity formation during this time is necessary, and a lack of proper transition could lead to role confusion. Much of the literature on identity development is founded on these principles, as traditional college students are likely to fall within these two phases.

Chickering and Reisser's Seven Vectors build on Erikson's work. The seven vectors represent ever-changing, unidirectional dimensions of identity development and include achieving competence, managing emotions, moving through autonomy toward interdependence, developing mature interpersonal relationships, establishing identity, developing purpose, and developing integrity (Chickering & Reisser, 1993). Psychosocial theories are useful working with students as well as athletes, offering ideas on how successful students cope with changes that often occur during the college years. While athletes' experiences create challenges that are unique to their individual population, these theories still apply and help us better understand the various stages of identity development experienced by students during college. Harris (2003) applied Chickering and Reisser's vectors to help guide athletic trainers in navigating injured students' development. Trainers can use Chickering and Reisser's vectors to predict how students will respond at the onset of injury and what support they will need to successfully rehabilitate (Harris, 2003). These seminal theories highlight the importance of building relationships during the formation of identity.

Cognitive-Structural Theory

Cognitive-structural theories are rooted in the work of Piaget (1952) and examine the intellectual development of college students. These theories focus on how students process information, reason, and make sense of their experiences. The mind is thought to have structures or stages that "act as sets of assumptions by which persons adapt to and organize their environments" (Evans et al., 2010, p. 43). These structures are the filters of how we perceive and evaluate our experiences and how social interactions can assist students to develop their decision-making habits. Most consider Perry (1968) as the foundational theorist of college students' intellectual development. Moral reasoning is attributed to Kohlberg (1976), which was later refined by Rest, Narvaez, Bebeau, and Thoma (1999). Gilligan (1982/1993) challenged the male-dominated intellectual theory development and introduced gendered moral reasoning and an ethic of care. Belenky, Clinchy, Goldberger, and Tarule (1986) advanced a women's way of knowing, and Baxter-Magolda (1992) introduced gendered meaning making in college. Other notable theorists in this family include King and Kitchener (1994), who examined "ill-structured problems" (Evans et al., 2010, p. 45) or how students reason when there is no clear solution to a dilemma. This is especially applicable to athletes, as Howard-Hamilton and Watt (2001) noted the highly structured and rule-driven environment of college sports may prevent students from being challenged to develop their own understandings and values. By applying and understanding cognitive development theories' relationship to athletes, professionals working with this population can assist them to process information and better understand how students rationalize their actions, behaviors, and interactions with others.

Experiential Learning

Learning style theories describe how individuals approach learning. Among the most widely used, Kolb's (1984) work was born out of an interest in academic cultures and what areas would be the best fit for particular students. He describes learning as a cyclical process consisting of four stages "whereby knowledge is created through the transformation of experience" (p. 38) and learning style as a "habitual way of responding to a learning environment" (Evans et al., 2010, p. 139). The four learning styles include converging, or those whose strengths are problem solving and decision making; diverging strengths are imaginative abilities, awareness of meaning and values, and generating and analyzing alternatives; assimilating strengths are in inductive reasoning, creating theoretical models, and integrating observation; and accommodating strengths are carrying out plans and adapting to change (Kolb, 1984, pp. 78–79). Kolb (2000) stressed that learning styles can change and are not static in nature. Learning styles are influenced by the demands of the immediate environment and are individual in nature. King (2003) has also done extensive work on learning style theories. In relation to athletes, there is no one-size-fits-all approach; athletes demonstrate a variety of different learning styles. Instructors, advisors, and coaches should be prepared to work with and help students identify their individual styles, learn techniques for navigating other styles, and work to meet the needs of diverse learners (Perkins, 2010). Understanding how individuals process information can help professionals design programs with individual learning strengths in mind.

Integrative Theories

One of the criticisms of the theories and theorists described in the foundational section is that they separate developmental processes into discrete categories. New integrative classes of theories acknowledge the intersection of multiple aspects of the personality and environment that contribute to change.

Ecological Theory

The first set includes ecological models, or the relationship that the person has with the environment. Evans et al. (2010) offer three types of ecological models: human ecology, or the interaction of humans and their environment; developmental ecology, a psychological approach that examines how the environment influences development; and campus ecology, which focuses on the interaction with the student and the campus environment. Human ecology explains how humans need to adapt to an environment that existed before them and will exist after them (Bubolz & Sontag, 1993). Developmental ecology model pioneer, Bronfenbrenner (1979), advanced the equation $D = f(B * E)$: development is a function of the interaction of the person and the environment. His model advanced the concepts of process, person, context, and time and represents the interaction of these four components to promote or inhibit development and is often used to study peer cultures. Campus ecology is the intersection of human and developmental ecology except it is focused on the specialized context of the campus environment and was introduced by Banning and Kaiser (1974). Using campus ecology, Brenner and Swanik (2007) found that athletes were significantly more likely to report high-risk drinking than their nonathlete peers when surveyed during their noncompetitive seasons. The increase in unstructured time and decrease in guidance during off-seasons is one explanation for this finding. Campus ecology models can help inform how environments can be structured to meet desired developmental outcomes.

Transition Theory

A second integrative theory applicable to athletes is transition theory. Transition can be defined as "any event, or non-event, that results in changed relationships, routines, assumptions, and roles" (Goodman, Schlossberg, & Anderson, 2006, p. 33). Transition includes type, context, and impact. Types comes in three forms: anticipated transitions, which predictably occur such as moving from high school varsity athletic team to college athletics; unanticipated transitions or those that are not scheduled such as a career-ending injury; and nonevents or events that are expected to occur but do not happen (e.g., you are expecting to play professional sports but are not selected or drafted). Context refers to one's relationship to the transition and the setting where it occurs. Impact is the degree to which the transition affects one's daily life. Schlossberg's Transition Theory (1989) introduced the terms of *moving in*, *moving through*, and *moving out* and is a useful theory in relation to athletes and their experiences moving through college as the theory examines what "constitutes a transition, different forms of transition, the transition process, and the factors that influence transitions" (Evans et al., 2010, p. 214). Some scholars working with athletes often describe the process of transitioning from a college athlete identity to life without sport (see Harrison & Lawrence, 2004; Moreland-Bishop, 2009). When compared to peers who may not identify as strongly with their athletic roles, students with higher athletic identities are reported to transition to nonathlete with greater ease as they report excitement about experiencing college as a traditional student. Still, these college athletes' transitions out of sport are often accompanied by a loss of identity, motivation, structure, and social network (Moreland-Bishop,

2009). Goodman et al. (2006) extended transition theory to include factors that affect the ability to cope with transitions and introduced the four Ss: situations, self, support, and strategies. This list could include counseling for athletes after terminating their sport.

Social Identity Theory

College allows students to begin to cultivate and navigate through their multiple identities. The application of identity development theories are relevant to athletes, as they help us to better understand the students as individuals and the personal growth and development they are experiencing. While no two students are likely to endure identical development, these theories provide a foundation for understanding and supporting students. Social identity issues in the mainstream United States have their roots in the civil rights movement of the 1960s. During the 1970s and 1980s, we witnessed a growth in scholars theorizing about social identity issues, including race, ethnicity, sexual identity, and gender. The 1990s witnessed additional scholarship in multiple social identity frameworks and by the early twenty-first century, issues of power, privilege, and oppression made their way to the forefront of student development theory. We share a brief overview of the main social identities that arise on college athletic teams but recognize other salient identity issues that may surface such as ability or "ableism" privilege (Evans & Herriott, 2009) or Christian privilege (Schlosser, 2003).

Racial/Ethnic Identity Development

Race and racialized analyses are one of the most highly discussed topics in college athletics. Racial and ethnic identities similarly find their way into the student development literature. While race and ethnicity are often used interchangeably, they represent different constructs and theorists typically distinguish racial identity models as those that frame identity in relation to the dominant group's status and position from ethnic identity models that tend to detail how cultural characteristics are acquired and maintained (Evans et al., 2010; Helms, 1996). In the late 1970s, Atkinson, Morten, and Sue (1979) introduced the minority identity model, which was revised and renamed by Sue and Sue in 2003 as the racial and cultural identity development model (RCID). The RCID includes five stages that describe how students of color view themselves in relation to white students. The RCID has served as the groundwork for models that examine the racialized experiences of students including Native American (Horse, 2005), Asian (Kim, 2001), black (Cross & Fhagen-Smith, 2001), Latina/o (Ferdman & Gallegos, 2001), and white (Helms, 1995) student identity development. Multiracial identity frameworks are also making their way into student development literature (see Renn, 2004).

In contrast, ethnic identity frames examine how students "understand the implications of their ethnicity and make decisions about its role in their lives"

(Phinney, 1993, p. 64). Phinney (1993) proposed that understanding ethnic identity was critical for positive self-concepts among students of color and identified a three-stage model where students move from having their ethnic identity unexamined to ethnic identity achievement where students establish a healthy identity status and accept their own and others' identity similarities and differences. Other ethnic identity frameworks include Torres's (2003) model of Hispanic identity development or Ibrahim, Ohnishi, and Sandhu's (1997) South Asian identity model and challenge earlier limited conceptions that ethnic minorities desire to be similar to white people. White ethnic identity models are also being developed (Helms, 1996).

The frameworks are important for college athletic teams as students are likely working through how their own racial or ethnic identity influences the perceptions others have for their performance both in the classroom and within their sport. Brueing, Armstrong, and Pastore (2005) demonstrate the role identity plays in African American female athletes' experiences. Having multiple overlapping marginalized identities, these students often find their voices silenced and their identities underrepresented in sport. These frameworks can be applied to students of varying identities to help understand their experiences, and help inform practices aimed at supporting their identity development (Bruening et al., 2005; Lawrence, 2005; Singer, 2005).

Sexual Identity and Gender Identity Development

Another group of theories relevant to athletes are theories on sexual identity and gender identity. It is important to clarify that sexual identity models refer to more than just sexual activity and include the "emotional, lifestyle, and political aspects of life" (Evans et al., 2010, p. 307). One of the first lesbian, gay, bisexual (LGB) identity models was Cass's (1996) model of sexual orientation identity formation. The six stages of development range from minimal awareness to an integration of the lesbian or gay self with other aspects of the self, including how others view the self. Alternative models better incorporate the role of contextual influences on development and challenge the notion that acceptance of self is necessarily equated with activism (Fassinger & Miller, 1997). Other prominent theorists on identity development include D'Augelli's (1994) model of lesbian, gay, and bisexual development that introduced a life-span model, which recognizes that people's identities are shaped by the context of time. Cunningham (2012) uses essays and stories from activists, coaches, and scholars to explore athletes' experiences navigating sexual identities. By highlighting the various issues faced by athletes through the lens of different constituents, Cunningham offers potential strategies to increase sexual identity inclusiveness within athletic environments. Today, theorists are also examining heterosexuality and norms (Worthington, Savoy, Dillon, & Vernaglia, 2002). It is important to better understand how to work with and support students to explore their own sexual identity development in healthy and developmental ways (Cunningham, 2012; Wolf-Wendel, Toma, & Morphew, 2001).

Gendered identities differ from one's sexual orientation and refer to norms and socialization of particular genders. While sex is typically considered a biological construct, gender is viewed as a culturally constructed concept shaped by how men and women should behave. While sex and gender are closely related, one cannot assume gender identity is based on sex alone. Contemporary developmental theory also recognizes transgender identity, when gender identity differs from sex ascription (Bilodeau, 2009). Much work is left to be done in this area.

College Athlete Identity Development

The bulk of research on college athletes focuses on how participation affects educational outcomes. Athletic identity is defined as the extent to which a person identifies with the role of an athlete (Brewer, van Raalte, & Linder, 1993). One shortcoming of athlete identity development is that rather than acknowledge the multidimensional aspects of athletes' respective identities, the literature concerning intercollegiate sports most often depicts athletes as navigating only two worlds as they strive to succeed both on the playing field as athletes and in the classroom as students (Adler & Adler, 1991; Person & LeNoir, 1997). Brewer et al. (1993) acknowledge the "multidimensional self-concept" of athletic identity and developed the Athletic Identity Measurement Scale (AIMS) to measure both the strength and exclusivity of athletic identity. The AIMS is one of the most widely used and cited instruments for assessing athletic identity.

It is not surprising that, as a result of their social interactions, demanding training schedules, and differing values, athletes often develop a strong salient athletic identity (Adler & Adler, 1991). The challenge exists when students' identities as athletes significantly overshadow their other identities; or when a life event (e.g., an injury or termination of athletic involvement) forces students to reconsider their identities. College athletes enter college with similar academic aspirations to their peers, but as students become more invested in their athletic roles, they often find themselves unable to meet their previously high academic aspirations while fulfilling their athletic responsibilities. This sometimes results in prioritizing one role over the other (Adler & Adler, 1991). Stronger salience of their identities as athletes puts them at risk of neglecting their student identity (Adler & Adler, 1991). Students with strong athletic identities also run the risk of psychological obstacles in the event of injury or transition away from their athletic careers (Brewer et al., 1993).

By understanding the implications of this research, we can better understand students' experiences, and use the opportunity to minimize the potential negative effects students may face. A strong salient athletic identity is accompanied by many positive attributes: opportunity for athletic skill development, greater understanding of self-identity, and a commitment to performance (Brewer et al., 1993). Similarly, a strong student identity is accompanied by many rewards, including retention, personal development, and drive for academic achievement (Evans et al., 2010). Some of the challenges that impact the roles students identify with include socialization, time commitments, responsibilities, and psychosocial development. Theory can be used to better inform practices that directly impact these students. Student services offices may offer time management workshops aimed specifically toward college athletes to help them better navigate their various commitments. We move now to a review of models used to understand how the environment affects the college athlete experience.

College Impact Models

The second major sets of theories reviewed in this chapter are college impact models or theories. College impact models "emphasize change associated with the characteristics of the institutions students attend . . . or with the experiences students have while enrolled" (Pascarella & Terenzini, 2005, p. 18). Pascarella and Terenzini (2005) show that there is a time dimension that can be applied to understanding the growth, change, and development of college students—one semester, after the first college year, after exposure to a particular program, and after exposure to four years of college, which also should be accounted for when examining athlete experiences. We present the most salient college impact models found in higher education scholarship.

Astin's I-E-O Model

Astin's I-E-O model (1977, 1991) and theory of involvement (1984) posit that to understand the impact of the college environment, one must also understand the student's characteristics upon entrance to college. The "I" refers to the inputs or students' background abilities and dispositions, the "E" is the environment to which the student is exposed during college, (e.g., faculty, peers, and diverse views), and "O" is the outcome of college or what the college hopes to produce or develop in students. Included in the I-E-O model is that students get out of college proportionally to what they put into the college experience. Astin's framework has been widely used as a conceptual guide in designing studies related to the impact of college on students, accounting for the characteristics of students before they entered college. See Comeaux (2005) for utility of the I-E-O model on college athletes.

Tinto's Theory of Student Departure

One of the most widely used frameworks on the decision of students to remain enrolled in or depart from college is Tinto's (1993) student departure theory. This theory posits that students enter college with particular goals and institutional commitments, which are influenced by their background and academic preparation. External factors such as family or work obligations also affect decisions. Students' initial commitments influence their ability to be socially or academically integrated into college. If students fail to become academically or socially integrated, they risk leaving college before completion. This theory can be useful in work with college athletes to understand in what subcultures they need to academically and socially integrate to successfully complete college.

Nora's Student Engagement Model

The third college impact model we review is a model of student engagement. Nora (2002) identifies college experiences that help students to acculturate into the campus culture. This model draws on Tinto's work but describes how validating and mentoring experiences from faculty and staff influence students' commitment, engagement, and sense of belonging to the campus. The model also includes intermediate outcomes of college as a result of meaningful engagement such as valuing diversity and knowledge of global issues. This work can be useful in working with athletes

From the Classroom to the Playing Field: How Research Informs Healthy Student Development

Susan Rankin is a former Division I coach and retired associate professor of higher education at the Pennsylvania State University. With more than thirty years of professional experience informing our discussion, Dr. Rankin offered her perspective on why there is an increased need to understand theory when working with college athletes. Dr. Rankin opened by stating that historically coaches' educational training was in education, so they entered the coaching profession with some understanding of basic human development theory. Increasingly coaches' are hailing from communications and business backgrounds and thus may not have been introduced to human development theory. Additionally, they may have a limited understanding of the breadth of scholarship available on how students experience college. Today, coaches expect that athletic advisors or counseling staff will assist athletes with their academic

and personal development, but research suggests that athletes prefer to talk to their coaches. Hence, some exposure to theory on how students from various social identities experience college can assist coaches with a better understanding of how well athletes from different backgrounds will transition to and adjust to college.

When addressing the role of faculty in athletes' lives, Dr. Rankin explained that faculty necessarily need to understand the time demands of athletes. Faculty should offer some flexibility with their athletes and be proactive with athletes and their development. Dr. Rankin shared that each semester she met with athletes in her courses and worked through the class syllabus and their competition schedule. She explained that it is not that athletes cannot or will not do the required work; it is just that their schedules may require some flexibility on the faculty member's

part with regard to tests and assignments. She advocates for the use of training for faculty in athletic identity development, emphasis on athlete success models, and attention to the effects of campus climates on the athlete experience. Despite scholarship that indicates that positive student-faculty interactions for athletes result in greater classroom engagement and strong academic classroom success, stereotypes and poor perceptions of athletes persist and these may create roadblocks to athlete success. Overall, Dr. Rankin's work with athletes as a former coach and college professor explains that knowledge of the college athlete experience but even college student development more generally can help guide the interactions and expectations between coaches and players and faculty and their students. ■

because it acknowledges those staff members that encourage a well-rounded academic and athletic experience.

Comeaux and Harrison's Conceptual Model of Academic Success for Student-Athletes

One comprehensive college impact framework advanced specifically for college athletes is Comeaux and Harrison's (2011) conceptual model of academic success for student-athletes. The model adds to the previously underresearched area of factors that influence college athlete academic success. The model contains four stages: precollege (family background, educational experiences, preparation, and individual attributes); initial commitments (goal, sport, and institutional commitment); college environment factors (social and academic systems); and commitments (goal, sport, and institutional commitment). The stages outline prevailing forces in student matriculation and present a framework for understanding students' academic success. The model suggests that both individual experiences and interactions within their college environment play a predominant role in athletes' academic success. Conceptual models are particularly useful in providing a clearer lens to view the various influences on student matriculation. Staff and administrators can use this model to guide interventions and programs, helping athletes appropriately navigate each of the stages evidenced to promote matriculation.

CRITICAL THEORY

Student development theory and college impact models seek to describe and understand individual student experiences. Critical theories go beyond understanding power but also critique how power operates in society. Critical theory seeks to identify, analyze, understand, and transform oppressive structural and cultural aspects of society that maintain marginal statuses of groups. Critical theory is primarily rooted in sociology but has been used to study sport (Eitzen & Sage, 2009). We highlight three main critical theories used in the study of sport: hegemony theory, feminist theory, and critical race theory. Hegemony theory (Sage, 1998) evaluates power and dominance in society and "sensitizes us to the role dominant groups play in American government, economic system, mass media, education, and sport in maintaining and promoting their interests" (p. 10). This theory can be used to understand how college athletics relates to the production and control of resources (Whisenant, Pedersen, & Obenour, 2002). Feminist theory is useful in examining athletes and college athletics. Historically, feminist theory made two basic assumptions: that people's experiences are gendered and that because women have been devalued in many contexts, there is a need to change those conditions. Today, feminist theories go beyond male versus female oppression and roles and "emphasize the need to challenge sexism, racism, colonialism, class, and other forms of inequalities in the research process" (Naples, 2003, p. 13). Feminist theory is useful in the study of college ath-

Navigating Multiple Identities: The Application of Theory to Practice

You are the academic coordinator responsible for ensuring the success of college athletes. You are assigned to work with the women's basketball and women's gymnastics teams. Your colleague works with men's wrestling and men's baseball. You both work primarily with first-year students but also work with returning college athletes who have not been able to secure a GPA of 3.0 or above (the grade point average needed for athletes who are not working with an academic coordinator). You just took a class about student development theories and campus climate, and you feel confident applying your knowledge to assist athletes with their academics and navigation of their identities and the campus environment. Your colleague working with men's teams is struggling with how to advise a young man who is questioning his sexual orientation. She also asked you for advice on how you work with students who do not seem to be academically successful.

Moreover, the issue of racial insensitivity has been heightened on your campus after a fraternity hosted a party depicting Asian and Pacific Islander populations negatively. Several current athletes are members of this fraternity and along with its sister sorority, have a history of initiating athletes as members. How might you use your knowledge of student identity development to support the athletes during this time and what advice can you provide your colleague to help her work with those students under her supervision? ■

letics to better understand inequities such as funding, individual player experiences, hiring of coaches and senior athletic administrators, and other related avenues to forefront power relations (Bruening et al., 2005). Finally, critical race theory (CRT) acknowledges the need to emphasize race in research and does so unapologetically. CRT is a framework used to understand how race and racism impact structures, processes, and discourses within an educational context. CRT challenges the dominant theoretical paradigms that offer deficit understandings of the educational ability of students of color or athletes of color (Comeaux, 2010; Donnor, 2005; Singer, 2005). CRT in education also theorizes and examines that place where racism intersects with other forms of discrimination, such as sexism and classism. CRT is transdisciplinary and draws on many other schools and methods of progressive scholarship. CRT attempts to link theory with practice, scholarship with teaching, and the academy with the community (Solorzano & Delgado-Bernal, 2001). Today, scholars have expanded upon critical race theory to examine specific populations and are further developing CRT such as LatCrit, TribalCrit, WhiteCrit, AsianCrit, QueerCrit, and FemCrit to name a few.

CAMPUS CLIMATE

Members of different social groups experience campus climate differently depending on group membership and group status (Rankin & Reason, 2005). Positive campus climates contribute to students' academic performance, social adjustment, and interpersonal skill development, while negative campus climates adversely affect those outcomes, particularly for groups with marginalized social identities. Campus climate is defined as the "current attitudes, behaviors and standards and practices of employees and students of an institution" (Rankin & Reason, 2008, p. 264).

Based on work by Smith et al. (1997), Rankin (2003), and Rankin and Reason (2008), the student-athlete climate conceptual framework (Rankin et al., 2011) was one of the first studies to comprehensively explore the perceptions and experiences of college athletes with regard to campus climate. This framework suggests that individual and institutional characteristics directly influence how athletes experience climate and a variety of educational outcomes unique to athletes. At the same time, athletes' experiences of climate can also influence these educational outcomes. Highlighted variables include demographic characteristics (e.g., race, gender), characteristics unique to athletes (e.g., sport affiliation), and characteristics unique to the array of participating institutions (e.g., divisional classification). Climate constructs include measures of athletes' experiences, attitudes, perceptions, and reports of institutional actions relevant to the campus, athletic department, and team climates. The outcome measures included academic success, athletic identity, and athletic success. The authors found evidence of the effect of positive climates on college athletes' outcomes in the study.

ORGANIZATIONAL THEORY: COLLEGE ATHLETICS AND CULTURE

In many ways, understanding the athletic organization as an enterprise is just as important as understanding the student within it; these organizations play a predominant role in institutional culture and success, and often have deeply embedded histories that dictate the ways in which the units—and in many cases, the institutions—function (Clark, 1972). This section provides a modest introduction to athletics as an organization and the theories that can be applied to athletic organizations as an enterprise.

The study of organizations refers to the environment, strategies, goals, work, and formal and informal structures present in organizations (Scott & Davis, 2007). Scott and Davis (2007) assert that various aspects of membership influence organizations, including individuals' needs and their demographics. The literature on organizational theory allows us to assess the unique cultures present in these collegiate athletic organizations and how those cultures affect the students involved. Organizations are complex structures; therefore, studying the ways organizations are framed and operate can be useful, because it provides information on what works or does not in achieving outcomes. Organizational theory allows us to understand leadership, enact change, or create new traditions within a unit (Bolman & Deal, 2008; Clark, 1972). Useful organizational theories for the study of sport and intercollegiate athletics specifically include Bolman and Deal's (1991) multi-frame perspective; Pelled's (1996) intervening process theory; Barney's (1991) or Richard's (2000) resource-based theory.

Sack (2009) identified three conceptual models that guide the contrasting views associated with college athletics while exploring the issues and assumptions prevalent in big-time college sports. The first, intellectual elitism, refers to the argument that college athletics represents a negative force in higher education. Some reformers are concerned with the threat presented by athletics to academic values, especially the resources allocated to athletic programs that could otherwise support educational needs. The second, academic capitalism, emphasizes the benefits of the commercialism of college athletics and the ways in which athletics align with the institution's missions and values. Finally, the athletic rights model advocates for the rights of college athletes, continually posing questions about students' educational and financial aid opportunities (Sack, 2009). Sack's conceptual models are useful in exploring the various assumptions institutions and athletes regularly navigate.

Additional theory textbooks and related work to understand sport include Coakley and Dunning's *Handbook of Sport Studies* (2000); Eitzen and Sage's *Sociology of North American Sport* (2009); Schroeder's model for assessing organizational culture (2010); and Giulianotti's *Sport and Modern Theorists* (2004).

CONCLUSION

College athletes possess various identities, affiliations, challenges, and opportunities that shape the way in which they approach both their academic and athletic experiences. Professionals working in higher education should exercise sensitivity to the complex needs of athletes. Knowledge and theory of the multiple facets of athletes' identities can equip scholars and practitioners with more nuanced understandings of diverse athlete experiences. Theory on college athletes and college athletics, while growing, still has many areas ripe for additional research and improved understandings.

College athletes interact with individuals in many different environments, from coaches and athletic directors to faculty and administrators. Each professional has the opportunity to assist students in their learning and engagement, and when possible, collaboration and communication among these various individuals is beneficial. While it may be challenging to encourage different groups to foster collaboration, the outcome is one that is beneficial for both the student and the institution: a student's goals and achievement will become more aligned with the institution's goals. From an identity standpoint, this collaboration will also likely minimize the role confusion that athletes experience.

QUESTIONS FOR DISCUSSION

1. What is theory, and why is it important to the study of college athletes and athletic organizations?

2. Identify specific times in an athlete's college experience when theory might be particularly useful. What theory might be useful in navigating that experience, and how would you apply it in your work with students?

3. If you developed a theoretical model for college athlete experiences, what outcome would you focus on and what areas would you include in your framework?

References

Adler, P. A., & Adler, P. (1991). *Backboards and blackboards: Colleges and role engulfment*. New York: Columbia University Press.

Astin, A. W. (1977). *Four critical years: Effects of college on beliefs, attitudes, and knowledge*. San Francisco: Jossey-Bass, 1977.

———. (1984). Student involvement: A developmental theory for higher education. *Journal of college student personnel, 25*, 297–308.

———. (1991). *Assessment for excellence: The philosophy and practice of assessment and evaluation in higher education*. New York: American Council on Education/Macmillan.

Atkinson, D. R., Morten, G., & Sue, D. W. (1979). *Counseling American minorities: A cross-cultural perspective*. Dubuque, IA: William C. Brown.

Banning, J. H., & Kaiser, L. (1974). An ecological perspective and model for campus design. *The Personnel and Guidance Journal, 52*, 370–375.

Barney, J. (1991). Firm resources and sustained competitive advantage. *Journal of Management, 17*(1), 99–120.

Baxter Magolda, M. B. (1992). *Knowing and reasoning in college: Gender-related patterns in students' intellectual development*. San Francisco: Jossey-Bass.

Belenky, M. F., Clinchy, B. M., Goldberger, N. F., & Tarule, J. M. (1986). *Women's ways of knowing*. New York: Basic Books.

Bilodeau, B. L. (2009). *Genderism: Transgender students, binary systems, and higher education*. Saarbrücken, Germany: VDM Verlag.

Bolman, L. G., & Deal, T. E. (1991). Leadership and management effectiveness: A multi-frame, multi-sector analysis. *Human Resource Management, 30*, 509–534.

———. (2008). *Reframing organizations: Artistry, choice, and leadership* (4th ed.) San Francisco: Jossey-Bass.

Brenner, J., & Swanik, K. (2007). High-risk drinking characteristics in collegiate athletes. *Journal of American College Health, 56*(3), 267–272.

Brewer, B. W., van Raalte, J. L., & Linder, D. E. (1993). Athletic identity: Hercules' muscles or Achilles heel? *International Journal of Sport Psychology, 24*, 237–254.

Bronfenbrenner, U. (1979). *The ecology of human development: Experiments by nature and design*. Cambridge, MA: Harvard University Press.

Bruening, J., Armstrong, K., & Pastore, D. (2005). Listening to the voices: The experiences of African American female athletes. *Research Quarterly for Exercise and Sport, 76*(1), 82–100.

Bubolz, M. M., & Sontag, M. S. (1993). Human ecology theory. In *Sourcebook of family theories and methods* (pp. 419–450). New York: Springer.

Cass, V. (1996). *Sexual orientation identity formation: A Western phenomenon*. In R. P. Cabaj & T. S. Stein (Eds.), *Textbook of homosexuality and mental health* (pp. 227–251). Washington, DC: American Psychiatric Press.

Chickering, A., & Reisser, L. (1993). *Education and identity* (2nd ed.). San Francisco: Jossey-Bass.

Clark, B. (1972). The organizational saga in higher education. *Administrative Science Quarterly, 17*(2), 178–184.

Coakley, J., & Dunning, E. (Eds.). (2000). *Handbook of sports studies*. Thousand Oakes, CA: Sage.

Comeaux, E. (2005, Summer). Environmental predictors of academic achievement among student-athletes in the revenue-producing sports of men's basketball and football. *Sport Journal, 8*(3) (ISSN: 1543–9518).

———. (2010). Racial differences in faculty perceptions of collegiate student-athletes' academic and post-undergraduate achievements. *Sociology of Sport Journal, 27*, 390–412.

Comeaux, E., & Harrison, C. K. (2011). A conceptual model of academic success for student athletes. *Educational Researcher, 4*, 235–245.

Cross, W. E., Jr., & Fhagen-Smith, P. (2001). Patterns of African American identity development: A life span perspective. In C. L. Wijeyesinghe & B. W. Jackson III (Eds.), *New perspectives on racial identity development: A theoretical and practical anthology* (pp. 243–270). New York: New York University Press.

Cunningham, G. B. (2012). *Sexual orientation and gender in sport: Essays from activists, coaches, and scholars.* College Station, TX: Center for Sport Management Research and Education.

D'Augelli, A. R. (1994). Identity development and sexual orientation: Toward a model of lesbian, gay, and bisexual development. In E. J. Trinkett, R. J. Watts, & D. Birman (Eds.), *Human diversity: Perspectives on people in context* (pp. 312–333). San Francisco: Jossey-Bass.

Donnor, J. (2005). Toward an interest-convergence in the education of African-American football student athletes in major college sports. *Race Ethnicity and Education, 8*(1), 45–67.

Eitzen, D. S., & Sage, G. H. (2009). *Sociology of North American sport* (8th ed.). Boulder, CO: Paradigm Publishers.

Erikson, E. H. (1968). *Identity: Youth and crisis.* New York: Norton.

Evans, N. J., Forney, D. S., Guido, F. M, Patton, L. D., & Renn, K. A. (2010). *Student development in college: Theory, research, and practice* (2nd ed.). San Francisco: Jossey Bass.

Evans, N. J., & Herriott, T. K. (2009). Disability theory and its implications for student affairs practice. In J. Higbee & A. Mitchell (Eds.), *Making good on the promise: Student affairs professionals with disabilities* (pp. 27–40). Lanham, MD: American College Personnel Association.

Fassinger, R. E., & Miller, B. A. (1997). Validation of an inclusive model of sexual minority identity formation on a sample of gay men. *Journal of Homosexuality, 32*(2), 53–78.

Ferdman, B. M., & Gallegos, P. I. (2001). Racial identity development and Latinos in the United States. In C. L. Wijeyesinghe & B. W. Jackson III (Eds.), *New perspectives on Racial Identity Development: A theoretical and practical anthology* (pp. 32–66). New York: New York University Press.

Gaston-Gayles, J. L., & Hu, S. (2009). The influence of student engagement and sport participation on college outcomes among Division I student athletes. *Journal of Higher Education, 80*, 315–333.

Gilligan, C. (1982/1993). *In a different voice: Psychological theory and women's development.* Cambridge, MA: Harvard University Press.

Giulianotti, R. (2004). *Sport and modern social theorists.* New York: Palgrave Macmillan.

Goodman, J., Schlossberg, N. K., & Anderson, M. L. (2006). *Counseling adults in transition* (3rd ed.). New York: Spring.

Guba, E. G. (Ed.). (1990). *The alternative paradigm dialog.* In E. G. Guba (Ed.), *The paradigm dialogue* (pp. 17–30). Thousand Oaks, CA: Sage.

Guba, E. G., & Lincoln, Y. S. (1994). Competing paradigms in qualitative research. *Handbook of qualitative research, 2*, 163–194.

Harris, L. L. (2003). Integrating and analyzing psycho-social and stage theories to challenge the development of the injured collegiate athlete. *Journal of Athletic Training, 38*(1), 75–82.

Harrison, C. K., & Lawrence, S. M. (2004). Female and male student athletes' perceptions of career transition in sport and higher education: A visual elicitation and qualitative assessment. *Journal of Vocational Educational and Training, 56,*485–506.

Helms, J. E. (1995). An update of Helms's white and people of color racial identity models. In J. G. Ponterotto, J. M. Casas, L. A. Suzuki, & C. M. Alexander (Eds.), *Handbook of multicultural counseling* (pp. 181–198). Thousand Oaks, CA: Sage.

———. (1996). Toward a methodology for measuring and assessing racial identity as distinguished from ethnic identity. In G. Sodowsky and J. Impara (Eds.), *Multicultural assessment in counseling and clinical psychology* (pp. 143–192).

Horse, P. G. (2005). Native American identity. *New directions for student services, 109*(1), 61–68.

Howard-Hamilton, M. F., & Watt, S. K. (Eds.). (2001). Student services for athletes. *New Directions for Student Services* (No. 93). San Francisco: Jossey-Bass.

Ibrahim, F., Ohnishi, H., & Sandhu, D. S. (1997). Asian American identity development: A culture specific model for South Asian Americans. *Journal of Multicultural Counseling and Development, 25*(1), 34–50.

Kim, J. (2001). Asian American identity development theory. In C. L. Wijeyesinghe & B. W. Jackson III (Eds.), *New perspectives on racial identity development: A theoretical and practical anthology* (pp. 67–90). New York: New York University Press.

King, P. M. (2003). Student learning in higher education. In S. R. Komives, D. B. Woodard Jr., et al., *Student services: A handbook for the profession* (4th ed., pp. 234–268). San Francisco: Jossey Bass.

King, P. M. & Kitchener, K. S. (1994). *Developing reflective judgment: Understanding and promoting intellectual growth and critical thinking in adolescents and adults.* San Francisco: Jossey Bass.

Kolb, D. A. (1984). *Experiential learning: Experience as the source of learning and development* (Vol. 1). Englewood Cliffs, NJ: Prentice-Hall.

———. (2000). *Facilitator's guide to learning.* Boston: Hay/McBer.

Kohlberg, L. (1976). Moral stages and moralization: The cognitive-developmental approach. In T. Lickona (Ed.), *Moral development and behavior: Theory, research, and social issues* (pp. 31–53). New York: Holt, Rinehart and Winston.

Lawrence, S. M. (2005). African American athletes' experiences of race in sport. *International Review for the Sociology of Sport, 40,* 99–110.

McEwen, M. K. (2003). The nature and uses of theory. In S. R. Komives & D. B. Woodard Jr. (Eds.), *Student services: A handbook for the profession* (4th ed., pp. 203–233). San Francisco: Jossey-Bass.

Moreland-Bishop, L. A. (2009). *The impact of transition out of intercollegiate athletics* (Unpublished doctoral dissertation). Clemson University.

Naples, N. A. (2003). Epistemology, feminist methodology, and the politics of method. In N. A. Naples (Ed.), *Feminism and method: Ethnography, discourse analysis, and activist research* (pp. 13–33). New York: Routledge.

Nora, A. (2002). *A theoretical and practical view of student adjustment and academic achievement.* In W. G. Tierney & L. S. Hagedorn (Eds.), *Increasing access to college: Extending possibilities for all students.* Albany: SUNY Press.

Parker, C. A. (1977). On modeling reality. *Journal of College Student Personnel, 18,* 419–425.

Pascarella, E. T., & Terenzini, P. T. (2005). *How college affects students: A third decade of research.* San Francisco: Jossey-Bass.

Pelled, L. H. (1996). Demographic diversity, conflict, and work group outcomes: An intervening process theory. *Organization Science, 7*(6), 615–631.

Perkins, K. R. S. (2010). *Assessment of freshmen varsity student-athletes' learning style preferences* (Unpublished doctoral dissertation). Auburn University.

Perry, W. G., Jr. (1968). *Patterns of development in thought and values of students in a liberal arts College: A validation of a scheme.* Final Report. Bureau of Study Counsel. Harvard University.

Person, D. R., & LeNoir, K. M. (1997). Retention issues and models for African American male athletes. *New Directions for Student Services, 80,* 79–91.

Phinney, J. S. (1993). A three-stage model of ethnic identity development in adolescence. In M. E. Bernal & G. P. Knight (Eds.), *Ethnic identity: Formation and transmission among Hispanics and other minorities* (pp. 61–79). Albany: SUNY Press.

Piaget, J. (1952). *The origins of intelligence in children.* New York: International University Press.

Rankin, S. R. (2003). *Campus climate for gay, lesbian, bisexual, and transgender people: A national perspective.* Washington, DC: National Gay and Lesbian Task Force Policy Institute.

Rankin, S. R., Merson, D., Sorgen, C. H., McHale, I., Loya, K., & Oseguera, L. (2011). *Student Athlete Climate Study (SACS) Final Report.* Center for the Study of Higher Education. Pennsylvania State University.

Rankin, S. R., & Reason, R. D. (2005). Differing perceptions: How students of color and white students perceive campus climate for underrepresented groups. *Journal of College Student Development, 46*(1), 43–61.

———. (2008). Transformational tapestry model: A comprehensive approach to transforming campus climate. *Journal of Diversity in Higher Education, 1*(4), 262–274.

Renn, K. A. (2004). *Mixed race students in college: The ecology of race, identity, and community on campus.* Albany: SUNY Press.

Rest, J., Narvaez, D., Bebeau, M. J., & Thoma, S. J. (1999). *Postconventional moral thinking: A Neo-Kohlbergian approach.* Mahwah, NJ: Erlbaum.

Richard, O. C. (2000). Racial diversity, business strategy, and firm performance: A resource-based view. *Academy of Management Journal, 43*(2), 164–177.

Sack, A. (2009). Clashing models of commercial sport in higher education: Implications for reform and scholarly research. *Journal of Issues in Intercollegiate Athletics, 2,* 76–92.

Sage, G. H. (1998). *Power and ideology in American sport: A critical perspective* (2nd ed.). Champaign, IL: Human Kinetics.

Schlossberg, N. K. (1989). Marginality and mattering: Key issues in building community. *New Directions for Student Services, 48*(48), 5–15.

Schlosser, L. Z. (2003). Christian privilege: Breaking a sacred taboo. *Journal of Multicultural Counseling and Development, 31*(1), 44–51.

Schroeder, P. J. (2010). A model for assessing organizational culture in intercollegiate athletic departments. *Journal of Issues in Intercollegiate Athletics, 3*, 98–118.

Scott, W., & Davis, G. (2007). *Organizations and organizing: Rational, natural, and open system perspectives.* Upper Saddle River, NJ: Pearson.

Singer, J. N. (2005). Understanding racism through the eyes of African American male student-athletes. *Race Ethnicity and Education, 8*, 365–386.

Smith, D. G., Gerbick, G. L., Figueroa, M. A., Watkins, G. H., Levitan, T., Moore, L. C., & Figueroa, B. (1997). *Diversity works: The emerging picture of how students benefit.* Washington, DC: Association of American Colleges and Universities.

Solorzano, D. G., & Delgado-Bernal, D. D. (2001). Examining transformational resistance through a critical race and LatCrit theory framework Chicana and Chicano students in an urban context. *Urban Education, 36*, 308–342.

Sue, D. W., & Sue, D. (2003). *Counseling the culturally diverse: Theory and practice* (4th ed.). New York: Wiley.

Tinto, V. (1993). *Leaving college: Rethinking the causes and cures of student attrition* (2nd ed.). Chicago: University of Chicago Press.

Torres, V. (2003). Influences on ethnic identity development of Latino college students in the first two years of college. *Journal of College Student Development, 44*, 532–547.

Whisenant, W. A., Pedersen, P. M., & Obenour, B. L. (2002). Success and gender: Determining the rate of advancement for intercollegiate athletic directors. *Sex Roles, 47*, 485–491. doi:10.1023/A:1021656628604

Wolf-Wendel, L. E., Toma, J. D., & Morphew, C. C. (2001). How much difference is too much difference? Perceptions of gay men and lesbians in intercollegiate athletics. *Journal of College Student Development, 42*, 465–479.

Worthington, R. L., Savoy, H. B., Dillon, F. R., & Vernaglia, E. R. (2002). Heterosexual identity development a multidimensional model of individual and social identity. *Counseling Psychologist, 30*, 496–531.

PART THREE

The College Athlete Experience

Both college athletes and their nonathlete peers are faced with stresses and expectations in the academic and social environment, but college athletes also encounter tremendous sport demands that create substantial challenges to the quality of their college experience. In chapter 6, Joy Gaston Gayles sketches the college experience of Division I athletes and summarizes some of the most common challenges they encounter. Community college athletes—a critically important student group that is often underresearched and overlooked in American higher education—are the focus of chapter 7. David Horton Jr. examines their experiences, with a particular focus on predictors of four-year transfer for athletes. In chapter 8, Janet Lawrence and Jon McNaughtan highlight issues associated with the conceptualization and assessment of campus climate as it relates to intercollegiate athletics more generally. They develop a conception of the intercollegiate athletics climate and use it to anchor a discussion of its effects on individual behavior (e.g., college athletes) and organizational performance. ∎

TODAY'S COLLEGE ATHLETE

Joy Gaston Gayles

When describing the experiences of athletes on Division I college campuses, most scholars compare athletes to nonathletes (Simons, Van Rheenen, & Covington, 1999; Watt & Moore, 2001). Such a comparison illuminates the unique ways in which participation in college sports impacts athletes and the additional responsibilities and requirements that must be managed for success in the classroom and on the field or court. In addition to taking classes, athletes must maintain academic eligibility requirements, take a full load of classes, make progress toward degree completion each year, practice, travel, compete, attend study hall, sustain injuries, and manage the psychological stress of winning and losing (Carodine, Almond, & Gratto, 2001). Although athletes make a conscious choice to endure these additional challenges, such experiences set them apart from their peers and require support from the university and athletic department in order achieve success both on the field and in the classroom.

Many of the ways in which the experiences of athletes are unique compared to their nonathlete peers are a result of the rules and regulations designed to govern and control college sports. The National Collegiate Athletic Association (NCAA), the athletic conference to which the institution belongs, and the college or university have regulations in place to which athletes must adhere in order to participate in college sports each year. The rules and regulations are designed to ensure that athletes make progress toward their degree and maintain a fair and equitable play across institutions within the NCAA.

College athletes who desire to compete in intercollegiate athletics must go through the NCAA Eligibility Center (formerly known as the

KEY TERMS

college athletes ◄

intercollegiate athletics ◄

higher education ◄

athletes on Division I ◄
campuses

NCAA Initial-Eligibility Clearinghouse). Initial eligibility requires that athletes graduate from high school and earn a minimum grade point average and test score based on a sliding scale. For example, under the current rules an athlete with a high school grade point average of 2.0 must have a SAT score of 1010 or a cumulative ACT score of 86. The relationship between grade point average and test score is inverted, such that lower grade point averages require higher test scores. In 2016 the sliding scale for initial eligibility will change for athletes at Division I institutions. In order to compete as a freshman in college, athletes will be required to earn a 2.3 grade point average in core courses. Further, athletes must successfully complete 10 of the 16 total required core courses before the start of their senior year of high school and 7 of the 10 courses must be in science, mathematics, and English. The sliding scale for test scores and GPA will increase. For example, a SAT score of 820 will require a grade point average of 2.5 in core courses. High school athletes who do not meet the initial eligibility standards cannot compete as a freshman. College athletes not in compliance will be allowed to practice and receive athletic grant-in-aid. If non-eligible athletes are successful in their first academic term, they may continue to practice during their freshman year of college.

Scholarship athletes are required to attend college full-time in order to participate. On most campuses this equates to taking 12 hours (four classes) per semester. To make sure students maintain 12 hours academic advisors often schedule athletes for 15 to 18 credit hours in the event that the student needs to drop a class in which he or she is performing poorly. In addition to taking a full load of classes, there are grade point average requirements that athletes must meet in order to participate each semester. In general, athletes cannot fall below a grade point average of 2.0.

College athletes are also unique because they have to balance the demands of academic requirements with practicing and competing in their sport. The NCAA mandates athletic departments to provide academic support and counseling services for athletes. Support services such as tutoring, supplemental instruction, computer labs, and course supplies must be provided to help athletes succeed in the classroom. In addition, NCAA rules state that athletes are not allowed to practice more than 20 hours per week; however, reports indicate that some athletes practice more than 40 hours per week on average, volunteering their time to review game tapes and condition for their sport (Wolverton, 2008).

CHALLENGES FOR ATHLETES AND HIGHER EDUCATION

The many rules and regulations, pressures, and scrutiny associated with intercollegiate athletics in higher education have created challenges for athletes and higher education institutions. Reports of scandals involving academic and social misconduct in intercollegiate athletics flood the media each year. The accusations and incidents have increased in severity over the years, and these scandals bring shame to the institution and spark distrust within the community. Some of the major challenges concerning athlete welfare include academic performance and graduation rates, balancing academic and athletic tasks, and the pay-for-play issue.

Academic Performance and Graduation Rates

The 1980s represents a period of increased concern about academic standards and performance for athletes. It was the first time that the NCAA enforced regulations for academic performance that were actually adhered to by member institutions. Proposition 48 and the Student Right to Know Act are two major reform efforts that set the foundation for academic standards.

NCAA member institutions have reported graduation rates since the mid-1980s under the Student Right to Know Act, which requires that higher education institutions make public graduation rate data as well as data on crime statistics so that

STAKEHOLDER PERSPECTIVE

Pay-for-Play: A Moral Dilemma

Darin Moss is the director for compliance at Big Time University, USA. Big Time University is one of the top land-grant universities in the country with highly ranked athletic programs for the majority of the 14 sports offered. The basketball program has clinched two national championships in the past 7 years and is ranked number 1 in the country. Darin has worked in compliance for 10 years. He spent the first few years of his career working in compliance at the National Collegiate Athletic Association before becoming the compliance director at Big Time University. During his time at the NCAA he worked in investigations and is very familiar with the rules and regulations, infractions, and penalties associated with breaking the rules.

Working at Big Time University, Darin understands that students are under a great deal of pressure to manage their affairs both on and off the playing field. At the beginning of every academic year Darin and his staff meet with all athletes by sport to remind them of the rules and regulations associated with participating in intercollegiate athletics. Some of the major issues for athletes in high-profile sports are accepting gifts from agents, boosters, and others in the community. The NCAA is very strict concerning athletes accepting monetary gifts, making deals with agents, and academic misconduct.

The pay-for-play issue is one that Darin struggles with. On one hand, Big Time University generates large sums of revenue largely based on the athletic prowess of athletes. Yet athletes do not receive a direct share of the profit for their labor. Moreover, Darin knows that some of the most talented players come from poor backgrounds where the families of athletes in high-profile sports are depending on their loved one to "go pro." However, while the athletes are competing at the college level, they do not have enough money to cover daily living expenses, such as washing clothes, going to the movies, or buying a bus ticket home for the holidays.

The associated press recently interviewed Darin about this issue as Big Time University is currently under investigation for allegations of university basketball players accepting money from boosters. Darin Moss told the Associated Press that pay-for-play is a major issue plaguing college sports. As commercialism and revenue generation increase without consideration of the overall well-being of athletes, misconduct and scandals involving rule infractions will continue to escalate and burden higher education institutions. ■

students can make informed decisions about the institutions they desire to attend. The latest graduation rate data show that athletes graduate at higher rates compared to students in the general population (Christianson, 2012). In 2012 the NCAA reported that athletes who entered as freshmen during the 2004–2005 academic year graduated at a rate of 81%. The NCAA also reported that in 2012 athletes in football and men's basketball showed remarkable improvement compared to past years. Men's basketball players graduated at 74%, a 6-point increase from the previous entering class. Further, football players had a graduation rate of 70%, 1-point increase over the previous entering class. Moreover, across an 11-year period of data collection graduation rates for men's basketball increased 21 percentage points and graduation rates for football players increased 7 percentage points.

Scholars and critics have questioned why the graduation rate data reported by the NCAA are so high (Southall, Eckard, Nagel, & Hale, 2012). One of the major reasons why the data vary so widely is because the NCAA and the federal government use different metric systems. The NCAA developed the Graduation Success Rate (GSR) to better account for transfer students who leave the institution in good standing. Thus, outgoing transfer students in good standing are included in the receiving institutions cohort of athletes. The current GSR is based on four cohorts of entering classes from 2002 to 2006. The GSR reported by the NCAA is usually about 20 percentage points higher than the rate reported by the federal government, which excludes transfer students from the calculation (Steinbach, 2012). Using the Federal Graduation Rate, athletes who entered in 2005 graduated at a rate of 65%, two percentage points higher than students in the general population did. Another reason why the GSR is higher than the Federal Graduation Rate is that for the first time Ivy League institutions were included in the calculations. It is important to note that Ivy League institutions are not like other Division I institutions because they do not award athletic scholarships.

Without probing any further, the fact that graduation rates have increased, particularly for high-profile sports, is good news. However, further examination of graduation data unmasks major differences in academic performance and successful degree completion. For example, disaggregating graduation rates by race and ethnicity shows major disparities. According to the GSR, African American athletes graduated at a rate of 54%. Although this represents an increase of 19% over time, the rate still lags behind students in the general population. More alarming is that African American males graduated at a rate of 49%—an increase of 16 points over time. However, like African American females this rate lags behind the average rate for all African American athletes and students in the general population. African American female athletes, however, are faring well graduating at a rate of 64%, which is on par with the average graduation for athletes in the general student population.

Balancing Academics and Athletics

Perhaps one of the most challenging and stressful tasks faced by athletes is the act of balancing academic, athletics, and social demands (Adler & Adler, 1991; Comeaux

& Harrison, 2011; Gaston-Gayles, 2004; Simons, Van Rheenen, & Covington, 1999). On most days athletes wake up early, take a full day of classes, attend practice, eat dinner, and then go to study hall. By the time study hall is over late in the evening it is time to rest and prepare to do it all over again the next day. Such a rigid schedule leaves limited time for social activities and in some cases not enough time to meet with professors during office hours and tutors for supplemental instruction. Moreover, balancing academic and athletic demands can be even more strenuous for athletes who enter college academically underprepared.

Scholars have studied the challenges athletes face balancing academic and athletic roles and responsibilities. Adler and Adler (1991) conducted one of the first studies on the topic using ethnographic techniques to study the basketball team at a major Division I institution. Overall they found that the male basketball players in the study had high aspirations toward academic performance in college; however, the demands of participating in their sport led to overinvolvement in athletics as early as the first and second semester of their college career. Adler and Adler coined the term *role engulfment* to characterize athletes who became overinvolved with athletic demands and as a result devoted little time to academic and social experiences during college.

A major problem resulting from overinvolvement in athletics is isolation from the general student body. Critics have argued that athletes form a separate subculture on college campuses that isolates them from the student body and impacts the extent to which they benefit from the college experience in ways similar to their peers (Bowen & Levin, 2003; Shulman & Bowen, 2001). Parham's (1993) study on the experiences of athletes supports that they have difficulty balancing academic and athletic tasks and experience social isolation from spending so much time in the athletic domain. The study also found that athletes experience mental and emotional stress from dealing with the pressures of winning and losing and managing relationships among competing groups, such as coaches, friends, and family. Parham concluded that the demands of balancing so many stressors make the athlete population vulnerable to other issues, such as lower gains in learning and personal development.

Other studies have examined the issue of balancing academic and athletic demands using motivation theory. It is quite natural for athletes to enter college highly motivated in the athletic domain because the university recruits and awards scholarships based on athletic talent. The problem is when students enter the university without the same level of motivation in the academic domain. Lack of academic motivation seems to be most problematic for high-profile athletes (Gaston-Gayles, 2004; Simons, Van Rheenen, & Covington, 1999). Gaston-Gayles (2004) developed a scale to measure athletes' motivation toward sports and academics and found that what mattered most in terms of academic performance was the extent to which athletes were motivated academically. Having high aspirations to excel in the athletic domain did not influence academic performance; however, lack of academic motivation, regardless of athletic motivation, had a negative influence on academics.

Other studies have examined motivation using self-worth theory to understand differences in motivation for the student athlete population. Simons, Van Rheenen, and Covington (1999) examined achievement motivation for athletes using self-worth theory and found that most athletes in revenue sports were failure avoiders—motivated to achieve success in one domain while avoiding failure in another. Moreover, failure avoiders are characterized by attitudes and behaviors that result in low academic performance such as use of self-handicapping excuses, low academic self-worth, higher problem levels in reading and studying, and less intrinsic motivation.

When athletes place too much emphasis in the athletic domain and become isolated from the student body, the question is raised as to whether athletes benefit from the college experience similar to their nonathlete peers. The idea that athletes make up a separate subculture on college campuses leads to discussion about possible negative consequences of participating in college sports. Gayles and Hu (2009) examined the athlete experience using national data from the NCAA and found that athletes interacted with peers other than athletes more commonly than any other form of engagement measured in the study. However, athletes participated in student organizations least frequently. In addition, interacting with peers other than teammates was one of the most influential factors in outcomes such as personal self-concept and learning and communication skills. A unique finding in this study, however, was that these effects were more beneficial for athletes in low-profile or Olympic sports. More investigation is needed to understand what factors matter relative to cognitive and affective gains for athletes in high-profile sports.

Pay-for-Play

The debate over whether to compensate athletes for their participation in college sports is a growing area of concern for intercollegiate athletics and higher education. College athletes, particularly those who participate in revenue sports such as football and men's basketball, generate large sums of revenue for athletic departments; yet athletes do not receive any share of the profit from the revenue they help generate. Further, athletic departments generate revenue from merchandise sales using the number and image of high-profile athletes.

Commercialism associated with college sports is a growing problem that institutions will have to address in the near future. As commercialism increases in the form or television contracts, ticket sales, high-salary coaches, and advertising endorsements, so does the pressure to produce winning teams and generate revenue. Over the years, cases of academic and social misconduct have increased in frequency and severity. Further, the commercialized values of intercollegiate athletics run contrary to the goals and values of higher education institutions. Institutions of higher education will need to figure out the proper role and function of intercollegiate athletics in higher education and take steps to align the values and goals of educating students to the goals and values associated with participation in college sports.

Pay-for-Play

The pay-for-play issue is predicated on the question of whether athletes should receive monetary compensation for their participation in college sports. The commercialism associated with college sports has increased exponentially over the years and institutions generate millions of dollars annually from television contracts, ticket sales, tournaments, and advertising deals. At the heart of the pay-for-play issue is the tension between the fact that athletic departments generate large sums of revenue and the individuals responsible for generating the revenue do not receive a direct share of the profit. In fact, athletes represent the only stakeholders who do not receive a direct share of the profit.

Some have argued that college athletes do receive payment in the form of an athletic scholarship. However, others have questioned if $40,000 to $50,000 over a total of 4 years is equivalent to the billions of dollars generated annually by athletic departments. Moreover, if athletes in high-profile sports are not successfully graduating from college, then is the promise of earning a college degree enough to compensate athletes for their labor?

Institutions of higher education adhere to the principle of amateurism as it allows for a peculiar institution such as college sports to exist within higher education institutions (Thelin, 2012). Compensating athletes directly would go against the values and principles of higher education and would change the face of college sports as we know it. Questions about how much athletes should be paid, should all athletes receive the same amount, should all athletes be paid or just athletes in revenue-producing sports are some of the questions that will have to be addressed if such a policy were enacted.

The NCAA recognizes the academic, financial, and social pressures faced by college athletes but remains strictly against compensating athletes for participation in the college sports. The collegiate model dates back to the 1950s and implies that athletes are also students (not employees of the institution). The NCAA recently passed legislation for institutions to award athletes up to $2,000 over the cost of attendance. However, this legislation was put on hold because athletic departments complained that they did not have enough revenue to do so. Further athletes are allowed to work no more than 20 hours per week and cannot be compensated more than $2,000 beyond the cost of attendance. Although this would allow athletes to earn additional money for daily living expenses, working a part-time job further complicates the issue of balancing academic and athletic demands.

About 300 athletes participating in high-profile sports across several Division I institutions recently filed a law suit against the NCAA for rights and royalties associated with marketing jerseys with players' names and numbers on them. College athletes feel that they should benefit from advertising and merchandise sales that use their names and numbers. The lawsuit indicates that they want direct compensation for and rights to merchandise sales. ■

The NCAA has taken a firm stance against pay-for-play and has held true to the amateur status of college sports. A few reform efforts that address the pay-for-play issue have been approved, but the NCAA has made clear that the measures taken are not a form of pay-for-play. In the 1990s the NCAA allowed athletes to work no more than 20 hours per week and earn no more than $2,000 above the cost of tuition. In 2011 the NCAA also approved a rule allowing athletic departments to add up to $2,000 above the cost of tuition to athletic grant-in-aid for athletes in an effort to close the gap between tuition and fees and the full cost of attendance. Because of complaints from athletic departments across the country, the NCAA has since tabled the rule until a solution is reached concerning how athletic departments can afford to increase scholarships for athletes. The following questions remain:

Should athletes be compensated beyond athletic grant-in-aid, and what does this mean for intercollegiate athletics on college campuses?

CONCLUSION

Although there are many challenges and problems with college sports on college campuses, intercollegiate athletics serves a unique purpose that should not be overlooked. If governed and controlled properly, intercollegiate athletics can serve as a bridge that connects the university to the community, provide opportunities for students to receive a quality education and develop character, and unite the campus community around a common goal. Reform agendas led by groups such as the Knight Commission on Intercollegiate Athletics and The Drake Group call for better alignment between the values and goals and intercollegiate athletics and institutions of higher education. For example, a recent Knight Commission Report (2010) entitled *Restoring the Balance* calls for greater transparency concerning spending in intercollegiate athletics, putting into place practices that lead to making academics a priority, maintaining the amateur status of college sports, and treating athletes as students first. At the heart of all reform efforts should be the welfare of the student athlete. Policy recommendations and rule changes must consider what is in the best interest of students and how can we better educate and support the athlete population in ways that support the mission of higher education institutions.

QUESTIONS FOR DISCUSSION

1. What are some of the major issues facing intercollegiate athletics in American higher education today?

2. Do you think that athletes at Division I institutions should be paid for their participation in intercollegiate athletics? Why or why not?

3. What are the pros and cons for institutions of higher education concerning paying athletes for participating in intercollegiate athletics?

References

Adler, P. A., & Adler, P. (1991). *Backboards and blackboards: College athletes and role engulfment*. New York: Columbia University Press.

Bowen, W. G., & Levin, S. A. (2003). *Reclaiming the game: College sports and educational values*. Princeton, NJ: Princeton University Press.

Carodine, K., Almond, K. F., & Gratto, K. K. (2001). College student athlete success both in and out of the classroom. In M. F. Howard-Hamilton & S. K. Watts (Eds.), Student services for athletes, *New Direction for Student Services*, 93, 19–33. San Francisco: Jossey-Bass.

Christianson, E. (2012, October 25). DI men's basketball, FBS football graduation rates highest ever. *NCAA News*.

Comeaux, E., & Harrison, C. K. (2011). A conceptual model of academic success for student-athletes. *Educational Researcher, 40*, 235–245.

Gaston-Gayles, J. (2004). Examining academic and athletic motivation among student athletes at a Division I university. *Journal of College Student Development, 45*(1), 75–83.

Gayles, J. G., & Hu, S. (2009). The influence of student engagement and sport participation on college outcomes among Division I student athletes. *Journal of Higher Education, 80*, 315–333.

Knight Commission on Intercollegiate Athletics. (2010). *Restoring the balance: Dollars, values, and the future of college sports*. Miami, FL: Author.

Parham, W. (1993). The intercollegiate athlete: A 1990s profile. *Counseling Psychologist, 21*, 411–429.

Shulman, J. L., & Bowen, W. G. (2001). *The game of life: College sports and educational values*. Princeton, NJ: Princeton University Press.

Simons, H. D., Van Rheenen, D., & Covington, M. V. (1999). Noncognitive predictors of student-athletes' academic performance. *Journal of College Student Development, 40*, 151–162.

Southall, R. M., Eckard, E. W., Nagel, M. S., & Hale, J. M. (2012). *Adjusted graduation gap report: NCAA Division-I football*. Chapel Hill, NC: College Sport Research Institute.

Steinbach, P. (2012). Record NCAA graduation rates don't tell the whole story. Retrieved from http://www.athleticbusiness.com/Governing-Bodies/record-ncaa-graduation-rates-don-t-tell-the-whole-story.html

Thelin, J. R. (2012). College athletics: Continuity and change over four centuries. In G. S. McClellan, C. King, & D. L. Rockey, *The handbook of college athletics and recreation administration* (pp. 3–20). San Francisco: Jossey-Bass.

Watt, S. K., & Moore, J. L. (2001). Who are student athletes? In M. F. Howard-Hamilton & S. K. Watts (Eds.), Student services for athletes, *New directions for student services*, 93, 7–18. San Francisco: Jossey-Bass.

Wolverton, B. (2008). Athletes' hours renew debate over college sports. *Chronicle of Higher Education, 54*(20), A1.

MVP

Predictors of Four-Year Transfer for Community College Athletes

David Horton Jr.

Intercollegiate athletics is a popular student activity at community colleges, especially at institutions situated in rural locales. Approximately 60% of all public community colleges in the United States sponsor at least one varsity athletic team (Castañeda, Katsinas, & Hardy, 2006; Kissinger & Miller, 2007). Between the three major athletics governing associations for community colleges (California Community College Commission on Athletics, National Junior College Athletic Association, and Northwest Athletic Association of Community Colleges), more than 75,000 individuals annually participate. At rurally located institutions athletes can compose as much as 22% of the total full-time enrolled student population (Castañeda et al., 2006). Though much research has been conducted on community college students, little is known about athletes or the factors that impact their academic experiences (Horton, 2009; Kissinger & Miller, 2007). Specifically, what is not fully understood is the impact of athletic participation on students' academic experiences.

The objective of the larger study from which this chapter was derived was to test empirically the effect of athletic participation and institutional and individual factors on the academic performance of community college athletes. This chapter is intended to answer the following two questions: To what extent do the academic experiences of athletes differ from their nonathlete peers; and what effect do academic performance and individual, precollege and institutional characteristics have on four-year transfer for athletes, compared to their nonathlete peers?

ATHLETICS AT THE COMMUNITY COLLEGE

Athletics at community colleges provide many benefits to students, institutions, and the communities they serve. For instance, athletics provide students with a true collegiate experience, contribute to the institution's efforts to recruit a more diverse student body, and address the missing male phenomenon (Bush, Castañeda, Hardy, & Katsinas, 2009). Institutions also benefit from increased enrollment of nonscholarship athletes that have been recruited by other institutions that do not permit athletic aid (Castañeda, et al., 2006). In their 2012 study, Barreno and Traut examined factors that influence individuals to choose to attend a community college. The authors found that female and black students in general were more likely than their peers to be influenced to attend a community college because of the availability of athletic teams and sports. Athletic programs are also likely to have a positive impact on the local economy (McCullough, 2000). For college athletes, athletics is a viable way to gain access to higher education, especially for students of color and those from minimal to modest financial means (Horton, 2011). Participation, in many states, also affords students access to athletic aid, which helps with tuition costs, and substantially provides upward social mobility for students through degree attainment, four-year transfer, or job placement (Hawkins, 1999).

STAKEHOLDER PERSPECTIVE

The Importance of Collaboration in the Best Interest of College Athletes

Christopher M. Mullin is the program director for policy analysis at the American Association of Community Colleges (AACC). In this capacity, his chief responsibility is to provide analysis and supporting data to guide and enhance AACC's advocacy efforts while also playing a central role in shaping AACC's long-term federal policy agenda. He earned a Ph.D. in Higher Education Administration at the University of Florida in 2008.

Mullin's work, especially a policy brief focused on the issue of transfer, notes that the research literature on transfer student success is varied. He also notes that rarely does the research acknowledge that success for students post-transfer may be due in part to the actions of the receiving institution. When unaccounted for, institutional inaction skews comparisons between the experiences of those who initially enroll in four-year colleges and those who start at community colleges. Put in another context, a team cannot win a relay race if subsequent runners drop the baton.

A real inequity exists for community college athletes, who now, as the result of policy changes by the National Collegiate Athletic Association (NCAA), must have a higher college grade point average to transfer and participate in Division I athletics than those students who transfer laterally. The data to justify the decision are severely limited, their legitimacy questionable, and the impact on community college athletes—especially students of color—is substantial. ■

STUDENT SUCCESS AND TRANSFER

Throughout the higher education literature diverse examples can be found of varying criteria that have been used to define transfer, identify possible transfer students, and calculate student transfer rates. In general, the term transfer encompasses various transitions students are likely to make between institutions and institutional types (Jones-White, Radcliffe, Huesman, & Kellogg, 2010). One of the most studied and perhaps most understood form of transfer is linear transfer. In this linear form the community college serves as the entry point to higher education for students who wish to eventually earn a bachelors degree (Townsend, 2002). Berkner, Horn, and Clune (2000) suggest the transition from community college to a four-year institution is one of the most important forms of transfer, "because its success (or failure) is central to many dimensions of state higher education performance, including access, equity, affordability, cost effectiveness, degree productivity, and quality" (p. 3). For the purposes of this study, four-year transfers were defined as any full-time first-time (FTFT) enrolled student who attended a community college and later enrolled in a four-year college or university (Romano & Wisniewski, 2003).

THEORETICAL APPROACH TO EXAMINING COLLEGE ATHLETE SUCCESS

Within the context of this study, a student's decision to participate in athletics at the collegiate level and an institution's role in providing access to higher education and awarding athletically related financial aid to athletes are viewed as investments in human capital. The basic tenets of human capital theory include the benefit of investments in activities that increase job-specific skills and academic credentials that generate income for future benefit (Becker, 1964, 1993). Human capital theory views increases in job-specific training and academic credentials as capital that yields higher wages, opportunities for personal and professional advancement, and upward social and economic mobility (Becker, 1964, 1993; Blaug, 1976). Becker (1964) primarily focused on the economic return that increased education yields over an individual's lifetime, compared to returns for those who choose not to invest in additional education beyond high school or specialized job training. The internal rate of return to costs associated with participation in higher education or other training opportunities is quantified by the net difference between investment costs (i.e., forgone earning, expenses for tuition, books, and other supplies) and future gains in income (Becker, 1964; Perna, 2006).

Participating in intercollegiate athletics requires a substantial commitment on behalf of the athlete. Comeaux (2011) asserts that "student-athletes devote more than 40 hours a week to sport-related activities, not to mention the mental fatigue, physical exhaustion, and nagging injuries that accompany those who participate in college sports" (p. 75). Across the United States, two-year institutions allocate nearly $50 million annually for athletically related financial aid. The desired and ultimate product of this investment, I argue, is the students' successful completion of a credential at a community college, accumulation of tools and skills necessary to enter the work force, or the opportunity to further their academic studies at a four-year institution. Accordingly, this study explores the impact and product of this investment.

RESEARCH DESIGN

Data for this study were provided by the Florida Department of Education's PK-20 Education Data Warehouse (EDW) and Community College and Technical Center MIS (CCTCMIS). The EDW has been the single repository of student-level data for public secondary schools, community colleges, career and technical education institutions, adult education, and four-year institutions since 1996 (Hansen, 2006). For the purposes of this study, a student was deemed "academically successful" if he or she transferred to a four-year institution within a maximum of 11 semesters. As such, a maximum of 11 semesters was set as the parameter for this study owing to limitations in the availability of data regarding the disbursement of athletically related aid to students in the state of Florida before the 2003–2004 academic year. Institutional level data from the National Center on Education Statistics Integrated Post-secondary Education Data System (IPEDS) 2005 survey were also incorporated in the present analysis.

Sampling

The institutional sample consisted of two-year institutions within the Florida community college system that sponsored athletic programs and teams during the 2004–2005 academic year. At the time of this study Florida's community college system consisted of 28 institutions. Because of the preceding criteria, three institutions and students who matriculated at one of these three institutions were excluded from this analysis. Five additional institutions and students attending these institutions were also excluded because of missing data. Students included in the nonathlete and athlete samples were limited to individuals who began their academic studies at 1 of 20 institutions in the state that sponsored intercollegiate athletics, and who were enrolled full-time (enrolled in 12 credit hours or more during the 2004 fall term) and members of 2004–2005 student cohort. The athlete sample was limited to students in the 2004–2005 cohort who were awarded athletically related aid during at least one academic term during their enrollment.

Methodology

The preliminary data analysis stage included descriptive analysis and independent t-tests. Findings from this stage are discussed alongside the discussion of independent and dependent variables provided in the next section. The second step of data analysis employed logistic regression methods to explore the effect of selected variables on four-year transfer propensity for athletes and nonathlete students. Within higher education research, logistic regression is the preferred statistical method when developing statistical models that incorporate dichotomous dependent variables, such as persistence, transfer, major and degree attainment, and both dichotomous and continuous independent variables (Cabrera, 1994).

Independent variables in the regression models were placed in blocks and added in succession to the baseline models. The baseline equation for model I (all students) included the group of variables representing student background characteristics: $Y_1 = \beta_0 + \beta_1(\text{Athletic status}) + \beta_2(\text{Race}) + \beta_3(\text{Gender}) + \beta_3(\text{SES}) + \varepsilon_1$, where Y_1 represents four-year transfer, β_j the coefficient, and ε_1 the constant or error term. The baseline equation for model II (athletes) included similar background characteristics as found in model I but was tailored to the athlete sample. Specifically, in model II, athlete status was replaced with sports team participation in order to capture the effect of athletic team participation. The regression model was represented as follows: $Y_1 = \beta_0 + \beta_1(\text{Sport}) + \beta_2(\text{RACE}) + \beta_3(\text{Gender}) + \beta_4(\text{SES}) + \varepsilon_1$, where Y_1 represents four-year transfer, β_j the coefficient, and ε_1 the constant or error term.

Independent Variables and Descriptive Statistics

Independent variables were placed in groups (i.e., athlete status, sports team participation, individual background characteristics, precollege characteristics, academic experience, and institutional characteristics). College athlete status was a binary variable based on the award of athletically related financial aid and was used to identify athletes in the student sample. The sample included 568 athletes. Sports team participation incorporated three binary variables, which included basketball (n = 173), baseball (n = 149), and golf, soccer, softball, swimming/diving, tennis, and volleyball (n = 246). Golf, soccer, swimming/diving, tennis, and volleyball were combined in the original dataset received from EDW, and thus were combined into one binary variable. The latter group was selected as the reference group in regression model II owing to a high concentration of ethnic majority students represented on these sports teams. Table 7.1 illustrates team participation by race.

Individual background characteristics consisted of race, gender, and socioeconomic status (SES). Because of a low representation of athletes from Asian or Pacific Islander (1.1%), Hispanic (6.4%), and American Indian (0.2%) racial/ethnic groups, a dummy variable for race was created where 0 = white and 1 = students of color. White students composed 59.2% (n = 8,646) of the nonathlete student sample and 61.7% (n = 345) of athlete sample. Students with missing data for race/ethnicity were excluded from analysis. Gender was coded with males serving as the reference group. Gender was reported for a total of 15,457 students (nonathlete and athletes combined). Female students had the highest representation across samples. Specifically, 61% (n = 9,087) of nonathletes and 56.1% (n = 317) of athletes were female.

To explore the impact of SES on student success, a proxy variable based on the receipt of a Pell Grant was created. Pell Grants are need-based awards given to un-

TABLE 7.1

Crosstabs for Sport Participation by Race/Ethnicity

	RACE/ETHNICITY		
SPORT	STUDENTS OF COLOR	WHITE STUDENTS	TOTAL
Basketball	153	17	170
Baseball	26	122	148
Golf, soccer, softball, swimming, diving, tennis, and volleyball	35	206	241
Total	214	345	

dergraduate and postbaccalaureate students from low-income backgrounds attending public and proprietary colleges and universities (U.S. Department of Education, 2009). For classification purposes that were based on the criteria for receiving a Pell Grant, grant recipients were classified as low SES; students in the sample that did not receive grant aid were classified as high SES. Low-SES students totaled 68% of all students. When delineated by athletic status, 69% (10,307) of nonathlete students and 36% (207) of athletes were categorized as low SES.

A dummy variable was created to capture the impact of time elapsed between high school completion and college entrance, where 0 = students that entered college within one calendar year of receipt of their high school diploma and 1 = students that delayed entry for more than one calendar year. Approximately 59% (n = 8,776) of nonathlete students enrolled in college within one year. A substantially higher percentage of athletes (89%) enrolled in college within a year.

Level of college readiness is of particular importance to the conversation of student success in general, and the discussion of athletes more specifically as little is known about its impact on athletes. Accordingly, a dummy variable was constructed for college readiness using a multiple-step process. First, student scores for the ACT were converted to SAT scores using the "ACT/SAT Conversion Table" provided by *The Princeton Review*. Next, student scores from the College Placement Test (CPT) were converted to SAT scores using the Florida Department of Education "Remedial Cutoff Score table" (Florida Department of Education, 2005). The table was used to determine students' academic readiness for college-level math, reading, and writing, where 0 = college ready and 1 = not college ready. Additionally, a categorical variable was created that was based on the number of content areas remediation where was needed. This variable was coded as 0 = if no remediation was needed, 1 = remediation in one content area was necessary, 2 = remediation in two content areas was required, and 3 = remediation was necessary in reading, writing, and math. Only 36% of all students (athletes and nonathletes combined) were college ready in all three content areas. Twenty-six percent of all

TABLE 7.2

Analysis of Mean GPA for Athletes and Nonathlete Students

COMPARISONS	LEVENE'S TEST OF EQUAL VARIANCE	
	F	SIG.
Nonathletes vs. athletes	134.01	0.000
Nonathletes (SOC) vs. athletes (SOC)	71.16	0.000
Nonathletes (female) vs. athletes (female)	90.95	0.000
Nonathletes (low SES) vs. athletes (low SES)	62.07	0.000

Note: Mean difference is significant at the $p \le .001$ significance level.

students required remediation in at least one content area, 18.6% in two content areas, and 19.1% in all three content areas.

Students' academic experiences were operationalized using three continuous variables (overall GPA, course credit hours enrolled, and course credit hours earned). Students' cumulative GPAs were calculated from transcript data obtained from EDW. Table 7.2 presents *t*-tests for comparisons conducted for GPA between students and athletes, and groups of athletes and nonathletes, and was based on race, gender, and SES. College athletes had a mean GPA of 2.59 compared to nonathlete students, who had a mean GPA of 2.29. These differences between athletes and nonathletes were found to be significantly different. Moreover, athletes enrolled in and earned more credit hours per semester than nonathlete students. Specifically, athletes enrolled in 12.53 credit hours and earned 10.08 credit hours per semester. In comparison, nonathletes enrolled in 9.00 credit hours and earned 6.18 credit hours (SD=3.69) per semester.

A categorical variable was created to represent institutions located in suburban, urban, and rural geographic locales. Dummy variables were then created for each category with suburban institutions serving as the reference group. Institution's full-time-equivalent (FTE) enrollment size provided another index in which to examine the impact of institutional characteristics on student success. Institutional FTEs were categorized as small (500–1,999), medium (2,000–4,999), large (5,000–9,999), and very large (at least 10,000). Categorical variables were recoded into three separate binary variables (e.g., 1=small, 0=medium, large, very large). Large institutions served as the reference group. Eleven institutions (55%) were classified as urban, four (20%) as rural, and the remaining institutions as suburban, according to IPEDS definitions. Ten (50%) of the included institutions had an enrollment size of 10,000 FTE or more, and five (25%) between 2,000 and 4,999, and two institutions had an enrollment size between 200 and 1,999 FTEs.

FINDINGS

Findings from this study are discussed in term of odds-ratios ($Exp(\beta)$), which represent the odds change for a one-unit change in the predictor factor when all other predictor variables in the equation are held at a constant value (Peng, So, Stage, & St. John, 2002). Additionally, probability values, another term commonly used throughout this chapter, are used to explain the likelihood of an event occurring for one designated group over another group and are discussed within this section as a percentage ($Exp(\beta) \times 100$) or decimal value ($Exp(\beta) = .469$). For instances where results are discussed for continuous variables (i.e., GPA and credit hours earned), the odds-ratios of transfer occurring were calculated at different values of the continuous variable, using the following formula:

$$\frac{Exp\{\beta_1(\chi+1)\}}{Exp\{\beta_1\chi\}} = Exp\{\beta_1(c)\},$$

where, β_1 is the coefficient's beta weight, χ and is the selected value of the independent continuous variable. Both model I and model II were significant at $p < 0.001$. Model I (all students) correctly predicted four-year transfer for 98.4% of the students in the samples and model II (athletes) correctly predicted 97.3%. Table 7.3 presents an illustration of findings from the regression analyses.

Regression Model I: All Students

Nine variables in model I were found to be significant predictors of four-year transfer (athlete status, gender, SES, delayed entry to college, math readiness, writing readiness, GPA, credit hours earned, and institutional enrollment size [large]). College athletes and students from low SES were found to be less likely to transfer. Females were found to be nearly two times more likely than males to transfer. Precollege characteristics had a significant impact on transfer. Specifically, students who delayed entry to higher education beyond one year and those who were not college ready in math or writing were less likely to transfer. Moreover, students' academic experiences were also highly significant predictors of four-year transfer for first-time students. As would be expected, students who maintained higher GPAs and those who earned more credit hours per semester were more likely than their peers to transfer. Lastly, only one factor within institutional characteristics, enrollment size (large), was found to impact transfer.

Regression Model II: College Athletes

Only three factors were found to be significant in model II (gender, GPA, and sports team participation). Females were nearly 14% more likely than males to transfer to a four-year institution. When holding all other predictor variables constant, athletes' GPAs were highly significant. For example, athletes with a mean GPA of 3.30 were

TABLE 7.3

Likelihood of Four-Year Transfer by Individual and Institutional Factors

VARIABLES	NONATHLETES (MODEL I)		ATHLETES (MODEL II)	
	BETA	EXP(B)	BETA	EXP(B)
Individual background characteristics				
Student athlete	−.587	.556*		
Female	.553	1.738***	−1.982	.138*
Students of color	.187	1.206	−.739	2.094
Low SES	−.655	.519***	−.003	.997
Precollege characteristics				
Delayed entrant	−.587	.556**	.735	2.085
Not math ready	−.709	.492***	−.065	.937
Not reading ready	−.271	.763	.395	1.483
Not writing ready	−1.241	.289**	−1.122	.326
Academic experiences				
Cumulative GPA[a]	1.231	3.425***	1.508	4.516*
Credit hours earned[a]	.232	1.262***	.028	1.028
Institutional characteristics				
Enrollment size (small)	.635	1.888	.215	1.240
Enrollment size (medium)	−.067	.935	−.352	.703
Enrollment size (large)	−.466	.628*	−.340	.712
Locale (urban)	.259	1.296	.065	1.067
Locale (rural)	−.104	.901	.002	1.002
Athletic participation (sport)				
Basketball			−19.32	.000
Baseball			−2.418	.089**

[a]Independent variable is continuous.
*$p < .05$
**$p < .01$
***$p < .001$

found to be 26 times more likely to transfer than students with a 2.30 average GPA. When considering specific sport participation, students who participated in baseball were less likely to transfer than students participating in golf, soccer, softball, swimming/diving, tennis, and volleyball.

CONCLUSION

Continued research on community colleges, student success, and four-year transfer more specifically, has broad implications for higher education. As the rising cost of college continues to be debated, athletics and athletes continue to be an easy target as many stakeholders in the academic community hold athletics partially responsible for these rising costs. Gaining a better understanding of the impact athletics plays in athletes' academic success is of utmost importance in these times. Two main issues regarding athletes and athletics were addressed in this study. First, differences in individual characteristics, precollege characteristics, and the academic experiences of athletes and nonathlete students were addressed. Second, the impact of risks factors as predictor of academic success for athletes, and for select racial, gender, and SES subgroups was tested.

The title of this chapter is "MVPs: Predictors of Four-Year Transfer for Community College Athletes." The title MVP, most valuable player, is given to a person who has the greatest instrumental value toward the goal of winning. It is clear which factors stand above the rest in making athletes at community colleges the MVPs. In sum, findings corroborate previous research that women are more likely to be successful than men; and students who exhibit positive academic behaviors, such as earning a majority of the credit hours they attempt and maintaining at least a "B" GPA are likely to transfer. Furthermore, students who enter college underprepared and those from low socioeconomic backgrounds are less likely to be successful with institutional intervention.

One practice employed by athletic programs at community colleges is to recruit students from disadvantaged socioeconomic or academic backgrounds to attend and participate in sponsored sports at their institution. Many lament that such institutional practices do more harm than good to students. It appears, however, that one's decision to participate in athletics and the institution's investment in students by providing college access does positively impact outcomes at the community college level. As Becker (1964; 1993) suggested, opportunities to earn academic credentials and job specific skills afford individuals higher wages, opportunities for personal and professional advancement, and upward social and economic mobility. Specifically, findings indicate that several predictors that have been found in previous research (e.g., Crisp & Nora, 2010; Dougherty & Kienzl, 2006) to negatively affect students' ability to be successful at community colleges do not similarly affect athletes. These findings suggest that institutions should give credence to the fact that athletics may not only provide access to higher education but also serve as an impetus for students to excel in their academic studies.

Despite the maturation of research on student outcomes, few studies have examined these or other factors and their impact on athletes' academic performance. This is especially surprising considering that many have long argued that collegiate athletes are at-risk students, less likely to complete a college degree, and inclined to perform at a lower level academically than their nonathlete peers. As debates have

Using Data to Support College Athlete Success

Travis County College (TCC) is a public two-year institution located in a large urban city in the state of Maryland. TCC offers low-cost, state-supported educational programs to individuals from within its service district, across the state of Maryland, and a few out-of-state and international students. TCC offers 107 accredited academic programs leading to an Associates of Arts (A.A.), Associates of Science (A.S.) or Associates of Applied Science (A.A.S.).

Travis County College annually serves more than 30,000 full-time and part-time students. Three-quarters of all students commute, are adult learners, or attend only part-time. Though viewed as a commuter campus, TCC does maintain four residence halls on campus with space to comfortably house 550 students. Mostly athletes and out-of-state and international students reside on campus.

TCC sponsors six women's (soccer, basketball, cheerleading, volleyball, softball, and track) and four men's (baseball, basketball, soccer, and track) sports. Most athletes at TCC receive partial athletic aid to cover their tuition and fees, books, meals, and on-campus or off-campus living expenses. The athletic program has been very successful over the past decade. The men's basketball and baseball and women's basketball and volleyball teams have won a total of eight national championships over the past five years.

Travis County College currently has an overall three-year graduation rate of 15% (full-time, first-time, and degree- or certificate-seeking undergraduates). More than 60% of new students intend to graduate or transfer to a four-year institution, but few actually complete one or both within three years. Dr. Claire Jackson, president of TCC, has recently refocused her attention on developing programs and services to increase the number of students that leave the institution with a certificate or associates degree. Specifically, she is interested in gaining a better understanding of how athletes have historically performed at the institution.

You have just been promoted to vice president for student affairs and director of athletics. In this position you have been tasked with putting together a plan for collecting, reporting, and utilizing data on athletics to make informed decisions about the future direction of athletics at your institution. Your specific goal is to better understand how athletes are performing and to find ways to increase graduation and transfer rates for this particular group. The president would like to have a draft of your plan within two weeks. ■

Questions to Consider

1. What information or data would you need to accomplish the given task and how would you obtain this information given the culture of your institution is not one that supports collecting this type of data?

2. You have been asked to put in place a system to measure the success of athletes at your institution, where there has never been such a system in place. What strategies would you employ to convey the importance of collecting data and to get support and buy-in from the college community (e.g., coaches, other administrators, and staff)?

transpired throughout the higher education community and within political circles regarding degree completion and four-year transfer rates for community college students, some of these debates have centered on the paradoxical expectations placed on institutions to maintain open access while also producing large quantities of academically prepared students.

Given the gap in higher education literature on athletics and athletes at community colleges, additional research is essential. The following list provides undergraduate and graduate students topics that can serve as a guide for future investigation.

- Best practices for advising athletes at community colleges

- Impact of new eligibility requirement for international students (Article V, sect. 3c) on the recruitment of international students by sports and region

- Curricular and co-curricular experiences of athletes who attend and participate in athletics at historically black two-year colleges

- Trend analysis of big-time sports program's recruitment of community college athletes: Have large athletics programs changed recruitment practices in recent years? Which factors have impacted these practices?

QUESTIONS FOR DISCUSSION

1. Community colleges and athletics governing boards do not collect or report data on athletes with the same frequency or rigor as their four-year counterparts. Accordingly, what criteria should community colleges use to measure and evaluate the academic performance of their athletes?

2. What types of support programs or campus services would be beneficial for community colleges to develop or enhance the success of athletes? What are some challenges community colleges would need to overcome in order to implement these new or enhanced programs and services?

3. In what specific ways can athletics programs at community colleges involve faculty and staff to support the academic success of athletes?

References

Barreno, Y., & Traut, C. A. (2012). Student decisions to attend public two-year community colleges. *Community College Journal of Research and Practice, 36,* 863–871.

Becker, G. S. (1964). Human capital: A theoretical and empirical analysis, with special reference to education. New York: National Bureau of Economic Research, Columbia University Press.

———. (1993). *Human capital: A theoretical and empirical analysis, with special reference to education* (3rd ed.). Chicago: Chicago University Press.

Berkner, L., Horn, L., & Clune, M. (2000). *Descriptive summary of 1995–96 beginning postsecondary students: Three years later.* Washington, DC: National Center for Educational Statistics (NCES 2000-154).

Blaug, M. (1976). The empirical status of human capital theory: A slightly jaundiced survey. *Journal of Economic Literature, 14,* 827–855.

Bush, B., Castañeda, C., Hardy, D. E., & Katsinas, S. G. (2009). What the numbers say about community colleges and athletics. In L. S. Hagedorn & D. Horton Jr. (Eds.), *New directions for community colleges* (Vol. 147, pp. 5–14). San Francisco: Jossey-Bass.

Cabrera, A. F. (1994). Logistic regression analysis in higher education: An applied perspective. In J. C. Smart (Ed). *Higher education: Handbook of theory and research* (Vol. 10, pp. 225–256). New York: Agathon Press.

Castañeda, C., Katsinas, S. G., & Hardy, D. E. (2006). *The importance of intercollegiate athletics at rural-serving community colleges.* A policy brief by the

Education Policy Center at the University of Alabama for the MidSouth Partnership for Rural Community. Retrieved from http://www.rural communitycolleges.org/ docs/MSPBRIEFATHLETICS .pdf

Comeaux, E. (2011). Examination of faculty attitudes toward Division I college student athletes. *College Student Affairs Journal, 30*(1), 75–87.

Crisp, G., & Nora, A. (2010). Hispanic student success: Factors influencing the persistence and transfer decisions of Latino community college students enrolled in developmental education. *Research in Higher Education, 51*, 175–194.

Dougherty, K. J. & Kienzl, G. S. (2006). It's not enough to get through the open door: Inequalities by social background in transfer from community colleges. *Teachers College Record, 108*, 452–487.

Florida Department of Education (FDOE). (2005). *Report for the Florida community college system*. Tallahassee, FL: Florida Department of Education.

Hansen, J. S. (2006). Education data in California: Availability and transparency. Retrieved from http:// irepp.stanford.edu/documents/GDF/STUDIES /15-Hansen/15-Hansen(3-07).pdf

Hawkins, B. (1999). Black student athletes at predominantly white National Collegiate Athletic Association Division I institutions and patterns of oscillating migrant laborers. *Western Journal of Black Studies, 23*(1), 1–9.

Horton, D., Jr. (2009). Class and cleats: Community college student athletes and academic success. In L. S. Hagedorn & D. Horton Jr. (Eds.), *New directions for community colleges* (Vol. 147, pp. 15–27). San Francisco: Jossey-Bass.

———. (2011). "Man-to-man": An exploratory study of coaches' impact on black male student-athlete success at HBCUs. In R. T. Palmer and J. L. Wood (Eds.), *Black men in college: Implications for HBCUs*

and beyond (pp. 138–147). New York: Routledge, Taylor and Francis.

Jones-White, D. R., Radcliffe, P. M., Huesman, R. L., Jr., & Kellogg, J. P. (2010). Redefining student success: Applying different multinomial regression techniques for the study of student graduation across institutions of higher education. *Research in Higher Education, 51*, 154–174.

Kissinger, D. B., & Miller, M. T. (2007). Profile of community college athletes in selected sports. *Community College Enterprise, 13*(2), 51–60.

McCullough, J. W. (2000). *The economic impact of an athletic program at a rural public community college on the local economy* (Unpublished doctoral dissertation). Texas A&M University.

Peng, C. J., So, T. H., Stage, F. K., & St. John, E. P. (2002). The use and interpretation of logistic regression in higher education Journals: 1988–1999. *Research in Higher Education, 43*, 259–293.

Perna, L. W. (2006). Studying college access and choice: A proposed conceptual model. In J. C. Smart (Ed.), *Handbook for Theory and Research* (pp. 99–157). New York: Springer.

Romano, R. M., and Wisniewski, M. (2003) Tracking community college transfers using national student clearinghouse data (CHERI Working Paper #36). Retrieved from Cornell University, ILR School site: http://digitalcommons.ilr.cornell.edu/cheri/16/

Townsend, B. K. (2002). Transfer rates: A problematic criterion for measuring the community college. In T. Bers and H. Calhoun (Eds.), *Next steps for the community college* (pp. 13–23). New Directions for Community Colleges, No. 117. San Francisco: Jossey-Bass.

U.S. Department of Education (2009). *Federal Pell grant program*. Retrieved from http://www2.ed.gov/finaid /prof/resources/data/pell-data.html

INTERCOLLEGIATE ATHLETICS CLIMATE

Effects on Students, Faculty, and Administrators

Janet H. Lawrence and Jon L. McNaughtan

There's a saying in New England, "If you don't like the weather, wait a minute!" Despite years of research in nonacademic settings, conceptions of organizational climate continue to vary—just like the weather (Dickson, Resick, & Hanges, 2006; Moran & Volkwein, 1992). Because the sport management literature draws heavily on organizational research, we begin with a brief overview of conceptual and measurement issues relevant to studies of intercollegiate athletics climate (IAC).

WHAT IS INTERCOLLEGIATE ATHLETICS CLIMATE?

Organizational climate research encompasses several branches of inquiry into peoples' perceptions of their environments (Schneider, Ehrhart, & Macey, 2013). Broadly speaking, the focus is on the cognitive representations of organizational conditions (e.g., goals, policies, practices, procedures, processes) that individuals construct and that guide their behavior (Dickson et al., 2006). Higher education researchers define campus climate as the perceptions of a college or university that constituents (e.g., students, faculty, administrators, alumni, boards) develop through their interactions and as they strive to interpret events at their institution (Allen, 2003; Moran & Volkwein, 1988).While organizational culture is conceptually similar to climate, and the two concepts are sometimes conflated (Kuenzi & Schminke, 2009), they are theoretically distinct. Organizational culture is the "shared basic assumptions, values, and beliefs that characterize a setting and are taught to newcomers as the proper way to think and feel, communicated by the myths and stories people tell about how the organization came to be the way it is as it solved problems associated with external adaptation and internal integration" (Schneider et al., 2013, p. 362). These assumptions are deeply held beliefs that govern behavior, a form of tacit knowledge or "taken for granted reality" (Moran & Volkwein, 1992, p. 39).

Both organizational climate and culture help people make sense of their environments. However, culture evolves slowly and is based on a known history of considerable duration. Climate forms more rapidly and in response to situational contingencies, such as changes in personnel, finances, or policies. Whereas, culture is an enduring organizational characteristic, a view of reality that is "embedded in a kind of collective consciousness that exists quite apart from [individual perceptions]" (Moran & Volkwein, 1988, p. 371), organizational climate can differ across individuals and campus subgroups depending on their experiences. Consequently, multiple climates may exist within a single organization (Kuenzi & Schminke, 2009; Schneider et al., 2013). Returning to the earlier example of New England weather, climate is akin to hikers' subjective interpretations of current environmental conditions, which vary across individuals. Culture is analogous to the accumulated knowledge about weather that is generally assumed to be true and influences all the hikers' interpretations.

A full discussion of the theoretical and measurement issues related to organizational climate is beyond the scope of this chapter. However, several concerns are germane to the intercollegiate athletics literature. One key theoretical issue is captured in debates about the multilevel nature of organizational climate, whether it is an individual, group, or organizational phenomenon. Does it exist only in the minds of individuals, as a result of personal efforts to understand particular situations? Is it a group attribute representing a common set of beliefs about environmental conditions that is co-constructed through interactions? Or is climate a distinct organizational feature that members comprehend as they repeatedly experience the same environmental conditions (e.g., policies and practices) (Kuenzi & Schminke, 2009; Moran & Volkwein, 1992)?

Answers to these questions guide the measurement of organizational climate in nonacademic and academic settings. Some proxies consist of an *individual's perceptions* of conditions within an organization or in the external environment within which an organization is situated. Others combine individual perceptions statistically (e.g., cluster analysis) or draw together the perceptions of organizationally defined groups (e.g., students, faculty, administrators) to form indicators of *subgroup perceptions*. Yet others aggregate individual data to create an index representing the *collective view of all organization members*. There is little consensus regarding what level of agreement constitutes group consensus, whether climate is value neutral or has positive and negative valences, if the reference point is a specific facet (e.g., supportiveness) or multiple aspects of climate (e.g., supportiveness, communication), and what contextual and individual characteristics account for differences in climate perceptions between and within groups (Dickson et al., 2006; Kuenzi & Schminke, 2009).

These disparities in the conceptualization and measurement of climate permeate the research on intercollegiate athletics and complicate the task of integrating this body of work. IAC can be an athlete's perception of professors' treatment of athletes and nonathletes (e.g., Simmons, Bosworth, Fujita, & Jensen, 2007); an index representing a common group perception, for example, athletic directors' opinions about the valued characteristics of revenue and nonrevenue generating sports (e.g., Cooper & Weight, 2011); or a list of features that researchers develop and respondents rank order (e.g., Trail & Chelladurai, 2002). Whereas a strict definition of IAC includes campus constituents' perceptions of intercollegiate athletics on their own campuses (e.g., Lawrence, Hendricks, & Ott, 2007), many inquiries ask people about their beliefs regarding intercollegiate athletics in general. For example, people assess the importance of winning athletic events and other outcomes in hypothetical situations (e.g., Putler & Wolfe, 1999). Sometimes the presence of a high-profile team like football is used to represent the athletic dimension of campus climate (e.g., Warner, Shapiro, Dixon, Ridinger, & Harrison, 2011). Controls on contextual variables, such as NCAA Division, and sociodemographic variables, such as faculty governance experience and students' race and gender, also vary (e.g., Engstrom, Sedlacek, & McEwen, 1995; Kuga, 1996; Weaver, 2010).

While we acknowledge the issues raised in reviews of organizational climate research, we define the IAC broadly to include the perceptions of an individual, subgroup members (e.g., students, faculty, administrators), or all campus constituents regarding the goals, policies, and practices related to college sports developed as they interpret events primarily at their own university. The definition emphasizes the subjective nature of IAC but assumes these orientations to athletics are influenced by external environmental factors, such as regional norms and NCAA divisional policies and practices; internal factors, such as campus mission, resources, and culture; and individual differences in sociodemographic characteristics and organizational roles (Baxter, Margavio, & Lambert, 1996). By way of illustration, imagine two individuals at the same university, one employed by athletics and the other by an academic department. Both understand that their campus culture values winning athletic contests; they have heard the legends passed down through generations. Nonetheless, given the contexts in which they interact, they may differ in whether they believe winning athletic events is a legitimate campus goal and how they perceive the policies and practices implemented to achieve this goal.

What are the key features of IAC? Historical accounts and reform reports suggest a key component of IAC is the institutional emphasis given to select goals: winning records, commercialization, branding, amateurism, broad-based student participation in sports, access to college, and academic success (Flowers, 2007; Thelin, 1994). Baxter et al. (1996) conclude campus constituents typically fall into one of two groups depending on whether they believe amateurism and academics or commercialization and professionalization of intercollegiate athletics are primary goals.

Eight distinct aspects of IAC emerge from quantitative studies: goals, policies, and practices related to college athletes' education (e.g., academic and social/ethical development), college athletes' health (e.g., substance abuse), campus image/visibility (e.g., branding), governance (e.g., decision making), winning (e.g., records), revenue/commercialization (e.g., costs and profits, professionalization of athletes), entertainment value (e.g., media interest), and ethics (e.g., compliance, policy equity, attention to diversity) (Cooper & Weight, 2011; Fink, Pastore, & Riemer, 2003; Mahony, Hums, & Riemer, 2002; Putler & Wolfe, 1999; Schroeder, 2010; Trail & Chellandurai, 2000). The discussion that follows summarizes studies of administrator, faculty, and student perceptions and behaviors related to these dimensions of IAC.

PERCEIVED IAC EFFECTS ON ADMINISTRATORS

Given questions raised by reformers and the press (Estler & Nelson, 2005; Morgan, 2008; Pine, 2010), we focus on college presidents' and athletic administrators' views of campus visibility, revenue, governance, and ethics.

Campus Administrators

Campus Visibility

Since the beginning of intercollegiate competition, presidents have used athletics as a marketing tactic (Flowers, 2007). Some administrators still believe joining athletic conferences with peer institutions, or ones they would like to associate with, will elevate their universities' standings (Cunningham & Ashley, 2001). However, presidents' perceptions vary (Duderstadt, 2000; Williams & Pennington, 2006).

The sport management literature is replete with inquiries into the role of intercollegiate athletics in campus "branding"—the strategic use of media to create a university image that it wants groups to recognize (Bouchet & Hutchinson, 2010; Brand, 2006; King & Slaughter, 2004). Despite empirical evidence indicating winning sports teams do not necessarily contribute to these outcomes (Fulks, 2011; Zimbalist, 2010), a key assumption is images that incorporate intercollegiate athletics achieve campus goals like increasing student applications, strengthening relationships with state legislators, and attracting gifts (Alexander & Kern, 2010). Researchers find "branding" assumptions prompt administrative decisions such as the reclassification of athletic programs and large financial investments in athletics (Bouchet & Hutchinson, 2010; Weaver, 2010).

Governance and Revenue

Few large-scale empirical studies are conducted with sitting presidents, and most tend to focus on leaders of NCAA Division I Football Bowl Subdivision (FBS) schools. One highlights presidents' perceptions of the governance and financial aspects of IAC (Knight Commission on Intercollegiate Athletics, 2009). Most were aware of the "insidious" divide between athletics and academics and alleged conflicts between athletic goals and institutional missions but felt their power to govern athletics on their own campuses is diminished by lucrative contracts with external organizations. Two-thirds were convinced that they can continue their current levels of operation but were unsure that other FBS institutions have the finances. Despite these circumstances, presidents held fast to the belief that participation brings tangible (financial) and intangible (sense of community, visibility) benefits to their campuses. The report concludes that "*personal experience* (emphasis added) plays a much more powerful role in defining presidents' attitudes toward athletics than do the results of [empirical] studies" (p. 13).

Ethics

Although presidents feel they have little control over the "athletics arms race," case studies suggest they play important roles in setting positive ethical and educational climates. A president's strong position, communicated through his charge to a committee, eliminated an offensive athletic mascot (Easter & Leoni, 2009). Administrators helped establish an environment that supports academic achievement among athletes at historically black colleges and universities (HBCUs) (Charlton, 2011).

Athletic Administrators

Critics of intercollegiate athletics assert coaches care most about winning, and athletic directors about generating revenue (Telander, 1989). However, studies show that athletic department staff members attend to multiple aspects of IAC.

Education

Administrators at one NCAA Division I institution rated the successfulness of hypothetical athletic departments (Putler & Wolfe, 1999). Win-loss records, athlete graduation rates, violations of regulations, home game attendance, gender equity, number of intercollegiate teams, and athletic department finances were manipulated. Across scenarios, athletic administrators' assessments of success gave more weight to education factors. Researchers find, however, the growing emphasis on winning fosters academic fraud (Powers, 2007). To keep players eligible, coaches and athletic staff game the system using tactics like academic clustering, placing athletes in select majors (Christy, Seifried, & Pastore, 2008; Martin & Christy, 2010.

Revenue

Although Division I FBS presidents believe they will have sufficient revenue, they report they may need to discontinue certain varsity sports to contain costs (Knight Commission on Intercollegiate Athletics, 2009). This dilemma raises questions about athletic administrators' beliefs that drive decision making (Cooper & Weight, 2011).

Supporting College Athletes

Carl had been the athletic director for almost five years. The university had 15 Division I athletic programs and recently joined a new conference that would save the university money on travel costs, enhance completion, and hopefully open up some new revenue opportunities. Despite all of the good things that had happened during his tenure, Carl sat at his desk concerned and frustrated. He had just received another email from an anxious athlete who had just gotten the following email from a faculty member:

> Dear Ms. Smith,
> You are more than welcome to enroll in my class but I would advise against it. Athletes have never, and likely will never, do well in my class. I have a strict attendance policy and I have a hard time believing that you will be able to succeed.
> Sincerely,
> Dr. Andersen

This was not the first email like this that Jana Smith, one of the gymnasts, had received. Carl decided it was time to visit with Jana. They emailed back and forth, and Carl finally set an appointment with her for later that week.

When they got together they talked about Jana's experience at the university.

CARL: Jana, this is the third professor that you received an email like this from. Why do you think they are so concerned about your ability to succeed?

JANA: I think it's because I am an engineering major. Most of the math professors don't have many athletes in their upper division classes, so they don't think I can handle the workload on top of my hectic schedule.

CARL: Do you think it is only because you are an athlete?

JANA: Oh yeah. I only sent you these emails because I wanted you to know how faculty view athletes. I hear things like this all the time, and, honestly, I'm about ready to change my major.

CARL: Are there many faculty members out there who are concerned with how athletes perform in their classes?

JANA: More than you would think. I know other athletes who changed their majors or took courses from more "athlete friendly" faculty just to lower their stress.

CARL: Are faculty the only ones who verbalize these concerns?

JANA: No. My academic advisor also told me that I could have a hard time finishing my degree in the four years of my scholarship. He told me that I would be better off to take something less time intensive. I also have had my coaches tell me that I need to focus more on improving my game. They would never tell me to not focus on school, but still I'm getting the message.

Carl's conversation with Jana raised several questions for him. It appeared that Jana was experiencing a campus that was not conducive to her success as an engineering major. He wondered how many other athletes shared her perceptions and had just given up and changed their major or not taken the classes they loved because they did not feel supported. ■

Questions to Consider

1. What advice do you think Carl should give to Jana?

2. How do you think Carl should follow up this conversation?

Senior members of athletic departments in NCAA Division I institutions identified features of revenue-producing and nonrevenue sports that they value (Cooper & Weight, 2011). Exemplary sportsmanship during competition and individual and team academic and athletic success were highly ranked features of both. Strong relationships between coaches and administrators and community involvement were valued characteristics of nonrevenue sports only. Fan support, revenue production, and fundraising were important characteristics of revenue-producing sports only. Administrators from FBS schools assigned significantly greater value to athletic success, fan support, revenue production, and fundraising.

Ethics

The perceived fairness of policies and practices is an important aspect of IAC (Hums & Chelladurai, 1994). Patrick, Mahoney, and Petrosko (2008) examined how senior women administrators and athletic department directors across all NCAA Divisions rated the fairness of resource allocation decisions. They were given four scenarios: two were situations where campus funds increased (because of gifts or good seasons among revenue-producing sports), and two were situations where funds decreased (because of campus-wide cuts or poor seasons among revenue-producing sports). Across scenarios, females preferred decisions that provided for equal distribution across sports. Males ranked options as most fair when allocations were based on operating costs. Administrators from NCAA Division I institutions were more likely to think decisions based on revenue production and the costs of competing were fairest.

Since the passage of Title IX, many athletic policies and practices have garnered attention (Agathe & Billings, 2000), among them the perceived equity of career opportunities (Sartore & Cunningham, 2006). A key question is whether IAC, particularly in Division I schools, constrains advancement among women and minorities. Women often describe an IAC that favors Caucasian males, noting the selection criteria for athletic directors emphasize experiences as top-level staff, with fundraising, and with management of football coaches. Hoffman (2011) explains that senior associate teams rarely include more than one woman, and hence valued experiences are more available to men.

PERCEIVED IAC EFFECTS ON FACULTY

Faculty members, for the most part, value academics and amateurism over the commercialization and professionalization of intercollegiate athletics (Baxter et al., 1996). They believe athletic programs should emphasize students' academic and social-moral development and support policies designed to achieve these goals (e.g., GPA standards for eligibility). They dislike practices catering to media and athletic performance (e.g., adjusting competitions to fit with TV schedules, awarding athletic scholarships) (Trail & Chelladurai, 2000). Academic-oriented situations where male athletes appear to be privileged as compared to students in general (e.g., when those with lower SAT scores were admitted) evoke anger (Engstrom et al., 1995).

While they prioritize the fit between academic mission and intercollegiate athletics, faculty views are not homogeneous. Professors' characterizations of the policies, practices, and athlete behavior on their own FBS campuses varies in relation to experiences teaching athletes and serving on governance committees (Lawrence et al., 2007). Analyses reveal discrepancies between faculty members who believe intercollegiate athletics is not integrated within their campuses and presidents who see athletics as integral to their campus brand (Lawrence & Ott, 2013). However, most think that athletics are treated differently from academic departments; the entertainment industry exercises undue influence over decisions; athletics is a low-priority faculty governance issue; football and basketball players are not adequately compensated; and time demands on athletes are escalating.

PERCEIVED IAC EFFECTS ON STUDENTS

Many researchers have asked how colleges affect students (Astin, 1999; Kuh, 1995; Pascarella & Terenzini, 2005). They find that students engage with their campus communities in different ways, that how they spend their time leads to different outcomes, and that engagement is often affected by perceived climate (e.g., Cabrera, Nora, Terenzini, Pascarella, & Hagedorn, 1999; Hurtado & Carter, 1997; Marsh & Kleitman, 2002).

As regards IAC, the perceptions and actions of individuals who self-identify as athletes, nonathletes, or fans are often compared (e.g., Clopton, 2008a; Yopyk & Prentice, 2005). Studies contrasting athletes and nonathletes yield conflicting results (Menon, Loya, & Rankin, 2012). Umbach, Palmer, Kuh, and Hannah (2006) found athletes are more academically engaged and more likely to believe their campuses provide academic and social support. Pascarella, Bohr, Nora, and Terenzini (1995) showed participation in athletics was negatively associated with academic engagement in the first year. Within the nonathlete subgroup, comparisons of fans and nonfans are common (Clopton, 2008b). Students who regularly attend football games are more positive about their impact on students' sense of campus community (Warner et al., 2011). Fans believe winning records enhance public perceptions of their campus, but students in general do not (Clopton & Finch, 2012).

Differences between athletes and nonathletes and among subgroups of nonathletes are informative across a range of issues. However, given athletic departments responsibilities for athletes, the focus here is on their climate perceptions and behavior. In particular, athlete beliefs about four aspects of IAC: athlete education, winning, athlete health, and ethics.

College Athlete Education

Academic challenges arise because of structural features of college sports, particularly intensive practice and competition schedules (Watt & Moore, 2001). Because athletes find it difficult to schedule group work with nonathletes, they often form groups with teammates and fail to acquire important information presented when they are traveling. However, published inquiries focus largely on the disparaging images of classroom environments that athletes cognitively construct. Many report they internalize negative remarks faculty members or fellow students make and that they come to believe they will always be viewed as academically inept, regardless of their ability (Simons, Bosworth, Fujita, & Jensen, 2007). One athlete (male) explained: "If a professor knows you are an athlete, you are assumed to be stupid." Adler and Adler (1991) suggest that repeated negative interactions combine with athletic department practices to undermine athletes' academic performance. Initially, members of a men's basketball team were optimistic about their academic careers and expected to graduate. However, over four years, coaches made most of their academic decisions. Players had little interaction with faculty, came to feel coaches would care for them academically, became detached from academics, and failed to graduate.

Climate perceptions, however, can vary among athletes (Melendez, 2006). Compared to individuals in "low-profile sports," those in "high-profile" sports (e.g., football and basketball) report more positive relationships with coaches and claim that these interactions contribute more than relationships with team academic advisors to their academic performance (Menon et al., 2012). Racial subgroups' perceptions of academic support differ (Comeaux & Harrison, 2007). Within a national sample, after controlling for precollege characteristics, white athletes more frequently than their black peers said they benefited from their interactions with faculty, and within the same team, perceptions of IAC varied by race (Beamon & Bell, 2006).

STAKEHOLDER PERSPECTIVE

The Loneliness of Being Part of a Team

When I was playing high school basketball, I never felt the amount of pressure that I feel playing in college. It isn't the pressure to perform well or win games. I have always felt that. I feel like everyone expects different things from me, and I can't be what all of them want me to be. Coaches treat you like they own you because you have a scholarship, and even though we keep being told that academics come first, we are still expected to make basketball our top priority. I can't miss a practice or team meeting no matter how short or "not mandatory" it may be. My professors treat me differently from other students. It doesn't matter how I perform in class: I will always be an athlete to them first and student second. Other students (nonathletes) also just don't understand what it is like when you work over 20 hours a week for your scholarship and still struggle financially to make ends meet. They think we have way more money than we actually do. The way I am treated makes it difficult to make real friends outside of the team or other athletes. I always thought being an athlete in college would make me popular. I guess in some ways it has: no one ever forgets what I do, but no one really knows who I am. To the other students, I am and always will be an athlete. Honestly, it is very isolating. ■

Winning and Commercialization

The growing emphasis on team standings and the commercialization of intercollegiate athletics contribute to higher levels of stress (Kimball & Freysinger, 2003) and social isolation among athletes (Broughton & Neyer, 2001; Riemer, Beal, & Schroeder, 2000; Toma, Wolf-Wendel, & Morphew, 2001). High expectations result in longer practices, more team meetings, weight training sessions, required study halls, and team building social outings. Each of these activities also separates athletes from nonathletes. Lisa, a tennis player, captures the climate perceptions of many: "I really like my tennis team and I really like friendships with them but I spend so much time playing tennis and weight training and running and classes . . . we are like such a closed group" (Riemer et al., 2000).

College Athletes' Health

College athletes often form ego identities based on how they perform in their sport (Harris, 1993), and there is a risk to their health if self-worth is tied exclusively to their athletic ability (Howard-Hamilton & Sina, 2001). College athletes' self-image can interact with performance expectations that underlie their financial assistance and heighten stress (Mazanov, Huybers, & Connor, 2011). Stress, in turn, affects their opinions about whether the use of performance-enhancing drugs is acceptable (Smith et al., 2010). College athletes are more likely to use drugs if they believe they will help them win, or if their scholarship or sponsorship is tied to performance (Mazanov et al., 2011).

Alcohol abuse and eating disorders are also prevalent (Lisha & Sussman, 2010; Juhn, 2003; Millman & Ross, 2003; Nelson & Wechsler, 2001). However, links to IAC are unclear. Doumas, Turrisi, and Wright (2006) posit unhealthy behaviors may already be ingrained in athletes before they arrive and are not due to college environments. Martens, Dams-O'Connor, and Beck, (2006) claim that substance abuse can be attributed to athletes' high-risk-taking personalities. Doumas et al. (2006) proposes that social isolation leads to alcohol consumption whereas Grossbard et al. (2008) believe a strong attraction to one's team increases alcohol and marijuana use.

Ethics

Athletic scholarships democratize higher education, facilitating interactions between students with different social and ethnic backgrounds (Duderstadt, 2000; Schulman & Bowen, 2001). However, athletes often encounter overt racism during the recruitment process. A case study of Ole Miss describes campus traditions and celebrations that minority students believe have negative racial overtones and explains how these perceptions influenced their college choices (Fondren, 2010). The study also raises questions about the ethics of athletic department and booster practices that use a rival campus's racial climate as a recruiting tool.

CONCLUSION

Our brief overview of the literature underscores both the variability of climate perceptions around intercollegiate athletics and the profound effects they can have on behavior. Campus leaders' orientations toward intercollegiate athletics shape their budget decisions, faculty beliefs influence the positions they take regarding the place of intercollegiate athletics in higher education, and athletes' climate perceptions influence how they engage the broader campus community. At the same time, mixed and often-conflicting study findings highlight the need to consider differences in campus contexts and individual experiences that inform these subjective interpretations of intercollegiate athletics goals, policies, and practices.

Why, then, might campus administrators be interested in IAC? Perhaps the university governing board wonders how integral intercollegiate sports are to campus life. Or the chief academic officer may want to know if perceived academic clustering of athletes affects campus-wide judgments about the quality of particular degree programs. An athletic department director may seek to understand the perspectives of campus advisory group members so that he or she can anticipate different positions and craft effective arguments in support of a particular decision option. Knowing the perspectives of staff in other campus departments can help senior women administrators initiate and sustain conversations about coordinating and improving support for athletes.

We have identified many critical features of campus IAC and factors internal and external to a university that may shape it. The notion of IAC that we propose provides insights into why campus constituents respond differently to established athletic department goals, policies, and practices. It also offers a way to structure discussions of proposed changes. However, we recognize the limitations of our framework and encourage readers to critique it and build a stronger conceptualization.

QUESTIONS FOR DISCUSSION

1. What are your personal beliefs about the goals of intercollegiate athletics today? What policies and practices do you think facilitate and detract from the attainment of these goals?

2. Consider a proposed policy change at your university or college. What potentially different responses to this proposal might follow from people's perceptions of your campus's intercollegiate athletics climate?

3. As an administrator in an athletic department, what steps can you take to position yourself to test the intercollegiate athletics climate prior to recommending changes in policies and practices?

References

Adler, P. A., & Adler, P. (1991). *Backboards and black-boards: College athletes and role engulfment.* New York: Columbia University Press.

Agathe, D., & Billings R. (2000). The role of football profits in meeting Title IX gender equity regulations and policy. *Journal of Sport Management, 14,* 28–40.

Alexander, D. L., & Kern, W. (2010). Does athletic success generate legislative largess from sports-crazed representatives? The impact of athletic success on state appropriations to colleges and universities. *International Journal of Sport Finance, 5,* 253–267.

Allen, D. K. (2003). Organizational climate and strategic change in higher education: Organizational insecurity. *Higher Education, 46,* 61–92.

Astin, A. W. (1999). Student involvement: A developmental theory for higher education. *Journal of College Student Personnel, 25,* 297–308.

Baxter, V., Margavio, A. V., & Lambert, C. (1996). Competition, legitimation, and the regulation of intercollegiate athletics. *Sociology of Sport Journal, 13,* 51–64.

Beamon, K., & Bell, P. A. (2002). "Going Pro": The deferential effects of high aspirations for a professional sports career on African-American student athletes and white student athletes. *Race and Society, 5*(2), 179–191.

Bouchet, A., & Hutchinson, M. (2010). Organizational escalation to an uncertain course of action: A case study of institutional branding at Southern Methodist University. *Journal of Issues in Intercollegiate Athletics, 3,* 272–295.

Brand, M. (2006). The role and value of intercollegiate athletics in universities. *Journal of the Philosophy of Sport, 33,* 9–20.

Broughton, E., & Neyer, M. (2001). Advising and counseling student athletes. In M. F. Howard-Hamilton & S. K. Watt (Eds.), Student services for athletes, *New directions for student services,* 93, 47–53. San Francisco: Jossey-Bass.

Cabrera, A. F., Nora, A., Terenzini, P. T., Pascarella, E., & Hagedorn, L. S. (1999). Campus racial climate and the adjustment of students to college: A comparison between white students and African-American students. *Journal of Higher Education, 70,* 134–160.

Charlton, R. (2011). The role of policy, rituals and language in shaping an academically focused culture in HBCU athletics. *Journal of Issues in Intercollegiate Athletics, 4,* 120–148.

Christy, K. Seifried. C., & Pastore, D. (2008). Intercollegiate athletics: A preliminary study examining the opinions on impact of the academic performance rate. *Journal of Issues in Intercollegiate Athletics, 1,* 1–10.

Clopton, A. W. (2008a). From message to messenger? Assessing the impact of athletics on a college campus. *Journal for the Study of Sports and Athletes in Education, 2,* 299–320.

———. (2008b). Examining the relationship between college sport and sense of community. *Research Quarterly for Exercise and Sport, 79,* 90–91.

Clopton, A. W., & Finch, B. (2012). In search of the winning image: Assessing the connection between athletics success on perceptions of external prestige. *Journal of Issues in Intercollegiate Athletics, 5,* 79–95.

Comeaux, E., & Harrison, C. K. (2007). Faculty and male student athletes: Racial differences in the environmental predictors of academic achievement. *Race Ethnicity and Education, 10*(2), 199–214.

Cooper, C. & Weight, E. (2011). Investigating NCAA administrator values of NCAA Division I athletic departments. *Journal of Issues in Intercollegiate Athletics, 4,* 74–89.

Cunningham, G., & Ashley, F. (2001). Isomorphism in NCAA athletic departments: The use of competing theories and advancement of theory. *Sport Management Review, 4*(1), 47–64.

Dickson, M. W., Resick, C. J. & Hanges, P. J. (2006). When organizational climate is unambiguous, it is also strong. *Journal of Applied Psychology, 91,* 351–364.

Doumas, D., Turrisi, R., & Wright, D. (2006). Risk factors for heavy drinking in college freshmen: Athletic status and adult attachment. *Sports Psychologist, 20,* 419–434.

Duderstadt, J. (2000). *Intercollegiate athletics and the American university.* Ann Arbor: University of Michigan Press.

Easter, B., & Leoni, E. (2009). Stakeholder salience and elements in decisions to retain or change American Indian nicknames and symbols at American universities. *Journal for the Study of Sports and Athletes in Education, 3,* 307–334.

Engstrom, C., Sedlacek, W., & McEwen, M. (1995). Faculty attitudes toward male revenue and nonrevenue student-athletes. *Journal of College Student Development, 36*(3), 217–227.

Estler, S. E., & Nelson, L. (Eds.). (2005). Who calls the shots? Sports and university leadership, culture, and decision making. *ASHE Higher Education Report, 30*(5), 1–152.

Fink, J., Pastore, D., & Riemer, H. (2003). Managing employee diversity: Perceived practices and organizational outcomes in NCAA Division III athletic departments. *Sport Management Review, 6*(2), 147–168.

Flowers, R. D. (2007). "Win one for the Gipper": Organizational foundations of intercollegiate athletics. *Journal for the Study of Sports and Athletes in Education, 1*(2) 121–140.

Fondren, K. (2010). Sport and stigma: College football recruiting and institutional identity of Ole Miss. *Journal of Issues in Intercollegiate Athletics, 3*, 154–175.

Fulks, D. L. (2011). Revenues and expenses, 2004–2010. NCAA Division I intercollegiate athletics programs report. Retrieved from http://www.ncaapublications.com/productdownloads/2010RevExp.pdf

Grossbard, J., Hummer, J., LaBrie, J., Pederson, E., & Neighbors, C. (2009). Is substance use a team sport? Attraction to team, perceived norms, and alcohol and marijuana use among male and female intercollegiate athletes. *Journal of Applied Sport Psychology, 21*, 247–261.

Harris, M. M. (1993). Developmental benefits of athletes. In W. D. Kirk and S. V. Kirk (Eds.), *Student-athletes: Shattering the myths and sharing the realities* (pp. 3–12). Alexandria, VA: American Counseling Association.

Hoffman, J. (2011). The old boys' network: Women candidates and the athletic director search among NCAA Division I programs. *Journal for the Study of Sports and Athletes in Education, 5*(1), 9–28.

Howard-Hamilton, M. F., & Sina, J. A. (2001). How college affects student athletes. In M. Howard-Hamilton & S. Watt (Eds.), Student services for athletes, *New directions for student services*, 93, pp. 35–45. San Francisco: Jossey-Bass.

Hums, M. A., & Chelladurai, P. (1994). Distributive justice in intercollegiate athletics: The views of NCAA coaches and administrators. *Journal of Sport Management, 8*(3), 200–217.

Hurtado, S., & Carter, D. F. (1997). Effects of college transition and perceptions of the campus racial climate on Latino college students' sense of belonging. *Sociology of Education, 70*(4), 324–345.

Juhn, M. (2003). Popular sports supplements and ergogenic aids. *Sports Medicine, 33*, 921–939.

Kimball, A., & Freysinger, V. J. (2003). Leisure, stress, and coping: The sport participation of collegiate student-athletes. *Leisure Sciences, 25*, 115–141.

King, S., & Slaughter, S. (2004). Sports "R" Us: Contracts, trademarks, and logos. In S. Slaughter & G. Rhoades (Eds.), *Academic capitalism and the new economy: Markets, state, and higher education* (pp. 256–278). Baltimore: Johns Hopkins University Press.

Knight Commission on Intercollegiate Athletics. (2009). *FBS Presidents Study*. Retrieved from http://www.knightcommissionmedia.org/images/President_Survey_FINAL.pdf

Kuenzi, M., & Schminke, M. (2009). Assembling fragments into a lens: A review, critique, and proposed research agenda for the organizational work climate literature. *Journal of Management, 35*, 634–717.

Kuga, D. J. (1996). Governance of intercollegiate athletics: Perceptions of faculty members. *Journal of Sport Management, 10*, 149–168.

Kuh, G. D. (1995). The other curriculum: Out-of-class experiences associated with student learning and personal development. *Journal of Higher Education, 66*(2), 123–155.

Lawrence, J. H., Hendricks, L. A., & Ott, M. C. (2007). *Faculty perceptions on intercollegiate athletics: A national study of faculty at NCAA Division I Football Bowl Subdivision institutions*. Retrieved from http://www.knightcommission.org/images/pdfs/faculty_perceptions_final.pdf

Lawrence, J. H., & Ott, M. (2013). Faculty perceptions of organizational politics. *Review of Higher Education, 36*(2), 145–178.

Lisha, N. E., & Sussman, S. (2010). Relationship of high school and college sports participation with alcohol, tobacco, and illicit drug use: A review. *Addictive behaviors, 35*, 399–407.

Mahony, D. F., Hums, M. A., & Riemer, H. A. (2002). Distributive justice in intercollegiate athletics: Perceptions of athletic directors and athletic board chairs. *Journal of Sport Management, 16*, 331–356.

Marsh, H. W., & Kleitman, S. (2002). Extracurricular school activities: The good, the bad, the nonlinear. *Harvard Education Review, 72*, 464–514.

Martens, M. P., Dams-O'Connor, K., & Beck, N. C (2006). A systematic review of college student-athlete drinking: Prevalence rates, sport-related factors, and interventions. *Journal of Substance Abuse Treatment, 31*, 305–316.

Martin, K., & Christy, K. (2010). The rise and impact of high profile spectator sports on American higher education. *Journal of Issues in Intercollegiate Athletics, 3,* 1–15.

Mazanov, J., Huybers, T., & Connor, J. (2011). Qualitative evidence of a primary intervention point for elite athlete doping. *Journal of science and medicine in sport, 14*(2), 106–110.

Melendez, M. C. (2006). The influence of athletic participation on the college adjustment of freshmen and sophomore student athletes. *Journal of College Student Retention, 8,* 39–55.

Menon, I., Loya, K., & Rankin, S. (2012). *The influence of climate & athletic personnel on the academic success of students-athletes in high profile sports.* Unpublished paper presented at AERA, Vancouver.

Millman, R. B., & Ross, E. J. (2003). Steroid and nutritional supplement use in professional athletes. *American Journal of Addiction, 12,* 48–54.

Moran, E. T., & Volkwein, J. F. (1988). Examining organizational climate in institutions of higher education. *Research in Higher Education, 28,* 367–383.

———. (1992). The cultural approach to the formation of organizational climate. *Human Relations, 45*(1), 19–47.

Morgan, W. J. (2008). Markets and intercollegiate sports: An unholy alliance? *Journal of Intercollegiate Sport, 1,* 59–65.

Nelson, T. F., & Wechsler, H. (2001). Alcohol and college athletes. *Medicine and Science in Sports and Exercise, 33,* 43–47.

Pascarella, E. T., Bohr, L., Nora, A., & Terenzini, P. (1995). Intercollegiate athletic participation and freshman–year cognitive outcomes. *Journal of Higher Education, 66,* 370–387.

Pascarella, E. T., & Terenzini, P. T. (2005). *How college affects students: A third decade of research.* San Francisco: Jossey-Bass.

Patrick, I. S., Mahony, D. F., & Petrosko, J. M. (2008). Distributive justice in intercollegiate athletics: An examination of equality, revenue production, and need. *Journal of Sport Management, 22*(2), 165–183.

Pine, N. (2010). The role of athletics in the academy: An alternative approach to financial investment. *Journal of Sport and Social Issues, 34,* 475–480.

Powers, E. (2007). Academic fraud in collegiate athletics. [Electronic version]. *Inside Higher Ed.* Retrieved from http://www.insidehighered.com

Putler, D. S., & Wolfe, R. A. (1999). Perceptions of intercollegiate athletic programs: Priorities and tradeoffs. *Sociology of Sport Journal, 16,* 301–325.

Riemer, B. A., Beal, B., & Schroeder, P. (2000). The influences of peer and university culture on female student-athletes' perceptions of career termination, professionalization, and social isolation. *Journal of Sport Behavior, 23*(4), 364–378.

Sartore, M. L., & Cunningham, G. B. (2006). Stereotypes, race, and coaching. *Journal of African American Studies, 10*(2), 69–83.

Schneider, B., Ehrhart, M., & Macey, W. (2013). Organizational climate and culture. *Annual Review of Psychology, 64,* 361–388.

Schroeder, P. J. (2010) A model for assessing organizational culture in intercollegiate athletic departments. *Journal of Issues in Intercollegiate Athletics, 3,* 98–118.

Schulman, J., & Bowen, W. (2001). *College sports and educational values: The game of life.* Princeton, NJ: Princeton University Press.

Simons, H. D., Bosworth, C., Fujita, S., & Jensen, M. (2007). The athlete stigma in higher education. *College Student Journal, 41,* 251–273.

Smith, A. C., Stewart, B., Oliver-Bennetts, S., McDonald, S., Ingerson, L., Anderson, A., & Graetz, F. (2010). Contextual influences and athlete attitudes to drugs in sport. *Sport Management Review, 13*(3), 181–197.

Telander, R. (1989). *The hundred yard lie: The corruption of college football and what we can do to stop it.* New York: Simon and Schuster.

Thelin, J. R. (1994). *Games colleges play: Scandal and reform in intercollegiate athletics.* Baltimore: Johns Hopkins University Press.

Toma, J. D., Wolf-Wendel, L., & Morphew, C. C. (2001). There's no "I" in "team": Lessons from athletics on community building. *Review of Higher Education, 24,* 369–396.

Trail, G., & Chelladurai, P. (2000). Perceptions of goals and processes of intercollegiate athletics: A case study. *Journal of Sport Management, 14,* 154–178.

———. (2002). Perceptions of intercollegiate athletic goals and processes: The influence of personal values. *Journal of Sport Management, 16,* 289–310.

Umbach, P. D., Palmer, M. M., Kuh, G. D., & Hannah, S. J. (2006). Intercollegiate athletes and effective educational practices: Winning combination or losing effort? *Research in Higher Education, 47,* 709–733.

Warner, S., Shapiro, S., Dixon, M., Ridinger, L., & Harrison, S. (2011). The football factor: Shaping community on campus. *Journal of Issues in Intercollegiate Athletics, 4*, 236–256.

Watt, S. K., & Moore, J. L. (2001). Who are student-athletes. In M. F. Howard-Hamilton & S. K. Watt (Eds.), Student services for athletes, *New directions for student services*, 93, 7–18. San Francisco: Jossey-Bass.

Weaver, A. (2010). Reevaluating prestige: The influence of history on the decision to reclassify to Division I: A case study. *Journal of Issues in Intercollegiate Athletics, 3*, 131–153.

Williams, M. R., & Pennington, K. (2006). Community College Presidents' Perceptions of Intercollegiate Athletics. *Community College Enterprise, 12*(2), 91–104.

Yopyk, D. J. A., & Prentice, D. A. (2005). Am I an athlete or student? Identity salience and stereotype threat in student-athletes. *Basic & Applied Social Psychology, 27*, 329–336.

Zimbalist, A. (2010). Dollar dilemmas during the downturn: A financial crossroads for college sports. *Journal of Intercollegiate Sport, 3*, 111–124.

PART FOUR

The Business Enterprise of College Athletics

Considerable attention has been given to the changing and complex context of collegiate athletics, where business practices and increasing commercialism can compromise the mission and philosophy of higher education. In chapter 9, Andrew Zimbalist outlines the nature of the tax privileges enjoyed by the multibillion-dollar industry of college sports and reviews the basis in the tax laws for this favorable treatment. Chapter 10, by Rodney Fort, explores Division I college athletics spending and the degree to which it is consistent with the fundamental academic mission of colleges and universities. Next, in chapter 11, Scott Hirko and Kyle Sweitzer discuss the business model in NCAA Division I athletics, in turn considering the "haves" and the "have-nots" in major college sports. They also outline several alternatives for reforming the current business model. In chapter 12, Murray Sperber and Vincent Minjares describe the questionable nature of investing millions of dollars in coaches and the effects of this practice on the university's mission. Likewise, they highlight the ways in which millionaire coaches emphasize team performance and winning over the academic and personal needs of their college athletes. ■

TAXATION of COLLEGE SPORTS

Policies and Controversies

Andrew Zimbalist

On October 2, 2006, U.S. House Ways and Means Committee chairman Bill Thomas sent National Collegiate Athletic Association (NCAA) president Myles Brand a long letter questioning why the NCAA and intercollegiate athletics should be able to retain their plethora of tax privileges. Thomas pointedly inquired how the hypercommercialized activities of Division I athletics supported the tax-exempt educational mission of U.S. colleges and universities. This chapter seeks to understand this issue, both from the perspective of tax law and from that of public policy.

Before one can meaningfully answer the question of why intercollegiate athletics should have tax privileges, it is necessary to understand what those privileges are as well as the legal basis for them. There are three principle areas of tax privileges for college sports:

1. The ability for donors to deduct 80% of "contributions" to athletic departments that are required for them to be able to purchase season's tickets to either football or men's basketball games

2. The ability of college sports programs to issue facility bonds, which has tax-exempt interest to the holders

3. The ability to avoid taxation on activities that are unrelated to the purpose of the tax exemption held by U.S. colleges and universities

These tax privileges are based on a broader tax exemption that is afforded U.S. colleges and universities. The exemption, in turn, is based for *public universities* on the assumption that the state is providing a service that may otherwise have to be produced by the federal government and for *private universities* on the assumption that education is a

KEY TERMS

unrelated business ◀
income taxation

functionally related ◀

deductible donation ◀

tax-exempt bonds ◀

501(c)(3) ◀

private inurement ◀

public good whose development promotes the general welfare and functioning of our democratic government. Public universities, as state enterprises, are automatically exempt, while private universities fall under the 501(c)(3) category that provides exemption for charitable, nonprofit organizations. In 1976 the U.S. Congress passed an amendment to 501(c)(3) that explicitly classified the promotion of amateur sports as a charitable activity. Hence, the NCAA was able to obtain 501(c)(3) status and therefore is covered by the tax exemption, as are private universities and colleges. According to Internal Revenue Service (IRS) code, however, both public and private nonprofit universities are explicitly made subject to unrelated business income taxation (UBIT); and, as we shall see, some key questions in connection to the UBIT arise about the relationship of intercollegiate athletics to the educational mission of universities that form the basis for the frequently heard call for college sports to be taxed.

DEDUCTIBILITY FOR DONATIONS

Let us now consider the three tax privileges that benefit intercollegiate athletics. Most of the 124 schools in the Football Bowl Subdivision (FBS, formerly D I-A) in 2013 require their supporters and fans to make a sizable donation to the athletic department in order to be able to purchase season's tickets to the home games of the school's football or basketball team. One of the first schools to do this was the University of Texas in the early 1980s. However, in 1984, Texas got some bad news from the IRS. The IRS ruled that since these "donations" to the university were a payment for purchasing part of a ticket for their personal enjoyment, they would not be deductible (as a gift to a charitable organization). Fortunately for the Texas athletic department, it had some powerful friends. In particular, its alumnus U.S. representative Jake Pickle happened to be a member of the House Ways and Means Committee. He wrote a bill, cosponsored by U.S. senator from Louisiana Russell Long, that stipulated 100% of the preticket "contributions" was tax deductible for fans buying tickets to the University of Texas and Louisiana State University football games (Dexheimer, 2007; Eichelberger & Babcock, 2012). Other schools quickly picked up on the favoritism and lobbied for the provision to be made general. In 1988, the U.S. Congress obliged, passing a bill that made 80% of all such ticket "donations" deductible for all universities (Gaul, 2012).

When Congress passed this deductibility provision, it was estimated that it would cost the U.S. Treasury $0.5 million annually. In 2012 *Bloomberg News* made open-record requests of FBS schools, but only 34 of the 120 FBS schools at the time responded with data on the donations collected in order to purchase season's tickets. Ohio State University collected the most, with $38.7 million, followed by LSU with $38.0 million and Texas with $33.9 million, and the 34 schools together collected $467.2 million. At 80% deductibility, this amounted to $373.8 million; and, at a top tax rate of 39.6%, this amounted to individual tax savings (or cost to the federal government) of $148 million. And this sum refers to only 34 schools. There are 124 FBS schools and 340 Division I schools (Eichelberger & Babcock, 2012).

It seems reasonable to view these upfront "contributions" as similar to permanent seat licenses (PSLs) that are sold by professional sports teams. PSL are essentially the first part of a two-part tariff to purchase a season's ticket: the total market price of the ticket is the prorated PSL (or "contribution") plus the nominal ticket price. For any given total market ticket price, university athletic departments can increase their ticket revenue by increasing the first part of the tariff and lowering the second part. By raising the first part, the net (after tax) ticket price to the fan is lower and, hence, the university can sell more tickets or charge a higher final price. There is no conceivable economic or efficiency justification for the federal government to sacrifice tax revenues in order to subsidize the purchase of season tickets (almost entirely by higher-income individuals) for big-time college sporting events. To the extent that there are ancillary benefits from such a policy, these could be obtained through a more direct approach.

ISSUANCE OF TAX-EXEMPT BONDS FOR FACILITY CONSTRUCTION

Athletic departments in either public or nonprofit, private universities are able, through their schools, to finance facility construction or renovation through the issuance of bonds, the interest on which is tax-exempt to its holders. Bond buyers are generally high-income individuals. Consider the following example. If a bond buyer, in the highest 39.6% tax bracket, buys a nonexempt corporate bond, with, say, a 7% interest rate, the net (after tax) interest rate is 4.23%. For a tax-exempt bond to be competitive with this corporate bond, the interest would have to be only 4.23% (or lower, given that there may also be an exemption from state income tax.) In this example, a bond to finance the construction or renovation of a college football stadium would save 2.72%, which on a $200 million bond, amounts to a $5.44 million annual saving on the bond's debt service, or a yearly federal subsidy to the stadium of $5.44 million.

Since 1995, U.S. universities have spent more than $30 billion on sports facilities. Many observers believe there is an arms' race among schools, wherein the forces of competition push these expenditures on modernized structures, replete with luxury boxes, club seating, signage boards, restaurants, and more. The federal subsidy encourages this lavish spending.

Given that a university's tax-exempt status is meant to underwrite its central purpose of education, there is a legitimate question of whether the hypercommercialized business of big-time intercollegiate athletics is sufficiently related to this central purpose to justify extending the exemption to the construction of sports stadiums, arenas, training facilities, and tutoring buildings for athletes.

In his 2006 letter to the U.S. Congress, NCAA president Myles Brand wrote: "Athletics facilities, state-of-the-art or otherwise, are necessary for the support of the activity for which there is a tax exemption. These facilities, often paid for through bonds or charitable contributions, also generate revenue that offsets the operational cost of athletics that might not otherwise be provided through institutional funds." If, however, these facilities generate sufficient funds to justify the investment in them, then there is no reason for the federal government to subsidize them. In the end, the modern stadiums and arenas raise the revenue level of big-time college sports. Since there are no stockholders to profit from successful sports programs and athletes are not remunerated beyond the basic grant-in-aid, a substantial part of the additional revenue flows to the coaches and administrators of the system. Thus, critics ask: Why should the taxpayer be called upon to support fancy facilities for college sports?

AVOIDANCE OF UBIT LEVIES

When a public or nonprofit institution sets up its own commercial enterprise, the net income of this operation may be subject to taxation. This principle was established by the UBIT legislation passed by the U.S. Congress in 1950. Before 1950, and dating back to a Supreme Court decision in 1924, charitable entities were permitted to run a commercial business and not have to pay taxes on its profits if the profits were used to support the entities' charitable activities. In 1950, however, out of concern that such businesses would have an unfair competitive advantage over independent businesses producing the same product or service and that the policy reduced government tax revenues, Congress enacted the UBIT. In 2004, the government collected more than $192 million in UBIT revenue from 501(3)(c) entities. This collection was based on reported gross income of $5.5 billion, constituting a tax rate of only 3.5%. The low rate is a product of the 501(c)(3) entities' ability to shift revenues and costs to lower the taxable income of their unrelated entities (Colombo, 2010).

Understanding how the UBIT applies to big-time intercollegiate athletics is not a simple matter and, like much of the law, is subject to interpretation. The basic criterion is whether or not the commercial entity's output is functionally related to and in furtherance of the basic mission of the charity (in this case, either education or the provision of amateur sports), and IRS interpretation of this criterion over the years has tended to be narrow. For instance, in 1968 the IRS ruled a hospital's charitable purpose was providing health care to the patients in the hospital; accordingly, a pharmacy within the hospital that provided drugs to patients in the hospital was functionally related to the charitable purpose, but the sale of drugs to the general public by such a pharmacy was not. In 1973 the IRS ruled that the sale of science books in an art museum bookstore was subject to UBIT but the sale of reproductions or postcards was not. In the context of the university, a Treasury Department regu-

NYU and C. F. Mueller Co.

In 1946, the owner of the renowned C. F. Mueller Co. passed away. Through a variety of personal connections, the entire company was made available for purchase to the NYU Law School at the heavily discounted price of $3.5 million, along with a low-interest loan. Under the Law School's ownership, the company flourished and the loan was paid off after some 20 years. By 1975, out of the Law School's total budget of $9 million, almost one-third came from the profits of its pasta company. The fact that Mueller's profits went untaxed was not overlooked by other pasta companies. They pressured Congress to level the playing field, which it did with the UBIT law of 1950.

Mueller's success met with another obstacle. The rest of NYU was in dire financial straits, running an operating deficit of $4.4 million during 1974–1975 and was projected to grow in the coming years. NYU began an austerity plan that included selling off its undergraduate campus in the north Bronx. The law school believed that its own health was tied to that of the university and, ultimately, was persuaded to sell its Mueller operation and, in exchange for greater law school budgetary autonomy, to share the proceeds with the university on a 59/41 basis. The company was sold in 1976 for $115 million, for a capital gain of over $110 million (Brooks, 1977). ■

lation stipulates that "the presentation of . . . drama and music events contributes importantly to the overall educational and cultural function of the university" and, hence, is not subject to UBIT (Colombo, 2010). Following this logic, a case can be made to the Treasury to apply the same reasoning to intercollegiate athletics.

The IRS briefly contemplated taxing television revenues in intercollegiate sports back in 1977, but reversed itself, and in 1980 ruled that TV revenues were not subject to UBIT (Colombo, 2010). In 1991 the IRS ruled that corporate advertising/sponsorship revenue in college sports was subject to UBIT, but in 1997 Congress voted to exempt such income from UBIT provided that it was not comparative and promotional in nature.[1] Thus, Coca-Cola could have a sign at the Camp Randall Stadium in Madison, Wisconsin, that simply stated "Coke" or " Coca-Cola Supports Badgers' Football," but it could not have a tax exempt sign that stated "Coke Is No. 1" or "Nothing Beats Coke for Satisfying Refreshment."[2] Similarly, buying naming rights to a facility does not involve explicit promotion and is exempt from UBIT Taxation.

Current law also excludes all passive income from UBIT, such as royalty or licensing income from the sale of logos, images, or game highlights. In 2005 licensing and royalty revenue in college sports was estimated at $203 million (Weisbrod, Ballou, & Asch, 2008).

For an entity to retain its 501(c)(3) status and, hence, its eligibility to remain tax exempt, it must also meet certain limitations. One such limitation is that there can be no "private inurement," or siphoning of surplus to the benefit of an employee of the entity. In order to meet this standard it is required that employees be paid a fair, market-based compensation for their services. The question has been raised about the high salaries of head coaches of Division I football and men's basketball teams and whether these constitute private inurement.

Another limitation is that there can be no "private benefit." Private benefit refers to an outsider to a 501(c)(3) organization gaining excessively from its relationship with the charitable entity, whether or not the payment is at a market rate. Consider how the NFL and the NBA gain excessively from the development and promotion of players in college sports. In baseball, the average major league team spends roughly $25 million on player development within its minor league systems, while the NBA's development league expenses are diminutive, and the NFL has no minor league or development system. In this way, college sports serve as a minor league and development system for the NBA and NFL, with the added bonus that Division I teams get enough media coverage so that the players come to the pros with substantial public resumes and notoriety.

Finally, it is appropriate to inquire whether applying UBIT to college sports would make a difference. If college athletic departments can shift costs and benefits among various college departments (e.g., buildings and grounds, dance, music, dining services, general administration) and thereby avoid showing any net income; or if there is truly no net income in most programs anyway, would it matter if college sports were subject to an income tax? The short answer is that UBIT law also contains a fragmentation principle that allows the IRS to view the separate parts of a 501(c)(3) entity independently. Thus, in theory at least, the IRS could consider net income from football, basketball, or corporate sponsorships, even though the entire athletic department did not generate a surplus. We turn now to consider the debate around this aforementioned question.

STAKEHOLDER PERSPECTIVE

Myles Brand, Former NCAA President

The NCAA organizes intercollegiate athletics. Its officers and employees benefit when college sports flourish economically. The president of the NCAA is a stakeholder in the system. Between 2002 and 2009, Myles Brand was the association's president.

In November 2006, Myles Brand wrote a 25-page response to the questions of U.S. Representative Bill Thomas of California about why the NCAA and intercollegiate athletics merit the tax privileges they enjoy. Among Brand's comments, he wrote: "The lessons learned on the football field or men's basketball court are no less in value or importance to those athletes than the ones learned on the hockey rink or softball diamond — nor, for that matter, than those learned in theater, dance, music, journalism or other non-classroom environments." At a general level, few would disagree with this assertion. Critics, however, would ask whether the commercialization of college sports is congruent with the educational goals to which Brand alludes.

Brand also wrote: "If the educational purpose of college basketball could be preserved only by denying the right to telecast the events, students, university faculty and staff, alumni, the institutions of higher education themselves and even the American taxpayer would ultimately lose. The scale of popularity and the media attention given to football and men's basketball do not forfeit for those two sports the education purpose for which they exist." Here Brand suggests that limiting commercialization would not promote educational goals, but it would reduce the consumer and financial benefits of big-time college sports. ■

JOINING THE DEBATE

Both at a technical level regarding the details of tax policy and at a political or philosophical level, a fundamental question is whether commercialized intercollegiate athletics is functionally related to the educational mission of U.S. colleges and universities. On the one hand, it can be argued that engagement in college sports by students provides a salutary balancing of an otherwise largely cerebral and sedentary lifestyle. Participation in intercollegiate athletics also can help athletes develop constructive personality traits, including the development of leadership skills, teamwork, tenacity, good time management, and positive self-esteem. These qualities of college sports appear to be functionally related to the educational mission of colleges and universities and, indeed, to provide an important complement to help create a well-rounded and healthy college experience.

On the other hand, it can be argued that these positive attributes apply to college sports in intramural form or in the less commercialized form of intercollegiate athletics of Divisions II and III. But at the highly commercialized level of Division I, and particularly FBS, the time demands on the athletes, the intrusive, television-driven scheduling of games, the frequent and increasingly distant travel, the lowering of admissions and classroom standards, the transformation of college culture, the incentives to transgress NCAA rules, and the outsized payments to the football and men's basketball head coaches all detract from the central charitable and educational purpose of the university.

The U.S. Congressional Budget Office (CBO) conducted a study in May 2009 that considered this issue, finding that 82.3% of the revenues for FBS college sports came from commercial sources. This share fell to 28.8% in FCS and to 27.9% in Division I without football. For universities as a whole, this share was only 10.9%, excluding hospitals and athletics (Congressional Budget Office, 2009). The implication of the CBO finding is that big-time college sports operate in a distinct fashion from higher education generally and, thus, could logically be given a different tax status.

The NCAA has justified the commercial growth of FBS football and Division I basketball, in part, on the grounds that the surplus generated by these sports helps to fund dozens of nonrevenue sports for both men and women. After all, in 1976 Congress explicitly denominated the promotion of amateur sports to be a charitable activity, and the revenue from big-time sports appears to be helping to fund these amateur teams.

Critics point to several problems with this argument. First, according to the 2012 Revenue and Expenses Report of the NCAA, only about one-fifth of the football and men's basketball teams in Division I generate an operating surplus. During the academic year 2010–2011, 68 of 120 FBS football teams reported an operating surplus, and, of these teams, the median surplus was $10.26 million. Also during 2010–2011, 66 FBS basketball teams reported a surplus, with a median surplus of $3.36 million. In FCS, far fewer programs operate in the black: during 2010–2011, only 2 of 122 football teams generated an operating surplus, and only 8 of 121 basketball teams had a surplus. In Division I without football, only 5 of 96 men's basketball teams generated a surplus. So, the first observation is that most Division I schools do not generate an operating surplus in either football or men's basketball, and, hence, in these schools, the big-time sports detract from the funds available for the promotion of the nonrevenue sports.

Second, even in those programs where there is an operating surplus in football or men's basketball, the actual financial picture is less sanguine. When capital expenses (e.g., debt service on football stadiums, basketball arenas, tutoring buildings, or training facilities) and administrative overhead (e.g., a pro rata charge for the school president's time spent on football) are included, the actual surplus generated is either diminished greatly or nonexistent. In a study for the NCAA, Jonathan and Peter Orszag (2005) estimated that the average FBS program had yearly capital expenses of more than $20 million.[3]

Third, even in those football and men's basketball programs where a true surplus is generated and some of this surplus is meaningfully transferred to support the nonrevenue sports, there is still evidence of substantial siphoning of the surplus. Consider the support given to exorbitant salaries of the head coaches of football and men's basketball teams, their assistant coaches, the athletic directors, and the conference commissioners. While the NCAA and others have attempted to justify these elevated levels of compensation on the basis of market competition, the underlying market forces are artificially created. Hence, there is good reason to believe that these salaries constitute private inurement that could disqualify athletic departments from 501(c)(3) treatment.

PRIVATE INUREMENT AND THE COMPENSATION FOR HEAD COACHES AND OTHERS

Today, there are more than 100 college football coaches with compensation packages exceeding $1 million; there are more than a dozen exceeding $3 million, and several exceed $4 or $5 million in monetary compensation alone. Men's basketball coaches' compensation packages are similar; indeed, the highest paid basketball coaches generally outdo their football counterparts. During the 2011 calendar year, Duke's coach Krzyzewski earned nearly $9.7 million (Berkowitz, 2013). Louisville's Rick Pitino earned $7.5 million during the academic year 2010–2011 (Upton, 2011).[4]

In 2009 the University of Kentucky agreed to pay John Calipari a guaranteed $31.65 million (plus incentives) over eight years. These figures exclude bonuses as well as extensive perquisites, including free use of cars, housing subsidies, country club memberships, private jet service, exceptionally generous severance packages, and more. The coaches also have handsome opportunities to earn outside income via apparel or sneaker endorsements, the lecture circuit, summer camps on campus, and book contracts. For some coaches' contracts, the buyout is the most lucrative element: former Notre Dame head football coach, Charlie Weis, is enjoying a nearly $19 million buyout after his release, even though he is currently employed as the University of Kansas head coach (Hamilton, 2013).

Not surprisingly, assistant coaches have also experienced an explosion in their pay packages in recent years. For instance, Tennessee lured its new defensive coordinator in 2009, Monte Kiffin, with a $1.2 million salary, a $300,000 bonus for staying through the end of the regular season, up to another $100,000 in incentives, and the use of two cars. The average salary for the nine assistant football coaches at Tennessee was $369,000 in 2009. *USA Today* identified more than 100 assistant coaches in the FBS who received over $250,000 in base compensation in 2009. Bob Stoops, Oklahoma's head football coach, is guaranteed $4.3 million in 2009, and his nine assistants earned nearly $2.5 million before bonuses. Alabama and LSU also boasted $6 million-plus for staff compensation (Wieberg, 2009).

Athletic directors and conference commissioners are also wealthy beneficiaries of the system. According to the *USA Today* Athletic Director Salary Database, in 2012–2013, there were eight college athletic directors who earned guaranteed pay over $1 million, one of whom earned more than $3 million. Bonuses ran as high as $760,000 and were paid on top of the guaranteed salaries. There is a clear pattern for schools with higher coach compensation to also have higher athletic director compensation.

Conference commissioners earn even more. Larry Scott, the Pac-12 commissioner, earned $3.1 million in calendar year 2011, while Jim Delaney, commissioner of the Big 10, earned $2.8 million and Mike Slive of the SEC pulled down $1.6 million.

This pattern began long ago. Back in 1924, Centenary College in Shreveport, Louisiana, the nation's first liberal arts college west of the Mississippi, was denied accreditation by the Southern Association of Colleges and Schools because the school placed an "undue emphasis on athletics." The primary evidence of Centenary's misplaced priorities by the Southern Association was that the college paid its football coach more than it paid its college president. The next year the football coach was gone, and the college gained accreditation (Johnson, 2008).

The legendary head football coach at the University of Alabama (1958–1982), Bear Bryant, adhered to a firm policy of always keeping his salary $1 below that of the school president. Bryant believed that it was symbolically important for the university president to be paid more than the head football coach (Barra, 2005).

Defenders of the multimillion-dollar head coaches' salaries often argue that coaches' compensation packages are driven by market forces. This may be true, but what drives the market forces? The market for coaches is sustained by several artificial factors: (a) there is no compensation paid to the athletes; (b) intercollegiate sports benefit from substantial tax privileges; (c) there are no shareholders demanding dividend distributions or higher profits to bolster stock prices; (d) athletic departments are nourished by university and statewide financial support; and (e) coaches' salaries are negotiated by athletic directors whose own worth rises with the salaries of their employees.

In a normal competitive market, college football coaches would not be getting compensated almost at the same level as NFL coaches. During the 2011–2012 season, the highest paid NFL coach was Bill Belichick of the Patriots at $7.5 million, and the tenth-highest-paid coach was Andy Reid of the Eagles at $5.5 million (Weir, 2012). The top 32 college football programs generate revenues in the $40–90 million range; the average NFL team generates around $270 million. The same logic applies to the NBA and its coaches. During 2011–2012, the top paid NBA coach was Doc Rivers of the Celtics at $7 million (nearly $3 million below Mike Krzyzewski's compensation at Duke), and the tenth highest paid was Scott Skiles of the Bucks at $4.5 million (Van Riper, 2012). The revenue range for the 30 top college basketball teams is $15–40 million, while the average NBA team generates $130 million.

If there were a rule that college head coaches could be paid no more than three times as much as the average salary of a full professor, it would not affect the quality of coaching or the level of intercollegiate competition. This is because the next best alternative for top college coaches (the reservation wage) is likely to be well below this level—perhaps coaching in Division II or III, or in high school, and earning between $20,000 and $100,000, without perks. Anything above the reservation wage is what economists call economic rent. Economic rent does not affect the allocation of resources. Thus, the argument that college coaches' compensation packages appear to constitute private inurement appears to be strong.

CONCLUSION

In this chapter I have presented the nature of the tax privileges enjoyed by college sports and reviewed the basis in the tax laws for this favorable treatment. The foundation for these privileges is the fact that athletic departments are housed within public colleges and universities or within private universities which are considered 501(c)(3) entities. Because it is not clear that the activity of big-time college sports is functionally related to the purpose of the university (education) or to the promotion of amateur sports, and because there is a compelling argument that there is private inurement and possibly private benefit in the operation of big-time college sports, there is a case to be made that college sports do not deserve favorable treatment. The IRS has attempted to capture some tax revenue from parts of the intercollegiate sports business, but it has backed off as a result of either political pressure or new legislation.

We have also seen that some believe that trying to tax college sports is a paper tiger. That is, even if the IRS or the U.S. Congress decided to tax the net income of college sports, athletic departments would find a way to manipulate their books to show no profit. While efforts at manipulation may occur, accounting rules could limit this ability. Further, if intercollegiate athletics were subjected to the UBIT, then activities like corporate sponsorships could be treated as separate entities under the fragmentation principle. The direct costs of obtaining corporate sponsorships are minimal and it would be difficult to hide the net income generated.

Further, I examined the policy to allow seat purchasers to deduct from their taxable income 80% of the "donation" or down payment on their season's tickets. For the better seats, the required "donation" often exceeds $10,000 per year per seat, and some schools earn tens of millions of dollars annually from these "donations" and the government loses out on hundreds of millions of dollars of tax revenue.

Finally, there is the issue of whether athletic departments should be allowed to use the university's tax-exempt bonding privileges, especially if their activity is judged not to be functionally related to the school's educational mission. It appears that this bonding privilege has only encouraged an arms' race to build bigger and better athletic facilities, foisting major funding costs of hundreds of millions of dollars on schools throughout the country.

QUESTIONS FOR DISCUSSION

1. Why did Congress pass the UBIT law in 1950?

2. Do you think that intercollegiate athletics is functionally related to the mission of the university?

3. Do you believe that the NFL and NBA enjoy excessive benefits from the operation of big-time college sports?

Notes

1. In the same bill, Congress lifted the previous $150 million limit on tax-exempt bonds for college facility construction.

2. The NCAA estimated that in 2004–2005 corporate sponsorship payments to college athletic programs totaled $275 million.

3. Sometimes it is argued that athletics departments support the overall educational mission of the university by generating a surplus, which is then transferred to the university's central budget. While it appears to be true that a handful of departments transfer a modest surplus to their university's central fund, in all but a dozen or so of the 340 Division I schools there is a deficit (when properly accounted) in the athletics department. In 2010–2011, the median FBS school athletic department ran an operating deficit of $10.3 million, according to the NCAA's own figures, and this was before the consideration of capital and indirect expenses. Further, sometimes it is claimed that a strong athletics programs attract student applications and increase donations to the school. While this is a complicated matter to assess, suffice it to state the scholarly evidence on each is ambiguous at best.

4. In 2012, in 41 of the 50 states, a head coach of a college football or basketball team was the highest paid public employee in the state.

References

Barra, A. (2005). *The last coach: A life of Paul "Bear" Bryant*. New York: W. W. Norton Press. Retrieved from www.bloomberg.com

Berkowitz, S. (2013, May 16). Duke's Krzyzewski credited with $9.7 million in pay for 2011. *USA Today*. Retrieved from www.usatoday.com

Brand, M. (2006). Response to survey letter to NCAA re. tax exempt status. Retrieved from http://www.nacua.org/documents/NCAALetter_TaxExempt_ResponsetoHouseWaysMeansCmte.pdf

Brooks, J. (1977, December 26). The law school and the noodle factory. *New Yorker*. Retrieved from www.newyorker.com

Colombo, J. (2010). The NCAA, tax exemption and college athletics. *University of Illinois Law Review, 109*, 111.

Congressional Budget Office. (2009, May). *Tax preferences for collegiate sports*. Congress of the United States. Report from the Congressional Budget Office.

Dexheimer, E. (2007, October 1). Some question tax breaks that help fill coffers. *Austin American-Statesman*. Retrieved from www.statesman.com

Eichelberger, C., & Babcock, C. (2012, October 25). Football-ticket tax break helps colleges get millions. *Bloomberg*. Retrieved from www.bloomberg.com

Gaul, G. (2012, October 18). College football gets tax breaks. *McClatchy*. Retrieved from www.mcclatchydc.com

Hamilton, B. (2013, May 23). Notre Dame Weis' buyout may approach $19 million. *Chicago Tribune*. Retrieved from www.chicagotribune.com

Johnson, J. (2008, September 4). The suicide season. *Shreveport Times*. Retrieved from www.shreveporttimes.com

Orszag, J. M., & Orszag, P. R. (2005). *The empirical effects of collegiate athletics: An update*. Indianapolis: National Collegiate Athletic Association.

Upton, J. (2011, May 19). Salary analysis: NCCA tournament coaches cashing in. *USA Today*. Retrieved from www.usatoday.com

Van Riper, T. (2012, May 15). The highest paid coaches in sports. *Forbes*. Retrieved from www.forbes.com

Weir, T. (2012, May 16). Bill Belichick tops Forbes list of 10 best-paid coaches. *USA Today*. Retrieved from www.usatoday.com

Weisbrod, B., Ballou, J., & Asch, E. (2008). *Mission and money: Understanding the University*. Cambridge: Cambridge University Press.

Wieberg, S. (2009, November 10). Top assistants command big pay. *USA Today*. Retrieved from www.usatoday.com

COLLEGE SPORTS SPENDING DECISIONS and the ACADEMIC MISSION

Rodney Fort

The two main themes in this chapter are the approach universities take to college sports, which explicitly documents college athletics spending; and the degree to which this spending is consistent with the fundamental mission of American higher education. Both topics are fundamental to an understanding of college sports outcomes.

The university approach to athletics is demonstrated with a fairly general descriptive model of hierarchical oversight using concepts mainly from economics. The model is based on well-used "principal-agent" (PA) logic applied to college sports. This general model helps make sense of spending data that are so confusing to many observers of the college sports scene.

This chapter does not cover everything. First, what follows is pretty much restricted to "big-time" college sports; lower NCAA divisions may have similar *qualitative* results but surely will have different *quantitative* results. Second, topic and space constraints also allow only cursory coverage of the remaining hierarchy; conference organizations, like the Southeastern (SEC) or Big Ten, and the National Collegiate Athletic Association (NCAA) are noted only in passing.

Whether observed spending is consistent with the fundamental academic mission of the university is a crucial question that economic assessment can only inform, not decide. As with all policy issues, the determination of the level of any public spending goes hand in hand with the determination of just what it is that the spender desires. And that is a truly difficult question, deserving of extensive treatment, because there are so many different spenders with so many different ambitions for universities.

Universities, by their very nature and because they are all at least partly publicly funded, should always be engaged in the exercise of assessing both their chosen purposes and how they are spending money toward those purposes. That discussion will always be best served by *less* rhetoric, *more* process recognition, and *more* data-driven analysis.

UNIVERSITY ADMINISTRATORS AND THEIR ATHLETIC DIRECTORS

While there will be variations, the generally descriptive model of university administrators (UAs) and their athletic directors (ADs) that is presented in this section borrows heavily from my textbook (Fort, 2011, chap. 13) and from my book with economist Jason Winfree (Fort & Winfree, 2013, chap. 2). Remember the limitations of the presentation; while both operate in their university structure, their conference structure, and as members of the NCAA, UAs and ADs in the "micro" look presented in this chapter are considered only in light of their eventual university interaction.

The first thing to observe about these relationships is that both the level of competence and the level of experience of UAs and ADs are empirical issues, directly observable, and not the subject of assumptions before the fact. All UAs and ADs "come up through the ranks" and satisfy quite stringent versions of what social scientists refer to as "selection mechanisms." Years of training and experience, in an extremely competitive employment area, are prerequisites for both UAs and ADs. So there need be no presumption that UAs and ADs are inept or naive.

The second part of our descriptive model is an assumption that is hardly controversial: all actors pursue their own self-interest. UAs and ADs care about their income and upward career mobility. In the context of their environment, enhanced welfare of UAs and ADs depends upon the performance of their respective organizations.

Note that an extremely important possibility presents itself here. There may be areas of conflict between the self-interested pursuits of UAs and the self-interested pursuits of ADs. In the operational environment of the university, the welfare of UAs depends on the performance of all of the units on campus along well-known dimensions—research, teaching, and service. The ability of UAs to overcome conflicts with their ADs will depend on two things: the net value of independent action to ADs and the costs of monitoring to UAs.

This is the "principal-agent" setting that is well known to economists: namely, UAs are "principals" to their university "agents." The agents are academic leaders like college deans and nonacademic leaders like ADs. The president of the university (most typically, but with some exceptions) controls the AD's employment and pay subject to market forces and does his or her level best to monitor the performance of the AD subject to the costs of doing so. Along this well-known line of PA reasoning, UAs have every incentive to create and manage methods of oversight that harness the self-interested behavior of ADs to the enhancement of UA welfare.

All well and good, but what do these observations so far suggest about how UAs will actually organize their academic and other units on campus? The answer is that UAs, over the history of universities, have organized different university functions into separate departments, with an oversight structure from department, to college, to UAs, for two reasons. First, people in all units on campus generate the largest total output when they are all able to pursue their comparative advantages along the lines of research, teaching, and service. Second, this type of hierarchical organization facilitates monitoring of the various units given the costs of doing so.

Given that the monitoring problem for UAs is essentially similar across its departments, it is no wonder that all units at the university, including the athletic department, are similarly structured. (At a few universities, athletic departments are separate entities reporting directly to an oversight board and the board of regents, but this is still oversight.) In athletic departments, all of the assistant coaches in a given sport are specialists in different areas, just like individual faculty members are on the academic side (e.g., in football, strength and conditioning, position coaches, offensive and defensive coordinators). These specialists are organized under the head coach similar to an academic department and its chair.

Then, the collection of sports is organized into the larger unit, the athletic department. To keep the analogy truly complete, we could refer to this as the "school of athletics," since, at the top of the athletic department, the AD is the equivalent of an academic dean (at least in terms of oversight and authority). There are associate ADs to handle the day-to-day operations of the department, freeing the AD to engage in fundraising and external relations for the athletic department. The AD answers to the president (rather than the provost on the academic side) and up the ladder to the regents and governor.

Some claim that ADs have the power over UAs in this relationship, a belief that engenders the view that the athletic department tail wags the university dog. It seems to them that ADs get whatever resources they want and should be predicted to run amok at times to the complete embarrassment of UAs. These observers point to the most heinous of episodes as cases in point. One example was behavior in the Southern Methodist University athletic community (all the way up to the governor) that led to the "death penalty" in 1987. The most recent example was behavior at Penn State University in 2011 that led to severe restrictions in 2012 as well as the firing of revered coach Joe Paterno and the resignation of president Graham Spanier and some of his staff.

From the perspective of the general descriptive model, instead, all of this is explained in terms of the chances for oversight failure. Interestingly, as long as oversight is costly, the model allows that sometimes ADs will create situations counter to the best interests of UAs. Depending on the opportunity cost of monitoring time and resources, minor problems with oversight should be expected occasionally, and in only rare situations will extreme examples like Southern Methodist and Penn State

The Failure of Oversight at Penn State

The child abuse sex scandal that engulfed an entire administration at Penn State in 2011 is well known and instructive for those plying principal-agent models of college sports. Former Penn State defensive coordinator Jerry Sandusky was arrested in November 2011 on numerous counts of child sexual abuse alleged (at that time) to have occurred from 1994 to 2009, including incidents on campus. Sandusky was found guilty of all but a few of the charges and is serving 30–60 years in prison. But this is only the beginning of the matter from the principal-agent perspective.

An investigation commissioned by the Penn State governing board, conducted by former FBI director Louis Freeh, found that Penn State president Graham Spanier, legendary head coach Joe Paterno, athletic director Tim Curley, and vice president for finance Gary Schultz had all known about Sandusky's behavior since 1998. The report also named them complicit in failing to disclose their knowledge and take proper action. All but Paterno, now deceased, have been ordered to stand trial on cover-up accusations. The NCAA also imposed sweeping sanctions on the Penn State athletic department just short of the "death penalty" and the university remains under investigation by the Department of Education.

All of this proves importantly instructive from the perspective of a principal-agent model of college sports. It is the essence of such a model that oversight design will not be foolproof; some ability to pursue independent objectives will be enjoyed by agents as long as oversight is costly. The challenge for principals in this situation is to minimize both the chances for oversight failure and the consequences.

If it were just a matter of catching problems, the Penn State oversight design, typical of college sports, actually worked quite well. Sandusky's behavior was observed, reported, and apparently moved up the chain of command from an assistant coach, to the head coach, to the AD and VP for finance (in charge of the University Police), and finally all the way to the university president. But once at this level, oversight eventually failed. For whatever reason—some said ineptness, others said panic, and still others blamed it on "sports culture"—neither denizens of the athletic department nor university administrators took the action dictated by law in such a situation. On the whole, then, oversight in this instance failed miserably.

While oversight failures are a fact of life in principal-agent situations, it is clear that there are a variety of other factors that contribute to the degree of oversight failure and the consequences. In the Penn State case, the welfare of university administrators (the president and VP of finance) was too closely intertwined with that of the athletic department. Administrators apparently decided that protecting the vaunted position of Penn State athletics was worth the potential costs of attempting to cover up Sandusky's behavior. While Sandusky's deeds were tragic enough, the ensuing impacts on Penn State University were the result of basic oversight failure. ■

occur. But this should all be taken in totality, and it appears that in general the oversight methods function satisfactorily.

If ADs do not contribute to UA goals, or if the athletic department becomes costly to the university in embarrassing ways, then UAs do have recourse. For one, all but a handful of athletic departments receive a budget allocation from UAs commonly referred to as "institutional support." And what UAs give they can also take away: budget allocations to the athletic department can simply be reduced. And they have done so repeatedly through the history of college sports. UAs can also take a much more dramatic action familiar to all who follow college sports: AD firings or forced resignations are common practice.

And then there are interesting current and historical observations where athletic departments are simply closed down altogether by UAs. One historical example is the elimination of the storied football program at the University of Chicago. Recently, UAs at Northeastern University (the Huskies) cut its football program in November 2009, and UAs at Hofstra University (the Flying Dutchmen) followed suit the next month. So there need be no presumption that ADs act completely independently.

The basics of the descriptive model so far are portrayed in Figure 10.1. Services from all areas of the university flow out, under the three major headings of research, teaching, and service, and money and political support come back to UAs. In turn, hierarchically, through deans and directors, including *athletic* directors, UAs allocate rewards back to departments. Deans and ADs are rewarded when they contribute to UA goals and punished when they do not (always a relative statement—rewards could just be smaller).

As with all things, not all departments are equally adept at each of the research, teaching, and service areas and an effective organizational structure would allow the pursuit of comparative advantage. Among academic departments, some are more about teaching and others are more about research. Compared to academic departments, the mix is different still for the athletic department. While athletic departments do not actually create research agendas or initiate research, they do participate in research, especially in sport medicine (recently, in the assessment of concussion mechanics and their impacts on players). Thus, their research "mission" is rather research cooperation. Even more clearly, there is teaching and service

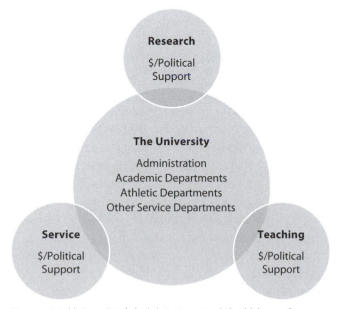

Figure 10.1. University Administrators and the Values of Campus Hierarchy.

performed by the athletic department. Athletic training students hone their skills on college athletes, and the athletes themselves often become teachers of their sport (coaches). A very few continue on in their sport at the professional level (a parallel here would be with the fine arts).

Some academic departments also have a service-entertainment contribution, but it is here that athletic departments truly shine. Members of the athletic department, from the AD through the associate ADs, on down to coaches and assistants, and finally the athletes themselves, provide entertainment services. Students have demanded and enjoyed these entertainment services practically since universities were formed. More important, these entertainment services are also enjoyed by millions of others throughout society. Some of them are boosters who then also contribute resources to their favorite university. UAs see these as resources that contribute to the pursuit of their own goals of research, teaching, and service.

Academic departments indeed contribute to the UA goals of research, teaching, and service (Figure 10.1). Athletic departments also generate resources used to achieve UA goals. Part of the value comes back through tuition dollars paid on the part of scholarship athletes by the athletic department. In addition, other values accrue to the rest of the university, beyond the athletic department bottom line. These are typically grouped as follows (Fort & Winfree, 2013, chap. 3):

- Greater giving by alumni and other boosters to the general university fund

- A larger and better set of student applicants

- Favorable general budget treatment by legislators

- Better faculty and administrators

- Value added to athletes, many of who would not be at the university without athletics

Thus, we get another implication of the model: *The value of the AD's efforts will be found in places other than the athletic department bottom line.*

One final observation on the monitoring problem rounds out the implications of this general descriptive theory. In the same way that UAs are flexible in terms of facilitating the comparative advantages of units on campus (contributions vary by research, teaching, and service), they also allow ADs more flexibility over revenues than typically deans of academic departments are allowed. But there is a valid economic reason why ADs are allowed this flexibility. While it is easier to observe athletic department success than academic department success, there is much more fluctuation in the former than in the latter. For athletic departments, there can be little disagreement in the final tally of wins and losses, but just which year the department will enjoy great success is much more uncertain than in the academic part of the university.

As a result of this fluctuation, UAs find that athletic departments are most valuable if ADs are allowed to spend the unexpected money they might generate during successful years. Academic deans do not have this discretion. They determine the needs of their departments, put them together in a budget request, and turn it over to the university administration. If spending is lower or revenues are greater than anticipated, UAs retain control over any positive balance.

Combined with the result of the institutional design described earlier, a reasonable conclusion is: *"Institutional support" to athletics is not a subsidy, it is an incentive reward*, and *it should be expected that spending would always rise to meet revenues.*

BIG-TIME COLLEGE SPORTS SPENDING

Rather than just looking at spending results as a simple measured statistic, there is also an opportunity to seek understanding of those outcomes using the implications of a descriptive model. (For a description of the data sources on college sports revenues and expenses, see Fort & Winfree, 2013, chap. 1).

The Value of the AD's Efforts Is Not Just in the Athletic Department Bottom Line

Fort and Winfree (2013, chap. 3) assess the work in the literature that estimates the values across the university generated by athletics but not found on the athletic department's bottom line. Typically, these values are small but statistically detectable. They then go on to show that looking only at the absolute size of the values generated by the athletic department to the rest of the university cannot be the end of the economic story. The rest of the economic story of the values created for UAs by college sports begs the question: Do UAs get their money's worth from their investment in college sports?

The first thing to notice is that the size of the investment in athletics by UAs, compared to the rest of the investments they make across the entire university, is really quite small. Here is an easy comparison for 2012, the most recent aggregate data reported through the NCAA (Fulks, 2013). The median of reported generated revenues, that is, not including institutional support, is $40.6 million. The median of total reported revenues from all sources, that is, including institutional support, is $56.0 million. Simple subtraction shows that institutional support at the median is about $15.4 million, or around 26% of total revenues. Rest assured that this $15.4 million median investment is a very small percentage of the "median" university total budget. So, while the conclusion from the literature is that the values generated by college sports are small, so is the investment made in athletics compared to the investment decisions made by UAs across all of the units at their university.

On the question of the return on this small investment, Fort and Winfree (2013, chap. 3) offer the following insight. For the most recent publicly available data at the level of individual institutions, 2010–2011, the smallest athletic department budget was at Washington State University. The total 2010–2011 Washington State budget was $843.7 million, and the athletic department budget was $40.6 million. But it is not the entire athletics budget that is of interest—UAs earn their return on just the part that they invest, that is, "institutional support." That investment was $9.9 million at Washington State, a truly trivial 1.2% of the total university budget. Now, 73% of that $9.9 million investment, or $7.2 million, came back directly to the university from the athletic department to cover athletic scholarships. If, in addition to that $7.2 million, there were only another $3.2 million generated in other values across the rest of the university, then UAs at Washington State would earn a 5% return on their investment. And that $3.2 million would be a small amount indeed to find in the university total budget of $843.7 million, just 0.38%.

Fort and Winfree also provide the same comparison for the median-sized athletics budget at the University of North Carolina and for the largest budget department, the University of Texas. The results there were simply startling in terms of the return earned on the investment in the athletic department by UAs. But the main point is that investments are small, returns are too, but the percentage return is quite healthy.

Not a Subsidy but an Incentive

The descriptive model tells us that ADs will always spend all that they get; revenues will equal expenses. To put it a bit more precisely, the correlation between revenues and spending should be unity. And this comparison should include *all revenues*, including the investment by UAs. Further, budget deficits can occasionally occur in the real world for the usual reasons of mistakes under uncertainty, but they cannot persist. After all, budget deficits under the descriptive model serve nobody's best interest. So, what do the data say?

Our insight comes from the NCAA's own report of annual operating revenues and expenses (Fulks, 2013). (Examining annual operations ignores capital, that is, facilities spending, but not everything can be covered in a single chapter; the student is referred to Orszag and Orszag [2005a, 2005b].) Figure 10.2 combines the data from those NCAA reports for FBS athletic departments (Fort, 2010, also produced a figure like this in a presentation at the NCAA Convention in 2009). The first thing to observe in Figure 10.2 is the steady increase in both revenues and expenditures over time. The real (adjusted for inflation) annual growth rates in the median of reported revenues and the median of reported spending were both 4.6% (quite large relative to the typical real growth rate in the economy at large). The second thing to notice is that spending rises over time to meet rising revenue. For fully 50 years, median reported revenues equal or exceed median reported spending, consistent with the implication of the descriptive model. Putting just a little more precision to it, at the median of revenues and the median of spending, the correlation between revenues and expenses is 0.995. Essentially, the "median" athletic department has enjoyed tremendous revenue growth and spent every dollar.

Figure 10.2 shows only a bit of a variation on this same theme for the departments reporting the largest revenues and expenses to the NCAA (the former have been re-

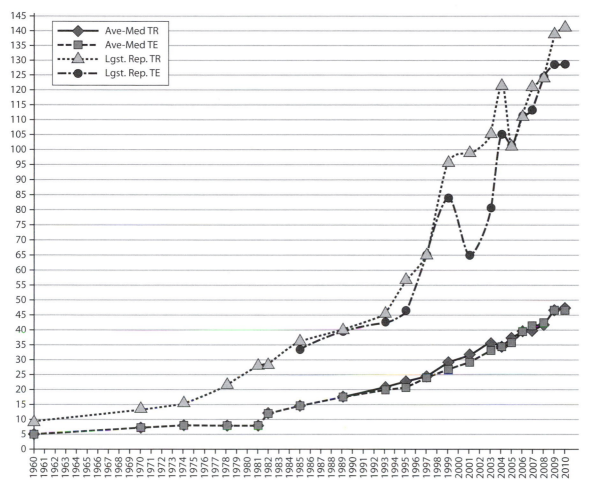

Figure 10.2. FBS Operating Revenues and Expenses (2009). TR = total revenue; TE = total expenses. (*Source:* Calculated from the data in Fulks (2011). *Note:* Largest Reported Total Revenue omits 2006 because the report that year is just not believable ($260.7 million $2009). Upon inquiry by the author, the NCAA responded that a particularly large gift to that program was responsible. But gifts are not operations so the figure omits this anomaly.)

ported only since 1985). First, the real annual growth rate in the largest reported spending is 5.8% (and essentially the same at 5.5% for revenues). Again, this rate is quite large relative to the typical real growth rate in the economy and also relative to the growth rate for the median program reports. Second, for fully 25 years, revenues equal or exceed spending, again, consistent with the prediction of the descriptive model. Another interesting comparison concerns the correlation, a bit lower 0.946 for the largest reports. Unlike their median counterparts, the largest athletic departments do not spend everything they bring in. We know that the observed surplus amounts typically go to athletic department endowment funds for future construction projects.

Of course, this is only part of the story. They may be doing it effectively, but are UAs choosing the *right level* of college sports activity? We now turn to that question.

IS SPORTS SPENDING CONSISTENT WITH ACADEMIC MISSION?

Economically, it appears the returns, also small, generate a reasonable return on that investment. But is even this small level somehow the "right" level? And here simple economic lessons end. In the policy arena, all concerned will have their opinion and rightfully so, since universities hold a special place in society (and most of them are at least partly publicly funded). The remainder of the chapter asks, "What is a modern university expected to do in the first place and how is it to cover the costs of doing so?"

Figure 10.1 detailed what universities do—research, teaching, and service. Research is pretty straightforward, and we will not spend much more time on this one. Revenues to do research come in the form of legislative budget allocations and, more importantly, outside research grants and contracts. Controversies arise occasionally over the types of research done at universities (a recent example is stem cell research) but not over the idea that one of their fundamental academic missions is to do research in the first place.

Teaching, at first blush, also seems straightforward. Undergraduate and graduate students are exposed to varieties of thought processes, trained to do particularly

Reflections on Managing College Sports

James Duderstadt is a past president of the University of Michigan (1988–1996). He was a nuclear engineer of renown and dean of the Engineering School at Michigan before taking the post, so he is clearly a capable and intelligent person. In his book *Intercollegiate Athletics and the American University: A University President's Perspective* (2003), he shares his insights into managing big-time college sports at one of the nation's premiere academic and athletic institutions.

The book offers an interesting perspective since Duderstadt's story is often cast in terms of relative risk—the medical school can threaten the institution financially, while the athletic department can threaten its integrity and reputation. He notes that athletic directors and coaches long for autonomy but simply cannot have it. Such autonomy (quoting from the introduction) "is a prescription for disaster in the complex political environment of the contemporary university." He also notes that, despite these potential problems and complexities, there is a place for sports on campus (although he laments their overcommercialization). Most importantly, he puts his finger right on the main points behind this chapter. Duderstadt clearly states and enumerates that the cause of any illness found, and the remedy as well, lies within the institutions governing college sports. He is quite specific that it is university administrators, at their own institutions and through both their athletic conferences and their membership in the NCAA, who bear primary responsibility for college sports outcomes.

Duderstadt pulls no punches and freely admits that there can be problems with college sports. But in the same breath he is quick to point out that the culprit is not really ambitious coaches, or thoughtless greedy athletes, or single-minded athletic directors. To blame them is to ignore the fact that most people in intercollegiate athletics are people of integrity trying to do their best to succeed within the rules. In addition, to blame them distracts attention from the true source of any remediation—governing boards and university presidents. ∎

challenging vocational activities, and also allowed the freedom to explore issues on their own. But the university mission here is not so simple as just providing faculty, classrooms, labs, and a forum. The undergraduate and graduate "college experience" is multidimensional; one dimension is students demand to be entertained.

Originally, students wanted to participate in sports, and universities quickly figured out how to make it available to them safely. In the modern context, students participate in intramural sports and as fans of sports played at a higher level than they can play themselves. Once, student-fans simply wore raccoon coats, sang "Boola Boola," cheered, and waved pennants. Now student-fans pay 24-hour TV and social media attention to their college teams. On this dimension at least, sports spending is in keeping with the academic mission—students want sports.

The reader at this point almost certainly says to himself or herself, all well and good but surely national TV broadcasts with immense rights fees go beyond the requirement to entertain students? Fair enough, but let's look closer at the provision of entertainment by universities. Universities provide a variety of entertainment services under the academic umbrella, from guest lectures on a range of topics to fine arts entertainment not otherwise provided by private promoters. But they also host popular superstars promoted privately but hosted in public university facilities simply for the notoriety—for example, Drake's appearance at the University of Texas, Arlington, and Ke$ha's at Southern Methodist University.

So it is with big-time sports. They are another demand on the university by clientele that contribute money and support, collected by UAs along the service dimension, that further its research, teaching, and service goals. The binding nature of long-term alumni and other booster relations makes the provision of sports entertainment a service that pays in currency important to UAs. It is, then, quite in keeping with the academic mission that these types of services also are provided.

But observing that the provision of services is in keeping with the academic mission still does not settle the issue of whether these entertainment offerings occur at the "right" level. So let's get to the heart of the criticism that the attention paid to athletics is overblown, almost always coupled with skepticism over its academic contribution. The dominant argument goes that sports pull students away from their studies without adding anything academically legitimate. But to what extent is that simply an observation about the particular niche that sports has been driven to at the university rather than an invitation to open discussion about the academic legitimacy of college sports?

CONCLUSION

By and large, oversight in the principal-agent relationship between UAs and their ADs produces benefits that appear to be worth the dollar investment. As with any oversight system, there will be failures. Most are small. Catastrophic results like those at SMU and Penn State have been few and far between. But whether the attention to college sports is at the right level is a complex issue that can only be informed, not solved, by the application of economic logic and data analysis. As with everything at the university, the level of attention and resources devoted to college sports is deserving of careful consideration. That discussion in the policy community concerned with universities will always be best served by less rhetoric, more process recognition, and more data-driven analysis. Using models like the one presented here is a good step in that direction.

QUESTIONS FOR DISCUSSION

1. What is a "principal-agent" model in general? (You may wish to consult an economics textbook.) What is the fundamental source of the tension between the principal and his or her agent(s)? How does the principal harness the pursuit of agent self-interest to be consistent with his or her own objectives? Is there an "optimal level" of failure in the designs of the principal? Why?

2. Rather than the principal-agent/oversight model presented in this chapter, other observers suggest that the athletic department is the tail that wags the university dog. Find an example of this "tail wagging the dog" belief in the popular media and explain the same outcome using the college sports principal-agent model in this chapter. Which is more convincing to you?

3. Why can economics not answer the question of whether sport spending is consistent with the academic missions of universities? How does economics inform this question?

References

Duderstadt, J. J. (2003). *Intercollegiate Athletics and the American University*. Ann Arbor: University of Michigan Press.

Fort, R. (2010). An economic look at the sustainability of FBS athletic departments. *Journal of Intercollegiate Sport, 3*, 3–21.

———. (2011). *Sports economics* (3rd ed.). Upper Saddle River, NJ: Prentice Hall.

Fort, R., & Winfree, J. (2013). *15 sports myths and why they're wrong*. Stanford: Stanford University Press.

Fulks, D. L. (2013). *2004–2012 NCAA revenues and expenses: NCAA Division I intercollegiate athletic programs report*. National Collegiate Athletic Association. Retrieved from http://www.ncaapublications.com/productdownloads/2012RevExp.pdf.

Knight Commission on Intercollegiate Athletics. (2009). Quantitative and qualitative research with football bowl subdivision university presidents on the costs and financing of intercollegiate athletics: Report of findings and implications. Retrieved from http://www.knightcommissionmedia.org/images/President_Survey_FINAL.pdf

Orszag, J. M., & Orszag, P. R. (2005a). *The physical capital stock used in collegiate athletics*. National Collegiate Athletic Association. Retrieved from http://www.ncaa.org/wps/portal/ncaahome?WCM_GLOBAL_CONTEXT=/ncaa/ncaa/research/financial_research.html

———. (2005b). *The empirical effects of collegiate athletics: An update*. National Collegiate Athletic Association. Retrieved from http://www.ncaa.org/wps/portal/ncaahome?WCM_GLOBAL_CONTEXT=/ncaa/ncaa/research/financial_research.html

THE BUSINESS MODEL of INTERCOLLEGIATE SPORTS

The Haves and Have-Nots

Scott Hirko and Kyle V. Sweitzer

In 1984 college football fans would rarely watch their alma mater play football on television more than twice per year. But leaders at the University of Oklahoma (OU) and the University of Georgia (UGA) believed they could earn more money and exposure by having their teams on television more frequently. OU and UGA sued the organization of which they were members, the National Collegiate Athletic Association (NCAA), which owned the rights to put college football on television (Lee, 2012). The football powers won the case before the U.S. Supreme Court, starting the "arms race" of massive spending and revenues in college sports. There was a prophetic moment before the court. In his dissent, Justice Byron White noted that significant revenues from televising football may change college sports: "NCAA's television plan seems eminently reasonable [because it] fosters the goal of amateurism by spreading revenues among the various schools and reducing the financial incentives toward professionalism" (*NCAA v. Oklahoma Board of Regents*, 1984).

College football today is far closer to professionalism than in 1984. Since *NCAA v. Oklahoma*, the money the media gives the big-time football powers has increased exponentially. For instance, in 1984 the Big Ten conference earned approximately $4.8 million annually from ABC television (Siegfried & Burba, 2003) compared to $232 million from several media partners in 2011 (Knight Commission on Intercollegiate Athletics, 2011). As of 2013, the revenue the "Big Five" athletic conferences with automatic qualification into the football Bowl Championship Series[1] (BCS) will make over the life of their television contracts is projected at nearly $21 billion (Dosh 2012; Knight Commission on Intercollegiate Athletics, 2011; Smith & Ourand, 2013). In other words,

KEY TERMS

Big Five ◄

Bowl Championship ◄
Series Automatic
Qualifier (BCS AQ)

exploitation ◄

Flutie effect ◄

revenue-producing sport ◄

subsidy ◄

membership in a Big Five conference with access to BCS games is lucrative and prestigious.

This chapter discusses the business model in NCAA Division I athletics. We illustrate two ways to consider the "haves" versus "have-nots" in major college sports. First: the "haves" are universities with a *commercial* athletics spending model because of access to major revenues that help pay for their athletic programs. The "have-nots" are schools with a *subsidization* athletics spending model because they pay for athletics primarily from other funding sources (e.g., student fees, general fund transfers, or other sources diverted from academic spending). The intent of the "haves" (*commercial*) is to be the best. The intent of the "have-nots" (*subsidization*) is to be perceived as being in the same league as the best. Second: the "haves" are the athletic teams considered major revenue sources (the "revenue sports"), specifically football and men's basketball. The "have-nots" are all of the other nonrevenue sports, many of which are referred to as Olympic sports, all of which are funded in part by the revenue generated by the football and men's basketball teams. Whether one looks first at the institutions or second at the teams, a dichotomy exists in big-time college sports primarily because of the money being generated by America's passion for football and men's basketball.

It is important to note that only a few of the "haves" actually make a profit from athletics. What is concerning is the incredible spending on athletics, in addition to conference shifting, as institutions try to become one of the "haves" and receive a larger share of major conference media contracts and football revenue.

Even though athletics is expensive, and most athletic departments fail to generate enough money to pay their costs, schools still invest in athletic teams to boost school pride and identity (Toma, 2003). One of the best examples occurred, coincidentally, in 1984. Boston College (BC) quarterback Doug Flutie completed a desperation touchdown pass on the last play of the game to defeat defending national champion University of Miami on national television. The media attention from the victory, combined with BC's subsequent significant increase in admissions applications, came to be known as the "Flutie effect."

The prophecy from Justice White in 1984 has proved accurate. Consider the money raised and shared by the "haves," which are the roughly 60 institutions in the Big Five athletic conferences with major football programs and access to huge football and basketball media revenues. The amount raised by the "haves" is massive compared to the money raised by the "have-nots," which are the roughly other 290 members of NCAA Division I with a minimal share of NCAA men's basketball championship media revenue.

The money generated in big-time athletics also raises questions about whether those creating the product, the college athletes, receive proper compensation. Athletics' imposition on the academic mission of higher education raises concerns about the future role of college sports. Scholars have chronicled how colleges use football and basketball players by prioritizing athletics over the athletes' academic and personal well-being in order to win for old alma mater (Sack & Staurowsky, 1998; Sperber, 2000). In return for full or partial athletic scholarships that help pay for their education, athletes at the most competitive level may decrease their opportunity to learn, and some encounter debilitating injuries. Be it greater publicity to the institution, enhanced revenues from more student applications, enhanced donations to athletics from winning, or just being the best on the playing field, each of these tenets create greater disparity between those who "have" and those who "have not."

ABOUT THE MONEY

The notion that colleges make money from their athletic program is debatable, and it depends on how one measures the dollars and what is included in the count. Few athletic programs break even from their athletic-related income versus what they spend on athletics. Almost all college athletic programs lose money and receive some form of subsidy from student fees, state government, or the institution's general funds, even in NCAA Division I (Berkowitz, Upton, & Brady, 2013).

The disparity between athletic-related expenditures and revenues manifests itself in various ways, often to the detriment of students. Former University of Michigan president James Duderstadt (2003) noted: "If we illuminate hidden costs and subsidies, we find that all intercollegiate athletics burden the university with considerable costs, some financial, some in terms of the attention required of university leadership, some in terms of the impact to the reputation and integrity of the university, and some measured only in the impact on students and staff" (p. 146).

Consider the expenses and revenues of 228 public NCAA Division I institutions in 2012. When one subtracts expenses from generated revenue (money earned from athletics with no subsidy), only 19 athletic programs earned more money than they spent. Student fees, money from a school's general fund, or other financial support was required to pay the athletics expenses at 209 of the 228 Division I public colleges and universities. In 2012 all Division I institutions spent more than $2.1 billion beyond generated revenue to pay for athletics (*USA Today*, 2013). Table 11.1 displays the primary expense and revenue categories among NCAA Division I athletic programs.

EXPENSES

College athletic programs operate a financial model in which costs are relatively fixed for planning purposes, such as coach and staff salaries, athletic scholarships, team travel, and facilities maintenance. The institutions with the wealthiest athletic programs ("haves") tend to spend more money on facilities and coaching salaries, thus driving up the cost and making it less affordable for the "have-nots" to compete.

The athletic governing body (e.g., NCAA, National Association for Intercollegiate Athletics [NAIA], National Junior College Athletics Association [NJCAA]) and

TABLE 11.1

Most Significant Drivers of Expenditures and Revenues in College Sports

EXPENDITURES	REVENUES
Salaries	Ticket sales
Athletic scholarships	Guarantees*
Travel and recruiting	Payouts from bowls and tournaments
Equipment, supplies, medicine	Television
Insurance	Corporate sponsorships, advertising, licensing
Legal, public relations, administrative	Unearned revenues
Capital expenditures (debt service and maintenance)	Booster club donations Student fees and assessments State or other government support Hidden university subsidies

Sources: Duderstadt (2003); Knight Commission on Intercollegiate Athletics (2013a, 2013b), NCAA (2013a).

*NCAA Financial Report forms define guarantees as "revenue received from participation in away games" (NCAA, 2013a, p. 11).

divisional level in which an institution competes are partly what drives the cost. For example, the NCAA requires certain standards that each school must follow as a member, such as the number of sports an institution must sponsor, especially if the institution awards athletic scholarships. The NCAA also limits the number of scholarships a school can offer in each particular sport for the purpose of creating a more equal playing environment—otherwise schools with more money would offer more scholarships. However, because scholarships are among the most expensive costs, not all institutions provide the full number of allowable athletic scholarships in all their sports.

While NCAA Division I football is the most profitable sport, it is also the most expensive. It requires the greatest number of participants. It requires the greatest number of coaches and support staff. Football's participation numbers mean more expenses for athletic scholarships, staff salaries and benefits, and travel costs for away contests. Football also necessitates the greatest expense in facilities, such as a stadium, practice, and training. Football also has the most significant NCAA requirements to be a member of the most competitive division, Division I-FBS (Football Bowl Subdivision): schools must offer football among at least 16 sports (eight all-female), draw more than 15,000 actual or paid attendance per football contest, schedule at least 60% of football games against fellow FBS opponents, and pay for at least 76 football scholarships (NCAA Bylaw 20.9.7) (NCAA, 2012). Football also drives the bulk of other costs for athletic departments, such as marketing and media relations (Duderstadt, 2003).

Institutions account for the debt to pay for athletics facilities differently. As an example, "have not" athletic programs may rely more on facilities used by all students, not just athletes. These athletic programs may not report the debt on those facilities. Some of the "have" athletic programs own their facilities and fully account for their debt. Some schools may take on more debt to build better facilities to be more competitive in a sport. For instance, in 2012 Division I schools reported to the NCAA athletics debt ranging from as little as nothing for the least wealthy athletic programs to more than $200 million for the wealthiest programs (Smith, 2013). The extent to which the success of a team is due to new facilities has not been well determined. Institutions must often help to pay the debt outside of what the athletic department can pay.

When it comes to expenses, level of competition matters little. As a percentage of the overall athletics budget, most institutions pay about the same for specific needs to run a college sports program. Figure 11.1 provides an understanding of the costs by categorizing institutions according to the level of athletic competition as well as the size of their athletics expense budget. Dividing FBS into quartiles further demonstrates expenses by the size of athletics budgets within the most competitive division. As stated earlier, coaching and administrative salaries, scholarships, team travel, and facilities are fixed costs to what the market demands. Therefore, the amount athletic programs pay to compensate coaches as a percentage of their overall budget is relatively the same at the wealthiest programs such as the University of Florida (see Quartile 1) as at the much less wealthy programs, such as Central Michigan University (see Quartile 4). Costs for facilities and game travel are similar. The percentage of scholarship costs predictably varies by the size of the athletics budget: since scholarships are fixed, the larger the overall athletics budget, the less scholarships are a percentage of the budget.

REVENUES

Unlike expenditures, certain revenue sources are variable and depend partly on the success of the teams. These revenue sources include ticket sales, appearances in football bowl games or the NCAA men's basketball tournament, licensing revenue, and donations (Duderstadt, 2003; Knight Commission on Intercollegiate Athletics, 2013). Figure 11.2 categorizes athletics revenues the same way as in Figure 11.1, demonstrating a stark reality of the difference between the "haves" and the "have-nots." Ticket sales for the "haves" (the top two FBS quartiles) come mainly from football and basketball attendance in huge stadiums and arenas that command high ticket prices. Fundraising and other contributions for the "haves" come from massive alumni bases and selling seat licenses for tickets, which fans can deduct on their tax returns.

Where the Money Goes...
Distribution of Athletic Expenditures for Division I Institutions, 2010

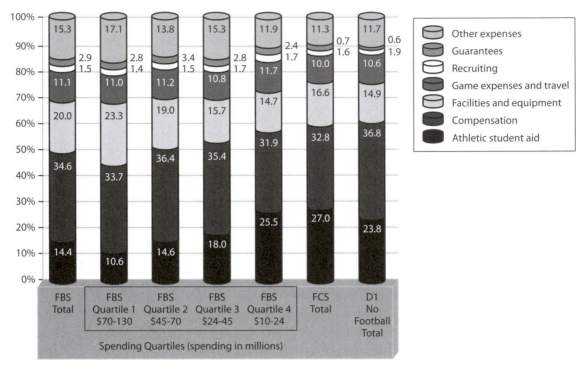

Figure 11.1. Expenses for Public Athletics Programs in NCAA Division I, 2010. (*Data Source:* USA Today's NCAA Athletics Finance Database (2013); *Source:* Knight Commission on Intercollegiate Athletics (2012a; 2012b); from www.knightcommission.org.)

The "haves" also command large revenues from media rights, primarily conference television packages and multimedia opportunities. The influence of football television coverage, primarily through the creation of the BCS and conference television packages, allowed some of the lesser-known institutions in football to become among the nation's most competitive programs. In 2009–2010, BCS automatic qualifying conferences received 82% of the $155 million BCS bowl revenue (NCAA, 2012). Furthermore, member schools of the Big Five conferences (with access to the BCS) are the "haves" because such media coverage allows them to recruit higher-level athletic prospects from high school; thus, the better athletic talent of the Big Five widens its gap between the "have-nots," which are not members of the BCS. Big Five conference athletic programs are the wealthiest (see Quartiles 1 and 2), generating 75% to 80% of the revenue necessary to pay their expenses.

By contrast, FBS schools in the bottom two quartiles as well as those at Division I Football Championship Subdivision (FCS) and Division I non-football schools received roughly 50% to 80% of their revenue from either government or institutional funding (such as student fees or other payments from the university's general fund).

Where the Money Goes...
Sources of Athletic Budget Revenue for Division I Institutions, 2010

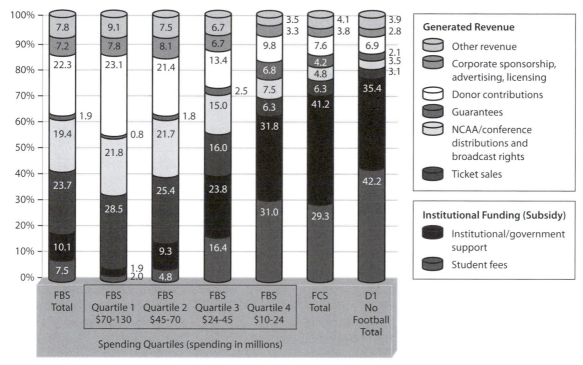

Figure 11.2. Revenues for Public Athletics Programs in NCAA Division I, 2010. (*Data Source:* USA Today's NCAA College Athletics Financial Database (2013); *Source:* Knight Commission on Intercollegiate Athletics (2012a, 2012b); from www.knightcommission.org.)

The differences in revenue in Figure 11.2 show how the wealthiest "have" programs generate revenues that are not available to the "have-nots." The majority of college athletic programs rely on student fees, institutional support, and government support as their primary source of revenue. Such differences drive the "have-nots" to spend more money from these nonathletics resources to keep up, thus escalating the "arms race."

CONFERENCE AND DIVISION MOVEMENT

Despite the well-documented reality that athletic programs are rarely self-sustaining, schools in less competitive divisions (Division II, Division I-FCS) decide to move up to more competitive divisions (Division I, Division I-FBS). Within Division I-FBS, schools in lesser-known conferences move into better-known leagues. Many institutional leaders assume that despite the cost, such an upward move in athletic status will result in increased publicity and notoriety for the institution as a whole

(Knight Commission on Intercollegiate Athletics, 2009; Toma, 2003). However, it is debatable that notoriety from athletic leads to a "Flutie effect" of increased admissions of students who are not athletes, including more out-of-state students (Orszag & Orszag, 2005).

Conference realignment in college athletics is due to schools' desiring to move to more prestigious, greater revenue-generating conferences. These more prosperous conferences typically welcome the institutions that are better established athletically and more marketable in order to garner a larger television market. For example, the University of Maryland at College Park, which in 2012 decided to move from the Atlantic Coast to the Big Ten, cited its need to have greater sustainability from extensive media dollars (Johnson, 2012). In turn, conferences that have had member schools leave decide to raid lesser-established conferences in order to retain some of their market share and maintain their television contracts (McMurphy & O'Neil, 2012).

In 2005 the University of Louisville, Rutgers University, and the University of South Florida joined the Big East Conference, which had its own television contract

---

TABLE 11.2

Expected Annual Long-Term Increase of Media Contractual Revenue (in millions) to Athletics as a Result of Conference Shifts into a "Big Five" Conference (announced shifts between 2010 and 2012)

INSTITUTION	BEFORE	AFTER*	INCREASE
Utah (Mountain West to Pac-12)	$1.2	$20.8	$19.6
Texas Christian (Mountain West to Big 12)	1.2	15.0	13.8
Pittsburgh (Big East to ACC)	10.3	17.1	7.2
Syracuse (Big East to ACC)	10.3	17.1	6.8
Colorado (Big 12 to Pac-12)	15.0	20.8	5.8
Nebraska (Big 12 to Big 10)	15.0	20.7	5.7
West Virginia (Big East to Big 12)	10.3	15.0	4.7
Texas A&M (Big 12 to SEC)	15.0	19.5	4.5
Missouri (Big 12 to SEC)	15.0	19.5	4.5
Maryland (ACC to Big 10)	17.1	20.7	3.6
Rutgers (ACC to Big 10)	17.1	20.7	3.6

Sources: Dosh, 2012; Knight Commission on Intercollegiate Athletics, 2011; Smith & Ourand, 2013.

*Before renegotiation of Big Ten Network on addition of Maryland and Rutgers. Also, before new independent Southeastern Conference television network. Amounts do not include exit fees from switching conferences or other third-party or independent school media revenue.

It Is Expensive to Chase the Haves

We provide revenue and expense data from three institutions to demonstrate the cost of trying to become a "have." We chose the University of Texas, San Antonio (UTSA), the University of Massachusetts, Amherst (UMass), and Boise State University because each switched its athletic affiliation (competitive division or athletic conference) after 2010. The most recent year (2011–2012) and the most distant year (2004–2005) of available data are presented in Table 11.3.

Between 2005 and 2012, more athletes participated at each institution, which required more money (particularly at UTSA, which added football, the sport with the most participants and scholarships). The student population increased between 10 and 12% at each of the three institutions. During the same period, the average size of the undergraduate population across all NCAA Division I institutions increased by 10% (U.S. Department of Education, IPEDS, 2013), diminishing a potential "Flutie effect." In other words, the undergraduate population likely would have grown about the same regardless of change in athletic conference or division. Athletic expenditures also increased significantly, even after adjusting for inflation (176% at UTSA, 36% at UMass, 118% at Boise).

UTSA generated $1.8 million more in ticket sales in 2012 than in 2005. Football was played in the Alamodome, averaging 29,226 paid attendees per game (NCAA, 2013b), leading the Western Athletic Conference. However, the $4.3 million increase in ticket sales, contributions, and conference revenues did not cover the $13.6 million increase in expenses. The $13.6 million subsidy in 2012 primarily covered the difference.

UMass's move into the "have-not" Mid-American Conference (MAC) created more revenue, primarily due to a $24 million subsidy. UMass struggled to meet the NCAA's football attendance requirement, with an average of 10,901 paid attendees in 2012 (NCAA, 2013b). While ticket sales and donations increased, athletics relied on 82% of its budget from the school's general fund, student fees, and state government. UMass athletics generated only 18% of its revenue. The rationale for the move was provided by UMass athletic director, John McCutcheon: "It's going to take four or five years to see a change for us. But a football team with a national profile can have transforming effects on a university" (Pennington, 2012).

From 2005 to 2012, a pair of BCS football bowl appearances helped boost Boise State's athletics prestige and revenue, doubling its annual ticket sales to $8.3 million and increasing yearly donations by nearly 300%. However, the expenses to become a "have" cost the athletic department an additional $25 million each year. Generated revenues from becoming a "have" were far less than the expense. To pay for the costs, the institution increased its subsidies by $4 million. ■

and greater football revenues as a member of the BCS. Over time, these institutions realized increased revenues to the point they became perceived by the public as members of the "haves." While the Big East is an indicator of how television has changed football since the 1990s (Oriard, 2009), the success from big media money also spelled its demise, as its football teams struggled while its men's basketball teams succeeded. From 1989 to 2013, Big East members sported a mediocre 8-7 record in BCS football bowl games. In men's basketball, Big East members had 11 Final Four appearances and 5 national champions. However, college football drives the media's interest and financial investment. Because of the mediocre football success, the seven successful men's basketball programs at private, Catholic member schools (i.e., Providence College, Marquette University, DePaul University, Georgetown University, Seton Hall University, St. John's University, and Villanova University) decided

TABLE 11.3

Select Revenue and Expense Data Reported by Three NCAA Division I-FBS Institutions in 2005 and 2012

	CONFERENCE	UNDERGRADUATE STUDENTS	ATHLETES	REVENUES LESS SUBSIDIES AND EXPENSES	EXPENSES
2005					
UTSA	No football	20,296	207	−$3,293,307	$7,675,714
UMass	A-10	18,031	586	−$14,393,280	$18,502,005
Boise St.	WAC	12,625	333	−$6,255,130	$16,852,312
2012					
UTSA	WAC	22,346	303	−$12,546,722	$21,223,077
UMass	MAC	20,338	623	−$24,079,190	$29,465,734
Boise St.	MWC	14,236	436	−$10,572,343	$43,172,225

Sources: USA Today NCAA College Athletics Financial Database (USA Today, 2013) and U.S. Department of Education Equity in Athletics Data Analysis Cutting Tool Website (EADA, 2013).

Note: Figures presented are from the 2004–2005 and 2011–2012 academic years. The financial data were reported by each institution to the U.S. Department of Education and to the NCAA. Data were obtained by USA Today through Freedom of Information Act requests.

to part ways and create a new Big East. The remaining FBS football schools formed their own conference, the American Athletic Conference, but lost their status to automatically qualify to participate in BCS bowl games. The loss in BCS status led to a significant decrease in the amount from media contracts: from $10.3 million annually per institution as a Big East member to $1.8 million per year per school as an American Athletic member. The new Big East, made up of only the Catholic basketball powers, will earn $3 million per year (McMurphy, 2013). FBS members with access to the BCS have repeatedly switched conferences to chase significantly more money from televising football (Table 11.2).

Transitioning from a lower division to Division I, particularly to the FBS, requires a large increase in athletics expenditures. While university and conference administrators negotiate, institutional rivalries are sometimes lost, the general student body may pay more in student fees, and college athletes may miss an increasing number of classes owing to increased travel. Academics seem to increasingly take a back seat to athletics as schools switch to conferences that are geographically a stretch.

WHAT ABOUT THE COLLEGE ATHLETES?

Historically, the increase in revenue and exposure in college athletics led the NCAA to create rules that placed the corporate needs of commercial sport over the academic needs of athletes (Sack & Staurowsky, 1998). Many refer to this as an exploitation of

REVENUES	TICKET SALES	CONTRIBUTIONS	NCAA AND CONFERENCE DISTRIBUTIONS	TOTAL SUBSIDIES
$9,828,305	$80,671	$221,373	$113,735	$5,445,898
$19,344,591	$1,032,637	$705,500	$873,855	$15,235,866
$16,912,927	$3,556,301	$2,390,045	$2,298,468	$6,315,745
$22,308,205	$2,266,444	$2,726,303	$622,446	$13,631,850
$29,762,217	$1,160,807	$1,174,767	$1,441,965	$24,375,673
$43,440,905	$8,306,921	$9,261,601	$4,167,536	$10,841,023

athletes to benefit college athletic programs. An example is allowing freshmen to compete instead of ensuring their first year is more focused on acclimating themselves to college. And many equate athletic scholarships to employment contracts. Sack and Staurowsky (1998) and Zimbalist (2001) argue college athletes are employees of their institutions, not amateurs. Such critics believe the NCAA continues to perpetuate the amateur myth for the NCAA's own benefit, primarily to preserve its nonprofit (and tax-exempt) status. However, consider the dichotomy of the "haves" and "have-nots" in discussions about amateur athletes. The exploitation of college athletes to benefit athletic programs is almost exclusively related to NCAA Division I-FBS football and Division I men's basketball because of the amount of money generated by these two sports (see Table 11.3). Thus, the dichotomy of the "haves" and "have-nots" at the institutional level (big-time Division I) is also realized at the college athlete level (those in football and men's basketball).

Keeping athletes eligible to compete is a top priority for institutions, particularly in the revenue-generating sports of football and men's basketball. The typical model is for NCAA Division I athletic departments to hire academic counselors to work with athletes to help them maintain eligibility. These counselors help athletes choose courses in which they are most likely to succeed, and which are least likely to interfere with practice times. Many counselors also monitor athletes' grades and check that athletes are attending their scheduled classes. Some wealthy programs spend millions of dollars on athlete academic centers equipped with computers and workstations available only to athletes (Wolverton, 2008). Meanwhile, despite the academic necessity of college athletes to attend class, the number of football and men's basketball games on weeknights has increased dramatically over the past several years, with games on television practically every night of the week. More weeknight games forces athletes to miss more time in the classroom.

In addition, there are many televised basketball tournaments during holiday breaks. Some schools compete in tournaments located far from their campus. The tourneys may benefit a school's image but result in missed class time for athletes, which is troubling considering that television networks market these tournaments in order to make money from commercials. Likewise, if an institution qualifies to participate in a postseason men's or women's basketball tournament, the contests may not fall during spring break. In NCAA Division I, all conferences but one (Ivy League) conduct both a men's and a women's basketball tournament at the conclusion of the regular season. Conference tournaments are held solely for the purpose of generating more revenue, which is why institutions agree to participate. To help increase viewership and guarantee a television time slot, all Division I conferences

---

STAKEHOLDER PERSPECTIVE

For Michigan, Winning Can Never Mean "At Any Cost"

Andrea Fischer Newman has served on the University of Michigan Board of Regents since 1994, including her election for a second term as chair in 2013. This perspective frames Newman's thoughts on the economic and financial landscape of big-time college athletics.

As a governing board, our primary responsibility is to protect and advance the academic environment for our students and faculty. No college student, or college athlete, should ever be a "have-not." Michigan's eight members of its Board of Regents take seriously the oversight of the resources raised and spent for our 29-sport athletic program . . . Our job is to keep the bar raised high—not on winning at any cost, but with vigilance to win with integrity and with the student experience at the core of our decision-making.

Intercollegiate athletics is a source of enormous pride at our university. Yes, our athletic program is one of the few that is entirely self-sustaining. We take pride from the athletic department sharing some of its revenues with the university to support student scholarships and toward renovation of recreational sports facilities. This is part of a shared university understanding that athletic activities cannot take away from the across-the-board excellence that defines the University of Michigan.

Athletics issues can also take up immense energy with risk to institutional reputation. But the same kind of oversight is necessary in our research arena, and our enormous health care operation. Institutional leaders must be conscious of the potential for harm. When something goes wrong, be open, honest, but swift in response.

NCAA reforms are necessary and important due to the tremendous pressures in today's changing world. If our guiding principles are student-centered, we can address "have/have-not" issues across many dimensions including financial resources and academic success. Previous NCAA reforms resulted in greater academic progress for our country's varsity athletes. When our governing boards and presidents set the bar high and associate with other like-minded institutions, we can address modern-day vulnerabilities while preserving a cherished intercollegiate tradition. ∎

mandate the winner of their conference tournament is guaranteed to represent their conference in the NCAA tournament. The winner of the months-long regular season is provided no such guarantee (even if the conference's regular season champion is undefeated). Conference postseason tournaments result in even more missed class time for athletes. Notably, the Ivy League does not have postseason conference basketball tournaments because of its academic mission in favor of the best interests of the athletes.

A switch in athletic conference affiliation may also impact the lives of athletes. Often, the switch results in a school competing against teams located much farther away compared to old conference foes, which sometimes results in athletes missing more class time than previously. Once again, the dichotomy between the "haves" and the "have-nots" comes into play, as schools decide to switch conferences to earn potentially greater publicity and revenue from the "have" teams of football or men's basketball, without consideration of the "have-not" athletes in the other 14 or more sports at the school.

CONCLUSION

This chapter is primarily about intercollegiate athletics at the NCAA Division I level. It is worth noting that discussions of making a profit from college athletics are practically nonexistent in NCAA Divisions II and III, the NAIA, and at two-year institutions. These institutions never make a profit on their athletic programs. However, in NCAA Division I, the amount of money on both the expenditure and revenue sides of the ledger precipitate the discussion of profits, paying players, and institutional subsidies. The revenue generated via media contracts and ticket sales in football and men's basketball, and the spending on coaches' salaries, is phenomenal in size. The salaries of football and men's basketball coaches often far exceed those of faculty salaries at many NCAA Division I schools, but not at schools in NCAA Divisions II and III, the NAIA, and junior colleges.

Similar to interscholastic athletics at the K–12 level, many would argue that the purpose of an educational institution having an athletic program is to enhance the educational experience of the student and to boost institutional identity and school pride, not to make a profit. Institutions should investigate if their spending on athletics is in line with their educational mission. Decision makers at "have-not" Division I schools should critically ask if the current financial model is worth the expense, particularly as it relates to whether the benefit is for all athletes and for the entire university. From the context of these perspectives, there are several alternatives to the expensive financial model that pits the "haves" versus the "have-nots":

1. Institutions, or the NCAA, can decide not to permit financial aid (scholarships) based on athletic ability. Rather, base financial aid strictly on need, as

it is for most other students, and as it is in NCAA Division III. Many of the nation's most talented high school prospects in football and men's and women's basketball, as well as in other sports, come from families of lower socioeconomic status and are categorized as "needy" in financial aid terms. This move would help lower the escalating costs of intercollegiate athletics as scholarships would not be awarded to those students who can afford college and play sports. A need-based aid policy would help reinforce the amateur model of college sports. Likewise, doing away with merit-based aid may help instill in college athletes that their primary concern must be academics rather than athletics.

2. Reinstate the rule that freshmen are ineligible for competition. Freshmen could practice with the team, and receive athletic scholarships, but they would not be allowed to compete in intercollegiate contests until their second year. This proposed model would allow freshmen to better adjust to the collegiate environment and could improve their academic standing.

3. Reduce the number of football scholarships in Division I-FBS from 85. For instance, Division I-FCS allows only 63 scholarships and National Football League professional rosters have only 53 players. The significant cost savings from fewer scholarships would also better align athletic departments with federal Title IX requirements of equal opportunity for both male and female athletes.

4. Leaders at colleges and universities should limit their athletics spending to a set percentage of the overall budget at their school. Limiting spending would force athletic departments to make decisions on coaching salaries, number of coaches, scholarship costs, facilities, travel, and other needs more in line with expenses in other areas of the institution.

5. Do not allow participation in any preseason or postseason tournaments beyond NCAA-sanctioned championship tournaments. Limiting game time beyond the regular season would give athletes more time to study, would reduce expenses to travel, and potentially would reduce the interest of "have-nots" to attempt to climb the ladder to be a "have" and participate in prestigious tournaments.

6. As advocated by the Knight Commission on Intercollegiate Athletics (2001, 2010), all colleges and universities participating in athletics as an NCAA member should make their finances public, as are most departments in higher education institutions. Publicizing athletics finances can help media and external stakeholders to scrutinize athletics' profits and losses, hold decision makers accountable, and help to further engage in a discussion on the cost and benefits of athletics in higher education.

QUESTIONS FOR DISCUSSION

1. Is the experience for those athletes in revenue-producing sports different from the experience in other sports? Should it be?

2. Is the purpose of athletics in colleges and universities different from that in high schools? If so, should it be? Likewise, is the purpose of athletics in NCAA Division I different from that in Division II, Division III, NAIA, or two-year colleges? If so, should it be?

3. Should the general student body subsidize intercollegiate athletic programs as is currently the case at the majority of institutions? Why or why not?

Note

1. The Big Five conferences are Atlantic Coast (ACC), Big 10, Big 12, Pacific 12, and Southeastern (SEC) (Knight Commission on Intercollegiate Athletics, 2011).

References

Berkowitz, S., Upton, J., & Brady, E. (2013, July 1). Most NCAA Division I athletic departments take subsidies. *USA Today*.

Dosh, K. (2012). College TV rights deals undergo makeovers. ESPN.com. Retrieved from http://espn.go.com/blog/playbook/dollars/post/_/id/705/college-tv-rights-deals-undergo-makeovers

Duderstadt, J. J. (2003). *Intercollegiate athletics and the American university: A university president's perspective*. Ann Arbor: University of Michigan Press.

Johnson, J. (2012, November 26). U-Md. president: Big Ten move deliberate. *Washington Post*.

Knight Commission on Intercollegiate Athletics. (2001). *A call to action: Reconnecting college sports to higher education*. Miami, FL: Knight Commission on Intercollegiate Athletics.

———. (2009). *College sports 101: A primer on money, athletics, and higher education in the 21st century*. Miami: John S. and James L. Knight Foundation.

———. (2011). Media contracts for 5 major conferences in place by or before 2012–13. Retrieved from http://www.knightcommission.org/images/pdfs/2009data/2011_tv_contract_big5.png

———. (2012a). Figure #2: Where the money goes. Retrieved from http://www.knightcommission.org/resources/press-room/787-december-3-updated-financial-data

———. (2012b). Figure #3: Where the money comes from. Retrieved from http://www.knightcommission.org/resources/press-room/787-december-3-updated-financial-data

———. (2013). NCAA Division I academic and athletic financial database. Retrieved from http://www.knightcommission.org

Lee, A. (2012). NCAA vs. Regents of the University of Oklahoma: History, aftermath, implications (and where we go from here). *Student papers: Sports stories*, from University of California School of Law.

McMurphy, B. (2013). Big East, ESPN agree to TV deal. Retrieved from http://espn.go.com/college-sports/story/_/id/8977673/big-east-conference-espn-agree-tv-rights-deal

McMurphy, B., & O'Neil, D. (2012, November 20). Maryland accepts Big Ten invite. *ESPN*. Retrieved from http://espn.go.com/college-sports/story/_/id/8651934/maryland-terrapins-rutgers-scarlet-knights-join-big-ten-sources-say

Myerberg, P. (2013, February 15). Big Ten proposal gives FCS worry. *USA Today*, p. 5C.

National Collegiate Athletic Association. (2012). *2012–2013 NCAA Division I manual*. Indianapolis.

———. (2013a). Agreed upon procedures: September 11, 2012. Retrieved from http://www.ncaa.org.

———. (2013b). 2012 national college football attendance. Retrieved from http://fs.ncaa.org/Docs/stats/football_records/Attendance/2012.pdf

NCAA v. Oklahoma Board of Regents, 478 U.S. 85 (United States Supreme Court 1984).

Oriard, M. (2009). Bowled over: Big-time college football from the sixties to the BCS era. Chapel Hill: University of North Carolina Press.

Orszag, J. M., & Orszag, P. R. (2005). *The physical capital stock used in collegiate athletics*. Indianapolis, IN: National Collegiate Athletic Association.

Pennington, B. (2012, December 29). Big dream, rude awakening. *New York Times*.

Sack, A. L., & Staurowsky, E. J. (1998). *College athletes for hire: The evolution and legacy of the NCAA's amateur myth*. Westport, CT: Praeger.

Siegfried, J., & Burba, M. (2003). *The college football association television broadcast cartel*. Nashville, TN: Vanderbilt University.

Smith, M. (2013, January 28). At Tennessee, Big orange battles red ink. *Sports Business Journal*.

Smith, M., & Ourand, J. (2013, May 6–12). With new swagger, ACC moves ahead on network. *Sports Business Journal*.

Sperber, M. (2000). *Beer and circus: How big-time college sports is crippling undergraduate education*. New York: Henry Holt.

Toma, J. D. (2003). *Football u: Spectator sports in the life of the American university*. Ann Arbor: University of Michigan Press.

USA Today. (2013). NCAA college athletics financial database. Retrieved from http://www.usatoday.com/sports/college/schools/finances/

U.S. Department of Education National Center for Education Statistics. (IPEDS). (2013). Integrated postsecondary education data system. Retrieved from http://nces.ed.gov/ipeds/datacenter

U.S. Department of Education Office of Postsecondary Education. (EADA). (2013). The equity in athletics data analysis cutting tool. Retrieved from http://ope.ed.gov/athletics/

Wolverton, B. (2008, September 5). Rise in fancy academic centers for athletes raises questions in fairness. *Chronicle of Higher Education*. Retrieved from http://chronicle.com/article/Rise-in-Fancy-Academic-Centers/13493/

Zimbalist, A. (2001). *Unpaid professionals: Commercialism and conflict in big-time college sports*. Princeton, NJ: Princeton University Press.

MILLIONAIRE COLLEGE COACHES and the SCHOOLS THAT PAY THEM

Murray Sperber and Vincent Minjares

Twenty-five years ago, one of the authors of this chapter, Murray Sperber, conducted research on coaches' compensation for his book, *College Sports Inc.: The Athletic Department versus the University* (1990). Sperber (1990) noted that Jackie Sherrill, head football coach at Texas A&M, received $267,000, and Rick Pitino, the head men's basketball coach at the University of Kentucky at the time, made roughly $850,000 (because of the multifaceted contracts given to coaches, nailing down exact numbers is often difficult).

To date, Sherrill has long-retired from coaching; however both Nick Saban of the University of Alabama, Tuscaloosa and Mack Brown of the University of Texas, Austin receive more than $5 million a year, and 12 head football coaches make more than $3 million (DeRamus et al., 2013). Rick Pitino, currently head men's basketball coach at the University of Louisville, earns close to $5 million annually (Berkowitz, Upton, Dougherty, & Durkin, 2013). Inflation in the U.S. economy has occurred in the past 25 years, but in no way does it come close to the increase in pay for college football and men's basketball coaches in that time span. And the increase has gone far beyond the charmed circle of star coaches like Saban and Pitino.

Sperber (1990) pointed out that a slight majority of National Collegiate Athletic Association Division I football and men's basketball coaches topped $100,000 a year, and a few were over $200,000. In contrast, in 2011, journalists found that the average for the current equivalent of a Division I head football coach was $1.47 million (Bishop, 2011), and a breakdown of the annual income of the 2013 NCAA Men's Basketball Tournament coaches revealed 36 over $1 million, as

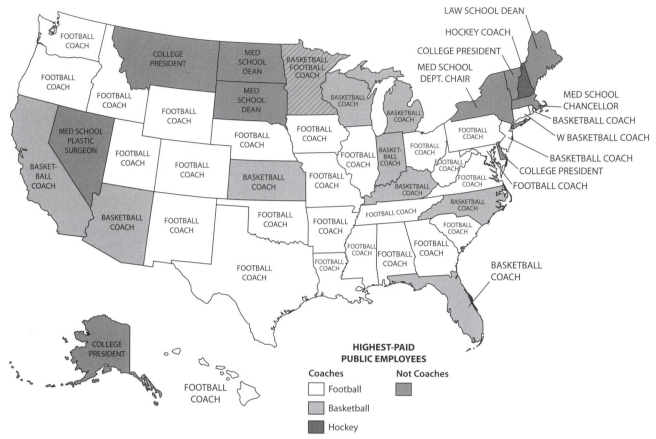

Figure 12.1. Your State's Highest Paid Public Employee. (Courtesy of Reuben Fischer-Baum and Deadspin.com.)

were some coaches whose teams did not make the tournament (Berkowitz et al., 2013).

Coaches' large pay packages occur within the context of the enormous financial constraints upon the universities that pay the coaches, raising the issue of whether coaches' high annual compensation is justified or not (see fig. 12.1).

COACHES' COMPENSATION WITHIN THE CONTEXT OF HIGHER EDUCATION ECONOMICS

One of the most important findings in Sperber (1990) was that most NCAA athletic departments, contrary to popular belief, operate at deficits; moreover, the studied schools covered their annual college sports deficits with funds that could have been allocated to academic units as well as to financial aid for students. Since that time, many studies, including some done by the NCAA, have tracked and updated athletic department deficits (Sperber, 2008). Researchers, using freedom-of-information (FOI) laws to obtain university financial records, drew the connecting line between coaches' pay and athletic department deficits : "Among public schools in the NCAA's top-level Division I, coaches' compensation is now the biggest hit on the budget" (Berkowitz, Upton, McCarth, & Gillum, 2010a, para. 5). In all probability, the same situation occurs at private schools in big-time intercollegiate athletics, but researchers cannot use the FOI laws to see their numbers.

If higher education institutions were wonderfully wealthy, possibly they could afford all the athletic department deficits. However, most public and many private universities have been in dire financial shape for many years, rattling the tin cup in front of unsympathetic legislators and other government officials, skeptical taxpayers, and ungenerous foundations and other potential donors. The 2008 stock market crash and subsequent major recession greatly exacerbated the problem.

In 2013 Moody's, the financial rating agency, called the economic situation in higher education "bleak" (Troop, 2013) and predicted a "gloomy future," particularly for public universities (Kelderman, 2013). That year, Jeff Orleans, a former director of the Ivy League athletic group and a proponent of intercollegiate athletics, told an audience at the NCAA Convention that, in higher education today, there is a "new status quo of financial weakness" (Wolverton, 2013, para. 6).

Yet big-time college football and men's basketball coaches have continued to receive their fabulous deals. When, in 2011, Ohio State University signed football coach Urban Meyer to a $4 million dollar annual package, an important journalist noted that "the big business of college football is undeterred by the nation's broader economic woes or by concern about the prominence of sports on campus" (Bishop, 2011, para. 1).

A symbol of that prominence is the discrepancy between coaches' pay and the salaries of faculty members. Various studies have offered the numbers: for example, Tsitsos and Nixon (2012) pointed out that in 2005–2006, the average salary of full professors at Division I-A Football Bowl Subdivision schools was $101,774 and the average pay for football coaches at these schools was over $900,000. A few years later, a researcher provided a graph showing head football coaches' pay averaging over $1 million versus $95,199 for tenured male professors (full and associates); untenured earned an average of $70,005, and graduate student assistants, on average, made $17,784 (Rampell, 2008). Big-time football and men's basketball coaches have long averaged ten times more in pay than tenured faculty, and well over twenty times more than graduate student assistants—who, in fact, do the bulk of college teaching and grading (Sperber, 2000). Even assistant football and basketball coaches as well as head women's basketball coaches receive pay packages worth many times more than those of academic personnel (Berkowitz & Upton, 2011a).

ARE COACHES WORTH THEIR HUGE PAY PACKAGES?

If we put aside the philosophical questions of whether a university should pay its athletic coaches much more than its teachers and researchers, and focus on the narrow economic questions of the supply and demand for and production results of coaches, we discover some surprising answers. We can begin by asking: Does the labor market for coaches justify the lucrative salaries?

A longtime NCAA Division I men's basketball coach, Sonny Smith, described big-time college coaching as "a make-it-while-you-can thing. You can be replaced at the drop of a hat. If I quit tomorrow, there'd be three hundred names in the ring" (as cited in Sperber, 1990, p. 150). Indeed, for every open college coaching position, there are many qualified candidates: coaches who have succeeded at the same level; coaches with excellent records at lower levels and ready to move up; and a large number of successful assistant coaches willing and able to take a head coaching position. Most importantly, most of these coaching candidates would be willing to work for far less than the million-plus dollars that the winning candidate will currently receive. On the other hand, universities hire faculty and other personnel according to supply and demand. And the reason that university faculty in English make far less than faculty in the Business School and associated fields is the huge supply of English instructors and the relatively smaller number of business faculty. But pay packages for athletic coaches defy these basic economic rules.

Tsitsos and Nixon (2012) in an article, "The Star Wars Arms Race in College Athletics: Coaches' Pay and Athletic Program Status," argued that schools "feel compelled to spend 'whatever it takes' to hire and retain coaches with records or prospects of major success" because schools believe that offering a coach a huge pay package is "the ultimate key to competitive success," that is, winning (p. 71).

To emphasize winning, almost every school includes bonus incentives in a head football and basketball coach's contract. For example, Alabama's Nick Saban receives $75,000 if his team plays in the SEC Championship and $50,000 if they win. Likewise, Saban makes $110,000 if his team plays in the BCS Championship game and $200,000 if they win (Berkowitz & Upton, 2012b). But even mid-major football coaches have bonus clauses. Kent State's Darrell Hazel earned $5,000 for a MAC Division Championship, $10,000 for a bowl game appearance, and $5,000 for each victory over a FBS opponent (Berkowitz & Upton, 2012b). And if a mid-major coach collects all his bonuses, it is likely that he will attract higher ranked schools who are willing to offer much larger pay packages (in 2013, Purdue hired Darrell Hazell at a significantly larger salary and bonuses than he earned at Kent State).

But do new coaches win and actually earn their huge pay compensation? Tsitsos and Nixon (2012) took the cohort of "top-paid football and men's basketball coaches" (pp. 73–74) and followed their teams through six seasons (starting in 2003), measuring their success or failure in terms of "rankings and mobility into and out of the [media's] 'Top 25' teams" (p. 75).

In terms of "short-term mobility"—moving into the Top 25 within a year or two of the new hire's taking charge—only 16% of teams in both football and men's basketball accomplished this for 2003–2007, and 24% and 28% for 2007–2011. However, most new, highly paid coaches achieved "no short-term change," that is, they either took over teams already in the Top 25 and stayed there or never got there: for 2003–2007, 64% of football and 68% of men's basketball teams did not change status, and for 2007–2011, 56% and 52%. But the news for schools becomes even more depressing with the statistic that for all the years studied and for the two sports, 20% of the new hires produced teams with "short-term downward mobility," that is, they got worse or dropped out of the Top 25.

Other studies reveal similar results. Peter Orszag, now a White House economic advisor, was involved in two of them (2005, 2009). Recently, Adler, Berry, and Doherty (2013) conducted a large longitudinal study comparing teams with new hires to those that did not make a change at the top. Tracking 120 FBS programs from 1997 through 2010, Adler and colleagues (2013) found that "a total of 263 [head coaching] changes occur in our data set, affecting football programs at 115 universities" (p. 3).

The results contradicted the sports cliché that firing a losing coach is always necessary. Adler, Berry, and Doherty (2013) found that schools with losing teams that did not change their coaches had won-loss records for the following seasons—and for many seasons—similar to those schools with losing teams that hired new head coaches. In addition, the schools that did not change coaches saved lots of money.

An Administrator Who Questioned the College Sports System

As associate chancellor at University of California, Berkeley for more than 25 years, John Cummins maintained oversight of the campus's athletic department. In the mid-2000s, Cummins played a key role in the administration's response to rapid growth in athletic department spending on coaching salaries. The following quotation is from a personal communication from Cummins, June 28, 2013:

Beginning in 2001, new Athletic Director Steve Gladstone vowed to change the athletics culture at Cal "so that we can win." One of his first major decisions was to hire a new football coach: Jeff Tedford. Whereas prior administrations were unwilling to pay a coach more than a professor, Gladstone was not. Tedford's first contract in 2001 was

for $600,000 plus incentives and, by 2012, Tedford's package (under new Athletic Director Sandy Barber) grew to more than $2 million per year. For Cummins, the subsequent high pay for a coach matched the philosophy of the new Chancellor at the time. Despite the Cal administration's spending millions to "subsidize" deficits in athletic spending, the Chancellor approved the coach's package because "football was the key to funding a successful [athletics] operation."

However, Cummins and his fellow administrators could not escape the pressure to balance the athletics budget. Given Berkeley's academic reputation, many of them questioned "athletics' privileged status in the university," with "angst about" coaches' high pay (the new men's

basketball coach, Mike Montgomery, also received a $1 million-plus package). Cummins believed that the best way forward was to open the athletics budget to campus faculty. Historically, the budget was very tightly held, and the faculty did not know its details. Cummins felt that opening the budget was an effort to "rein in spending on athletics and to hope that the university comes to a consensus" on the issue.

Cummins's push proved fateful. By 2009, in the midst of drastic state cuts to higher education, a working group of professors drafted a faculty resolution demanding cuts in athletics spending. The result: the decision to terminate five sports, and specific plans to balance the athletics budget. Private donations later saved the five teams, but the budget plans remain in place. ■

Moreover, "among teams where entry conditions appear to be most favorable" for short-term and long-term mobility, "the choice to replace leadership is detrimental, rather than helpful, to team performance" (p. 4). Adler and colleagues pointed out: "The significant costs universities typically incur by choosing to replace a head football coach, suggest that universities should be cautious in their decision to discharge their coach for performance reasons" (p. 28).

But like losing gamblers who keep doubling down, universities keep paying more to hire new coaches. For the past few years, researchers have tracked the pay packages offered to new coaches; the titles of their articles outline the situation: "Salaries Rising for New College Football Coaches" (Berkowitz & Upton, 2012a); and "Pay Rises Yet Again for College Football's New Hires" (Berkowitz & Upton, 2013b).

Berkowitz and Upton (2011c) have also tracked the increasing pay raises for assistant coaches in football and men's basketball. In 2011 they declared, "Major college football assistant coaches now have something on their bosses: their pay is increasing faster" (para. 1). They pointed out that "23 assistants were making at least $500,000 this season and 48 making at least $400,000" (para. 9). By 2013, these same researchers indicated that "college football assistants [are] seeing salaries surge" even more than in the past, and they calculated that the average pay for an assistant was "roughly $200,000" (Berkowitz & Upton, 2013a, para. 1).

Setting the pace was national champion Alabama, and because "The Tide" had won three of the last four national championships, it is the school most imitated in college football. In 2013 it raised its defensive coordinator to $1.28 million a year, its offensive coordinator to $680,000, and the pay of four other assistants to between $300,000 and $400,000 each (Scarborough, 2013). Alabama also led the way in hiring assistants beyond the nine full-time allowed by the NCAA. Calling the extras "support staff," "analysts," and other vague titles, the school now has twenty-four specialists to assist the regular coaching staff in "player personnel" (mainly recruiting), "football analysis" (analyzing the current team and opponents), "strength and conditioning," "video," and various other football program activities (Mandel & Staples, 2013). Alabama paid these 24 assistants a total of $1.6 million in salary: that averages to $66,666, but some earned more than $100,000 (Mandel & Staples, 2013). As long ago as 2007, one observer noted that some "support staff" football recruiters in the SEC earned more than $200,000 a year (Adams, 2007).

College basketball has fewer assistant coaches than football does; the NCAA allows three basketball assistant coaches and two graduate student assistants. But head basketball coaches—men and women—have created many "support staff" positions. Almost all big-time programs have staff for "basketball operations" (including recruiting), "performance enhancement" (assisting the strength coach), "basketball technology" (assisting the videotape guys), and "player personnel" (often a euphemism for baby-sitting the players, among other tasks). Increasingly, the total number of basketball assistants is greater than the total number of varsity players (Branch, 2013). Berkowitz and colleagues have also shown that the regular basketball assistants average well over six figures a year in earnings and the support staff personnel does very well (Berkowitz et al., 2013).

COACHES' PAY AND UNIVERSITY AND ATHLETIC DEPARTMENT MISSIONS

Often college presidents and athletic directors justify the high pay of their athletic coaches by claiming that big-time college football and basketball are businesses similar to the entertainment industry. And just as movie and television stars receive huge pay packages, so should the ongoing stars of college sports, the coaches. This frank admission of commercialism has worried some educators. While Myles Brand was president of the NCAA, he talked about the need for member schools to "ensure that their commercial activities related to athletics align with the university's educational mission" (Brand, 2006). Unfortunately, this is easier said than practiced, and Brand admitted that "there is no algorithm or set of rules that would . . . automatically determine whether a commercial activity"—offering a coach millions of dollars is a prime example—"is consistent with the values of higher education" and a university's mission (Brand, 2006).

The research for this chapter included examining the mission statements of many universities in big-time college sports, as well as the mission statements of their athletic departments; unfortunately, maybe intentionally on the part of the universities, the researchers found nothing that could apply to the high salaries of coaches. Quite obviously, universities and their athletic departments do not want to engage this subject, and so, finally, researchers have to leave it to the public to decide this question.

However, the mission statements of athletic departments do discuss the role of coaches in the formation of their athletes. Stanford University is typical, particularly in its use of inflated rhetoric to state its high-minded ideals. It fulfills its athletic department mission "by hiring and retaining the best coaches and staff members available and arming them with the tools to achieve at the highest level . . . [and] by fostering and nurturing a coaching . . . staff that is committed to teaching with integrity and ambition and that performs in a manner which is consistent with the academic priorities of Stanford University" (Stanford University, 2012, para. 1). All of the mission statements proclaimed high ideals similar to Stanford's, but what occurs when these ideals collide with the reality of contemporary big-time college sports?

COACHING PRIORITIES IN A CLIMATE OF ASTRONOMICAL SALARIES

An increasing body of research indicates that coaches' extremely high pay and the pressure to win creates a climate where they have to focus their athletes mainly on sports performance and secondarily on academic and personal concerns. Coaches always talk about sports as character building, but the daily reality of big-time college sports indicates little time for this activity. As Lyle (2002) asserts, a coach's potential to support an athlete's academic and personal growth is inversely proportional to the pressure on the coach to win.

No researcher disputes the fact that coaches work very long hours every day of the week. In addition to team activities, including practices and games, the contract of a current big-time football and basketball coach requires him or her to spend time in activities to build the program and also allows time to accumulate personal profit. The two elements often intertwine: paid and unpaid media shows and interviews; speech making to and appearances at various groups, both often personally lucrative; endorsing products of sponsors of the athletic program as well as products for his or her own profit; working with and for apparel and equipment companies that provide institutional equipment; conducting summer camps and sports clinics for institutional or personal profit; and fundraising and many other tasks on behalf of the athletic department and charitable organizations and for personal gain (Gentry & Alexander, 2011).

Whereas the twentieth-century ideal for college coaches included being teachers, advisors, and father figures for all of their athletes, in the twenty-first century, a head coach's multitude of activities and responsibilities undermine his or her availability for traditional duties.

Big-time coaches devote painstaking attention to work that directly improves their team's chances to win. More than ever, they do so through recruiting future players, and the intense competition for top talent now requires a coach's year-round commitment to it. Feldman (2007) profiles this phenomenon with the football team at the University of Mississippi, a school where, according to head coach Ed Orgeron, "Recruiting isn't some kind of heavy-duty hobby, it's my lifestyle" (p. 1). One big-time coach lamented, "We don't coach anymore . . . This job isn't about coaching. It's about acquiring talent" (O'Neil, 2010, p. 1). But acquiring that talent comes at a price: it takes time and energy away from current athletes whom the coach has already brought to campus. As one head coach admits, "You walk into a living room and promise a mother that you'll be there for her son, and as soon as they get on campus, you're gone" (O'Neil, 2010, p. 2).

College athlete responses to a NCAA study (2011) reinforce the logic of coaches' placing such a high priority on recruiting. Two-thirds of Division I men's basketball and football players agreed or strongly agreed that the recruiting process, particularly their relationships with the recruiting coaches, impacted their college choice decision. Only a minority of men's basketball players agreed or strongly agreed that they would have attended their particular school if a different head coach were there. These data reinforce the anecdotal evidence that many elite prospects sign with the athletic program and coaching staff that can best help them to achieve their dream of becoming a professional athlete.

Coaches fully understand that they must spend enormous amounts of time recruiting these "blue chip" professional prospects, even if, in college basketball, they may have them for as few as one year of their four years of playing eligibility. As University of Kansas men's basketball coach Bill Self says, "Bottom line, I don't know anybody who would not want to recruit guys who are good enough to play in the league [NBA]. Guaranteed. They win" for you (Prisbell, 2013, para. 6).

The Good, the Bad, and the Ugly of a Multimillionaire College Coach

When Urban Meyer signed a contract in 2011 to become head football coach at Ohio State University, his family asked him to also sign a contract with them. Nikki Meyer (2012), his eldest daughter, crafted a list demanding that Meyer not take the OSU job unless, among other things, he "eat three meals a day, sleep with the cell phone on silent . . . [and] answer his daughters' calls no matter what he is doing." Her demands were inspired by the negatives of her father's years as head coach at the University of Florida: work-life imbalance, insurmountable pressure, ill health, and athlete misconduct. Urban Meyer's story indicates the reality that surrounds big-time coaches in higher education.

In his tenure at Florida, 2005–2010, Meyer achieved outstanding success, compiling a 65-15 win-loss record that included two SEC championships, two BCS National Championships, a Heisman Trophy winner, and 26 NFL draft picks. Without question, Meyer benefited financially along the way. He originally signed a six-year, $14 million dollar contract but later gained a seven-year extension worth $24 million.

However, Meyer has openly acknowledged the disastrous effect that his coaching intensity had on his family and his health while at Florida: "I was always fearful I would become 'That Guy,' the guy who had regret. Yeah, we won a couple of championships, but I never saw my kids grow up. Yeah, we beat Georgia a couple of times, but I ruined my marriage" (Thompson, 2012). For Meyer, the effects were severe. He lost 35 pounds in his final season, was hospitalized for recurring chest pain, and retired not once, but twice.

Questions also surround Meyer's role in the lives of his athletes. While Tim Tebow generated acclaim for Meyer as an Academic All-American, others were less successful. In light of the very public murder charges against former Florida tight end Aaron Hernandez, Meyer has come under scrutiny for his players' conduct during his time in Gainesville. A *New York Times* report found that between 2005 and 2010, 31 Florida football players were arrested (Bishop, 2013). Meyer has deflected criticism by referring to his academically successful athletes, his annual contributions to the community, and his efforts to mentor troubled team members, including Hernandez.

Nonetheless, revelations from Meyer's time at Florida suggest the reality of exceptionally successful college coaches: win, no matter the costs. St. Louis Rams cornerback Janoris Jenkins—a star on the Gators under Meyer but removed from the team because of multiple arrests by Meyer's successor—offered a revealing comment: "If Coach Meyer were still coaching [at Florida], I'd still be playing for the Gators . . . Coach Meyer knows what it takes to win" (Bishop, 2013). ∎

Along with full-time recruiting, coaches engage in an exhaustive effort to prepare for games. While Division I football and men's basketball players report spending more than 40 hours per week in-season on their sport, coaching staffs often double that number. Accounts of coach burnout, such as Urban Meyer's at the University of Florida, reveal a hypercompetitive culture with coaches working as much as 100 hours in a week, watching video of their team and opponents into the early morning, and sleeping in their offices.

And what are the consequences of the coach's behavior on the growth and well-being of athletes? In an NCAA survey (2011), one-third of men's basketball players agree or strongly agree that their coach "put them down" in front of others. Roughly one-half of men's basketball and football players admit that winning was more important than sportsmanship. And, significantly, more than half of Division I men's basketball players do not agree that their head coach could be trusted. The recent firing of Rutgers University men's basketball coach Mike Rice for verbally and physically abusing his players offers a disturbing reminder of the reality of these athlete experiences.

When Rice's treatment of his players became public knowledge, two Rutgers faculty members, Belinda Edmondson and Beryl Satter (2013), issued a statement, in fact, a heartfelt plea, for sanity in college sports. They wrote:

> Public universities . . . are not [corporate] sports franchises. They are not dysfunctional families in which the powerful can abuse the less powerful. As faculty members, we were deeply dismayed to learn that some Rutgers University administrators had known for months about Mike Rice Jr. and his assistant coach's physical and verbal abuse of student athletes, yet remained silent. Homophobic slurs and physical abuse teach students a deformed version of athletic masculinity. (para. 1)

The Rutgers professors were referring to the school president's and athletic director's awareness of Rice's behavior and doing very little about it. Of course, these were the officials who had hired Rice at typically high pay and had tolerated his behavior. (Rice had a mediocre win-loss record; and this is not surprising considering the research we have cited.)

CONCLUSION

The Mike Rice case at Rutgers can serve as a symbol for much that has gone wrong in big-time college sports. The enormous and unjustified pay packages given to coaches have spawned a win-at-all-costs mentality and have mainly benefited the coaches themselves and the small cohort of players who actually make it to the professional leagues. Far too many of the other athletes feel that they have had negative athletic experiences in college and also did not receive much of an education.

Finally, for all its glitter and apparent wealth, big-time college sports face serious systemic problems. If the result of the current lawsuit brought by former UCLA athlete Ed O'Bannon against the NCAA moves the courts to allow open professionalism in college sports, then the current system will crumble and intercollegiate athletics will closely resemble professional sports. Coaches will still have large pay packages but so will many players. At that point, universities will have to decide whether they want to fund very expensive and mainly money-losing professional franchises or go to a genuinely amateur-based system resembling the current NCAA Division III. The past 25 years in college sports have been fascinating; the future might be even more interesting.

QUESTIONS FOR DISCUSSION

1. Is it fair to compare the pay of head football and men's basketball coaches to that of university faculty and other teachers? If yes, why? If no, why not?

2. According to the research cited in this chapter, when a school hires a new coach, how well does the team of that coach do?

3. Is the high pay of assistant coaches justified? If yes, why? If no, why not?

References

Adams, R. (2007, January 6). The new big shots of the gridiron: Top recruiters are now the subject of bidding wars. *Wall Street Journal*. Retrieved from http://online.wsj.com/article/SB116805290671669041.html

Adler, E. S., Berry, M. J., & Doherty, D. (2013). Pushing "reset": The conditional effects of coaching replacements on college football performance. *Social Science Quarterly, 94*(1), 1–28. http://onlinelibrary.wiley.com/doi/10.1111/j.1540-6237.2012.00929.x/abstract

Berkowitz, S., & Upton, J. (2011a, April 4). Salaries dramatically rise for top women's basketball coaches. *USA Today*. Retrieved from http://usatoday30.usatoday.com/sports/college/womensbasketball/2011-04-04-coaches-salaries-increase_N.htm

———. (2011b, December 19). Auburn, LSU, Alabama, Texas among highest-paid staffs. *USA Today*. Retrieved from http://usatoday30.usatoday.com/sports/college/football/story/2011-12-19/college-assistant-salaries-package/52123650/1

———. (2011c, December 21). Assistants outpace bosses in raises. *USA Today*. Retrieved from http://usatoday30.usatoday.com/sports/college/football/story/2011-12-19/college-assistant-salaries-package/52123650/1

———. (2012a, January 16). Salaries rising for new college football coaches. *USA Today*. Retrieved from http://usatoday30.usatoday.com/sports/college/football/story/2012-01-16/College-football-coaches-compenstion/52602734/1

———. (2012b, November 27). Which coaches in BCS contention have the best bonuses. *USA Today*. Retrieved from http://www.usatoday.com/story/sports/ncaaf/2012/11/27/college-football-coaches-bonuses/1728007/

———. (2013a, June 24). College football assistants seeing salaries surge. *USA Today*. Retrieved from http://www.usatoday.com/story/sports/ncaaf/2012/12/18/assistant-coaches-salaries-bowl-subdivision/1777719/

———. (2013b, July 1). Pay rises yet again for college football's new coaching hires. *USA Today*. Retrieved http://www.usatoday.com/story/sports/ncaaf/2013/02/11/college-football-coach-salary-changes-ncaa/1907359/

Berkowitz, S., Upton, J., Dougherty, S., & Durkin, E. (2013, April 3). Methodology for college basketball coaches salary database. *USA Today*. Retrieved from http://www.usatoday.com/story/sports/ncaab/2013/04/03/college-basketball-coach-contracts-database-methodology/2048865/

Berkowitz, S., Upton, J., McCarthy, M., & Gillum, J. (2010a, April 12). Rising salaries of coaches force schools to seek budget patches. *USA Today*. Retrieved from http://usatoday30.usatoday.com/sports/college/mensbasketball/2010-04-01-coaches-salaries-cover_N.htm

———. (2010b, October 6). How student fees quietly boost college sports. *USA Today*. Retrieved from http://www.usatoday.com/sports/college/2010-09-21-student-fees-boost-college-sports_N.htm

Brand, M. (2006, April 24). Commercialism controlled when activity aligns with mission. *NCAA News*. Retrieved from http://fs.ncaa.org/Docs/NCAANewsArchive/2006/Editorial/commercialism%2Bcontrolled%2Bwhen%2Bactivity%2Baligns%2Bwith%2Bmission%2B-%2B4-24-06%2Bncaa%2Bnews.html

Bishop, G. (2011, November 28). For new coach at Ohio State, it's first down and $4 million. *New York Times*. http://www.nytimes.com/2011/11/29/sports

/ncaafootball/for-new-coach-at-ohio-state-its-first
-down-and-4-million.html?pagewanted=all&_r=0

———. (2013, July 6). Hernandez among many who found trouble at Florida in the Meyer years. *New York Times*. Retrieved from http://www.nytimes.com/2013/07/07/sports/ncaafootball/hernandez-among-many-arrested-at-florida-in-the-meyer-years.html?ref=sports&_r=3&

Branch, J. (2013, March 15). Here, there and everywhere: Assistant coaches. *New York Times*. Retrieved from http://www.nytimes.com/2013/03/16/sports/ncaabasketball/theyre-here-there-and-everywhere-college-basketball-assistants.html?pagewanted=all

Chronicle of Higher Education. (2013). Table: Average faculty salaries, 2011–12 [Data file]. Retrieved from http://chronicle.com/article/faculty-salaries-table-2012/131433

Daughters, A. (2013, May 5). Why we would never be a college head coach. *Bleacher Report*. Retrieved from http://bleacherreport.com/articles/1629795-why-we-would-never-be-a-college-football-head-coach

DeRamus, K., Frasier, D., Linders, P., Price, B., Schnaars, C., Thomassie, J., & Upton, J. (2012, November 19). Sports college football coaches salaries database [Data file]. *USA Today*. Retrieved from http://www.usatoday.com/story/sports/ncaaf/2012/11/19/ncaa-college-football-head-coach-salary-database/1715543/

Edmondson, B., & Satter, B. (2013, April 8), The university will not be sold. *Chronicle of Higher Education*. http://chronicle.com/blogs/conversation/2013/04/08/the-university-will-not-be-sold/

Feldman, B. (2007). *Meat market: Inside the smash-mouth world of college football recruiting*. New York: ESPN Books.

Gentry, J. K., & Alexander, R. M. (2011). From the sideline to the bottom line. *New York Times*. Retrieved from http://www.nytimes.com/2012/01/01/sports/ncaafootball/contracts-for-top-college-football-coaches-grow-complicated.html?pagewanted=all&_r=1&

Kelderman, E. (2013, August 14). Moody's report forecasts a gloomy future for public universities. *Chronicle of Higher Education*. Retrieved from http://chronicle.com/blogs/bottomline/author/ekelderman/

Knight Commission on Intercollegiate Athletics. (2013). *College sports 101: A primer on money, athletics and higher education in the 21st Century*. Retrieved from

http://www.knightcommission.org/collegesports101/chapter-2

Lyle, J. (2002). *Sports coaching concepts: A framework for coaching behavior*. New York: Routledge.

Mandel, S., & Staples, A. (2013, June 10). Go for it on fourth and multiply. *Sports Illustrated-CNN Magazine*. Retrieved from http://sportsillustrated.cnn.com/vault/article/magazine/MAG1207744/index.htm

National Collegiate Athletic Association. (2011, January 13). *Examining the student-athlete experience through the NCAA GOALS and SCORE studies*. Slides from the 2011 NCAA Convention. Retrieved from http://www.ncaa.org/wps/wcm/connect/5fb7ac004567f21ead40bfc8c7999200/Goals10_score96_final_convention2011_public_version_01_13_11.pdf?MOD=AJPERES&CACHEID=5fb7ac004567f21ead40bfc8c7999200

———. (2012). *Revenues & expenses, 2004–2011: NCAA Division I intercollegiate athletics programs report*. Indianapolis, IN. Retrieved from http://www.ncaapublications.com/productdownloads/D12011REVEXP.pdf

Office of Postsecondary Education. (2013). The equity in athletics data cutting tool [Data file]. Retrieved from http://ope.ed.gov/athletics/

O'Neil, D. (2010, July 22). What's wrong with college basketball. *ESPN*. Retrieved from http://sports.ESPN.go.com/ncb/columns/story?columnist=oneil_dana&id=5398415

Orszag, J. M., & Orszag, P. R. (2005, April). *The empirical effects of collegiate athletics: An update* (Commissioned by the National Collegiate Athletic Association). Retrieved from http://216.197.120.83/webdocs/90.pdf

Orszag, J., & Israel, M. (2009, February). *The empirical effects of collegiate athletics: An update based on 2004–2007 data* (Commissioned by the National Collegiate Athletic Association). Retrieved from http://fs.ncaa.org/Docs/DI_MC_BOD/DI_BOD/2009/April/04,%20_Empirical_Effects.pdf

Prisbell, E. (2013, March 25). Championship coaches round table: Team with three one-and-dones. *USA Today*. Retrieved from http://www.usatoday.com/story/sports/ncaab/2013/03/25/championship-coaches-roundtable-team-with-three-one-and-done-players/2018779/

Rampell, C. (2008, October 22). Academic vs. football coach salaries. *New York Times*. Retrieved from http://economix.blogs.nytimes.com/2008/10/22 /academic-vs-football-salaries/

Scarborough, A. (2013, April 16). Alabama approves coach contracts. *ESPN.com*. Retrieved from http:// ESPN.go.com/college-football/story/_/id/9180008 /alabama-crimson-tide-makes-kirby-smart-highest -paid-college-defensive-coordinator

Sperber, M. (1990). *College sports Inc.: The athletic department versus the university*. New York: Henry Holt.

———. (2000). *Beer and circus: How big time college sports is crippling undergraduate education*. New York: Henry Holt.

———. (2008, May 23). Stop hiding the financial truth about college athletics. *Chronicle of Higher Education*. Retrieved from http://chronicle.com/article /Stop-Hiding-the-Financial/12198/

Stanford University. (2012). Athletic department mission statement. Retrieved from http://www .gostanford.com/school-bio/

Thompson, W. (2012, August 12). Urban Meyer will be home for dinner. *ESPN.com*. Retrieved from ESPN http://ESPN.go.com/ESPN/otl/story/_/id/8239451 /ohio-state-coach-urban-meyer-new-commitment -balancing-work-family-life

Troop, D. (2013, January 16). Near-term outlook is bleak for all of higher education, Moody's says. *Chronicle of Higher Education*. Retrieved from http://chronicle .com/blogs/bottomline/near-term-outlook-is-bleak -for-all-of-higher-education-moodys-says/

Tsitsos, W., & Nixon, H., II (2012). The star wars arms race in college athletics: Coaches' pay and athletic program status. *Journal of Sport & Social Issues, 36*, 68–88.

Upton, J., Gillum, J., & Berkowitz S. (2012, April 12). Rising salaries of coaches force colleges to seek budget patch. *USA Today*. Retrieved from http:// usatoday30.usatoday.com/sports/college /mensbasketball/2010-04-01-coaches-salaries -cover_N.htm

Wolverton, B. (2013, January 17). In time of budget austerity, athletics programs need a reset. *Chronicle of Higher Education*. Retrieved from http://chronicle .com/blogs/players/in-austere-times-athletics -programs-need-a-reset/32403

PART FIVE

The Significance of Race and Ethnicity Issues

Race and ethnicity have raised important issues in intercollegiate athletics, and scholars have employed a wide range of frameworks and theoretical perspectives to study their effects. In chapter 13, Eddie Comeaux and Marcia Fuentes introduce and summarize diversity-related research on college athletes and their nonathlete peers and place the findings within a framework for understanding campus racial climate. They offer strategies that coaches and student affairs professionals can use to foster interaction across diverse racial groups in order to promote athletes' racial understanding and pluralistic perspectives. In chapter 14, John Singer employs a critical race theory framework to discuss how societal, organizational, and individual-level factors contribute to the miseducation of African American male athletes at predominantly white institutions of higher education. Robin Hughes explores the experiences of African American female college athletes in chapter 15, giving special attention to the intersectionality of race and gender. In chapter 16, Earl Smith and Angela Hattery provide an overview of conference realignment, the motives and challenges of conference expansion plans among various NCAA division I conferences, and the potential impact of expansion on African American male athletes. ■

CROSS-RACIAL INTERACTION of DIVISION I ATHLETES

The Campus Climate for Diversity

Eddie Comeaux and Marcia V. Fuentes

Several recent demographic and social trends provide the stimulus for higher education institutions to prepare students to lead and compete in an increasingly complex and diverse society. First, the number of racial and ethnic "minority" individuals in the United States increased from 86.9 million to 111.9 million between 2000 and 2010 (U.S. Census Bureau, 2011). Second, the landmark Supreme Court decisions in *Gratz v. Bollinger* (2003) and *Gutter v. Bollinger* (2003) provided incentives for colleges and universities to develop authentically responsive intervention strategies that could make the most effective use of diverse campus learning environments. Third, the business community has affirmed the need for cross-culturally competent college graduates with the ability to lead in a global society or a "plurality nation" (Bikson & Law, 1994). In light of these trends, it is clear that the extent to which college students who interact across diverse racial groups can develop cognitive, intrapersonal, and interpersonal skills that prepare them to view the world from someone else's perspective, tolerate others with different beliefs, and negotiate controversial issues with conviction will be critically important (Newman, Couturier, & Scurry, 2004).

Most diversity-related studies have focused primarily on students in the general population, which limits our understanding of the cross-racial interactions Division I athletes experience and the resulting benefits of diversity. It is important to have this discussion with Division I athletes as the population of interest because their college experiences typically differ in important ways from those of the general student population (Watt & Moore, 2001). This population of students is additionally of interest because of evidence that suggests intercollegiate

KEY TERMS

college athletes ◀
cross-racial interaction ◀
campus climate ◀
campus race relations ◀
diversity ◀

athletic teams may provide an ideal environment for positive intergroup relations with diverse teammates. Extant research and anecdotal evidence suggest Division I athletes are likely to have more frequent interactions with diverse student groups than their nonathlete peers (Brown, Brown, Jackson, Sellers, & Manuel, 2003; Potuto & O'Hanlon, 2007). In fact, athletes tend to constitute a unique and highly diverse subset of most student populations in the higher education community, which allows them contact with diverse teammates. They often live, eat, and socialize together and are sometimes even tracked into the same majors, all of which enhance their chances for cross-racial interaction with each other (Brown et al., 2003). Likewise, college coaches in team sports encourage their athletes to build team chemistry and cohesion, to focus on commonalities and shared goals, and to look beyond racial/ethnic differences in order to achieve desirable outcomes (Brown et al., 2003). Coaches may even go as far as to say that they will not tolerate the existence of a racially hostile team environment.

This chapter explores the cross-racial experiences of Division I athletes at predominantly white institutions (PWIs). A deeper understanding of their experiences can have a significant impact on the specific intervention strategies that can engage and re-engage athletes in racially diverse learning environments. In this chapter we assert that, beyond understanding the cross-racial experiences of athletes, it is important to comprehensively deduce elements of the broad campus climate that can shape the quality of these experiences.

We begin by synthesizing the diversity-related research on college athletes and their nonathlete peers. Then, drawing from and expanding upon the work of Hurtado, Milem, Clayton-Pederson, and Allen (1998), we discuss a framework for understanding the campus racial climate in order to explain how dimensions of the institutional context can influence the quality of college athletes' experiences. Finally, we conclude with suggestions for concrete intervention strategies and co-curricular activities that, in light of the diversity-related research and campus climate framework, coaches and student affairs professionals can employ to foster interaction across diverse racial groups with the goal of promoting racial understanding for college athletes.

RESEARCH ON THE EDUCATIONAL BENEFITS OF DIVERSITY

Only a few studies have sought to explore the impact of cross-racial interaction among college athletes. Brown et al. (2003), for example, used data provided by white athletes during their first semesters at 24 predominantly white colleges and universities and found a significant relationship between their contact with black teammates and racial attitudes. Importantly, the relationship varied by type of sport played; white athletes who played team sports with a higher percentage of black teammates reported more positive attitudes toward blacks in general, as compared to white athletes who played individual sports. Another study surveyed athletes from 18 Division I universities, in part to understand the extent to which they had rich multicultural experiences (Potuto & O'Hanlon, 2007). Overall, the research study indicated 60.5% of athletes reported their athletic participation had significantly contributed to their understanding of people of racial or ethnic backgrounds different from their own. Moreover, 79% reported their tolerance for people of other races or backgrounds was positive.

Building on the work of Jayakumar (2008), Comeaux (2013a) examined the extent to which cross-racial interaction influenced postcollege pluralistic orientation and leadership skills for Division I white athlete graduates, and the degree to which engagement effects were conditional on their precollege neighborhoods. The author surveyed 310 white athlete college graduates representing 16 Division I Football Bowl Subdivision conferences. The findings suggest cross-racial interaction during college had continuing benefits on pluralistic orientation and leadership skills for white athletes from racially diverse neighborhoods, and long-term effects on leadership skills for white athletes from segregated precollege neighborhoods.

While the literature examining the influence of cross-racial interaction specifically for college athletes may be incomplete, the growing body of research related to the general student population, inclusive of athletes, can provide additional insight. Scholars have found increasing the number of students of color on campus allows for higher levels of cross-racial interaction among college peers (e.g., Chang, 1999; Saenz, Ngai, & Hurtado, 2007), including interracial friendships (Antonio, 2001). Two decades of social science research have linked engagement with diverse peers, which racially diverse student bodies make possible, to a range of desirable college outcomes (e.g., Astin, 1993; Hurtado, 2001; Jayakumar, 2008).

Numerous studies demonstrate quality cross-racial interactions, both inside and outside the classroom, are associated with positive learning outcomes, including college satisfaction (Astin, 1993; Chang, 1999), leadership skills and cultural awareness (Antonio, 2001; Astin, 1993), critical thinking skills (Gurin, 1999), and higher levels of positive academic and social self-concept (Chang, 1999; Gurin, Dey, Hurtado, & Gurin 2002). Other studies have shown a positive relationship between higher levels of cross-racial interaction and civic interest (Gurin et al., 2002; Hurtado, 2001), cognitive development (Astin, 1993; Gurin et al., 2002), and pluralistic orientation or students' thinking and social interaction skills in an increasingly diverse society (Jayakumar, 2008). Thus, as this body of literature continues to grow, it is becoming evident that there are important educational benefits associated with a racially diverse student body.

CAMPUS RACIAL CLIMATE FOR ATHLETES

Current studies are encouraging, but they also remind us, as Allport (1954) noted nearly six decades ago, that certain conditions facilitate the type of intergroup contact that can lessen racial prejudice. In other words, while it is increasingly evident that there are unique benefits associated with a racially diverse student body, these positive effects are contingent upon the specific nature of the interactions (Chang, Denson, Saenz, & Misa 2006; Gurin et al., 2002). Therefore, in order to facilitate our understanding of the cross-racial experiences of Division I athletes, it is important to identify factors that contribute to a more positive campus climate. While increasing the proportion of nonwhite students on campus is necessary and important, scholars contend that it is insufficient for fostering a supportive campus environment or for maximizing the benefits associated with diversity (Hurtado et al., 1998). There are interrelated challenges or forces that confront students in diverse learning environments, and these can influence the quality of campus experiences and educational outcomes. Thus, institutions that do not account for other aspects of the campus racial climate are likely to increase opposition and hostility among racial groups (Hurtado et al., 1998).

To understand these institutional forces, we draw from the empirical framework developed by Hurtado and colleagues (1998), which describes an institution's climate for racial/ethnic diversity. Four interrelated elements shape the campus racial climate: compositional diversity,[1] the level of racial diversity in a student body; psychological climate, defined by perceptions and attitudes between groups; behavioral climate, the quantity and quality of intergroup relations; and the institution's historical legacy of exclusion of racial/ethnic groups, history that continues to perpetuate inequity across racial lines (Hurtado et al., 1998). Later, Milem, Dey, and White (2004) included a fifth dimension of climate: organizational/structural, which "represents the organizational and structural aspects of colleges and the ways in which benefits for some groups become embedded into these organizational and structural processes" (Milem, Chang, & Antonio, 2005, p. 18). For the purposes of this chapter, we primarily focus on three elements of the institution's climate for racial/ethnic diversity—compositional diversity, organizational/structural aspects, and psychological climate. For this chapter, compositional diversity is conceptualized as the numerical representation of racial/ethnic minority athletes across team sports. In addition, the organizational/structural aspect is related to the limited access and underrepresentation of minority football coaches (or exclusionary hiring practices) at Football Bowl Subdivision schools. Finally, psychological climate involves the extent to which athletes tend to perceive group relation and discriminatory acts by members of the campus community, which can have a significant impact on the likelihood of diverse interactions.

Influence of Compositional Diversity

As described earlier in the chapter, it is well documented that increasing compositional diversity on college campuses is an important step in providing students with more opportunities for interracial interactions and improving the climate (e.g., Antonio, 2001; Chang et al., 2006). For example, Hurtado and colleagues (1998) asserted that when campuses lack diverse environments, the dominant or majority student group will likely shape various forms of interaction and limit its own chances of benefiting from interactions with students of different races. Hurtado and colleagues (1998) also reported that when campuses lack compositional diversity, underrepresented student groups tend to be viewed as tokens.

The relevance of these findings to athletes is evident when we consider the demographics of college athletics. According the National Collegiate Athletic Association's (NCAA) race and ethnicity report (2010), white athletes constitute a disproportionate number of participants in certain team sports: lacrosse for men (90.2%) and women (90%); women's field hockey (86.5%); baseball (83.4%); swimming/diving for men (83.7%) and women (85.8%); rowing for men (82.9%) and women (81.7%); and water polo for men (79.5%) and women (77%). As a result, these students have fewer opportunities in the athletic realm to exchange views with students of other races, particularly when they devote more than forty hours per week to sport-related activities (Wolverton, 2008). A lack of racial diversity can heighten racial tension among teammates, lending support to the aforementioned work of Brown and colleagues (2003). Thus, increasing the racial diversity of participants in certain team sports has the potential to enhance opportunity for intergroup contact and, importantly, for desirable outcomes.

Organizational/Structural Dimension of Climate

The racial and ethnic representation of head coaches in major college football has received public and scholarly attention (e.g., Lapchick, Anjorin, & Nickerson, 2012; Walker, 2005). Specifically, concerns have been raised about the low number of black football coaches. In the 2012 season, blacks made up roughly 46% of college football players at Football Bowl Subdivision (FBS) schools, yet they made up just 12% of head coaches in this sport. And, according to Lynch (2013), "only 312 of 1,018 of college football assistant coaches are Black, and only 31 of 255 offensive and defensive coordinators are African-American." FBS schools have a historical legacy of exclusion, hiring a disproportionate number of white coaches while denying access and opportunities to deserving black coaches (Agyemang & DeLorme, 2010; Sagas & Cunningham, 2005).

In large measure, coaches are central figures in the lives of athletes, and consequently shape their academic, social, and athletic priorities (Jayakumar & Comeaux, 2011). It appears, then, that the college experiences of nonwhite football athletes at FBS schools are influenced to a significant degree by white males (see Lapchick et al., 2012). Further, when racial/ethnic minority football coaches are not appropriately represented at these schools, it may give nonwhite athletes the impression that the campus climate is not supportive or inclusive of these racial/ethnic groups.

The Psychological Element of the Climate

The psychological element of the campus racial climate framework speaks to the importance of individual perceptions and attitudes. Evidence reveals students from different racial/ethnic backgrounds tend to view intergroup relations on campus and instances of racism differently (Hurtado et al., 1998). Studies affirm athletes experience the campus climate differently depending on their race/ethnicity, sex, and sport (Simons, Bosworth, Fujita, & Jensen, 2007; Comeaux, 2012). Perceptual differences can lead to varying levels of social integration and institutional commitment. For example, students who perceive a hostile and discriminatory campus racial climate are less likely to feel connected with the institution (Locks, Hurtado, Bowman, & Oseguera, 2008).

While numerous studies have addressed general student perceptions of campus racial climate, there is a growing body of related work on athletes. Studies reveal that the campus climate can be perceived as quite hostile, particularly for black athletes (e.g., Bruening, Armstrong, & Pastore, 2005; Comeaux, 2012; Simons et al., 2007; Singer, 2005). For example, Bruening et al. (2005) qualitatively examined the collective experiences of black female Division I students in the college community, and their findings indicated that collectively the mass media, coaches, athletic administrators, and other athletes all played a role in virtually ignoring the experiences of these participants, thereby silencing them. More recently, Comeaux (2012) used a qualitative survey to explore 122 athletes' perceptions of discriminatory acts by professors and other students at a Division I university. The majority of respondents reported either positive or neutral experiences with other campus community members, but a small number described instances where professors and other students questioned their intellectual abilities, academic motivation, or treatment by the university. In short, it appears that for athletes generally—and black male and female athletes more specifically—the campus environment is, to a significant degree, unwelcoming, unsupportive, alienating, and racially hostile.

INTERVENTION STRATEGIES FOR COACHES AND STUDENT AFFAIRS PROFESSIONALS

It is clear from the literature that athletes have particular experiences that can both improve and impede their ability to engage in positive cross-racial interactions. In this section, we propose several intervention strategies for coaches, student affairs professionals, and others who desire to improve the interaction and communication of athletes across racial groups. These proposed strategies are aligned with the ideas we have presented in the earlier sections of the chapter.

Assessment of Team, Athletic Department, and Campus Climate

An important first step in any effective intervention strategy designed to improve the cross-racial experiences of athletes is a comprehensive assessment of the climate of the athletic teams, athletic department, and broader campus community. Few, if any, athletic departments hire personnel or independent researchers to assess the climate, but there is no better time than now. Attention should be given to the framework developed by Hurtado and colleagues (1998), with a particular focus on the assessment of the compositional diversity, an athletic department's organizational/structural dimension, and the psychological climate that sets the tone for the broader campus racial climate. A deeper understanding of these elements will help stakeholders within athletic departments make precise observations about and recommendations for athletic teams, the athletic department, the campus community, and individual stakeholders.

For example, through focus groups or targeted interviews with various campus stakeholders (including athletes), athletic department personnel can collect rich data

STAKEHOLDER PERSPECTIVE

Kenny Donaldson, Assistant Director of Academic Services at the University of California, Los Angeles (UCLA)

From his perspective as coordinator of academic support services for the Bruins' men's and women's basketball teams, Donaldson discussed the cross-racial interactions of these athletes. He explained that most 17-, 18-, and 19-year-olds seek a comfort zone in college with respect to their engagement with peers. What athletes deem comfortable in college is largely dictated by their high school experiences. In other words, the high school context matters; athletes who attended highly segregated high schools may have a hard time coming to UCLA where team compositions (compositional racial diversity) are different, whereas teammates who came from less segregated high schools are likely to have an easier transition.

The degree to which athletes feel comfortable in their new college peer group is reflected in their level of engagement with different-race peers off the court. For example, African American basketball players tend to find a community with African American athletes on other teams. Racial cliques, thus, form when there are enough numbers to have one; this dynamic is especially salient among African American athletes. The safe peer space and community African American athletes seek may also be linked to the extreme underrepresentation of African American undergraduate male students on the UCLA campus (3.33% incoming fall 2012) juxtaposed with a high representation of African American male athletes in the revenue-generating sports of basketball and football (48.8%, as cited in Harper, Williams, & Blackman, 2013), statistics that Donaldson has presented to his staff colleagues.

Thus, while basketball and football teams bring a racially diverse peer group together, this level of cross-racial interaction may not translate off the field. Donaldson theorizes that African American athletes (like different race peers) "have frequent interactions with racially diverse teammates because of shared experiences, i.e., athletics and often being together in close quarters. They often travel, shower and compete together so in a way, they are forced to interact with (each other). It's not always genuine or deep, but (engagement) is necessary to build a bond as teammates. However, off the field, that shared experience isn't necessarily there, many times because of prejudice or stereotypes that exist on both sides of the racial fence, whether real or assumed." In order to address the cultivation of an environment that is welcoming and safe for everyone in the athletic department, students and staff, Donaldson led the creation of the Diversity Ad Hoc Committee at UCLA. Donaldson also coordinated with the Intergroup Relations Program at UCLA to provide a facilitated workshop, in the near future, for incoming Bruins' men's and women's basketball teams. Donaldson believes more intergroup dialogue is needed inside and outside of the classroom, on and off the court, and the athletic staff needs to provide the environment and encouragement for this to occur. ■

that will identify strengths and problem areas as well as increase their own and others' awareness about specific campus conditions that impact athletes. Likewise, such data will enable stakeholders in athletic departments to move beyond anecdotal evidence and to offer feedback and practical solutions that enhance athletes' campus experience. Without proper assessment, practitioners in academic support centers are less likely to be fully aware of the types and magnitude of academic and personal issues that athletes encounter. Moreover, they are less likely to respond to these issues in meaningful ways. In the absence of assessment data, practitioners generally rely on assumptions and in some cases develop internalized biases about athletes that too often present them through a deficit lens (Comeaux, 2013b). A deficit-minded perspective may include attributing differences in educational outcomes for athletes generally and black athletes specifically to cultural stereotypes, low cognitive ability, or a lack of motivation on their part (Simons et al., 2007).

Assessment data should be shared with key athletic leaders and the broader academic community. In this way, the athletic department can demonstrate transparency, which, in turn, leads to greater trust from stakeholders of the campus community and beyond. Further, this approach enables campus units to collectively strategize ways to optimize diverse learning environments for athletes and provide direction for future inquiry.

Developing Diversity Competency among Stakeholders

Colleges and universities have an obligation to prepare athletic leaders for the realities they will encounter. In the context of steady racial/ethnic demographic shifts over the past decade, coaches and student affairs professionals need ongoing professional training to develop knowledge and behavior competencies that allow them to effectively respond to the challenges and opportunities posed by the presence of sociocultural diversity (or lack thereof) within athletic organizations. With this focused preparation, they will be better equipped to engage and re-engage a racially diverse group of athletes in a way that leads to positive outcomes.

Increased Compositional Diversity

A critical step toward improving the campus racial climate is to increase the representation of athletes of color in certain team sports. As the statistics above make clear, there is a dearth of athletes of color in such team sports as baseball, field hockey, and swimming/diving. It would be prudent for coaches to find innovative ways to actively recruit more racially diverse athletes in these team sports.

One major obstacle to increasing the representation of athlete participants of color in these team sports is that there are not enough of them in the pipeline, in part because there are limited opportunities for athletes of color to participate in sports other than track and field, football, and basketball (Coakley, 2008). A long-term goal is to provide training grounds for the development of young athletes to increase the number of competitive athletes of color in certain team sports. These facilities would require professional sports leagues and private donors to support their operations.

Inclusion of Minority Football Coaches

The underrepresentation of black head football coaches at Football Bowl Subdivision schools has been an ongoing debate. Hence, NCAA policy must ensure head football coaching positions are available to more blacks and other racial/ethnic minorities. The NCAA should establish a policy similar to the Rooney Rule, which requires National Football League (NFL) teams to interview at least one racial/ethnic minority candidate for all vacant head coaching positions. The NFL has witnessed an increase in the number of black head coaches since the rule was implemented in 2003 (Harrison, 2013).

It would also be helpful for the NCAA to initiate comprehensive mentorship programs and other educational initiatives for aspiring racial/ethnic minority head football coaches. This approach would allow aspiring leaders not only to develop their talents but also to expand their social networks in the sports industry. Increasing the number of black head football coaches and athletes of color in certain team sports is important. This measure alone, however, is not likely to improve the campus racial climate of athletic organizations unless other elements of climate are addressed—in particular, the racial diversity of participants in certain team sports and the psychological climate of perceptions and attitudes between groups.

Improving Psychological Climate

Several studies have documented that athletes generally, and black athletes specifically, attest to negative experiences on their campus community, which to a significant degree can impact their sense of belonging and overall satisfaction in college. Documenting the campus climate and giving voice to discriminatory practices are certainly important first steps in remedying this. In doing so, student affairs professionals can respond meaningfully to issues that affect the campus racial climate.

Interventions designed to combat these racial inequalities and to address the social significance of race and racism in the lives of black male athletes and other students of color is imperative, especially on predominantly white campuses. With this in mind, it would be instructive for student affairs professionals to work closely with scholars who study race and racism to initiate and design professional development trainings and workshops that include sessions on specific cultural groups, including black male and female collegians who have experienced some of the most detrimental stereotypes and negative labels by members of the campus community (Bruening et al., 2005; Comeaux, 2010; Edwards, 1984). An interactive and experiential session on racial stereotypes, for example, would facilitate intergroup dialogue and foster cross-cultural understanding of the types of conscious and unconscious

Changing the Game: BCA Hiring Report Card

The severe underrepresentation of African American and other racial or ethnic minority head football coaches at Division I colleges and universities has been interrogated intensely for several decades. Over the course of eight years, from 1996 to 2004, there were 142 openings for new head coaching positions in Division IA football, yet only one African American was hired each year (Hill, 2004). Richard Lapchick, professor and director of the DeVos Sport Business Management program, called the head coaching position in football "the most segregated position in all of college sport" (Harrison, 2004).

Different theories exist to explain the lack of racial diversity of head college football coaches. Some scholars theorize that stakeholders in the affairs of athletics who make hiring decisions, such as athletic directors and boosters, conform to racist stereotypes, believing racial or ethnic minority football coaches do not have the intellectual capacity to lead teams, as compared to their white counterparts (Agyemang & De-Lorme, 2010). Others argue the racial or ethnic disparities in head coaching positions are related to institutional racism and likewise a lack of established professional networks among minorities in the sport industry (e.g., Sagas & Cunningham, 2005).

In response to inequities of hiring head football coaches in college, the Black Coaches and Administrators (BCA) initiated its first Hiring Report Card starting with the 2003–2004 academic year. The Report Card was created by Dr. C. Keith Harrison with the primary purpose to assure accountability in the hiring process and to study, over time, the methodological approach or process for hiring new head football coaches rather than solely focusing on the hiring outcome at Football Bowl Subdivision (FBS) and Football Championship Subdivision (FCS) schools. All schools with open coaching positions during the football hiring cycle are included in the Report Card and are graded based on a four tier model: number of communications with the executive director of the BCA or the chair of the Minority Opportunity Interest Committee; number of racial or ethnic minorities on the search or hiring committee; number of racial or ethnic minorities who received on-campus interviews; and length of time to hire a candidate. The BCA affirms that a more transparent and objective process will ultimately lead to more opportunities for racial or ethnic minority head coaches in college football.

Since the inaugural Report Card in 2003–2004, Harrison and Yee (2009) reported some enthusiasm for the hiring practices of new head football coaches largely because of the record number of coaches of color in the 2009 season. Nonetheless, this keen interest was tempered by the decline in both the percentage of people of color on search committees and the percentage of racial or ethnic minority candidates interviewed compared to previous years.

Recently, the 2011–2012 Hiring Report Card revealed that coaches of color were selected in 10 of the 29 searches during the football hiring cycle for the 2012 season. As a result, there were a total of 28 racial or ethnic minority head football coaches in NCAA Division I football for this season, an all-time high. Since the initial 2003–2004 BCA Hiring Report Card, "there has been a 600% increase in the number of FBS head football coaches" (Lapchick, Anjorin, & Nickerson, 2012).

According to Floyd Keith, BCA executive director, improvement in the ratio of racial or ethnic minority head football coaches stems from the accountability of the Hiring Report Card, NCAA football professional development academies for aspiring head coaches, and the passion of activists and scholars who want to effect change in college sports (Lapchick, Jackson, & Lilly, 2011).

Since the first Hiring Report Card, Keith has also recognized a positive change in the attitudes and behaviors of participating schools. Contrary to early Hiring Report Cards, there appears to be a greater level of comfort among participating schools, and as such, fewer issues have emerged because of their willingness to fully participate in the process. ■

prejudices and discriminatory attitudes that are directed toward certain student groups.

Implementation of Co-Curricular Activities

It is imperative that college and universities create ideal conditions for quality cross-racial interaction and communication among a diverse student body. Several studies have revealed that co-curricular activities such as participation in leadership training and living and working on campus have the potential to foster interaction across diverse racial groups (Chang, 1996; Saenz et al., 2007). As such, initiatives facilitated by student affairs professionals to create optimal conditions for athletes to communicate across racial lines could include (but should not necessarily be limited to) studying with a racially diverse group of peers, including teammates and nonathletes; diversity workshops and structured leadership training during the off-season; and meaningful cross-racial exchanges that challenge students to think about their own and others' worldviews through purposeful team activities and comprehensive educational programs initiated by personnel in academic support services for athletes.

CONCLUSION

This chapter described the cross-racial experiences of Division I athletes while accounting for dimensions of the broad campus racial climate that can shape the quality of these experiences. Considering the diversity-related research on athletes, it seems that participation in intercollegiate athletics may not always foster ideal conditions for cross-racial interaction. Additionally, athletes tend to have diverse views of the campus climate owing to their varying positionalities and experiences with racism. Efforts aimed to promote a positive climate for all athletes should consider compositional diversity, the organizational/structural aspects of college as well as perceived racial conflict and discrimination on campus (i.e., the psychological dimension). The ability of institutions generally—and stakeholders in the affairs of athletics, specifically—to holistically assess the dynamic aspects of the campus racial climate will likely create optimal conditions and unique opportunities for higher levels of quality cross-racial interaction for all athletes.

While some progress has been made and insights have been gained about the nature and influence of campus racial climate for athletes, there is much that remains unknown. For example, few empirical studies (e.g., Brown et al., 2003; Comeaux, 2013a) have examined the behavioral dimension of racial climate or the nature of cross-racial interaction among athletes, and this must be explored in greater depth. In addition, future efforts should examine a wider spectrum of athletic stakeholders, including coaches and athletic administrators of various racial/ethnic groups, and the extent to which they view and experience the campus environment. In spite of limited extant empirical research, this chapter can serve as a foundation on which to build. A multidimensional understanding of the experiences of athletes and athletic stakeholders can offer a unique perspective on campus diversity that helps to prepare all students for life and work in a pluralistic society.

QUESTIONS FOR DISCUSSION

1. What additional factors, beyond those discussed in this chapter, should athletic leaders and educators consider in implementing strategies to encourage positive and meaningful cross-racial experiences for athletes?

2. If a majority of the student body at predominantly white institutions racially identifies as white, what role do white athletes and nonathletes have in shaping climate that affects their willingness to engage meaningfully with racially diverse peers?

3. What role can athletic departments play to address the persistence of campus racism, which impacts the ability to create supportive environments and to maximize the benefits associated with diversity? What educational programs and activities can help campus members confront negative stereotypes and prejudices against both black or African American athletes and students different from themselves?

Note

1. Although Hurtado et al. (1998) use the term *structural diversity* to describe a dimension of campus climate, this chapter uses *compositional diversity*, which is consistent with Milem et al. (2004).

References

Agyemang, K., & DeLorme, J. (2010). Examining the dearth of black head coaches at the NCAA football bowl subdivision level: A critical race theory and social dominance theory analysis. *Journal of Issues in Intercollegiate Athletics, 3*, 35–52.

Allport, G. (1954). *The nature of prejudice*. Cambridge, MA: Addison-Wesley.

Antonio, A. L. (2001). The role of interracial interaction in the development of leadership skills and cultural knowledge and understanding. *Research in Higher Education, 42*, 593–617.

Astin, A. W. (1993). *What matters in college: Four years revisited*. San Francisco: Jossey-Bass.

Bikson, T. K., & Law, S. A. (1994). *Global preparedness and human resources*. Santa Monica: Rand.

Brown, K. T., Brown, T. N., Jackson, J. S., Sellers, R. M., & Manuel, W. J. (2003). Teammates on and off the field? Contact with black teammates and the racial attitudes of white student athletes. *Journal of Applied Social Psychology, 33*, 1379–1403.

Bruening, J., Armstrong, K., & Pastore, D. (2005). Listening to the voices: The experiences of African American female athletes. *Research Quarterly for Exercise and Sport, 76*, 82–100.

Chang, M. J. (1996). *Racial diversity in higher education: Does a racially mixed student population affect educational outcomes?* (Unpublished doctoral dissertation). University of California, Los Angeles.

———. (1999). Does racial diversity matter? The educational impact of a racially diverse undergraduate population. *Journal of College Student Development, 40*, 377–394.

Chang, M. J., Denson, N., Saenz, V., & Misa, K. (2006). The educational benefits of sustaining cross-racial interaction among undergraduates. *Journal of Higher Education, 77*, 430–455.

Coakley, J. (2008). *Sports in society: issues and controversies*. New York: McGraw-Hill.

Comeaux, E. (2010). Racial differences in faculty perceptions of collegiate student-athletes' academic and post-undergraduate achievements. *Sociology of Sport Journal, 27*, 390–412.

———. (2012). Unmasking athlete microaggressions: Division I student-athletes engagement with members of the campus community. *Journal of Intercollegiate Sport, 5*, 189–198.

———. (2013a). The long-term benefits of cross-racial engagement on workforce competencies for Division I white student-athletes. *Journal of Student Affairs Research and Practice, 50*(1), 37–55.

———. (2013b). Rethinking academic reform and encouraging organizational innovation: Implications for stakeholder management in college sports. *Innovative Higher Education, 38*, 281–293.

Edwards, H. (1984). The black "dumb jock": An American sports tragedy. *College Board Review, 131*, 8–13.

Gratz v. Bollinger, 539 U.S. 244 (2003).

Grutter v. Bollinger, 539 U.S. 306 (2003).

Gurin, P. (1999). *Expert report. Gratz et al. v. Bollinger et al., No. 97-75321 (E.D. Mich.) Grutter et al. v. Bollinger et al., No. 97-75928 (E.D. Mich.)*. Ann Arbor: University of Michigan.

Gurin, P., Dey, E. L., Hurtado, S., & Gurin, G. (2002). Diversity in higher education: Theory and impact on educational outcomes. *Harvard Educational Review, 72*, 330–366.

Harrison, C. K. (2004). The score: A hiring report card for NCAA Division IA and IAA football head coaching positions. This report was supported and funded by the Black Coaches and Administrators (BCA). Retrieved from www.bcasports.org/images/pdf/04-hiring-report-card.pdf

———. (2013). *Examining coaching mobility trends and occupational patterns: Head coaching access, opportunity and the social network in professional and college sport*. A report presented by the National Football League.

Harrison, C. K., & Yee, S. (2009). *Protecting their turf: The head football coaching hiring process, and the practices of FBS & FCS colleges and universities*. This report was supported and funded by the Black Coaches and Administrators (BCA). Retrieved from www.bcasports.org/images/pdf/09-football-hrc.pdf

Hill, F. (2004, March). Shattering the glass ceiling: Blacks in coaching. *Black Issues in Higher Education, 21*, 36–37.

Hurtado, S. (2001). Linking diversity and educational purpose: How diversity affects the classroom environment and student development. In G. Orfield & M. Kurlaender (Eds.), *Diversity challenged: Evidence on the impact of affirmative action* (pp. 187–203). Cambridge, MA: Harvard Education Publishing Group.

Hurtado, S., Milem, J. F., Clayton-Pedersen, A. R., & Allen, W. R. (1998). Enhancing campus climates for racial/ethnic diversity: Educational policy and practice. *Review of Higher Education, 21*, 279–302.

Jayakumar, U. M. (2008). Can higher education meet the needs of an increasingly diverse and global society? Campus diversity and cross-cultural workforce competencies. *Harvard Educational Review, 78*, 615–651.

Jayakumar, U. M., & Comeaux, E. (2011). *A perpetual (un)balancing act: The role of an athletic organization in shaping student-athlete identities*. Paper presented at the annual meeting of the American Educational Research Association, New Orleans, LA.

Lapchick, R., Anjorin, R., & Nickerson, B. (2012). *Striving for sustained positive change: The black coaches and administrators (BCA) hiring report card for NCAA FBS and FCS football head coaching positions*. This report was supported and funded by the Black Coaches and Administrators (BCA). Retrieved from www.tidesport.org/Grad%20Rates/BCA/2012%20BCA%20Football%20Report%20Card.pdf

Lapchick, R., Jackson, S., & Lilly, A. (2011). Building positive change: The black coaches and administrators (BCA) hiring report card for NCAA FBS and FCS football head coaching positions. This report was supported and funded by the Black Coaches and Administrators (BCA). Retrieved from www.bcasports.org/images/pdf/bca_fb_hiring_final_11.20.2011.pdf

Locks, A. M., Hurtado, S., Bowman, N. A., & Oseguera, L. (2008). Extending notions of campus climate and diversity to students' transition to college. *Review of Higher Education, 31*, 257–285.

Lynch, M. (2013). Missing men: The lack of African-American head coaches in college football. *Huffington*

Post. Retrieved from http://www.huffingtonpost
.com/matthew-lynch-edd/missing-men-the-lack-of
-a_b_2439944.html

Milem, J. F., Chang, M. J., & Antonio, A. L. (2005).
*Making diversity work on campus: A research-based
perspective.* Washington, DC: Association American
Colleges and Universities.

Milem, J. F., Dey, E. L., & White, C. B. (2004). Diversity
considerations in health professions education. In
B. D. Smedley, A. S. Butler, & L. R. Bristow (Eds.), *In
the nation's compelling interest: Ensuring diversity in
the health care workforce* (pp. 345–90). Washington,
DC: National Academies Press.

National Collegiate Athletic Association. (2010).
*1999-2000-2009-2010 NCAA student-athlete
ethnicity report.* Indianapolis: NCAA Research.
Retrieved from http://fs.ncaa.org/Docs/library
/research/ethnicity_report/2001-02/2001-02
_ethnicity_report.pdf

Newman, F., Couturier, L., & Scurry, J. (2004). *The
future of higher education: Rhetoric, reality, and the
risks of the marketplace.* San Francisco: Jossey-Bass.

Potuto, J. R., & O'Hanlon, J. (2007). National study of
student-athletes regarding their experiences as
college students. *College Student Journal, 41,*
947–966.

Saenz, V. B., Ngai, H. N., & Hurtado, S. (2007). Factors
influencing positive interactions across race for
African American, Asian American, Latino, and
white college students. *Research in Higher Education, 48*(1), 1–38.

Sagas, M., & Cunningham, G. B. (2005). Racial differences in the career success of assistant football
coaches: The role of discrimination, human capital,
and social capital. *Journal of Applied Social Psychology, 35,* 773–797.

Simons, H. D., Bosworth, C., Fujita, S., & Jensen, M.
(2007). The athlete stigma in higher education.
College Student Journal, 41, 251–273.

Singer, J. N. (2005). Understanding racism through the
eyes of African American male student-athletes.
Race Ethnicity and Education, 8, 365–386.

United States Census Bureau. (2011). *2010 Census shows
America's diversity.* Washington, DC: Author.
Retrieved from http://www.census.gov/2010census
/news/releases/operations/cb11-cn125.html

Walker, M. A. (2005). Black coaches are ready, willing—
and still waiting. *Black Issues in Higher Education,
22*(6), 26–29.

Watt, S. K., & Moore, J. L. (2001). Who are student
athletes? In M. F. Howard-Hamilton & S. K. Watt
(Eds.), *Student services for athletes: New direction for
student services, 93,* 7–18. San Francisco:
Jossey-Bass.

Wolverton, B. (2008, January 25). Athletes' hours renew
debate over college sports. *Chronicle of Higher
Education.* Retrieved from http://chronicle.com
/article/Athletes-Hours-Renew-Debate/22003

THE MISEDUCATION of AFRICAN AMERICAN MALE COLLEGE ATHLETES

John N. Singer

In this chapter, I draw primarily from critical race theory (CRT) and my experiences as a black male, former aspiring athlete, university summer bridge program advisor and academic mentor, college professor, and scholar to discuss how certain macro- (i.e., societal), meso- (i.e., organizational), and micro- (i.e., individual) level factors contribute to the miseducation of African American[1] male athletes at predominantly white institutions of higher education (PWIHE) in the United States of America. By *miseducation* I am referring to a process that often occurs when one is given a wrong or faulty education and where, oftentimes, external forces restrict or impair students' ability to explore the totality of who they are, what they are, and their options and possibilities in various life domains (Marks, 2000). In using CRT as the overarching framework to explore this issue, I focus first and foremost on what is "wrong" with American society and the educational and sports enterprises, as opposed to what is "wrong" with African American male athletes and their interactions with these social systems. Doing so allows me to keep the primary focus on the broader structural issues at the societal and organizational levels and, likewise, critically examine the role these athletes as individuals play in their own educational experiences and outcomes.

As an academic and activist movement that is rooted in the social missions and political struggles of the civil rights movement of the 1950s and 1960s, CRT first emerged in the field of law/legal studies (see Crenshaw, Gotanda, Peller, & Thomas, 1995) and was eventually adopted by scholars in other fields such as education (see Ladson-Billings & Tate, 1995). In general, CRT scholars have emphasized "the many ways that

KEY TERMS

race and racism were fundamentally ingrained in American social structures and historical consciousness and hence shaped U.S. ideology, legal systems, and fundamental conceptions of law, property, and privilege" (Lynn & Adams, 2002, p. 88). CRT scholars view "race" as a category, identity, or designation that has been legally and socially constructed by human beings (particularly "white" elites) for the purposes of establishing permanent power and privileges for certain groups of people, and justifying the perpetual denigration and marginalization of the non-white, racialized "other" (see Haney Lopez, 1996). Given this reality, most CRT scholars are particularly concerned with *understanding* how a regime of white supremacy and the subordination of people of color have been created and maintained in American society, and *changing* the bond that exists between American social systems and racial power and privilege. The ultimate goal of the CRT movement is not only to understand and address race and racism but, in so doing, also to understand and address other forms of subordination based on gender, class, language, and other differences (Parker & Lynn, 2002).

Both African American male and female athletes at PWIHE have been encumbered by race and racism, as well as other challenges related to their various identities and diverse backgrounds. However, since the early pioneering work of noted scholar and activist Harry Edwards (1969, 1973), a great deal of the attention has been paid specifically to the educational plight of African American males, who constitute a significant portion of the labor force in the high-profile, revenue-producing sports of Division I football and basketball at PWIHE (see Singer, 2013, for brief overview). In comparison to other subpopulations of students (athletes) in both the higher education context (see Harper, 2012; Harper, Williams, & Blackman, 2013), as well as the pre-K–12 school context (see Howard, 2014), African American males are at the very bottom with respect to educational attainment and most indicators of academic performance (e.g., grade point average, graduation rates), and this group seems to be the most severely and disproportionately affected by the schooling process.

These points are not to suggest that all African American males are lagging behind or enter PWIHE underprepared academically or otherwise. In line with one of the major tenets of CRT, there are many counterstories or counternarratives to the dominant discourse that we typically see concerning the educational problems and challenges of African American male college students in general and African American male college athletes in particular (Bimper, Harrison, & Clark, 2012). Indeed, several African American male "scholar-ballers" (see Comeaux & Harrison, 2011) have accomplished great things not only on the playing field and court but also in the classroom and in their communities. These gifted and talented individuals graduate and advance to graduate or professional school and to successful careers (as professional athletes and other professionals) as well as productive lives as citizens in the United States and beyond. The story of Dr. Albert Bimper, a former college and professional football player turned college professor and athletic administrator at his college alma mater is a case in point (see Stakeholder Perspective on page 197).

Reading Is Fundamental to the Education of African American Male Athletes

In an article in *Black Issues in Higher Education*, "The James Brooks Illiteracy Scandal," Downton (2000) discussed the story behind James Brooks, former National Football League (NFL) and University of Auburn running back, and his problems with illiteracy. Despite the fact he graduated from high school in 1977 and spent four years on a football scholarship at Auburn, this highly gifted and talented African American male athlete was functionally illiterate throughout his college career. He left the university for the NFL without having graduated, and his problems with illiteracy continued during his NFL playing career and into retirement. In a similar case, *Ebony* magazine highlighted the story of Dexter Manley, a former All-Pro, two-time Super Bowl champion in the NFL and standout at Oklahoma State University. Unlike James Brooks, Manley did receive a college degree; however, like Brooks, he too was illiterate during his college playing career and most of his playing days as an NFL player (see Randolph, 1989). Kevin Ross, a former basketball standout at Creighton University, was also functionally illiterate. And like the athletes highlighted here, Ross was admitted into the university and passed through the system because of his athletic gifts and talents (see Donnor, 2005). These three cases are just a few of the many examples where the educational interests of African American male athletes at predominantly white institutions of higher education (PWIHE) have been manipulated in favor of the interests of other educational stakeholder groups (see Ganim, 2014, for more examples pertaining to the issue of illiteracy and the African American male athlete). Each case demonstrates how their experiences in the American educational system (i.e., elementary, secondary, higher education) have not necessarily served them well.

What is particularly interesting about these cases is that at the core of these African American male athletes' educational challenges is the issue of literacy, which is the foundation of learning and knowledge production. In particular, reading is fundamental to the educational process. Historically, it was illegal during slavery for African Americans to learn how to read and write (Anderson, 1988; Woodson, 1919). White elites went to great lengths to keep slaves from learning to read and write because they realized "the more you cultivate the minds of slaves, the more unserviceable you make them" (Woodson, 1919, p. 9). In this regard, keeping slaves from learning how to read and write was the key to maintaining the system of white dominance and black subordination that had become institutionalized in American society. Forbidding the slave from reading was at the heart of the miseducation of black people in America; white elites realized that once the slaves learned how to read it would allow them to come into the knowledge of self, others, and the world, putting them on a path to take ownership of their destiny (see the autobiography of former slave, Frederick Douglass [1854], as an example).

In reflecting on the foregoing cases and the historical roots of the miseducation of black people in American society, there are some critical questions one could ponder in the examination the educational plight of the African American male college athlete today: Why do many of these African American male athletes struggle with reading and writing today? What role has the American educational system played in the creation of this problem of illiteracy and the so-called black "dumb jock" (Edwards, 1984)? What role has the black male athlete played in his own miseducation? This chapter is concerned with these and many other questions. ■

But despite the many "success" stories we can point to and the potential benefits the African American male college athlete derives from his involvement and investment in intercollegiate athletics (Singer, 2008), there still remain many of these young men who continue to be negatively exploited during their time on campus and are leaving these PWIHE ill-equipped to fully function in life after their playing days have ended. Further, it is important to note that while I certainly acknowledge the potential value in the pursuit and attainment of a college degree, *graduation* from a college or university does not necessarily equate to receiving a true *education* (Edwards, 1984). The case study at the beginning of this chapter bears witness to this point and calls for further exploration of the miseducation of African American male athletes from a macro-, meso-, and microperspective. I draw from CRT and other relevant literature, and build on the work of scholars who have critically analyzed the educational plight of college athletes in general, and African American male college athletes in particular. In the sections that follow, I lay out the key components of this multilevel framework and discuss the implications for research, policy, and practice in higher education and intercollegiate athletics.

MACROLEVEL FACTORS: SYSTEMIC RACISM

In the foreword to Carter G. Woodson's (1998) book, John Henrik Clarke notes, "Unfortunately, African people in the United States still have some prevailing misperceptions about their education and education in general. We were not brought to the United States or the so-called New World to be educated. We were brought as a massive labor supply . . . What the slave masters permitted was training and not education" (p. 1). Clarke's quote captures the essence of this section on broad societal factors that impact the miseducation of African American male college athletes. In particular, a discussion of *systemic racism* and how it has become institutionalized in the American educational system and big-time college sports is particularly relevant.

One of the primary tenets of CRT is that racism is endemic in American society and has become entrenched in American law, culture, and social institutions. In discussing the permanence of racism in American society, CRT pioneer Derrick Bell (1992) describes black people in the United States as "faces at the bottom of the well," and he discusses the unparalleled history of oppression and continuous struggle this racial minority group has faced in American society. Similarly, in his book, *Systemic Racism: A Theory of Oppression*, sociologist Joe Feagin (2006) discussed the history and legacy of white-on-black oppression (e.g., chattel slavery, legal segregation, contemporary racism) and how systemic, institutionalized, covert forms of racism and white supremacy have been created and sustained across a broad array of institutions and social settings over time.

The American educational system is one such institution and social setting. Woodson's (2000 [1933]) indictment of the American educational system provides a strong foundation for other scholars to discuss the negative, harmful impact this system has had on the black community in general and black males in particular. Shujaa (1994) makes the distinction between *schooling* and *education*, describing the former as "a process intended to perpetuate and maintain the society's existing power relations and institutional structures that support those arrangements" and the latter as "the process of transmitting from one generation to the next knowledge of the values, aesthetics, spiritual beliefs, and all things that give a particular cultural orientation its uniqueness" (p. 15). Shujaa's distinction suggests, on the one hand, that when black people engage in the schooling process, they are being trained to acquiesce to the dominant social order, where they frequently amass the cultural orientations of elite whites, oftentimes to their own detriment. On the other hand, when black people are engaged in the process of education they are in learning environments that recognize their cultural history and heritage, facilitate the transmission of cultural knowledge, and affirm their cultural identity.

In his historical investigation into the political and ideological foundations of the "miseducation of the Negro" and how schooling, not true education, is often what black people have been subjected to in American society, William Watkins (2001) builds on the work of Woodson (2000 [1933]) in arguing that when slaves were

STAKEHOLDER PERSPECTIVE

Countering the Miseducation of African American Male Athletes at PWIHE: Recognizing "Race Matters"

Dr. Albert Bimper holds a joint appointment as an assistant professor of ethnic studies and senior associate athletic director of diversity and inclusion at his alma mater, Colorado State University, where he was a four-year starter at center for the football team. He also had a brief stint in the NFL, earning a Super Bowl ring as a member of the 2006 Indianapolis Colts. Dr. Bimper earned his Ph.D. in curriculum and instruction (with a cultural studies in education concentration) at the University of Texas and served as an assistant professor in the Department of Special Education, Counseling, and Student Affairs and as an academic mentor to athletes at Kansas State University before returning to his alma mater.

As can be seen from his bio, Bimper has important experiences

as a student, athlete, mentor, educator, administrator, and researcher. In reflecting on his initial experiences as a college athlete, Bimper indicated he was being led down the wrong path and it took the intervention of faculty and mentors outside athletics to help him tap into his inner gifts and talents beyond his athletic prowess. He began to acknowledge the significance of race and the impact it could have on his educational experiences and future success: "I was challenged to consider how issues of race were impacting my experience and development. I believe race had an impact on how my athlete experience was constructed. But I was also encouraged to develop a sense of awareness and agency that gave me the confidence and capital to create opportunities that could lead to

success. Maybe more than anything, by considering the impact that race was having and would continue to have on my life, I actually broadened my definition of what success could mean for me."

As Bimper's statement implies, this recognition of race empowered him to expand his horizons and think more about who he was, what he could become, and the myriad possibilities for success in life beyond the playing field. This example certainly speaks to the important role that race consciousness plays in helping to counter and deal with issues of racism and its impact on the educational experiences of African American male athletes at predominantly white American institutions of higher education (PWIHE). ■

"emancipated," a system for "educating" them was put into place to discipline, exploit, and supposedly civilize them. He discusses how America's colonization of black people employed the educational system as often as the bullet or other destructive tactics. Moreover, he highlighted and interrogated the prominent role that powerful, wealthy white men have played in the establishment of educational institutions (e.g., historically black colleges and universities) and vocational training for black people. Watkins's critical analysis suggests that while these white power brokers might appear to have been benevolent by providing "educational" opportunities for black people, they were particularly concerned with doing so in the interest of controlling and limiting the knowledge production and acquisition of black people. In this way, black people might continue to be serviceable to and manipulated by white elites.

This sentiment is consistent with the interest-convergence principle tenet of CRT, which posits that white elites will often tolerate and even support potential opportunities for racially marginalized groups, particularly when it substantially and disproportionately supports their own self-interests (Bell, 1980, 2004). Scholars have utilized CRT and the interest convergence principle to discuss the integration of athletic departments at PWIHE and how these institutions have exploited the athletic prowess of African American male athletes often to this group's detriment (see Davis, 1995; Donnor, 2005; Singer, 2009b, 2013). A central feature of CRT is the notion of race as a property interest (Harris, 1993). Ladson-Billings (1998) discusses how African Americans were historically constructed as property in the sense that they were owned, and although Africans Americans eventually were legally granted citizenship, they "represent a unique form of citizenship in the United States—property transformed into citizenship" (p. 16). Relatedly, some scholars have suggested African American male college athletes have been treated like valuable property on a metaphorical plantation (e.g., Hawkins, 2010). In revisiting the quote by John Henrik Clarke, this begs the rhetorical questions: Were African American male athletes brought to PWIHE to serve primarily as a "massive labor supply?" Are they being trained to serve the interests of the NCAA, member institutions, and other powerful stakeholders as opposed to being properly educated to serve their own interests and the interests of their communities?

MESOLEVEL FACTORS: ORGANIZATIONAL CULTURE, STRUCTURE, AND PRACTICES

According to Chesler, Lewis, and Crowfoot (2005), "Organizations are the key intermediaries between the larger society and the lives of individuals and groups. They typically mirror the larger society and are in the position of either passing on or sometimes challenging dominant patterns and their effects . . . While the people and groups in an organization work together for overarching goals and purposes, they also have different interests—based on their identity, role, functional unit—and these interest groups often compete for limited resources" (p. 47). Their words capture the essence of this section because it allows for a critical reflection on how institutions and organizations (e.g., universities and their athletic departments) subordinate low-status groups (e.g., college athletes) by erecting barriers to their access to resources, opportunities, and full participation in certain processes. In particular, by focusing on aspects of the culture, structure, and practices of athletic departments at PWIHE, we can better understand how the miseducation of African American male athletes unfolds at the organizational level of analysis.

Unfortunately, college sport organizations have, for the most part, been in the business of passing on dominant societal patterns and their effects. Chesler and colleagues (2005) mentioned the competing visions athletic departments and academic units within colleges and universities often have about how athletes should spend their time, energy, and efforts. Interestingly, Frey (1994) described the athletic department as a "deviant subunit" of the larger university culture and structure and discussed how its relationship with and dependence on resources from external stakeholder groups (e.g., boosters, media, corporations) allows it to effectively resist control by internal university mechanisms. In this regard, it can be viewed as an organization on campus that has a unique culture focused on commercial development, which is oftentimes in direct conflict with the educational values and academic mission of the broader university (Bowen & Levin, 2003).

In discussing the inherent contradictions between the cultures of universities and their athletic departments, Comeaux (2007) argues that athletes are entering into a "culture of academic disengagement" beginning with the recruitment process: the neglect of academic and other educational matters and the overemphasis on athletics perpetuate a culture of low academic expectations. While this athletics subculture creates a myriad of challenges for athletes from all backgrounds, these challenges may be even more pronounced for African Americans in football and men's basketball, particularly those highly touted prize recruits who come to PWIHE from disadvantaged economic backgrounds and pre-K–12 educational environments that lack resources to fully prepare them for the academic rigors and challenges of higher education (Kozol, 2005). Indeed, research reveals how and why so many African American male college athletes in particular, while thoroughly immersed in the athlete role, have become detached from the academic role, often to their own detriment (Adler & Adler, 1991; Benson, 2000; Hawkins, 2010).

In addition, my formal research (see Singer, 2005, 2008, 2009a, 2009b, 2013), general observations, and several conversations with African American male athletes (and other athletic department stakeholders) have allowed me to glean insight into how the culture, structure, and practices in these athletic departments can negatively impact this group. For example, I served as a summer graduate advisor and was primarily responsible for working with highly recruited, academically "at-risk" African American male football and basketball players in a ten-week transition bridge program. During one particular summer, the head football coach, according to one of the players, told these athletes in a meeting during their first day on campus that "school and academics come first [as he held up two fingers], and football comes second [as he held up one finger]." When highly paid powerful coaches communicate these types of contradictory messages, it can often create cognitive dissonance and difficult challenges for athletes who might be truly interested in a holistic educational experience during their time on campus.

As big-time college sports has continued to grow and PWIHE have continued to recruit athletes from various backgrounds, colleges and universities have invested in state-of-the-art academic support centers and intensified the scope and services these centers offer over the years (Pickeral, 2012). However, the role and effectiveness of these centers in addressing the unique needs of black athletes have been questioned. Spigner (1993) asserts these centers might be "aiding and abetting a racial status-quo by emphasizing more of a social desire for sports entertainment" (p. 144). More than two decades later, these same concerns still exist but are even more pronounced, given how drastic the commercialism in college sports has become. My research with African American male athletes and other experiences as an academic mentor and college professor reveal that, while African American male athletes have garnered some benefits from these support programs, many of the academic support personnel in these programs have (un)wittingly assisted in perpetuating racism and reproducing the status quo. The pressures often put on academic support personnel to keep athletes eligible to play encourages many of these individuals to engage in practices that are often detrimental to athletes' overall educational development.

Comeaux and Harrison (2011) discuss various forces and processes confronting Division I college athletes' academic success and other educational outcomes. One aspect of these scholars' conceptual model particularly relevant here is the academic and social integration of these athletes into the organizational (school) environment, which involves activities such as interactions with faculty and nonathlete peers in and out of class, community service work, and engagement in extracurricular campus activities besides athletics. While these activities are often facilitated through academic support programs and affiliated staff members, Comeaux and Harrison caution that these activities and opportunities have been severely limited for black athletes because of "a hostile campus racial climate and reinforcement of low academic expectations by significant members of the campus community" (p. 241). Unfortunately, many of these significant members of the campus community have included faculty, coaches, student peers, administrators, academic advisors and learning specialists or tutors, and the athletes themselves.

MICROLEVEL FACTORS

Individual level factors can also impact the miseducation of the African American male athlete. Harry Edwards (1984) points out, "It is the black student-athletes themselves who must shoulder a substantial portion of the responsibility for improving their own circumstances. Education is an activist pursuit and cannot in reality be 'given.' It must be obtained 'the old fashion way'—one must earn it . . . the bottom line here is that if black student-athletes fail to take an active role in establishing and legitimizing a priority upon academic achievement, nothing done by any other party to this American sports tragedy will matter—if for no other reason than the fact that a slave cannot be freed against his will" (p. 13). In this section, my focus is on identity development and personal ethics.

Identity Development

Harry Edwards (2000) notes that for decades he has contended "that the dynamics of black sports involvement, and the blind faith of black youths and their families in sport as a prime vehicle for self-realization and socio-economic advancement, have combined to generate a complex of critical problems for black society" (p. 9). Edwards has long argued black students' aspirations and motivation to pursue athletic careers and identities has too often been at the expense of other critically important areas of personal and cultural development. Several scholars have studied the career aspirations and identity development of African American males in particular and found that this group, in comparison to other groups, is more likely to play sports in school with the goal of it leading to a college athletic scholarship or professional football or basketball career (see Harrison, Sailes, Rotich, & Bimper, 2011). Unfortunately, while the pursuit of fame and fortune as a professional athlete is not necessarily something that should be discouraged, in far too many instances African American male athletes' "aspirational capital"[2] prevents them from developing a more realistic, holistic identity profile as human beings (Singer & May, 2011).

Scholars have also discussed the effect negative stereotypes can have on the identity development and educational experiences of African American male athletes at PWIHE (Hodge, Burden, Robinson, & Bennett, 2008; Sailes, 1993). Historically, these individuals have been stereotyped as athletically superior but intellectually inferior to other racial groups (Hodge, Burden, Robinson, & Bennett, 2008), and as Hughes, Satterfield, and Giles (2007) explained, they have been "athleticized" as dumb jocks and campus entertainment, not as serious students. Steele and Aronson (1995) described this outcome of stereotyping as a stereotype threat, which involves "being at risk of confirming, as self-characteristic, a negative stereotype about one's group" (p. 797). Self-stereotyping most certainly can have an adverse effect on the self-esteem and motivation of black male athletes to pursue other important identities and developmental experiences outside of sports excellence.

Personal Ethics

DeSensi and Rosenburg (2003) describe *personal ethics* as a set of morals and values that an individual brings to a particular organization or situation, and *social responsibility* as the legal and moral responsibility we have to ourselves and other human beings. Comeaux and Harrison (2011) discuss the importance of precollege characteristics and how the commitments (i.e., goal, institutional, and sport) of Division I college athletes impact their academic success and educational experiences. In discussing the miseducation of African American male athletes it is certainly important to understand how their precollege lived experiences in the home, school, and other contexts could impact the educational goals they set for themselves, and their commitments to sporting endeavors and the educational institution.

What is it about the personal ethical profiles of former black male college athletes at PWIHE such as Isaiah Thomas, Robert Smith, Myron Rolle, Albert Bimper, and several others who have been able to struggle through their individual circumstances and successfully traverse the educational terrain while challenging a flawed educational system and corrupt athletic enterprise? As Harry Edwards suggests, these athletes viewed their education as an activist pursuit, and they took an active role in establishing and legitimizing a priority upon academic achievement and other aspects of their education outside of their athletic identities. From a CRT perspective, these black male athletes, in many ways, serve as that counternarrative to the all-too-familiar stereotypic image of the black male "dumb jock" that Edwards (1984) has always insisted is not born but rather has been systematically created in American society and the educational system.

CONCLUSION

In his book, *Race Matters*, Cornell West (1993) argued that when discussing issues of race in America it is imperative that we begin not with the "problems of black people" but with "the flaws of American society—flaws rooted in the historic inequalities and longstanding cultural stereotypes" (p. 6). I began this chapter with a case study that highlighted historic flaws of American society, and suggested these flaws and deep-seated injustices against black people have contributed greatly to some of the contemporary problems and issues we have observed regarding the educational plight and miseducation of African American male college athletes. While the case study focuses specifically on the issue of illiteracy and its negative impact on the African American male athletes, the focal point of this chapter is on the role that certain macrolevel, mesolevel, and microlevel factors can play in understanding this complex, multifaceted educational problem. While other scholars have certainly offered provocative insights into the educational plight of African American male athletes at PWIHE, I have attempted to add to this body of work by focusing on the relationship between and among societal, organizational, and individual factors contributing to the miseducation of this important stakeholder group.

There are significant implications for research, policy, and practice. From a research perspective, there is a need for critical race-based, participatory action research (PAR) projects conducted with African American male athletes in institutions of higher education of all types. This approach would allow researchers to help empower and give "voice" to African American male athletes at each step of the research process, from the identification of the research problem to the write-up and dissemination of the results. These athletes' participation in such an educational process, although time-consuming and potentially difficult, can be a liberating experience for this group. It could allow African American males to define for themselves the kinds of issues and concerns that are likely to impact their educational experience. Moreover, athletes' active engagement in this research process could set the tone for further pursuit of knowledge and ambitions beyond the playing fields and courts and give them a better appreciation for the true purpose of higher education, which according to Clarke (1991) is to prepare the student to handle power responsibly.

Indeed, African American male athletes' (and other athlete groups) participation in PAR and other qualitative research projects (e.g., case studies, ethnographies) related to their educational experiences could certainly enhance their understanding of the power dynamics at play in big-time college sports. Although college athletes have certain privileges and perks that are not afforded to many of their non-athlete peers, college athletes today have very little voice in determining policies that directly affect them. Athletes often subjugate themselves to the rules, regulations, and directives that have been established by powerful governing bodies and organizations, and they are ostracized if they refuse to conform. From a social reproduction perspective, athletes in general, and black male athletes in particular, have been relegated to the bottom of a social class order that in many ways is diametrically opposed to their economic, academic, and other educational interests. Interestingly, in the early days of college athletics the athlete played a significant role in the control and administration of this enterprise (Covell & Barr, 2010); but today, outside of the involvement of a few athletes on advisory committees at the NCAA and member institution levels, this type of power has been severely limited. This lack of voice for athletes in general and black male athletes in particular is certainly a policy issue that should be addressed.

Finally, from a practical standpoint, faculty, coaches, administrators, and other educational stakeholders of higher education and intercollegiate athletics must do more to implement and fully support (financially and otherwise) programs and learning opportunities that help empower college athletes in general to engage more in the process of self-discovery (e.g., "scholar-baller paradigm"; see Comeaux & Harrison, 2011); and in the case of African American male athletes at PWIHE, there is a need for a focus on culturally relevant programs (Singer, 2013). But, perhaps more important, athletes must take it upon themselves to seek higher learning opportunities by aligning themselves with programs, coalitions, alliances, and people (particularly outside of athletics) who will serve to enlighten them and provide support for their educational experiences beyond the athletics playing court and field.

QUESTIONS FOR DISCUSSION

1. What are other potential factors at the macro-, meso-, and microlevels that can be added to the multilevel framework presented in this chapter?

2. How might your definitions of education and miseducation be similar to and different from the ones presented in this chapter?

3. In reflecting on the case study at the beginning of this chapter, what thoughts come to mind?

Notes

1. The terms *African American* and *black* are sometimes used interchangeably, but they can have different meanings. The term *black* is typically seen as a broader term that describes a diverse array of people of African descent within the African Diaspora (e.g., African Continent, North America, and the Caribbean). "African American" is a term that describes people of African descent who were born in the United States and whose ancestral lineage is rooted in the American chattel slavery system.

2. Yosso (2005) described this as "the ability to hold onto hope in the face of structural inequality and often without the means to make such dreams a reality" (p. 77).

References

Adler, P. A., & Adler, P. (1991). *Backboards and blackboards: College athletes and role engulfment*. New York: Columbia University Press.

Anderson, J. D. (1988). *The education of blacks in the south, 1860–1935*. Chapel Hill: University of North Carolina Press.

Bell, D. (1980). Brown vs. Board of Education and the interest-convergence principle. *Harvard Law Review, 93*, 518–533.

———. (1992). *Faces at the bottom of the well: The permanence of racism*. New York: Basic Books.

———. (2004). *Silent covenants: Brown v. Board of Education and the unfulfilled hopes for racial reform*. New York: Oxford University Press.

Benson, K. F. (2000). Constructing academic inadequacy: African American athletes' stories of schooling. *Journal of Higher Education, 71*, 223–246.

Bimper, A. Y., Jr., Harrison, L., Jr., & Clark, L. (2012). Diamonds in the rough: Examining a case of successful black male student athletes in college sport. *Journal of Black Psychology, 39*(2), 107–130.

Bowen, W. G., & Levin, S. A. (2003). *Reclaiming the game: College sports and educational values*. Princeton, NJ: Princeton University Press.

Chesler, M., Lewis, A., & Crowfoot, J. (2005). *Challenging racism in higher education: Promoting justice*. Lanham, MD: Rowman & Littlefield.

Clarke, J. H. (1991). *Africans at the crossroads: Notes for an African world revolution*. Trenton, NJ: Africa World Press.

Comeaux, E. (2007). The student(less) athlete: Identifying the unidentified college student. *Journal for the Study of Sports and Athletes in Education, 1*(1), 37–44.

Comeaux, E., & Harrison, C. K. (2011). A conceptual model of academic success for student-athletes. *Educational Researcher, 40*, 235–245.

Covell, D., & Barr, C. A. (2010). *Managing intercollegiate athletics*. Scottsdale, AZ: Holcomb Hathaway Publishers.

Crenshaw, K., Gotanda, N., Peller, G., & Thomas, K. (Eds.) (1995). *Critical race theory: Key writings that formed the movement*. New York: New Press.

Davis, T. (1995). The myth of the superspade: The persistence of racism in college athletics. *Fordham Urban Law Journal, 22*, 615–698.

DeSensi, J. T., & Rosenburg, D. (2003). *Ethics and morality in sport management*. Morgantown, WV: Fitness Information Technology.

Donnor, J. (2005). Towards an interest-convergence in the education of African-American football student athletes in major college sports. *Race Ethnicity and Education, 8*(1), 45–67.

Douglass, F. (1854). *Narrative of the life of Frederick Douglass: An American slave*. New York: Signet.

Downton, J. (2000, January 6). The James Brooks illiteracy scandal: Auburn University's and the Cincinnati Bengal's secret little "problem" unveiled. *Black Issues in Higher Education*, 18–20.

Edwards, H. (1969). *The revolt of the black athlete*. New York: Free Press.

———. (1973). *Sociology of sport*. Homewood, IL: Dorsey Press.

———. (1984). The black "dumb jock": An American sports tragedy. *College Board Review*, 8–13.

———. (2000). Crisis of black athletes on the eve of the 21st century. *Society, 37*, 9–13.

Feagin, J. R. (2006). *Systemic racism: A theory of oppression*. New York: Routledge.

Frey, J. H. (1994). Deviance of organizational subunits: The case of college athletic departments. *Journal of Sport & Social Issues, 18*(2), 110–122.

Ganim, S. (2014, January 8). *CNN analysis: Some college athletes play like adults, read like 5th-graders*. Retrieved from http://www.CNN.com

Haney Lopez, I. F. (1996). *White by law: The legal construction of race*. New York: New York University Press.

Harper, S. R. (2012). *Black male student success in higher education: A report from the national black male college achievement study*. Philadelphia: University of Pennsylvania, Center for the Study of Race and Equity in Education.

Harper, S. R., Williams, C. D., & Blackman, H. W. (2013). *Black male student-athletes and racial inequities in NCAA Division I college sports*. Philadelphia: University of Pennsylvania, Center for the Study of Race and Equity in Education.

Harris, C. (1993). Whiteness as property. *Harvard Law Review, 106*, 1707–1791.

Harrison, L., Sailes, G., Rotich, W. K., & Bimper, A. Y. (2011). Living the dream or awakening from the nightmare: Race and athletic identity. *Race, Ethnicity and Education, 14*(1), 91–103.

Hawkins, B. (2010). *The new plantation: Black athletes, college sports, and predominantly white NCAA institutions*. New York: Palgrave Macmillan.

Hodge, S. R., Burden, J. W., Robinson, L. E., & Bennett, R. A. (2008). Theorizing on the stereotyping of black male student-athletes: Issues and implications. *Journal for the Study of Sports and Athletes in Education, 2*(2), 203–226.

Howard, T. C. (2014). *Black male(d): Peril and promise in the education of African American males*. New York: Teachers College.

Hughes, R. L., Satterfield, J. W., & Giles, M. S. (2007). Athletisizing black male student-athletes: The social construction of race, sports, myths, and realities. *NASAP Journal, 10*(1), 112–127.

Kozol, J. (2005). *The shame of the nation: The restoration of apartheid schooling in America*. New York: Crown Publishers.

Ladson-Billings, G. (1998). Just what is critical race theory and what's it doing in a nice field like education? *International Journal of Qualitative Studies in Education, 11*(1), 7–24.

Ladson-Billings, G., & Tate, W. F. (1995). Toward a critical race theory of education. *Teachers College Record, 97*, 47–68.

Lynn, M., & Adams, M. (2002). Introductory overview to the special issue critical race theory and education: Recent developments in the field. *Equity & Excellence in Education, 35*(2), 87–92.

Marks, B. T. (2000). The miseducation of the negro revisited: African American racial identity, historically black institutions, and historically white institutions. In L. Jones (Ed.), *Brothers of the Academy* (pp. 53–69). Sterling, VA: Stylus.

Parker, L., & Lynn, M. (2002). What's race got to do with it? Critical race theory's conflicts with and connections to qualitative research methodology and epistemology. *Qualitative Inquiry, 8*(1), 7–22.

Pickeral, R. (2012, August 7). *Pressure on academic support staffs*. Retrieved from http://espn.go.com/college-sports/story/_/id/8242892/

Randolph, L. B. (1989, October). Dexter Manley's incredible story: "I broke down and started crying . . . how did I get through school when I couldn't read?" *Ebony*.

Sailes, G. A. (1993). An investigation of campus stereotypes: The myth of black athletic superiority and the dumb jock stereotype. *Sociology of Sport Journal, 10*, 88–97.

Shujaa, M. J. (Ed.). (1994). *Too much schooling, too little education: A paradox of black life in white societies*. Trenton, NJ: Africa World Press.

Singer, J. N. (2005). Understanding racism through the eyes of African American male student-athletes. *Race, Ethnicity, and Education, 8*, 365–386.

———. (2008). Benefits and detriments of African American male athletes' participation in a big-time college football program. *International Review for the Sociology of Sport, 43*, 399–408.

———. (2009a). Preparing African American male student-athletes for post-secondary education: Implications for educational stakeholders. In H. R. Milner (Ed.), *Diversity and education: Teachers, teaching, and teacher education* (pp. 31–50). Springfield, IL: Charles C. Thomas.

———. (2009b). African American football athletes' perspectives on institutional integrity in college sport. *Research Quarterly for Exercise and Sport, 80*(1), 102–116.

———. (2013). Stakeholder management in big-time college sport: The educational interests of African American male athletes. In D. Brooks & R. Althouse (Eds.), *Racism in College Athletics* (3rd ed.) (pp. 345–362) Morgantown, WV: Fitness Information Technology.

Singer, J. N., & May, R. A .B. (2011). The career trajectory of a black male high school basketball player. *International Review for the Sociology of Sport, 46*, 299–314.

Spigner, C. (1993). African American student-athletes: Academic support or institutionalized racism? *Education, 114*(1), 144–150.

Steele, C. M., & Aronson, J. (1995). Stereotype threat and intellectual test performances of African-Americans. *Journal of Personality and Social Psychology, 69*, 797–811.

Watkins, W. H. (2001). *The white architects of black education: Ideology and power in America, 1865–1954*. New York: Teachers College Press.

West, C. (1993). *Race matters*. New York: Vintage Books.

Woodson, C. G. (1919). *The education of the Negro prior to 1861* (2nd ed.). Washington, DC: Associated Publishers.

———. (1998). *The education of the Negro*. Brooklyn, NY: A&B Publishers Group.

———. (2000). *The mis-education of the Negro*. Chicago: African American Images. (Originally published in 1933, Associated Publishers)

Yosso, T. J. (2005). Whose culture has capital? A critical race discussion of community cultural wealth. *Race, Ethnicity, and Education, 8*(1), 68–91.

FOR COLORED GIRLS WHO HAVE CONSIDERED BLACK FEMINIST THOUGHT WHEN FEMINIST DISCOURSE and TITLE IX WEREN'T ENOUGH

Robin L. Hughes

A growing body of research explores the experiences of African Americans who participate in sports. While somewhat rich in quantity, too frequently the focus tends to lean toward negative and deficit models of what it means to be both an African American and an athlete (Hatcher, 2004). This is particularly true for the exploration of African American males who participate in sports. Much of the research focuses on athletic exploitation, inadequate role models, and black males' "so-called" incessant emphasis on sports rather than schooling (Edwards, 1984). Other literature about black athletes tends to overemphasize their athletic prowess and achievement, while at the same time underemphasize the importance of their academic success (Hughes, Satterfield, & Giles, 2007). Because such research articles are so frequently published, they may serve to reinforce and shape how university faculty, administrators and students might view athletes of color and their athletic ability in general (Comeaux, 2010; Comeaux & Harrison, 2007; Hughes et al., 2007).

Media also plays a role in what the *world* learns and purports to "know" about sporting and sport participation. Media's often myopic, somewhat naive, and negative depictions of black athletes can serve to reify what the rest of the world, which rarely encounters athletes, actually understands about athletes, athletics, and sporting (Hughes et al., 2007). Media's often narrow focus on dismal graduation rates, violence, and drugs in sports can leave a lasting and persistent, yet misleading construction of athletes, athletics, and sport participation general.

More recent literature, however, tends to use more critical and reflective lenses from which to study the experiences of athletes of color (Comeaux, 2010; Comeaux & Harrison, 2011). There are a number of

KEY TERMS

African American ◄
females

African American female ◄
athletes

black feminist thought ◄
and athletics

African American female ◄
athletes and Title IX

studies that use critical race theory, constructivism and critical theory to more accurately describe the experiences of black athletes and how they are socially constructed (Comeaux, 2010; Hughes et al., 2007; Singer, 2005). Those studies in particular take into consideration the importance of cultural, historical, and racial contexts in order to better understand social and political influences in athletics and how naive knowledge about particular groups may be socially constructed. Nevertheless, when we (scholars in general) do inform the intellectual works and the academic field about athletes, those contents tend to place an overwhelming focus on African American males who participate in revenue-generating sports (i.e., football and men's basketball in most regions of the country). This is troubling for a number of reasons. First, when data are collected and reported in such a way that excludes women, it may increase the likelihood that stakeholders make assumptions about how the experiences of both groups may be identical. Second, if we assume that the experiences are similar or identical, there may be little interest and greater inclination to overlook women who participate in collegiate athletics.

This chapter focuses on African American women, what it means to participate in athletics in American society, and the intersectionality between race and gender. To frame the discourse about women of color, it draws from black feminist thought. Also explored are the ways in which the black female athlete is socially constructed, how those constructions impact the way they experience university life, and the role Title IX legislation has played in supporting women of color. Finally, how black female athletes experience university life is discussed.

CONSTRUCTING AFRICAN AMERICAN WOMEN IN LITERATURE

While the literature regarding African American females is sparse at best, the work regarding African American males appears to have stimulated some interest over the past 10 or so years. In 1997 Sellers, Kupermine, and Damas noted that only two empirical studies focused specifically on the college experiences of African American female athletes. During my own literature review, studies regarding African American female athletes were scant at best. A quick and nonscientific search in Google Scholar for the specific terms, "African American female student athletes" yielded only 25 articles. A similar search substituting the word females for males yielded almost 10 times that number. This "research" merely suggests that neither area of exploration has been exhausted by any means. Yet it also might suggest that little attention has been paid to the exploration of African American women who participate in intercollegiate athletics.

The examination of African American females who attend colleges and universities (those who do not participate in sports) seems to have become more prevalent in recent years. This research is particularly interesting given that many studies suggest that African American females are in general, more "resilient" as a group, and in some writings black women have been donned with the "arrogant" status of "model minority"—arrogant frankly, because the backhanded term is often misappropriated to some groups of color suggesting that racialized groups outperform other racialized groups. This clearly patronizing description pays little attention to the complexity of context and historical underpinnings of oppression with which the group may have encountered and still faces. In addition, the celebration of a model minority's exaggerated success is traditionally based on stereotypes and myths about racialized groups (Takaki, 1989; Wise, 2002).

More unsettling, conferring "model" status to any particular group insinuates a troubling subtext—that other racialized or gendered groups perform less well and fail under similar or identical social contexts, structures, and challenges. The consequence can easily pit one group against the other by subtly suggesting that it "get over" its challenges like the model group, which has been more successful at facing similar challenges (Wise, 2002). Most importantly, it provokes the reckless and pathological question, What is the matter with that other group? Descriptors such as hardworking, even-tempered, knows how to handle situations with dignity and class, and articulate, scripts African women and other model groups as "different" without really exploring or understanding much about their own unique historical context, positionality, or life circumstances at all.

For instance, regarding ahistorical knowledge and quasi context, Tim Wise (2002) notes that "the Black population represents a cross-section of all Black people in America" (para. 6). Voluntary minorities tend to have the skills and the money needed to leave their countries in the first place. In essence, the immigrant populations most often regarded as "model" are largely a skewed representation of a subset of multiple countries. Indeed, according to Takaki (1989), Asian and Pacific Island groups that are not doing as well, according to United States pundits' and politicians' standards, are still considered "model" simply because of phenotype. In essence, they are lumped together—rendering the unemployed Hmong, the downtown Chinese, the elderly Japanese, the old Filipino farm workers, and others, as invisible.

Similar rhetoric places black women at odds with black men and ignores the historical, Eurocentric, patriarchal power structure in America. The experiences of black women and black men and how they are positioned in American culture are dissimilar. The context and circumstances of such context in which any group lives overwhelmingly determine their discourse and how each group is constructed and reified in American society. "African American men are often positioned and perceived as posing a greater threat to the power structure of a white social order more so than Africana American women, so it makes sense that they may be at greater risk in white social context" (Sellers et al., 1997, p. 716). Further, America's penchant for upholding a system steeped in hegemony, control, congratulatory inequities, and capitalism tends to drive who becomes a "model" and juxtaposes it with the economic demands and exploitation. America's need to control groups— without the equity, of course, and opportunistic economic structure (economic exploitation)—serves as incubator for the creation of a "model" minority when "America" feels it necessary.

Ultimately, however, the rhetoric is similar: that a lauded, hardworking, fill-in-the-gap group's success is contrasted with the performance of an ill-prepared and failing fill-in-the-gap group. The new discourse includes comparing hardworking and, in particular, "resilient" African American women with African American males. Indeed, "model" rhetoric creates the "new black"—African American women—absent the reality that people of color face persistent barriers relative to whites and that they struggle tremendously throughout American life (Wise, 2002).

FRAMING AFRICAN AMERICAN FEMALES IN SPORT

Patriarchy and hence feminism alone do not adequately describe the social space or positioning that black women occupy in America. Black women find it difficult to separate race, class, and sexual oppression because they are most often experienced at the same time. Black women have to redefine and deconstruct the complexity of race within such a society that continuously reifies race. The historical context and uniquely peculiar historical institution of slavery and racism assures us that black men neither live in the same nor do they have the similar relations to patriarchal or capitalist hierarchies as white men. And white women's experiences are also unique to their own epistemologies, which are far different from that of black women. White women have been oppressed by white men, and white men hold institutionalized power and currency throughout the world. Therefore, it is normal that black women feel solidarity with progressive black men and do not advocate the fractionalization from their experiences and reality (Combahee River Collective, 1977). The lived experience of both black men and women, as people of color, necessitates solidarity around the constructions of race and gender (Hill Collins, 1989; Moraga & Anzaldua, 1981). Together, black women struggle with black men against racism, while struggling with black men and sexism (Morga & Anzaldua, 1981). Black women and men of the African diaspora have also been overwhelmingly impacted by racism, thus making them partners in the struggle against racialized oppression (Combahee River Collective, 1977; Moraga & Anzaldua, 1981).

Black feminist thought recognizes the differences in the experiences of black women in the United States. It describes the experiences of black women who exists within a structure of patriarchy and racist hegemony and supplants thinking about universal feminism with the accepted wisdom that black women and men struggle together against racism, while they also struggle about sexism (Combahee River Collective, 1977).

Patricia Hill Collins suggests that black women in particular should consider alternative epistemologies for assessing a black woman's perspective. In particular they should employ those epistemological stances that use standards and realities that are more consistent with the ways in which black women come to understand their own existence in the world. In particular, using an Afrocentric frame of reference makes most sense when considering black women's common experience of oppression (Hill Collins, 1989) because, in spite of the varying histories, black societies reflect elements of a core African value system that existed prior to and independent of racial oppression (Hill Collins, 1989). While black women share a history of patriarchal oppression with their feminist sisters, because of race and the black males' position in racist America, feminism does not do an adequate job of framing the African American women's perspective (Combahee River Collective, 1977; Moraga & Anzaldua, 1981).

Because there is some overlap between Africanist and feminist perspectives, Hill Collins (1989) suggests that black women consider both epistemological realties. In fact, "much of what it termed women's culture which was created in the context of and produced by oppression is unlike African America culture" . . . In essence, those who argue for a women's culture," Hill Collins states, "are electing to value, rather than denigrate, those traits associated with females in white patriarchal societies" (p. 756).

Title IX was created from such a feminist framework. Feminist groups have made significant strides in bringing to fruition upward mobility for women in general. Yet, more specifically, Title IX has provided the momentum needed in order to disproportionately increase gains for white women in the world of sport and athletics.

This should come as no surprise, given the manner in which the legislation was framed. While the women who were most instrumental worked from a feminist framework, the senators' introduction of the bill clearly set the stage for whom the legislation was created. In his remarks on the Senate floor, Birch Bayh generalized the experiences of all women and sealed the legislation that was to support "universal" womanhood. He stated:

> We are all familiar with the stereotype of women as pretty things who go to college to find a husband, go on to graduate school because they want a more interesting husband, and finally marry, have children, and never work again. The desire of many schools not to waste a "man's place" on a woman stems from such stereotyped notions, but the facts absolutely contradict these myths about the "weaker sex" and it is time to change our operating assumptions. (Michaelson, 2012)

Importantly, while this description seemed to have fully resonated with feminist and white women, it did little to describe the experiences and positionality of women of color. In fact, black women have never been presented nor have they been constructed in American society as the weaker sex, looking for husbands to support them while staying at home and never having to work. To the contrary, African American women have been stereotypically described and denigrated as mammies, auntie's (as in Aunt Jemima), Jezebel, the bad, vexing, seductive, black-girl, and Sapphire, the head-snaking, smart and loud black woman who lets everyone know that she is running things (Yarbrough & Bennett, 2000), in addition to more contemporary markers including ho, welfare queen, and mannish. Even historic discourse reveals the negative depiction of African American women. In her 1851 speech "Ain't I a Woman," Sojourner Truth contrasts the intersectionality of race and gender: "That man over there says that women need to be helped into carriages and lifted over ditches, and to have the best place everywhere. Nobody ever helps me into carriages, or over mud-puddles, or gives me any best place!" (Truth, 1851).

The point is this: the universal description that Baye put forth on the legislative floor had little to do with the experiences, descriptions, or social constructions of black women. Given his testimony, he and others assumed a collective identity and constructive of what it means to be "female" in the United States—giving little credence to the experiences and political and economic status of women of color and black women specifically (Hill Collins, 1989).

HISTORICAL ANTECEDENTS OF TITLE IX

It is impossible to engage in a discourse centered on women in sports and athletics and not engage in discussion of about Title IX. The legislation has been celebrated as "monumental" in protecting the rights of women and girls who participate in sports (Musil, 2007; Valentin, 1997). Title IX originated from the 1965 presidential Executive Order that prohibited federal contractors from discrimination in employment on the basis of race, color, religion, or national origin and later amended to include discrimination based on gender (Valentin, 1997).

The feminist movement played a large role in the advancement of Title IX. The legislation would purportedly impact how women and girls would be influenced in educative space. Title IX, section 1681, (a) states that: "No person in the United States shall, on the basis of sex, be excluded from participation in, be denied the benefits of, or be subjected to discrimination under any education program or activity receiving federal financial assistance" (Title IX, 1972).

Has Title IX been successful? Reports regarding the impact of Title IX legislation on the upward mobility of women (Hatcher, 2004) send a clear message—women, in general, have received some benefits—some of the support systems could be considered staggering. However, rarely do those progress reports disaggregate benefits by race. For instance, when reporting presidential and administrative trends in higher education, Musil (2007) notes that "by 1986 the number of women college presidents had tripled from 1970 to almost 10 percent, and by 2006 it reached 23 percent, with a large proportion serving as presidents of community colleges" (p. 44). However, when those figures are disaggregated by race, the story becomes more telling.

King and Gomez (2007) found that black women were only 3.9% of the number of all woman presidents in 1986. That number almost doubled in 2006—but to a mere 7.1%. White women, on the other hand, occupied 89.4% of those positions in 1986, and in 2006 held 81% of the positions of all women presidents. Ultimately, disag-

Eric Ware, Consultant and Motivational Speaker

Eric Ware is the father of a soon-to-be high school athlete. He is also partial owner of a newly created high performance athletic training organization. I was able to sit in during a conversation that he had with three young African American girls about what it means to demonstrate sportsmanlike behavior, uphold a positive attitude, and learn to be accountable to themselves as athletes and to each other as teammates. All three girls participated in club sports and were selected to play as high-ability athletes on an elite team.

As the meeting progressed, Mr. Ware explained that African American girls are particularly rare in some sports. He asked the girls whether they noticed anything about themselves in comparison to the other girls who played club ball. The girls seemed puzzled. I was unable to discern whether the confusion came from a lack of understanding of the question or some hesitancy on their part to answer a question about a taboo topic or whether it, the question, resonated with them at all. Following a few prompts, Eric conveyed that club ball is a very unique way to engage in sports and that, in fact, club ball can be a racialized sporting event. The girls appeared to be puzzled, confused, and a bit nervous. He went on to explain that it is available to those families who can afford to play. "What does that have to do with people of color?" he asked. "How many black girls have you noticed playing this sport? How many people look like you?" While the girls indicated that they had some knowledge of the number of African American girls who played the sport, they did not seem to pay much attention to why.

Eric reminds the girls that they must be thankful to their ancestors and parents for their own hard work, because it was exactly that, hard work that might help support their movement from high school, to college, and on to become whatever professional that they wanted to become. True to the theme of African American uplift and community, Eric talked about giving back and becoming good role models to their teammates and giving back to their communities. Perhaps most interesting was that Eric not only noticed that the girls were particularly talented but also encouraged them to be more accountable for the work that they did on the court and to hold each other accountable. During this meeting, he devised a way for the young girls to "check" on each other. He referred to the process, as "I'm ok." During this exercise the girls were to check each other to make sure that they are working to their fullest potential, staying focused, and mentally in tune to the game and to their coaches. Following the talk with the girls, the girls communicated that Mr. Ware's insight was helpful because that conversation taught them not only how they should become better participants in sports but also how they might go about conducting themselves in school and at home. ■

gregating by race tells a different story about black women. If we extrapolate those figures, this would mean that 7.1% of the 23% of women are African American or only about 1%. Further, 8.1% of the 2,148 college presidents in the authors' 2006 survey were African American women, which translates to 174 of more than 2,000 college presidents, and of those 174 the majority are located at junior colleges or historically black colleges and universities (King & Gomez, 2007).

Title IX has provided some benefits for women of color regarding sport participation. However, we still have a long way to go. While the "legislation has been monumental in women's and girls' sport participation the focus of the legislation has been gender equity, not racial equity in women's sports. The most glaring outcome of the legislation is that white woman—as athletes and administrators—have been the overwhelming beneficiaries" (Rhoden, 2012, para. 4). The impact can be seen from all levels of sport participation beginning with club sports, which tend to be where girls first become acclimated into sports, and throughout high school; subsequently, white women are disproportionate beneficiaries at the collegiate level in all sports except for basketball.

In a 1972 report regarding gender equity, women held 90% of the coaching positions for women's collegiate teams, and in 2010 they held only 65% of these positions. However, disaggregating those numbers reveals that African American women held only 35 of the 300 positions in 2010 while white women occupied around 165. Ultimately women in general and black women specifically still face challenges 40 years beyond legislation. While there have been some significant changes for women over the years, there is still need for more nuanced and introspective interpretations and action that would include viewing legislation from multiple equity lenses gender and race.

THE EXPERIENCE

In general athletes experience college differently than those who do not participate in sports (Comeaux, 2010; Hughes et al., 2007). Athletes spend a significant amount of time participating in sport-related activities and therefore are far less likely to be able to find time to participate in activities outside of their own sport. African American females in particular find themselves uniquely positioned in their athletic environment, juxtaposed within their institutions of higher education. Not only do they encounter uncomfortable gendered incidences within the sporting context; African American females are also fraught with racialized incidences during their collegiate careers (Bruening, Armstrong, & Pastore, 2005; Corbett & Johnson, 2000).

While there have a been a few scholars who have explored the experiences of African American women who attend college, there have been only a few that have provided the world of intercollegiate athletics and higher education in general with a rare look at the African American female athlete's experience. Bruening et al. (2005) is a unique study that uses black feminist thought to examine what role, race, class, and gender and their intersectionality might play in the experiences of African American female athletes throughout their intercollegiate careers.

Some findings have surfaced regarding African American females who participate in athletics. Black women athletes suggest that men's sports seem to be more important than women's sports and that in general they were not respected as athletes (Bruening et al., 2005). For instance, one participant in their study described in great detail how her body was objectified by coaches, who requested that she "put on more clothing" because her body was distracting to the males. The males on the other hand, routinely worked out without shirts. While gendering and objectifying the athlete's body mattered in the Bruening and colleague's study, just a half century earlier African American women who were beginning to dominate American track and field teams were considered mannish and brutish, so they were pushed to participate into sports that were constructed as "mannish" such as track (Cain, 2001, p. 349).

Given America's unique history of slavery and subjugation, it comes as no surprise that positions and entire athletic disciplines have been scripted as feminine or masculine or racially categorized as a black or white sport or position (Cain, 2001). Even today, black female athletes are subjected to racialized sports positions. In fact, not only are black women stereotyped and pushed to play particular sports, they are also stereotyped into certain types of sporting positions (Bruening et al., 2005; Cain, 2001; Hughes et al., 2007). This is not new—similar positional stereotyping occurs in men's sports whereby African American males are routinely placed into various sports positions or roles (Adesioye, 2008). For instance, in male-dominated sports such as football, the coveted role of quarterback has routinely been racialized (Schalter, 2012).

Similar stereotypes occur in women's sports. Black females have been racially and sexually objectified throughout history (Cain, 2001), and in the twenty-first century, African American female athletes still suggest that communications to and

STAKEHOLDER PERSPECTIVE

Mrs. Kent, Mother of an African American Female Youth Who Participates in Club and High School Sports

Mrs. Kent has a daughter who participates in club sports. She noted that the first day that she walked into the sports venue, the playing field was overwhelmingly white. Mrs. Kent finds it interesting that the resources required to participate in some club sports are fairly inexpensive. As she stated, "You only need a net and a ball—just like basketball." Yet, the participation fees in club sports generally are expensive and often considered to be part of a great divide. Most parents with children in club sports are those who not only are wealthy and middle class (Rohwer, 1994) but seem to be determined to find any route to collegiate scholarships, including through club sports (Rohwer, 1994). Similarly, Mrs. Kent stated that, "There is a way to isolate oneself in sports in order to get an advantage, and I expect that from parents." However, it's a problem when you eliminate the competition by opening it up only to those who have the ability to pay—not on purpose necessarily. Either way, you create a hidden, in some cases, classist sporting arena. Those parents who are able to pay and shuttle their children from one state event to another are the ones who reap benefits, thus creating a classist and racist structure. They, the moneyed, are creating yet another income stream for the future. Their children are living investments in sports.

Mrs. Kent was conflicted during the meeting. "Don't get me wrong," she stated, "I want my child to do well. However, I am African American. I honor my collective identity. I want all African American girls to have similar or equal chances. It's just not right. It is hard for me to believe that the only people who notice that the sport is predominantly white and female are black parents. In addition, while I am black, I do know that particular black families can afford to play—me, for instance. We fit a certain profile. We are part of this so-called middle class. So, in essence, I am a part of this classist, racist structure. Certainly If I don't say something or do something, then what does that message convey to our children and to the future of sport?" ■

about them have done little to change the discourse (Bruening et al., 2005). For instance, in the Bruening et al. (2005) study, while it would seem more appropriate that a coach might reference a player on an opposing team vis-à-vis jersey number, the team name, mascot, or even a name, an athlete explains how the opposing team's coach screamed at his team to "get the black girl."

Ultimately, during the time spent on the university campuses, college athletes become part and parcel of a new social order, a new social context so to speak. Those environments, including the players, coaches, parents, and campus in general have the will to determine just how those athletes will fare as team member, student, and social human being. Some things we know about black female athletes, and many other things we have yet to learn, and there are even more things that we should be doing. While we know that Title IX was created to support opportunities for women in general, we know that African American women's access to benefits have been disproportionate. We know that African American women must still negotiate challenging educational and sporting environments on college campuses. The question is what are universities and all of its stakeholders willing to do to assure that all aspects of educational and professional environment are equitable? To be sure, Title IX was guided by women who wanted equity in educative spaces for all women. However, the reality is that women of color are less likely to realize the full benefits from that legislation.

CONCLUSION

Multiple possible remedies would assure that all women might realize equitable beneficiaries of Title IX. The most important might include revisiting Title IX and what the legislation has to offer and to whom it has benefited in all sectors. For instance, reauthorization of Title IX might include specifically addressing the intersectionality of race and gender and the unique needs of women of color who represent a multiplicity of diasporadic spaces. Other analysis may include simply reviewing and deconstructing policy and reinterpreting policy from a different lens—most notably that of black feminist thought. This might require that upper administrative bodies be open to women who would lend an authentic voice to policy interpretation. Far too many times organizational spaces that have become racially stagnant and male dominated exist because people, quite frankly, are more comfortable "permitting a few Black women to acquire positions of authority in intuitions that legitimate already existing knowledge and policy. This 'act' encourages them work and accept the already shared community take-for granted assumption that Black females are inferior" (Hill Collins, 1989, p. 753). It is no surprise that "safe" outsiders are rewarded tremendously on college campuses and are ultimately used by institutions to legitimize long-existing racist and patriarchal structures. Simply hiring critical faculty members of color, who tend to see and interpret the world through a different lens, might steadily shift the somewhat skewed balance of equity in sporting spaces.

QUESTIONS FOR DISCUSSION

1. What role might the context of sport play for different groups of students who are athletes? I am specifically and intentionally referring to race and gender and how the context may play a role in sporting environment.

2. How, if at all, do we all participate in the social construction of athletes? Think specifically about athletes who participate in different athletic "realms" such as tennis, golf, swimming, basketball, football. Who participates in those sports? Why? Discuss racial and gender demographics.

3. Why would certain sports, which are typically not expensive, tend to resemble "country club sports"? For instance, what are the demographics of sports like volleyball?

References

Adesioye, L. (2008, August 25). *Is race a factor in sports success?* Retrieved from http://www.theguardian .com/commentisfree/2008/aug/25/race.olympics 2008#start-of-comments

Bruening, J. E., Armstrong, K. L., & Pastore, D. L. (2005). Listening to the voices: The experiences of African American female student athletes. *Research quarterly for exercise and sport, 76*(1), 82–100.

Cain, P. (2001). Women, race, and sports: Life before Title IX. *Journal of Gender, Race and Justice, 4,* 337–351.

Combahee River Collective. (1977). *The Combahee River Collective Statement.* Retrieved from http:// historyisaweapon.com/defcon1/combrivercoll.html

Comeaux, E. (2010). Racial differences in faculty perceptoins of collegiate student athletes' academic and undergraduate achievements. *Sociology of Sport Journal, 27,* 390–412.

Comeaux, E., & Harrison, C. K. (2007). Faculty and male student athletes in American higher education: Racial differences in the environmental predictors of academic achievement. *Race, Ethnicity and Education, 10*(2), 199–214.

———. (2011). A conceptual model of academic success for student-athletes. *Educational Researcher, 40*(5), 235–245.

Corbett, D., & Johnson, W. (1993). The African-American female in collegiate sport: Sexism and racism. *Racism in college athletics: The African*

American athlete's experience. Morgantown, WV: Fitness Information Technology.

Edwards, H. (1984). The black dumb jock: An American sports tragedy. *College Board Review, 131,* 8–11.

Hatcher, K. (2004). *Making the grade* (Unpublished doctoral dissertation). University of Texas at El Paso.

Hill Collins, P. (1989). The social contruction of Black feminist thought. *Signs: Journal of Women in Culture and Society, 14,* 745–773.

Hughes, R. L., Satterfield, J., & Giles, M. S. (2007). Athletisizing black male student-athletes: The social construction of race, sports, myths, and realities. *NASAP Journal, 10*(1), 112–127.

King, J., & Gomez, G. (2007). The American college president: 2007 edition. *ACE Center for Policy Analysis. doi, 10,* 2649160.

Michaelson, L. (2012, June 23). *Full Court.* Retrieved from http://www.fullcourt.com/lee-michaelson /21403/title-ix-former-texas-longhorn-reflects -era-change

Moraga, C., & Anzaldua, G. (1981). This bridge called my back: Writings by radical women of color. Water-town, MA: Persephone.

Musil, C. (2007, Fall). The triumphs of Title IX. *MS. Magazine*, pp. 42–46.

Rhoden, W. (2012, June 10). *Black and white women far from equal under Title IX.* Retrieved from http:// www.nytimes.com/2012/06/11/sports/title-ix-has

-not-given-black-female-athletes-equal-opportunity
.html?_r=0

Rohwer, B. (1994, February 2). Prep voices: Club sports
provide polish, but at what cost? *Los Angeles Times*.
Retrieved from http://articles.latimes.com/1994-02
-02/sports/sp-18109_1_club-sports

Schalter, T. (2012, March 5). *Bleacher Report*. Retrieved
from http://bleacherreport.com/articles/1089725
-why-african-american-qbs-are-systemically
-trained-to-abandon-mechanics

Sellers, R. M., Kuperminc, G. P., & Damas, A. (1997). The
college life experiences of African American women
athletes. *American Journal of Community Psychology, 25*, 699–720.

Singer, J. (2005). Understanding racism through the
eyes of African American male student-athletes.
Race and Ethnicity in Education, 8, 365–386.

Takaki, R. (1989). Asian Americans: The myth of the
model minority. In *Strangers from a different shore:*
A history of Asian-Americans (pp. 1–6). Boston: Little
Brown.

Title IX of the Education Amendments of 1972, 20 U.S.C
§ 1681 (1972).

Truth, S. (1851, May). Ain't I a woman? In *Ain* (Vol. 1,
p. 129).

Valentin, I. (1997). *Title IX: A brief hisotry*. Newton:
Women's Educational Equity Act (WEEA) Resource
Center at EDC.

Wise, T. (2002, October 7). *Con-Fusion ethic: How whites
use Asians to further anti-black racism*. Retrieved
from http://www.timwise.org/2002/10/con-fusion
-ethic-how-whites-use-asians-to-further-anti-black
-racism/

Yarbrough, M., & Bennett, C. (2000). Cassandra
and the "Sistahs": The peculiar treatment of
African American women in the myth of women
as liars. *Journal of Gender, Race and Justice, 24*,
626–657.

CONFERENCE REALIGNMENT and the DEMISE of the ACADEMIC MISSION

Earl Smith and Angela J. Hattery

The path to all of this shake-up and confusion was paved in dollar bills, not academic prestige, collegiality or any other faux virtue anyone in an ivy-covered office tries to peddle.

Dana O'Neil, ESPN.com

KEY TERMS

exploitation ◀

African American male ◀
athletes

conference realignment ◀

We analyze the question posed by Edwards (1979) and others (Greene, 2012; Olson, 1968) about the mechanisms that allowed for the exploitation of the African American athlete (primarily male athletes), especially at the level of intercollegiate competitive sports. The impact of this research has been powerful in making this claim, yet there is limited research some 40 years later to see if it is still valid (Smith, 2014). In fact, Rhoden (2007) argues that African American athletes are "forty million dollar slaves," raising the bar on the question of exploitation. In this chapter, we examine the recent and dramatic conference realignment that has taken place in intercollegiate sports and analyze the ways in which this movement contributes to both the exploitation of African American male athletes and the racialization of the athletic experience for men playing both the revenue-generating sports of football and basketball and the Olympic sports. Conference realignment offers an illustration of the continued exploitation of black bodies.

THE SOCIAL CONSTRUCTION OF RACE

One of the key arguments among sport sociologists is the role that race plays in athletic performance. Scholars like Jon Entine (2000) and John

Hoberman (1997) argue that there are biological advantages that people of African origin or African descent have that may contribute to their overwhelming success in sports like football and track and field. We do not have the space here to explore this argument (see Smith 2014, for a lengthy discussion of this debate), but for our purposes here we summarize the sociological perspective on race.

In contrast to scholars like Entine and Hoberman, sociologists argue that race is not biological but rather is a social construct. This is not to deny that racial groups have biological traits that can be grouped together—including complexion, hair texture, the shape of the eyes or nose, and so on. When sociologists argue that race is a social construct, what they mean is that the categories of race are not based on hard and fast biological traits but are constructed by the social world primarily for the purposes of creating dominant and minority groups and controlling access to power and resources.

One easy way to understand how the social construction of race works is to examine the U.S. Decennial Census, wherein Americans are enumerated every 10 years. Some of the best illustrations of the social construction of race come from analyzing the census categories over time.

For example, in the 1860 census, there were three racial categories: "white," "negro," and "mulatto." Immediately following the U.S. Civil War, a special census was taken in 1865. In this census, those who identified as "negro" or "mulatto" were asked again to confirm their racial identity. Part of the purpose of this special census was to offer "negroes" a chance to be returned to Africa, although by this date most had been born in the United States and only a small percentage had ever been in Africa. What this examination of census categories reveals is that, though individual people did not change, the official construction of their race did.

This pattern of changing racial designations in the U.S. census has continued up to the present day. For example, the category "mulatto" disappeared in both terminology and sentiment until 2000. In the 2000 census, for the first time since the mid-1800s 1800s, individuals could choose more than one race. To be clear, there is no racial category "mixed" or "bi" but people can choose "White" and "Black" or "White" and "Asian." As a result, in the 2010 census approximately 13% of the U.S. population identified as multiracial or as belonging to more than one race (Figure 16.1). The 2000 census was also important because the census moved the designation "Hispanic" out of the set of racial categories and into a special designation of "ethnicity." Interestingly "Hispanic" is currently the *only* ethnic category in the U.S. census.

What does this mean? Consider a case that should be familiar to scholars and consumers of sports. Imagine someone like Sammy Sosa or Albert Pujoles. According to the 1990 census, both men's race was "Hispanic." In 2000 and again in 2010, they now had to decide if they were "black," "white," "Asian/pacific islander," or "native American/Alaskan native." Racially, they were no longer Hispanic, at least in terms of race according to the U.S. government though they were able to choose the designation "Hispanic" as their ethnicity. Both Sammy Sosa and Albert Pujoles are the same people in 1990 and 2000 and again in 2010, the traits we identify as

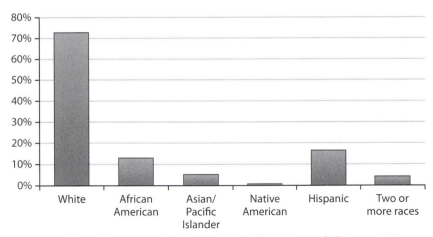

Figure 16.1. Racial distribution in US population (2010 Census). (*Source:* U.S. Census Bureau, *2010 Census Redistricting Data.*)

"racial"—skin tone, hair texture, and so forth—did not change, but their racial identity did.

Not surprisingly, in 2000 and again in 2010 the majority of "Hispanics" left the racial category blank. It did not make sense to them that they were anything other than "Hispanic." All of these are examples of what sociologists mean when they say that race is a social construct (Lopez, 2000).

Finally, as one of the authors argues extensively elsewhere (see Smith, 2014), race matters. Race matters in terms of what sports you play; race matters in terms of the positions played in some team sports; and it matters whether you can coach or own a team (Smith, 2014).

EXPLOITATION AND THE SPORTS WORLD

Exploitation in the strict sense of the term—whether analyzing manufacturing workers, males and females, or college athletes or professional athletes—is centered on two core issues that are relevant to our discussion of the exploitation of athletes: (1) the relationship between owners and workers and (2) paying the worker—in this case, the athlete—less than he is worth.

For those readers who have plowed through Marx's (2000) *Theories of Surplus Value* and other work on labor theory of value, we know that in the United States at least African American laborers and athletes share a similar fate (Meek, 1956). The point of the matter is that just as Marx spelled out theoretically, hundreds of years ago, unless you own the means of production, you are working for someone who does. That person has the power to set the values of one's labor and therefore one's salary as well as the working conditions, length of the contract, and so on. Marx (2000) uses his *Labor Theory of Value* to derive his theory of exploitation under capitalism:

The worker becomes all the poorer the more wealth he produces, the more his production increases in power and range. The worker becomes an ever-cheaper commodity the more commodities he creates. With the increasing value of the world of things proceeds in direct proportion to the devaluation of the world of men. Labor produces not only commodities; it produces itself and the worker as a commodity—and does so in the proportion in which it produces commodities generally. (p. 169)

We employ this explanation to address conference realignment and the exploitation of African American male athletes. McCormick and McCormick (2010) have argued that the bulk of the revenue generated for athletic departments at the nation's colleges and universities is generated on the backs of African American athletes. They further suggest that because the recipients of this revenue and those who set the labor standards and compensation—which amounts to access to a college scholarship—are almost exclusively white men that college football and to a lesser extent college basketball operate like a slave plantation.

Although we can debate the degree to which the college scholarship is an adequate compensation for the labor of these mostly African American young men, and although, as one of the authors has argued extensively elsewhere (see Smith, 2014), while revenue is indeed generated, few athletic departments make a *profit*, conference realignment shines a light on the nature of the exploitation of the African American athlete by white institutions.

CONFERENCE REALIGNMENT

Intercollegiate athletic conferences were originally established to organize schools by both size and geography. Conference realignment has been going on for decades but has exploded in the past year. In short, conference commissioners—who are all white men—are scrambling to assemble and reconfigure conferences in ways that give them the most potential to make money. Although most, if not all, of the institutions engaged in realignment argue that they will profit from such moves, there is very little in these discussions about the ways which money would be distributed to each individual school.

Rather, as we suggest, this movement is about making the conference lucrative and the conference commissioners wealthy and powerful. Conference commissioners have become so powerful that they are more powerful than college presidents and athletic directors. This movement is also an attempt on the part of the conference commissioners to effectively remove the influence and power of the National Collegiate Athletic Association over college football. Not surprisingly, completely absent in the discussion is any consideration of the impact of conference realignment on athletes. Indeed, noted sports writer Buzz Bissinger (2012) wrote an article whose title provides a summary for our argument here: "Why College Football Should

Be Banned: The Costs Are High, the Benefits to Students Are Low, and Academics Pay the Price."

In the limited discussions of the costs of conference realignment to athletes, there is virtually no discussion of the ways in which the impact is shaped by race. In fact, if race matters so much in intercollegiate sports, why has no one stepped back from the euphoria that money causes for university presidents, NCAA officials, athletic directors, and coaches to seriously consider the unintended and unanticipated consequences of the race implications of conference realignment?

In the social sciences, unintended consequences (sometimes referenced as unanticipated consequences or unforeseen consequences) are outcomes that are not the ones intended by a purposeful action (Merton, 1936). The concept has long existed—at least since Adam Smith's *The Wealth of Nations* (Tribe & Mizuta, 2000)—but was named and popularized in the twentieth century by the American sociologist Robert K. Merton. This "law" of unintended consequences is what happens when a simple system tries to regulate a complex system, and this is what we see happening with what we call the conference realignment movement.

According to sociologist Merton (1936), unintended consequences can be roughly grouped into three types:

1. A positive, unexpected benefit (usually referred to as luck, serendipity, or a windfall)

2. A negative, unexpected detriment occurring in addition to the desired effect of the policy (e.g., while irrigation schemes provide people with water for agriculture, they can increase waterborne diseases that have devastating health effects, such as schistosomiasis)

3. A perverse effect contrary to what was originally intended (when an intended solution makes a problem worse), such as when a policy has a perverse incentive that causes actions opposite to what was intended

Theoretically, we employ Merton's schema to identify the unintended and unanticipated consequences in intercollegiate football as it moves toward superconferences as a way to both own and control the growing profits embedded in the hypercommercialism of media rights to broadcasting college football games and to control access to the lucrative system of elite bowl games.

The driving impetus for what we see in the conference realignment movement is the consummation of a 24-hour radio and TV deal that the University of Texas made public on January 19, 2011. This arrangement, with ESPN and the University of Texas IMG College, a company that handles marketing and licensing contracts for the university, is for 20 years and for as much as $300 million (Haurwitz & Maher, 2011).

Once Texas opened the door for establishing independent and lucrative television contracts, other institutions and entire conferences followed suit. Schools began jockeying for positions in the conferences with the most lucrative television contracts. At the same time as the television contracts were being negotiated, the Bowl Championship Series was establishing the first playoff system in college football and negotiated this playoff outside of the auspices of the NCAA. This contributed to conference jumping, as every major athletic program understood the importance of being in a conference that would be included by the BCS commissioners in the playoff system. Once conference realignment got started it would not stop. Schools were jumping all over the map, many illogically.

The Racial Implications

There are many consequences of conference realignment, including significant budgetary increases associated with travel but also fees to join and exit conferences; and the disruption of natural rivalries. In this discussion, we focus on two key issues related to conference realignment and race:

1. Conference realignment is expected to further the exploitation of African American athletes.

2. The complete and final disruption of the academic mission of colleges and universities as these apply to athletes is assured. We simply can no longer say that athletes, at least those playing Football Bowl Subdivision (FBS) football and basketball, can realistically earn an education, and this is especially detrimental to many African American athletes whose singular route to an education is via an athletic scholarship.

An examination of conference realignment lays bare these realities. However, because this movement is so recent (as noted, 49 teams were "realigned" on July 1, 2013), there is not yet a scholarly literature on this issue. Thus, our discussion here is theoretical and is based on examination of news accounts as well as scholarly literature that focuses on exploitation of African American athletes. Scholarship by researchers such as Harry Edwards and Amy and Robert McCormick and our own previous research have clearly demonstrated that increasing exploitation of African American male athletes by institutions governed almost entirely by white men continues into the twenty-first century (Edwards 1979; Smith 2014).

One of our main concerns is that with all of this conference movement, extensive travel will keep the athlete away from class, which makes meeting their academic requirements more difficult. We have reviewed decades' worth of graduation rate data (see Smith, 2014) that documents disturbingly low graduation rates for African American men who play football and basketball. We anticipate that one unintended consequence of conference realignment is to push even lower the graduation rates for African American men.

Why do we care if African American athletes graduate or not? First of all, we should care. As the NCAA is fond of advertising, there are more than 4,000 athletes, and most will "go pro" in something other than sports. Whether they want to believe it or not, this applies to both the vast majority of African American male athletes as well. Thus, getting a college education is still their primary route to accessing the American Dream. Why? Because so few of these athletes will ever make it to the professional leagues (Beamon & Bell, 2002).

Second, all of the debates about the exploitation of the African American male athlete focus on the fact that it is primarily *their* labor that generates enormous revenues for athletic departments (McCormick & McCormick, 2010). Despite the fact that most of these revenues do not become profits, they do contribute to the ability—or at least the justification—for paying enormous salaries to head football coaches and athletics directors (see Greene, 2012). Head football coaches make salaries that are often 10 times higher than college presidents and 100 times greater than full professors. A sore point for many of us. In short, the argument is that the labor of African American men generates the profits for white men (McCormick & McCormick, 2010)—the very exploitation Marx wrote about.

Defenders of this system, including the NCAA, argue that the reward or "pay" that college athletes receive for their labor are the scholarships they receive: full scholarships that range in value from $20,000 to 60,000 per year, and the ability to earn a college education that may otherwise remain elusive to many of these athletes (see Pennington, 2008). Thus, when African American male athletes fail to graduate, they fail to receive the reward that is believed to be the promise for their labor.

If we are right, and conference realignment decreases the likelihood of graduating from college—because athletes are away from campus more days, which

Men's Basketball Coaches

The key stakeholders in conference realignment would appear to be the NCAA, the conference commissioners, the athletic directors, athletes, and the head coaches of football and men's basketball. Why, then, we wondered, would Syracuse leave the Big East? According to Coach Jim Boeheim, "If conference commissioners were the founding fathers of this country, we would have Guatemala, Uruguay, and Argentina in the United States . . . The audience knows why we are doing this. There are two reasons: Money and football."

The decision indeed by Syracuse to leave the Big East was based on what was best for the football program. Though Syracuse football has not been as successful in the past decade as it was in the past, the Orangemen and fans hold out hope that the team will return to glory. As storied as the Big East is in college basketball, it is perhaps the weakest of the power conferences in college football. And it is due to become weaker when Rutgers leaves in 2014. Thus, Syracuse made a decision that was ideal for football but tragic for

basketball (and presumably all other sports). That is, at least until the Big East was dismantled. Today that decision looks to be a winner for Syracuse.

The only stakeholders that matter are the conference commissioners who stand to make millions of dollars through television contracts and through the administration of the first ever playoff in elite college football. Most everyone else, especially athletes, will lose. ■

results in more days of missed classes and missed work and additional pressures to make up work—then clearly the exploitation of these men and their labor increases in proportion. According to legal scholars Robert and Amy McCormick (2011), "Today a largely African-American work force generates extraordinary wealth by creating the product of college sports, but those players are forbidden to share in that wealth. Instead, NCAA amateurism rules guarantee that the money will be reserved to benefit the overwhelmingly European-American managers of the college-sports industry" (para. 4).

The Impact on Everyone except Football: In Other Words, White Men

Conference realignment is about money. What will be the impact of conference realignment on white athletes, who participate at the highest rates in the Olympic sports, including baseball, soccer, tennis, golf, swimming and diving, and lacrosse?

As we have noted, conference realignment will require many athletic departments to identify and funnel a greater amount of resources (e.g., money), to football programs in order to accommodate the increased travel costs that are almost always associated with conference realignment. Although conference commissioners and athletic directors may suggest that the creation of a power conference will increase revenue, there is no indication of exactly how this might happen or even if it will.

Conference realignment will increase travel costs for the football team. Where will the money come from? Even now, most FBS football programs are not profitable; they lose money and thus require subsidies from the general operating budget in order to bring them into the "black" (see Smith, 2014). Inside the athletic department itself, the competition for resources will be even more intense.

Another concern we have is that conference realignment may further exacerbate the different types of athletic experiences that African American and white athletes often already have. For example, resource differences can also create experiential differences. Athletes playing in the revenue-generating sports of football and men's basketball are far more likely to travel by air, on chartered flights, and stay in more upscale hotels than their Olympic sports counterparts, who are far more likely to travel by van, even long distances, and often report staying in substandard motels.

Conference realignment has the potential to have devastating consequences for Olympic sports. Most likely, these sports—which are dominated by white men—will see their budgets trimmed as a result of the increased cost of travel for the football team. These teams will likely have their travel budgets remain flat or they could even be cut, which will prohibit the types of long-distance travel that the football team will participate in. For example, they might be able to schedule fewer nonconference games—which is critically important for rankings—or they might see the conference split into north and south or east and west with teams only playing those on their "side."

Other strategies to funnel more money toward football may lead to other types of budget cuts to the Olympic sports, which could impact coaches' salaries, the number of assistant coaches, equipment budgets, food budgets, and so on. All of these restrictions will create a different—and inarguably inferior—experience for Olympic sports athletes.

Conference realignment could thus have several significant outcomes:

1. Realignment will increase the quality of the exploitation of African American male athletes. Specifically, the added travel, perhaps accumulating up to six lengthy trips per season, will make it harder for the athletes to complete academic work, earn credit, and ultimately graduate. This failure to attain an academic degree, which is the express "payment" for their performance on the field and the enormous revenues they generate, creates a system that can only be characterized as exploitation.

2. The movement of teams between conferences alone coupled with increased exploitation completes the disruption of the academic mission of the university and renders the professed educational mission of the NCAA a total sham, despite NCAA president Mark Emmert's claims that "the association's mission is to be an integral part of higher education and to focus on the development of our student athletes" (NCAA, 2012).

3. Conference realignment will inevitably "racialize" the athlete experience. The racialization of these experiences will further racial antagonisms and produce even more segregation. Not only will the athlete be separated from the rest of the campus but also an internal segregation will occur in which football and men's basketball players, with heavy travel requirements, will frequently be off campus, while the other athletes will be limited to partial conference competition or even insignificant nonconference play.

CONCLUSION

Conference realignment is perhaps the most significant shaper of the future of intercollegiate sports and also the most unpredictable. Even just two or three years ago there were whispers about the possibility of massive conference realignment and the probability of individual conferences negotiating lucrative television contracts separately from the NCAA's gaze and control. Though several of the teams involved in this realignment play basketball only, specifically the schools that now compose the "new" Big East (the American Athletic Conference), this constitutes nearly 15% of all basketball teams that moved to a new conference on July 1, 2013.

Big East Conference

The most compelling situation in all of conference realignment has to be the case of the Big East. The Big East has a long and storied history in college basketball. The Big East tournament, played in Madison Square Garden, is considered by many to be not only the premier conference tournament but also as big a deal as all of March Madness. Over the years, 80% to 90% of Big East teams have received a bid to the NCAA tournament, and in many years more than one team survived to play in the Final Four.

The Big East has never been a powerful football conference; in fact, about half of the institutions in the Big East do not field football teams, but they have had a few football programs that have had some success over the years, notably Syracuse, the University of Pittsburgh, and, most recently, Rutgers. As conference realignment shifted into high gear, the Big East saw its "football" schools being offered opportunities (or being poached, depending on your vantage point) in conferences with more significant football histories. Both Syracuse and Pitt were offered opportunities to join the ACC, along with Louisville, and Rutgers was invited to join the Big 10. As the Big East member institutions assessed the landscape and saw that the conference was losing members, institutions knew they had to do something. In a bold move, the group that came to be known as the Catholic Seven—a collection of Catholic schools that were competitive programs in Big East basketball and do not field football teams—decided to secede from the Big East and form their own basketball-only conference. Along with their exit, they managed to negotiate the ownership of the conference name, the Big East.

Simultaneously the former Big East, now the American Athletic Conference, had been adding football members, including Houston, but the history and prestige of the conference were clearly gone. UConn, a premiere basketball program, having won the national championship three times in the last ten years, likely did not anticipate this decimation and dragged its heels and did not jump quickly in pursuing its own move to the ACC.

UConn is perhaps the biggest loser in all of conference realignment. Because UConn did not have a powerful football program, it was not recruited in this realignment away from the Big East. And when the Catholic Seven was able to broker a joint leave from the Big East and take the conference name with it, UConn remained stranded in the new American Athletic Conference. Lost are its historic rivalries with Syracuse, Georgetown, St. Johns, and others, only to be replaced by potential new rivals such as Houston and the University of South Florida. Another "loser" will likely be Boise State, which, like UConn, dragged its heels and did not join the Big East before it became a basketball-only conference.

Perhaps the biggest winners in conference realignment are teams like Houston and South Florida, which by joining a major conference now have the access they need to compete in more prestigious bowl games and possibly for the national championship. ∎

We are certain that conference realignment will have consequences that are racialized. Although some of the impact may appear on the surface to be positive for some African American male athletes, we are concerned that there will be a price to pay for many African American men and that there will be an even lower probability that they will exit their playing careers either with a chance to play professionally or with a college degree. In the end, their labor will yet again be exploited by the machine that is college sports.

All of the Olympic sports—both men's and women's—will also suffer as athletics budgets that are already operating in "the red" will shift even more resources away from these programs that are typically grossly underfunded. Of course, the real loser in all of this may be the student attending the university who is now faced with higher fees that are now the "go to" method for generating revenue to keep athletic departments afloat.

The impact of conference realignment on the Olympic sports will be even greater as a two-tiered system will emerge with the NCAA governing the Olympic sports and independent commissions governing and regulating the most lucrative sports, football and men's basketball. Not only would the NCAA lose the majority of its revenue and power, it would essentially become meaningless.

Furthermore, a system might emerge that looks more like the club and minor league systems we see in Europe, Latin America, and Asia. Again, this will have significant racial implications as well. If football and men's basketball exit the university, significant numbers of African American men will be removed from college campuses, eliminating their opportunity to earn a college degree and decreasing the overall diversity for all students.

QUESTIONS FOR DISCUSSION

1. Given the authors' argument about the impact of conference realignment on Olympic Sports, what would you speculate would be the impact on women's athletics?

2. If you were a head football coach, would you argue to join the "new" American Athletic Conference (where the top basketball teams left to form their own conference) or would you prefer to stay where you are?

3. Do you believe that conference realignment will have negative consequences for African American male athletes? Why or why not?

References

Beamon, K., & Bell, P. (2002). Going pro: The differential effects of high aspirations for a professional sports career on African-American student-athletes and white student-athletes. *Race and Society, 5*, 179–192.

Bissinger, B. (2012). Why college football should be banned: The costs are high, the benefits to students are low, and academics pay the price. Retrieved from http://online.wsj.com/article/SB1000142405270230474370457738229237619422O.html

Edwards, H. (1979). The Olympic project for human rights: An assessment ten years later. *Black Scholar, 10*, 2–8.

Entine, J. (2000). *Taboo.* New York: Public Affairs.

Greene, L. S. (2012). Head football coaches: Ending the discourse of privilege. *Wake Forest Journal of Law & Policy, 2*(1), 115–142.

Haurwitz, R. K. M., & Maher, J. (2011, January 20). UT sets new standard with $300 million ESPN deal: Few if any other schools could match such a TV network arrangement, officials say. *American-Statesman.* Retrieved from http://www.statesman.com/news/local/ut-sets-new-standard-with-300-million-espn-1197020.html

Hoberman, J. (1997). *Darwin's athletes.* New York: Houghton Mifflin.

Lopez, I. (2000). The social construction of race. In R. Delgado & J. Stefancic (Eds.), *Critical race theory: The cutting edge* (pp. 163–175). Philadelphia: Temple University Press.

Marx, K. (2000.) *Theories of surplus value*. New York: Prometheus Books.

McCormick, R., & McCormick, A. (2010). Major college sports: The new apartheid. *Texas Review of Entertainment & Sports Law, 12*, 1533–1903.

———. (2011, May 15). Amateurism rules benefit whites at blacks' expense. Letter to the Editor, *Chronicle of Higher Education*. Retrieved from http://chronicle.com/article/Amateurism-Rules-Benefit/127544/

Meek, R. (1956). *Studies in the labor theory of value*. New York: Monthly Review Press.

Merton, R. (1936). The unanticipated consequences of purposive social action. *American Sociological Review, 1*, 894–904.

National Collegiate Athletics Association. (2012). *On the collegiate model of athletics*. Retrieved from http://www.ncaa.org/wps/wcm/connect/public/NCAA/NCAA+President/On+the+Mark

Olson, J. (1968, July 1). The black athlete—A shameful story. *Sports Illustrated*. Retrieved from http://sportsillustrated.cnn.com/vault/article/magazine/MAG1081325/

O'Neil, D. (2012). *When stardom ends in college*. Retrieved from http://espn.go.com/mens-college-basketball/story/_/id/8079374/college-players-see-failure-their-future-reach-nba-college-basketball

———. (2013). Realignment not as bad as we think: From retro big east to the new-look ACC, plenty of positives with realignment. *ESPN.com*. Retrieved from http://espn.go.com/mens-college-basketball/story/_/id/9458453/how-college-basketball-emerged-conference-realignment

Pennington, B. (2008, March 10). The scholarship divide: Expectations lose to reality of sports scholarships. *New York Times*. Retrieved from http://www.nytimes.com/2008/03/10/sports/10scholarships.html?pagewanted=all

Rhoden, W. C. (2007). *$40 million slaves: The rise, fall, and redemption of the black athlete*. New York: Crown.

Smith, E. (2014). *Race, sport and the American dream* (3rd ed.). Durham, NC: Carolina Academic Press.

Tribe, K., & Mizuta, H. (2002). *A critical bibliography of Adam Smith*. London: Pickering & Chatto.

PART SIX

Gender Equity and Compliance Issues

Signed into law more than four decades ago, Title IX of the Education Amendments of 1972 bars sex discrimination in all aspects of federally funded education programs. The statute is perhaps best known for barring sex discrimination in intercollegiate athletics, and a subset of Title IX compliance standards has been designed specifically for this purpose. The chapters in part VI address various dimensions of the resulting dynamic. Chapter 17, by Nancy Lough, describes the history of Title IX and its impact on women's participation in intercollegiate athletics. In chapter 18, Jennifer Lee Hoffman, Jacqueline McDowell, and Valyncia Raphael examine several legal cases that have influenced athletics for women in American higher education. Chapter 19 presents Barbara Osborne's discussion of the standards used to determine whether intercollegiate athletic programs are in compliance with current gender equity requirements, as well as the implications of these standards. She also examines the enforcement of Title IX through litigation and by the Office for Civil Rights of the U.S. Department of Education. In chapter 20, Erin Buzuvis explores growing trends related to women's representation in leadership positions in intercollegiate athletics, including coaching, administration, and management, and the reasons for women's representation (or lack thereof) in some arenas. ■

EFFECTS OF TITLE IX on INTERCOLLEGIATE ATHLETICS, 1972–2012

Nancy Lough

When Title IX was passed as a section of the Education Amendments that President Richard M. Nixon signed in 1972, it was intended as an education law to remedy sex discrimination within American educational institutions. Bernice Sandler has been credited with drafting portions of the legislation, spurred by her personal experience of being denied a tenure-track position in the late 1960s because she "came on too strong for a woman" (Edwards, 2010, p. 303). Sandler began studying the issue, resulting in the accumulation of 250 complaints of sex discrimination against colleges receiving federal contracts. This list of complaints served as the impetus for the initial introduction of a bill requiring gender equity in education. The bill changed over time, with language used replicating Title VI of the Civil Rights Act of 1964, in which "sex" was substituted for "race, color, or national origin," resulting in the following: "No person in the United States shall, on the basis of sex, be excluded from participation in, be denied the benefits of, or be subjected to discrimination under any educational program or activity receiving Federal financial assistance" (20 U.S.C. 1681).

Originators of the law purposely worked to draw as little attention as possible during the process, concerned attention would weaken the chances of the law passing. As Sandler indicated, "We had no idea how bad the situation was—we didn't even use the word sex discrimination back then—and we certainly had no idea the revolution it would start" (Wulf, 2012, para. 4). The resulting significance of Title IX has been the profound increase in opportunities for women, both in sports and in higher education. While gains for women in college sports have been impressive, with a 622% increase in participation numbers from 1971–1972

KEY TERMS

gender equity ◄

grant-in-aid ◄

proportionality ◄

sex discrimination ◄

Equity in Athletics ◄
Disclosure Act (EADA)

to 2009–2010, gains in education have been equally impressive. In 1972 women earned less than 10% of both law and medical degrees and only 13% of doctoral degrees. By 2012, nearly half of all law and medical degrees and more than half of all doctoral degrees were earned by women.

As a result, some have pointed to Title IX as the most important step toward gender equality, beyond the Nineteenth Amendment giving women the right to vote. Yet the original intent to provide equal educational opportunity for women quickly became lost within a high-profile debate centered on football. Sports became the lightning rod for those opposed to Title IX. Both the National Collegiate Athletic Association (NCAA) and the College Football Association expressed alarm, as they contended Title IX would harm college football.

Two divergent points of view prevailed throughout the decades following Title IX's passage. On one side, Title IX was credited with creating improved gender equity within U.S. colleges and universities, by empowering generations of women to successfully pursue higher education. Contrastingly, those who opposed the law blamed Title IX for the elimination of men's sports programs. Opposition to Title IX never declined, requiring continued vigilance on the part of those who support the law.

WHY WAS TITLE IX NEEDED?

In the decades leading up to Title IX, discrimination against women who sought degrees and careers in higher education was common. For example, during a three-year period in the state of Virginia prior to Title IX, 21,000 female applicants were denied admission to college, while all male applicants were accepted. Several barriers existed throughout the United States for women interested in higher education. Admissions criteria were often 30 to 40 points higher for women applicants than men. Quotas admitting one or two women were an accepted standard within law schools, medical schools, and even doctoral-degree-granting programs, where classes of men could be upwards of 100 or more. This culture of discrimination was also evidenced by requirements for women to live on campus, while men were free to select where they would live. The on-campus housing requirement often was an additional expense, thus acting to impede the opportunity for those women without financial means for the added cost.

While these barriers restricted access to higher education for women, the situation in college sports was no different. Before Title IX, athletic opportunities at the collegiate level were often in the form of "play days" organized by women physical educators. Perhaps most telling, the legendary Billie Jean King, who won multiple Grand Slam titles, was not provided an athletic scholarship, labeled grant-in-aid by the NCAA, to compete in tennis at UCLA. This example points out how the first steps toward a remedy for sex discrimination were awareness and acknowledgment a problem existed.

The congressional passage of Title IX demonstrated the highest level of support toward seeking gender equality in federally funded educational programs. Yet initial interpretations of the law questioned whether it applied to intercollegiate athletics. While the Department of Health & Human Services delayed the initial deadline for institutional compliance until 1978, the Office of Civil Rights (OCR), charged with enforcement of Title IX, did not issue a policy interpretation statement until 1979. The most critical aspect of the 1979 interpretation was labeled the three-prong or three-part test (Johnson, 1994).

Compliance with Title IX requires an institution demonstrates *one* of the following:

Part One: Substantial Proportionality. Satisfaction of this part occurs when participation opportunities are "substantially proportionate" to the respective undergraduate enrollment for men and women.

Part Two: History and Continuing Practice. Satisfaction of this part occurs when an institution can show a history and continuing practice of expanding programs in response to developing interests and abilities of the underrepresented sex.

Part Three: Effectively Accommodating Interests and Abilities. Satisfaction of this part occurs when the interests and abilities of female students have been met by the institution, even where there are disproportionately fewer females than males participating in sport. (U.S. Department of Education, 1997)

Despite this clarification, many institutions were unclear to what degree they were expected to comply with Title IX. The first true legal test required resolution by the Supreme Court in 1984, which for a time meant Title IX did not apply directly to intercollegiate athletics. There have been four distinct stages in the evolution of Title IX, including resistance, marginalization, advocacy, and backlash (Lough, 2012). In each of these stages, major milestones contributed to development of the law as it is understood today.

STAGE 1: RESISTANCE

In the initial period following the passage of Title IX, the rhetoric was often divisive. The conflict was centered primarily on the NCAA's contention that a choice needed to be made between football and women's sports. The NCAA petitioned Congress to be considered "exempt" from Title IX on multiple occasions. The perception was that allocating funding to support women's sports would compromise the established men's programs. During the initial grace period given for implementation and clarification, several amendments were drafted by the NCAA to make men's revenue-producing college sports exempt from Title IX. All were rejected. Then in 1975, final regulations were issued, establishing a three-year time frame for institutions to become compliant with the law. This regulation was reviewed by Congress and signed into law with additional provisions banning sex discrimination. Similarly, the 1979 Policy Interpretation provided the three-prong test for determining compliance, which provided guidance on the requirements for sport participation opportunities. With this, the Office for Civil Rights was assigned oversight authority for Title IX.

The time period from the passage of Title IX through the end of the 1970s, was one marked by limited understanding resulting in a lack of enforcement. One estimate suggested NCAA women's Division IA sports accounted for 14% of the overall athletics budgets in 1977, which meant 86% of all expenditures were on men's sports. For decades the men's programs had benefited from receiving mandatory student fees with this revenue allocated exclusively to men's athletics operating budgets. This was one of many practices demonstrating gender discrimination, yet among college sports leaders it was perceived as fair. Widely accepted practices such as this point to the crux of the struggle for acceptance that women's sports faced in this initial stage of resistance. Change is most often met with resistance, which is one partial explanation for reluctance to share resources. Finally in 1981, after numerous failed attempts to avert Title IX, the NCAA officially adopted women's sports.

STAGE 2: MARGINALIZATION

The marginalization stage is noted for the milestone litigation resulting in suspended operation of women's sports programs among athletic departments from 1984 through 1988. The landmark case of *Grove City College v. Bell* questioned whether programs had to be in *direct* receipt of federal funds to be held to Title IX compliance. The resulting U.S. Supreme Court decision provided two instructive points. First, indirect federal funding did result in Title IX jurisdiction, but in this ruling "the jurisdiction of Title IX applied only to the subunit within the institution that was the *direct* recipient of the federal funding" (Carpenter & Acosta, 2005, p. 195). The second part of this decision resulted in athletic departments no longer falling within the scope of Title IX. In essence, federal funding was linked mostly to grants and financial aid for students; however, in the case of athletics, if an athlete received this type of funding, it was not via the athletic department. Since athletic departments did not directly receive federal funding, there was no need for compliance with Title IX. This case is particularly instructive even today, as the ruling demonstrated that many athletic and institutional leaders were willing to stop the progress that had been made and, in some cases, take steps backward.

During this same period the rapid decline in women's athletic programs and departments led by women, and concomitantly the dissolution of the Association for Intercollegiate Athletics for Women (AIAW), was unfolding. The AIAW had served in the leadership role for women's college sports for decades, offering 41 national championships in 19 sports for more than 6,000 teams representing 960 member institutions (Carpenter & Acosta, 2005). The AIAW had been successful in obtaining television contracts for its women's basketball national championship, which unfortunately led to the NCAA perceiving the AIAW as a competitor. Given the influence the NCAA had with the media, it effectively blocked the AIAW from acquiring new television contracts, which compromised a key revenue source. The AIAW then sued, but lost its antitrust case against the NCAA. The AIAW then dissolved, due largely to an inability to compete with the money the NCAA offered to member schools who qualified for national championships.

The advocacy stage came about largely as a result of the Civil Rights Restoration Act, which in effect restored the original intent of Title IX. Throughout the next decade, the lack of investment in women's sports and failures to focus on Title IX compliance by universities resulted in several lawsuits. The need for litigation to begin the progress toward Title IX compliance marks the beginning of the advocacy stage.

STAGE 3: ADVOCACY

After the first 20 years of Title IX, more opportunities for women's sport participation existed, but sex discrimination continued. The Office of Civil Rights was admittedly reluctant to punish institutions, largely because removal or elimination of federal funding from an institution of higher education was simply too harsh a consequence to levy. The ramifications would be far reaching and clearly beyond the scope of problems existing in the athletic program. As a result, those advocating for change turned to litigation.

One of the most crucial court decisions came from the *Franklin v. Gwinnett County Public Schools* in 1992. While this case was not centered on sports, it was illuminating because it demonstrated that monetary awards, in the form of punitive and compensatory damages, could be awarded to successful Title IX plaintiffs. In this case, the actual issue involved sexual harassment. Initially, Franklin filed a complaint with the OCR, but the result did not meet her expectations. By exercising her private right of action, the case reached the Supreme Court, where a unanimous decision affirmed monetary damages may result from a Title IX lawsuit. This was an important point, since it served as a wake-up call to higher education institutions. In essence, noncompliance with Title IX now posed the threat of substantial financial loss. Some institutions realized the most fiscally appropriate action would be to adhere to compliance standards. However, the male model of college sports was a deeply gendered subculture, which meant advocacy would be met with resistance.

With little help from the OCR, female athletes increasingly pursued litigation to remedy the discrimination in college sports. As higher education began to feel the challenge of an economic downturn in the early 1990s, athletics budgets were reduced and a common response was to eliminate sports, often focusing on women's programs. Multiple lawsuits challenged universities that chose to eliminate women's sports. Perhaps one of the most notable was the case in which the National

Organization for Women (NOW) sued the entire California State University system (19 schools at the time). In this case the Cal State system lost, resulting in a settlement that forced it to develop a plan to provide women sport participation opportunities more closely reflecting the student body ratio of females to males. To achieve the new targets, some institutions chose to eliminate men's sports, instead of adding women's sports. This practice led to media accounts repeatedly blaming Title IX and women's sports for elimination of men's nonrevenue sport programs. Rhetoric around gender equity was typically framed as "battle of the sexes," a "dispute," "fight," or "tug of war" (Staurowsky, 1998, p. 7).

Still the most definitive case to date was *Cohen v. Brown University*. Initiation of the lawsuit was in response to Brown's decision to cut sports for both men and women. Cohen represented the female athletes suing to reinstate their sports. Brown believed the cuts were fair. However, at the time of the cuts, the ratio of male to female athletes was 63.3% to 36.7%. This case is particularly illustrative of a practice many institutions pursued, which was to eliminate an equivalent number of female and male sports. Brown University spent millions of dollars defending its position, which led to more clarity on a number of issues tied to gender equity. First, terminating the same number of sports for men and women is not a "safe passage" to compliance. Second, the "relative interests" theory was pursued as a key argument by Brown. The idea was that by surveying students regarding their interest in sports, the ratio of responses could then be used as a gauge to measure proportionality and thereby demonstrate compliance with Title IX. The courts rejected this approach.

In addition to striking down the "relative interests" argument, the court also rebuked the use of "quota" and "affirmative action" language when pursuing Title IX compliance. Additionally the ruling clarified that actual participants, not participation opportunities, need to be reported. Similarly, using ratios acquired from a survey would freeze opportunity levels and thereby sustain past discriminatory practices. Because a new group of students can potentially represent a new level of interest, a survey of interests typically captures only one moment in time, as opposed to developing interests and abilities.

Cutting men's sport was suggested by the Supreme Court as one potential remedy to discrimination, noting the OCR had deemed proportionality as a "safe harbor." With mounting pressure following the *Brown* ruling, The NCAA Gender Equity Task Force created the most comprehensive definition to guide institutions toward Title IX compliance: "An athletics program can be considered gender equitable when the participants in both the men's and women's sports programs would accept as fair and equitable the overall program of the other gender. No individual should be discriminated against on the basis of gender, institutionally or nationally, in intercollegiate athletics" (NCAA Gender Equity Task Force). Put in clearer terms, if the men's basketball team would trade all aspects of its program, including coaches, travel, uniforms, practice, and competitive facilities with the women's basketball program, then gender equity has truly been achieved. Also, around this time, the task force recommended the creation of emerging sports, to address growing interest and continue the development of sport opportunities for women.

Perhaps one of the most impactful steps was creation of the Equity in Athletics Disclosure Act (EADA) in 1996, which was a federal mandate for disclosure of data by every NCAA athletic department and included categories such as operating expenses for all sports, per capita expenses for all sports, recruiting and scholarship allocations, salaries for head and assistant coaches, and revenues and expenses for basketball and football. The EADA was proposed to provide an avenue for parents and athletes to assess the level of commitment each school provides for its athletic programs. The notion was that a more informed decision could be made when selecting a college or university. Also, the belief was athletic programs would be held more accountable through this annual disclosure of data. Yet, in a study examining EADA data, Hattery, Smith, and Staurowsky (2007) found gender inequities have clearly continued, even as the fourth decade of the law was unfolding.

STAGE 4: BACKLASH

While each prior stage involved aspects of backlash against Title IX, the thirtieth anniversary of the law marked the beginning of a period of significant challenges. In 2002 the Bush administration formed a commission to study Title IX. Spurred on by critics such as the National Wrestling Coaches Association (NWCA), the Commission on Opportunity in Athletics held hearings across the country over a period of eight months. Ultimately, Title IX was not reformed in any significant way, although proponents were reassured that the progress made over the past 30 years could easily be reversed if the law was weakened or eliminated. Following the commission hearings, in 2003 the OCR issued further clarification indicating Title IX does not encourage or expect reduction of men's sport programs, as many had suggested the proportionality test advocated.

Similarly, criticism of prong three continued, with the primary concern being that universities fail to meet either the spirit or intent of Title IX when using manipulative strategies to demonstrate "interest" among women has been met. Following a 2005 clarification debacle, the OCR issued new guidelines in 2010 regarding the use of interest surveys. Notably, the OCR indicated a survey cannot stand alone, and its evaluation will focus on both the content and target population of the survey. In essence, prong three can be used to determine compliance but only if the demonstration of interest employs sound survey methods and seeks information from the underrepresented population.

In total there are 13 areas for compliance including equipment and supplies, scheduling, travel and per diem, tutors, coaches, facilities, medical care and training, housing, publicity, support services, and recruiting. To demonstrate a disparity in any of these areas the differences must be based on sex with a negative impact on athletes of one sex, and the disparity must be so substantial as to deny equal

Sport Media Guides

Messner (2002) argued sport media is the primary vehicle that legitimizes "unequal power relations between the sexes" and makes female athletes and their bodies "contested ideological terrain." Following Title IX, media portrayals of female athletes replicated social norms, even though sports was believed to empower women and serve as a means to foster change. Guided by the notion "media coverage of sport offers fertile ground for any investigation that explores images, symbols, and myths related to power," Kane and Buysse (2005) analyzed Division I media guide covers from the 1990s to the early 2000s seeking differences in gender portrayals. Media guides from 12 sports at 68 colleges in six major Division I athletic conferences, resulted in 528 guides for analysis. Media guides were chosen because they are considered a marketing tool used to advertise teams to sponsors, donors, alumni, and key stakeholders, while also used as a recruitment tool for future college athletes. Three aspects were examined: Were the athletes in or out of their uniforms, on or off the court, and in active or passive poses? In earlier studies, women's teams were often depicted as "ladylike" being portrayed in dresses, in passive poses, and in a nonsports environment.

The authors found males and females were portrayed in uniforms on most media guide covers. Approximately 80% of the women and 86% of the men were portrayed in their competitive venue. Females were portrayed in active poses in 71% of the media guides compared to 78% for men. The results "clearly indicate strong and consistent trends regarding the seriousness with which male and female athletes were portrayed" (Kane & Buysse, 2005, p. 223). A visual analysis also revealed women in hockey, softball, basketball, and tennis were most likely to be in active poses, compared to sports of golf and gymnastics. Not surprisingly, traditionally feminine sports were sometimes portrayed in a passive pose, adhering to gender stereotypes. This analysis demonstrated "significant shifts in the representations of sportswomen from the early 1990s to 2004, shifts that led to the construction of females as serious, competent athletes" (p. 231). Notably, Kane and Buysse found these recent portrayals of college sportswomen represented a stark contrast to the images found in mainstream media. They concluded:

> The impact of Title IX, and its relationship to higher education, is behind our second suggestion for why stereotypic narratives did not rule the day . . . In large measure because of Title IX, more and more girls are exposed to formalized, competitive sports at an early age. This not only creates a greater interest in sports among females but also produces a sense of entitlement that is often expressed in the expectation of an athletic scholarship . . . consequently, colleges and universities are now required to make meaningful athletic opportunities and experiences available to women. One way to do this is to structure women's athletics around the highly competitive and commercialized "male model" of sports. Women's intercollegiate athletics have thus become more commercialized and, as a result, institutions of higher education now have a stake in making them more appealing to a broader audience. (pp. 234–235) ■

Questions to Consider

1. Given the 13 areas for Title IX Compliance, in which area(s) would this issue reside? Why?

2. Given the need for college sports programs to generate revenue and garner media attention, discuss the need for women's athletic programs to emulate the commercialized "male model."

opportunity to athletes of the one sex. This is not to say that all areas must be exactly equal or equivalent. Permissible differences are recognized by the OCR based on the unique aspects of each sport. For example, event management costs are far higher for football than any other sport, as are equipment costs for all sports requiring protective equipment. While there is not room here to discuss each of the 13 areas, scholars have shown disparities in a number of these areas. Yet Staurowsky and Weight (2011) found Title IX knowledge is lacking among both athletes and coaches. Without a full understanding of gender equity, all 13 areas covered by Title IX, discriminatory practices are likely to go unchallenged.

UNINTENDED CONSEQUENCE

Paradoxically, growth in sport participation opportunities for women occurred as the numbers of women coaches and administrators diminished. For more than 30 years, Acosta and Carpenter (2012) kept track of these trends. Despite a record number of sports offered, the representation of female coaches has remained below 50% for decades. Women athletic directors, also few in number, have seen little growth even though the pipeline for leadership should be filled with an unprecedented number of former college athletes. For a better understanding of this issue, readers are encouraged to access Acosta and Carpenter's (2012) full report.

STAKEHOLDER PERSPECTIVE

NCAA Emerging Sports for Women

In 1994 the NCAA's Gender-Equity Task Force recommended a list of emerging sports as a way to continue to grow opportunities for women. During the past 17 years, rowing, ice hockey, water polo, and bowling have become championship sports. To remain on the list, emerging sports are required to attain a minimum of 40 varsity programs within 10 years or show steady progress toward the goal. Marilyn Moniz-Kaho'ohanohano, chair of the NCAA's Committee on Women's Athletics (CWA), indicated the CWA was supportive of forwarding triathlon for consideration as an emerging sport. Triathlon is believed to be a natural fit for colleges and universities, with more than 150 campuses currently supporting triathlon clubs. At the 2013 national collegiate championship, triathletes from 46 states participated, including more than 400 women. USA Triathlon's data further support interest, with women representing more than 40% of all collegiate participants. Moniz-Kaho'ohanohano said the CWA was impressed with the level of support offered by USA Triathlon, including a coach's certification program and events in 50 locations utilized to introduce triathlon to new communities while developing future participants.

Marymount University is one of a list of institutions adding the sport, which will increase to 15 the sports offered in the 2012–2013 seasons.

Dr. Chris Domes, Marymount's vice president for student development and enrollment management, said "We're very excited because these will be the first sports added at Marymount since 2003, when we launched men's and women's cross country. More sports mean more opportunity for athletes; in our experience, these are students who tend to do well academically and who serve as leaders and role models on campus. As an NCAA Division III school, Marymount values athletics as part of a well-rounded educational experience; we also recognize the important role that sports can play in building community and promoting school spirit." ■

Relatedly, some believe the decline in women coaches is reflective of a climate that does not value women. For decades, women's sports coaches were fired for speaking out regarding gender inequities. Yet the scope of Title IX regarding retaliation for whistle blowers did not reach the Supreme Court until 2005 in *Jackson v. Birmingham Board of Education*. This case, pursued by a male girls' basketball coach, resulted in the court expanding the range of permissible plaintiffs. In essence, the ruling indicated that Title IX protects victims of retaliation, even when the plaintiff was not a direct victim of the discrimination. This watershed ruling opened the door for coaches who had lost their jobs as a result of advocating for gender equity in their programs. The numbers of coaches and administrators who fell victim to this form of discrimination is unknown, but clearly the backlash would have continued had this critical ruling not come about in 2005.

Most recently the scope of Title IX has been broadened within higher education, as this educational law has also been utilized to address inequities in access to higher education, career education, employment, the learning environment, math, science and technology, sexual harassment, and standardized testing, as well as treatment of pregnant and parenting students. As further evidence of how college sports continues to be predominantly a male model, the NCAA failed to recognize the need to protect athletes during pregnancy until 2005. For many women, the protection provided by Title IX also presented various forms of backlash.

THE FORTIETH ANNIVERSARY AND EMERGING FIFTH STAGE

Forty years of Title IX has not resulted in the elimination of sex discrimination, even within college sports, where it has received the most attention. Instead, Title IX as applied to intercollegiate athletics has been deemed "the most visible gender controversy" (Suggs, 2005). Even recent accounts continue to illustrate the divergent views initiated in the 1970s. Title IX has been credited with increasing sport participation opportunities for women, while also being blamed for cuts to men's collegiate sport teams. Upon examining narratives regarding Title IX's impact, Hardin and Whiteside (2009) confirmed the notion that many believe women do not deserve the equality Title IX affords them.

CONCLUSION

Twenty years after the initial passage, a shift toward gender equity began due largely to litigation pursued by women athletes interested in restoring or improving athletic opportunities. To date, the OCR has never used its authority to penalize a school for noncompliance, and at the same time, every institution of higher education sued for noncompliance with Title IX in intercollegiate athletics has lost in court. From the beginning, college football proponents pointed to Title IX as the cause for financial challenges, which has been refuted consistently in scholarly work. Examples over the past 40 years lead many to believe that the eradication of Title IX would result in the elimination of women's programs and thereby educational opportunities. At the heart of this legislation created to eliminate sex discrimination is the fact that each opportunity to participate in athletics is in fact an educational opportunity. Few would argue that men deserve more opportunities to pursue a degree in higher education than women. Yet this is the essence of the arguments used to privilege men's sports over women's. Continued advocacy and education are needed as accurate knowledge of Title IX remains limited, even among coaches of women's sports, athletes, and athletic administrators.

QUESTIONS FOR DISCUSSION

1. Do you think the spirit and intent of the federal law written in 1972 is a reality today? Why or why not?

2. Why has a law written to improve educational opportunities become known primarily as a "sport law"?

3. Of the three methods to demonstrate compliance, which appears to be most effective? Why?

References

Acosta, R. V., & Carpenter, L. J. (2012). *Women in intercollegiate sport: A longitudinal, national study thirty-five year update 1977–2012*. Retrieved from http://www.acostacarpenter.org

Brown, G. (2013). CWA asks to add triathlon as an emerging sport. NCAA.org. Retrieved from http://www.ncaa.org/wps/wcm/connect/public/NCAA/Resources/Latest+News/2013/May /CWA+asks+to+add+triathlon+as+an+emerging+sport

Carpenter, L., & Acosta, V. (2005). *Title IX*. Champaign, IL: Human Kinetics.

Civil Rights Restoration Act of 1987, 20 U.S.C. section 1687 (1988).

Cohen v. Brown University, 991 F. 2d 888 (1st Cir. 1993); 101 F. 3d 155 (1st Cir. 1996), cert. denied 520 U.S. 1186 (1997).

Edwards, A. R. (2010). Why Sport? The development of sport as a policy issue in Title IX of the Education Amendments of 1972. *Journal of Policy History, 22*, 300–336.

Franklin v. Gwinnett County Public Schools. Retrieved from http://caselaw.lp.findlaw.com/scripts/getcase.pl?court=us&vol=503=60

Grove City College v. Bell. Retrieved from http://caselaw.lp.findlaw.com/scripts/getcase.pl?court=us&vol=465&invol=555

Hardin, M., & Whiteside, E. E. (2009). The power of "small stories": Narratives and notions of gender equality in conversations about sport. *Sociology of Sport Journal, 26*, 255–276.

Hattery, A., Smith, E., & Staurowsky, E. (2007). They play like girls: Gender equity in NCAA sports. *Journal for the Study of Sports and Athletes in Education, 1*(3), 249–272.

Johnson, J. K. (1994). Title IX and intercollegiate athletics: Current judicial interpretation of the standards for compliance. *Boston University Law Review, 74*, 553–589.

Kane, M. J., & Buysse, J. A. (2005). Intercollegiate media guides as contested terrain: A longitudinal analysis. *Sociology of Sport Journal, 22*, 214–238.

Lough, N. (2012, April). *Equity in education: 40 Years of Title IX; A panel discussion*. Sponsored event held in the Hendrix Auditorium, UNLV College of Education, Las Vegas. http://wrinunlv.org/2211/equity-in-education-celebrating-40-years-of-title-ix/.

Messner, M. (2002). *Taking the field: Women, men and sports*. Minnesota: University of Minnesota Press.

NCAA Gender Equity Task Force. *Gender equity*. Retrieved from http://www.ncaa.org/about/resources/inclusion/gender-equity

Staurowsky, E. (1998). Critiquing the language of the gender gap equity debate. *Journal of Sport & Social Issues, 98*(22), 7–26.

Staurowsky, E., & Weight, E. (2011). Title IX literacy: What coaches don't know and need to find out. *Journal of Intercollegiate Sport, 4*, 190–209.

Suggs, W. (2005). *A place on the team: The triumph and tragedy of Title IX*. Princeton, NJ: Princeton University Press.

U.S. Department of Civil Rights Office. Retrieved from www.ed.gov/about/offices/list/ocr/index.html

U. S. Department of Education. (1997). Title IX: 25 years of progress. Retrieved from www.ed.gov/pubs/TitleIX/

U.S. Department of Justice. Retrieved from www.usdoj.gov/crt/cor/coord/titleix.htm

Wulf, S. (2012, March 26). Title IX: 37 words that changed everything. *ESPNW.com*. Retrieved from http://w.espn.go.com/espnw/title-ix/7722632/print

KEY CASE LAW and LEGISLATION SHAPING WOMEN'S OPPORTUNITY in INTERCOLLEGIATE ATHLETICS

Jennifer Lee Hoffman, Jacqueline McDowell, and Valyncia Raphael

> *Equal athletic treatment is not a luxury. It is not a luxury to grant equivalent benefits and opportunities to women. It is not a luxury to comply with the law. Equality and justice are not luxuries. They are essential elements, which are woven into the very fiber of this country. They are essential elements now codified under Title IX.*
>
> Cook v. Colgate University (1992)

When Title IX of the Educational Amendments of 1972 (Title IX) was passed, it fundamentally changed women's access for equal opportunity in all educational programs, and women reemerged in the competitive landscape of sports in colleges and universities. Born in a climate of social change that focused on individual rights and fairness and the emergence of liberal feminism that advocated for giving women equal access to the same opportunities as men, Title IX policies reflect these themes. Modeled after Title VI of the Civil Rights Act of 1964, Title IX promotes gender equity efforts by mandating equal access and equitable treatment of men and women in educational institutions: "No person in the United States shall, on the basis of sex, be excluded from participation in, be denied the benefits of, or be subjected to discrimination under any education program or activity receiving federal financial assistance" (Title IX, 1972). Most schools receive federal support directly or indirectly via student loans or federal research funding; hence this component of the law extends Title IX application to nearly all public and most private educational institutions.

Although Title IX is highly associated with women's sports, this legislation has broader coverage and has significantly helped increase equity in men's and women's educational opportunities in college and career preparatory programs; science, technology, engineering, and math (STEM) fields; and technical fields. Moreover, Title IX offers protection against sex- and gender-based harassment and violence and discrimination against pregnant and parenting students, and it promotes equity in admissions, financial aid, housing, employment, and other educational services and benefits (Office of Civil Rights, 2012).

Unlike other educational areas, in interscholastic and intercollegiate sports Title IX permits a gender-separate system of opportunity. This structure of gender-separate opportunities is known as the dilemma of difference and presents a unique legal framework in which to interpret and implement the law (Brake, 2010). Although enacted after the 1954 *Brown v. Board of Education* decision wherein justices asserted in the field of public education the doctrine of separate but equal has no place, Title IX solidified a separate but equal doctrine. The adoption of this philosophy, presents questions about how to pursue equality for women's opportunity without unquestioningly accepting sameness based on men's athletics (Festle, 1996).

In athletics an overall determination of compliance in Title IX includes effectively accommodating students' interests and abilities by the types and quality of sport opportunities provided; requiring athletic scholarships to be awarded substantially proportionate to the participation rates of male and female athletes; and requiring males and females to receive equivalent treatment, benefits, and opportunities in coaching, academic assistance, travel and per diem expenses, equipment and supplies, practice and competitive facilities, recruitments, housing and dining services, locker rooms, medical, training facilities, publicity, and scheduling of games and practices and support services (O'Shea, 1998). Moreover, in 1979 the Office of Civil Rights' (OCR) Intercollegiate Athletics Policy Interpretation of Title IX established a three-part test to assess whether institutions were providing equitable participation opportunities. Specifically, intercollegiate athletic departments must provide participation opportunities for male and female students substantially proportionate to their undergraduate enrollment, show a history and continuing practice of program expansion for men and women, *or* demonstrate that the interest and abilities of the underrepresented sex are fully and effectively accommodated. OCR has consistently reinforced that schools needed to satisfy only one of the three alternatives, but the proportionality test has become the salient, and sometimes controversial, face of Title IX (Reynolds, 2003).

Similar to other civil rights laws, Title IX has a litigious history characterized by successes and setbacks. Title IX legislation and cultural shifts in gender ideologies have resulted in significant increases in women's sport opportunities at the interscholastic and intercollegiate levels; but these improvements, however, were not achieved without struggles. As noted by Hogshead-Makar and Zimbalist (2007), "The strength of civil-rights laws hinges on the ability and willingness of our citizens to prevent and expose violations and to bring the goal of equality to fruition" (p. 187); and after futile efforts to address inequities and discrimination, legislation would prove to be instrumental in opening up, and sometimes closing, opportunities for women in sport.

Title IX has been an evolving law, dynamic and changing with each generation, as it is interpreted through decisions by the courts, Congress, and executive order. This chapter highlights key court cases that illustrate the tensions and dilemmas in the contemporary sporting context in education: athletic programs are separated by a gender-separate model of participation, yet opportunity must remain equal under the law. This chapter does not present an exhaustive description of how Title IX has been shaped but highlights themes of opportunity through several prominent legal cases that have influenced athletics for women in higher education.

THE LINK BETWEEN OPPORTUNITY AND INTEREST:
COHEN V. BROWN UNIVERSITY

In 1993, citing budgetary problems, Brown University demoted women's volleyball and gymnastics and two other men's teams to club status. The women athletes sued citing discrimination and not promoting equal opportunities for women to participate in intercollegiate athletics. Before the cutbacks, Brown University was already offering only 36% of its participation opportunity to women. The three-part test for participation equity became a key feature of the *Cohen v. Brown University* case and became the legal test for this method of determining participation equity (Brake, 2010). Not only was the three-part test upheld, but substantial proportionality became the standard for calculating equity in participation.

The *Cohen v. Brown University* case reveals several important issues in equity in participation. First, cutting women's teams is legally risky (Estler & Nelson, 2005). Repeatedly, the courts and OCR rulings have upheld the three-part test as constitutional. Second, when Brown University attempted to cut the women's varsity gymnastics team and demote it to an unfunded club team, it revealed other inequities in the athletic program that were detrimental to cultivating interest among women athletes. These inequities contributed to an environment in which participation and interest are interrelated. The court in *Cohen* found that "because interest is developed and not inherent, disparities in sport opportunities themselves suppress women's interest in sports" (Brake, 2010, p. 78).

From 1991 to 1997, Brown University repeatedly argued against the three-part test as reverse discrimination against men because "men are more interested than women in intercollegiate athletic participation" (Brief, *Cohen v. Brown University*, 1996, p. 1). Brown University's position was that less interest in athletics participation among women is "unrelated to disparities in opportunities" (Brief, *Cohen v. Brown University*, 1996, p. 1). Brown University maintained that women were less interested in participating in sports and the three-part test itself was a quota that forced discrimination against men (Brake, 2010).

One of the unintended outcomes of securing the three-part test as constitutional and highlighting the relationship between interest and opportunity was solidifying rhetoric that Title IX creates opportunities at the expense of men—particularly among the Olympic or non-revenue-producing sports. Title IX's three-part test prescribes not how to increase opportunity for women, only that one of the three parts must be satisfied. The strategy of cutting some men's teams rather than creating new opportunity pits the participation interests of women athletes against the financial interests of big-time football and basketball. The themes of women's interests and football interests resonate in other gender equity cases.

CALCULATING EQUITY IN A GENDER-SEPARATE PROGRAM: *BLAIR V. WASHINGTON STATE UNIVERSITY*

In the fall of 1979, women athletes and coaches sued Washington State University, claiming the school discriminated against women's athletics in violation of Washington State's Equal Rights Amendment (*Blair v. Washington State University*, 1983). In the lower-court decision, the state found that football operated "for profit under business principles" (*Blair*, 1983). To achieve equity in funding women's scholarships required increases in yearly increments until the university's financial support for women's scholarships "reaches a level representing the same percentage as women represent of the total undergraduate population at the university . . . excluding football" (*Blair*, 1983, 1987; see also Reynvaan, 1992, p. 28). Additionally, the court found that football would be excluded from the calculation of equity in participation because football is a "largely self-sustaining sport" (Reynvaan, 1992, p. 28; see also *Blair*, 1983).

The trial court ruling that self-generated funds from football are program specific and designated the operation of football as a business endeavor rather than an educational endeavor was reversed. The Washington State Supreme Court ruled that football would not be eliminated in football revenues, scholarships, or participation opportunities (*Blair*, 1987). Thus, football could not be separate from the rest of the department and still considered educational.

In deciding the case, the state Supreme Court observed that the state equal rights amendment "contains no exception for football" (*Blair*, 1987; see also Kaplin & Lee, 1995, p. 564). Despite football's unique commercial characteristics, it could not be excluded from the educational interests of the university and must be included in determining equity between men's and women's athletics. The reinforcement between football and education is notable in the Blair case. In *Blair*, the lower court attempted to differentiate football as a business model, citing that "football is operated for profit under business principles" (*Blair*, 1983; see also Graff, 1988). However, with the State Supreme Court reversing this decision, it clarified football as an educational endeavor noting, "Football is a large and essential part of intercollegiate athletics at the University" (*Blair*, 1987). This ruling under state-level gender equity law reveals the legal connection between athletics and education for all aspects of the athletic program. It also strengthens the interdependence between women's athletic participation and big-time football in the educational interests of college sports programs.

IN THE PURSUIT OF FAIRNESS: *KELLMEYER ET AL. V. NATIONAL EDUCATION ASSOCIATION ET AL.*

Fern Lee "Peachy" Kellmeyer was a star tennis player, who competed in the U.S. Tennis Open at the age 15 and became the first woman to compete for a men's college team at the University of Miami (Rykoff, 2011). She was also the first person hired full time by the Women's Tennis Association. However, the biggest mark she left on women's sports was the class-action lawsuit filed against the Association for Intercollegiate Athletics for Women (AIAW), the former governing body for collegiate women's athletics, challenging the rule that women on athletic scholarships could not compete in AIAW-sponsored competitions (Rykoff, 2011).

AIAW rules prohibited women from obtaining athletic scholarships out of concerns over commercialization, professionalization, pressure recruiting, and financial burdens (Sack & Staurowsky, 1998). However, after Title IX passed the legality of this gendered policy was challenged in *Kellmeyer et al. v. National Education Association et al.* (U.S. District Court, Southern District of Florida, no. 73, 21 Civ NCR).

In January 1973, Kellmeyer, director of physical education at Marymount College and a group of female tennis players and coaches from Marymount College and Broward Community College argued that the prohibition on scholarships denied them equal protection of the law, citing violations of the Fourteenth Amendment and Title IX. The case did not proceed to court. Instead, AIAW abrogated the scholarship rule preemptively.

This landmark change in the AIAW's scholarship rule did more than provide women athletes with equitable opportunities to obtain financial assistance—it was instrumental in changing the structure and governance of women sports. This move was seen as the first step away from the AIAW's education-based philosophy and toward the National Collegiate Athletic Association's (NCAA) commercialized sports model (Wu, 1999). Moreover, by "exposing the traditional sex-separate philosophy of women's sport to the law of equal protection, the *Kellmeyer* litigation paved the way for the NCAA's initiative in women's sports" (Wu, 1999, p. 47). This ruling was among the catalysts that resulted in the control of women's sports shifting from women leaders in the AIAW to the men's NCAA governing association.

ALL SPORTS ARE NOT CREATED EQUAL: *STANLEY V. UNIVERSITY OF SOUTHERN CALIFORNIA*

Title IX has created more participation opportunities for women in sports, and the law has led to substantial increases in resources being allocated to women's sports. Title IX extends beyond obtaining equal opportunities for college athletes to coaches' compensation but is specific in its scope. Protection from employment discrimination is limited to differences where the coaching compensation impacts the availability or quality of coaching "due to the sex of the team rather than the sex of the coach" (Weiss, 2002, p. 154). In addition, many coaching contracts include compensation from third parties, such as apparel companies or athletic associations, and are not subject to Title IX regulations (Gentry & Alexander, 2012).

Marianne Stanley was hired as head coach of the University of Southern California's women's basketball team in 1989 with a four-year contract. Her salary was $60,000 per year with a $6,000 housing stipend (O'Brien, O'Brien, & Sarfo-Kantanka, 2009). Two months before the contract expired in 1993, Stanley and the athletic director, Michael Garrett entered into contract negations for a three-year contract. Stanley wanted a base salary comparable to that of the men's basketball coach's $135,000 annual base salary (Ryan, 1999). Garrett denied her request and when negotiations failed after her first contract expired, Garrett informed her that he would start looking for a new coach (*Stanley v. University of Southern California*, 1994).

In response Marianne Stanley filed a 1993 lawsuit against the University of Southern California and the athletic director, Michael Garrett, claiming sex-based discrimination and retaliatory discharge. The court ruled that there was not a violation of the Equal Pay Act, FEHA, the Constitution, or Title IX because Stanley failed to show discriminatory conduct. The men's basketball coach was deemed to have sufficiently more relevant experience and qualifications than Stanley, warranting the pay difference. The court ruled that since Stanley's contract expired and she had not successfully renegotiated a contract that was acceptable to her, it was not retaliation or wrongful discharge. Moreover, no violation of express employment contract or good-faith and fair-dealing violations occurred because Garrett offered her a multiyear deal during contract negotiations, and it was Stanley's choice to not accept the offered terms (*Stanley*, 1994).

In the 1993 *Stanley* case, the court asserted that there were significant differences between the men's and women's basketball coaching positions, in relation to public relations and promotional activities. It was also opined that Coach Raveling, the men's basketball coach, had more experience and higher qualifications than Stanley. In the eyes of the court, these differences were sufficient to support differential compensation packages. These findings set precedent for future EPA and Title IX rulings regarding university coaches. Repeatedly since *Stanley*, the courts have affirmed that a revenue-generating sport (versus a nonrevenue one) constitutes a sufficient difference in job duties to allow a pay difference due to further obligations, such as media appearances and public relations that are required of those coaches. They have also held years of coaching experience, level of education, and service to the university as distinguishing markers that can merit a pay difference (O'Brien et al., 2009).

COMPETITIVE CHEERLEADING AND EQUITY: *BIEDIGER V. QUINNIPIAC UNIVERSITY*

Cheerleading began before World War II, with men who were yell leaders, but it later developed into feminized hallmark of men's sports. As other women's opportunities for sport participation have grown, rather than calling into question the presence of cheerleading, the number of girls in cheering activities has expanded. Contemporary sideline rally and entertainment-style cheerleaders are a prominent feature at most college football and men's basketball games and are accepted as an important role in the formation of community around spectator sports. Cheerleaders contribute to the collegiate ideal (Toma, 2003; Toma & Kezar, 1999), just the same as the mascot, colors, logos, songs, and other rituals and ceremonial practices common at intercollegiate events that are traditionally male gendered (Figure 18.1). The role of cheerleaders in the support of athletic events falls under the guidelines for equal program support required by Title IX.

Figure 18.1. Cheerleaders are under the guidelines for equal program support required by Title IX but raise questions about their gendered role at athletic events. (Photo, Department Defense, Cherie Cullen.)

Cheerleaders are present at many women's basketball events as well. But the highly feminized role of cheerleaders at women's events raises questions about what constitutes the cultivation of traditions and customs at sporting events when the participants and the cheerleaders are both women. The presence of cheerleaders equally dispatched to boys and girls athletic contests was the subject of a 2007 Title IX complaint in New York State (Hu, 2007). A complaint filed by the parent of a girls' high school basketball player was that boys' teams regularly had cheerleaders and girls' basketball teams only had occasional support from cheerleaders, such as during the play-offs or championship contests. Yet when cheerleaders appeared at girls' basketball games, they were met with resistance from the girls' basketball players.

In addition, a new form of competitive cheerleading has emerged that includes strenuous tumbling, complicated jumps, and tossing maneuvers. These acrobatic skills and performances are an organized activity where the primary goal is competition; complete with scoring, judges, and a national champion-type award structure. Like gymnastics, figure skating, or synchronized swimming, cheering teams are judged on elements that require strength, skill, and agility found only in highly athletic activities.

Cheerleaders or Gymnasts?

State University, a school with a Division II athletic program, was hit hard by the recent economic downturn. Budgets for many academic units were cut. Because the athletic department received a reduction in student fees for athletics, it has a deficit of approximately $500,000 and has been unable to close the budget gap.

After several years of deep cuts, all teams have been retained, but the only options at this point are to begin cutting teams. Despite the strong interest in gymnastics across the state, the ability to attract many of the region's gymnasts to State University, and a record of earning national academic honors and individual and team championships, the gymnastics programs are slated for elimination. Transferring to another program is not likely for most of the gymnasts, as the schools in the region with gymnastics programs are Division I, and the rate of transfer to these programs has historically been very low. State University will honor the scholarships of all current scholarship gymnasts—women and men—who would like to remain at State University and complete their degrees.

The athletic department is considering an unusual move in this decision. The university has a strong commitment to athletic participation, and several other conference members are considering adding competitive cheerleading to comply with Title IX. Interest in competitive cheerleading has grown around the state, with club teams in almost every city, and many of the state's women gymnasts are opting to participate in these clubs instead of continuing in gymnastics as they approach high school age. The university is exploring this option; and if a new competitive cheerleading squad is started, any current woman gymnast can join the new competitive cheerleading team permanently until her eligibility is exhausted.

The campus athletics board has been notified and asked to weigh in on the possibility of adding competitive cheerleading. The board knows of the growing popularity of competitive cheerleading in the state and how it has created more opportunities for women students to do something they love after they can't perform in a sport that favors only a small portion of the population. Despite the growing interest, the view of cheerleading, no matter how competitive, is mixed among the board members. What should their recommendation be to the athletic department? ∎

Competitive cheer has been tested as a sport under Title IX. In March 2009 Quinnipiac University cut the women's volleyball team and replaced it with competitive cheerleading. In July 2010 the U.S. District Court ruled that competitive cheerleading did not meet the requirements as a sport under Title IX and upheld on appeal. To qualify as a sport under Title IX, the ruling suggested several guidelines for competitive cheerleading to be met before being recognized as a sport under Title IX law. The guidelines set specific criteria for qualifying competitive cheerleading in colleges and universities as a sport. For cheerleading to be considered a sport under Title IX, it must be a fully developed and organized activity characterized by:

1. Competitions against other squads in a defined season

2. Coaches and practices

3. Resemblance to all other varsity sports at an institution in structure and operation

4. A governing organization

In addition, the primary goal of the cheerleading activity must be competition. Although competitive cheer meets some of the requirements, it lacks sufficient development in others: number and quality of competitions; availability of conference; and state-, regional-, and national-level competition. In addition, the NCAA does not yet sanction competitive cheerleading with emerging sport or championship status. Without the competitive opportunities or governance structure, meeting the quality of competition and governing organization standards remains a challenge. Until these requirements are consistently met, competitive cheerleading will not be considered a sport for Title IX purposes.

FIGHTING FOR THE RIGHT TO PLAY: *RICHARDS V. UNITED STATES TENNIS ASSOCIATION*

During Title IX's inception years, fears prevailed that the law would result in athletic opportunities becoming coeducational (Ware, 2007). Instead Title IX legislation resulted in high school and college sports becoming highly defined and divided by sex and gender. Title IX's legitimization and encouragement of a gender binary has resulted in ambiguity about transgender and intersex athletes' access to sport participation opportunities. Transgender athletes' fight for equal access to competition in *Richards v. United States Tennis Association* (USTA) paved the way for transgendered athletes to be granted equal access and rights to compete.

The lawsuit against the USTA was brought about by Dr. Renée Richards, who was born a male but in 1975 underwent sex reassignment surgery (Kozlowski, 2009). Prior to the operation, Richards competed in professional tennis tournaments; but upon becoming a woman, the United States Open Committee (USOC) and Women's Tennis Association prevented her from qualifying and participating in the 1976 women's singles U.S. Open by instituting a sex-chromatic test. The USTA and USOC's contention was that men who had undergone "sex change" surgery have a competitive advantage over biological females because of the physical training and development that they experienced as a male (*Richards*, 1977). Richards claimed the test violated her rights under the New York State Human Rights Law (NY Exec. Law §297(9)) and the Fourteenth Amendment to the U.S. Constitution and sought a preliminary injunction prohibiting the USTA from subjecting her to a sex verification test. In an unprecedented judgment, the New York's trial court lifted USTA's testing policy and opined that the defendants intentionally targeted Richards and discriminately instituted the Barr body test to prevent her from participating. Moreover, the court found USTA's requirement that Richards pass a chromosomal test was "grossly unfair, discriminatory and inequitable, and violative of her rights under the Human Rights Law of this State" (*Richards*, 1977).

The *Richards* case was pivotal in bringing about social change for transgender athletes at the collegiate and professional levels of sport. Since the *Richards* lawsuit, governing associations have changed their policies to allow transgender athletes to compete. In 1999 the IOC eliminated its mandatory gender testing; and in 2004, it adopted the Stockholm Consensus that allowed transgender athletes to compete in the Olympic games. The United States Golf Association in 2005 and the Washington Interscholastic Activities Association in 2007 (Zeigler, 2011) followed IOC's precedent and passed their own policies permitting transgender people to compete. In 2010 the LPGA preemptively voted to remove the "female at birth" requirement, and in 2011 the increased emergence of transgender athletes and concerns about potential constitutional and Title IX lawsuits prompted the NCAA to approve a policy to allow athletes to participate on teams based on their gender identity (Lawrence, 2011). Despite the gender binary that Title IX preserves in sports, the protection against gender-based harassment this policy provides offers a possible "legal recourse" for transgender athletes (Griffin & Carroll, 2010, p. 51).

CONCLUSION

This chapter has highlighted several lawsuits that helped create social change and gender equity in competitive sports. These lawsuits exemplify progress in advancing women's opportunities in sports, but even after 40 years of Title IX policy there

STAKEHOLDER PERSPECTIVE

Putting Equity into Practice

Marie Tuite is the deputy director for internal operations and chief operating officer for San Jose State University Spartan Athletics. She previously held athletic administration positions at the University of California, the University of Washington, the Pacific 12 Conference, and the National Collegiate Athletic Association. She was a member of the women's field hockey and basketball teams at Central Michigan University and is the third woman athlete inducted into Central Michigan University Hall of Fame.

Tuite has experienced firsthand the opportunities Title IX provided as an athlete and has worked to promote gender equity for athletes and coaches throughout her athletic administration career. She has seen the resistance to change in the early years of Title IX and how some departments used this policy to cut men's programs. She has also navigated the challenges of implementing fair and equitable treatment in a gender-separate system under Title IX law. "Title IX is about equality. Often it can be difficult to take a 'fairness' position when faced with decisions in athletics that are simply not fair."

As an administrator she also questions the influence Title IX has had over the years on opportunities for women in athletics. "We have always followed the path of men's athletics. We've spent resources the way men's sports have allocated resources. Perhaps that has not been the most efficient way to advance women's programs. Would women's programs benefit more from the redirecting of our resources to those sports that continue to grow or should we be offering new sporting opportunities to more women? Would we be better off redirecting some of our resources from women's basketball to other women's sports? Would we better off putting more emphasis on women's volleyball, soccer, or softball or offering new sporting opportunities for more women?" ■

were a record number (900) of complaints alleging Title IX violations in athletic programs between 2009 and 2011 (Office for Civil Rights, 2012). These complaints exemplify the systemic inequities and discriminatory behaviors that continue to prevent girls and women from fully participating in interscholastic, intercollegiate, and professional athletics.

As a result of lawsuits, guidelines, and policy interpretations since 1972, Title IX can be described by the discourses of advocacy, resistance, and accommodation (Estler & Nelson, 2005). Title IX has been a touchstone for advocacy for women's opportunity in intercollegiate athletics, yet this advocacy has not been unified or without consequences.

Advocacy for equity has been met with resistance since the law was first passed. From challenges in the courts to the three-part test, to how football would be accounted for in measuring women's participation, to rhetoric over highly publicized accusations that men's sports were cut to comply with Title IX, the resistance to fully developing women's interests and opportunities is part of Title IX's discourse (Estler & Nelson, 2005). The continued litigation over the elimination of women's athletic opportunity and the continued discriminatory treatment of coaches who advocate for women's athletics remind us that achieving equity in opportunity for women in intercollegiate athletics is controversial (Brake, 2010; Buzuvis, 2010; Porto, 2012). Despite several high-profile cases at Fresno State University where women coaches and administrators received substantial monetary awards over retaliation for gender equity advocacy, the Fresno State cases "may paint a unduly positive picture for Title IX advocates because they reflect only the circumstances in which a coach or administrator challenged opportunity by filing a lawsuit" (Porto, 2012, p. 2). Many coaches still fear retaliation, and the burden remains largely with women athletes to protest discrimination (Porto, 2012).

However, the realities of advocacy and resistance discourses over cutting men's teams in favor of women's opportunity divert our attention from other themes of equal opportunity for all women. In attempting to create policy and legislation that mandate equity based on gender, themes of the gender-binary in sports and white privilege are left out of the discourses on women's participation. Title IX has largely benefited white women who participate in intercollegiate athletics (Rhoden, 2012). National Collegiate Athletic Association participation data indicate that the while overall athlete population is only 43% women, 76.2% of women athletes are white. Women of color have not benefited from Title IX's progress in sports at the same rate (Lapchick, Augusta, Kinkopf, & McPhee, 2012).

The capacity of FBS member athletics programs to generate revenue provides an important funding source for women's athletics. Within this economic model of Title IX, a persistent theme of gender and race in American society emerges (Hawkins, 2010). These deeply held social and structural themes go unnoticed in most discourses of women's opportunity in intercollegiate athletics. Furthermore, when evaluated from the economic context of intercollegiate athletics, where black male athletes constitute the majority of the revenue-generating labor force that funds big-time athletics departments, most women athletes are white. Division I Football Bowl Subdivision (FBS; formerly Division I-A) member schools have the lowest proportionality gap of all NCAA schools (Anderson, Cheslock, & Ehrenberg, 2006).

Future opportunities for all women to participate in sports, coach teams, and lead college athletic departments must incorporate a broader ethic of equity that accommodates many more women. The dilemmas of providing equitable opportunity in the gender-separate context of intercollegiate athletics reveal inequities and limitations in what Title IX law can provide. It is up to higher education's other social and economic interests to provide the leverage that is needed to promote equity for all women in intercollegiate athletics.

QUESTIONS FOR DISCUSSION

1. Given that Title IX permits a gender-separate legal structure for athletic participation, can women's sports achieve equal social status in the athletic department and the campus community?

2. What are the economic, structural, and cultural campus contexts that foster or deter women's interest, and subsequent opportunities, in athletic participation?

3. Given the increased commercial growth of women's basketball and other women's sports such as soccer, volleyball, and softball, are salary differences justified between compensation of coaches of women's and men's athletic programs?

References

Anderson, D., Cheslock, J., & Ehrenberg, R. (2006). Gender equity in intercollegiate athletics: Determinants of Title IX compliance. *Journal of Higher Education, 77,* 225–250.

Blair v. Washington State University, No. 28816 (January 3, 1983).

Blair v. Washington State University, 108 Wash. 2d 558, 740 P.2d 1379 (1987).

Brake, D. L. (2010). *Getting in the game: Title IX and the women's sports revolution.* New York: New York University Press.

Brief for National Women's Law Center et al. as Amicus Curiae Supporting Plaintiff- Appellees, *Cohen v. Brown Univ.,* 101 F.3d 155 (1st Cir. 1996).

Buzuvis, E. (2010). Sidelined: Title IX retaliation cases and women's leadership in college athletics. *Duke Journal of Gender Law & Policy, 17*(1), 1–46.

Cook v. Colgate Univ., 802 F. Supp. 737 (N.D.N.Y. 1992).

Estler, S. E., & Nelson, L. J. (2005). *Who calls the shots? Sports and university leadership, culture, and decision making* (Vol. 5). San Francisco: Wiley Subscription Services.

Festle, M. J. (1996). *Playing nice: Politics and apologies in women's sports.* New York: Columbia University Press.

Gentry, J., & Alexander, R. M. (2012, April 2). Pay for women's basketball coaches lags far behind men's coaches. *nytimes.com.* Retrieved from http://www .nytimes.com/2012/04/03/sports/ncaabasketball /pay-for-womens-basketball-coaches-lags-far -behind-mens-coaches.html?pagewanted=all& _r=0

Graff, D. (1988). Blair v. Washington State University: Making state era's a potent remedy for sex discrimination in athletics. *Journal of College and University Law, 14,* 575–589.

Griffin, P., & Carroll, H. (2010). *On the team: Equal opportunity for transgender student athletes.* National Center for Lesbian Rights. Retrieved from http://www.nclrights.org/site/DocServer /TransgenderStudentAthleteReport.pdf?docID =7901

Hawkins, B. (2010). *The new plantation: Black athletes, college sports, and predominately white NCAA institutions.* New York: Palgrave Macmillan.

Hogshead-Makar, N., & Zimbalist, A. (Eds.). (2007). *Equal play: Title IX and social change.* Philadelphia: Temple University Press.

Hu, W. (2007, January 14). Equal cheers for boys and girls draw some boos. *New York Times,* p. 1.

Kaplin, W. A., & Lee, B. A. (1995). *The law of higher education* (3rd ed.). San Francisco: Jossey-Bass.

Kellmeyer, et al. vs. National Education Association, et al. (U.S. District Court, Southern District of Florida, no. 73, 21 Civ NCR, 17 Jan. 1973).

Kozlowski, J. C. (2009). Transsexual advantage in women's competition? *Parks & Recreation, 44*(8), 34–37.

Lapchick, R., Agusta, R., Kinkopf, N., & McPhee, F. (2012). *The 2012 racial and gender report card: College sport.* The Institute for Diversity and Ethics in Sport. Retrieved from http://www.tidesport.org /RGRC/2012/2012_College_RGRC.pdf

Lawrence, M. (2011, September 13). Transgender policy approved. *NCAA.org.* Retrieved from http://www .ncaa.org/wps/wcm/connect/public/NCAA /Resources/Latest+News/2011/September /Transgender+policy+approved

O'Brien, D., O'Brien, T., & Sarfo-Kantanka, V. (2009). Pay equity among college coaches: A summary of case law since *Stanley* and administrative guidance. *Willamette Sports Law Journal, 6*(1), 29–43.

Office for Civil Rights. (2012). *Title IX enforcement highlights.* Washington, DC: U.S. Department of Education.

O'Shea, M. F. (1998, July 23). Dear colleague letter: Bowling Green State University. "A policy interpretation: Title IX and intercollegiate athletics." Retrieved from http://www2.ed.gov/about/offices/list/ocr/docs /bowlgrn.html

Porto, B. (2012). You'll never work (or play) here again: A lingering question in Title IX retaliation claims brought by coaches and athletes after Jackson v. Birmingham Board of Education. *Marquette Sports Law Review, 22*(553). Retrieved from http:// scholarship.law.marquette.edu/sportslaw/vol22 /iss2/7

Reynolds, G. (2003, July 11). *Further clarification of intercollegiate athletics policy guidance regarding Title IX compliance.* Washington, DC: Unites States Department of Education.

Reynvaan, J. A. (1992). *Sex discrimination in Washington State University's intercollegiate athletics program: An examination of Washington State University's administrative response to Blair v. WSU from an organizational culture perspective.* Washington State University, Pullman.

Rhoden, W. (2012, June 10). Title IX has not given black female athletes equal opportunity. *New York Times.* Retrieved from http://www.nytimes.com/2012/06/11 /sports/title-ix-has-not-given-black-female-athletes -equal-opportunity.html

Richards v. United States Tennis Association, 400 NYS 2d 267 (NY Sup Ct 1977).

Ryan, J. (1999, June 13). Playing field is still not level. *San Francisco Chronicle.* Retrieved from http://www .sfgate.com/education/article/Playing-Field-Is-Still -Not-Level-2923808.php

Rykoff, A. (2011, August 9). Kellmeyer: "Title IX was what I'm most proud of." *ESPNW.* Retrieved from http://espn.go.com/espnw/features-profiles /6843871/title-ix-was-most-proud-of

Sack, A. L., & Staurowsky, E. J. (1998). College athletes for hire: The evolution and legacy of the NCAA's amateur myth. Westport, CT: Praeger.

Stanley v. University of Southern California. 13 F. 3d 1313 (9th circuit 1994).

Title IX of the Education Amendments of 1972, 20 U.S.C § 1681 (1972).

Toma, J. D. (2003). *Football U.: Spectator sports in the life of the American university.* Ann Arbor: University of Michigan Press.

Toma, J. D., & Kezar, A. J. (Eds.). (1999). *Reconceptualizing the collegiate ideal* (Vol. 105). San Francisco: Jossey Bass.

U.S. District Court, Southern District of Florida, no. 73, 21 Civ NCR.

Ware, S. (2007). *Title IX: A brief history with documents.* Boston: Bedford/St. Martin's.

Weiss, M. (2002). Pay equity for intercollegiate coaches: Exploring the EEOC enforcement guidelines. *Marquette Sports Law Review, 13*(1), 149–171.

Wu, Y. (1999). Kellmeyer: The lawsuit that ruined women's control of intercollegiate athletics for women. Proceedings of the 28th Annual Conference of the North American Society for Sport History, Banff Alberta.

Zeigler, C. (2011, July 13). Moment #89: Washington becomes first state to adopt high school trans athlete policy. Retrieved from http://www.outsports.com/2011/7/13/4051532/moment-89-washington-becomes-first-state-to-adopt-high-school-trans moment-89-washington-becomes-first-state-to-adopt-high-school-trans

TITLE IX COMPLIANCE and INTERCOLLEGIATE ATHLETICS

Barbara Osborne

FUNDAMENTALS AND INSTITUTION-WIDE REQUIREMENTS

Thirty-seven words in the U.S. Code impact every aspect of federally funded education programs, including access to higher education, career education, and math and science: "No person in the United States shall, on the basis of sex, be excluded from participation in, be denied the benefits of, or be subjected to discrimination under any education program or activity receiving Federal financial assistance" (20 U.S.C. § 1681(a)). These words prohibit sexual harassment and sexual violence and differential treatment on the basis of sex in standardized testing or for pregnant and parenting students. School-based sports programs, such as intercollegiate athletics (as well as intramurals and recreation programs), are subject to Title IX because they are extracurricular activities.

Although the legislation was passed by Congress and signed into law in 1972, it was not until 1975 that Code of Federal Regulations were promulgated that provided notice to colleges and universities as to the expected standards to achieve for compliance (34 C.F.R. §106). All institutions are required to designate a Title IX coordinator and establish nondiscrimination policies and grievance procedures (34 C.F.R. §106.8 and 106.9). There is a section in the Regulations that specifically addresses athletic programs (34 C.F.R. §106.41); other sections that intercollegiate athletic administrators need to be aware of for compliance include admissions and recruitment of students (34 C.F.R. §106.21 et al.), financial assistance (34 C.F.R. §106.37), and marital or parental status

Figure 19.1 A women's basketball tournament played at then Moorhead State University, now Minnesota State University Moorhead in Moorhead, Minnesota, on February 20, 1975. Note the lack of championship amenities, the small gym, very few fans, and mismatched uniforms. (Photo courtesy of St. Paul Pioneer Press.)

(34 C.F.R. §106.40). Also, subpart E addresses sex discrimination and employment at educational institutions (34 C.F.R. §106.51). Almost 40 years later, many colleges and universities still do not comply with the Regulations (Figure 19.1).

Every educational institution is required to designate a Title IX coordinator, and to notify students and employees of the name, title, and contact information of this person. The Title IX coordinator is expected to have adequate training regarding Title IX requirements, has supervisory and communications responsibilities for Title IX compliance, and should not have a conflict of interest (34 C.F.R. §106.8(a)). A savvy college athletic administration will seek out and build a strong relationship with the institution's Title IX coordinator. Many athletic administrators and athletes assume that the senior woman administrator (SWA) in the athletic department is the Title IX coordinator. Although the SWA may be a logical choice for an assistant Title IX coordinator role in athletics, given the broad responsibilities for Title IX compliance for all programs and activities across the university, it is unlikely that the SWA has the requisite training or time to serve in the Title IX coordinator role for the entire campus. The SWA role also may present a conflict of interest as it may be impossible to represent an athlete or coach's interest against the athletic department or university.

Another fundamental Title IX requirement for every educational institution is to develop and publish a nondiscrimination policy that expressly states that the school does not discriminate on the basis of sex (34 C.F.R. §106.9). The policy must be distributed broadly to all students and employees and include the contact information for the Title IX coordinator. Similarly, grievance procedures that identify how to report Title IX violations and whom to report them to are also required (34 C.F.R. §106.9). These procedures should be written in plain language and widely distributed as well. As these are institution-wide requirements, there is no need for the athletic department to develop its own policies and procedures. However, best practices dictate that athletic administrators, employees, and athletes should all be informed and that the policies and procedures be included in employee and athlete handbooks and on departmental websites.

TITLE IX AND EQUAL ATHLETICS OPPORTUNITY

In 1979, the Office for Civil Rights (OCR) of the U.S. Department of Education issued a Policy Interpretation specifically targeted at intercollegiate athletic programs to provide additional guidance on the requirements for compliance with Title IX (45 C.F.R. Part 26). The Policy Interpretation focused on three areas—equal participation opportunities, equal treatment, and athletic scholarships—and provided guidance regarding the factors and standards required by the Regulations. It also established that OCR will compare the entirety of the men's athletic program to the entirety of the women's athletic program to determine whether disparities are discriminatory or justifiable.

MEETING THE INTERESTS AND ABILITIES OF MALE AND FEMALE COLLEGE ATHLETES

A significant focus of Title IX compliance has been on providing equal athletic participation opportunities for female athletes, as male athletes have historically enjoyed preferential entitlement to play college sports. From the 1975 Regulations, equal opportunity was to be determined by examining whether "the selection of sports and levels of competition effectively accommodate the interests and abilities of members of both sexes" (34 C.F.R. 106.41(c)(1)). This broad mandate was further clarified in the 1979 Policy Interpretation, which explained that compliance could be achieved by measuring the interest in participation and the abilities of the participants in a variety of ways, and examining the selection of sports and levels of competition offered for each sex (45 C.F.R. Part 26 VII (C)(2)).

Colleges and universities are not required to provide the exact sports for male and female athletes, but they do have to show that they effectively accommodate the underrepresented sex. If a school does not offer both a men's and a women's team in a contact sport, it is expected to add a team if "the opportunities for members of the excluded sex have historically been limited; and there is sufficient interest and ability among the members of the excluded sex to sustain a viable team and a reasonable expectation of intercollegiate competition for that team" (45 C.F.R. Part 26 VII (C)(4)). For noncontact sports, the institution must minimally allow the excluded sex to try out for the team but may still be required to add a team if opportunities have been historically limited and there is sufficient interest and ability to sustain a viable team.

The 1979 Policy Interpretation also introduced the three-part test to measure whether the participation opportunities offered effectively accommodate the interests and abilities of both male and female athletes. Institutions have three options to show compliance:

1. Whether participation levels for men and women in intercollegiate athletics are substantially proportionate to the respective enrollments;

2. Whether there has been a history and continuing practice of program expansion which is demonstrably responsive to the interest and abilities of the underrepresented sex; or

3. Whether it can be demonstrated that the interest and abilities of the members of the underrepresented sex have been fully and effectively accommodated by the present program. (45 C.F.R. Part 26 VII(C)(5)(a))

In addition to these three ways to show nondiscriminatory participation opportunities, athletic departments must also show that both the men's and women's teams on a program-wide basis offer equity in their competitive team schedules.

The three-part test has attracted considerable attention—so much so that many people mistakenly believe that the three-part test is Title IX, or alternatively, that compliance with the three-part test equals compliance with Title IX. Although the federal courts have uniformly upheld the three-part test, critics continued to decry it as an unfair quota system. In response, OCR issued a clarification on the three-part test in 1996. The first option, proportionality, requires that the institution provide comparable athletic opportunities for male and female athletes within 1–2% of the proportion of male to female students in the undergraduate student body. This option has been called a "safe harbor" because it is a simple equation: an institution does not have to fully accommodate the interests and abilities of either sex as long as the provided participation opportunities are proportionate. In determining whether the institution has continued to expand opportunities for the underrepresented sex, the entire history of the athletic program is examined, focusing on the responsiveness of the institution in adding or elevating teams to varsity status. It is important for athletic programs to have a nondiscriminatory policy in place that explains the procedure for requesting the addition or elevation of sports, and that the policy and procedures are clearly communicated to the student body. The third part, full and effective accommodation of the underrepresented sex, is the most flexible for institutions to achieve. Although an athletic program may have significantly disproportionate participation by male and female athletes, the institution only has to show that the imbalance is not due to discrimination. This option gives full consideration to the critics that claim women are not as interested

Adding Men's Sports and Title IX Compliance

Georgia State University is a public university with 18,000 undergraduate students. Like the majority of colleges and universities across the country, the undergraduate enrollment is 58% female and 42% male. The university offers 16 varsity sports—6 for men and 10 for women. The athletics program has experienced tremendous growth, moving from NCAA Division I non-football to Football Championship Subdivision (FCS) to Football Bowl Subdivision (FBS) in just five years. Georgia State provides an example of an institution that is striving to meet the needs of its student body while satisfying Title IX requirements.

In 2006 Georgia State conducted a feasibility study to add intercollegiate football. The university is on a strong growth trajectory, which includes increasing the residential student population and providing a full college experience in downtown Atlanta. An integral part of this plan is to build a stronger athletics program that includes football. The primary funding for the football team came from an increase in student fees, which was approved by the student body. A consultant was hired to coordinate the football launch, and the program was officially approved and announced on April 17, 2008.

In February 2009, Cheryl Levick was hired as athletic director. At the time she was hired, the university had seven football coaches, one player and two helmets, so getting the football program operational was a major focus. Seventy-one players reported for practice in August, just six months after Levick's arrival, and the Georgia State football team played its first official game in September 2010 as a member of the Colonial Athletic Association, an NCAA FCS conference. The university has accepted an offer to become a member of the Sun Belt Conference and began playing as an FBS institution in fall 2013.

When Levick was hired, Georgia State did not have a comprehensive gender equity plan in place. To address immediate needs, the addition of sand volleyball was announced in September 2011. Sand volleyball is currently recognized as an emerging sport by the NCAA. Constructing a new sand volleyball facility took almost a year, and Georgia State's sand volleyball team completed its first season in spring 2013.

Also in fall 2011, the university hired a consultant to do a comprehensive Title IX assessment. The evaluation took a full year to complete, examining every area of Title IX from scholarships to participation opportunities to equal treatment in all program components. From the data gathered through the assessment, a formal Gender Equity Plan was established, including recommendations to add women's swimming and diving and women's lacrosse to Georgia State's varsity sports offerings. The plan was approved by the Faculty Subcommittee on Athletics in the spring of 2012.

In addition to increasing participation opportunities for women, Georgia State's athletics program is also working on addressing some of the inequities identified in the examination of program components from the Title IX assessment. Efforts have already been made to increase marketing efforts for women's sports. Similarly, gender-neutral travel policies have been established to eliminate past disparities in travel accommodations.

Few, if any, intercollegiate athletics programs are in complete compliance with all of the Title IX regulations. Georgia State Athletics demonstrates that diligent efforts to achieve compliance can include adding athletic opportunities for both men and women. ■

in sports as men. However, if the underrepresented sex can show interest in a sport that is not offered, there are sufficient numbers of students with appropriate competitive ability to sustain a team, and competition is available to create a comparable schedule, the institution will not be able to prove compliance with this option. Rather than mandate a one-size-fits-all quota, the three-part test provides significant flexibility for athletic administrators to choose the best method for compliance for each institution.

While organizations such as the American Sports Council (formerly the Collegiate Sports Council) complain that men's teams are being cut because of Title IX, and some institutions have discontinued teams citing Title IX as a reason, OCR issued a clarification in 2003 stating that "nothing in Title IX requires the cutting or reduction of teams in order to demonstrate compliance with Title IX, and that the elimination of teams is a disfavored practice" (para 11).

Contrary to claims that Title IX is unnecessary, or that it is hurting men's sports, intercollegiate athletics is experiencing its highest levels of participation for both male and female athletes. Although schools have cut men's programs, particularly wrestling, women's teams have been cut as well. However, many of the opportunities that were eliminated were replaced by adding men's and women's soccer, men's and women's lacrosse, and even more football teams, reflecting the current interests of students. Currently, increases in male participation in intercollegiate athletics are outpacing new opportunities for female athletes (Irick, 2012).

STAKEHOLDER PERSPECTIVE

Dick Rasmussen, Executive Secretary of the University Athletic Association

The University Athletic Association (UAA) is a NCAA Division III athletic conference comprising eight of the leading private liberal arts research universities in the United States. When the UAA was formed in 1988, the founding presidents articulated that "women's programs must be included in the new association with the same degree of support as men's programs." One of the fundamental principles articulated in the UAA Constitution states: "Equal opportunities in athletics shall be provided for men and women." This commitment to equity and excellence throughout the athletic enterprise is found in the Association's Statement of Philosophy as well.

Dick Rasmussen, executive secretary of the UAA, explains how the conference operates in order to achieve equity:

From its inception, men's and women's teams across the UAA have traveled and competed together. Soccer and basketball teams play a unified schedule in which both teams play the same institutional opponents on the same day at the same venue. The order of contests are alternated in a manner that women's and men's coaches, as well as athletic and academic administrators, agree makes sense for their athletes and provides equitable competitive

experiences. Championships in cross country, swimming and diving, and track and field have always been conducted as joint championships, alternating men's and women's events.

The UAA's commitment to gender equity is also reflected in the organization of the leadership and the sports committees of the association. Two of the founding presidents were women, and four women have served as athletic directors on member campuses. The head coaches of men's and women's teams meet together on sports committees to govern their respective sports. ■

ATHLETIC SCHOLARSHIPS

The Regulations require that athletically related financial assistance, otherwise known as athletic scholarships or athletic grants-in-aid, be allocated in proportion to the numbers of male and female students participating in intercollegiate athletics (34 C.F.R. §106.37). The scholarships proportion is calculated by measuring the amount of scholarship funding provided to each sex and dividing it by the number of male and female participants in the athletic program. There may be legitimate, nondiscriminatory reasons for differences, such as in-state versus out-of-state tuition, but the guiding principle under Title IX is that access to higher education in the form of financial assistance cannot be discriminatory on the basis of sex.

Research indicates that colleges and universities may be confused about the scholarships requirement. Using data that institutions are required to report under the Equity in Athletics Disclosure Act, Osborne and Anderson (2011) found that only 24% of National Collegiate Athletic Association (NCAA) Division I institutions were substantially in compliance (defined as within 2%). Just over a quarter (26%) of the schools were substantially overfunding men's athletic scholarships, and surprisingly, half (50%) were overfunding women's athletic scholarships. There were significant differences between FBS, FCS, and nonfootball members of Division I. The majority of FBS schools (58%) were overspending on men's scholarships, and only 22 schools (18%) were spending too much on women's scholarships. Scholarship spending at FCS schools was more evenly distributed with 31% overspending on men's scholarships, 33% in substantial compliance, and 36% overspending on women's scholarships. Only six institutions without football (6%) were overspending on men's scholarships, while 77% were overspending on women's athletic scholarships. One possible explanation is that athletic departments may be trying to compensate for sex-based inequities in other parts of the program by spending more on women's scholarships, which unfortunately is not considered within the Title IX compliance framework. Another explanation lies within the NCAA rules regarding scholarship limitations. Institutions that provide scholarships funding for all sports at maximum NCAA levels may find themselves out of compliance because of head count versus equivalency sports depending upon the various teams that school offers (Osborne & Anderson, 2011). It is important to note that compliance with NCAA rules is not equivalent with Title IX compliance.

EQUAL TREATMENT

Beyond providing athletic participation opportunities, and funding those opportunities with athletic scholarships, equal opportunity also requires that male and female athletes are treated equally. The 1975 Regulations identify nine specific athletic program components as well as a catchall "other factors" category to be evaluated to determine whether the availability, quality, and types of benefits, opportunities,

TABLE 19.1

Program Components to Determine Equal Treatment: The "Laundry List"

PROGRAM COMPONENTS	FACTORS TO CONSIDER TO DETERMINE EQUAL TREATMENT AND BENEFITS
Provision and maintenance of equipment and supplies	Availability, quality, quantity, and suitability of equipment and supplies; maintenance and replacement schedules
Scheduling of games and practice times	The number of competitive events per sport; number and length of practice opportunities; time of day competitive events and practices are scheduled; opportunities for pre-season and post-season participation.
Travel and per diem expenses	Quality of transportation vehicle(s), hotel accommodations, and dining options; length of pre- and post-game stay; amount of per diem allowances
Opportunity to receive coaching and academic tutoring	Relative availability of full-time/part-time coaches, assistant coaches, and graduate assistants (measured as full-time equivalency ratios to number of student-athletes); criteria for obtaining academic tutoring/assistance; quantity of tutors available
Assignment and compensation of coaches and tutors	Determine whether compensation or assignment policies or practices deny male and female athletes coaching or tutors of equivalent quality, nature, or availability; equivalent assignment examines training, experience, professional standing, and qualifications of coaches and tutors; equivalent compensation considers rate of compensation per sport, per season, duration of contracts, experience, duties, working conditions, and conditions related to contract renewal or other terms of employment
Provision of locker rooms, practice and competitive facilities	Quality and availability of facilities; exclusivity of use; maintenance and upkeep; facilities preparation and breakdown for practices and competition
Provision of medical and training services and facilities	Availability and qualifications of doctors, athletic trainers, and other medical personnel; provision of health, accident, or injury insurance; availability and quality of strength and conditioning facilities
Provision of housing and dining services and facilities	Access to and assignment of housing; quality of housing provided; amenities or special services provided (e.g., laundry facilities, housekeeping service, parking); access to dining services; quality and quantity of meal plans or services provided
Publicity	Availability and quality of sports information/athletics communications personnel; availability and access to publicity resources; quality and quantity of publications and other promotional devices including conventional and digital media
Other factors affecting equal opportunity, such as support services	Availability, quality, and quantity of administrative, clerical, and operational support personnel
Recruitment (§106.21ff.)	Availability of personnel and opportunities to recruit; resources available for recruiting; limitations that may impact recruiting

and treatment provided to male and female athletes are equivalent when comparing the men's program as a whole to the women's program as a whole. Table 19.1 identifies the various program components and provides information about the various ways that equivalence is determined.

Compliance does not require that the school provide identical benefits or treatment, as each sport has unique aspects that may justify differential treatment (45 C.F.R. Part 26(B)(2)). In evaluating whether an athletic program is in compliance with this requirement, the men's program as a whole is compared to the women's program as a whole for each line item. A single disparity within a component may be substantial enough to deny equal treatment. For example, all men's and women's teams at an institution share the same practice and competitive facilities, with the exception of baseball and softball. These sports are unique and require different fields. If the baseball field is on campus, has been recently renovated, and provides state-of-the-art amenities for both athletes and spectators, but the softball field is off-campus, is very old, and is poorly maintained by the local parks department, this disparity may be enough for a finding of noncompliance. A simple way to conceptualize equal treatment is to imagine giving everything that the women's program has to the men, and vice versa. If both your male and female athletes are still happy with what they now have, both programs are probably being treated equally.

PREGNANCY

Title IX Regulations also prohibit discrimination against any student on the basis of pregnancy, childbirth, false pregnancy, termination of pregnancy, or recovery from these conditions (34 C.F.R. § 106.40(b)(1)). In 2007, ESPN's *Outside the Lines* aired a segment titled "Pregnant Pause" about female athletes who terminated their pregnancies because they feared losing their athletic scholarships. These athletes were forced to sign team contracts that threatened dismissal from the team and revocation of athletic scholarships if they became pregnant. All of these actions are prohibited under Title IX.

In 2008 the NCAA published a model policy to provide intercollegiate athletic programs guidance in assisting athletes who become pregnant (Hogshead-Makar & Sorensen, 2008). Medically, most pregnant athletes can continue to participate without restrictions through the first 14 weeks and then may continue participation based on the advice of an obstetrician. Some athletes, such as golfers, may be able to practice and compete throughout the entire pregnancy. It is important to remember that pregnancy is a temporary medical condition, not a moral dilemma that requires punishment. The Regulations mandate that pregnant athletes be treated like any other athlete with a temporary medical condition—they can't be kicked off the team, prevented from attending practices, dressing for games, or traveling to games, *unless* that is the same way that other athletes who are medically unable to play are treated (34 C.F.R. §106.40(b)(4)). Similarly, decisions regarding safe participation should be made by a physician, not by the coach.

SEXUAL HARASSMENT AND SEXUAL VIOLENCE

Sexual harassment, unwelcome conduct of a sexual nature, is a serious problem in U.S. schools. Over 80% of students have experienced sexual harassment at some time during their school years, and approximately 20% of college women and 6% of college men are victims of sexual assault or attempted assault (Dear Colleague Letter, 2011). Sexual harassment is discrimination based on sex, and when it negatively impacts or limits a student's ability to equally receive the benefits of an educational program or activity, it is a violation of Title IX. Title IX protects students from harassment by employees (such as administrators or coaches), peers (other students or athletes), and even third parties who are engaged in school activities or do business on campus such as officials or media.

All schools are required to have policies and procedures in place that eliminate harassment, prevent its recurrence, and address its effects (Dear Colleague Letter, 2011). The athletic program should not create its own policies and procedures. Instead, all athletic program personnel, as well as athletes, should be educated about the institution's procedures and how to report incidents. This information should also be easily accessible on the athletic department website, and in employee and athlete handbooks. It is critically important for athletes and employees to know whom to report to if there is a complaint. The university is responsible for ensuring that university personnel are able to recognize when harassment has occurred and then take prompt and effective action to end the harassment. The institution must also prevent recurrence of harassment and retaliation against the victim or any others who reported the issues. Support services should be available to remedy the effects of the harassment (Revised Guidance, 2001).

Participation in athletics is both physical and emotional, and athletes and personnel spend a significant amount of time together building close personal relationships. Sexual harassment occurs when conduct of a sexual nature is "unwelcome." However, intercollegiate athletes are adults who may choose to engage in consensual sexual relationships with athletic department personnel. The NCAA strongly encourages its members to create athletic department policies that prohibit romantic or sexual relationships between department personnel and athletes, without exception (Brake & Nelson, 2012). There is a significant power differential between athletes and coaches, which puts consent at issue. Even if both parties do consent, the relationship is likely to have a negative impact on the rest of the team, compromising the athletes' ability to fully receive the benefits of their participation, which is a violation of Title IX.

Schools may also have liability under Title IX for acts of sexual harassment and sexual violence committed by athletes. While sexual assault and rape are criminal matters and the criminal justice system has responsibility for determining guilt and punishing the perpetrator, properly addressing sexual violence is a responsibility for schools as well. The majority of acts involving sexual violence on campus do not involve athletes, but research indicates that masculine-dominated environments promote objectification of women (Crosset, 2000). This, combined with the athletes' expectation of entitlement, peer support and approval, rewards for engaging in aggressive behavior, and failure of coaches or administrators to discipline athletes, has been found to increase the likelihood that athletes will commit acquaintance rape, sexual violence, and sexual assault (Crosset, 2000; Dear Colleague Letter, 2011). The institution is responsible when it creates a culture that promotes sexual violence (i.e., by demeaning women or recruiting athletes with a history of sexual violence) or allows that culture to perpetuate by not disciplining athletes, covering up the incidents, or pressuring the victim to keep quiet. Schools that have not upheld their responsibilities under Title IX have paid millions in damages to the victims of sexual violence (*Simpson v. University of Colorado*, 2007; *Williams v. Board of Regents*, 2007).

TITLE IX ENFORCEMENT

Title IX has been the law for more than 40 years, but many schools have either willfully or negligently disregarded their obligations to comply. The Office for Civil Rights of the U.S. Department of Education is responsible for administrative enforcement of Title IX. Anyone who believes a school is not complying with the law may file a complaint with OCR. Once a complaint is filed, OCR will notify the school of the complaint and request information to begin an investigation. At this time, schools have several options to resolve the matter. Before completing the investigation, OCR may act as a facilitator between the complainant and the institution to settle the matter. If the parties cannot settle their differences, the school may attempt to settle directly with OCR. Settlements generally will include establishing or revising nondiscriminatory policies and procedures related to the specific claim, education and training of all school-related personnel regarding the compliance requirements under Title IX and the new policies and procedures (if any), and some sort of restitution to make the complainant whole. If OCR and the school are not able to come to terms for a settlement, OCR will complete the investigation and issue a formal record of findings, including a plan for the institution to become Title IX compliant and monitoring progress toward, and achievement of, compliance. While most OCR investigations remain narrowly focused on the complainant's claims, the agency does have the authority to initiate comprehensive compliance reviews whether a complaint has been made against a school or not.

People who believe they have personally suffered discrimination under Title IX also have the option of filing a civil lawsuit; a full range of judicial remedies including injunctions and monetary damages are available to plaintiffs that litigate successfully. Lawsuits are costly and time consuming, for both the plaintiff and the institution. Our judicial system encourages settlement between parties, and many lawsuits are settled. However, those cases that are not settled may take several years to be resolved. Institutions that have been found in violation of Title IX have been ordered to pay plaintiff's attorney's fees and damages of millions of dollars. Ironically, the cost to the institution to treat all athletes (and employees) fairly is generally much less than the investment made to litigate the matter.

CONCLUSION

While much of the media focuses on the business of college sports and the commercialization of football and men's basketball, it is important to remember that the core of college sport participation is access to education. Girls who participate in sports are academically more successful, complete more education, are more likely to work full-time and pursue nontraditional careers (Staurowsky et al., 2009). All of these traits are consistent with the mission of higher education to prepare productive citizens in a democratic society.

QUESTIONS FOR DISCUSSION

1. After 40 years, why have schools been so slow to become compliant with Title IX?

2. Title IX was enacted to address sex discrimination in education, and women have constituted the majority of college students for more than a decade. Is Title IX still necessary?

3. How are the requirements under the Regulations and the three-part test related?

References

Brake, D. L., & Nelson, M. B. (2012). *Staying in bounds: A model policy to prevent inappropriate relationships between student-athletes and athletic department personnel*. Indianapolis, IN: NCAA Publications.

Clarification of Intercollegiate Athletics Policy Guidance: The Three-Part Test. (1996). Retrieved from http://www2.ed.gov/about/offices/list/ocr/docs/clarific.html#two

Crosset, T. (2000). Athletic affiliation and violence against women: Toward a structural prevention project. In J. McKay, M. Messner, & D. Sabo (Eds.), *Research on men and masculinities: Masculinities, gender relations, and sport* (pp. 147–162). Thousand Oaks: Sage.

Dear Colleague Letter. (2011). Retrieved from http://www2.ed.gov/print/about/offices/list/ocr/letters/colleague-201104.html

Further Clarification of Intercollegiate Athletics Policy Guidance Regarding Title IX Compliance. (2003). Retrieved from http://www2.ed.gov/about/offices/list/ocr/title9guidanceFinal.html

Hogshead-Makar, N., & Sorensen, E. (2008). *Pregnant and parenting student-athletes: Resources and model policies*. Indianapolis, IN: NCAA Gender Equity.

Retrieved from http://www.nacua.org/documents/NCAAParentingHandbook.pdf

Irick, E. (2012). *NCAA sports sponsorship and participations rates report 1981-1982-2011-2012.* Indianapolis, IN: NCAA. Retrieved from http://www.ncaapublications.com/productdownloads/PR2013.pdf

Osborne, B., & Anderson, P. (2011, March). *Scholarship equity: A new look at an old requirement.* Paper presented at the annual meeting of the Sport and Recreation Law Association, Savannah, GA.

Policy Interpretation. 45 C.F.R. Part 26 (1979). Retrieved from http://www2.ed.gov/about/offices/list/ocr/docs/t9interp.html

A Policy Interpretation; Title IX and Intercollegiate Athletics, 45 C.F. R. Part 26 (1979). Retrieved from http://www2.ed.gov/about/offices/list/ocr/docs/t9interp.html

Regulations. (1975). 34 C.F.R. Part 106.41. Retrieved from http://www2.ed.gov/policy/rights/reg/ocr/edlite-34cfr106.html

Revised Sexual Harassment Guidance: Harassment of Students by School Employees, Other Students, or Third Parties. (2001). Washington, DC: US Department of Education, Office for Civil Rights. Retrieved from http://www2.ed.gov/about/offices/list/ocr/docs/shguide.pdf

Simpson v. University of Colorado, 2007 U.S. App. LEXIS 21478 (10th Cir. 2007).

Staurowsky, E. J., DeSousa, M. J., Ducher, G., Gentner, N., Miller, K. E., Shakib, S., Theberge, N., & Williams, N. (2009). *Her life depends on it II: Sport, physical activity, and the health and well-being of American girls and women.* East Meadow, NY: Women's Sports Foundation.

Staurowsky, E. J., & Weight, E. (2011). Title IX literacy: What coaches don't know and need to find out. *Journal of Intercollegiate Sport, 4,* 190–209.

Title IX of the Education Amendments, 20 U.S.C. § 1681 et seq. (1972).

U.S. Department of Education, Office for Civil Rights. (2013). *Supporting the academic success of pregnant and parenting students under Title IX of the education amendments of 1972.* Washington, DC. Retrieved from ttp://www2.ed.gov/about/offices/list/ocr/docs/pregnancy.pdf

Williams v. Board of Regents of University System of Georgia, 477 F.3d 1282 (11th Cir. 2007).

BARRIERS to LEADERSHIP for WOMEN in COLLEGE ATHLETICS

Erin E. Buzuvis

Today there is an enormous gender disparity among collegiate head coaches and athletic administrators in the United States. Women fill less than a quarter of head coach and athletic director positions in college athletics and are even minorities among coaches of women's teams (Acosta & Carpenter, 2012). Few other professions are as impervious to gender integration. Leadership in college athletics is, in the words of one scholar, one of the "few male bastions remaining" (Kane, 2001, p. 115), which raises the question: Why are women so starkly underrepresented in leadership positions within college athletics? There is no easy answer, but rather a variety of factors that exclude, deter, or cause an early exit for women who would have otherwise pursued careers in college athletics. After presenting the demographics of leadership in college athletics to illustrate this gender disparity, this chapter considers the unique barriers women face when seeking entry to the profession, the ways in which athletic departments operate to constrain women's advancement and retention in their jobs, and the combined effect of these and other factors on women's interest and motivation to pursue or remain in leadership positions in college athletics.

THE CHANGING DEMOGRAPHICS OF COLLEGE ATHLETICS

Today the number of female college head coaches is at an all-time high. According to the most recent update by Acosta and Carpenter (2012) to their 35-year longitudinal study of the gender demographics of college athletics, there are 3,974 women serving as head coaches of women's teams, plus another estimated 200–300 women who coach men's teams.

Yet despite the gains by women in absolute terms, two comparisons suggest that the number of female head coaches is not as high as it could or should be. First is the comparison to the number of men serving in similar positions. The 3,974 women coaching women's teams constitute only 42.9% of head coaching positions in women's college sports. More than 5,300 women's teams (57%) have a male head coach. Men outnumber women as head coaches of women's teams in all three athletic divisions, but are particularly overrepresented in Division II, where they coach 62.5% of women's teams. Male dominance in head coaching positions also varies by sport. Men are the extreme minority among coaches of women's sports like synchronized swimming (0%), field hockey (6.2%), equestrian (10.0%), and lacrosse (14.9%). Men are also outnumbered—though considerably less so—among coaches of women's softball (37.9%), basketball (40.5%), and volleyball (46.7%). Yet men dominate as head coaches of women's sports like rowing (63.1%), soccer (67.8%), tennis (70.1%), swimming and diving (73.8%), ice hockey (75.5%), cross country (78.8%), and track and field (80.8%). In contrast, the number of female head coaches of men's teams amounts to only 2%, demonstrating that cross-gender coaching is almost entirely the domain of men.

The second relevant comparison is to the percentage of female head coaches over time. According to Acosta and Carpenter's (2012) data, the percentage of female head coaches in women's college sports has been declining since the passage of Title IX. In 1972, when Congress passed the law prohibiting sex discrimination in education, there were far fewer women's teams than there are today; yet women coached a vast majority (90%) of them. By 1978, the year the federal government initially designated as the deadline for compliance with Title IX, the number of women's athletic teams more than doubled—from an average of about 2.5 teams to 5.6 teams per school—creating many new coaching positions in women's sports. Correspondingly, the percentage of women coaching women's teams decreased to 58.2% in that short time. The percentage has dropped fairly steadily since then, reaching its lowest in 2006 (42.4%) and recovering slightly between then and 2012 (42.9%).

Acosta and Carpenter (2012) have also reported on the gender demographics of college athletic administrators. In 2012 there were 215 female athletic directors—36 in Division I, 46 in Division II, and 133 in Division III. Expressed as a percentage, 20.3% of college athletic directors are female. For historical perspective, it is important to note that in 1972, men's and women's athletic programs were separate, and the vast majority of women's programs were led by a female director. Today, nearly all colleges have merged once-separate programs into a single department. The fact that only 1 in 5 athletic directors are women suggest that mergers more often expanded the jurisdiction of male administrators of men's athletics at the expense of female administrators of women's athletics than the other way around (Hoffman, 2011).

Looking more broadly at college athletics administration, women have somewhat higher levels of representation but are still a minority, constituting about a third of athletic administrators overall. Acosta and Carpenter (2012) have kept tabs on the percentage of colleges in which there is not a single woman serving in the athletic department administration and report that figure to be at an all-time low of 9.2%. Yet many schools employ female administrators in a token capacity, as suggested by the fact that the average number of female administrators per administration is 1.41. While their longitudinal study does not indicate the types of jobs women are more likely to hold within college athletics, others report that women who serve in athletics administration are relegated to support positions such as academic advising, compliance, marketing, life skills, and sports information (Coakley, 2008). They are also assigned to oversee women's sports and excluded from oversight of revenue-producing sports (Inglis, Danylchuk, & Pastore, 2000).

Acosta and Carpenter's longitudinal data should also be considered in conjunction with others that examine the racial demographics of college athletics. The National Collegiate Athletic Association (NCAA) regularly reports such data for its member institutions, most recently, for the 2009–2010 academic year (Irick, 2011). At that time, there were 208 female athletic directors, 21 of whom were black and 3 Asian, 1 Hispanic, and 1 who responded "two or more races." In that same year, women held 4,214 head coaching positions (23%) overall. Of those women, 87% were white, 9% were black, and the remaining 4% reflect the combined percentage of Hispanic, Asian, Native American/Pacific Islander, and those who reported "two or more races." A deeper examination of the data suggests that these low percentages of minority female coaches are disproportionately low in some contexts. For instance, black women constitute 10.7% of head coaches of women's basketball despite making up 50.1% of the athletes participating in that sport (Borland & Bruening, 2010).

HEGEMONIC MASCULINITY IN SPORTS

To understand the gender gap in college athletics, we must first understand the interconnected nature of sport, power, and gender in our society. Sport has, from its origins, operated as a means to ascribe power to men, by creating the highly visible, symbolic linking of power with masculinity in a way that makes that association appear natural and legitimate (e.g., Messner, 1988; Willis, 1982). As a result, the ways in which women are denied access to sports and its associations with power are largely unquestioned and unseen. In fact, the hegemonic nature of this phenomenon means that men and women alike perpetuate the association of masculinity and power through sports. Women are excluded from opportunities within sports, whether through lawful or unlawful means, or their interest suppressed by external social forces that make their actions appear to be internal and agentic, or their opportunities to engage in the sporting enterprise are constructed on different terms so as to pose no threat to the gender order. Evidence of hegemonic masculinity in sports can help explain the imperviousness of college athletic departments to leadership of women (Whisenant, Pedersen, & Obenour, 2002), as it offers a framework to explain the barriers to entry, job constraints, and the construction of women's athletic interest and motivation that all contribute to the gender imbalance of leadership in college athletics.

BARRIERS TO ENTRY

Women's representation among the ranks of coaches of collegiate women's teams dropped precipitously in the early years of Title IX, as the new law motivated colleges and universities to rapidly expand and improve athletic opportunities for women. Before the statute's passage in 1972, women's sports was, in the words of one historian, "a small time venture, hardly noticed by anyone but the participants" (Festle, 1996, p. 99). Women had opportunities to engage in intercollegiate competition, but these opportunities were less numerous, less visible, and received considerably fewer resources than the athletic opportunities afforded to men. Women with backgrounds in physical education organized and coached athletic opportunities for women, and did so through organizations like the Commission on Intercollegiate Athletics for Women (CIAW) (1966–1972) and the Association for Intercollegiate Athletics for Women (1971–1983). These organizations provided opportunities for women's leadership of women's athletics, and they espoused an athlete-centered model of sports rooted in educational values that was distinctly different from the competitive, commercial model of the NCAA (Staurowsky, 2011). But Title IX's passage brought changes to women's sports. The law's mandate for equal treatment and equal opportunity meant that women's sports could no longer be treated like a little stepsister by university athletic departments. To university leaders, this meant striving to conform existing women's sports programs to the dominant, competitive, and commercial model of sports espoused by the NCAA, which had begun holding women's championships in 1981–1982. Perceiving the NCAA to be the more legitimate governing body for what would now be competitive programs in women's sports, colleges and universities withdrew their affiliations with the AIAW, causing its demise, and established the male-dominated NCAA as the premier athletic association for both men's and women's sports (Drago, Hennighausen, Rogers, Vescio, & Stauffer, 2005).

These rapid changes in the early years of Title IX explain the precipitous decline in the ranks of female leaders in women's sports. The integration of women's sports into the prevailing, high-stakes commercial model of college athletics squeezed out women leaders, with their athlete-centered, educational approach. Some left head coaching and other leadership positions rather than compromise their values, while others were likely seen as unqualified to coach newly created women's teams that were expected, like their men's counterparts, to win at all cost (Hasbrook, Hart, Mathes, & True, 1990). Men, in turn, were likely attracted to the new positions of leadership in women's sports now that those positions were infused with Title IX's promise of support and the NCAA's venire of legitimacy.

Since that time, men have been successfully competing with women for positions in women's sports, but the reverse is rarely true. Discrimination, motivated by stereotypes about women and their compatibility for leadership in competitive athletics, is believed to erect significant barriers for entry to women seeking to advance into head coaching or senior administrative positions in athletics.

Homologous Reproduction

Researchers have offered several theoretical lenses through which to examine and explain these barriers to entry. One is homologous reproduction, the tendency for the dominant group to preserve that dominance by "systematically reproducing themselves in their own image" (Stangl & Kane, 1991, p. 50). The theory helps explain why athletic departments led by men have fewer women in other positions of leadership, as several studies have shown (Acosta & Carpenter, 2012; Stangl & Kane, 1991; Welch & Sigelman, 2007). The homologous character of a dominant group of insiders is reproduced by extending a presumption that those of the same sex or race as the insider group are qualified to be insiders, and requiring others to prove their qualification for membership. As applied to athletics, this may explain other research findings that women who are hired for head coaching positions are in some ways better credentialed than their male counterparts (Hasbrook et al., 1990), why those credentials do not help women in the pipeline for head coaching positions as much as they help men (Cunningham & Sagas, 2002), and why "social capital" (stronger interpersonal networks) is more predictive of job success for male than for female administrators (Sagas & Cunningham, 2004). It could also explain why male athletic directors are generally hired younger and at more prestigious institutions than their female counterparts (Whisenant et al., 2002). Without access to the same favorable presumptions of legitimacy, it takes women longer to reach the top.

Social Role and Role Congruity Theories

Another set of related theories, social role theory and role congruity theory, also explain how stereotypes and biases hamstring women's entry into leadership positions in college athletics. Social role theory is the idea that society has different expectations for men and women. While women are expected to be communal in nature—described with such adjectives as "affectionate, helpful, kind, sympathetic, interpersonally sensitive, nurturing, and gentle"—men are ascribed "agentic" characteristics, such as " being aggressive, dominant, forceful, self-confident and self-sufficient" (Burton, Grappendort, & Henderson, 2011). Therefore, jobs that society associates with characteristics expected of women are viewed as incompatible for men, and vice versa. Known as role congruity theory, this idea explains why jobs deemed to require communal characteristics are seen as more appropriate for women, while jobs seen to require agentic characteristics are deemed appropriate for men. Role congruity theory also explains prejudice against both men and women who hold or aspire to positions that are inconsistent with their perceived roles.

Researchers have found evidence suggesting that role congruity theory operates in college athletic departments. For example, participants in one study perceived certain managerial qualities to be masculine, as well as associated with the expectations of an athletic director (Burton, Barr, Fink, & Bruening, 2009). These associations could contribute both to bias against female applicants for athletic director positions, a possibility supported by a follow-up study in which college athletic administrators predicted that a hypothetical male candidate was much more likely to be selected for an athletic director position and that a hypothetical female candidate was more likely to be selected for the position of life skills director. Internalized perceptions of gender roles and expectations about role congruity may also explain why women would engage in self-limiting behavior, such as choosing not to apply for an athletic director position or expressing disinterest in leadership (Sartore & Cunningham, 2007).

Pervasive gender roles also create the expectation that women serve as the primary caretaker of children. This expectation leads many hiring decision makers, consciously or otherwise, to assume that a female applicant for a leadership position in college athletics is less capable of succeeding in demanding job like head coach or athletic director. A male applicant may be seen as less encumbered by family responsibilities, and thus more likely to be devoted to the job (Dixon & Bruening, 2005). Expectations that women are not competitive or aggressive may also disadvantage women aspiring to head coaching positions. These expectations may also explain why positions coaching men are largely off-limits to women, and why when women are hired to coach men it is usually in men's sports with the least prestige and in the least competitive divisions (Kamphoff, Armentrout, & Driska, 2010).

Intersectionality

Stereotypes about race and sex orientation intersect to magnify the barriers to entry experienced by those who are or are perceived to be minorities in additional ways than sex. People of color are also underrepresented among positions of power in college athletic departments, so the tendency of homologous reproduction puts women of color at a double disadvantage. Women of color also report serving a "token" candidate to help hiring committees create the appearance of inclusivity and cover for the fact that a nonminority candidate had the inside track all along (Borland & Bruening, 2010).

Heterosexism and antilesbian bias suppress the hiring of women as well, due to the perception that lesbians do not comply with expected social roles for women and are thus destabilizing to male-dominated culture (Griffin, 1998). Lesbians are saddled with negative stereotypes such as sexually seductive and predatory, masculine, aggressive, and harmful toward children (Sartore & Cunningham, 2007). "In general, it is perceived that lesbians are bad for the 'image of women's sport.' Lack of sponsorship, fan support, and respect for women's sport is often blamed on the 'lesbian presence'" (Krane & Barber, 2005, p. 68). These stereotypes and negative attitudes force female applicants who are lesbian to remain closeted and privilege indicia of heterosexuality. As one research participant told Borland and Bruening (2010), "The easiest way to get a head coaching position is to be married" (p. 413). A strong bias operating against a large subset of women—that is, those who are not married to male partners or can otherwise claim heterosexuality—cuts significantly into the pool of women deemed hirable by athletic departments trading in such concerns and surely contributes to women's overall underrepresentation in coaching and leadership hires.

CONSTRAINTS TO WOMEN'S ADVANCEMENT AND RETENTION

College athletic departments may be structured in ways that constrain women's opportunities to advance or remain in head coaching positions and in positions of administrative leadership. One such constraint is due to the fact that women's athletic programs, the programs to which women's coaching opportunities are effectively limited, in general receive less support than men's programs, which can set female coaches up to appear less successful than their male counterparts. A female coach with comparatively fewer assistant coaches, a lower operating budget, fewer resources for recruiting, and diminished access to quality equipment and facilities does not have the same potential for success as her well-supported male counterpart (Inglis et al., 2000). Yet, especially at the most competitive institutions, a coach's ability to produce wins is highly influential in the decision to renew her job contract. The fact that more female head coaches are found in prestigious institutions that devote more resources to women's sports (Welch & Sigelman, 2007) supports the notion that resource allocation is essential to the success of female coaches.

Another set of constraints to retention and promotion of women in athletics can be found in the way job responsibilities are distributed. Women report being "set up to fail" by the assignment of "hidden" job responsibilities and expectations that do not appear on paper (Inglis et al., 2000). Women are also more likely to be saddled with the responsibilities that are not as valued within the department. Gender equity, for example, is marginalized as an issue of concern for female staff, not the entire department (Inglis et al., 2000). Yet women who take on this responsibility may be targeted for retaliation for advancing an agenda that may conflict with the objective of the dominant group, which has a stake in men's athletics (Buzuvis, 2010).

Women's job responsibilities may also position them outside the track to advanced levels of leadership. For example, black female assistant coaches in basketball reported that they must also serve as "token recruiters" (i.e., of black female athletes) and, as a result, are not exposed to other facets of the job that would enable

Sex Discrimination in College Athletics

In 2006 two former head coaches and one former associate athletics director filed lawsuits against California State University, Fresno. The three plaintiffs, all women, alleged that they had lost their jobs in retaliation for having spoken out against sex discrimination within the athletics department. The facts of their cases demonstrate how dangerous it can be for female coaches and administrators to challenge hegemonic masculinity in athletics. At the same time, however, the outcomes of these cases should serve as a cautionary tale to deter other athletics departments from behaving similarly in the future.

One plaintiff was Associate Athletic Director Diane Milutinovich, a 22-year department veteran who in 2002 filed a complaint with the Department of Education's Office for Civil Rights, alleging that Fresno State was violating Title IX by failing to devote sufficient resources and opportunities to female athletes and by discriminating in the compensation of employees of women's athletics. Soon after filing this complaint, Milutinovich learned that her position had been eliminated and that she was being transferred outside the department. When she continued to advocate for gender equity in athletics, she was terminated from that position as well.

Head volleyball coach Lindy Vivas also filed a complaint about Title IX violations stemming from the department's lack of support for her program. In addition, she blew the whistle on the department's practice of awarding shorter employment contracts to female coaches. In apparent response, the athletics director decided not to renew Vivas's contract, despite her success as a coach for 14 years. Soon thereafter, the director terminated another female head coach, Stacy Johnson-Klein, who was threatening to complain publicly about sexual harassment and discriminatory treatment of the women's basketball team.

All three women filed Title IX lawsuits challenging these acts of apparent retaliation. In October 2007, Fresno State settled with Milutinovich for $3.5 million. But Vivas's and Johnson-Klein's lawsuits both went to trial, where they produced not only multimillion-dollar verdicts for the plaintiffs but volumes of testimony about the department's hostile and homophobic environment and discriminatory treatment of female coaches and staff. For example, one witness in Vivas's trial testified about the athletics director's vilification of those he perceived to be lesbians and his preference for hiring female coaches who were "straight and attractive." And the testimony in Johnson-Klein's case revealed how attractive, feminine coaches were vulnerable to sexual harassment and exploitation.

The jurors in both cases agreed that the plaintiffs were unlawfully terminated. In Johnson-Klein's case, this verdict came notwithstanding the fact Johnson-Klein had suffered from an acknowledged drug addiction, the university's stated reason for firing her. The jury nevertheless believed that her termination was retaliatory, because known drug problems in the men's basketball program were not punished as severely.

In the end, both coaches won multimillion-dollar verdicts that were the largest ever in a Title IX case. Fresno State had to pay $4.5 million to Vivas and will pay another $9 million to Johnson-Klein over the course of 23 years, the largest compensation ever in a Title IX case. Because of all three Fresno State plaintiffs, university athletic departments everywhere are on notice that Title IX protects those who challenge sex discrimination in athletics and that retaliation doesn't pay. ■

them to be strong, well-rounded candidates for head coaching positions (Borland & Bruening, 2010). A similar tendency was reported by women who serve as senior associate athletic directors at Division I institutions, who were kept at arms' length when it came to the facets of the job that serve as a proving ground for future athletic directors (Hoffman, 2011). A gendered division of labor among senior administrators operates to deny women the opportunity to cultivate business credentials—by working on football and men's basketball and in such areas as fundraising, development, and contract negotiation. The areas in which women's leadership is welcome, while crucial to the department, are not valued as strongly by those setting hiring priorities (Hoffman, 2011).

Negative recruiting is another way in which female coaches are constrained in their abilities to succeed and stay or advance in their jobs (Krane & Barber, 2005). Negative recruiting is when a coach uses the perception of another coach's lesbianism during the recruiting process, in an effort to undermine her with potential players and their parents (Griffin, 1998). This tactic relies on the susceptibility of recruits and parents to the antilesbian bias, which studies show is still present in significant ways despite the improving public perception of gays and lesbians (e.g., Gill, Morrow, Collins, Lucey, & Schultz, 2006; Sartore & Cunningham, 2008). Relatedly, married male coaches are able to use their wives and children to help construct the image of their team as "family" in order to enhance their recruiting efforts. This tactic trades in heterosexual and marital privilege as it is unavailable to unmarried female coaches. These gendered recruiting practices have the potential to put many female coaches at a distinct professional disadvantage, especially in programs with high expectations for head coaches to recruit a winning team.

STAKEHOLDER PERSPECTIVE

Success Coaching Men: A Product of Belief

Jennifer Kolins is the head coach of the men's and women's tennis teams at Western New England University in Springfield, Massachusetts. She is among the small minority of women who coach male athletes at the college level. Though she did not set out to coach men, she attributes her unique position to her own playing experience growing up with mostly male opponents and teammates in high school and in the National Junior Tennis League. Having played successfully with and against boys, it never occurred to Kolins that she could not coach them. In 2001 Western New England hired Kolins to head coach both the established men's and the then-fledgling women's teams.

Today, the athletic department's website touts Kolins's .591 winning percentage for the men's team, .689 winning percentage for the women's teams, among the highest of coaches in the region. But to Kolins, success is the cultivation of her athletes' self-confidence, a cornerstone of their overall development as students. This attitude underscores her strong, athlete-centered coaching philosophy, which she modeled after that of her tennis hero, Arthur Ashe, who taught that success is an outcome of believing in oneself.

As a female coach of male athletes, Kolins certainly faces challenges that men in her position would not. Opposing coaches and parents of recruits have, on initial contact with Kolins, questioned her knowledge, ability, and authority. But it is hard for anyone who knows Kolins to hold onto these negative stereotypes for long. Kolins's athletes, successful on and off the court, reflect well on her coaching and convey respect for her and the program she leads. Kolins also benefits from a supportive department, strong mentors, and an understanding partner. But at the root of Kolins's success is the same philosophy that she espouses to her athletes. To succeed—whether as a student, a player, or a coach—you've got to believe you can. And Kolins certainly believes. ■

Female coaches who coach men are also constrained in their jobs by the unique challenges they face to cultivating credibility and respect among athletes, parents, and officials. These women have also reported difficulty cultivating mentors in the profession, since they have virtually no female colleagues within their sport and because many male coaches may be deterred by pride or ego from extending professional support to a female opposing coach (Kamphoff et al., 2010).

WOMEN'S MOTIVATION AND INTEREST

The biases and job constraints not only operate as formal barriers to women's entry, retention, and advancement in college athletic leadership but influence women's desire to pursue or stay in those careers as well. Female athletes have reported less interest in pursuing coaching careers than male athletes for reasons that include many that are gendered in nature, such as the perception that female and minority coaches are treated differently than male and white coaches and that they are held back by exceeding pressure to win (Kamphoff & Gill, 2008).

Researchers examining why female coaches have reported less desire to remain in coaching than their male counterparts have found compelling evidence to suggest that these desires are constructed by the constraints of the workplace. For example, a survey of assistant coaches revealed that women who experience the workplace of the athletic department to be inclusive—that is, free from sexual and racial harassment, accepting of all sexual orientations, striving for equal representation of men and women, and supportive of female coaches' career longevity—are more likely to desire a long career in college athletics (Cunningham, Sagas, & Ashley, 2003). And former coaches interviewed by another researcher suggested that inequitable allocation of resources, facilities, compensation, job duties, and administrative support strongly motivated their desires to the leave the profession (Kamphoff, 2010).

Due to gendered cultural norms around caretaking, women are more likely to be required to engage in stressful contortions to balance professional and family responsibilities. Coaching is a particularly challenging career to balance with parenting, as it requires availability evenings and weekends when children are not in school and when day care is not readily available (Dixon & Bruening, 2007). This conflict can deter women from continuing on in coaching careers (Bruening & Dixon, 2007), and indeed former coaches with children have reported that they were motivated to leave the profession in part by the lack of support for their caregiving responsibilities (Kamphoff, 2010).

Homophobia and negative recruiting also detrimentally affect women's desires to remain in coaching. Both create internal pressure on women of all sexual orientations to suppress their homosexuality or conform to a heterosexual norm. Both those who can conform and those who cannot can experience this requirement as a source of stress and dissatisfaction and may be influenced by it to abandon career aspirations in college coaching (Kamphoff, 2010; Krane & Barber, 2005).

CONCLUSION

As many sport scholars have acknowledged, the gender imbalance in coaching and athletic leadership is an important social problem because it is rooted in the hegemonic masculinity of sport. The stereotypes, role conflicts, and job constraints discussed in this chapter all operate to construct the appearance that women are less qualified, and less interested, in positions of athletic leadership, so that the narrow associations between sport, leadership, and masculinity remain unchallenged. Women are underrepresented in athletic leadership because their presence there is destabilizing to the patriarchy. But it is precisely because of their destabilizing potential that women must be seen in positions of athletic leadership (Kane, 2001). Not only does their presence suggest "that the field of coaching is a legitimate option with respect to employment, but the visibility and responsibility associated with coaching implies that women are capable of leadership positions of any kind" (Stahura & Greenwood, 2002, p. 2). Therefore, efforts must continue to expose and suppress the bias and stereotypes that infect hiring decisions, to eliminate double standards and job constraints, to affirmatively address and compensate for women's greater family demands and unique vulnerability to homophobia and negative recruiting, and to compensate for women's lack of existing power and social capital that is necessary for advancement and success in college athletic leadership.

QUESTIONS FOR DISCUSSION

1. Why is it important that women are adequately represented among leaders in college athletics?

2. Does hegemonic masculinity explain how and why biases, stereotypes, and job constraints operate to suppress women's entry and advancement in athletic leadership?

3. What should athletic department and other university officials take away from this chapter?

References

Acosta, R. V., & Carpenter, L. J. (2012). *Women in intercollegiate sport: A longitudinal, national study 35-year update: 1977–2012*. Retrieved from www.acostacarpenter.org

Borland, J. F., & Bruening, J. E. (2010). Navigating barriers: A qualitative examination of the underrepresentation of black females as head coaches in collegiate basketball. *Sport Management Review, 13,* 407–420. doi:10.1016/j.smr.2010.05.002

Bruening, J. E., & Dixon, M. A. (2007). Work-family conflict in coaching II: Managing role conflict. *Journal of Sport Management, 21,* 377–406.

Burton, L. J., Barr, C. A., Fink, J. S., & Bruening, J. E. (2009). Think athletic director, think masculine? Examination of the gender typing of managerial subroles within athletic administration positions. *Sex Roles, 61,* 416–426. doi:10.1007/s11199-009-9632-6

Burton, L. J., Grappendort, H., & Henderson, A. (2011). Perceptions of gender in athletic administration: Utilizing role congruity to examine (potential) prejudice against women. *Journal of Sport Management, 25*(1), 36–45.

Buzuvis, E. E. (2010). Sidelined: Title IX retaliation cases and women's leadership in college athletics. *Duke Journal of Gender Law & Policy, 17*, 1.

Coakley, J. J. (2008). *Sports in society: Issues and controversies*. New York: McGraw-Hill.

Cunningham, G. B., & Sagas, M. (2002). The differential effects of human capital for male and female Division I basketball coaches. *Research Quarterly for Exercise and Sport, 73*, 489–495. doi:10.1080/02701367.2002.10609051

Cunningham, G. B., Sagas, M., & Ashley, F. B. (2003). Coaching self-efficacy, desire to become a head coach, and occupational turnover intent: Gender differences between NCAA assistant coaches of women's teams. *International Journal of Sport Psychology, 34*(2), 125–137.

Dixon, M. A., & Bruening, J. E. (2005). Perspectives on work-family conflict in sport: An integrated approach. *Sport Management Review, 8*, 227–253. doi:10.1016/S1441-3523(05)70040-1

———. (2007). Work-family conflict in coaching I: A top-down perspective. *Journal of Sport Management, 21*, 377–406.

Drago, R., Hennighausen, L., Rogers, J., Vescio, T., & Stauffer, K. D. (2005). Final report for CAGE, the Coaching and Gender Equity Project. Retrieved from http://lsir.la.psu.edu/workfam/CAGEfinalreport.doc

Festle, M. J. (1996). *Playing nice: Politics and apologies in women's sports*. New York: Columbia University Press.

Gill, D. L., Morrow, R. G., Collins, K. E., Lucey, A. B., & Schultz, A. M. (2006). Attitudes and sexual prejudice in sport and physical activity. *Journal of Sport Management, 20*, 554–564.

Griffin, P. (1998). *Strong women, deep closets: Lesbians and homophobia in sport* (paperback ed.). Champaign, IL: Human Kinetics.

Hasbrook, C. A., Hart, B. A., Mathes, S. A., & True, S. (1990). Sex bias and the validity of believed differences between male and female interscholastic athletic coaches. *Research Quarterly for Exercise and Sport, 61*, 259–267. doi:10.1080/02701367.1990.10608688

Hoffman, J. L. (2011). Inside the huddle: Gender stereotyping work among senior level women athletic administrators. *International Journal of Sport Management, 12*, 255–274.

Inglis, S., Danylchuk, K. E., & Pastore, D. L. (2000). Multiple realities of women's work experiences in coaching and athletic management. *Women's Sport and Physical Activity Journal, 9*(2), 1–26.

Irick, E. (2011). *NCAA race and gender demographics, 1995–2011*. Indianapolis, IN: National Collegiate Athletic Association. Retrieved from http://web1.ncaa.org/rgdSearch/exec/main

Kamphoff, C. S. (2010). Bargaining with patriarchy: Former female coaches' experiences and their decision to leave collegiate coaching. *Research Quarterly for Exercise & Sport, 81*, 360–372.

Kamphoff, C. S., Armentrout, S. M., & Driska, A. (2010). The token female: Women's experiences as Division I collegiate head coaches of men's teams. *Journal of Intercollegiate Sport, 3*, 297–315.

Kamphoff, C. S, & Gill, D. (2008). Collegiate athletes' perceptions of the coaching profession. *International Journal of Sports Science and Coaching, 3*(1), 55–72. doi:10.1260/174795408784089351

Kane, M. J. (2001). Leadership, sport, and gender. In S. J. Freeman, S. C. Bourque, & C. M. Shelton (Eds.), *Women on power: Leadership redefined* (pp. 114–146). Boston: Northeastern University Press.

Krane, V., & Barber, H. (2005). Identity tensions in lesbian intercollegiate coaches. *Research Quarterly for Exercise and Sport, 76*(1), 67–81. doi:10.1080/02701367.2005.10599263

Messner, M. (1988). Sport and male domination: The female athlete as contested ideological terrain. *Sociology of Sport Journal, 5*, 197–211.

Sagas, M., & Cunningham, G. B. (2004). Does having "the right stuff" matter? Gender differences in the determinants of career success among intercollegiate athletic administrators. *Sex Roles, 50*, 411–421. doi:10.1023/B:SERS.0000018895.68011.fa

Sartore, M. L., & Cunningham, G. B. (2007). Explaining the under-representation of women in leadership positions of sport organizations: A symbolic interactionist perspective. *Quest, 59*, 244–265. doi:10.1080/00336297.2007.10483551

Stahura, K. A., & Greenwood, M. (2002). Sex of head coach as a function of sport type prestige and institutional structure. *Applied Research in Coaching and Athletics Annual, 17*, 1–25.

Stangl, J. M., & Kane, M. J. (1991). Structural variables that offer explanatory power for the underrepresentation of women coaches since Title IX: The case of homologous reproduction. *Sociology of Sport Journal, 8*(1), 47–60.

Staurowsky, E. J. (2011). A radical proposal: Title IX has no role in college sport pay-for-play discussions. *Marquette Sports Law Review, 22*, 575–595.

Welch, S., & Sigelman, L. (2007). Who's calling the shots? Women coaches in Division I women's sports. *Social Science Quarterly, 88*, 1415–1434. doi:10.1111/j.1540-6237.2007.00509.x

Whisenant, W. A., Pedersen, P. M., & Obenour, B. L. (2002). Success and gender: Determining the rate of advancement for intercollegiate athletic directors. *Sex Roles, 47*, 485–491. doi:10.1023/A:1021656628604

Willis, P. (1982). *Women in sport in ideology.* In J. Hargreaves (Ed.), *Sport, culture and ideology* (pp. 117–135). London: Routledge.

PART SEVEN

NCAA and Member Institution Policy Concerns

In many ways, the established rules, policies, and principles of the NCAA and its member institutions remain at the heart of ardent debates about athletes' rights and well-being. Ellen Staurowsky uses chapter 21 to explore some of the limitations imposed on college athletes. She discusses the degree to which NCAA rules undermine the purposes of higher education and impose a chilling effect on the ability of college athletes to exert their rights as students, workers, and citizens. In chapter 22, David Ridpath examines the significance of recruiting processes, rules and restrictions on recruiting, and the future of recruiting in intercollegiate athletics. Amateurism may be the issue currently receiving the most public and scholarly attention in intercollegiate athletics. In chapter 23, Billy Hawkins, Ashley Baker, and Velina Brackebusch examine this concept and its initial application to intercollegiate athletics, including its philosophical and ideological applications. Chapter 24 focuses on the growth of the internet and social media. Specifically, Eric Snyder offers an overview of "inappropriate" college athlete use of social media that has resulted in disciplinary action by the NCAA or specific institutions. He also summarizes differing social media policies and legislation at the NCAA, institutional, state, and federal levels. In this part's final chapter, chapter 25, Timothy Davis examines both the National Letter of Intent and the Financial Aid Agreement and makes a compelling case that the contractual relationship between college athletes and their institutions unfairly benefits colleges and universities. ■

COLLEGE ATHLETES' RIGHTS

Ellen J. Staurowsky

THE COLLEGE SPORTS PARADOX

Evan Joseph, a football player at the University of Richmond, had collaborated with three teammates to create an apparel company that they called "Loaded." After the harsh realities of two knee injuries diminished Joseph's hopes for a career in the NFL, he began contemplating his future after college was over and testing the waters to pursue a career in business. The tangle of NCAA rules would affect the approach that he and his teammates, who were his business partners, would take to manage and market Loaded. Avoiding the spotlight for fear that he might inadvertently trigger a National Collegiate Athletic Association (NCAA) issue, Joseph said, "To not be able to put my face on it [the promotional materials for Loaded] on campus, to be in that spotlight, I was upset" (Hruby, 2013). He went on to comment: "We actually had some of our coaches who wanted some shirts. We didn't know if *that* would be an infraction. We had this operation going—first athletes supporting us, then students, then faculty—and at the same time we sort of hid from the NCAA" (Hruby, 2013).

Noting the irony in the fact that he was a member of the University of Richmond football team that won a national title his first year and the men's basketball team made it into the Sweet 16 of the NCAA men's basketball tournament, Joseph found the contradictions around his situation difficult to reconcile. While his professors were advising him to grow and explore new vistas and horizons, his participation as an athlete was curbing his ability to do just that. Joseph observed, "We helped the school get publicity" but were unable to generate publicity for the fledgling

The Case of Jonathan Benjamin

From all indications, Jonathan Benjamin was the kind of student who any college or university would want to admit and enroll. Highly motivated and optimistic, he battled his way onto the University of Richmond men's basketball team as a first-year athlete. Described as an unsung member of the team who had the ability to make things happen ("Senior walk-on . . . ," 2013), the will that Benjamin exhibited in earning a place on the team was a quality that he displayed in his relationships with other students and in his coursework.

An attentive student in the Robins School of Business, Benjamin would catch a glimpse of his future as an entrepreneur and executive while taking a marketing class with Professor Adam Marquardt during the summer of 2011. Out of a class project, Benjamin developed the idea to create a clothing line, called Official Visit Activewear (OVAW). Benjamin's sense of possibility was fueled as he watched a video of Kevin Plank, a former walk-on football player at the University of Maryland, who went on to become the founder and chief executive officer of sports apparel company, Under Armour (Hruby, 2013). His enthusiasm would grow with encouragement from Professor Adam Marquart, who helped guide him through the process of taking an idea and strategically building it into a company. In turn, Professor Marquardt characterized Benjamin as one of his favorite students, who was the "picture of what we hope for in academia—somebody who is not relying on us to give them all of the answers, but using what they find in class as a springboard to learn and do and experience and more" (Hruby, 2013).

Returning home in the summer of 2011, Benjamin began implementing his business plan. He opened a business account, chose a company logo, strategized about how to use social media to leverage his company, and started to build inventory for the t-shirts he was selling (Hruby, 2013). Over the course of a year, his company began to thrive. In the beginning, Benjamin was unaware that NCAA regulations prohibited him from marketing his selection of t-shirts and apparel using his own image. In November 2011, he would be featured in a story in the *Richmond Collegian*, the school paper. Offering insight into why he formed the company, he said, "A lot of us [athletes] like to get dressed up. When we go to class, we look tired in our sweats, and I want to help athletes across the country with our day-to-day wear" (Martin, 2011). Influenced by a sense of social responsibility, 20% of the funds generated through merchandise sales were donated to a local shelter for children (Martin, 2011). Coaches and teammates praised Benjamin for his initiative, drive, and commitment to making the venture work. Consistent with his stated goals for the company, Benjamin had begun to reach out to students at other institutions including the University of Florida, Santa Clara, Bentley, UCLA, and Rutgers.

A good student whose interests were ignited by something that he learned in the classroom was barred from playing basketball for a time because he was fulfilling his promise as a student and that promise was in conflict with NCAA rules. In his efforts to create and build a brand, a specific issue arose when his t-shirt supplier asked if they could feature Benjamin in a company newsletter. Uncertain if the request would fall under a news story or promotional piece, Benjamin sought assistance from his schools' athletics compliance office. In turn, they sought assistance from the Atlantic 10 Conference office.

In the course of that inquiry and as a result of Benjamin's good-faith effort to follow NCAA rules, he found himself in the improbable position of being declared ineligible to play (Hruby, 2013). Researching OVWA's Facebook and Twitter accounts, the Atlantic 10 compliance office found photos of Benjamin wearing the apparel. When he learned that posting images of him modeling his own clothing line was a violation of NCAA rules, and the penalty he would pay was banishment from the team, Benjamin said, "I thought it was a joke at first. I didn't really think they would kick me off of the team because of this. It was then that I realized how serious this was" (Riddick, 2013). After filing an appeal, the NCAA reinstated him but not before Benjamin scaled back his sales efforts and agreed to remove his name and image in association with the company. ■

business venture. Pointing to the intrusion into his development as a student, he said, "And some of us were studying marketing!" (Hruby, 2013). The predicament of Jonathan Benjamin, a walk-on with the Richmond men's basketball team, offers a striking parallel to that of Joseph.

While the source of the restraints placed on college athletes relative to their capacity to run their own businesses may elude the average person, college sports insiders would most likely point to the *2012–2013 NCAA Division I Manual*, a rulebook of roughly 450 pages, and cite bylaw 12.4.4, which pertains to self-employment.[1] That bylaw notes, "A student-athlete may establish his or her business, provided the student-athlete's name, photograph, appearance or athletics reputation are not used to promote the business" (p. 70). The Benjamin and Joseph cases highlight the intersections that exist between the business of college sports and the central goals of higher education that are often in conflict.

Why does the NCAA have such a concern over whether college athletes grab hold of an idea and make money off of it using their own image? Why does the NCAA care if a college athlete like Benjamin, a marketing major, were to recognize his own value in promoting a line of sports apparel and promoting the product to his own economic benefit?

College athletes are certainly not experiencing economic windfalls from their participation in the college sports system. While the salaries of head coaches in the major revenue-producing sports of football and men's basketball have risen 650% from 1986 to 2010 (Clotfelter, 2011), limits on what college athletes can earn remains defined largely by the athletic scholarship as adopted in the mid-1950s. Research from Huma and Staurowsky (2010, 2011) demonstrate that even college athletes who receive full-ride scholarships do not have all of the expenses associated with their college education covered. Due to the composition of the full athletic scholarship, which provides for tuition, room and board, and books, there is a financial shortfall between the cost of attendance and a full scholarship, generally between $3,000 and $5,000 per year. While college athletes are permitted, if they demonstrate financial need, to receive additional support up to the full cost of attendance through federal programs such as Pell grants and other funding, the ability of Joseph and Benjamin to close that gap through their own initiative and business skill is foreclosed. As a matter of scale, the scholarship shortfall that exists for entire college football teams would cost less to cover than what a coach might earn in bonuses in a given year (Huma & Staurowsky, 2010).

Lessons from the Benjamin and Joseph cases suggest that, within the framework of NCAA rules, a college athlete's entrepreneurial spirit and capacity to recognize commercial opportunities and monetize them have the potential to threaten the NCAA's conception of amateurism. Considered a defining principle of college sports, the NCAA Bylaw 12.01.1 states that "only an amateur student-athlete is eligible for intercollegiate athletics participation in a particular sport" (NCAA, 2012–2013, p. 59). In Benjamin's case, his amateur standing and eligibility to play were threatened because he violated a prohibition that athletes may not use their athletic skill (directly or indirectly) for pay in any form in that sport (NCAA, 2012–2013, p. 59).

NCAA CONTROL OF COLLEGE ATHLETES' LIVES

An answer to the question as to why the NCAA reaches into the lives of college athletes and imposes rules regarding the use of their names, images, and likenesses may be found, in part, in the observations of Walter Byers, the first full-time executive director of the NCAA. In his memoir, Byers referred to amateurism as economic camouflage for monopoly practice where the NCAA reserved the right for itself to make money off of the names, likenesses, and images of athletes, precluding others from doing so. If the NCAA were to relax the limitations on college athletes to earn money from their images and likenesses, that would then open the door for athletes to access a share of college sports revenue or compete with the NCAA for sponsors and financing. Such a potentiality would threaten the ability of the NCAA to monopolize the college sports industry in service to its own economic interests.

The NCAA rules governing who gets to use the names, likenesses, and images of college athletes has become the substance of several lawsuits, one of the most widely discussed being *O'Bannon v. NCAA*. In 2009, a former UCLA basketball player Ed O'Bannon sued the NCAA and its business partners, EA Sports and Collegiate Licensing Company (CLC) alleging that they had conspired to deny athletes compensation for the use of their names and likenesses in an array of commercial ventures, including but not limited to video games and television broadcasts (McCann, 2013). Through this conspiracy, the NCAA was alleged to have violated antitrust law by preventing athletes from entering into group licensing agreements. O'Bannon further contended that the accumulated effect of NCAA amateurism rules designed to deceive athletes into signing away their rights to their own images and names has been a violation of athletes' right of publicity (a property interest in one's image, voice, or other characteristics). The NCAA maintained in its defense that it neither licenses the likenesses of athletes nor prevents athletes from doing so (McCann, 2013).

In September 2013, two of the defendants in *O'Bannon*, EA Sports and CLC, settled for the sum of $40 million, leaving the NCAA as the remaining sole defendant. On the same day that the EA Sports and CLC settlement was announced, the NCAA's legal counsel, Donald Remy, said, "We're prepared to take this all the way to the Supreme Court if we have to. We are not prepared to compromise on this case" (Berkowitz, 2013).

The dispute over the value of college football and men's basketball players in revenue-producing sports and the right of an individual to have control of his or her image and who can profit from it was at the heart of the *O'Bannon* case. In August 2014, a complicated finding was issued in *O'Bannon* that allows schools to offer athletic scholarships up to the full cost of attendance and provides for schools to set aside a limited amount of revenue generated from licensing to be held in trust for players until they graduate or their eligibility expires (Wilken, 2014). As of the time of this writing, the NCAA expressed an intention to appeal the decision, asserting that it does not believe that its business practices violate antitrust laws (Tracy, 2014). Much remains to be resolved in terms of the legal issues relative to what the *O'Bannon* ruling means. While the NCAA continues to argue that the rules in place are put there to ensure that college athletes are treated like all other members of the student body and are designed to create a clear line of demarcation between college and professional sports, and while *O'Bannon* has challenged some of those assertions, the impact of the rules at present continues to intrude on the commercial spheres in which college athletes may be able to profit off of their own labor and celebrity, and as the cases of Benjamin and Joseph illustrate, NCAA rules limit the ability of college athletes to lead full lives as students, entrepreneurs, and citizens.

THE NCAA MYTH OF THE STUDENT-ATHLETE

The contradiction in the stated position of the NCAA that "graduating from college is as important as winning on the playing field" is borne out in a number of ways in the relationship between colleges and universities and scholarship athletes.[2] Despite claims that academics are the first priority, college athletes are awarded athletic scholarships on the basis of their ability to perform athletically and must perform athletically in order to retain their athletic scholarships.

In the fall of 2013, four NCAA Division I athletic directors groups under the banner of 351 Division I Athletic Directors—One Voice pledged that college athletes would never be paid. This obfuscation denies the fact that college athletes are paid.

NCAA Controls in Conflict with Athlete Interests

A former two-time Minnesota state high school champion in the sport of wrestling with a promising future at the University of Minnesota's wrestling program, Joel Bauman, found himself facing an opponent who would not yield. That opponent would be the NCAA. As a sophomore redshirt, Bauman was found to be in violation of NCAA rules governing the use of his name, likeness, and image when he performed as a singer under his own name in online videos. By so doing, Bauman violated the NCAA's principle of amateurism by allowing his name to be used in the promotion of a commercial entity and subsequently lost his eligibility. Bauman learned that if he used an alias and made no reference to himself as a Minnesota wrestler, he would have retained his eligibility. Confronted with the choice of presenting an inauthentic image of himself in his videos or losing his eligibility to compete in his sport, Bauman opted for his music career. In explaining his reasoning, he said, "I'm Joel Bauman—it's my message. It's not Little Joel or MC Joel. It's me." He went on to say, "The way you fight a movement is by being a movement yourself. I need to show people I'm serious about inspiring people. When that happens, it will speak for itself." ■

What is under dispute is whether they are compensated adequately for what they do. Emblematic of this continual form of verbal bait and switch is the discussion regarding the "miscellaneous expense allowance" or "stipend." The NCAA Division I Board of Directors passed a proposal in the fall of 2011 approving the addition of a stipend up to $2,000 to scholarship athletes up to the full cost of attendance. Pushback from the membership resulted in a reversal regarding the stipend with officials representing the major conferences within the NCAA urging its adoption. A stipend, as defined by *Merriam-Webster's Dictionary* is "a fixed regular sum paid as a salary or allowance."

College athletes live in a world where linguistic subterfuge is common currency. In August 2013, the Twitter feed for the NCAA's National Student-Athlete Advisory Committee (NSAAC) featured an image of actor James Van Der Beek with the caption in bold block letters "YOU KNOW OPTIONAL MEANS MANDATORY."[3] College athletes are told that they are only playing their sports 20 hours a week in season when the NCAA rules alter the meaning of the term "one hour." On a competition day, no matter how many hours an athlete may be involved in his or her sport, only three hours will be recorded.[4] Thus, on a game day that might take up nine hours of an athlete's life, only three hours are reported. Further manipulations around the amount of demands placed on a college athlete's time and energies are found in the labeling of some activities as "countable" (practice, games, meetings called by coaches) and "uncountable" ("voluntary" practices, training room visits, meetings that athletes call with coaches).[5]

Such a system does not, by itself, support a determination that the mission of higher education, which holds as a core principle the importance of intellectual honesty and a search for the truth, is upheld by the athletics enterprise (American Council on Education, 2005). College athletes in general, and scholarship athletes in particular, have few meaningful ways to challenge this system or decline to participate in it without jeopardizing their ability to play.

The NCAA points to the National Student-Athlete Advisory Committee (SAAC) structure as a mechanism for athletes to express their views. Notably, while the SAAC concept has been around for more than 25 years, the number of lawsuits filed by college athletes alleging that the NCAA has imperiled their health and safety and worked to suppress their access to just compensation have grown substantially. According to reporter Jon Solomon (2014), "At least 65 former college athletes are suing the NCAA over its handling of concussions" (para. 1). Apart from organizations such as the National College Players Association (NCPA), which has represented the interests of roughly 17,000 college football and men's basketball players through advocacy efforts targeting health and safety, education, and compensation for more than 15 years, athletes have had to resort to lawsuits and public pressure to effect change, efforts that are costly, that often require more years than their playing time as college athletes to resolve, and that threaten their security because of the potential for them to be labeled troublemakers.

The careful and calculated language of the "student-athlete" and its attendant vocabulary is that it defines a certain hybrid status for college athletes where it is difficult for them to access their rights as students and they are denied any access to rights as employees, because they are not viewed as either (Staurowsky, 2014). In 2014 the NCAA announced a new governance structure that granted autonomy to the five most powerful conferences in college sport: the Atlantic Coast Conference (ACC), Big Ten, Big Twelve, Pac-12, and the Southeastern Conference (SEC). Because college athletes have been afforded few avenues to offer feedback on the rules that govern their lives and have no capacity to vote on rules that have previously been imposed unilaterally, the new structure provides representation for athletes throughout the governance structure, providing them the opportunity to vote for the first time in NCAA history. Whether this system genuinely addresses the diverse issues experienced by athletes remains an open question. The percentage of representation at each level is as follows:

- NCAA Board of Directors (BOD): The chair of the National SAAC sits on the BOD, the only athlete on a 24-member board (representing 4%).

- NCAA Council: Of the 40-member council, there are two athletes. Votes made by athletes represent 3.1% of the total due to the variable weighting assigned to various representatives on the council.

- NCAA Autonomous Power Five Conferences: Out of 80 representatives in total from these conferences, 15 are athlete representatives, 20% of the vote at this level (Hosick, 2014).

With such limits, and with limited voting in the rule-making process within the NCAA, they are trapped in a system that appears benign but routinely strips them of rights that others have as a matter of their place in society.

Arguably, in the cases discussed, Benjamin and Joseph had difficulty exercising their rights under the U.S. Constitution to work and to access an education that was free of intimidation under university student conduct codes. There will be those who argue that college athletes, by virtue of their agreement to play college sports at an NCAA institution, are obligated to play by the rules as approved by the NCAA's membership. However, college athletes working under this kind of system, without the benefit of collective bargaining and an advocacy group, such as a players association or union, that is fully funded to represent the interests of athletes external to the NCAA, are limited by the structure imposed on them by college sport administrators who have significant conflicts of interests.

COLLEGE SPORTS REFORM

Between 2008 and 2014, the college sports industry has undergone an unprecedented amount of upheaval. As the financial stakes grow ever greater, and as the effects of 24-hour, 7-day-a-week television coverage leads to increasing scrutiny, charges of hypocrisy and calls for reform have been persistent. Some have taken the form of legal challenges, new legal theories, and recommendations for the U.S. federal government to intervene.

Selected Legal Challenges

The proliferation of lawsuits and calls for federal government intervention into the college sports industry attests to increasing awareness that old pronouncements regarding the NCAA's principle of amateurism have lost their valence as current college sports marketplace reality catches up with its fictional past. Legal challenges to the NCAA allege that those in the college sports industry engage in practices that violate antitrust laws harming athletes in the process through limitations in levels of compensation and inadequate protections to player health. In *White v. NCAA* (2006), former NCAA Division I football and men's basketball players argued that the NCAA engaged in an unlawful restraint of trade by limiting their compensation to tuition, room and board, and books, creating a shortfall between what a grant-in-aid or athletic scholarship covered and the full cost of attendance. Sidestepping an antitrust ruling that would have resulted in the NCAA paying triple damages, it agreed to a settlement that provided for eligible former athletes to be reimbursed up to $2,500 (the average amount of the scholarship gap at that time) for school expenses associated with undergraduate, graduate, or professional certificate education or a one-time payment of $500 (Hosick, 2008).

The year 2009 brought a ruling from a judge in the Court of Common Pleas in the state of Ohio in favor of Oklahoma State baseball player Andy Oliver (Fitzgerald, 2009). Oliver was accused of receiving improper representation from attorneys in violation of NCAA bylaw 12.3.1 when Oliver was trying to determine if he was going to sign with a professional team or accept an offer to play at the college level. The court determined that the NCAA rule, which allows for athletes to have attorneys or advisors but prohibits them from being in the room when athletes are considering offers from professional teams, interfered with the attorney-client relationship. On appeal, the case was eventually settled, and the NCAA rule remained intact (Weiner, 2012). As Lockhart (2010) notes, however, regardless of the NCAA's insistence on retaining it, members of the legal community are aware of the persuasiveness of the court's determination to discourage its enforcement due to the prospect of future lawsuits should the NCAA attempt to do so. Lawyer Jeff Kessler, credited with bringing free agency to the National Football League (NFL), has said, "Another court can come to exactly the same conclusion and hold the policy unlawful, and the fact that the decision has been vacated does not make its reasoning any less persuasive" (as cited in Lockhart, 2010, p. 179).

In *John Rock v. NCAA* (2012) a former college football player from Gardner Webb alleged that he was stripped of his scholarship by a newly hired head football coach contrary to promises made to Rock by the previous coach. Rock asserted that he was told by his previous coach that as long as he maintained athletic and academic eligibility, he would retain his scholarship. Troubles arose, according to Rock, after he missed several spring practices because he was completing an off-campus internship required for his academic degree in the spring of 2010. As related by Rock, the new coach viewed the player's absences as evidence of a lack of commitment to the team, providing grounds for the scholarship to be withdrawn. Rock sued the NCAA, questioning whether NCAA restrictions on the number and amount of athletic scholarships constitutes an illegal restraint that limits the ability of college athletes to market their services in a free and open market (*John Rock v. NCAA*, 2012; Weiner, 2012). Although his initial suit was thrown out, he refiled it, and it recently survived a motion to dismiss (*John Rock v. NCAA*, 2012).

While Rock, O'Bannon, and Oliver have contested NCAA rules limiting compensation and access to player representation, a lawsuit filed by former Eastern Illinois football player Adrian Arrington accused the NCAA of endangering the health and safety of college athletes by failing to establish a clear policy regarding the handling of concussions. In a request for class-action certification in the case, plaintiffs included a report by Robert Cantu, medical director of the National Center for Catastrophic Sports Injury Research, who cited an internal NCAA survey that found that "nearly half of college athletic trainers had put athletes showing signs of concussion back in the same game in contradiction of well-settled practices within the scientific community that an athlete should never be permitted to return to play on the same day after a concussion diagnosis" (Axon, 2013).

In August 2014, the NCAA offered to settle the *Arrington* case (and others that were consolidated with it) for $70 million, an amount that would create a fund to provide medical monitoring to all current and former athletes who played NCAA-sponsored sports on or prior to the date of the settlement but offer nothing to the athletes who brought the suit (McGuire, 2014). The proposed settlement of these cases has been controversial, characterized by Jay Edelson, one of the plaintiffs lawyers, as "truly a rarity: a settlement where the class members get nothing but are forced to give up everything. Injured student athletes will be . . . left in the dust" (as quoted in Tarm, 2014, para. 4).

Whether pressure from lawsuits will permanently change the way athletes are treated in the college sports industry remains to be seen. In *White*, *Oliver*, and *Arrington* the NCAA opted to settle rather than alter its rules structure. In *O'Bannon*, the ruling may take months and possibly years to sort out, especially if the NCAA proceeds with the planned appeal of that ruling.

The Possibility of College Athletes Being Designated as Employees

Despite the historical fact that NCAA decision makers in the 1950s were aware that they were establishing a pay-for-play system by creating the athletic scholarship and by the NCAA's subsequent adoption of the term *student-athlete* (Byers, 1995; Sack & Staurowsky, 1998), "the NCAA has repeatedly prevailed in workers' compensation claims brought by severely injured college athletes," thus foreclosing on opportunities for athletes to gain access to rights as employees and to unionize (Fram &

Frampton, 2012; Sack & Staurowsky, 1998). Legal scholars have searched for ways under the National Labor Relations Board (NLRB) for athletes to be designated as employees under federal labor law. Fram and Frampton (2012) suggest: "Labor law has articulated theoretical frameworks (in certain jurisdictions at least) that would likely encompass college athletes as "employees." In at least a dozen states, we believe college athletes would be among those individuals entitled to certain statutory protections, should they collectively undertake to alter the conditions under which they labor" (p. 1078).

In January 2014, Northwestern football players, led by former quarterback Kain Colter, petitioned the NLRB seeking recognition as employees with the right to form a labor union (Borden, 2014). Within two months, NLRB regional director Peter Sung Ohr had determined that football players at Northwestern who received full grants-in-aid were employees based on a common-law definition of an employee as "a person who performs services for another under contract for hire, subject to the other's control or right of control and in return to payment" (Vary & Dubin, 2014, para. 6). In the ruling, Ohr noted that athletic scholarships are awarded solely for athletic performance and may be withdrawn for nonperformance; that the scholarship agreement is itself a "tender" of employment; that there was value in the services provided to Northwestern by football players as evidenced in the $235 million generated by the team between 2003–2012; and that the array of rules that govern a Northwestern football player's life from the necessity of registering a car with the athletic department to policies pertaining to activity on social media to conduct codes to regimented training and practice schedules offered support for a conclusion that certain college athletes deserve the protections that come with the designation of employment status.

While Northwestern University opted to appeal and as of this writing that appeal is pending, reaction around the country to the ruling varied widely. Because the NLRA applies only to private institutions, some have wondered if the Northwestern ruling presents a threat to the college sports system (Staurowsky, 2014). In an attempt to avert the question entirely in the state of Ohio, legislatures have moved a proposal that would bar college athletes from being recognized as employees. In a further development, the State Employees Association of North Carolina extended a welcome to college athletes who are on scholarship to become members and to receive the benefits that being employees might afford.

Calls for U.S. Government Intervention

During the past five decades, the U.S. Congress has held approximately 30 separate formal hearings on the NCAA or amateur or collegiate athletics and has produced 17 reports regarding the NCAA and the related topics of amateur or collegiate athletics. To date, Congress has remained unmoved to enact legislation to regulate the NCAA (Johnson, 2013). *Bloomberg News*'s Washington editor, Albert Hunt (2011), wrote about the necessity for the federal government to intervene in college sports, given the "corrosive corruption" that existed in "top level intercollegiate athletics," evidenced by "cheating, paying players under the table and taking advantage of other athletes, while turning a blind eye to criminal activities." Recognizing Congress's interest in college sports but its failure as yet to intervene, Johnson (2011) proposed the Collegiate Athlete and Employee Fairness Act (CAEFA) as a potential solution to many of the recurring and seemingly irresolvable issues that have plagued college sports by inserting the free market into system.

The major elements of CAEFA would require that the NCAA and any related associations be designated not as IRS 501(c) (3) charitable entities but rather as 501(c) (6) trade association entities (similar to the NFL) and that revenue derived from athletic programs be operated from within higher education institutions, audited in accordance with generally accepting accounting principles, and reported separately with its annual IRS Form 990. Under CAEFA, provisions would be made to provide college athletes with disability, health, and life insurance and to have rights and privileges accorded to students and employees at their institutions. CAEFA also calls for Congress to "establish an administrative law system within the Department of Education to adjudicate any enforcement of any rules or regulations of any entities purporting to regulate colleges and universities and their college athletes," with appeals to be heard by the Federal Circuit Court of Appeals and the U.S. Supreme Court if granted cert (Johnson, 2013).

An alternative approach to a federal enforcement agency for college sports is the adoption of an antitrust exemption for the NCAA and college conferences that proposers, like The Drake Group, believe will allow for greater ability to rein in excesses in the college sports system. In October 2013, The Drake Group announced that it is developing the College Athlete Protection Act with the goal of turning the NCAA "back into something more academic oriented, rather than just going all out professional" (Grasgreen, 2013). According to a preliminary draft form as of this writing, the act would seek an antitrust exemption to rules that have commercial consequences, such as limiting games to weekends and school vacation periods; provide for a restructuring of NCAA governance by replacing the Executive Committee with a Board of Directors with more equal balance between the association's competitive divisions; and include due process protections for athletes (Grasgreen, 2013). It is expected that the proposal will be submitted to Congress as an amendment to the Higher Education Act of 1965.

CONCLUSION

College athletes in the twenty-first century have been born into a system not of their own making where rules and regulations passed by college sports authorities are brought to bear on their lives in ways that distinguish them from the rest of the student body. In the absence of a viable advocacy group, such as a players association or other collective bargaining entity, college athletes are vulnerable to the impact of college sports business practices that restrict their rights as students, citizen, and athletes. As court cases roll on and calls for reform continue, a model of college sports reform that places the athlete at the center, not as a commodity but as a human being, would be important in rectifying the persistent problems that plague the enterprise.

QUESTIONS FOR DISCUSSION

1. One of the arguments that have been used to defend recognizing college athletes in the revenue-producing sports of big-time college football and men's basketball as employees is that college games would no longer be marketable because "students" were not playing. In the modern university, do you think that it would be possible for schools to sponsor profit-making college sports that had paid employees and that college sports fans would still buy tickets and watch and television?

2. Should college athletes be able to profit off of their own names, images, and likeness through individual endorsement deals?

3. Should college athletes have a group similar to a players association so that they have an advocate for their needs and interests?

Notes

1. The *2012–2013 NCAA Division I Manual* was consulted because the case is from that year. The bylaw, 12.4.4., appears the same in the *2014–2015 NCAA Division I Manual*.

2. The statement from the NCAA website can be found at http://www.ncaa.org/wps/wcm/connect /public/ncaa/about+the+ncaa#sthash.wElzPCZE.dpbs

3. Retrieved from https://twitter.com/Div1SAAC /status/365302371548528641/photo/1

4. 17.1.6.3.2 Competition Day. All competition and any associated athletically related activities on the day of competition shall count as three hours regardless of the actual duration of these activities.

5. 17.02.1 Countable Athletically Related Activities. Countable athletically related activities include any required activity with an athletics purpose involving student-athletes and at the direction of, or supervised by, one or more of an institution's coaching staff (including strength and conditioning coaches) and must be counted within the weekly and daily limitations under Bylaws 17.1.6.1 and 17.1.6.2. Administrative activities (e.g., academic meetings, compliance meetings) shall not be considered as countable athletically related activities.

References

American Council on Education. (2005). Statement on academic rights and responsibilities. Retrieved from http://www.chea.org/pdf/ACE__Statement_on _Academic_Rights_and_Responsibilities_%286_23 _2005%29.pdf

Axon, R. (2013, July 25). Does NCAA face more concussion liability than the NFL? *USA Today*. Retrieved from http://www.usatoday.com/story/sports /ncaaf/2013/07/25/ncaa-concussion-lawsuit-adrian -arrington/2588189/

Berkowitz, S. (2013, September 26). NCAA vows to fight O'Bannon suit to the Supreme Court. *USA Today*. Retrieved from http://www.usatoday.com/story /sports/ncaab/2013/09/26/ncaa-ed-obannon-ea -sports-lawsuit-supreme-court/2877579/

Board of Regents. (2012, October). Student conduct code. Minneapolis: University of Minnesota. Retrieved from http://regents.umn.edu/sites /default/files/policies/Student_Conduct_Code.pdf

Borden, S. (2014, February 5). College athletes to unionize? More on the Northwestern University football players NLRB petition. *Labor Relations Today*. Retrieved from http://www.laborrelations today.com/2014/02/articles/bush-board-reversal /college-athletes-to-unionize-more-on-the -northwestern-university-football-players-nlrb -petition/

Byers, W., with Hammer, C. (1995). *Unsportsmanlike conduct: Exploiting college athletes*. Ann Arbor: University of Michigan Press.

Clotfelter, C. (2011). *Big-time sports in American universities*. New York: Cambridge University Press.

Fitzgerald, T. (2012, March 14). Here it is, March Madness by the numbers. *Media Life Magazine*. Retrieved from http://www.medialifemagazine.com /here-it-is-march-madness-by-the-numbers/

Fram, N., & Frampton, T. W. (2012). A union of ama- teurs: A legal blueprint to reshape big-time college athletics. *Buffalo Law Review*. Retrieved from http:// papers.ssrn.com/sol3/papers.cfm?abstract_id =2001027

Fitzgerald, D. (2009, February 25). Oliver v. NCAA: Court throws out NCAA baseball lawyer-agent rule. *Connecticut Sports Law*. Retrieved from http:// ctsportslaw.com/2009/02/25/oliver-v-ncaa-court -throws-out-ncaa-baseball-lawyer-agent-rule/

Grasgreen, A. (2013, October 11). Academics to propose federal legislation restructuring NCAA. *Inside Higher Education*.

Hosick, M. B. (2008, February 5). Court initially approves settlement in white case. *NCAA News*. Retrieved from http://fs.ncaa.org/Docs /NCAANewsArchive/2008/association-wide/ncaa %2Bagrees%2Bto%2Bsettlement%2B-%2B01-30 -08%2Bncaa%2Bnews.html

Hosick, M. (2014). Student-athletes will vote at every governance level. Retrieved from http://www.ncaa .org/about/resources/media-center/news/board -adopts-new-division-i-structure

Hruby, P. (2013, April 13). Unionize college athletes. *Sports on Earth*. Retrieved from http://www .sportsonearth.com/article/44209014/

Huma, R., & Staurowsky, E. J. (2010). *An examination of the financial shortfall for athletes on full scholarship at NCAA Division I institutions—2009–2010*. Riverside, CA: National College Players Association.

———. (2011). *The price of poverty: A comparison of big-time college athletes fair market value, their current compensation, and the U.S. federal poverty line*. Riverside, CA: National College Players Association.

Hunt, A. (2011, December 11). College sports need a government intervention. *Bloomberg News*. Re- trieved from http://www.bloomberg.com/news /2011-12-11/college-sports-need-a-government -intervention-albert-r-hunt.html

John Rock v. National Collegiate Athletic Association, Case No. 1:12-cv-1019 JMS-DKL (S.D. Ind. July 25, 2012).

Johnson, R. (2011, September 19). Solution to NCAA: Legislate free market into college sports. *Street & Smith's SportsBusiness Journal*. Retrieved from http://www.sportsbusinessdaily.com/Journal /Issues/2011/09/19/Opinion/Richard-Johnson.aspx

———. (2013, August 22). The NCAA has never been regulated by Congress, so will Congress finally man-up with proposed new legislation? *Sports Law Blog*. Retrieved from http://sports-law.blogspot .com/2013/08/the-ncaa-has-never-been-regulated -by.html?m=1

Lockhart, M. (2010). Oliver v. NCAA: Throwing a contractual curveball at the NCAA's veil of ama- teurism. *University of Dayton Law Review, 35*(2), 175–198.

McCann, M. (2013). NCAA v. O'Bannon class certifica- tion hearing primer. *Sports Illustrated*. Retrieved from http://sportsillustrated.cnn.com/college -football/news/20130619/ncaa-ed-obannon -hearing-primer/

McGuire, M. (2014). NCAA, student-athletes reach settlement in head-injury class action. Retrieved from http://www.lexisnexis.com/legalnewsroom /litigation/b/litigation-blog/archive/2014/07/29 /ncaa-student-athletes-reach-settlement-in-head -injury-class-action.aspx

National Collegiate Athletic Association. (2012). *2012–13 Division I manual*. Indianapolis, IN: National Collegiate Athletic Association.

O'Bannon v. Nat'l Collegiate Athletics Ass'n, Nos. C 09-1967 CW, C 09-3329 CW, C 09-4882 CW, 2010 WL 445190, at *8 (N.D. Cal. Feb. 8, 2010).

Ohr, Peter S. (2014, March 26). Northwestern University (employer) and College Athlete Players Association. Ruling in Case 13-RC-121359. Retrieved from http://www.nlrb.gov/news-outreach/news-story /nlrb-director-region-13-issues-decision -northwestern-university-athletes

Riddick, J. (2013, April 6). Former student-athlete can finally promote his clothing line. *University of Rochester Collegian*. Retrieved from http:// thecollegianur.com/2013/04/16/former-student -athlete-can-finally-promote-his-clothing-line /34723/

Sack, A. L., & Staurowsky, E. J. (1998). *College athletes for hire: The evolution and legacy of the NCAA's amateur myth.* Westport, CT: Praeger.

Senior walk-on contributes in his own way to UR. (2013, October 7). *Times Dispatch.*

Solomon, J. (2014, February 6). Who's suing the NCAA? AL.com database of concussion lawsuits by ex-players. *AL.com*. Retrieved from http://www.al.com /sports/index.ssf/2014/02/whos_suing_the_ncaa _alcom_data.html

Staurowsky, E. J. (2014, April 7). What does the Northwestern football ruling mean for college sports? Q & A. *Drexel Now*. Retrieved from http:// www.drexel.edu/now/features/archive/2014/April /Ellen-Staurowsky-Q-and-A/

Tarm, M. (2014, August 24). Athlete asks judge to reject NCAA head-injury deal. *YahooSports.com*. Retrieved from http://sports.yahoo.com/news/athlete-asks -judge-reject-ncaa-125445383—spt.html

Tracy, M. (2014, August 10). N. C. A. A. will appeal O'Bannon ruling. *New York Times*. Retrieved from http://www.nytimes.com/2014/08/11/sports /ncaabasketball/ncaa-will-appeal-obannon-ruling .html

Vary, N. & Dubin, A. (2014). NLRB gets in the game: Will decide whether Northwestern's football players can unionize. *Buck Consultants' Knowledge Resource Center*. Retrieved from https://www .buckconsultants.com/portals/0/publications/fyi /2014/FYI-2014-NLRB-gets-game-will-decide -whether-NW-football-plays-unionize.pdf?utm _content=5375143&utm_medium=social&utm _source=linkedin

Weiner, R. (2012, August 13). Ohio athletes sue NCAA in antitrust over scholarship allocations. *Akron Legal News*. Retrieved from http://www.akronlegalnews .com/editorial/4465

Wilken, C. (2014, August 8). O'Bannon v. National Collegiate Athletic Association: Findings of fact and conclusions of law. No. C 09-3329 CW. Retrieved from http://i.usatoday.net/sports/!Invesitgations -and-enterprise/OBANNONRULING.pdf

White v. NCAA, No. CV 06-999-RGK, slip op. at 4 (C.D. Cal. Sept. 21, 2006). Retrieved at http://www1.ncaa .org/eprise/main/administrator/white_v_ncaa/11.pdf

RECRUITING in INTERCOLLEGIATE ATHLETICS

B. David Ridpath

KEY TERMS

recruiting ◀

NCAA ◀

contacts ◀

evaluations ◀

phone call ◀

The system of intercollegiate athletics, specifically commercialism and the drive for winning and revenue generation, influences many areas in American higher education. One of the most evident influences is the recruiting of prospective athletes for college and university athletic teams. The teams with the most talented and athletically gifted athletes will likely succeed by winning more on the field or court of play. Recruiting for an elite prospective athlete by college and university teams is as competitive as the games themselves. The stakes are extremely high, as many institutions have decreed their respective athletic departments as the "front porch" or the cleanest and clearest window through which the public views the institution (Suggs, 2003). By extension, many claim that successful winning athletic teams will benefit the institution overall through greater funding, marketability, applications, fundraising, and even improved academic programs (Frank, 2004; Litan, Orszag, & Orszag, 2003). The proliferation of enhanced media opportunities through television, social media, and internet platforms also vastly increases the competition for the best recruits as it is believed that the enhanced multimedia exposure available to multiple institutions adds to the front-porch concept. This exposure is often called "free advertising" for not just the athletic program but the institution overall. Although the result of this exposure is difficult to quantify positively or negatively, institutions are constantly pushing for winning teams to generate that publicity. Many factors shape a winning athletic program, but in the end it starts with the recruited athlete.

Recruiting is mostly built on hope, but for those teams that do win consistently and compete for championships, there certainly can be lucrative benefits, specifically in coaching and administrative salaries, and although not guaranteed, some short term gains in finances, applications, and marketability (Frank, 2004). If it turns out that these aforementioned gains do not happen, then those same coaches may be terminated. In most cases, hope reigns supreme, and getting a superior athlete or athletes can make the hopes and dreams of coaches, fans, and administrators grow exponentially. The drive to recruit the best athletes that fit a certain institutional model and commitment to athletics is reflected in the National Collegiate Athletic Association (NCAA) three-division model and other intercollegiate athletics governing bodies. No matter the level or the size of school or conference, it all starts with the basic building block for any team

STAKEHOLDER PERSPECTIVE

Recruiting

John Infante of athletics scholarships.net and former Division I compliance director reflects on the recruiting process.

In all areas of NCAA rules, there is an interplay between monitoring and education. But nowhere is that more evident than in the NCAA's recruiting rules. Not only are the recruiting rules some of the most highly nuanced and technical; they are also applied most often by coaches in field, without ready access to a compliance officer or NCAA manual.

As a result, recruiting rules education has traditionally been about hammering the basics to make sure coaches internalize the most important rules. No contact with juniors. No letters or emails to sophomores. One call per week. No unofficial visits during a dead period.

For most of the history of modern NCAA enforcement, monitoring became increasingly labor-intensive. Infractions cases and NCAA interpretations drove best practices that normally resulted in having a human

being review more documents more often. Phone calls went from something coaches tracked with handwritten notes that the compliance office might review if accusation of a violation was received to include a complete accounting of all phone contact that was audited regularly against phone bills.

One of the biggest recent advancements in recruiting monitoring has been to automate the process. Phone calls are logged automatically via smartphone apps and audited against phone bills automatically by software programs. This has freed compliance offices to focus attention on other areas. In recruiting, the expectation for education has risen as the cost in terms of time of robust (even comprehensive) monitoring has gone down.

Expect this trend to continue as technology advances and expands into other areas. Mobile apps and web services could one day automate the process of logging evaluations, tracking recruiting calendars,

and documenting official visits. As with phone calls, this will create an expectation for compliance officers to expand their efforts in other areas.

Sooner rather than later, the cliché of the compliance professional staring at phone bills and travel receipts will become a thing of the past. If the pace of recruiting deregulation speeds up, compliance professionals will quickly find themselves doing far less recruiting monitoring than they do now.

But at the same time, reforms like the new head coach control philosophy will raise the stakes of every recruiting violation. Education will have to become more sophisticated, including teaching head coaches how to monitor recruiting activity. So while monitoring will become automated and education of individual rules will get easier, recruiting will still hold a large portion of a compliance professional's attention and anxiety. ■

or athletic program—the athlete. The recruited athlete will likely have choices where to go to school and participate in his or her sport. For schools that are enrollment-driven for the bulk of funding, such as smaller private schools at the NCAA Division II and III levels, recruiting the athlete that fits the school mission and model can often be as competitive as larger Division I schools. While the drive for winning and revenue generation might not be as acute, the pressure exists to win and field enough athletes to help the institution sustain itself. It is a different kind of pressure, but enough for coaches to recruit the best athletes they can.

With this in mind, this chapter focuses on the largest and best-known intercollegiate athletics governing body—the NCAA— at the Division I level. Using the NCAA as template, this chapter examines the history of the NCAA and recruiting, the relationship of academics and recruiting, the recruiting process, recruiting rules and definitions, and the future of recruiting in intercollegiate athletics using new technologies.

Recruiting is often called the "lifeblood" of American intercollegiate athletic programs (Belotti & Ley, 2011). This is certainly true at the highest levels of competition where simple economics rule. The teams with the best players and the most resources win more often and likely generate more revenue. Much of the revenue is spent on recruiting the best athletes available—so much so that many elite NCAA Division I programs have massive or even unlimited recruiting budgets. The University of Georgia spent over $600,000 on recruiting in 2011–2012, a figure that is close to 10% of the entire football budget (Ching, 2013). Those schools that must budget more effectively due to lesser revenue still spend a large portion of team budgets on recruiting the best-possible prospective athletes. Typical costs for recruiting are vast and can run into the thousands of dollars for a prospect who may not even attend a school that has invested a large amount of time and money in him or her. Such is the competitive game of recruiting. It is a game that you play—but you may not win.

HISTORY OF RECRUITING IN INTERCOLLEGIATE ATHLETICS

Intercollegiate athletics have been a part of higher education and university life since the early eighteenth century. Intercollegiate athletic competition in the United States is traced back as early as the 1820s to football and rugby games between Ivy League schools like Harvard, Yale, and Princeton (Crowley, n.d.; Falla, 1981). During that time, concerns were raised about the violent nature of sporting events, particularly football. In 1906 the Intercollegiate Athletic Association of the United States was officially established as an intercollegiate athletics governing body and was later renamed the National Collegiate Athletic Association (NCAA) in 1910.

At the first NCAA Convention in July 1946, the participants drafted the statement Principles for Conduct of Intercollegiate Athletics (Brown, 1999; Sack & Staurowsky, 1998). According to Falla (1981) and Brown (1999), the principles concerned topics such as adhering to the definition of amateurism and not allowing professional athletes to compete, holding athletes to the same sound academic standards as the student body, awarding financial aid without consideration for athletic ability, and developing a policy of "recruiting that basically prohibited a coach or anyone representing a member school from recruiting any prospective student athlete with the offer of financial aid or any equivalent inducement" (Falla, 1981). During this time, there was a major problem of athletes receiving compensation for their athletic services, which was in direct conflict with NCAA and U.S. amateurism rules. The athletic scholarship had not yet been introduced, and this effort, later known as the Sanity Code, was the first legitimate attempt to regulate academics, eligibility, and recruiting (Falla, 1981). Even though the Sanity Code was later repealed, it set a precedent for how academics, eligibility, recruiting, and financial aid would be governed in the future, all of which remain the core areas that intercollegiate athletics governing bodies regulate.

In 1982 the American Council on Education established an ad hoc group, the Committee on the Problems of Major Intercollegiate Athletics Programs, to address the problem of institutional initial eligibility standards versus establishing a national initial intercollegiate athletic eligibility standard and, as such, served as a political force to get the proposition adopted (The Crisis, 1990). In September 1982, committee members had written proposals that would toughen initial eligibility and academic progress rules for prospective recruited and nonrecruited athletes.

These proposals were later modified to require a prospective athlete to graduate from high school with at least a 2.0 grade point average on a 4.0 scale in a core curriculum of 11 academic courses, eventually becoming the foundation for future reform related to the controversial NCAA Proposition 48 legislation (Funk, 1991). The Proposition 48 standard, although passed in 1983, was not officially adopted for Division I colleges and universities until 1986. Under the newly proposed standards, a prospect needed a 2.5 grade point average (out of a possible 4.0) in 13 core high school units, along with a combined minimum SAT score of 700, or a minimum 17 score on the ACT. These new rules still allowed athletic programs to recruit athletes who are deemed academically deficient and encourage them to attend a junior college or prep school to improve their academic record.

In 1994 the NCAA Initial Eligibility Clearinghouse (now called the NCAA Eligibility Center) was established. The Clearinghouse was developed as a national center for determining initial eligibility of recruited athletes for all NCAA Division I and II institutions, thus eliminating member institutions themselves from the initial eligibility certification process. Prior to the creation of the Clearinghouse, colleges and universities, some under pressure from alumni and coaches, could conveniently change a basic math course into a core course with the stroke of a pen, thus aiding in the recruitment of the prospect regardless of academic deficiencies (McMillen, 1992). With these changes, the NCAA believed that if recruited athletes were better prepared for college-level work, they, in turn, would have a legitimate chance to graduate. These new initial eligibility requirements changed recruiting forever, as institutions were forced to take a closer look at whether prospective athletes could actually perform academically while competing athletically at a high level.

THE RECRUITING PROCESS

Recruiting athletes is considered almost an additional full-time job that involves coaches, staff, families, and other university personnel. It has evolved along with college sports to a very technical science that today uses all forms of multimedia platforms such as the internet, specific computer programs, a plethora of recruiting services, social media, texting—and still the standbys of letters, phone calls, and in-person visits. Most coaching staffs have a coach who is designated recruiting coordinator, and many large institutions have numerous employees working for their football and men's basketball teams in a pseudo–player personnel department. As hard as college teams fight in the swimming pool, the field, track, or court, the institution's fight for the best athlete can be just as intense. Some coaches may keep a visible wall-mounted sign that reads: "Recruiting is like shaving, if you don't do it every day you look like a bum." Balancing the desire to get a great athlete who will help the team with the evolving and changing academic requirements is a challenge, but institutions will do all that they can (hopefully within the rules of the governing body) to get a player that fits their program. Even then, it might not be enough, as oftentimes one school watches a prize recruit go to a rival institution.

To fully understand the recruiting process at all levels of intercollegiate athletics, it is important to understand the policies and consequences that the process entails. There is no one-size-fits-all approach when it comes to identifying and recruiting a prospective athlete to an institution, but it is considered an art form by some coaches. And, to some degree, the recruited athletes want to make sure they are going to the best team that can showcase their talents, while also earning a college education. It is important to note that stakeholders involved in this recruiting process must adhere to NCAA rules, otherwise, there are likely eligibility consequences before the athlete even puts on a uniform. The first citation in NCAA (2012–2013) Bylaw 13 states:

> The recruitment of a student-athlete by a member institution or any representative of its athletics interests in violation of the Association's legislation, as acknowledged by the institution or established through the Association's enforcement procedures, shall result in the student-athlete becoming ineligible to represent that institution in intercollegiate athletics. (p. 77)

Even with present technology and access to prospects through internet sites, television, and other multimedia, recruiting starts with prospecting for the perfect athlete to fit a specific team need. According to the *NCAA Manual* (2012–2013), a prospect is defined as a student who has started ninth-grade classes; before the ninth-grade year, a college can give him or her, relatives, or friends any financial aid or other benefits that the college does not provide to students generally in an attempt to get an early start on courting the prospect. Prospecting for an athlete can be a time-intensive process that starts with recruiting lists provided by recruiting services, contacts with high school coaches who give information on athletes to the colleges, information from the prospects themselves, and prior knowledge of a prospect through a previous evaluation of other recruited athletes. While not an exhaustive list, teams will start with hundreds if not thousands of prospects and begin to pare that list down by athletic position needs and academic ability. Prospecting starts early, and amazingly some college teams offer scholarships to prospects who have not even started high school (Smith, 2013).

If the prospective athlete is one that an athletic program wants, the institution generally will issue an agreement called the National Letter of Intent (NLI) on a predetermined signing day or during a permissible signing period. The NLI is a voluntary program administered by the NCAA Eligibility Center. An NCAA Division I or II institution does not have to participate in this program, but most do, as it generally protects the athlete and the institution. By signing an NLI, the college-bound athlete agrees to attend the college or university for at least one academic year in exchange for athletics financial aid for one academic year from the college or university (NCAA, 2012).

RECRUITING RULES AND DEFINITIONS

NCAA recruiting legislation is governed by NCAA Article 13 (NCAA, 2012–2013). Importantly, recruiting rules are different and distinct for football and men's and women's basketball. Most of the other sports operate under similar recruiting guidelines, but it is always important to check with the athletic compliance office, the conference office, or the NCAA itself. NCAA member schools have adopted important rules and definitions[1] for college-bound athletes, and several key rules are outlined:

1. *Contact*. A contact occurs any time a coach has any face-to-face contact with a student-athlete or his or her parents/guardian off the college's campus and says more than hello. A contact also occurs if a coach has any contact with a student-athlete at his or her high school or any location where the student-athlete is competing or practicing.

2. *Contact Period*. During this time, a college coach may have in-person contact with a college-bound student-athlete and/or his or her parents/guardian on or off the college's campus. The coach may also watch the student-athlete play or visit his or her high school. The student-athlete and parents/guardian may visit a college campus, and the coach may write and telephone the student-athlete during this period.

3. *Dead Period*. The college coach may not have any in-person contact with the college-bound student-athlete and parents/guardian at any time in the dead

period. The coach may write and telephone the college-bound student-athlete and parents/guardian during this time. It is often believed that a "dead period" means absolutely no recruiting activities at all, but phone calls and written correspondence are allowed.

4. *Evaluation*. An evaluation is an activity by a coach to evaluate the college-bound student-athlete's academic or athletic ability. This would include visiting the student-athlete's high school to review academic records or watching the student-athlete practice or compete.

5. *Evaluation Period*. The college coach may watch the college-bound student-athlete play or visit his or her high school, but cannot have any in-person conversations with the student-athlete and parents/guardian off the college's campus. The student-athlete and parents/guardian can visit a college campus during this period. A coach may write and telephone the student-athlete and parents/guardian during this time.

6. *Official Visit*. An official visit is any visit to a college campus by the college-bound student-athlete and parents/guardian paid for by the college. The college may pay the following expenses:

   ■ The college-bound student-athlete's transportation to and from the college

   ■ Room and meals (three per day) while the student-athlete visits the college

   ■ Reasonable entertainment expenses, including three complimentary admissions to a home athletic contest

   Before a college may invite the college-bound student-athlete on an official visit, the student-athlete will have to provide the college with a copy of his or her high school transcript (Division I only) and SAT, ACT, or PLAN score and register with the NCAA Eligibility Center.

7. *Quiet Period*. The college coach may not have any in-person contact with the college-bound student-athlete and parents/guardian off the college's campus. The coach may not watch the student-athlete play or visit his or her high school during this period. The student-athlete and parents/guardian may visit a college campus during this time. A coach may write or telephone the student-athlete and parents/guardian during this time.

8. *Unofficial Visit*. An unofficial visit is any visit by the college-bound student-athlete and parents/guardian to a college campus paid for by the student-athlete and/or parents/guardian. The only expense the student-athlete may receive from the college is three complimentary admissions to a home athletic contest. The student-athlete may make as many unofficial visits as he or she desires and may take those visits at any time. The only time the student-athlete cannot talk with a coach on campus during an unofficial visit is during a dead period.

9. *Verbal Commitment.* This phrase is used to describe a college-bound student-athlete's commitment to a school before he or she signs (or is able to sign) a National Letter of Intent. A college-bound student-athlete can announce a verbal commitment at any time. While verbal commitments have become very popular for both college-bound student-athletes and coaches, this "commitment" is not binding on either the college-bound student-athlete or the school. Only the signing of the National Letter of Intent accompanied by a financial aid agreement is binding on both parties. Thus, recruiting athletes in middle school does not mean they have to attend the school they verbally commit to.

10. *Telephone Calls/Written Correspondence.* Telephone calls and written correspondence, including recruiting materials such as brochures, are governed by different rules for different sports and depend on the year in high school. For instance, a high school sophomore may receive recruiting materials and initiate a phone call with a coach at his or her own expense, but a coach may not call a sophomore prospect or even return the call. As the prospect progresses into junior and senior year, the ability of the school to increase recruitment in the areas of phone calls and written correspondence increases exponentially.

   The NCAA regulation over texting (SMS) prospects has evolved over the years. Initially, enterprising coaches were allowed to send hundreds of texts per day to prospects as a necessary part of recruitment, and as such, many top prospects would receive text messages in the thousands. In 2007 unlimited texting to recruits was banned; and in 2012, the NCAA returned to the unlimited text messaging rule (NCAA, 2012–2013).

11. *New Technology/Social Media.* Nothing has vexed coaches and compliance staffs more than social media and recruiting. Compliance staffs must be diligent in monitoring social media and informing boosters, interested parties, and the recruits themselves what can and cannot be done with new media. Rules regarding recruiting change rapidly and with new media one can expect similar changes.

   The aforementioned aspects and terms of recruiting underscore the daily maintenance and monitoring of the process that must happen to ensure NCAA, conference, and institutional rules are not being violated. Every aspect of recruiting is thoroughly regulated. Correspondence, phone calls, visits, texting, and social media all have limitations and permissible time periods. To complicate things further, each sport has its own specific recruiting rules that govern the main areas of recruiting mentioned outlined here.

   Due to the competitive nature of recruiting, coaches often attempt to push the NCAA boundaries to gain a recruiting advantage for a prized prospect. While re-

Cutting Corners: Creativity in Recruiting Often Does Not Pay

Coaches are often looking for ways to push the boundaries of recruiting legislation. Most are not looking to outright break NCAA rules but simply want to maximize every advantage possible. A simple written letter can become a valuable weapon. For example, can the letter be larger, have more color, or in some other way be specially delivered? By rule, written correspondence has to be general and not excessive in nature. Still many enterprising coaches will look for ways to maximize the rules to their benefit to secure an athlete. Some notable cases, though, include coaches who try to stay within the rules but ultimately go a bit too far.

While the coach at the University of Colorado, Rick Neuheisel, a trained attorney, was cited for 51 recruiting violations, mostly involving impermissible contacts with recruits. Neuheisel perfected the art of "bumping." Bumping is defined as "inadvertent" contact between recruits and coaches. This is entirely understandable, but Neuheisel took it to a new level by planning out the "unintentional bumping" scenarios, attempting to make it look inadvertent, and using it to his advantage to gain access to recruits. While some might call him creative, the NCAA sanctioned Neuheisel, which restricted his ability to recruit off-campus for nearly a year in his new position as head coach at the University of Washington. Scenarios like this demonstrate how coaches will often try to manipulate the rules by thinking outside the box to gain a recruit.

Kelvin Sampson, former men's basketball coach at Indiana University, was accused in allegations stemming from a phone call scandal that occurred while Sampson was still under recruiting restrictions following a similar scandal while coaching at the University of Oklahoma. Sampson was accused of participating in a three-way phone call with recruits even though he was not permitted to make recruiting phone calls. Sampson, thinking he could be on the calls as a listener but not an initiator, soon found himself the subject of another NCAA investigation for similar violations:

- Sampson, and two assistant coaches, failed to comply with sanctions imposed on Sampson for impermissible recruiting calls he made at Oklahoma.

- Sampson jointly participated in telephone calls with his assistants when Sampson was prohibited from being present or taking part when assistant coaches or staff members made recruiting calls.

- Sampson "acted contrary to the NCAA principles of ethical conduct when he knowingly violated recruiting restrictions imposed by the NCAA Committee on Infractions.

Sampson might have been trying to be creative in recruiting and to minimize his sanctions so he would potentially not lose a player to a rival. However, this "creative strategy" backfired, and Sampson was eventually fired as men's basketball coach at Indiana on February 22, 2008. ∎

cruiting violations are quite common, oftentimes they are unintentional and due to poor oversight and record keeping, such as when a coach calls a prospect that another coach in the same program already called during a period where only one phone call is allowed. Beyond the mere oversight and the potential negative consequences associated with them, some coaches are willing to engage in unscrupulous behaviors to secure the player who will help them win games. Several notable cases of recruiting improprieties include the University of Kentucky men's basketball in 1988, University of Miami football in 2011, and the Indiana University men's basketball in 2006. These are just a few examples, as many schools have found themselves in trouble with the NCAA because of intentional and unintentional recruiting violations.

CONCLUSION

Recruiting will continue to be a highly competitive process, as coaches work to secure the best athletes that fit their athletic program. Recruiting deregulation, such as allowing unlimited text messages and social media contacts, has been attempted more in the past few years than ever before by NCAA membership. It is becoming increasingly difficult to monitor all aspects related to recruiting, especially given the number of available communication channels and ease at which coaches can contact recruited athletes. The costs to monitor all these activities are becoming astronomical in computer monitoring software, human resources, and other complicated monitoring situations. Since monitoring recruiting activities is becoming more challenging for NCAA membership, recent attempts to lessen restrictions surprisingly met resistance from coaches. However, the resistance from some coaches should not be unexpected given that any deregulation was viewed as a way that one school or coach might gain an advantage over another. Any drastic changes are something many coaches are zealously guarding against. Coaches may not like the rules, but if it does not appear to be a level playing field between schools in the recruiting wars, coaches will likely want even more rules.

QUESTIONS FOR DISCUSSION

1. As discussed in this chapter, what are the primary areas of the recruiting process? Define and describe each area. How are they interrelated?

2. What is the impact of new technology on the recruiting process? What does the future of recruiting in intercollegiate athletics look like?

3. Despite many coaches not favoring additional NCAA regulations, why do many coaches want more regulations in recruiting, and not less?

Note

1. For more details, see the *2012–2013 NCAA Manual* and the *2012–2013 Guide for the College Bound Student Athlete*.

References

Belotti, M., & Ley, B. (Host). (2011, April 4). *Outside the lines: The Nader Plan*. Bristol, CT: ESPN.

Brown, G. (1999, November 22). NCAA answers call to reform. *NCAA News*, pp. A1–A4.

Ching, D. (2013, August 11). Recruiting a major yet vital expense. *ESPN.com*. Retrieved from http://espn.go.com/college-football/story/_/id/9551775/georgia-bulldogs-recruiting-budget-shows-cost-importance-reaching-players

The Crisis in Intercollegiate Athletics: A Report by a Panel of Retired College Presidents. (1990). *Chronicle of Higher Education*. Retrieved from http://www.chronicle.com

Crowley, J. (n.d.). *In the arena: The NCAAs first century*. Retrieved from http://www.ncaapublications.com/p-4039-in-the-arena-the-ncaas-first-century.aspx

Falla, J. (1981). *NCAA: The voice of college sports*. Shawnee Mission, KS: National Collegiate Athletic Association.

Frank, R. (2004). *Challenging the myth: A review of the links among college athletic success, student quality, and donations*. Retrieved from http://www.knightcommission.org/index.php?option=com_content&view=article&id=73&Itemid=4

Funk, G. (1991). *Major violation. The unbalanced priorities in athletics and academics*. Champaign, IL: Leisure Press.

Litan, R., Orszag, J., & Orszag, P. (2003, August). *The empirical effects of intercollegiate athletics: An interim report*. Retrieved from http://www.sc.edu/faculty/PDF/baseline.pdf

McMillen, T. (1992). *Out of bounds: How the American sports establishment is being driven by greed and hypocrisy—and what needs to be done about it*. New York: Simon and Schuster.

National Collegiate Athletic Association. (2012). *2012–2013 guide for the college bound student athlete*. Indianapolis, IN: National Collegiate Athletic Association.

———. (2012–2013). *National Collegiate Athletic Association Division I manual*. Indianapolis, IN: National Collegiate Athletic Association.

Sack, A., & Staurowsky, E. (1998). *College athletes for hire: The evolution and legacy of the NCAA's amateur myth*. Westport, CT: Praeger.

Smith, C. (2013, June 13). Kentucky offers seventh grade DB prospect Jairus Brents a football scholarship. *Yahoo Sports*. Retrieved from http://sports.yahoo.com/blogs/highschool-prep-rally/kentucky-offers-seventh-grade-db-prospect-jairus-brents-233504532.html

Suggs, W. (2003, May 2). Sports as the universities front porch: The public is skeptical. *Chronicle of Higher Education*. Retrieved from http://chronicle.com/article/Sports-as-the-University-s/11599

INTERCOLLEGIATE ATHLETICS and AMATEURISM

Billy Hawkins, Ashley R. Baker, and Velina B. Brackebusch

KEY TERMS

▶ amateurism

▶ intercollegiate athletics

▶ National Collegiate Athletic Association

▶ commercialization

▶ athletes

It's been a long, a long time coming
But I know a change gonna come, oh yes it will

Sam Cooke (1964)

Judge Claudia Wilken's decision in the *O'Bannon v. National Collegiate Athletic Association (NCAA)* case stands to disrupt the commercial enterprise of Division I—and, more specifically, FBS college athletics—by cracking the foundation of amateurism that holds it in place. Under her ruling, the NCAA will have to share in the revenue it generates from licensing athletes' image, names, and likenesses. Furthermore, the concept of amateurism in college sports received a blow as a recent investigative reporting by *Yahoo Sports* revealed several SEC football players received benefits from NFL agents and financial advisors, and the five-part series produced by *Sports Illustrated* exposed Oklahoma State football program's bonus system that compensated players based on their on-the-field performances, academic fraud, and other indiscretions (Dohrmann & Evans, 2013; Robinson & Getlin, 2013). Finally, amateurism was tarnished in the EPIX Original Documentary, *Schooled: The Price of College Sports*, where Adrian Foster admits to receiving money while playing football for the University of Tennessee (Valentine, Muscato, Branch, & Foxworth, 2013).

Amateurism has been the bedrock that allows the NCAA, its member institutions, conferences, corporate sponsors, and television networks to create revenue and for some to profit from the athletic talents and likenesses of college athletes in the sports of football and men's basketball. Now that amateurism is being challenged once again, it appears that "change gonna come." Change may be in the form of modifying the concept of amateurism: it may apply only to non-revenue-generating sport athletes, be alleviated altogether, or develop into a new and improved model that best captures the intercollegiate athletic experience of athletes, especially those in the revenue-generating sports of football and men's basketball. Regardless of the evolution or metamorphosis of amateurism, this case ruling coupled with the continual exposure of abuses in the form of economic benefits from external stakeholders will change the landscape of intercollegiate athletics, especially as it relates to the ideology of amateurism.

Intercollegiate athletics is a unique aspect to the higher educational experience in the United States. Many of this nation's major public and private universities are situated within athletic conferences that offer elite-level athletic competition in a variety of sports. Most of these institutions' athletic departments do not generate enough revenue to offset operating expenses; thus, very few sports make a profit or break even (Fulks, 2010). Yet both the nonmonetary benefits and intangibles these sports bring to a university campus are significant. For example, Toma (2003) explains that spectator sports, especially football, are fundamental to institutional life, collegiate culture, fostering external relations (e.g., alumni, corporate sponsors), and "providing the campus with a distinctive identity and popular appeal" (p. 1).

Although these universities have a variety of competitive sports and several elite-level Olympic sports that supply the U.S. Olympic Team with valuable talent, the most visible sports are men's and women's basketball and football; and the most profitable are football and men's basketball. For example, according to the U.S. Department of Education, of the top 10 universities based on total athletics revenue, the University of Texas ranked number one and generated $163,295,114, while Auburn University was ranked number ten and generated $105,951,251. At these institutions, football and basketball revenue attributed the largest percentage to this total revenue; in the example of the University of Texas and Auburn University, football's contribution to the total revenue was 64% and 73%, respectively, and basketball contribution to the total revenue was 11% and 9% (cited in Finger, 2013) (Table 23.1).

Due to the commercial nature of these institutions, institutional control and oversight are imperative. Additionally, conference and national-level control and oversight are necessary. At the conference level, governance is performed by such conferences as the Southeastern Conference (SEC), Atlantic Coast Conference (ACC), Pacific Athletic Conference (Pac-12), and the Big East Conference. The NCAA performs governance at the national level. This chapter examines the origin of amateurism, how the NCAA initially applied it to intercollegiate sports, and how the concept of amateurism is evolving in the new college athletic model.

TABLE 23.1

2012–2013 Top Twenty Teams Based on Total Revenue and Expenses

INSTITUTIONS	TOTAL REVENUE	TOTAL EXPENSES	FOOTBALL REVENUE/ EXPENSES	BASKETBALL REVENUE/ EXPENSES
Texas	$163,295,114	$129,234,974	$103,813,684/$25,896,203	$18,478,466/$8,603,853
Ohio State	$142,043,056	$116,400,943	$58,112,270/$34,026,871	$18,872,400/$5,956,288
Michigan	$128,750,370	$100,973,238	$85,209,247/$23,640,337	$9,880,283/$5,933,437
Alabama	$124,129,127	$98,280,539	$81,993,762/$36,918,963	$11,770,736/$6,161,728
Florida	$120,267,106	$111,007,311	$74,117,435/$23,045,846	$10,186,778/$8,474,783
Texas A&M	$119,702,222	$81,792,118	$44,420,762/$17,929,882	$6,134,315/$5,855,031
LSU	$113,964,540	$94,201,202	$68,804,309/$24,049,282	$9,421,518/$5,050,811
Penn State	$108,252,284	$84,498,339	$66,210,503/$30,206,692	$9,612,001/$5,056,643
Oklahoma	$106,456,616	$98,160,767	$59,630,425/$24,097,643	$8,011,804/$6,813,149
Auburn	$105,951,256	$96,315,836	$77,170,242/$33,334,595	$9,493,646/$7,588,390
Wisconsin	$101,490,339	$99,962,504	$48,416,449/$24,231,297	$17,144,598/$6,839,111
Tennessee	$105,869,282	$105,869,282	$52,590,771/$19,786,617	$14,521,082/$5,689,254
FSU	$100,049,444	$90,278,878	$35,870,789/$18,689,809	$5,959,659/$5,959,659
Arkansas	$99,757,483	$83,579,973	$64,193,826/$24,325,173	$16,630,650/$8,041,317
Iowa	$97,415,941	$79,130,558	$50,460,344/$21,607,187	$8,731,784/$6,243,668
Notre Dame	$97,112,859	$78,526,028	$68,986,659/$25,757,968	$3,538,334/$4,622,255
Oregon	$94,635,829	$89,709,350	$27,713,278/$18,198,476	$4,120,198/$5,852,153
Michigan State	$93,946,707	$88,100,432	$49,754,373/$19,079,522	$19,228,130/$9,837,886
Georgia	$91,670,613	$88,923,561	$74,989,418/$22,710,140	$8,476,089/$5,599,447
Kentucky	$88,373,452	$84,929,819	$32,997,939/$13,368,099	$21,598,680/$15,119,088

Sources: U.S. Department of Education: http://ope.ed.gov/athletics/http://ope.ed.gov/athletics/; USA Today: http://www.usatoday.com/sports/college/schools/finances/

THE EARLY YEARS OF AMATEURISM

Amateurism dates back to 1784, when it was first used to denote individuals who nurtured or cultivated any activity as a pastime. According to Abe (1988), amateurism, around 1901, was defined as: "One who cultivates a particular study or art for the love of it, and not professionally: in general terms, one who plays a game for pleasure, as distinguished from a professional who plays for money—nearly every game has its special definition to meet its own requirements" (p. 9). Recently, Zimbalist and Sack (2013) defined amateurism as: "The belief that leisure activities are qualitatively superior to those associated with making a living or whose motive is material gain. The aristocrat had time to appreciate activities like literature, science, and sports merely for the love of it" (p. 2).

The early movement of amateurism originated in nineteenth-century Britain, where the upper class or aristocrats were enjoying sport activities for leisure. They were more interested in playing well and for the intrinsic values associated with leisure activities. Greater value was placed on individuals who were good at the activity by nature, as opposed to someone who attempted to become better in their ability through frequent practice (Sack & Staurowsky, 1998; Smith, 1993). According to Smith (1993), the intent of the British amateurism model was designed by the aristocracy to exclude the working-class people from participating. This meant that only certain groups of higher social status were forming the circle of partaking in amateur sports. Sports like cricket included one paid position, the bowler or pitcher, usually played by working-class athletes; however they were not allowed in the upper-circles gatherings after the game. This formation allowed the aristocrats to keep their amateur status; as the working-class athlete was being paid he did not fit the concept of an amateur. Also, the position of bowlers or pitchers was more physically demanding and required training; therefore, it conflicted with what the upper class viewed as amateur (Smith, 1993). When paying working-class athletes to fill those positions, the aristocracy was able to combine pleasure from playing the sport, excluding these athletes from entering its society, and avoiding the physical training that contradicted the idea of a natural athlete.

The two most-elite institutions in England—Oxford and Cambridge—became the main playgrounds where amateurism excelled (Smith, 1993). Students spent hours on the practice fields to stand out in sports like cricket, tennis, rowing, and soccer. These two institutions represented the offspring of the elites in the British society where amateur athletics were excelling. As students became increasingly involved in practicing sports, the traditional ideals of amateurism began to fade. Some students were recruited to play sports and were funded, yet these institutions and their students were praised for academic and scholastic achievements; athletics was not viewed as a tool to recruit or draw massive crowds to gain publicity or reputation (Sack & Staurowsky, 1998). The aristocratic ideal that excelling by simply being a "natural" and not putting effort into any single activity was slowly moving toward a new meaning of amateurism.

Amateur athletics began to make its transition from British universities to elite American academic institutions when in 1852 Yale University challenged Harvard University to a rowing race now marked as the first intercollegiate sporting event in the United States. Since the first rowing competition between Harvard and Yale, tremendous growth has taken place in American athletics, and the British view of amateurism has been immensely transformed on American soil. In the early 1900s questions of amateurism emerged, and the "Osborn problem" further exposed the differing views of what amateurism meant to the achievement-driven American society (Smith, 1993).

During a time when Harvard University's football program was experiencing an increase in support and American football was considered by some to be the most important college sport, Charles Osborn, a star goalie from Oxford University, was recruited to join Harvard's football team. As Smith (1993) explained, head football coach Bill Reid was highly upset with Osborn for his desire to play spring sports like cricket, tennis, and soccer as opposed to attending spring football practice. The coach believed that an athlete should concentrate on one sport and develop his strength and conditioning that best fits that sport. Osborn's "English attitude," or his aspiration to play multiple sports as a natural athlete, concerned Reid, as he believed this mind-set handicapped Osborn and challenged the American standard of athletics, which, at that time, meant concentrating on one sport. Reid wanted Osborn to be clear that his athletic responsibility was to the football team and not to the other sports.

The Osborne-Reid conflict illustrates the beginning of many challenges that the NCAA would face while modifying the concept of amateurism. The idea that athletes are amateurs but at the same time train and devote their time as professionals was just one of the first arguments raised in what was to become decades of debate on the topic. Today this matter has become much more controversial due to the financial commercialization of college athletics.

THE NCAA AND AMATEURISM

In 1906 the NCAA, formerly named the Intercollegiate Athletic Association of the United States, was founded, and its purpose in part was to restore amateur standards. The NCAA documented its position on amateurism in its 1906 bylaws, which closely reflected the same position taken by British universities (Sack & Staurowsky, 1998). According to NCAA (2013) Bylaw 2.9, the "Principle of Amateurism" states: "Student-athletes shall be amateurs in an intercollegiate sport, and their participation should be motivated primarily by education and by the physical, mental, and social benefits to be derived. Student participation in intercollegiate athletics is an avocation, and student-athletes should be protected from exploitation by professional and commercial enterprises" (p. 4). The principle, as currently stated does not greatly differ from the NCAA's stance when first formed. With this as a guiding principle, member colleges and universities were charged with the responsibility of monitoring amateurism in an effort to prevent violations.

The NCAA's stance in the early 1900s was that athletes were not allowed to receive financial incentives as a way to lure them to compete, and prominent athletes were not to be sought out and invited to participate in athletics. In 1906 the aforementioned activities were defined as violations; however, this is what we know today as athletic scholarships and the recruitment of athletes. With established amateurism rules in place, opposition still existed among NCAA membership, which led to concern as to how colleges and universities would uniformly enforce these rules. By the mid-1930s the NCAA reported major concerns regarding the recruitment and subsidization of athletes, two violations clearly defined in the acceptance of the 1906 bylaws. By the 1940s, "the violation of basic amateur principles was becoming formal policy in some schools and conferences" (Sack & Staurowsky, 1998, p. 40).

Member institutions were informed by the NCAA that any aid awarded to athletes should come from outside of the athletic department and follow the same criteria for any other student on campus. One criterion used to determine whether aid should be awarded was the financial need of the student. Even with this policy in place financial aid practices greatly varied between conferences, and colleges and universities were still primarily responsible for monitoring themselves. As a result the Sanity Code was presented at the 1947 NCAA convention and was approved the following year.

The Sanity Code was an attempt by the NCAA to create a comprehensive list of rules addressing amateurism, financial aid and eligibility, and a plan for the uniform enforcement of these rules. As part of this legislation, institutions were still permitted to offer athletes partial financial aid, if financial need was established, even though enticing talented athletes with financial aid offers was a direct violation of the principles of amateurism. The inclusion of regulations on the awarding of financial aid, recruiting, academic standards, institutional control, and amateurism still did not maintain support from the membership, and it was repealed in 1951 due to concerns over the limitations it placed on recruiting and financial aid (NCAA, 2011). By 1956, NCAA legislation permitted institutions to provide financial aid that covered educational costs to athletes, and need was no longer a requirement.

The NCAA was violating its own amateurism principle by implementing practices that resembled professionalism and, as such, went to great lengths to maintain the appearance that grant-in-aid was not an employee contract (Sack & Staurowsky, 1998). Over the next several years, while denying that scholarships were employment contracts, the NCAA sought ways to take away the scholarships of athletes who were not meeting required expectations. By 1967, scholarship athletes could have their four-year grants-in-aid reduced or canceled if they falsified information on an application or engaged in misconduct (Sack & Staurowsky, 1998). It was also at this time the standard practice of providing a four-year scholarship was challenged. Six years later, with the approval of the NCAA, scholarships were reduced to one academic year.

In the 1970s "need based" financial aid was back on the table for consideration as a way to cut costs. It was met with resistance for fear that it would again encourage rule violations. Proposals for need-based aid were brought before the NCAA six times over the course of a decade, and in 1981 the newest version of the proposal was defeated for the seventh time (Sack & Staurowsky, 1998). Schools now had to look for ways to cut costs and generate more revenue for their institutions.

It was during the 1960s and 1970s the NCAA received waiver requests, which it unfailingly denied, from athletes who wanted to retain their amateur status in one sport while being professionals in another, until major changes were made to the amateurism rules in 1974 (Hawes, 2000). Athletes were permitted to compete as a professional in one sport and maintain eligibility in another. Additionally, they could tryout with a professional team as long as they covered their own costs and did not accept any form of payment. The amateurism rules have seen a host of changes since its first inception; even today the NCAA has dedicated an entire section to the concept of amateurism in its *NCAA Manual* and on its website.

Furthermore, the NCAA established the NCAA Eligibility Center (formerly known as the NCAA Initial-Eligibility Clearinghouse) to verify the academic and amateur status of all prospective college athletes. Each college-bound athlete is required to answer a list of questions regarding previous participation in sports. The fall of 2007 marked the first time the NCAA was involved in certifying amateurism for college-bound athletes (NCAA, 2012a). Prior to 2007 each NCAA member institution was responsible for determining the amateur status of athletes it admitted. The primary purpose of a uniform amateurism certification was to create consistency among member institutions.

During the certification process, the NCAA Eligibility Center gathers information from the college athletes to fully understand the details of their amateur status. Cited examples of activities that may be reviewed include contracts with a professional team, salary for participating in athletics, prize money, play with professionals, tryouts, practice or competition with a professional team, benefits from an agent or prospective agent, and an agreement to be represented by an agent. Based on the results of this inquiry, the amateur-certification staff will likely take appropriate actions if a violation has occurred. According to the NCAA, less than 1% of college athletes seeking amateur certification receive penalties related to amateurism (NCAA, 2012a).

AMATEURISM AND THE NEW COLLEGIATE MODEL

Despite the controversy incurred in the evolution of amateurism, its application and effectiveness in maintaining a nonprofessional and competitive athletic experience is noteworthy. What is also noteworthy is that within the current configuration of intercollegiate athletics and the varying divisions of NCAA governance, there are sporting experiences that align with the amateurism model, theoretically and in practice, and likewise the intercollegiate sporting experiences that present a challenge to the ideals of amateurism. For example, most non-revenue-generating sports align themselves, in theory and practice, with amateurism, whereas revenue-generating sports, such as football and men's basketball, challenge amateurism's ideals. Consequently, in a 2006 presidential address the late Myles Brand informed NCAA Convention attendees, "Amateur defines the participants, not the enterprise" (Brand, 2006). Brand's concept of amateurism denotes a shift in the historic conception of amateurism to a concept that emphasizes no longer a privileged status or opportunity but rather, within the *new collegiate model*, a constraint, a forfeiture of athletes' rights, and a punishment.

To use Brand's statement as a conceptual framework for intercollegiate athletic divisions and sports governed by NCAA, again, there are divisions and sports that, on the one hand, fit neatly within his new collegiate model of amateurism and challenge the traditional model of amateurism, and then, on the other hand, there are those which fit into the traditional model of amateurism. For example, the structure of NCAA Division III athletics, without question, fits within the traditional model of amateurism where the requirements do not allow the following (as mentioned earlier):

- Contracts with professional teams

- Salary for participating in athletics

- Prize money

- Salary for participating in athletics

- Prize money above actual and necessary expenses

- Play with professionals

- Tryouts, practice, or competition with a professional team

- Benefits from an agent or prospective agent

- Agreement to be represented by an agent

- Delayed initial full-time collegiate enrollment to participate in organized sports competition (NCAA, 2012b)

Most of the problems involving violations of these rules or others where athletes have received some form of benefits (see The Ohio State's "tattoo-gate" or The University of Miami's "Shapiro-gate") or some form of compensation (see University of Georgia's "ring-gate" and "jersey-gate") have occurred in football and men's basketball at the FBS level (see, e.g., Cash, 2010; Robinson, 2011; Associated Press, 2003; Tucker, 2010). Therefore, the traditional model of amateurism does not align with the construction of the new collegiate model.

Intercollegiate sports at the FBS level, mainly football and men's basketball, challenges the traditional model because of the increased commercialization and athletic demands placed on the lives of collegiate athletes have created a labor

CASE STUDY

The Professionalization of College Athletes

The NCAA has addressed the issue of professionalization of college sports since the early1900s, when college players were being compensated for their athletic services in various forms. For example, during the turn of the twentieth century James Hogan played football at Yale, where he was given a scholarship, luxurious suite of rooms, free meals at the University Club, and profits from game-day program sales. He also had a deal with the American Tobacco Company according to which he would receive a commission for every package of cigarettes sold in that city. Finally, after the football season, he was afforded a 10-day paid vacation in Cuba (Lucas & Smith, 1978). This practice help spawn the creation of the NCAA to address the professionalization and compensation of college athletes. Thus, developing and implementing a model of amateurism suitable for college athletics was one of the original tasks of the NCAA.

Since the establishment of the NCAA, it has had to frequently enforced and uphold its principles of amateurism. Given the highly publicized episodes of college athletes receiving various forms of compensation because of their status as athletes on high-profile college teams, the NCAA has to once again enforce its rules regarding amateurism, including cases at Ohio State, University of Miami, and the University of Georgia.

Because amateurism anchors the college athletic experience within the context of higher education, its maintenance and enforcement is crucial. Furthermore, according to the NCAA, amateurism is critical to "preserving an academic environment in which acquiring a quality education is the first priority" (NCAA 2012b). Allowing athletes to share in the revenue generated from their images and likenesses completely changes both notions of amateurism and the way the concept was formerly applied. ■

Questions to consider

1. To ensure the NCAA assists its member institutions in creating an academic environment that fosters a quality educational experience, what additional strategies can the NCAA implement with the changes in the landscape of intercollegiate athletics as a result of the ruling in *O'Bannon v. NCAA*?

2. As an athletic administrator, in light of the highly publicized violations involving compensation, what measures would you put in place to prevent these types of violations?

relationship where the athletic scholarship is a form of payment for athletic services rendered. The NCAA (2012b) states: "Amateur competition is a bedrock principle of college athletics and the NCAA. Maintaining amateurism is crucial to preserving an academic environment in which acquiring a quality education is the first priority. In the collegiate model of sports, the young men and women competing on the field or court are students first, athletes second" (para. 1). When one examines the revenue generated by FBS level football and men's basketball programs, it is hard to conceive that "preserving an academic environment in which acquiring a quality education is the first priority" NCAA (2012b, para. 1) (see Table 23.1). Subsequently, the enormous physical and time demands placed on athletes to sustain these multimillion-dollar budgets challenge whether these athletes are purely engaged in their respective sports solely for educational attainment purposes. Furthermore, when we have testimonies like Bob DeMars, former USC player from 1997 to 2001, who was verbally assaulted by his then coach, Ed Orgeron, for leaving practice early to go to class, it raises awareness about the athletic demands placed on athletes (Ellis, 2013).

Within this configuration, what constitutes a student activity and amateur experience for athletes in non-revenue-generating sports has clearly become a profession to athletes in revenue-generating sports. The amateur sporting experiences of many athletes in non-revenue-generating sports are at the expense of a "professional" experience of a few athletes in revenue-generating or spectator-oriented sports. Thus, the "free ride," which is nomenclature often associated with scholarship amateur athletes, is not free.

PATERNALISM AND AMATEURISM

Despite this incongruence in experiences, what has allowed these athletes, with varying experiences, to function under the ideals of amateurism is a prevailing culture of paternalism where commercial interests are masked. Jackman (1994) captures the essence of paternalism when she stated:

> The traditional father-child relationship on which the term [paternalism] is based was one in which the father authoritatively dictated all the behaviors and significant life-decisions of his children within a moral framework that credited the father with an unassailable understanding of the needs and best interests of his children. They, in turn, accepted implicitly and absolutely the authority of their father—occasional bouts of independence were not

STAKEHOLDER PERSPECTIVE

Amateurism and Race

In *The New Plantation: Black Athletes, College Sports, and Predominantly White NCAA Institutions*, Billy Hawkins illustrates that less than 1% of the more than 480,000 college athletes generate over 90% of the NCAA's annual revenue; and, coincidentally, over 60% of the 1 percent are black male basketball athletes. A similar pattern is recognized when college football at the FBS level is examined: black male athletes make up the majority of the top 25 teams, many of which have budgets exceeding $70 million, with football generating over 50% of the athletic departments' budgets for these institutions. When critically assessed, amateurism takes on a different meaning within the context of the aforementioned data, and its application is more of a legal right to the image and athletic labor that is converted into products that generate revenue. The black body, once again, is used to advance the commercial agendas of white power structure. Thus, the "professional" athletic efforts of black male athletes, specifically, and white male athletes, in general, in revenue generating sports provide an amateur experience for 99% of intercollegiate athletes at the NCAA FBS level. The challenge with this arrangement is that for black male athletes their graduation rates are the lowest among all athletes. Therefore, a grave contradiction exists where amateurism, in theory, is designed to ensure attaining and obtaining a quality education as the first priority and ultimate objective, yet, in practice, it is negligent in assuring black male athletes excel academically. ■

unexpected, but never tolerated. Good children learned to comply with and defer to the wishes of their father. (p. 10)

The NCAA efforts of protecting the athlete from exploitation by professional and commercial enterprises denote its roles as father, protector, and provider. When "bouts of independence" are exhibited, generally in the form of rule violations pertaining to amateurism, it is the paternal nature of the NCAA to instill discipline and restore equilibrium to the system of amateurism. Under the auspices of paternalism, the administration, implementation, and adherence to amateurism seem feasible, logical, and, for some, more palatable.

What this paternal association has fostered is a unique relationship in which the athletes submit to the authority of the NCAA member institutions directly and the NCAA indirectly and the NCAA establishes the parameters of this relationship. Ideally, both parties are supposed to benefit mutually: athletes obtain education and perhaps play professionally, while the NCAA member institutions' athletic departments operate multimillion-dollar budgets and provide a variety of sporting opportunities. This paternal association has provided the NCAA, its member institutions, and the respective conferences with complete *rights* to the product produced from the athletic talent and image of collegiate athletes—again, mainly those in revenue-generating sports.

The new collegiate model seeks adherence to amateur ideals as a mechanism to protect college athletes from commercial exploitation, yet what is concealed is the NCAA's efforts to protect itself and its member institutions from litigations involving labor disputes or antitrust violations (e.g., *O'Bannon v. NCAA, 2010*; see Staples, 2013). As the "bedrock principle of college athletics and the NCAA," amateurism enables these institutions to operate an athletic commercial enterprise while minimally compensating its labor force. Especially, according to Huma and Staurowsky (2012), college athletes in the revenue-generating sports of football and men's basketball are definitely not receiving compensation based on their fair market value.

CONCLUSION

Amateurism has been at the disposal of the NCAA and its member institutions since 1906. It has been modified considerably from its original meaning when it was conceived in 1784. Amateurism has weathered many storms and, despite being modified and heavily scrutinized, has endured—until the court ruling in the *O'Bannon* case. Its fortitude, pliability, and applicability will be tested in this era when collegiate athletics are increasingly commercialized and athletes in revenue-generating sports can share in the profits generated from the use of their likenesses and images. How will the new amateurism model function in a system where the NCAA and its member institutions are capitalistic in revenue generation and accumulation while the athletic departments are egalitarian in revenue distribution? Can amateurism, once again, be modified to best capture the experiences of all college athletes, or will a new identity be given to those that mimic the practices of professional athletes—"elite amateurs" maybe? Will creating an additional division (Super Division I, as has been suggested by the Division I-A faculty athletics representatives) to expand the NCAA beyond the traditional three divisional classifications solve the threat to amateurism? According to the architects of this proposal, creating a super division for FBS institutions that are similar in regards to resources will provide them with autonomy needed to control their destinies (1A Faculty Athletics Representatives, 2013).

The ruling in the *O'Bannon v. NCAA* has created a need for the concept of amateurism to morph into something different and unique. Also, the work of the National College Players Association in highlighting the economic contribution of athletes in revenue-generating sports of football and men's basketball continues to stimulate debate about the usefulness of the term amateurism (Huma & Staurowsky, 2012).

The continued economic growth of intercollegiate spectator sports contributes to the need to develop new models of intercollegiate athletics. For example, one model could conceptualize amateurism that is applicable only to athletes in non-revenue-generating sports and classify athletes in revenue-generating sports as "elite" amateurs or paraprofessional athletes, similar to elite Olympic-level athletes. Under this proposed model, revenue-generating athletes would be able to earn revenue from endorsements, guest appearances, signing autographs, or receive additional stipends given their market value. This proposed model would maintain the current academic expectations, where athletes are expected to enroll in so many hours per semester and successfully progress toward a degree and graduation within four or five years.

Another model would entail the creation of an additional divisional classification; a Super Division I, for example. Athletes competing in this division would be compensated based on fair market value as if they were in a minor-league division. Because of the athletic demands, these athletes will have greater flexibility with their academic pursuits and options: they could continue along the tradition path of academic expectation (i.e., a certain number of hours per semester, per year, successfully progressing toward a degree, and graduating in four or five years), or they could select a reduced course-load during their respective seasons, have an extended period of time to obtain their degree, or have unlimited access to their scholarship—a type of "scholarship-banking" that allows the athlete to fully take advantage of educational opportunities later. Therefore, if the athlete decides to compete professionally for a few years, he or she always has the option of returning to complete a degree without cost; some universities currently have this system in place for athletes who retire or transition from professional sports.

These are loosely constructed models to ignite debate and discussion around intercollegiate athletics and amateurism. Clearly, legal, political, and market forces are presenting an opportunity for the NCAA to once again reframe how amateurism is defined and applied. Regardless of the historical fortitude of the concept of amateurism, "a change gonna come."

QUESTIONS FOR DISCUSSION

1. What is the origin of amateurism, and what is its original definition? How has the NCAA modified the term amateurism to apply to intercollegiate athletics?

2. What is the Sanity Code, and how was it a challenge to amateurism?

3. Given the various divisional classifications of the NCAA (i.e., Division, I, II, and III), which of these divisions best adhere to the definition of amateurism? Explain?

References

1A Faculty Athletics Representatives (FAR). (2013). Principles and model for new governance structure. Retrieved from http://www.oneafar.org/Governance_Proposal.pdf

Abe, I. (1988). A study of the chronology of the modern usage of sportsmanship in English, American, and Japanese Dictionaries. *International Journal of the History of Sport, 5*(1), 3–28.

Associated Press. (2003). Nine must buy rings after selling last year's. ESPN. Retrieved from http://sports.espn.go.com/ncf/news/story?id=1676582

Brand, M. (2006). The principles of intercollegiate athletics. *NCAA News Archive—2006*. Retrieved from, http://fs.ncaa.org/Docs/NCAANewsArchive/2006/Association-wide/brand%2Bcharts%2Bcourse%2Bfor%2Bcollegiate%2Bmodel_s%2Bnext%2Bcentury%2B-%2B1-16-06%2Bncaa%2Bnews.html

Cash, R. L. (2010). Pryor, four other OSU players suspended first five games in 2011 for accepting improper benefits. *SportingNews*. Retrieved from http://www.sportingnews.com/ncaa-football/feed/2010-12/osu-suspensions/story/reports-osu-investigating-tattoo-allegations

Cooke, S. (1964). *Change is gonna come*. Retrieved from http://www.metrolyrics.com/its-been-a-long-time-coming-lyrics-sam-cooke.html

Dohrmann, G., & Evans, T. (2013). Special report on Oklahoma State football: Part I—The Money. Retrieved from http://sportsillustrated.cnn.com/college-football/news/20130910/oklahoma-state-part-1-money/

Ellis, Z. (2013). Ex-USC player: Ed Orgeron berated me for going to class instead of practice. *SI.com*. Retrieved from http://college-football.si.com/2013/06/12/usc-trojans-bob-demars-ed-orgeron/?eref=sircrc

Finger, M. (2013). Dry spell puts onus on Dodds. *San Antonio Express*. Retrieved from http://www.tapmecontest.org/entries/assets/AAAA_13_SAEN_FingerMike01.pdf

Fulks, D. L. (2010). Revenues & expenses, 2004–2009: NCAA Division I intercollegiate athletics programs report. Indianapolis, IN: National Collegiate Athletic Association.

Hawes, K. (2000). Debate on amateurism has evolved over time. *NCAA News*. Retrieved from http://fs.ncaa.org/Docs/NCAANewsArchive/2000/association-wide/debate%2Bon%2Bamateurism%2Bhas%2Bevolved%2Bover%2Btime%2B-%2B1-3-00.html

Hawkins, B. (2013). *The new plantation: Black athletes, college sports, and predominantly white NCAA institutions*. New York: Palgrave Macmillan.

Huma, R., & Staurowsky, E. J. (2012). *The $6 billion heist: Robbing college athletes under the guise of amateurism*. A report collaboratively produced by the National College Players Association and Drexel University Sport Management.

Jackman, M. R. (1994). *The velvet glove: Paternalism and conflict in gender, class, and race relations*. Berkeley: University of California Press.

Lucas, J. A., & Smith R. A. (1978). *Saga of American Sport*. Philadelphia: Lea and Febiger.

National Collegiate Athletic Association. (2011). *NCAA enforcement*. Retrieved from http://www.ncaa.org/wps/wcm/connect/public/NCAA/Enforcement/Resources/Chronology+of+Enforcement

———. (2012a). *NCAA becoming eligible*. Retrieved from http://www.ncaa.org/wps/wcm/connect/public/NCAA/Eligibility/Becoming+Eligible

———. (2012b). *Remaining eligible: Amateurism*. Retrieved from http://www.ncaa.org/wps/wcm/connect/public/NCAA/Eligibility/Remaining+Eligible/Amateurism

———. (2012–2013). *2012–2013 NCAA Division I manual*. Indianapolis, IN: National Collegiate Athletic Association.

O'Bannon v. Nat'l Collegiate Athletics Ass'n, Nos. C 09-1967 CW, C 09-3329 CW, C 09-4882 CW, 2010 WL 445190, at *8 (N.D. Cal. Feb. 8, 2010).

Robinson, C. (2011). Renegade Miami football booster spells out illicit benefits to players. *Yahoo Sports*. Retrieved from http://sports.yahoo.com/investigations/news?slug=cr-renegade_miami_booster_details_illicit_benefits_081611

Robinson, C., & Getlin, R. (2013). Documents, text messages reveal impermissible benefits to five SEC players. Retrieved from http://sports.yahoo.com/news/ncaaf—documents—texts-reveal-impermissible-benefits-to-five-sec-players-202513237.html

Sack, A. L., & Staurowsky, E. J. (1998). *College athletes for hire: The evolution and legacy of the NCAA's amateur myth*. Westport, CT: Praeger.

Smith, R. A. (1993). History of amateurism in men's intercollegiate athletics: The continuance of a 19th-century anachronism in America. *Quest, 45*, 430–447.

Staples, A. (2013). Ed. O'Bannon v. the NCAA: A complete case primer. SI.com. Retrieved from http://sportsillustrated.cnn.com/college-football/news/20130402-ed-obannon-ncaa-case-primer/

U.S. Department of Education. (2011). The equity in athletics data analysis cutting tool. Retrieved from http://ope.ed.gov/athletics/

Toma, J. D. (2003). *Football U.: Spectator sports in the life of the American university*. Ann Arbor: University of Michigan Press.

Tucker, T. (2010). A. J. Green: I sold jersey for "extra cash" during spring break. *Atlanta Journal Constitution*. Retrieved from http://blogs.ajc.com/uga-sports-blog/2010/09/28/a-j-green-i-sold-jersey-for-extra-cash-during-spring-break/

USA Today: College sport finances. (2013). Retrieved from http://www.usatoday.com/sports/college/schools/finances/

Valentine, B., Muscato, A. J., Branch, T., & Foxworth, D. (2013). *Schooled: The Price of College Sports*. EPIX Original Documentary. Retrieved from http://press.epixhd.com/programming/schooled-the-price-of-college-sports/

Zimbalist, A., & Sack, A. (2013). Thoughts on amateurism, the O'Bannon case and the viability of college sport. Retrieved from http://thedrakegroup.org/2013/04/10/drake-group-report-obannon-amateurism-and-the-viability-of-college-sport

FREEDOMS LOST

*Exploring Social Media Policies
in Intercollegiate Athletics*

Eric M. Snyder

KEY TERMS

▶ social media

▶ social networking site(s)
(SNS)

▶ National Conference of
State Legislatures
(NCSL)

▶ legislation, social media
monitoring services
(SMMS)

▶ Facebook

A full 22 years after the first intercollegiate athletics event in America, President James McCosh of Princeton University reported multiple ethical issues that had permeated intercollegiate athletics to the Princeton Board of Trustees (Smith, 1983). In particular, students began to spend more time participating in intercollegiate athletics than academics. As such, President McCosh's concern was whether intercollegiate athletics could remain uncorrupted without any administrative oversight (Smith, 1983). Despite the president's report, students continued to collect athletics fees and organize games without intervention (Thelin, 2012). However, the freedom to operate as an unregulated student organization managed by the student body was short-lived. In 1881 Princeton began the process of reining in student control by forming the first faculty athletics committee (Smith, 1983). Over the past 133 years, the deterioration of student control of intercollegiate athletics has resulted in a plethora of rules and regulations, many of which eliminate certain rights that the general student population still enjoys.

Even though the concern of this chapter pertains precisely to social media policies and college athletes, it is important to note that policies diminishing the rights of athletes are nothing new. The following are examples of athletes' rights that have been lost over the past century: the exclusion of a player's ability to select what shoe brand to wear if the institution has signed an endorsement contract; the prohibition on athletes being able to transfer and participate in sports at their new institutions immediately; the prevention of athletes' choice to forgo college and participate in certain professional sports; the loss of scholarship security with the creation of the one-year renewable; and, finally, the evolution of social media policies that monitor, regulate, and even prohibit the social media activities of athletes (Snyder, 2013).

Because of the emergence of social media as a major form of communication, there have been an increased number of National Collegiate Athletic Association (NCAA) sanctions following athlete use of social media. The result is augmented pressure on institutions to address social media use by athletes. The issue, however, is whether the NCAA, the university, or government, whether state or federal, can produce a balanced social media policy for intercollegiate athletic departments to implement. Currently, athletic programs continue to create and adopt institution-specific social media policies. As of 2013, the NCAA has yet to institute a social media bylaw specific to monitoring, banning, or regulating athletes' social media accounts. Thus, an analysis of social media policies, bylaws, and regulations must now focus not only on the NCAA and universities but also on state and federal law.

BACKGROUND

Throughout history, the progression of technology has been closely linked to the evolution of intercollegiate athletics. Since the first intercollegiate athletics event at Lake Winnipesaukee in the mid-nineteenth century, there exists a cyclical progression, with the creation of a new communication medium followed by the creation of a new athletic department use. Intercollegiate athletic departments have capitalized on these forms of communication, including radio, television, the internet, and social media. Each communication technology has played a prominent role in intercollegiate athletics by decreasing the amount of time it takes to reach sports fans.

In 2004 the emergence of the social networking site (SNS) Facebook was particularly important. Since then, advances in social media have continued to permeate the athletic departments and completely change the way in which they operate. A SNS as defined by Boyd and Ellison (2007) consists of "Web-based services that allow individuals to construct a public or semi-public profile within a bounded system" (p. 211). Within this system, the user can add others with whom he shares a connection or common interest. Social media is defined as an electronic service or account, or electronic content, including, but not limited to, videos or still photographs, blogs, video blogs, podcasts, instant and text messages, email, online services or accounts, or internet web site profiles or locations. Social media has grown into one of the most popular forms of communication with roughly 67% of adult users participating in social media (Brenner, 2013). Facebook, the world's largest social media platform, registered over one billion accounts in October 2012 (Ortutay, 2012). Twitter, which has over 500 million registered users, generates over 340 million "tweets" daily (Whittaker, 2012).

It is apparent that these social media platforms have become critical communication tools in our society (Epstein, 2012). Because of their impact, many intercollegiate athletic departments incorporate social media into their business models for marketing, public relations, and recruiting. For example, the University of Michigan football team currently has 149,382 followers of its Twitter account (Twitter, 2013a). Since its adoption of Twitter, the team has released more than 8,460 tweets to fans providing them with accurate team news (Twitter, 2013a).

In addition to athletic departments, an individual athlete can bring increased attention and support to her sport and her school. Former Notre Dame University women's basketball player Skylar Diggins, for example, had more than 150,000 twitter followers during her college athletic career (McManus, 2012). Diggins social media presence has been credited with helping to promote the athletic department and to increase the popularity of women's intercollegiate basketball (Lopresti, 2013; McIntyre, 2012; Voepel, 2013).

SOCIAL MEDIA USE BY COLLEGE ATHLETES

When an athlete decides to join the virtual world, he or she is given the opportunity to share information with users of the same SNS. The evolution of social media, specifically Facebook and Twitter, created the opportunity for problems to arise by allowing almost all users access to other user accounts—even when accounts are set to private. The ability of athletes to easily access friends and post comments has sparked increased scrutiny by athletic department administrators as they have become concerned about the athletic department image and the well-being of athletes (Butts, 2008). This section highlights specific examples of "inappropriate" use of social media by athletes who, as a result, were suspended, stripped of their scholarship, or dismissed from the institution.

According to Brown (2008), an athlete was dismissed from the Wake Forest football team for posting on his Facebook wall that he would "blow up campus." In addition, the individual promised friends and fans logging onto his profile that he would bring a loaded Uzi for those left standing (Brown, 2008). Reporters of this story were unsure whether the athlete was expelled from the university or if he voluntarily withdrew (Brown, 2008). Regardless, his posting on social media caused panic for the athletic department and the entire university community.

In August 2011, the men's golf team at a Bethany college in Kansas was suspended for taking an inappropriate team picture and placing it on Facebook (Denver Channel, 2011). The photo allows the general public to see the golf team nude with clubs covering their private parts. As a result, the institution banned the players from the first three tournaments of the season. The institution, however, cannot block access to the image, which remains in the public domain indefinitely (Denver Channel, 2011).

More recently, an Ohio State backup quarterback sent the following message to his followers: "Why should we have to go to class if we came here to play FOOTBALL, we ain't come to play SCHOOL classes are POINTLESS." For this Twitter post, the backup quarterback was sidelined for one game and his twitter account was deleted (Clayton, 2012).

Finally, Florida State's football coach told his players they were prohibited from using their Twitter accounts for the entire 2012–2013 school year (Associated Press, 2012). The decision stemmed from players tweeting of allegedly inappropriate material, including rap lyrics about killing police officers. The coach believed that social media was an unnecessary distraction that would cause his players to lose their focus during the season (Associated Press, 2012).

SOCIAL MEDIA POLICIES, BYLAWS, AND LEGISLATION

Athletic Department Policies

Social media behavior by athletes has caused athletic departments to develop more stringent department policies. In particular, NCAA sanctions on the University of North Carolina (UNC) in 2010 changed the way in which many athletic programs regulate social media, by monitoring, regulating, and even banning its use by athletes. After an athlete revealed an inappropriate relationship with an agent at a club and posted other comments that indicated violation of the NCAA's amateurism rules (Giglio, 2010), the NCAA (2011) issued the following statement: "In February through June 2010, UNC did not adequately and consistently monitor the social networking activity that visibly illustrated potential amateurism violations within the football program." The NCAA's admonition to UNC proved that an NCAA member institution's failure to monitor an athlete's social media use can result in sanctions (e.g., 2-year bowl ban). Since the incident, the NCAA has not made any statement that requires universities to monitor the social media accounts of athletes; however, this investigation is proof that the NCAA may expect universities to monitor such usage.

In response to the NCAA sanction, UNC immediately changed its social media policy, which according to the UNC *Student Athlete Handbook* (2013) requires athletes to "identify at least one coach or administrator who is responsible for having access to and regularly monitoring the content of team members' social networking sites and postings" (p. 8). Like UNC, many institutions have adopted the practice of requiring athletes to allow access to their social media account by a coach or administrator (Oppenhuizen, 2008). Nonetheless, there remains an overabundance of differing social media policies at the institutional level.

Some athletic department social media policies utilize outsourced social media monitoring services (SMMS) such as UDiligence and Varsity Monitor. These companies were created in order to monitor the social media activities of athletes by "flagging" a list of keywords. The company uses software that notifies coaches, administrators, and the athlete when inappropriate or prohibited content is discovered (Meredith & Marot, 2010). In return, the athletic department personnel can further investigate the material in hopes of avoiding a public relations crisis.

As of 2010, more than two dozen schools, many at the Division I level, have contracted with SMMS (Littmann, 2010). For example, Louisiana State University *Student-Athlete Handbook* (2013) includes the following social media policy: "The LSU

Athletic Department has partnered with outside agencies to assist in monitoring social media databases. Currently enrolled athletes, managers, and trainers are required to register with the monitoring service and grant all requested information on the application" (p. 6). The costs associated with adopting these services range from $1,359 per year for 50 athletes to $5,000 for more than 500 athletes (Henry, 2010).

According to Havard and colleagues (2012), some institutions such as the University of Iowa rely on team leadership to pass along any inappropriate social media activity to athletic department personnel. In essence, the team captains monitor their fellow teammates and report any violation of athletic department rules.

Furthermore, the University of Arizona enforces a different policy to evaluate the social media usage of its athletes. Its *Student-Athlete Handbook* (2011) states: "If you choose to have a personal site, it is departmental policy to set your privacy settings as to not allow the public to view your page. You are in a very vulnerable position as an athlete and this policy is to protect your personal information" (p. 98). The language within University of Arizona's policy differs by requiring its athletes to place their privacy settings on "private" status.

To date, Sanderson (2011) offers the only study that explores athletic department social media policies. Drawing from 159 NCAA Division I institutions athlete handbooks via athletic department websites, he found that most policies emphasize re-

The Unintended Effects of Social Media Policies

David Puzak is a football player at an NCAA Division I school and political science major who envisions a future in politics. Given David's major and career goals, he decided to become an elected official of the College Republican National Committee. While his passion for politics is well known, David led all wide receivers with 108 receptions. Because of his athletic ability, David has developed a large fan following of 800,000 twitter friends.

During the spring of 2013, the institution implemented a new social media policy that requires David to download a software application that monitors the posts on his twitter account. The software sends an email message to both athletic personnel and David if it finds a word that has been "flagged" as inappropriate by the university. Many of the 380 words it flags are slang expressions connected to drugs, sex, and violence.

Like many athletes, David routinely tweets to his "friends." During the spring semester of 2013, David tweeted a comment that included the phrase: "They are KILLING OUR FREEDOMS." The post was immediately flagged by the institution because the term *killing* is used. As a result, an email message was sent to David requesting him to remove the post.

Because of David's political aspirations, he refused. The institu-tion took action and revoked David's scholarship privileges. David gave a quote to the local newspaper regarding the social media policy: "It is unfair that I cannot enjoy the same rights as the general student population in regard to posting a politically affiliated comment on social media. I feel this policy violates my constitutional right to free speech." As David's situation reveals, the social media policy may have a negative effect on the athletes they intend to benefit. It is important to remain cognizant of legitimate communications when implementing such policies. ■

stricting what content athletes could reveal via social media (e.g., personal contact information). In addition, many of the policies provided precautionary statements for the athlete to consider. These statements pertain to the fact that viewing of social media accounts by individuals within and outside of the athletic department may occur at any given time (e.g., school personnel, potential employers, law enforcement). Furthermore, 16 of the 159 policies required athletes to provide athletic department personnel access to their social media sites. It remains unclear what "access" to an account actually entails (e.g., will the athlete provide usernames and passwords to the athletic department?). Only one policy stated within the athlete handbook that the athletic department contracted with a social media monitoring service (e.g., Udiligence) to monitor the athlete (Sanderson, 2011).

These specific examples of the social media policies illustrate the vast differences that exist between NCAA Division I member institutions. Such policies are largely composed of restricting content, monitoring of accounts by athletic department personnel or SMMS, and requiring athletes to privatize their accounts. Analysis of each individual institution's policy at the NCAA Division I, II, and III levels would be necessary to provide an assessment of current policy approaches.

The NCAA Bylaws

Currently, the NCAA remains an inactive player when it comes to creating social media policies to monitor, ban, or require athletes to privatize their settings. However, the NCAA handbook does include bylaws related to athlete recruitment through the use of social media. It is important to note that these rules differ by divisional affiliation.

At the Division I level, Bylaw 13.4.1.2 "Electronic Transmissions" limits the forming of relationships with prospective athletes and parents through electronic emails (National Collegiate Athletic Association, 2013a). The Division II policy is strikingly similar. At the Division III level, the use of any SNS by athletic department personnel to contact an athlete is prohibited (National Collegiate Athletic Association, 2013b). In January 2012, Bylaw 13.02.11 changed Division III sports by adopting a new communication rule regarding text messaging, deeming texting the "new norm" and allowing coaches and enrolled athletes to contact recruits through text messaging (Brown, 2012). As for monitoring, restricting, and banning athletes' social media usage, the NCAA has placed the onus on the institution.

State Legislation

Over the past few years, various laws have specifically addressed the use of social media by athletes. In designing institution-specific social media policies for athletes, it is important to adhere to these laws.

In 2013, 36 bills were introduced with a majority awaiting approval from state legislators (National Conference of State Legislatures, 2013). These bills relate to employer-employee relations, the general student population, and the athlete sub-population as they relate to use of social media. However, only a few have become law at the state level. The National Conference of State Legislatures (NCSL) website tracks bills related to higher education institutions' access to SNS.

This resource is particularly helpful for athletic department personnel. In 2012 four states passed legislation that prohibits higher education institutions from accessing and monitoring social media accounts. Four additional states have followed in 2013. All eight have been signed by the state's governor.

In Delaware, H.B. 309 was signed on July 20, 2012: "Makes it unlawful for a academic institution to mandate that a student disclose account information, thereby granting the academic institution access to the student's social networking profile. Prohibits institutions from requesting that a student log onto a personal social media account" (NCSL, 2012, chap. 354).

In California, S.B. 1349 was signed on September 27, 2012: "Prohibits postsecondary educational institutions, from requiring or requesting a student or student group disclose personal social media information. Prohibits institutions from taking certain actions for refusal of a demand for such information. Requires certain actions by institutions to ensure compliance with provisions. Requires such institution to post social media privacy policy on its website" (NCSL, 2012, chap. 619).

In New Jersey, A.B. 2879 was signed on December 3, 2012: "Prohibits requirement to disclose user name, password, or other means for accessing account or service through electronic communications devices by institutions of higher education" (NCSL, chap. 75, 2012).

In Michigan, H.B. 5523 was signed on December 27, 2012: "Prohibits educational institutions from requiring certain individuals to disclose information that allows access to social networking accounts. Prohibits employers and educational institutions from taking certain actions for failure to disclose information that allows access to certain social networking accounts" (NCSL, 2012, Public Act 478).

In Utah, H.B. 100 was signed on March 26, 2013: "Modifies provisions addressing higher education to enact protections for personal Internet accounts; enacts the Internet Employment Privacy Act, including defining terms, permitting or prohibiting certain actions by an employer" (NCSL, 2013, chap. 94).

In Arkansas, H.B. 1902 was signed on April 8, 2013: "Prohibits an institution of higher education from requiring or requesting a current student from disclosing his or her username or password for a social media account" (NCSL, 2013, Act 998).

In New Mexico, S.B. 422 was signed on April 5, 2013: "Prohibits public and private institutions of post-secondary education from requesting or requiring a student, applicant or potential applicant to provide a password or access to the social networking account of the student or applicant for admission" (NCSL, 2013, chap. 223).

In Oregon, S.B. 344 was signed on June 13, 2013: "Provides that an educational institution may not require, request or otherwise compel a student to disclose or to provide access to a personal social media account" (NCSL, 2013, chap. 408).

Problematic Social Media Posts

After the rivalry game between Rich-Public University and Poor-Public University, two athletes of Rich-Public took to their Twitter accounts. Student A sings the praises of Coach Joe Doaks for his decision making during the closing minutes of the contest with the following post: "Coach Doaks is the best god damn coach ever. #RichPublicF—ingWins. Student B, who also has a Twitter page, has a differing opinion of Coach Doaks and posts the following: "Coach Doaks knows I am better than my teammates. Favoritism stinks" #DoaksStinks. In this instance, both athlete accounts were set to private; however, because of the large amount of followers, "re-tweeting" of the comments occurs. The institutions social media policy monitors the athletes' accounts, and likewise it prohibits offensive language, threatening remarks, and negative comments about athletics personnel and athletic departments. ■

Questions to Consider

1. Should any action be taken by athletic departments for the athletes' posts?

2. Should any action be taken by the NCAA?

The laws in these states will ensure that athletes will not have to give up their social media activities in order to participate in athletics at a college or university. It is imperative that athletic department personnel continue to monitor state legislation in order to ensure institutional policies are legal.

Federal Legislation

Given the increase in state legislation, it is not surprising that federal legislation was recently proposed. The Social Network Online Protection Act (SNOPA) was first introduced in May 2012 and died in Congress. In February 2013 the House of Representatives reintroduced the bill (H.R. 537). The bill "prohibits employers and certain other entities from requiring or requesting that employees and certain other individuals (i.e., college athletes) provide a user name, password, or other means for accessing a personal account on any social networking website" (Social Network Online Privacy Act, 2013). While this bill includes employee-employer relations, it also includes an amendment to the Higher Education Act of 1965 by adding the following:

> The institution will not (i) require or request that a student or potential student provide the institution with a user name, password, or any other means for accessing a private email account of the student or potential student or the personal account of the student or potential student on any social networking website; or (ii) discharge, discipline, discriminate against in any manner, or deny admission to, suspend, or expel, or threaten to take any such action against, any student or potential student. (Social Network Online Privacy Act, 2013)

It remains to be seen whether SNOPA will gain momentum or follow in the footsteps of the states to protect students, including athletes, who attend institutions of higher education. A concern with the language of SNOPA is whether monitoring by SMMS is included within the scope of the bill.

CONCLUSION

Since 1881, with the inception of faculty athletics committees, athletes have continued to lose rights otherwise enjoyed by the general student population. The loss of social media access through monitoring, banning, regulating, and prohibiting athlete use within certain institutions is the most recent example. In order to develop the athlete for life after college, we must maximize the benefits of social media by educating the athlete about the risks.

Athletic department personnel must be aware of the risks but not exaggerate them to the point that they deprive athletes from utilizing twenty-first-century communications. It would be counterproductive to protect athletes until they graduate and then expect them to be responsible digital citizens. The more social media education provided to athletes, the more successful they will be in avoiding inappropriate online behavior.

For example, athletic departments could take the following steps to provide social media education:

1. Move beyond traditional methods of communication with athletes and create an athletic department culture that embraces social media (instruct coaches and athletic personnel to tweet updates about practice, meetings, etc.).

2. Utilize problem-based learning as an early strategy. This student-centered approach provides real-life examples of other athlete misbehavior (and positive behavior) on social media.

3. Provide athletes with an arena to discuss social media policies with athletic department personnel.

Furthermore, it would be prudent for athletic department personnel to increase their awareness of other institutional policies and state and federal legislation while remaining cognizant of NCAA bylaws. As this chapter revealed, institutional-specific policies vary to a significant degree and should be revisited. Athletic department personnel should put forth extensive effort to create policies that balance the rights of the athletes in conjunction with protecting the athletic department brand. One way to achieve balance is through the use of democratic governance. For example, the athletic department can arrange for team representatives to discuss policies with the faculty athletics representative (FAR) or the Student Athletic Advisory Committee (SAAC). Providing athletes an avenue where they can express their concerns about policies is critical because the athlete is directly impacted by the decision of athletic administrators. The FAR and SAAC are appropriate resources because they serve the interests of the athlete, the athletic department, and the institution. Additionally, the FAR and SAAC have more ability than individual teams to navigate the bureaucracy of athletic departments.

The NCAA's lack of a social media monitoring bylaw creates ambiguity among member institutions. The absence of leadership resulted in a variety of institutional policies, many of which create institutional concerns regarding their image, legal liability, and athlete safety. It would be instructive for the NCAA to expedite basic uniform guidelines to institutions focusing on the balance between athlete rights and institutional objectives.

In all, it appears evident that states are leaning toward protective legislation for the rights of athletes. This movement is apparent not only from laws recently passed but also from pending legislation in several states. Both the NCAA and institutions should support state legislators in an ongoing effort to protect athletes. Support is equally important at the federal level in light of the proposed SNOPA bill.

The NCAA has a mantra that "there are over 400,000 student-athletes and most of them are going pro in something other than sports." Social media policies that impede the development of the "pro" skills needed to compete in life after college are inimical to the growth of the athlete. For example, a coach banning the use of social media during season prohibits athletes from creating a virtual identity that shares and endorses their brand to an online world. It is no longer optional for athletes to passively participate in social media. Many job opportunities pursued after graduation require the virtual skills one develops using SNS. Athletic departments should attempt to provide workshops to athletes regarding the importance of their brand development through virtual communication. These workshops should focus on how social media can be used by an individual to succeed in a variety of professions. Additionally, the creation of a virtual identity theory by researchers could help athletic departments further their understanding of social media use. In return, better policy at the federal, state, NCAA, and institutional level can be devised and implemented.

QUESTIONS FOR DISCUSSION

1. How do technological trends in intercollegiate athletics have consequences for a new generation of athletes and professionals in higher education and sport administration?

2. How do NCAA member institutions protect themselves from possible sanctions resulting from inappropriate athlete social media use?

3. Should athletes have a voice in creating social media policies within their institution?

References

Associated Press. (2012). FSU players banned from tweeting. *Fox Sports News.* Retrieved from http://msn.foxsports.com/collegefootball/story/florida-state-seminoles-players-banned-from-tweeting-072612

Boyd, D. M., & Ellison, N. B. (2007). Social network sites: Definition, history, and scholarship. *Journal of Computer-Mediated Communication, 13,* 210–230. doi: 10.1111/j.1083-6101.2007.00393.x

Brenner, J. (2013). *Pew internet: Social networking.* Retrieved from http://pewinternet.org/ Commentary /2012/ March/Pew-Internet-Social-Networking-full-detail.aspx

Brown, G. (2012, January 14). Text messaging adopted in Division III. Retrieved from http://www.ncaa.org /wps/wcm/connect/public/NCAA/Resources /Latest+News/2012/January/Text+messaging +adopted+in+Division+III

Brown, L. (2008). Luke Caparelli kicked off Wake Forest football for Facebook comments. Retrieved from http://larrybrownsports.com/tag/facebook

Butts, F. (2008). NCAA athletes and Facebook. *Sport Journal, 11*(1). Retrieved from http://www .thesportjournal.org/article/ncaa-athletes-and-facebook

Clayton, A. (2012). Ohio State third string QB Cardale Jones tweets that classes are 'pointless' . . . saying he went to college to play football. *NY Daily News.* Retrieved from: http://www.nydailynews.com /sports /college/ohio-state-player-tweets-classes -pointless-article-1.1176616

Denver Channel. (2011). College golf team suspended over racy photo: Bethany college picture posted on Facebook. ABC News. Retrieved, from http://www .thedenverchannel.com/news/college-golf-team -suspended-over-racy-photo

Epstein, T. L. (2012). Student-athlete.o: Regulation of student-athletes social media use; A guide to avoiding NCAA sanctions and related litigation. *Mississippi Sports Law Review 1*(1), 1–36.

Facebook. (2013). *KeyFacts.* Retrieved from: http:// newsroom.fb.com/Key-Facts

Giglio, J. P. (2010). UNC's Austin posted more than 2,400 Twitter updates. *News & Observer.* Retrieved from http://www.newsobserver.com/2010/07/21 /590713/austin-prolific-tweeter.html

Havard, C. T., Eddy, T., Reams, L., Stewart, R. L., & Ahmad, T. (2012). Perceptions and general knowl-edge of online social networking activity of university student-athletes and non student-athletes. *Journal of Sport Administration and Supervision, 4*(1), 14–31.

Henry, J. (2010). *Colleges do UDiligence to prevent social networking embarrassment.* Retrieved from http:// www.aolnews.com/2010/02/01/colleges-do -udiligence-to-prevent-social-networking -embarrassmen/

Littmann, C. (2010). New services strive to save schools from social media catastrophes. *SB Nation.* Re-trieved from http://www.sbnation.com/2010/5/14 /1646959/new-service-strives-to-save

Lopresti, M. (2013). Skylar Diggins' Notre Dame legacy goes beyond Twitter, Final Four. *USA Today.* Retrieved from http://www.usatoday.com/story /sports/ncaaw/bigeast/2013 /03/05/skylar-diggins -notre-dame-fighting-irish/1965359/

Louisiana State University. (2013). Student-athlete handbook: Social media. Retrieved from http:// compliance.lsu.edu/studentathletes/Pages /Introduction.aspx

McIntyre, J. (2012). Notre Dame football's secret recruiting weapon: Skylar Diggins. Retrieved from http://www.thebiglead.com/index.php/2012/06/25 /notre-dame-footballs-secret-recruiting-weapon -skylar-diggins/

McManus, J. (2012). Female athletes connect with twitter. *ESPN.* Retreived from http://espn.go.com /espnw/news-commentary/article/7727869 /female-athletes-connect-twitter

Meredith, L., & Marot, M. (2010). Software helps schools monitor posts by athletes. *Telegraph Herald.* Retrieved from http://www.thonline.com/article .cfm?id=285093

National Collegiate Athletic Association. (2011). NCAA notice of allegations to University of North Carolina, Chapel Hill. Retrieved from http://www.unc.edu /news/ncaa/NOA%20Response%20_%20redacted.pdf

———. (2013a). *NCAA Division I manual.* Retrieved from www.ncaapublications.com/productdownloads /D110.pdf

———. (2013b). *NCAA Division III manual.* Retrieved from http://www.ncaapublications.com /productdownloads/D313.pdf

National Conference of State Legislatures. (2012). Employer access to social media usernames and passwords. Retrieved from http://www.ncsl.org

/issues-research/telecom/employer-access-to-social
-media-passwords.aspx

———. (2013). Employer access to social media usernames and passwords. Retrieved from http://www
.ncsl.org/issues-research/telecom/employer-access
-to-social-media-passwords-2013.aspx

Oppenhuizen, K. (2008, July 27). Schools creating new
rules for social networking policies. *USA Today*.
Retrieved from http://www.usatoday.com/ sports
/college/2008-07-27-socialnetworks_N.htm

Ortutay, B. (2012). Facebook tops 1 billion users. *USA
Today*. Retrieved from http://www.usatoday.com
/story/tech/2012/10/04/facebook-tops-1-billion
-users/1612613/

Sanderson, J. (2011). To tweet or not to tweet: Exploring
Division I athletic departments' social media
policies. *International Journal or Sport Communication, 4*, 492–513.

Smith, R. A. (1983). Preludes to the NCAA: Early failures
of faculty intercollegiate athletic control. *Research
Quarterly for Exercise and Sport, 54*, 372–382.

———. (1988). *Sports and freedom: The rise of big-time
college athletics*. New York: Oxford University Press.

Snyder, E. (2013). Student-athletes and the freedoms
lost list. Retrieved from HigherEdJobs.com

Social Network Online Privacy Act. (2013). H.R. 537.
Amends U.S.C Section 487(a) of the Higher Education Act of 1965 (20 U.S.C. 1095(a).

Thelin, J. (2012). College athletics: Continuity and
change over four centuries. In G. S. McClellan,

C. King, & D. L. Rockey Jr. (Eds.). (2012) *The handbook of college athletics and recreation administration*. San Francisco: Jossey-Bass.

Twitter. (2013a). Umichfootball. *Twitter Website*.
Retrieved from https://twitter.com/ umichfootball

———. (2013b). About us: The fastest, simplest way to
stay close to everything you care about. *Twitter
Website*. Retrieved July 9, 2013 from https://twitter
.com/about

University of Arizona. (2011). *The University of Arizona
department of intercollegiate athletics: The student-
athlete handbook*. Retrieved from http://athletics
.arizona. edu/cats/2010-11_StudentHandbook
.pdf

University of North Carolina. (2013). *Carolina student
athlete handbook: 2012–2013*. Retrieved from http://
studentathletes.web.unc.edu/files/2013/02
/Student-Athlete-Handbook.pdf

Voepel, M. (2013). Diggins denied, but still a winner.
ESPN. Retrieved from http://espn.go.com/womens
-college-basketball/tournament/2013/story
/_/id/9146072/ women-final-four-2013-lack-title
-diminish-skylar-diggins-notre-dame-fighting-irish
-career

Whittaker, Z. (2012). Twitter turns six: 140 million
users, 340 million tweets daily, *ZDNet*. Retrieved
from http://www.zdnet.com/blog/btl/twitter
-turns-six-140-million-users-340million-tweets
-daily/72123

THE ATHLETE and UNIVERSITY CONTRACTUAL RELATIONSHIP

Timothy Davis

Pursuant to the National Letter of Intent (NLI) and the Financial Aid Agreement (FAA), an athlete agrees to participate in intercollegiate sports in exchange for his or her college's promise to provide athletic financial aid. Historically, these documents have produced a contract between athletes and their institutions that has disproportionately favored colleges and universities. This imbalance is arguably exacerbated by documents that the National Collegiate Athletic Association (NCAA) requires athletes to sign as a condition to their participation in intercollegiate athletics.

This chapter examines the terms of the contract documents that have given rise to the imbalanced relationship, including both the respective obligations arising out of these express contract documents and the limitations that the documents impose on athletes (e.g., the NLI transfer restrictions). It also explores efforts to create a more balanced relationship, including state disclosure legislation, the NCAA's adoption of legislation approving of multiyear scholarships, the absence of affirmative obligations assumed by institutions, and athletes' attempts to use antitrust laws to challenge NCAA regulations.

THE BASICS OF THE CONTRACTUAL RELATIONSHIP

A contract is an agreement that generally arises from an exchange of promises in which two or more persons make commitments to act or to refrain from acting in certain ways in the future. The contractual relationship between athletes and their institutions arises from promises set forth in a body of documents consisting, in part, of documents, such as catalogs and bulletins, which govern the legal relationship between all students and their colleges and universities. What differentiates the contractual relationship between athletes and their institutions are the NLI and the FAA (Davis, 1996).

By signing an NLI, a prospective athlete agrees to attend college and participate in intercollegiate athletics at the institution specified in the NLI (National Letter of Intent, 2013a). An NLI is legally ineffective unless, at the time it is signed, the athlete has received a written commitment from the institution named in the NLI to provide athletic financial aid for at least one academic year (National Letter of Intent, 2013b). Without an accompanying promise of financial aid from the signatory institution, the NLI does not bind an athlete to attend a particular institution, and other colleges and universities may recruit the athlete (National Letter of Intent, 2013b). Other important conditions to the validity of the NLI include requirements that the athlete comply with NCAA initial eligibility standards and that the athlete has been admitted as a student at the named institution (National Letter of Intent, 2013c).

Although the exact form of the FAA may vary in insignificant ways from one institution to another, they are substantively the same. FAAs articulate their purpose as providing financial aid to enable an athlete to pursue a program of study and to participate in the institution's educational process (Davis, 1991). Pursuant to the FAA, a college or university promises to provide athletic financial aid to an athlete to assist in covering the cost of tuition, fees, room, board, and books (National Collegiate Athletic Association, 2013). Thus, the FAA formalizes an institution's commitment to provide financial aid to an athlete in exchange for the athlete's commitment to play intercollegiate athletics.

LEGAL ISSUES ARISING FROM THE CONTRACTUAL RELATIONSHIP

College athletes and their advocates assert that the NLI, FAA, and other documents create an imbalanced contractual relationship that operates to the detriment of athletes. They assert this imbalance is a product of the adhesive nature of a contract that consists of form documents that athletes must sign without a meaningful opportunity to negotiate.

> Universities enjoy an enormous advantage in terms of bargaining power that allows them to dictate terms and conditions to student-athletes, who have no real voice in the negotiation. Not only do student-athletes lack equal bargaining power, they lack meaningful choice because if they do not agree to the terms put before them, they are declared ineligible to participate in intercollegiate athletic competitions sanctioned by the NCAA. Lack of choice is contractually problematic because the essence of contract is volition (free exercise of will). (Baker, Grady, & Rappole, 2012, p. 620)

Commentators further assert the detrimental effects of this adhesion contract manifest in multiple ways including: (1) limitations on athlete mobility; (2) the lack of meaningful restrictions on institutions' exercise of discretion to refuse to renew short-term athletic scholarships; (3) preventing athletes, particularly African Americans, from receiving a share of the ever increasing revenue streams generated largely by revenue-producing sports of Division I football and men's basketball (McCormick & McCormick, 2012); (4) the absence of effective means to hold prominent athletic programs accountable for failing to fulfill contractual obligations that institutions impliedly owe to their athletes (Smith & Millhiser, 2012); and, (5) requiring athletes to sign documents, without full knowledge of their legal implications, in which they relinquish important commercial rights (Baker et al., 2012). The chapter now turns to a discussion of certain of the legal issues raised by these assertions.

The National Letter of Intent and Transfer Restrictions

In arguing that the contract between the athlete and the university operates to the detriment of athletes, critics point to the NLI penalty provisions. Consider the following scenarios. A high school athlete signs a NLI but decides he or she wants to attend another institution and never enrolls at the named institution. Alternatively, suppose the athlete attends the named institution for less than a year and transfers and enrolls at another institution. Absent a waiver by the named institution, the athlete will not be permitted to participate in intercollegiate sports until he or she completes a full academic year in residence at the new institution (National Letter of Intent, 2013d). In addition, the athlete loses a year of eligibility to complete in intercollegiate athletics at the new institution.

Suppose further that prior to an athlete's matriculation or during the athlete's first year at the named institution, the coach who recruited an athlete departs to work at another institution or is fired. The NLI expressly states that it constitutes an agreement between the athlete and the institution rather than a coach (National Letter of Intent, 2013e). Therefore, the departure of a coach who recruited an athlete does not invalidate the NLI, and the athlete remains bound by its provisions. This holds true despite the important role that coaches play in an athlete's decision to attend a particular institution (see Davis, 2013).

The NLI permits an institution to release an athlete from his or her commitment (National Letter of Intent, 2013f). Fearing that it would set bad precedent and encourage other athletes to transfer, coaches are reluctant to exercise this option. Coaches willing to grant a release often prohibit an athlete from transferring to a competitor sports program as a condition to the athlete's ability to play sports and receive athletic financial aid from his or her new college (Bishop, 2013).

Coaches argue that the transfer limitations are necessary to prevent rival coaches from continually attempting to poach players. College athletes and their advocates counter that NLI transfer sanctions are a tool that vindictive coaches can use to penalize athletes who made important decisions when they were teenagers (Bishop,

2013). They also argue that the NLI has been transformed from a tool to restrict recruiting to a mechanism that harms athlete welfare. Finally, they add that the imbalance created by the NLI is intensified by NCAA rules.

Under NCAA bylaws, Division I baseball, basketball, men's hockey, and FBS football players who transfer to another four-year institution cannot participate in intercollegiate competition until they attend the new institution for a minimum of one academic year (National Collegiate Athletic Association, 2013). Athletes in other sports can transfer one time without being penalized if certain conditions are met. This limitation operates independently of the NLI penalty that restricts mobility within the first year. Therefore an athlete eligible for a one-time transfer restriction would still be subject to the NLI basic penalty if the athlete spent less than one academic year at the named institution (National Letter of Intent, 2013f).

Lack of informed consent underlies criticisms of the NLI's and NCAA's regulatory regime relating to transfers. The language of the NLI does not require that an athlete sign it in order for him or her to receive a scholarship to play intercollegiate sports. Yet the overwhelming majority of athletes will not follow the lead of Brandon Knight, a highly recruited athlete, who signed a scholarship agreement to play at the University of Kentucky but did not sign an NLI (Brennan, 2010). Factors that result in high school NLIs include lack of talent that would afford them the leverage to negotiate a scholarship without signing an NLI; language some colleges include in their FAAs mandating that athletes sign an NLI as a condition to receiving an athletic scholarship; athletes' desire to appease coaches; and lack of awareness by athletes and their parents of either the penalties imposed by the NLI or that signing an NLI is not mandatory. These concerns have led to such suggestions as permitting an athlete to transfer without being penalized if a coach leaves for another program or is placed on probation (Wolverton, 2013a).

Multiyear Scholarships

In 1973 the NCAA adopted legislation that restricted institutions to awarding one-year renewable athletic scholarships (Hakim, 2000). The one-year scholarship rule was adopted in response to a system under which the NCAA did not regulate the duration of athletic scholarships. Reasons offered in support of the 1973 legislation included achieving uniformity in the scholarship program so as to remove the length of athletic scholarships as a basis for competition for athletes and acceding to the wishes of coaches who sought to increase their authority over athletes (Hakim, 2000).

In October 2011 the NCAA Division I Board of Directors adopted nonmandatory legislation that permits institutions to award multiyear athletic scholarships for up to five years (National Collegiate Athletic Association, 2013). Opponents argue the new legislation will restore the competitive pressures that the one-year rule sought to eliminate inasmuch as athletes would more likely sign with schools financially better positioned to offer multiyear scholarships (Jessop, 2012). Critics also argue multiyear scholarships will bind the hands of new coaches who lose the discretion to refuse to renew the scholarship of an athlete who would not fit into a new coach's system of play; require institutions to renew scholarships of athletes whose injuries rendered them unable to play their sport; and create a disincentive for athletes to work hard from year to year (Jessop, 2012; Wolverton, 2012).

In contrast, proponents hail multiyear scholarships as infusing a modicum of balance in the relationship between the athlete and the university. Absent a formal or informal university policy that restricts nonrenewals of one-year scholarships (e.g., prohibiting nonrenewal of the scholarship of an athlete whose injury prevents him or her from playing sports), an athlete is placed at the mercy of the athletic department, which is vested with unlimited discretion to refuse to renew an athlete's scholarship. Thus proponents believe multiyear scholarships hold the potential to stymie practices that elevate athletics over academics, such as "running off," which occurs when a coach refuses to renew the scholarship of an athlete whom the coach perceives as a mediocre athletic talent and replaces him or her with an athlete perceived as athletically superior (see Segrest, 2011).

Other reasons offered in support of multiyear scholarships include precluding the termination of scholarship because injuries prevent an athlete from participating in his or her sport; developing a scholarship structure that comports with the expectations of athletes and their parents, most of whom assume that a one-year renewable scholarship is guaranteed for four to five years so long as the athlete follows the rules and maintains athletic eligibility (see Hakim, 2000); and concerns that the one-year durational limit violated antitrust law.

In the face of this new reality, there is a fear that coaches may engage in practices that will extricate them from their long-term scholarship commitments to athletes. Thus, institutions may seek to recapture the discretion the multiyear scholarship deprived them of by incorporating a myriad of nonathletic related conditions into their FAAs (DeCourcy, 2011).

Two recent studies suggest that, at least in the short term, some coaches have attempted to preserve their discretion. A 2013 survey of 82 Division I institutions found that 16 college and universities had offered more than 10 multiyear scholarships, 32 institutions had offered between 1 and 10 multiyear scholarships, and 34 institutions had offered no multiyear scholarships to athletes (Dent, 2013). According to the survey, Big-Ten Conference institutions had offered the most multiyear scholarships, a total of 633 (Dent, 2013). A representative at the University of Illinois noted that the university had also extended multiyear scholarships to athletes on partial scholarships and in non-revenue-producing sports without creating financial problems.

In contrast, the Big 12 Conference, which formally sought to override the NCAA's multiyear scholarship legislation, had offered the fewest, a total of 11 as of the date of the survey. Kansas State, Texas, Texas Tech, Iowa State, Oklahoma, and Oklahoma State had offered two or fewer multiyear scholarships over a two-year period (Dent, 2013). Officials at these institutions point to an unwillingness to make long-term commitments rather than financial considerations as the basis for their decision to forgo offering multiyear scholarships (Wolverton & Newman, 2013).

Whether institutions such as those within the Big 12 Conference will be able to maintain this posture in the long term is questionable. Doing so could place them at a competitive disadvantage. The University of Florida, an athletic powerhouse, has offered multiyear scholarships as a recruiting inducement. Mid-major institutions, such as Fresno State University (which as of 2013 had offered the most multiyear scholarships at 316), use longer-term scholarships as a tool to differentiate their athletic programs from those of other institutions (Wolverton & Newman, 2013). The market pressures on reluctant institutions to offer multiyear scholarships is likely to grow as parents, athletes, and high school coaches gain greater awareness that longer-term scholarships are available (Wolverton, 2013b). So long as efforts by coaches to circumvent the protections afforded by multiyear scholarship awards are held at bay, this NCAA reform measure holds promise as a significant advancement in athlete welfare.

State Legislation

Responding to concerns that athletes lack information to navigate the confusing and often complex world of athletic scholarships and to make wise decisions, legislatures in California and Connecticut enacted laws requiring institutions to be more forthcoming in disclosing the terms and conditions of their contracts with athletes.[1] Pursuant to the legislation, a hyperlink titled "Student Athletes' Right to Know" must be posted on the front page of an institution's official athletics website; institutions are required to explain the obligations that an athlete assumes when he or she signs an NLI and FAA.[2]

In regard to the NLI, neither statute requires an institution to clearly disclose that an athlete is not required to sign an NLI in order to get an athletic scholarship. Nevertheless, institutions must disclose information including the nonbinding nature of verbal commitments made by prospective athletes and coaches, conditioning of the validity of the NLI on an accompanying offer of an athletic scholarship, and penalties to which an athlete will be subjected for failing to comply with the terms of the NLI.[3]

The legislation also requires institutions to provide athletes with specific information regarding athletic scholarships.[4] Postsecondary institutions in California and Connecticut will be required to fully explain the duration of athletic scholarships, what expenses athletic scholarships cover, and other terms such as the circumstances under which an athletic scholarship can be terminated.[5]

Implied Contractual Obligations

The FAA expressly obligates an institution to provide athletic financial aid to an athlete. The express terms of the FAA impose, however, no other affirmative obligations on colleges and universities. Given this, athletes have requested that courts imply into the contract affirmative obligations on institutions including providing athletes with an educational opportunity,[6] the resources to enable athletes to develop athletically,[7] and competent academic counseling[8] and limiting a university's discretion to discontinue a sport that an athlete was recruited to play.[9]

A focus on one of the terms athletes have sought to have implied in their contracts with colleges and universities, an obligation on institutions to provide an educational opportunity to their athletes, illustrates both the theoretical bases on which athletes rely and the judiciary's response. College athletes theorize that the circumstances surrounding their relationships with colleges justify the implication of an educational obligation. According to athletes, these circumstances include an express contract that obligates athletes to participate in both intercollegiate athletics and the educational process at their colleges. Also NCAA regulations emphasize the educational value as a critical feature of the relationship between the athlete and the university and require athletes to comply with their institutions' academic standards in order to maintain athletic eligibility. According to athletes, the essential character of the relationship gives rise to a mutual understanding that an institution implicitly promises to afford athletes an educational opportunity and thereby protect athletes' reasonable expectations.

The leading case of *Ross v. Creighton University* illustrates courts' reluctance to impose affirmative obligations on universities that are not expressly articulated in the documents creating their express contract with athletes.[10] In *Ross*, an athlete argued that the duty of good-faith and fair dealing imposed an affirmative obligation on the institution to provide athletes with an educational opportunity. Relying on policy considerations, including the need to defer to institutions in educational matters, the court rejected Ross's efforts to impose, by implication, a duty on the university to provide athletes with an educational opportunity. A similar judicial response occurred in *Jackson v. Drake University*, where an athlete alleged that a university's failure to provide adequate tutoring and counseling and requiring that an athlete turn in plagiarized work impeded his ability to play basketball and to succeed academically.[11] According to the athlete, this amounted to a breach of the university's implied obligations to provide him with an educational opportunity and an opportunity to play basketball.

Notwithstanding the theoretical basis on which athletes rely in urging courts to imply terms into their contracts with universities, recent cases have adhered to the precedent established in *Ross* and *Jackson*. In *Hendricks v. Clemson University*,[12] an athlete resorted to a fiduciary duty theory as a basis for implying a term in his agreement with the university. The South Carolina Supreme Court rejected the athlete's assertion that the university breached an implied obligation when it rendered academic advice resulting in the athlete's being deemed academically ineligible to compete in intercollegiate athletics. In *Knelman v. Middlebury College*,[13] an athlete resorted to several theories in support of his claims that the university owed him obligations not expressly set forth in the parties' contract. The court refused to im-

Breach of Scholarship Commitment and Impeding Academic Progress?

CASE STUDY

Kathy was a highly regarded high school basketball player. Although numerous schools recruited Kathy, she decided to attend State University, her state's flagship university and a Division I women's basketball power. Kathy's high school grades and her SAT scores were unimpressive but were sufficient to meet NCAA initial eligibility standards and State's admission requirements. During the recruiting process, State's head women's basketball coach told Kathy that State athletes receive the support that they need to succeed academically. Kathy signed an NLI to play basketball at State and received a four-year athletic scholarship.

Kathy's college basketball career got off to a rough start because of her clashes with her coach who believed that Kathy never put forth maximum effort. On more than one occasion, the coach complained of the mistake she had made in giving Kathy a scholarship. Kathy also found the academics at State more challenging then she had anticipated. After her first semester, Kathy's grade point average was 1.9, which disappointed her but was sufficient to maintain her athletic eligibility.

Kathy's academic counselor advised her of specific steps, including increased tutoring assistance, that Kathy needed to take if she expected to improve academically. Kathy responded that getting more tutoring and studying more could be problematic because of her demanding practice schedule. Kathy's coach required her to devote more time to practice than other players because of what the coach perceived as Kathy's lackluster play. In fact, the coach would review Kathy's tutoring schedule and schedule additional practices at the same time. When Kathy complained, the coach remarked that Kathy was at State to play basketball and that if she could not abide by the athletics handbook, Kathy would be dismissed from the team and would lose her scholarship. The athletics handbook states that an athlete who refuses to adhere to team rules, including practice schedules set at the head coach's discretion, would fail to fulfill the terms of their athletic scholarship, which are conditioned, in part, on an adherence to team rules. Kathy's spring semester GPA was below the minimum required for her to continue to play basketball. The head coach terminated Kathy's athletic scholarship.

You are a member of the faculty athletics committee to which Kathy has appealed the termination of her scholarship. How would you rule on Kathy's appeal? What additional facts would you want to know before making a decision? ∎

ply terms into the contract requiring the college to permit the athlete to play his sport (hockey) and to take action against an allegedly abusive coach.

In Re NCAA Student-Athlete Name & Likeness Licensing Litigation

Although college athletes have failed to convince courts to expand their rights by implying terms in their contracts with colleges, antitrust litigation has yielded more positive results. In *Agnew v. NCAA*,[14] an athlete resorted to antitrust law to challenge the NCAA's then prohibition on multiyear scholarships. Before the case could be resolved on its merits, the NCAA changed its rules to permit multiyear scholarships. Some argue that the rule change was a consequence of the threat of a favorable ruling for the plaintiff in *Agnew* (see Erickson, 2012).

In *White v. NCAA*,[15] former Division I-A football players and Division I basketball players filed an antitrust lawsuit challenging the NCAA's rule limiting the maximum value of athletic scholarships to the value of tuition, fees, room and board, and books, which amounts to less than the true cost of attendance. In 2008, before the case went to trial, the parties entered into a settlement pursuant to which the NCAA agreed, among other things, to establish a $10 million fund to "provide "career development services and reimburse various educational expenses" of qualifying former football and basketball players.[16]

In addition to the NLI and FAA, an athlete signs documents that are not essential to his or her contract with a college or university. These documents, which the NCAA requires that athletes sign as a condition to their eligibility to participate in intercollegiate athletics, include the Student-Athlete Statement/Drug Consent form in which the athlete, inter alia, affirms his or her amateur status and eligibility to participate in intercollegiate athletics, waives his or her Buckley rights by agreeing to disclose his or her education record to the athletic department, and affirms he or she has not tested positive for substances banned by the NCAA.[17]

The NCAA's 2012–2013 Student-Athlete Statement/Drug Consent form, designated as NCAA Form 12-3a, also includes Part IV, Promotion of NCAA Champions, Events, Activities or Programs, which reads: "You authorize the NCAA [or a third party acting on behalf of the NCAA (e.g., host institution, conference, local organizing committee)] to use your name or picture in accordance with NCAA Bylaw 12.5, including to promote NCAA championships or other NCAA events, activities or programs."[18] This seemingly innocuous provision has spawned litigation that some argue could alter the relationship between athletes and the university and upend the amateurism principle, which is one of the pillars that undergird the NCAA's economic model.

The case, *In Re Student-Athlete Name & Likeness Licensing Litigation*,[19] is premised on the alleged misuse of athletes' images and likenesses by Electronic Arts (EA), a developer of interactive entertainment software, the NCAA, and Collegiate Licensing Company (CLC), an affiliate of IMG College that partners with approximately 200 colleges to manage their product licensing.[20] EA produces, among other products, an NCAA Football and Basketball series of interactive video games that permit consumers to simulate football and basketball games between college teams.[21] The games contain the images of virtual players that resemble real-life current and former athletes. The depiction of virtual players does not use athletes' names but contains information (e.g., jersey numbers, height, weight, home state, skin tone, and hair color) from which the identity of an athlete can be derived.[22]

The two lawsuits, which were subsequently consolidated into one action,[23] assert that the foregoing arrangement violates a range of statutory and common-law rights, including athlete publicity rights and federal antitrust laws. In 2009 Sam Keller, a former starting quarterback at Arizona State University and the University of Nebraska, filed a lawsuit on behalf of himself and similarly situated athletes, alleging that EA's use of his and other players' images misappropriated athletes' likenesses in football, basketball, and the NCAA March Madness Basketball Tournament.[24] In particular, the suit alleges that EA's use of players' likenesses violated EA's licensing agreement with CLC and the NCAA. The licensing agreement allegedly incorporated NCAA Bylaw 12.5, which Keller contends prohibits the commercial licensing of an athlete's "name, picture or likeness."[25] NCAA Bylaw 2.9 articulates the principle that athletes are considered amateurs and their "participation in intercollegiate athletics is an avocation" (National Collegiate Athletic Association, 2013). A loss of amateurism status renders an athlete ineligible to compete in an intercollegiate sport in which amateur status has been compromised.[26] Under certain circumstances, an athlete's or an institution's use of an athlete's image or likeness may result in a loss of amateur status and a corresponding loss of eligibility to compete in intercollegiate athletics. In a major victory for plaintiffs, a federal appellate court in July 2013 ruled that plaintiffs' right of publicity claim could move forward because EA's use of the players' likenesses was not protected activity under the First Amendment of the U.S. Constitution.[27]

Edward O'Bannon, who was a member of UCLA's men's basketball team from 1991 to 1995, initiated the other lawsuit on behalf of himself and former NCAA Division I basketball players and Football Bowl Subdivision football players. O'Bannon alleges that the language in a document that he signed, which is the equivalent of Part IV of form 12.3(a) and other NCAA provisions, violates federal antitrust and other laws. According to the lawsuit, Part IV in conjunction with NCAA Bylaw 12.5.1.1 grants the NCAA permission to enter into licensing agreements with companies that distribute products containing the images of athletes. These provisions also allegedly grant the NCAA and third parties with which it contracts to use the images of athletes without compensation and in perpetuity. Alleging that he did not give true consent to these provisions, O'Bannon asserts that defendants violated antitrust laws by "foreclos[ing] class members from receiving compensation in connection with

STAKEHOLDER PERSPECTIVE

The Value Derived by College Athletes

Richard is the athletic director of a Division I FBS athletic program. He is proud of the athletic and academic accomplishments of his university's athletes, particularly those in the revenue-producing sports. In fact, Richard's institution has been recognized for its athletics teams' academic achievement as demonstrated by their exceptionally high Academic Progress Rates. Richard takes issue with those who argue that there exists an inherent imbalance in the athlete/university relationship and that current athletes should receive compensation related to their athletic participation. "The student-athlete's contract with his or her university isn't unfair. The athlete receives the opportunity to acquire a college education worth tens of thousands of dollars and skills that lead to long-term tangible and intangible benefits. It's hard to place a dollar figure on the benefits of a quality education."

Richard's comments offer another perspective on the issue of whether the athlete/university relationship disproportionately favors institutions. ∎

the commercial exploitation of their images following their cessation of intercollegiate athletic competition."[28] In short, the plaintiffs argue that the NCAA conspired in violation of Section 1 of the Sherman Act[29] by requiring athletes, as a condition to their ability to participate in intercollegiate athletics, to sign Part IV which waives athletes' right to receive compensation from the use of their images and likenesses.

Historically, courts applying Section 1 of the Sherman Act tend to find that NCAA eligibility rules intended to preserve amateurism and foster academic values and competitive equity do not unreasonably restrain trade and therefore do not run afoul of Sherman 1. Where plaintiffs have established, however, that a NCAA rule or practice had a negative commercial impact and did not foster the aforementioned values, the likelihood of a Sherman Act violation increases. In *Agnew v. NCAA*,[30] the court noted this distinction. "The Bylaws at issue, especially the prohibition against multiyear scholarships, seem to be aimed at containing university costs, not preserving the product of college football, though evidence presented at a later stage could provide that the Bylaws are, in fact, a key to the survival of the student-athlete and amateurism." Therefore, the outcome of the consolidated litigation is likely to turn on this distinction.

The potential import of the consolidated litigation was significantly heightened when the plaintiffs requested that the court certify the class of plaintiffs as consisting of not only former but also current players (Farrey, 2013).[31] A certification of the class to include current players would create the potential for a ruling on the merits allowing current athletes to receive compensation for the use of their images, which would be antithetical to the NCAA's amateurism principle. Antitrust experts question the likelihood that the court will certify the class to include current players. Professor Matt Mitten distinguishes the rights of former and current players, asserting, "It's not necessary for the NCAA to enforce its rules on former athletes for the purposes of maintaining the amateur nature of its enterprise of promoting competitive balance" (Wolverton, 2013c, para 28). Professor Gary Roberts similarly states, "I don't see why, if the NCAA is infringing on former players' publicity rights in the production of video games, that would lead to a remedy of current players receiving TV rights. . . . I don't think there's any court that will jump that legal chasm" (Wolverton, 2013c, para 32).

CONCLUSION

The lack of a meaningful opportunity for most athletes to negotiate the terms of their contracts with colleges and universities gives rise to an adhesion contract that historically has operated to the detriment of athletes. Recent legislative developments, often the product of litigation initiated by athletes, have brought greater equity to the relationship. In particular, antitrust litigation has laid the groundwork for changes that have corrected certain of the imbalances extant in the athlete/university relationship. Although they represent progress toward equity, additional changes must occur, particularly in regard to the affirmative obligations institutions owe to their athletes before a more balanced relationship is a reality.

QUESTIONS FOR DISCUSSION

1. Does the contract an athlete signs with his or her college disproportionately favor the institution or does it represent a fair exchange given the benefits that could potentially be derived from an athlete attending school?

2. Should an implied duty be imposed on colleges and universities to provide athletes with an educational opportunity?

3. Should current athletes benefit financially from the use of their images and likenesses but have any compensation derived therefrom set aside in a trust fund accessible after the athlete's intercollegiate career ends?

Notes

1. Thus far, only California and Connecticut have enacted legislation requiring the online disclosure of information relating to athletic scholarships by postsecondary institutions situated in those states. See Cal. Educ. Code § 67365 (West 2013); see also Conn. Gen. Stat. Ann. § 10a-55k (West 2013).

2. Cal. Educ. Code § 67365 (West 2013); Conn. Gen. Stat. Ann. 10a–55k (West 2013).

3. Ibid. While the required language in the statutes differs slightly, the following information regarding the NLI must be included on athletics department websites:

   a. A verbal commitment is not binding on either the student-athlete or the institution.

   b. The National Letter of Intent is a binding agreement between a prospective student-athlete and an institution of higher education in which the institution agrees to provide a prospective student-athlete, who is admitted to the institution and is eligible for financial aid under NCCA rules, athletic aid for one academic year in exchange for the prospective student-athlete's agreement to attend the institution for one academic year.

   c. The National Letter of Intent must be accompanied by an institutional financial aid agreement.

   d. If the prospective student-athlete signs the National Letter of Intent but does not enroll at that institution for a full academic year, the student-athlete may be subject to specific penalties, including loss of a season of eligibility and a mandatory residence requirement.

4 Ibid.

5. Ibid.

6. *Ross v. Creighton Univ.*, 957 F.2d 410 (7th Cir. 1992).

7. *Jackson v. Drake Univ.*, 778 F. Supp. 1490 (S.D. Iowa 1991).

8. *Hendricks v. Clemson Univ.*, 578 S.E.2d 711 (S.C. 2003).

9. See, e.g., *Soderbloom v. Yale Univ.*, 1992 Conn. Super. LEXIS 256, at *8 (court rejects athlete's claim that school's termination of wrestling program breached implied contractual obligation to provide a varsity wrestling program as part of the four-year undergraduate educational program).

10. 957 F.2d 410 (7th Cir. 1992).

11. 778 F. Supp. 1490 (S.D. Iowa 1991).

12. 578 S.E.2d 711 (S.C. 2003).

13. 2013 WL 121026 (D. Vt. Jan. 9, 2013).

14. 683 F.3d 328 (7th Cir. 2012).

15. CV06-0999 (C.D. Cal., filed Feb. 17, 2007).

16. See http://www.ncaa.org/wps/wcm/connect /public/NCAA/Resources/White+v+NCAA

17. NCAA, *Form 12-3a Student-Athlete Statement- Division I, Academic Year 2012–13*, http://web.mit.edu/athletics/www/sa/forms/CompetitionForms_DI.pdf

18. Ibid.

19. 2011 WL 1642256 (N.D.Cal.).

20. *Keller v. Electronic Arts, Inc.*, 2010 WL 530108 (N.D. Cal. Feb. 8, 2010).

21. Ibid. at * 1.

22. Ibid.

23. *In re NCAA Student-Athlete Name & Likeness Licensing Litigation*, 2012 WL 1745593, *6 (N.D. Cal.).

24. Ibid.

25. Ibid. at * 6.

26. Ibid. at § 12.01.1.

27. *In re NCAA Student-Athlete Name & Likeness Licensing Litigation*, 2013 WL 3928293 (9th Cir.).

28. *In re NCAA Student-Athlete Name & Likeness Licensing Litigation*, 2012 WL 1745593, at *6.

29. Section 1 of the Sherman Act prohibits agreements that unreasonably restrain interstate trade or commerce and thereby have an adverse impact on competition. Specifically, it provides that "every contract, combination . . . or conspiracy in restraint of trade or commerce" is illegal (15 U.S.C. § 1).

30. 683 F.3d 328 (7th Cir. 2012). The case was settled before a determination was made on the merits of the plaintiff's antitrust claims.

31. To bolster their request for certification of a class including former and current players, in July 2013, six current football players were added as plaintiffs.

References

Baker, T. A., III, Grady, J., & Rappole, J. M. (2012). Consent theory as a possible cure for unconscionable terms in student-athlete contracts. *Marquette Sport Law Review, 22*, 619–650.

Bishop, G. (2013, June 7). Want to play at a different college? O.K. but not there or there. *New York Times*.

Brennan, E. (2010, April 27). Wave goodbye to the NLI? *Espn.com*. Retrieved from http://espn.go.com/blog/collegebasketballnation/post/_/id/11022/wave-goodbye-to-the-nli

Davis, T. (1991). An absence of good faith: Defining a university's educational obligation to student-athletes. *Houston Law Review, 28,* 743–790.

———. (1996). College athletics: Testing the boundaries of contract and tort. *UC Davis Law Review, 29*, 971–1017.

———. (2013). The coach and athlete recruitment: Ethical and legal dimensions. In R. L. Simon, C. R. Torres, & P. F. Hager (Eds.), *The ethics of coaching sports: Moral, social and legal issues* (pp. 235–252). Boulder, CO: Westview Press.

DeCourcy, M. (2011). Proposed NCAA reforms a mixed bag of genius, idiocy. *Sportingnews.com*. Retrieved from http://aol.sportingnews.com/ncaa-basketball/story/2011-08-11/proposed-ncaa-reforms-a-mixed-bad-of-genius-idiocy

Dent, M. (2013). Colleges, universities slow to offer multiyear athletic scholarships. *Pittsburg Post-Gazette*. Retrieved from http://www.post-gazette.com/stories/sports/pitt-big-east/colleges-universities-slow-to-offer-multiyear-athletic-scholarships-688205/

Erickson, J. A. (20012). A shift in college football recruiting has begun. *Columbus Ledger-Enquirer*. Retrieved from http://www.ledger-enquirer.com/2012/02/03/1918647/joel-a-erickson-commentary-a-shift.html

Farrey, T. (2013, July 22). 6 current players join NCAA lawsuit. ESPN.com. Retrieved from http://espn.go.com/espn/otl/story/_/id/9491249/six-current-football-players-join-ed-obannon-ncaa-lawsuit

Hakim, L. (2000). The student-athlete vs. the athlete student: Has the time arrived for an extended-term scholarship contract. *Virginia Journal of Sports and the Law, 2*, 145.

Jessop, A. (2012, February 13). Should Division I schools vote to overturn the NCAA's multi-year scholarship measure? *Business of College Sports.com*. Retrieved from businessofcollegesports.com

McCormick, A. C., & McCormick, R. A. (2012). Race and interest convergence in NCAA sports. *Wake Forest Journal of Law & Policy, 2*, 17–43.

National Collegiate Athletic Association. (2013). *NCAA Division I manual*. Retrieved from www.ncaapublications.com/productdownloads/D110.pdf

National Letter of Intent. (2013a). *Provisions of letter satisfied*. Retrieved from http://www.ncaa.org/wps/wcm/connect/nli/nli/nli+provisions/provisions+of+letter

———. (2013b). *Financial aid requirement*. Retrieved from http://www.ncaa.org/wps/wcm/connect/nli/nli/nli+provisions/financial+aid

———. (2013c). *Letter becomes null and void*. Retrieved from http://www.ncaa.org/wps/wcm/connect/nli/nli/nli+provisions/null+and+void

———. (2013d). *Provisions, basic penalty*. Retrieved from http://www.ncaa.org/wps/wcm/connect/nli/nli/nli+provisions/penalty-basic

———. (2013e). *Provisions, coaching changes*. Retrieved from http://www.ncaa.org/wps/wcm/connect/nli/nli/nli+provisions/coaching+change

———. (2013f). *NLI, FAQ*. Retrieved from http://www.ncaa.org/wps/wcm/connect/nli/nli/frequently+asked+questions/index.html

Segrest, D. (2011, October 23). The one-year itch: Some athletes lose their single-year grants to better players. *Birmingham News*. Retrieved from http://www.al.com/sports/index.ssf/2011/10/college_athletes_rights_some_a.html

Smith, R. K., & Millhiser, N. (2012). The BCS and big-time intercollegiate football receive an "F": Reforming a failed system. *Wake Forest Journal of Law & Policy, 2*, 45–68.

Wolverton, B. (2012, February 22). Who opposed multiyear athletics aid? You might be surprised. *Chronicle of Higher Education*. Retrieved from http://chronicle.com/blogs/players/who-opposed-multiyear-athletics-aid-you-might-be-surprised/29639

———. (2013a, June 5). Many big athletics programs fail to protect themselves from fickle recruits. *Chronicle of Higher Education*. Retrieved from http://chronicle.com/blogs/players/category/multiyear-scholarships

———. (2013b, May 20). I'm not sure why the NCAA and the coaches are keeping this secret. *Chronicle of Higher Education*. Retrieved from http://chronicle.com/blogs/players/category/multiyear-scholarships

———. (2013c, June 18). Lawsuit over athletes' rights challenges NCAA's principles of amateurism. *Chronicle of Higher Education*. Retrieved from http://chronicle.com/article/Dispute-Over-Athletes-Rights/139885/

Wolverton, B., & Newman, J. (2013, April 19). Few athletes benefit from move to multiyear scholarships. *Chronicle of Higher Education*. Retrieved from https://chronicle.com/article/Few-Athletes-Benefit-From-Move/138643/

Calls for academic reform focused on athletes have been made from inside and outside of colleges and universities. The extent to which institutions can identify new models of academic support and provide meaningful, authentically responsive strategies to enhance the academic talents of athletes remains an ongoing challenge. The chapters presented in this final section of the volume discuss a variety of approaches to improve the quality of the college experience of athletes and ultimately their desirable outcomes. In chapter 26, Derek Van Rheenen describes the University of Connecticut men's basketball program as a potential proactive intervention model for other Division I programs. Likewise, he outlines the challenges and opportunities of academic support for athletes in light of the commercially driven college sports enterprise. Keith Harrison and Scott Bukstein, in chapter 27, offer an overview of the Scholar Baller Program, describing its culturally relevant curriculum intervention and academic performance incentive initiatives and highlighting the impact of language, culture, and identity on participating college athletes. Finally, in chapter 28, Kristina Navarro discusses current literature on college athlete career transitions and offers recommendations for higher education practitioners to enhance the school-to-career development of athletes. ■

THE DILEMMA of ACADEMIC SUPPORT for COLLEGE ATHLETES

Advising to the APR

Derek Van Rheenen

Just as American teachers feel enormous pressure to increase student scores on high-stakes standardized tests, academic support staff for athletes also feels pressure to raise institutional scores on the NCAA's mandated Academic Progress Rate (APR). Under these circumstances, many educators and practitioners teach to the test or advise to the APR. Such rational yet educationally problematic decision making is an unintentional consequence of these national reforms. The National Collegiate Athletic Association (NCAA) established the APR as a measure intended to increase the retention and graduation rates of college athletes, with particular focus on the revenue-generating sports of football and men's basketball. While national educational and athletic reform programs have led to increased scores and rates overall, the heightened focus on student outcome has prompted serious questions, often politically charged and heightened by claims of racial discrimination. Critics argue that "academic progress" may not reflect academic performance or educational development (Comeaux, 2013; Gurney & Southall, 2012). Worse yet, efforts at achieving narrowly defined academic progress may come at the expense of academic integrity and genuine educational opportunity (Gurney & Southall, 2013; Smith, 2011).

This chapter seeks to highlight some of the competing values and priorities inherent in the academic support of Division I athletes, particularly in light of the high-stakes culture of American college sports today. To highlight the effects of the APR reform initiative since its inception a decade ago, I offer a case study of the University of Connecticut (UConn), the first program in a major conference to be publicly penalized under the APR reform initiative. In 2011, the Division I UConn men's basketball team won the national championship but simultaneously scored well below the minimum academic standards set by the NCAA. On the basis of its APR four-year average, the team was banned from postseason competition in 2013. Rather than being permanently tarnished by its academic failings, however, UConn basketball experienced a dramatic turnaround of its APR scores. UConn's academic rebound followed a particular path, one that may well serve as a successful intervention model for other Division I programs.

Several intervention strategies are available to institutions to raise APR scores and to avoid simply advising for eligibility. While critics have described ways that institutions can game the APR system, little has been written about best practices in advising athletes in light of these high-stakes metrics. Several policy recommendations for academic support, however, are available to practitioners to achieve desired (and federally mandated) student outcomes within an educational model of genuine student development.

ACADEMIC PROGRESS RATE LEGISLATION

In 2003 the NCAA initiated major academic reform legislation that revised initial eligibility standards and set more restrictive progress-toward-degree or continuing eligibility requirements. This legislation introduced the Academic Progress Rate and Graduation Success Rate (GSR). The basic premise of the APR is that retention and continuing eligibility provide the primary predictors for future graduation. In response to delayed graduation rate data, however, the APR provides a more real-time snapshot of an institution's progress toward graduating athletes by team and by year. As such, the APR is a term-by-term measure of athlete retention and eligibility. A maximum of two points are awarded for each athlete on athletic aid each academic term, one for maintaining academic eligibility and another for staying in school. The maximum APR score is 1,000. The APR score is the proportion of total possible points earned by a population of athletes (i.e., a team roster), multiplied by 1,000.

In response to the methodological limitations (and less favorable numbers) of the Federal Graduation Rate (FGR), a metric established as a result of the 1990 Student Right-to-Know and Campus Security Act, the GSR offers an alternative graduation rate methodology. The GSR credits colleges and universities for transfers and midyear admits who graduate, whereas the FGR does not account for these students in its calculations. And unlike the FGR, the GSR does not penalize institutions for athletes who leave prior to graduation if they are in good academic standing when they leave.[1] As such, the GSR is generally higher than the FGR (LaForge & Hodge, 2011).

NCAA preliminary statistical analyses set an APR score of 925 as a national benchmark, projected to predict a 50% FGR and a 60% GSR (Brown, 2005; Moltz, 2010). Initially, as part of its academic reform legislation, the NCAA threatened to penalize institutions with teams that scored below this mark. For teams with APR scores below 900, further sanctions included loss of athletic scholarships, as well as restrictions on practice time and postseason play. However, in 2010 only 137 of 428 teams with scores lower than 925 received sanctions, down from 177 and 213 teams penalized in 2009 and 2008, respectively (Sander, 2010).

Kevin Lennon, NCAA vice president for academic and membership affairs, has stated that "the main goal is not to penalize" (Moltz, 2010, Escaping the death penalty section, para. 5). As such, the NCAA grants reprieves from penalties on a case-by-case basis: teams (and the institutions to which they belong) who can demonstrate significant and continued academic improvement may receive conditional waivers in the hope that their APR scores will significantly improve. Critics have claimed that the liberal use of these waivers, as well as medical and missed term exceptions, exemplify institutional strategies for manipulating APR scores (Gurney & Southall, 2012).

In 2010 the low graduation rates of several high-profile basketball teams led U.S. secretary of education and former Harvard basketball player Arne Duncan to criticize the NCAA for being too lax in its academic standards. Duncan called on the NCAA to ban any team with a federal graduation rate below 40% from future NCAA Division I Men's basketball tournaments. Had Duncan's proposal been enacted that year, the NCAA would have banned 19% (12 of 64) of the men's teams and 5% (3 of 64) of the women's teams; over the past three years, these numbers have improved (Lapchick, Bukstein, & Harrison, 2013).

In a written statement, the NCAA argued that the APR is "a much better indicator of classroom success" of current athletes. "Imposing a ban on teams for the academic performance of athletes who entered as freshmen eight to eleven years ago is probably not the best course of action. Basing postseason bans on graduation rates penalizes the wrong students" (Fuller, 2010, para. 4). Instead, the NCAA argued, teams with low APR scores should be prohibited from postseason competition.

In 2011, the NCAA adopted policy recommendations from reports by the Knight Commission on Intercollegiate Athletics (2001, 2010) to ban any Division I athletic team from participating in postseason competition if the team is not on track to graduate at least half its players, as measured by the NCAA's APR. The NCAA Board of Directors raised the bar with this revised legislation, equating a four-year APR score of 930 to a 50% GSR.

Walter Harrison, president of the University of Hartford and the chair of the NCAA's Division I Committee on Academic Performance, noted that the APR "has now become the definitive academic-management tool on our campuses. Every coach, most of the players, every athletic administrator knows what an APR means. They know what they need to do to achieve a good one, and they're putting it in place" (Sander, 2009, para. 7). Indeed, institutions have invested in ways to score well on the APR, particularly given the potential negative consequences of not making the grade.

Those institutions that have been able to invest most in academic support services for athletes have often fared best in APR scores. Conversely, low-resource

The Rise and Fall and Rise Again of UConn Men's Basketball

Despite positive trends, several prominent athletics programs continue to struggle to retain and graduate their athletes. In 2012 the University of Connecticut men's basketball team became the first program in a major conference to be banned from postseason competition because of poor academic performance. This ban was particularly dramatic due to the team's athletic success, having won two national championships since the establishment of the Academic Progress Rate (APR) reform legislation. After winning the national championship in 2011, the NCAA banned the team from postseason play, highlighting the seriousness of the association's academic reform legislation. In 2009 UConn men's basketball scored an APR of 844, followed by a score of 826 in 2010, dropping its four-year APR average to 893. Even with a perfect score of 1000 in 2010–2011—the year the team won the national championship—the team would be ineligible for postseason competition the following year.

This national embarrassment set in motion an academic improvement plan focused on increasing the retention and graduation rates of the UConn men's basketball players. The school implemented a series of strategies, which resulted in a strong academic comeback that may serve as a model for other programs and institutions to emulate. Some of the changes implemented included mandated study hours, more effective monitoring of study hall, greater use of intersession courses during the winter, and pushing athletes to have more contact with faculty (Wolverton, 2013).

In particular, in November 2011, UConn president Susan Herbst named Sally Reis, a long-time professor of education and nationally recognized expert on student achievement, to take on a new administrative role in the provost's office. Part of this position was to oversee a revitalized balance between academics and athletics. In February 2012 UConn also hired a new athletic director, Warde J. Manuel, a former academic advisor who helped the University of Buffalo improve its athletic academic standing. Under new administration, UConn raised academic expectations for its athletes. In 2011, the program produced an APR score of 978; in 2012, the team scored 947, ensuring that UConn men's basketball would be eligible for post-season play once again in 2014. These changes and the increased academic expectations, in concert with excellent basketball performance, culminated in a tremendous tournament run and the 2014 Division I Men's Basketball national championship.

Part of UConn's turnaround apparently involved moving the academic support program for athletes out from under the provost to the Department of Intercollegiate Athletics, a move that gave the new AD "day-to-day contact with academic issues" (Wolverton, 2013, para. 5). The UConn case study cautions current practitioners: UConn also fired the director of Academic Support Services for athletes and the primary academic advisor for men's basketball during this academic turnaround. This may have been the right move, given the dramatic results since their dismissal, but it also reminds academic support staff for athletes that their jobs do depend, at least in part, on APR outcomes. ■

institutions, most commonly historically black colleges, have been far less successful at meeting the APR expectations set by the NCAA. In fact, all but 3 of the 18 Division I teams slapped with postseason bans in 2014 because of poor academic performance are historically black colleges, continuing a troubling pattern among less-wealthy institutions (Wolverton, 2013). These are also schools that compete in mid-major conferences, often defined as those conferences in Division I that do not belong to the prestigious Bowl Championship Series (BCS).

This trend may evidence a recurring pattern of racial discrimination within the NCAA's academic reform efforts. And yet, since introducing the APR a decade ago, the graduation success rate for all Division I African American athletes has increased by 19 points to 54%, 49% for African American males and 64% for African American females. African Americans at Division I Football Bowl Series schools have seen their GSR climb 9 percentage points, while the GSR for African American male basketball players has increased by 21 points (Peterkin, 2012).

BEST PRACTICES OF ACADEMIC SUPPORT FOR ATHLETES

The UConn case study offers anecdotal evidence of how an athletic team at one institution can improve its scores within a short amount of time. Though APR legislation was enacted more than a decade ago, limited scholarship and few empirical studies based on these new metrics exist; thus, practitioners have difficulty in setting institutional policy and creating best practices for supporting athletes academically. For schools serious about implementing strategies for improving their APR scores, several factors contribute to the complexity of providing academic support for athletes. This complexity is both practical and philosophical.

In addition to the individual traits of college athletes—age, sex, race/ethnicity, team affiliation, high school context, socioeconomic status, and educational history of their parents—each team possesses its unique culture. This team culture may be more or less focused on its academic accomplishments, relative to other sports teams. These teams nest within an athletic department that exists within an institution of higher learning. The priorities of an athletic department, realized in its policies and expenditures, reflect a larger cultural pattern and its relative commitment to genuine academic achievement. The level and degree of governance of athletic departments on a given college or university campus likewise impact policies and expenditures. Finally, there exists tremendous institutional variation in the size, control, diversity, wealth, and conference affiliation of colleges and universities. With these myriad factors in mind, perhaps it is not surprising that "the APR is related to institutional characteristics that also predict general student outcomes" (McLaughlin, 2013, p. 23).

In a widespread study of more than 5,000 teams from 325 Division I institutions, McLaughlin (2013) found that APR scores were higher at private schools than public institutions. APR rates were higher for women, lower for teams with larger squad sizes, and lower for football and men's basketball. Bowl Conference Series (BCS) schools had higher APR scores on average than non-BCS institutions. McLaughlin (2013) concluded that "programs and interventions aimed at improving academic eligibility rates should take into account specific institutional and team characteristics. When further examining athlete outcomes, it may be prudent for individual institutions to select additional predictors pertinent to their mission and goals" (pp. 25–26).

Similarly, LaForge and Hodge (2011) argue that institutional analyses of the underlying causes for lost APR points should be a regular and systematic exercise. These authors recommend that the athletic administration of colleges and universities should be responsible for balancing athlete welfare and the management of the APR/GSR, but that these efforts must be overseen by central campus administrators. In particular, LaForge and Hodge (2011) suggest that the APR should be used as a diagnostic tool for identifying institutional patterns that may need to be addressed. They highlight three areas of focus: recruiting, athletic admissions, and academic support services.

MORE SELECTIVE RECRUITING AND ADMISSIONS

One of the benefits of the APR legislation has been how it has changed the tenor of conversations about academics between coaches, academic support staff, and athletic and academic administrators (Brady, 2008; Sander, 2010). In many cases, these conversations have led to more selective recruiting and more selective admissions (Moltz, 2010). At a minimum, institutions have become ever more interested in finding screening methods to predict future academic success among prospective athletes. Even where the APR has not changed admissions policies, coaches and administrators are well aware that recruiting mistakes have become costlier.[2] Sports programs and institutions know which students have lost APR points, and officials must now seek to determine the reasons underlying an athlete's academic problems. While this heightened focus may be less about student welfare and more about the academic bottom line, these developments have forced institutions to individualize their academic support of athletes. As a result of the APR, therefore, the focus has shifted in part from simply getting students into school and keeping them eligible to now supporting them to matriculate and graduate.

Since 1991, when the NCAA adopted Rule 16.3.1.1, making academic support for athletes mandatory, there has been an exponential increase in tailored academic support for this student population. APR legislation since 2003 has only magnified this increase. Colleges and universities competing at the highest athletic levels, particularly those with the greatest financial resources, now employ a cadre of learning specialists, academic advisors, and class checkers. Academic support services and the facilities that house them have also become a major part of the competition for top recruits (Brady, 2008; Wolverton, 2008).

THE DOWNSIDE OF ACADEMIC SUPPORT SERVICES AND THE APR

As a result of the NCAA's APR initiative, the business of academic support for athletes has become a growth industry, leading critics to question whether this growth has helped or hindered the academic integrity of American college sports (Gurney & Southall, 2013; Hosick, 2009). Recent academic scandals at the University of North Carolina and Florida State might suggest that there actually exists a correlation between advising to the APR and a rise in academic rules violations. Critics also question whether academic support practitioners are more interested in maintaining APR scores than in genuinely supporting student development and the pursuit of education. As Gurney and Southall (2013) argue, "the academic reform program has led to an increased number of woefully underprepared athletes entering our universities being kept eligible on academic life support without the chance of a world-class education or a meaningful college degree" (Consequences section, para. 1).

Gurney and Southall (2012) refer to the rise of "creative academic advisors," a new breed of experts who successfully navigate the NCAA's APR legislation and seek solely to keep college athletes eligible. "Advising for eligibility" is not a new concept in the arena of academic support for athletes. Well before the establishment of the APR and GSR in 2003, critics of big-time college sports argued that academic advisors for athletes should more aptly be called "eligibility brokers" (Covell & Barr, 2001; Grasgreen, 2012). The field of academic support for athletes is commonly attacked for its lack of professional integrity, steering students into easy "jock" courses and majors held in low repute (Duderstadt, 2003; Shulman & Bowen, 2001), and for its complacency and tunnel vision (Comeaux, 2013).

In reality, these practitioners are perennially caught between a rock and a hard place. If they advise a student to stretch his or her academic and intellectual boundaries and he or she succeeds, the athlete might acknowledge the support and the belief in his or her potential. But if the same athlete fails in his or her academic

---

Integrity, Professionalism, and Balance

Kim Durand is responsible for the administration and supervision of a comprehensive academic support unit that provides academic advising, tutoring, career, and personal development to the 650 athletes from 19 Division I men's and women's varsity teams. Ms. Durand is also the president-elect of the National Association of Academic Advisors for Athletics (N4A), a diverse organization of practitioners who promote the integrity of the academic support profession. The N4A's mission seeks to empower athletes to become productive young adults through education and personal development.

In her leadership capacity, Durand understands how Academic Progress Rate (APR) has impacted academic support for athletes. She points out, "While our primary focus is to serve students and encourage independent academic initiative, we must also take into account the unintended consequences of APR legislation as we advise a student. The advisor often has to pause and calculate any APR ramifications of a student's academic decision on athletic eligibility or a team's APR score."

Durand believes that the successful navigation of the APR legislation must be a collaborative effort among campus and athletic administration, coaches, staff, and athletes. Success begins when coaches recruit and institutions admit academically capable and engaged students. Durand reflects that "student support services professionals must be relentless in their integrity, professionalism, and expertise as they balance the sometimes conflicting demands of the student and the APR. Most importantly, athletes must take ownership of their education and academic choices. The goal is to reap the benefits of increased academic standards while protecting student choice. ∎

effort and ends up athletically ineligible or costing his or her team an APR point or two, there is often a rush to blame those responsible for his or her failures—other than the individual athlete. In these cases, the coach, sport supervisor, athletic director, and other salient stakeholders in the affairs of athletics may question the academic advisor's abilities. Worse yet, the athlete may blame the advisor for poor course selection and a lack of support. Conversely, if advisors propose an easier approach and do not encourage academic exploration and risk taking among their advisees, advisors run the risk of creative advising or advising simply for eligibility. In these cases, critics of the current system, especially faculty, condemn academic advisors for athletes. While the rationale for the APR is well intentioned, the academic reform initiative heightens this educational dilemma.

Thus, a vigilant focus on monitoring college athletes runs the risk of undermining the mission of many academic support programs—to help athletes become independent, self-reliant learners, and vested, integrated members of the academic community.[3] Class checks and faculty progress reports contradict such a mission, implying a lack of trust in these young adults' ability to navigate their own educational experiences and take responsibility for their academic decisions. Despite national regulations that require that colleges and universities treat students as adults (e.g., FERPA),[4] APR legislation tends to infantilize college athletes, arresting their academic development. For many athletes, this hypermonitoring of their academic and degree progress feels patronizing. Others are convinced that they need it. Either way, the scrutiny reinforces a divide between college athletes and other students on campus.

Many of us in the field rationalize this level of monitoring as part of a developmental model of advising, providing academic support to first- and second-year students and then slowly removing this overly structured level of support. This educational plan provides scaffolding to students to fulfill the mission of creating academic self-reliance and independence. And yet, when this same kind of monitoring is in place for fifth-year seniors, the system has to be seen as something of a facade. Thus, a myopic focus on the APR, advising to the APR and GSR, encourages a system of co-dependence between academic support practitioners and athletes. More and more, academic advisors for athletes can ill afford to argue on principle in support of student independence. As the UConn case study attests, their jobs might now require specific APR outcomes. Athlete outcomes, narrowly defined by the APR, become a primary motive or raison d'être for academic support staff, often reflected in job security, career advancement, and salary bonuses.

CONCLUSION

These philosophical debates concern core educational values and why students attend college in the first place. Despite the lofty goals of learning for learning's sake and the intrinsic ideals of intellectual curiosity and exploration, extrinsic rewards win out more often on college campuses today. Of course, this is not just the case for college athletes. But, for this particular population of students, a focus on accountability and learning outcomes in the face of the APR only heightens the use of other extrinsic methods—requiring athletes to choose a major early in their college career and to continue with that major; monitoring class attendance, mandated study hall; and punishing those who deviate from these academic expectations. In the game of advising to the APR, the stick becomes a more effective tool than the carrot.

As educators and practitioners, we hope our students will learn critical thinking skills, earn meaningful degrees, and become educated, contributing members of society. As academic advisors, we want to believe that we helped our students develop into healthy young adults. The NCAA's academic reform legislation based on the APR and GSR has forced many academic support practitioners to wonder if we have to settle for retention and eligibility scores, while hoping that athletes realize loftier educational goals along the way.

Academic advisors can achieve both of these goals, simultaneously supporting the development of athletes and achieving high APR scores. As the UConn case study demonstrates, this balancing act requires regular, open conversations with key institutional stakeholders about realistic recruitment and admissions and about the academic support needed for these students. Critically, these conversations must also include athletes, helping them to set realistic goals related to their academic and degree plans. Ideally, these plans represent the students' own intellectual property, creative outcomes far more meaningful than simply remaining eligible. Monitoring these plans is essential, to be sure, but not at the expense of student independence and academic engagement.

QUESTIONS FOR DISCUSSION

1. While the establishment of the APR has led to increased retention and graduation rates for college athletes nationally, have the increased standards been in the best interests of athletes educationally?

2. Has the APR led to increased academic rules violations and therefore undermined the academic integrity of colleges and universities?

3. Is the UConn case study, combining an academic improvement plan with a 2014 Division I men's basketball championship, reflective of a national model of effective implementation in light of the APR or a cautionary tale for academic support practitioners in the field?

Notes

1. The NCAA has set an arbitrary grade point average of 2.6 to determine what constitutes *good academic standing*, despite the fact that most colleges and universities acknowledge that a C average or 2.0 GPA represents such standing at their respective institutions. Only those students who fall below this threshold

are placed on academic probation. Therefore, students who earn GPAs between 2.0 and 2.6 and then transfer are counted against their initial institution's APR and GSR, deemed in poor academic standing by the NCAA but not their own college or university. While many complain about grade inflation within American education broadly, there remains tremendous variation by institution and within institutions (e.g., by college major) in assigning grades. This arbitrary number may inadvertently encourage academic support staff to advise athletes to enroll in courses, majors, and schools with higher average GPAs simply to meet this mark. This process of steering athletes into easier courses and subjects may likewise lead to clustering, where a disproportionately larger number of athletes enrolls in certain majors (Fountain & Finley, 2009; Grasgreen, 2012; Schneider, Ross, & Fisher, 2012).

2. The NCAA created a database in 2010 that tracks the APR of coaches based on the college athletes they recruit. See the NCAA Division I Head Coach APR Portfolio Database at http://fs.ncaa.org/Docs/newmedia/public/rates/index2.html

3. For example, I am the director of the Athletic Study Center at the University of California, Berkeley, and we explicitly and intentionally use the language of student independence and self-reliance in our mission statement. See the ASC website at: http://asc.berkeley.edu/About/mission

4. The Family Educational Rights and Privacy Act (FERPA) is a federal law that protects the privacy of student education records. FERPA gives parents certain rights with respect to their children's education records. These rights transfer to the student when he or she reaches the age of 18 or attends a school beyond the high school level. For more information, see the U.S. Department of Education's website at http://www.ed.gov/policy/gen/guid/fpco/ferpa/index.html

References

Brady, E. (2008, November 20). Athletes' academic choices put advisers in tough balancing act. *USA Today*. Retrieved from http://usatoday30.usatoday.com/sports/college/2008-11-20-athletes-advisers-cover_N.htm?imw=Y

Brown, G. (2005, February 14). Implementation of penalty structure triggers new terminology, consequences, questions. Retrieved from http://fs.ncaa.org/Docs/NCAANewsArchive/2005/Division+I/apr%2B101%2B-%2B2-14-05%2Bncaa%2Bnews.html

Comeaux, E. (2013). Rethinking academic reform and encouraging organizational innovation: Implications for stakeholder management in college sports. *Innovative Higher Education, 38*, 281–293.

Covell, D., & Barr, C. A. (2001). The ties that bind: Presidential involvement with the development of NCAA Division I eligibility legislation. *Journal of Higher Education, 72*, 414–452.

Duderstadt, J. (2003). *Intercollegiate athletics and the American university: A university president's perspective*. Ann Arbor: University of Michigan Press.

Fountain, J. J., & Finley, P. S. (2009). Academic majors of upperclassmen football players in the Atlantic Coast Conference: An analysis of academic clustering comparing white and minority players. *Journal of Issues in Intercollegiate Athletics, 2*, 1–13.

Fuller, A. (2010, March 17). Arne Duncan and NCAA differ on how to score teams' academic success. *Chronicle of Higher Education*. Retrieved from http://chronicle.com/article/Arne-DuncanNCAA-Differ-on/64712/

Grasgreen, A. (2012, April 20). More credits, more clusters. *Inside Higher Education*. Retrieved from http://www.insidehighered.com/news/2012/04/20/football-advisers-predict-negative-athlete-outcomes-under-9-credit-rule

Gurney, G. S., & Southall, R. M. (2012, August 9). College sports' bait and switch. *Espn.com*. Retrieved from http://espn.go.com/college-sports/story/_/id/8248046/college-sports-programs-find-multitude-ways-game-ncaa-apr

———. (2013, February 14). NCAA academic reform has hurt higher ed's integrity. *Inside Higher Ed*. Retrieved from http://www.insidehighered.com/views/2013/02/14/ncaa-academic-reform-has-hurt-higher-eds-integrity-essay

Hosick, M. B. (2009, October 2). *Study shows increased DI spending on academics*. Retrieved from http://fs.ncaa.org/Docs/NCAANewsArchive/2009/Division+I/study%2Bshows%2Bincreased%2Bdi%2Bspending%2Bon%2Bacademics_10_02_09_ncaa_news.html

Knight Commission on Intercollegiate Athletics. (2001). *A call to action: Reconnecting college sport and higher education*. Miami, FL: Author.

————. (2010). *Restoring the balance: Dollars, values, and the future of college sports*. Miami, FL: Author.

LaForge, L., & Hodge, J. (2011, March–April). NCAA academic performance metrics: Implications for institutional policy and practice. *Journal of Higher Education, 82*, 217–235.

Lapchick, R. E., Bukstein, S., & Harrison, C. K. (2013, March 19). Keeping score' when it counts: Academic progress/graduation success rate study. Retrieved from http://www.tidesport.org/Grad%20Rates /2013%20Men's%20and%20Women's%20Basket ball%20Tournament%20Teams%20Study.pdf

McLaughlin, J. (2013). Student athlete academic progress: A multilevel analysis of team and institutional effects on academic eligibility at Division I institutions. Center for Leadership in Athletics, University of Washington. Retrieved from http:// sites.education.washington.edu/uwcla/sites /sites.education.washington.edu.uwcla/files /McLaughlin%202013_Full%20Document_Final% 20PDF.pdf

Moltz, D. (2010, June 10). NCAA levies academic penalties. *Inside Higher Ed*. Retrieved from http:// www.insidehighered.com/news/2010/06/10/apr

NCAA. Division I Academics. (2013, June 16). Student athletes continue academic success: Basketball and football teams meeting the mark. Retrieved from http://www.ncaa.org/wps/wcm/connect/public /ncaa/resources/latest+news/2013/june/student -athletes+continue+classroom+success

Peterkin, C. (2012, October 25). Graduation rates of football and men's basketball players reach new highs, NCAA says. *Chronicle of Higher Education*. Retrieved from chronicle.com/article/Graduation -Rates-of-football/135400/

Sander, L. (2009, May 7). One in 10 teams still fail to make the NCAA's grade. *Chronicle of Higher Education*. Retrieved from http://chronicle.com/article /One-in-10-Teams-Still-Fails-to/47238

————. (2010, June 9). Athletes' academic performance improves, but work is not finished, NCAA says. *Chronicle of Higher Education*. Retrieved from http:// chronicle.com/article/Athletes-Academic-Performa /65846/

Schneider, R. G., Ross, S. R., & Fisher, M. (2012, March). Academic clustering and major selection of intercollegiate athletic student athletes. *College Student Journal, 44*(1), 64–70.

Shulman, J., & Bowen, W. (2001). *The game of life: College sports and educational values*. Princeton: Princeton University Press.

Smith, R. (2011). *Pay for play: A history of big time college athletic reform*. Chicago: University of Illinois Press.

Wolverton, B. (2008, September 5). Rise in fancy academic centers for athletes raises questions in fairness. *Chronicle of Higher Education*. Retrieved from http://chronicle.com/article/Rise-in-Fancy -Academic-Centers/13493/

————. (2013, April 4). For UConn, lessons from a year of tournament exile. *Chronicle of Higher Education*. Retrieved from http://chronicle.com/blogs/players /for-uconn-lessons-from-a-year-of-tournament -exile/32811

COLLEGE ATHLETES in REVENUE and NONREVENUE SPORTS

Language, Culture, Identity

KEY TERMS

▶ scholar-baller

▶ Athletes Think

▶ academic success

▶ language

▶ culture

▶ identity

C. Keith Harrison and Scott Bukstein

In American higher education, an emphasis is all too often placed on the *athletic* abilities and accomplishments of athletes and the success of athletic teams rather than their *academic* goals and achievements. While most stakeholders of athletics agree that education, broadly defined, should be the core mission of colleges and universities, it is frequently overlooked, and the academic success of athletes is constantly overshadowed (see Harrison 2002a, 2002b). This lack of attention to and focus on marketing and branding athlete academic excellence impacts the external perception and self-identity of athletes. With this in mind, this chapter provides an overview of the Scholar Baller (SB) Program with a special focus on the culturally relevant curriculum intervention and academic success initiatives that empower athletes through strategically marketing, branding, and rewarding academic success. This chapter also explores the influence of language, culture, and identity on athletes who participate in the SB Program.

COLLEGE ATHLETE: THE IMPACT OF LABELS ON IDENTITY AND PERCEPTIONS

When a label is externally attached to a person, this creates a definition (identity) of that person based on external as well as internal (personal) perceptions (see Becker, 1963, for additional information on labeling theory). Identity relates to and is impacted by language and communicative behavior (see Riley, 2007). The label of *athlete* within the term *student-athlete* leads to pervasive issues and persistent problems as a result of frequent (over)emphasis by colleges and universities on "athlete" at the expense of "student" (see Comeaux & Harrison, 2004). Collegiate athletes "receive little positive reinforcement for academic accomplishments, but receive positive reinforcement for their athletic achievements" (Harrison & Valdez, 2004, p. 192). Role reinforcement and role conflict theories predict that athletes are more likely to invest time and energy (and prioritize) the self-identity of the particular role or label that is reinforced, which is generally the athletic role (see Adler & Adler, 1987).

As a result, some scholars have decided to avoid using the term *student-athlete* (see Shulman & Bowman, 2001). Staurowsky and Sack (2005) urged scholars and practitioners to reconsider its use because the term presents "inherent inconsistencies that are problematic" (p. 111). Therefore, it is imperative for scholars and practitioners to utilize language and culture to reframe, redefine, and reposition the role and identity of students who participate in athletics. Scholar Baller is one example of a culturally relevant program that values education and uses language and labels (with corresponding reinforcement and reward structures based on academic performance) to influence athlete identity and perceptions.

THE SB PROGRAM: MARKETING COLLEGE ATHLETE ACADEMIC SUCCESS

The SB Program, which was established in 1995 to help bridge the gap between education, sport, and popular culture, serves as an excellent example of a culturally relevant program that incentivizes athletes to excel academically and that also fosters positive and meaningful interaction between team members. The mission of the SB Program is to inspire youth and young adults to develop leadership skills and to excel in education and life by using their cultural interests in sport and entertainment. SB, which is a not-for-profit organization endorsed by the National Collegiate Athletic Association (NCAA), has developed an extensive curriculum and academic performance recognition program for high schools, NCAA member institutions, as well as for athlete development programs such as Major League Baseball Urban Youth Academies.

Scholarly research has driven the development of all Scholar Baller curriculum content and strategies with respect to recognizing athletes for academic performance (see Harrison, 2002a, 2002b; Harrison & Boyd, 2007). As former NCAA president Dr. Myles Brand explains, "The Scholar Baller Program . . . is a well-conceived successful way to recognize and reward academic achievement by student-athletes. It speaks to the contemporary student-athletes in their language and in their context" (M. Brand, personal communication, July 2006). Dr. Bernard Franklin, executive vice president of NCAA Membership & Student-Athlete Affairs/chief inclusion officer, described the SB Program as "a creative and unique approach to providing academic support for student-athletes. The program resonates with student-athletes because it addresses the challenges of balancing participation in a sport and academic achievement in a contemporary fashion" (B. Franklin, personal communication, 2006).

Scholar-ballers at participating schools and organizations—for example, students who participate in athletics or an extracurricular activity and who achieve at least a 3.0 grade point average (GPA)—are typically awarded academic performance recognition incentives such as jersey patches, helmet decals, t-shirts, shorts, hats, license plate holders, and flash drives. Some participating universities have created scholar-baller study lounges and recognition walls to further integrate the positive messaging about the importance of academic excellence.

The SB Program utilizes the following metrics to measure athlete academic success at participating schools and programs: pretest and posttest measures of academic and athletic identity and success, individual athlete GPA, team GPA, team graduation rates, academic probation numbers, community service, improved academic and athletic identity and self-concept, and significant academic improvement (e.g., the annual Academic Momentum Award presented by Scholar Baller and the National Consortium for Academics and Sports). Examples of success stories with respect to the Scholar Baller curriculum and incentive initiatives include the following:

- The average GPA for athletes on a Division I basketball team gradually increased from 2.3 to 2.8 to 3.1 to 3.3 during a four-semester period as a result of the Scholar-Baller of the Month Recognition and Incentive Model.

- An NCAA Football Championship Subdivision (FCS) football team went from an extremely low team GPA to the highest football team GPA in school history. The same school reached the highest athletic department GPA in school history and also achieved one of the highest graduation rates for African-American male athletes on the football team.

- A community college experienced an increase from 36 to 85 athletes with "Scholar Baller" status (benchmark was GPA of 3.0 or higher) over a two-year period.

College athletes at schools and within other extracurricular programs that have adopted the Scholar Baller curriculum have opportunities to compete academically both inside and outside of the classroom while simultaneously gaining the opportunity to interact with teammates of different races, ethnicities, and social classes—teammates who also have diverse personalities, perspectives and values (see Harrison, Bukstein, & Brock, 2012). The following narratives from select collegiate athletes who have participated in the SB Program demonstrate the effectiveness of marketing and branding athlete academic success through the development and implementation of culturally relevant initiatives:

Citrus College: Success Story Related to Scholar Baller Partnership with Campus Leaders

Citrus College officially began participation in the Scholar Baller Program in fall 2007, when 15 athletes were initially recognized as scholar-ballers for earning a cumulative GPA of at least 3.0. Two years later, during the 2009–2010 academic year, there were 55 scholar-ballers on Citrus College athletics teams. The growth continued over the next three years, with 69 athletes recognized in 2010–2011, 73 in 2011–2012, and a record high 89 athletes in 2012–2013.

This type of gradual achievement is the goal of Scholar Baller: to impact the academic performance culture through language and identity. While several universities have experienced this type of success in partnership with the Scholar Baller leadership team, Citrus College is the focus of the current case study. To quote the famous African proverb, "It takes a village to raise a child." This case study highlights some of the leaders and stakeholders of that village at Citrus College.

As explained in the *Citrus College News Magazine* (2013, Winter), "In the spring of 2007, Citrus College Dean of Kinesiology, Health and Athletics Jody Wise and Athletics Counselor Alicia Longyear attended a presentation on Scholar-Baller®, an academic achievement program for athletes, at the California Community College Athletic Association (CCCAA) Spring Conference. Shortly thereafter, Citrus College joined the nearly 100 community colleges and four-year institutions nationwide that utilize Scholar-Baller to help their athletes succeed in the classroom" (p. 16). The success of the Scholar Baller Program at Citrus College is a direct result of the hard work and academic effort of athletes combined with the leadership and vision of Jody Wise and Alicia Longyear.

In the words of Alicia Longyear, "Watching their numbers grow [since 2007] has been awesome. The program is a real motivating factor for our athletes . . . We adopted the program because the curriculum is very impressive and I knew it would resonate with our athletes . . . At the time, we didn't have anything that focused on academics, and the program provided a good opportunity" (Wheeler, 2013).

Citrus College administrators have consistently demonstrated an emphasis on academic achievement. According to Wise, "We needed a way to promote academics to our athletes because keeping up with their studies is the only way they are going to move on . . . Scholar-Baller stresses the important things about being a college student such as attendance, note taking and studying. It helps our students become more aware that we care about academics, and it's a way for our department to stress that success in the classroom is important" (Wheeler, 2013). When asked to describe the impact and meaning of the scholar-baller term and identity, Wise responded that "it means you're a champion in the classroom as well as in the sport that you're doing" (Lucero, 2011).

The Scholar Baller Program plans to continue motivating and recognizing academic champions throughout the world—one jersey patch, helmet sticker, t-shirt, or other academic performance incentive at a time. ■

- Football players usually never get noticed for what they do in the classroom, but after the Scholar-Baller patches came out, people started to notice it." (Arizona State University student and member of football team)

- It is an honor to be part of such a movement, emphasizing what we as student-athletes came to college to do: better ourselves." (Florida A&M University biology and pre-med major and member of football team)

- I feel honored to be able to display that I am a scholar-baller, and to express to the younger athletes that it is not only about on the field activity but also off the field." (Florida A&M University criminal justice major and member of football team)

- I take pride and honor that I perform better academically each term. I also take pride in wearing the Scholar-Baller patch during competition." (Portland State University health science and business major and member of football team)

- It was a true honor to wear the Scholar-Baller patch during the Valero Alamo Bowl. This patch showed my teammates that I am a hard worker. It also shows the coaches, competitors and fans that I excel on and off the field. Also, the patch gave me a special swagger about myself that I was not only representing the University of Arizona, but every kid who lives in a tough situation and has a hard life growing up and is trying to do the right thing. I wanted to thank the Scholar Baller program and committee for recognizing my accomplishments and hard work I have put in over the past years. Winning this award has opened up new doors to my life and my career." (University of Arizona interdisciplinary studies major and member of football team)

THE SB PROGRAM: BRANDING COLLEGE ATHLETE ACADEMIC SUCCESS

The SB Program has developed various terms, labels, and language to maximize the impact of curriculum intervention strategies and academic performance recognition incentives.

Label 1: Scholar-Baller

In the academic and athletics context and in other contexts such as entertainment, the urban term "baller" can function as a positive label that can be used as a noun, adjective, or verb to signify various aspects of achievement or success. In popular culture, baller has been mainstreamed on ESPN, Music Television (MTV), in major newspapers such as *USA Today*, and in speeches by President Obama and First Lady Michelle Obama. A "scholar-baller" is someone who succeeds academically and socially (or athletically). The scholar-baller label "challenges the meaning of [counterproductive] cultural messages by serving as a counter-strategy to intervene in representations and to reconstruct stereotypical images of student athletes with a new 'brand' and broader meaning(s) of what it means to be a student athlete" (Harrison & Boyd, 2007, p. 207).

As Jean Boyd, senior associate athletic director at Arizona State University, explains,

Baller is [a] term that young people today associate with and recognize as someone who achieves a high level in all that they do. We've tried to shift the negative stereotype and create an image of a scholar-baller as a positive . . . When I was growing up everyone wanted to be a baller, which meant status and you were at the top of your game. Education was often overlooked. It wasn't cool to be smart. If you were smart you were a nerd . . . By putting the word scholar with baller it creates a new meaning for individuals who don't value education. I know what a baller is. I want to be that so if something else is attached to being a baller, maybe I can be that too. (Boor, 2011, para. 9; 2012, para. 10)

Many of today's youth and young adults understand and identify with the term scholar-baller, which has the ability to transform how athletes define themselves and also how others (mis)perceive and define athletes. For example, a student formerly on the football team at Arizona State University noted: "When you wear that jersey people know you're not just a typical dumb jock. You have that Scholar-Baller patch, so they know you work hard in the classroom."

Professional sports leagues also comprehend the inherent value and impact of the term (label) scholar-baller. The SB Program collaborates with Major League

STAKEHOLDER PERSPECTIVE

Innovative and Impactful Academic Support for College Athletes

Mr. Jean Boyd is the senior associate athletic director for the Office of Student Athlete Development (OSAD) at Arizona State University (ASU). In this important leadership role, Boyd has developed strategies and programs to raise OSAD's graduation success rate and has worked closely with academic coaches to educate, train, and strategize about ways to improve the department's Academic Progress Rate (APR), which increased to a 976 average in 2011–2012 (second highest in the Pac-12 Conference). Boyd has also spearheaded a number of strategic changes in academic-support programming, including enhancing the first-year athlete experience and implementing cohort events, which provide relevant programs, speakers, and seminars for each athlete cohort.

As a result of his outstanding leadership, Boyd was selected as the 2012 Lan Hewlett Award winner at the 2012 National Association of Academic Advisors for Athletes Conference (N4A). The award is presented annually by the N4A for outstanding performance as an academic advisor for athletics and recognizes sustained professional service, a high level of competence in administrative skills, merited professional stature, innovation in meeting the needs of athletes, effectiveness in the development of junior staff, significant contributions to the field through publications and professional development, and leadership in university affairs.

Boyd has been responsible for implementing and overseeing the Scholar Baller Program at ASU since 2004. According to Boyd, the

Scholar Baller Program has resulted in "improvement in GPA, retention, and progress [regarding academic] probation. Our freshman class had a one-year jump from 1.54 to 2.54 in a single semester. We have also had an impact on changing the value of education, which is less measurable on paper, but it has been successful."

Boyd has created and maintained an "academics first" culture within the ASU athletic department. And he is extremely proud of the athletes he mentors on a daily basis. "I'm in awe of the young people graduating from Arizona State University who have competed at the very highest level in their sport," Boyd says. "They're All-Americans, they're first-round draft picks, they're Olympians—who, at the same time, have embraced education." ■

Baseball's Urban Youth Academies to develop and deliver a comprehensive curriculum to youth baseball players participating at various academy locations throughout the United States. SB is also working with the National Football League Player Engagement Department to create the Scholar-Baller of the Month Award in which at least one current or former NFL player and high school student who participates in football will be recognized for their academic performance and community involvement.

Label 2: Athletes Think

The SB Program recently launched a new academic performance incentive initiative to inform professors, coaches, academic and athletic administrators, teammates, and members of the general public that "Athletes Think." Athletes Think is a lifestyle. Athletes Think creates a positive and productive culture within an athletic program or team. Youth and young adults identify with and embrace this culturally relevant concept (label). The Athletes Think initiative encourages each participating organization, and each individual student who participates in athletics, to create his or her own definition of Athletes Think and likewise offer practical examples of how Athletes Think.

Label 3: Academic Swagger

Academic Swagger describes an attitude. It identifies students who participate in athletics and carry themselves with confidence inside and outside of the classroom and take pride in their academic obligations and accomplishments. The contemporary urban meaning of the term *swagger* has a much different meaning today compared to when the term was first used in Shakespeare's 1596 play, *A Midsummer Night's Dream*. A character once asked the question in this play: "What hempen homespuns have we swaggering here?" During that time, "swagger" generally meant displaying a sense of elitism and dominance and carrying oneself in an arrogant or condescending manner. Nonetheless, today "swagger" is generally understood to mean confidence, sophistication, and a general sense of being "cool." By adding the "academic" label, now it is cool to be smart—and to possess Academic Swagger.

Figure 27.1. Thinkman Image. (Photo courtesy of Scholar-Baller I.M.A.G.E., LLC.)

Label 4: Thinkman

The Thinkman image (Figure 27.1) portrays an athlete at a desk studying and listening to music. The Thinkman logo represents the three key pillars of the Scholar Baller concept: education, entertainment, and sport. The Thinkman logo is one of the primary graphics designed by the SB Program to recognize athletes for balancing playbooks and textbooks.

Label 5: Thinkwoman

The Thinkwoman image (Figure 27.2) embodies qualities such as intelligence, athleticism, true beauty, and respect of women: mind, body, and soul. The Thinkwoman logo also exemplifies support of Title IX policies, diverse body representations, and the creation of a positive label about women's health and physical activity. The SB Program is inclusive by enabling men's and women's athletic teams to equally participate in this cultural movement to encourage all athletes to excel in the classroom.

Label 6: Thinkkids

Marketing and branding the academic performance of students who are athletes must start at the K–12 level. For example, the SB Program has collaborated with youth basketball camps to create "education stations" at camps where sport business professionals discuss academic and career paths related to sports.

Figure 27.2. Thinkwoman Image. (Photo courtesy of Scholar-Baller I.M.A.G.E., LLC.)

CONCLUSION

In the final analysis, the SB Program has been able to motivate many athletes and athletic administrators to focus on academic excellence through its culturally relevant curriculum intervention and academic performance incentive initiatives, combined with its development of positive and purposeful "lifestyle labels" such as Athletes Think, Thinkwoman, and Academic Swagger. As illustrated by some of the result metrics and student narratives in this chapter, the SB Program has shifted the focus of numerous athletes and has changed the culture of numerous college athletic programs. Leaders of the SB Program plan to collaborate with even more high schools and colleges and universities in the future so that all athletes aspire to be a scholar-baller.

QUESTIONS FOR DISCUSSION

1. What is your personal definition of the following terms: Scholar Baller, Athletes Think, Academic Swagger, Thinkman, Thinkwoman, and Thinkkids?

2. What are some additional culturally relevant terms (labels) that relate to the general areas of learning, personal and professional development, and athlete academic success, and how can academic institutions and athletic programs strategically and effectively market and brand athlete academic success?

3. What is the Scholar Baller Program, and how does the program complement and supplement existing responsive intervention strategies aimed at improving athlete academic success and social integration?

References

Adler, P., & Adler, P. A. (1987). Role conflict and identity salience: College athletics and the academic role. *Social Science Journal, 24,* 443–455.

Becker, H. (1963). *Outsiders: Studies in the sociology of deviance.* New York: Free Press.

Boor, W. (2011). NCAA athletics: Putting the 'student' in student-athlete. *SB Nation.* Retrieved from http://www.houseofsparky.com/2011/5/3/2151576/putting-the-student-in-student-athlete

———. (2012). ASU student-athletes strive to break negative stereotypes. *The State Press.* Retrieved from http://www.statepress.com/2012/06/24/asu-student-athletes-excel-in-all-walks-of-life/

Comeaux, E., & Harrison, C. K. (2004). Labels of African American ballers: A historical and contemporary investigation of African American male youth's depletion from America's favorite pastime, 1885–2000. *Journal of American Culture, 27*(1), 1–14.

Harrison, C. K. (2002a). Scholar or baller: A visual elicitation and qualitative assessment of the student-athlete mindset. *National Association of Student Affairs Professionals Journal, 8*(1), 66–81.

———. (2002b). Scholar or baller in American higher education: A visual elicitation and qualitative assessment of the student-athlete's mindset. *NASPA Journal, 5*(1), 66–81.

Harrison, C. K., & Boyd, J. (2007). Mainstreaming and integrating the substance and spectacle of scholar-baller: A new game plan for the NCAA, higher education and society. In D. Brooks & R. Althouse (Eds.), *Diversity and social justice: Sport management and the student-athlete* (pp. 201–231). Morgantown, WV: Fitness Information Technology.

Harrison, C. K., Bukstein, S., & Brock, W. (2012). Dimensions of diversity. In G. McClellan, C. King, & D. Rockey Jr. (Eds.), *Handbook of college athletics and recreation administration* (pp. 321–335). San Francisco: Jossey-Bass.

Harrison, C. K., & Valdez, A. (2004). The uneven view of African American ballers, ball and ballin. In C. Ross (Ed.), *Race and sport: The struggle for equality on and off the field* (pp. 183–221). Oxford: University of Mississippi Press.

Lucero, R. (2011). Program emphasizes the "A" in athletics. *The Clarion Online.* Retrieved from http://www.theclariononline.com/program-emphasizes-the-a-in-athletics-1.2533327

Riley, P. (2007). *Language, culture and identity: Advances in sociolinguistics.* London: Continuum.

Shulman, J., & Bowen, W. (2001). *The game of life: College sports and educational values.* Princeton, NJ: Princeton University Press.

Staurowsky, E. J., & Sack, A. (2005). Reconsidering the use of the term student-athlete in academic research. *Journal of Sport Management, 19,* 103–116.

Wheeler, A. (2013, Winter). Scholar-athletes win in the classroom. *Citrus College News Magazine.* Retrieved from http://www.citruscollege.edu/pio/magazine/Documents/winter2013edition.pdf

BEST PRACTICES in CAREER TRANSITION PROGRAMMING for COLLEGE ATHLETES

Kristina M. Navarro

Today, higher education student affairs professionals are charged to understand the challenges and needs of a diverse student body. These professionals must also prepare a diverse group of students for the inevitable transition to career fields in life after their higher education experience. In turn, college career development programs now exist to assist students not only to develop their academic talents and transferrable skill sets during college, but also to prepare them for life after this transition (National Career Development Association, 2013). Today the National Career Development Association (NCDA) offers specific training to prepare higher education professionals as certified Career Development Facilitators. Current student affairs professionals who possess this certification demonstrate mastery in 12 core competencies to assisting individuals with transition from school to work or between career fields (NCDA, 2013).

Higher education professionals must seek to further understand the challenges that certain student populations experience during college to best prepare them for lifelong success as professionals in a volatile economy and competitive job market. Savickas et al. (2009) suggest competition in the contemporary job markets is exacerbated by the globalization of economies and rapid advances in information technology. In turn, it is of enhanced importance to understand how athletes navigate processes of career development throughout their higher education experience and how student affairs professionals can best prepare these individuals for impending challenges as they transition to the work force.

CAMPUS ENGAGEMENT AND CAREER DEVELOPMENT PROCESSES

Reason, Terenzini, and Domingo (2006) posit the college years are vitally important to processes of career development. The authors suggest students experience significant periods of cognitive and social development as they engage with the college environment. Consistently, research suggests that many students face multidimensional adjustment processes as they cognitively adjust to the rigor of college work, emotionally discover a new sense of identity, and psychosocially establish peer groups (Keup, 2007; Kidwell, 2005; Reason et al., 2006). Furthermore, Gaston-Gayles and Hu (2009) suggest athletes, a population nested within the general higher education student body, face unique challenges that influence their holistic development potential during college. In turn, Gaston-Gayles and Hu (2009) posit the level to which undergraduate students engage in educationally sound activities influences career readiness (i.e., identification with roles outside of sports and ability to transfer skill sets in college to the work force). Regardless of student group affiliation, higher education literature suggests universities need to support students via holistic campus-wide career development programming to lay the groundwork for long-term career success (Baille & Danish, 1992; Keup, 2007; Kidwell, 2005).

Considering students face multifaceted challenges during their higher education experience, scholars continue to the note the importance of student engagement to future career preparation. Jordan and Denison (1990) suggest engagement outside of the confines of the classroom can best prepare students for life after college in career fields as they are able to encounter and explore diverse career alternatives via experiential learning. Donahue (2004) and Reason et al. (2006) further support this notion and add that experiential exercises outside the classroom (i.e., practicum and experiential learning assignments) can help students to develop a sense of community and enhance consideration of diverse career alternatives. Such experiential learning activities enable students to develop interpersonal connections and network with potential employers early in their higher education experience. Overall, engagement outside of the classroom is viewed as beneficial to career exploration as students explore viable career alternatives outside of typical environments.

CAREER DEVELOPMENT AS AN EVOLUTIONARY PROCESS

Contemporary college career development practitioners continue to reflect Baldwin and Blackburn's (1981) foundational position that career development programming must be viewed as a process rather than an isolated program or experience. This framework is acknowledged today as a best practice in the field of higher education and career development (NCDA, 2013). While career development theorists differ in specific approaches to career development, findings generally support the notion that career development is a dynamic, psychosocial process rather than a static phase of life (Baldwin & Black, 1981; Hall & Nougaim, 1968; Osborn, Howard, & Leierer, 2007; Savickas, 2002, 2005). Since career development is a very individualized construct, career development programs and interventions are complex (Baldwin & Blackburn, 1981). Overall career development literature suggests career programming must consider the needs and interests of a diverse student population in order to be effective (Baldwin & Blackburn, 1981; Hall & Nougaim, 1968; Osborn et al., 2007). In turn, the National Career Development Association continues to consider this foundational literature and philosophy of career development being an evolutionary process as it presents guiding competencies and benchmarks for contemporary career programming (NCDA, 2013).

Contemporary Literature on Career Development Programs

Today scholars continue to grapple with how to best implement career programs across the higher education experience. In turn, best practices in career program delivery continue to be a highly debated issue in the current literature. Reese and Miller (2006) suggest that highly structured career development programs best reach diverse undergraduate populations. To assess the effects of specific programming designed to promote career decision-making efficacy, Reese and Miller (2006) studied

Best Practices in Career Transitions

Kelli Richards is a career development coordinator and academic advisor for Division I athletes at the University of Wisconsin, Madison. A former Division I college volleyball player at Northwestern University, she earned an undergraduate degree in human development and psychological services and a master's of education degree in counseling psychology from Wisconsin. She currently works with the Peer Mentorship and Freshmen Experience components of a formalized four-year athlete career development curriculum nested within the Badger Life Skills Academy.

Reflecting on her experiences with athletes, Kelli discusses the importance of college student affairs professionals taking a holistic approach to the development of athletes as they transition from high school to college and college to career fields. She notes athletes often come to campus unaware of the many career resources available to them. Kelli views her primary role as a career development coordinator in athletics as assisting athletes with processes of career exploration, choice, and preparation for a lifetime of success after sport. She highlights the Badger Life Skills Academy

as a crucial program to foster personal development and career decision-making skills over the course of the college experience. As well, she notes that maintaining athletic eligibility is a reality professionals in her field must be cognizant of as they advise athletes, but this approach cannot be the sole focus of decision-making processes. Kelli feels her foundational training as a student affairs and certified Career Development Facilitator enables her to assist students to develop a holistic action plan for success during college as well as in their aspiring career fields. ∎

a group of 30 undergraduate students enrolled in an introductory career development course. The results demonstrated that athletes who took the course perceived they had a higher level of career decisiveness, specifically with respect to setting career goals and creating a career trajectory plan. Similarly, Davis and Horne (1986) and Garis and Niles (1990) suggest that career courses enhance the educational experience and the transition from higher education to careers. Garis and Niles (1990) demonstrate students' desire for career development programming that is highly structured and intentional. Davis and Horne (1986) similarly demonstrate in a study on undergraduate students at four-year institutions that highly structured programming best prepares students for impending transitions to career fields. Clearly, undergraduate athletes reveal throughout these studies that intentional and structured career development programs are beneficial to their transition to life after college.

Building on this growing trend to develop intentional career programming, a study conducted by the National Association of College and Employers in 1998 concludes more than half of the four-year institutions surveyed support formal career development courses (Collins, 1998). According to Collin's research, this number continues to increase as faculty and administrators provide career development program opportunities in the form of courses for credit. As students demonstrate a need and desire for intentional career development programming, higher education student affairs practitioners must continue to develop and sustain such programming.

Career Theory

When focusing on how to design career development programming, the theoretical contributions of John Holland often guide higher education programmatic decisions. Holland (1997) draws a clear connection between one's personality and environment. His theoretical framework continues to be regarded as one of the most influential in the field of career counseling. Holland's theory is manifested in a career assessment tool that enables students to understand individual interests and obtain career clarity through categorization of strengths and weaknesses, as well as likes and dislikes. Gottfredson (1981) notes that while Holland's assessment tool is commonly used in organizational behavior disciplines, this framework and assessment tool is also beneficial to students during their higher educational experience. He further posits this tool enables students to reflect on strengths and weaknesses and to understand how their skill set fits certain majors and career fields. Many student affairs practitioners draw on this tool as they create and implement career development programming for students. However, this tool is not tailored to specific needs of diverse populations, namely, athletes. In addition, this tool is considered outdated according to Savickas's (2002) Career Construction Theory, in which students should not be classified into categories; rather, they should be seen as consistently growing and acquiring new tools in response to life experiences.

Additional research discussing career development as an evolutionary process notes the importance for students to develop self-efficacy or confidence in career decision making during their college experience. Paulson and Betz (2004) studied

627 undergraduate students measuring six variables of confidence. The findings revealed that low levels of confidence in career decision making among students can be tied to low levels of confidence in academic skills acquired during their educational process (Taylor & Betz, 1983). Paulson and Betz (2004) posit students who develop poor self-esteem in the classroom due to academic defeat can continue to experience difficulty with respect to career confidence in career decision-making processes (i.e., career decision exploration, choice, and preparation). Therefore, it is of heightened importance to engage students in career development skill set acquisition from the foundational first year and throughout their college years. Student engagement is not only related to academic-related endeavors but also career-related activities to enhance self-esteem; confidence is paramount to facilitate the multistage career decision-making process.

Overall, college students are placed in an environment that lends itself to development and change. The higher education experience is often referred to as a time of intense adaptation, life change, and a need to overcome challenges (Keup, 2007; Kidwell, 2005; Reason et al., 2006). Moreover, as students navigate this new environment and adapt to life experiences, they garner foundational transferrable skills for success in life after college. However, intentional career programming is also needed to guide students. In turn, it is beneficial for student affairs practitioners who work with diverse student groups to design career development programming while considering the multifaceted development that takes place during the college experience and the evolutionary process of career development (Baldwin & Blackburn, 1981; Hall & Nougaim, 1968; Osborn et al., 2007; Savickas, 2002).

CONTEMPORARY COLLEGE ATHLETES AND CAREER TRANSITIONS

For certain population subsets, namely, athletes, career transitions take on additional meaning. As athletes approach this transition from higher education to career fields, they also face an inevitable end to the college athletic experience. For many, nearing the end of one's athletic career further complicates the impending transition to life after sport. According to the NCAA's most recent study on the estimated probability of athletes pursuing professional sports, on average less than 3% of athletes who participate in college sports will eventually pursue professional careers in their sport (NCAA, 2011). Regardless of participation in intercollegiate athletics, the transition from college to the real world is viewed as both difficult and transformational for young adults (Harrison & Lawrence, 2004).

THE COLLEGE ATHLETE EXPERIENCE

For many students, college is a frightening and overwhelming experience, full of challenges and change. Kidwell (2005) notes that all college students must study for

Toward an Understanding of College Athlete Career Construction Processes

Researchers highlight college athletes, a specific subset of individuals nested within the general student body, who face additional challenges with respect to constructing meaningful career plans. As such, this qualitative case study employed a multiple semistructure interview method to explore the life experiences of 29 senior athletes at a large midwestern university. Framed from a constructivist epistemology, findings of this phenomenological study were guided by Savickas's (2005) Career Construction Theory. Personal narratives were collected via 29 semistructured individual interviews and analyzed by employing pattern and process coding techniques to develop cognitive mind maps for each participant. Collectively these cognitive mind maps illustrated how athletes construct individual career paths and engage in career decision-making processes during their higher education experience.

The findings demonstrated that all of the participants in this case study viewed undergraduate academic major choice as a fundamental component of career choice and preparation. For example, participants discussed the importance of an academic major to provide transferrable skill sets to career fields in life after sport. In addition, this case study confirmed previous findings in athlete development literature centering on themes of role conflict (Adler & Adler, 1987) and athletic eligibility concerns (Case, Greer, & Brown, 1987; Fountain & Finley, 2009, 2011). First, participants

stated they faced an internal psychosocial struggle to balance the dual roles of *student* and *athlete* during their higher education experience. This role conflict was most prevalent with individuals who participated in the revenue-generating sports of football, as well as men's hockey and basketball. Second, 59% of athlete participants discussed eligibility and time constraints during college limited their ability to fully engage in career construction process. Participants also discussed their difficulty in choosing academic majors that not only assisted with eligibility but also directly related to future career aspirations, and engaging in campus-wide career preparation programs. Likewise, participants noted the time commitment of Division I athletics was a primary reason to pursue less labor- and time-intensive majors and thus rely solely on athletic department career support.

Findings from this case study also confirm previous studies that suggest the time commitment of Division I athletics influences athletes' drive to pursue degree paths that often fail to align with future career aspirations (e.g., Case, Greer, & Brown, 1987; Fountain & Finley, 2009, 2011; Renick, 1974). Subsequently, these internal and external struggles athletes' face during college implicate how they construct career identities and prepare for life after sport. Continued analyses of athlete career construction processes can guide contemporary student affairs practitioners as they advise this special population of students. ∎

college-level exams, live away from home, and create new social networks. However, researchers who focus on the athlete population argue athletes' experiences in college are different from the experiences of nonathletes (Howard-Hamilton & Watt, 2001). Such challenges are posited to separate athletes from general population students. These include: the internal need to balance roles as student and athlete (Adler & Adler, 1987); a psychosocial affinity to identify with athletic roles (Adler & Adler, 1987); external feelings of isolation from the student body and faculty (Broughton & Neyer, 2001); and external pressure to maintain athletic eligibility in the big-business college sports environment at the expense of academic goals (Lapchick, 2006).

Blann (1985), Kennedy, and Dimmick (1987), Murphy, Petitpas, and Brewer (1996), and Sowa and Gressard (1983) argue athletes struggle to dedicate sufficient time and resources to further career and postgraduate plans throughout their higher education experience. They posit the lack of time dedicated to career exploration can result in a lower perceived level of career maturity upon graduation. This failure to explore opportunities outside of comfortable skill sets can limit the career construction process with respect to potential career choices.

Overall, literature on the college athlete experience suggests additional support is necessary for athletes to prepare for this life transition. Since athletes may rely to a greater extent on support services internal to athletic departments, it is imperative for higher education professionals to understand the complexities of this special population and develop intentional programs that best assist with this impending transition.

CONCLUSION

This chapter considers Division I athletes' preparation for life after their undergraduate programs of study. Discussion of the higher education literature presents clear themes and recommendations for practitioners. In this section, I highlight specific recommendations for higher education practitioners who work closely with athletes.

Astin (1999), Gaston-Gayles and Hu (2009), and Pascarella and Terenzini (2005) suggest that one of the most influential factors to the personal development of students during college is engaging in purposeful activities to facilitate a holistic student experience. In this sense, intentionally engaging with career preparation activities during the undergraduate experience is critically important. However, researchers must continue to probe just how athletes, who face these additional internal and external challenges during college, engage purposefully with campus career development resources to prepare for their respective career fields (Miller & Kerr, 2003). Scholars and practitioners alike continue to suggest intentional programming during college is necessary to prepare students for life after college in career fields. Three recommendations are presented for contemporary practitioners who work with athlete populations.

First, given the importance of intentional focus on career preparation for this population, practitioners who work with athlete populations must work to achieve a stronger balance between athletic-specific and campus-wide career development initiatives. As intercollegiate athletic practitioners seek to best incorporate evidence-based seminars, courses, and workshops into athletes' weekly routines, they should consider the athlete voice to determine how time can be best spent. Moreover, findings from Baille and Danish (1992), Gaston-Gayles and Hu (2009), Lally and Kerr (2005), Kennedy and Dimmick (1987), and Navarro (2012) illustrate that confining athletes solely to athletic-specific programming may inhibit networking opportunities and long-term career preparation. Moving forward, athletic practitioners may seek to engage in intentional professional development activities with both campus-wide student affairs professionals and potential employers to best serve athletes as they prepare for life after sport. For example, rather than athlete-specific career fair events, athletic student affairs professionals may seek to work with campus-based academic units to engage athletes in campus-wide career events.

Second, Baldwin and Blackburn (1981), Hall and Nougaim (1968), Osborn et al. (2007), and Savickas (2002) discuss the importance of viewing career development as an evolutionary process. Therefore, it is suggested that athletic practitioners work to provide career programming throughout the four-year experience as athletes will begin to cognitively understand the importance of preparing for the transition to life after sport at different times. While career development programs can often be of greatest focus for students in their senior year as the impending transition draws near, practitioners must emphasize the importance of gradual preparation for this life change. By modeling an evolutionary approach to career development, practitioners can assist students to cognitively process and prepare for transition to career fields. In turn, athlete populations may begin to understand the transition to life after sport is not just the end of their athletic participation but the beginning of a successful career as a contributor to society.

Third, findings from Adler and Adler (1987), Blann (1985), Kennedy and Dimmick (1987), Murphy et al. (1996), Sowa and Gressard (1983), and the included case study on career development patterns of athletes posit athletes' sense of urgency to prepare for this transition appears to be further complicated as athletic responsibilities often take precedence over personal and career development. In turn, practitioners may consider making select career development programming a mandatory educational experience for athletes to ensure some focus is given to this area amid other role expectations. For example, higher education professionals may consider exploring an undergraduate course for credit that facilitates personal assessments to understand personal strengths and weaknesses, as well as likes and dislikes. According to the findings from the case study, contemporary athletes continue to view academic major selection as a foundational component of career preparation. Yet Case, Greer, and Brown (1987) and Fountain and Finley (2011) argue that they fail to select majors that adequately align with career aspirations. In turn, a course for credit may also include a distinct focus on exploring possible academic majors across campus to ensure proper consideration of alternatives.

QUESTIONS FOR DISCUSSION

1. Considering the multiple roles contemporary higher education practitioners play, how might practitioners develop holistic career development programs for athletes that also compliment eligibility requirements?

2. How might these programmatic efforts differ at the Division I, II, and III levels?

3. In light of this chapter's recommendations for practitioners to continue to shape holistic career development programs for athletes, how would you suggest practitioners implement a multiyear career development program for college athletes?

References

Adler, P., & Adler, P. (1987). Role conflict and identity salience: College athletics and the academic role. *Social Science Journal, 24*, 443–450.

Astin, A. W. (1999). Student involvement: A developmental theory for higher education. *Journal of College Student Development, 40*, 518–529.

Baille, P. H. F., & Danish, S. J. (1992). Understanding the career transition of athletes. *Sport Psychologist, 6*, 77–98.

Baldwin, R. G., & Blackburn, R. T. (1981). The academic career as a developmental process: Implications for higher education. *Journal of Higher Education, 52*, 598–614.

Blann, F. W. (1985). Intercollegiate athletic competition and students' educational and career plans. *Journal of College Student Personnel, 26*(2), 115–118.

Broughton, E., & Neyer, M. (2001). Advising and counseling student athletes. *New Directions for Student Services, 93*, 47–53.

Case, B., Greer, S., & Brown, J. (1987). Academic clustering in athletics: Myth or reality? *Arena Review, 11*(2), 48–56.

Collins, M. (1998). Snapshot of the profession. *Journal of Career Planning & Employment, 58*(2), 32–36.

Cote, J. E. (2006). Emerging adulthood as an institutionalized moratorium: Risks and benefits to identity formation. In J. J. Arnett & J. L. Tanner (Eds.), *Emerging adults in America: Coming of age in the 21st Century* (pp. 85–116). Washington, DC: APA.

Davis, R. C., & Horne, A. M. (1986). The effect of small-group counseling and a career course on career decidedness and maturity. *Vocational Guidance Quarterly, 34*, 255–262.

Donahue, L. (2004). Connections and reflections: Creating a positive learning environment for first-year students. *Journal of the First-Year Experience & Students in Transition, 16*(1), 77–100.

Fountain, J. J., & Finley, P. S. (2009). Academic majors of upperclassmen football players in the Atlantic Coast Conference: An analysis of academic clustering comparing white and minority players. *Journal of Issues in Intercollegiate Athletics, 2*, 1–13.

———. (2011). Academic clustering: A longitudinal analysis of Division I football programs, *Journal of Issues in Intercollegiate Athletics, 4*, 24–21.

Gaston-Gayles, J., & Hu, S. (2009). The influence of student engagement and sport participation on college outcomes among Division I student athletes. *Journal of Higher Education, 80*, 315–333.

Garis, J. W., & Niles, S. G. (1990). The separate and combined effects of SIGI or DISCOVER and a career planning course on undecided university students. *Career Development Quarterly, 38*, 261–274.

Gottfredson, L. S. (1981). Circumscription and compromise: A developmental theory of occupational aspirations. *Journal of Counseling Psychology, 28*, 545–579.

Hall, D. T., & Nougiam, K. (1968). An examination of Maslow's need hierarchy in an organizational setting. *Organizational Behavior and Human Performance, 3*, 12–35.

Harrison, C. K., & Lawrence, S. M. (2004). Female and male student athletes' perceptions of career transition in sport and higher education: A visual elicitation and qualitative assessment. *Journal of Vocational Education and Training, 56*, 485–506.

Holland, J. L. (1997). *Making vocational choices: A theory of vocational personalities and work environments*. Odessa, FL: Psychological Assessment Resources.

Howard-Hamilton, M. F., & Watt, S. K. (Eds.). (2001). Student services for athletes. *New Directions for Student Services* (No. 93). San Francisco: Jossey Bass.

Jordan, J. M., & Denson, E. L. (1990). Student services for athletes: A model for enhancing the student-athlete experience. *Journal of Counseling and Development, 69*(1), 95–97.

Kennedy, S. R., & Dimick, K. M. (1987). Career maturity and professional sports expectations of college football and basketball players. *Journal of College Student Personnel, 27*, 548–559.

Keup, J. R. (2007). Great expectations and the ultimate reality check: Voices of students during the transition from high school to college. *NASPA Journal, 44*(1), 3–31.

Kidwell, K. S. (2005). Understanding the college first-year experience. *Clearing House: A Journal of Educational Strategies, Issues and Ideas, 78*(6), 253–256.

Lally, P. S., & Kerr, G. A. (2005). The career planning, athletic identity and student role of identity of intercollegiate student-athletes. *Research Quarterly for Exercise and Sport, 76*(3), 275–285.

Lapchick, R. E. (2006). *New game plan for college sport*. Westport, CT: Praeger Publishers.

Miller, P. S., & Kerr, G. A. (2003). The role experimentation of intercollegiate student athletes. *Sport Psychologist, 17*, 196–219.

Murphy, G. M., Petitpas, A. J., & Brewer, B. W. (1996). Identity foreclosure, athletic identity, and career maturity in intercollegiate athletes. *Sport Psychologist, 10*, 239–246.

National Career Development Association. (2013). Career development facilitator. Retrieved from http://ncda.org/aws/NCDA/pt/sp/facilitator_overview

Navarro, K. M. (2012). *Toward an understanding of career construction in the 21st century: A phenomenological study of the life experiences of graduating student-athletes at a large highly-selective Midwestern university* (Unpublished doctoral dissertation). University of Wisconsin. Retrieved from ProQuest, LLC. (UMI No. 3508437).

NCAA. (2003). CHAMPS/Life Skills Program. Retrieved from http://www.ncaa.org/wps/ncaa?key=/ncaa/NCAA/Academics+and+Athletes/CHAMPS++Life+Skills/ Program

———. (2010). *2010–11 NCAA Division I manual: Constitutional operating bylaws, administrative bylaws, effective August 1, 2010*. Indianapolis, IN: NCAA.

———. (2011). Estimated probability of competing in athletics beyond the high school interscholastic level. Retrieved from http://www.ncaa.org/wps/wcm/connect/public/NCAA/Issues/Recruiting/Probability+of+Going+Pro

Osborn, D. S., Howard, D. K., & Leierer, S. J. (2007). The effect of a career development course on the dysfunctional career thoughts of racially and ethnically diverse college freshmen. *Career Development Quarterly, 55*, 365–376.

Pascarella, E. T., & Terenzini, P. T. (2005). *How college affects students: A third decade of research*. San Francisco: Jossey-Bass.

Paulson, A. M., & Betz, N. E. (2004). Basic confidence predictors of career decision making self-efficacy. *Career Development Quarterly, 52*, 354–362.

Reason, R. D., Terenzini, P. T., & Domingo, R. J. (2006). First things first: Developing academic competence in the first year of college. *Research in Higher Education, 47*(2), 149–175.

Reese, R. J., & Miller, C. D. (2006). Effects of a university career development course on career decision-making self-efficacy. *Journal of Career Assessment, 12*(2), 252–266.

Renick, J. (1974). The use and misuse of college athletics. *Journal of Higher Education, 45*, 545–552.

Savickas, M. L. (2002). Career construction: A developmental theory of vocational behavior. In D. Brown & Associates (Eds.), *Career choice and development* (4th ed., pp. 149–205). San Francisco: Jossey-Bass.

———. (2005). *The theory and practice of career construction*. In S. D. Brown & R. W. Lent (Eds.), *Career development and counseling: Putting theory and research to work* (pp. 42–70). Hoboken, NJ: John Wiley & Sons.

Savickas, M. L., Nota, L., Rossier, J., Dauwalder, J. P., Duarte, M. E., Guichard, J., Salvatore, S., Van Esbroeck, R., & Van Vianen, A. E. (2009). Life designing: A paradigm for career construction in the 21st century. *Journal of Vocational Behavior, 75*, 239–250.

Sowa, C., & Gressard, C. (1983). Athletic participation: Its relationship to student development. *Journal of College Student Personnel, 24*, 236–239.

Taylor, K. M., & Betz, N. E. (1983). Applications of self-efficacy theory to the understanding and treatment of career indecision. *Journal of Vocational Behavior, 22*, 63–81.

THE CHANGING LANDSCAPE of ATHLETICS in AMERICAN HIGHER EDUCATION

Eddie Comeaux

During the past century, intercollegiate athletics at many Division I colleges and universities have gradually morphed into a highly commercialized business enterprise and, as such, the relationship between athletics and the fundamental mission and philosophy of higher education has been seriously questioned. Too often, this relationship is gauged by the extent to which, and the conditions under which, colleges and universities are able to provide viable opportunities for college athletes' personal and learning development and, more broadly, how the National Collegiate Athletic Association (NCAA) (2011) adheres to its stated purpose: "to integrate intercollegiate athletics into higher education so that the educational experience of the student-athlete is paramount" (para. 1).

As the chapters of this book make clear, there is a steadily growing body of literature on the study of athletics in American higher education. It is also clear, however, that much of the recent work does not focus extensively on the direct and intangible institutional benefits of college athletics or the opportunities gained and successes achieved by college athletes through sport participation. This absence is largely due to the changing and complex context of big-time collegiate sports in which business practices and rampant commercialism tend to receive significant attention, and thus increasingly undermine the positive benefits of college athletics.

Today, concerns seem to ring hollow, not only about the quality of educational experiences for college athletes, but also about the financial exploitations and abuses of athletes by power brokers who benefit quite handsomely from this commercial enterprise. Numerous scholarly articles and a handful of national reports have emerged, calling for greater accountability and leadership from stakeholders in the affairs of athletics, reduced athletics spending, improvement of athletes' well-being, and elimination of gender discrimination. Few of our prominent colleges and universities have responded substantively to these concerns. Long ago the Ivy League eliminated athletic scholarships with the Ivy Group Agreement of 1954 as a way to deemphasize athletics, to better integrate the athlete into the general student body, and to ensure that athletics adheres to the larger educational mission of the institution. More recently, though, Division I colleges and universities have done very little to change the tide and slow down the increasingly unmanageable and unsustainable arms race that is likely only to widen the chasm between higher education and athletics. In this epilogue, I outline in broad strokes three salient and interrelated issues with which stakeholders in the affairs of athletics are likely to contend over the next several years.

ATHLETICS SPENDING IN AN ACADEMIC CONTEXT

The Knight Commission on Intercollegiate Athletics (2010) released a report revealing that per student spending on athletics between 2005 and 2008 increased at a rate 4 to 11 times faster than per student spending on academics. More recently, Desrochers (2013) found that of public colleges and universities in the six major football conferences (i.e., Southeastern, Big 12, Pacific 10, Atlantic Coast, Big Ten, and Big East), 2010 median annual athletics spending was more than $100,000 per athlete—6 to 12 times the amount spent per student on academics. Indeed, athletics spending seems to be spiraling out of control. To further exacerbate this concern, 221 of 228 athletic departments at NCAA Division I public schools, according to a *USA Today* sports analysis, received subsidies in the form of student fees, institutional support, and state appropriations to cover their operating costs in 2012. And several of these schools have given more than $20 million from their budgets to help run their athletic programs, where, in most cases, they were not self-sufficient. Ironically, it is evident that additional spending in athletics does not necessarily equate to athletic success.

State and federal fiscal deficits are placing unwanted pressures on the budgets of many schools; faculty salaries are stagnant; new enrollment and course offerings have been cut back; vital student programs have been eliminated; tuition costs are on the rise. In this context, these ongoing funding practices have dire consequences for the future state of higher education—particularly when athletics, many have argued, compromise the core academic mission and values of colleges and universities. Not surprisingly, as I write, university faculty and other prominent groups have called for restraints on athletics spending and subsidies to athletic departments.

Given these trends, athletic stakeholders will have to work together with all deliberate speed to determine effective approaches for curbing excessive athletics spending. Athletic stakeholders are expected now and will be expected in future years to reconceptualize the value of intercollegiate athletics and demonstrate how it supports the educational mission and goals of their institutions. The Knight Commission calls for, among other changes, greater financial transparency among institutions, including delineating their athletics expenditures and revenue each year. I agree with the Knight Commission's approach and would also appoint ad hoc faculty committees at each institution to monitor financial information associated with athletic programs and to propose changes to their financial models when appropriate. In this way, athletic departments can ensure the public trust and work toward a more transparent system. Athletic stakeholders might also consider a cap on university subsidies for athletics. As well, continued research on and documentation of spending trends, including coaches' salaries in intercollegiate athletics, is imperative.

CONCEPT OF AMATEURISM

In recent years, the concept of amateurism has been highly debated within the academic community and in the popular press, and this is made particularly apparent by the number of pages devoted to amateurism in this textbook. The NCAA's (2012a) principle of amateurism states in part that "student participation in intercollegiate athletics is an avocation, and student-athletes should be protected from exploitation by professional and commercial enterprises" (p. 4). Although the NCAA amateurism definition attempts to draw a line of demarcation between collegiate and professional sports, many scholars and other advocates of college athletes are not convinced; they have argued that the NCAA uses this concept to protect itself and to justify athletic scholarships as sufficient compensation for the services of athletes (McCormick & McCormick, 2008). Other critics tend to believe the concept is archaic and that athletes in the revenue-generating sports of football and men's basketball, who are disproportionately African American, are not fairly compensated for their contributions to athletic programs and are being financially exploited. Despite these charges, NCAA officials continue to cling to the ideal of amateurism in college sports.

But recently, there were two significant rulings that may change the face of college athletics precisely by eroding the power of the NCAA and member institutions while empowering the athlete. First, the National Labor Relations Board (NLRB) ruled that Northwestern University scholarship football players were employees of the university and had the right to form a labor union and to bargain collectively. As part of its supporting evidence for its decision, the NLRB highlighted the amount of time athletes spend on sport-related activities and the incredible control and power that coaches have over scholarship athletes. Although the recent NLRB decision applies only to private schools, the precedent is likely to extend to public schools as well. Second, in *O'Bannon v. NCAA* (2010), a group of plaintiffs challenged the NCAA's use of names, images, and likenesses in television and other media products. On August 8, 2014, more than four years after the case was filed, U.S. District Judge Claudia Wilken ruled the NCAA's restrictions violated antitrust laws. Starting in 2016, schools will be able to provide athletes with deferred compensation from the licensing of their name, image, and likeness to companies that cannot be less than $5,000 for every year they remain academically eligible. As I write, the NCAA plans to appeal the decision and continue to make a case for *its* version of amateurism.

Meanwhile, researchers and advocacy groups have been actively exploring the fair market value for college athletes. Huma and Staurowsky (2012) reported that if revenue in college sports was distributed the same way as it is in professional sports, the average Football Bowl Subdivision player would be worth $137,357 per year, while the average basketball player at that level would be worth $289,031. Thus, it appears that college athletes in revenue sports are denied a significant amount of their fair market value. Huma and Staurowsky recommended that in addition to providing players their fair share of a multibillion-dollar enterprise, the NCAA, among other things, should relax its current rule and implement the Olympic amateur model, so that all amateur college athletes have access to the commercial free market.

Beyond antitrust lawsuits and national reports with reliable data and thoughtful recommendations to improve college athletics, in the near future other movements may gain momentum and force the NCAA to reconsider the concept that athletes are amateurs. The Drake Group, for example, is currently drafting a proposal that calls for a limited antitrust exemption for the NCAA, in part to redirect revenues toward educational and medical benefits for athletes and to better align athletic departments with the core academic mission of their colleges or universities (see Wolverton, 2013). This restructuring might be a worthy step forward to ensure the well-being of college athletes.

DATA-DRIVEN APPROACHES: THE ATHLETE AS STUDENT

The challenges to eligibility and retention of scholarship athletes in football and men's basketball persist. College athletes in these revenue-generating sports continue to perform less well academically than those in other team sports, as measured by graduation rates (see Harper, Williams, & Blackman, 2013; Southall, Eckard, Nagel, & Hale, 2012). The NCAA Board of Directors has passed several pieces of legislation over the years to help restore the proper balance between academics and athletics and, more precisely, to enhance the academic performance of Division I athletes overall. Most of these initiatives provide minimal systemic change within the structure of athletics, however.

Since 2005, the focal point of the NCAA's academic reform has been the Academic Progress Rate (APR) initiative. There are compelling educational benefits to the APR. For one, these standards place the onus on member colleges and universities to police themselves and to ensure that all athletes are progressing toward degrees. As a result, more and more athletic departments have both expanded their academic facilities for athletes and hired more specialized personnel such as life skills coordinators and academic coaches. In addition, the APR holds head coaches more accountable for the academic success or failure of athletes they recruit. For the 2012–2013 season, 35 teams faced APR penalties, but it is not clear how these schools responded to improve their academic success rates for athletes (National Collegiate Athletic Association, 2012b).

Looking ahead, while the APR has demonstrated some promise, this initiative would benefit from a supplemental component that includes more robust indicators and data-driven approaches that promote student learning and academic success at member institutions. The NCAA uses the APR to measure the eligibility and retention of athletes, which they consider a predictor of graduation rates, although the measure is rather ambiguous (Eckard, 2010). Moreover, the APR in its current form leaves much to be considered about the quality of educational experiences for athletes. For example, while we know that the APR includes graduation as a factor in its matrix, it would be wise to hold athletic stakeholders accountable for documenting and explaining, through reliable and valid assessment tools, how they create environments that influence the learning and personal development of athletes as well as subsequent desirable outcomes such as graduation. Linking the current APR matrix to a more comprehensive, data-driven framework at each member institution might contribute to greater transparency and understanding of athletes' educational patterns by race/ethnicity, gender, and type of sport, as well as enhancement of the quality of their school-to-career transitions (see Comeaux, 2013). With a thorough data-driven framework, organizational problems can be understood in radically different ways, including as a mechanism for social justice.

While some academic support centers for athletes are considered resource-starved, this should not be seen as a "free pass" to give up on this special population of students. Rather, financially constrained academic support centers should use this as an opportunity to rethink existing practices and to encourage incremental organizational innovations. Indeed, we need creative tools and ideas to address the current realities and the future directions of intercollegiate athletics in American higher education, and specifically to develop the academic talents of athletes. It would be prudent for salient stakeholders such as athletic directors to consider developing and offering incentives to academic practitioners who successfully engage in data-driven models and other "best practices." And athletes themselves can benefit from incentives that are linked to their academic performance (see Harrison & Boyd, 2007). In short, incentives and rewards can serve as an effective way to motivate behavioral change among both athletes and academic practitioners.

Without a doubt, the academic success of athletes is inevitably impaired by the increasing commercialism of college sports. Too often, priorities such as winning games and securing corporate sponsorship tend to trump academic obligations and the career goals of athletes. And new challenges for college athletes will likely emerge. As such, the future of intercollegiate athletics will be shaped by external forces, and likewise by the vision, knowledge, and competencies of those providing athletic leadership in this enterprise. It is imperative that athletic stakeholders redefine and refine the baselines in intercollegiate athletics, accounting for the issues and recommendations outlined in this epilogue and throughout this textbook. In this way, we can improve the compatibility of intercollegiate athletics with American higher education and ensure the college athlete, one of the most vulnerable institutional actors on campus, is given a fighting chance to successfully traverse the educational terrain as both student *and* athlete.

References

Comeaux, E. (2013). Rethinking academic reform and encouraging organizational innovation: Implications for stakeholder management in college sports. *Innovative Higher Education, 38*, 281–293.

Desrochers, D. M. (2013). *Academic spending versus athletic spending: Who wins?* Washington, DC: Delta Cost Project of the Association of Institutes for Research.

Eckard, E. W. (2010). NCAA athlete graduation rates: Less than meets the eye. *Journal of Sport Management, 24*(1), 45–58.

Harper, S. R., Williams, C. D., Jr., & Blackman, H. W. (2013). Black male student-athletes and racial inequities in NCAA Division I college sports. Retrieved from https://www.gse.upenn.edu/equity/sites/gse.upenn.edu.equity/files/publications/Harper_Williams_and_Blackman_%282013%29.pdf

Harrison, C. K., & Boyd, J. (2007). Mainstreaming and integrating the spectacle and substance of scholar-baller: A new blueprint for higher education, the NCAA, and society. In D. Brooks & R. Althouse (Eds.), *Diversity and social justice in college sports: Sport management and the student-athlete* (pp. 201–231). Morgantown, WV: Fitness Information Technology.

Huma, R., & Staurowsky, E. J. (2012). *The $6 billion heist: Robbing college athletes under the guise of amateurism.* A report collaboratively produced by the National College Players Association and Drexel University Sport.

Knight Commission on Intercollegiate Athletics. (2010). *Restoring the balance: Dollars, values, and the future of college sports.* Miami, FL: Author.

McCormick, A. C., & McCormick, R. A. (2008). The emperor's new clothes: Lifting the veil of amateurism. *San Diego Law Review, 45*, 495.

National Collegiate Athletic Association. (2011). *Core purpose.* Retrieved from http://www.ncaa.org/about/ncaa-core-purpose-and-values

———. (2012a). *Division I manual.* Indianapolis, IN: National Collegiate Athletic Association.

———. (2012b). *Most Division I teams deliver top grades.* Retrieved from http://www.ncaa.org

O'Bannon v. Nat'l Collegiate Athletics Ass'n, Nos. C 09-1967 CW, C 09-3329 CW, C 09-4882 CW, 2010 WL 445190, at *8 (N.D. Cal. Feb. 8, 2010).

Southall, R. M., Eckard, E. W., Nagel, M. S., & Hale, J. M. (2012). *Adjusted graduation gap report: NCAA Division-I football.* Chapel Hill, NC: College Sport Research Institute.

Wolverton, B. (2013). Watchdog's group proposal calls for antitrust exemption for NCAA. *Chronicle of Higher Education.* Retrieved from http://chronicle.com

INDEX

ABOUT THE EDITOR

Eddie Comeaux is an assistant professor of higher education in the Graduate School of Education at the University of California, Riverside. Dr. Comeaux's research interests are located in the broad field of higher education and include college student engagement, intercollegiate athletics, and diversity competence and leadership in student affairs using an explicit framework of social justice and activism. He has authored numerous peer-reviewed articles in the major journals for higher education and other related fields including *Educational Researcher*, *Journal of Intercollegiate Sport*, *Journal of College Student Development*, and *Sociology of Sport Journal*. He is the co-founder and former chair of the Research Focus on Education and Sport Special Interest Group of the American Educational Research Association. Dr. Comeaux has a forthcoming textbook, *Making the Connection: Data-Informed Practices in Academic Support Centers for College Athletes* (Information Age Publishing). Prior to earning his Ph.D. at UCLA, he was drafted out of the University of California, Berkeley in the amateur free draft by the Texas Rangers baseball organization—and spent four years playing professionally.

ABOUT THE AUTHORS

Ashley R. Baker is currently a doctoral student at the University of Georgia in the sport management and policy program. She received her M.Ed. in sport administration from Bowling Green State University where she served as the director of student-athlete services. Her research interests include race and sport as well as youth sport.

Evan Bates is a master's student in higher and postsecondary education at Arizona State University. His professional experience includes leadership roles in private for-profit, community nonprofit, and university settings. He is currently interested in investigating the effect organizational leadership has on institutional stakeholders in higher education.

Velina B. Brackebusch is a doctoral student in sport management and policy at the University of Georgia. Her research areas are sport for development, sport and ableism, international student-athletes, and qualitative methodology.

Scott Bukstein, J.D., is one of the program directors of the DeVos Sport Business Management Program at the University of Central Florida. Mr. Bukstein's research explores the intersection of sport and the law, the business of collegiate athletics and professional sport, the perceptions and academic performance of college student-athletes, and leadership and diversity/inclusion issues in sport.

Erin E. Buzuvis is a professor of law at Western New England University in Springfield, Massachusetts. She researches and writes about gender and discrimination in education and athletics, and is a co-founder and contributor to the Title IX Blog, an interdisciplinary resource for news and commentary about Title IX, which prohibits sex discrimination in education.

Timothy Davis is the John W. & Ruth H. Turnage Professor of Law at Wake Forest University, School of Law. He has published numerous casebooks and articles on sports related topics. Professor Davis is a graduate of Stanford University and the University of California, Berkeley, School of Law.

Rodney Fort is a professor of sport management at the University of Michigan. He is a recognized expert worldwide on all issues relating to the economics of both pro and college sports in the United States.

Marcia V. Fuentes (M.A./M.P.P.) is a doctoral candidate in the higher education and organizational change program at the University of California, Los Angeles. Her research engages critical social justice issues of policy and practice in higher education, including areas of affirmative action, cross-racial interactions, and campus racial climate.

Joy Gaston Gayles is an associate professor of higher education at North Carolina State University. Her research focuses on the college student experience, particularly for student-athletes and underrepresented populations in STEM fields. Dr. Gayles's work has been published in the *Journal of College Student Development*, the *Journal of Higher Education*, and *Research in Higher Education*.

Allison Goldstein is a Ph.D. student in the higher education program at Penn State University. She received her master's degree in post-secondary educational leadership and student affairs from San Diego State University. Her research interests include student identity development and the role of technology in education.

C. Keith Harrison is associate professor of business administration in the DeVos Sport Business Management program. A former NCAA scholar-athlete (center) on the football team at West Texas A&M University, Dr. Harrison has numerous peer-reviewed journal articles and book chapters. Currently, he is a researcher for the NFL.

Angela J. Hattery is professor and director of women and gender studies at George Mason University. Dr. Hattery's research and teaching focus on social stratification, gender, family, and race. She is the author of several books, including *African American Families: Myths and Realities* and *The Social Dynamics of Family Violence*.

Billy Hawkins is a professor at the University of Georgia in the Department of Kinesiology's Sport Management and Policy program. Dr. Hawkins is the author of *The New Plantation: Black Athletes, College Sports, and Predominantly White NCAA Institutions*; and coauthor of *Sport, Race, Activism, and Social Change: The Impact of Dr. Harry Edwards' Scholarship and Service*. He received his Ph.D. in Sport and Cultural Studies from the University of Iowa.

Scott Hirko is an assistant professor of sport management at Central Michigan University. Dr. Hirko also serves as Associate for Communications and Research to the Knight Commission on Intercollegiate Athletics. He earned a Ph.D. in Higher, Adult, and Lifelong Edu-

cation from Michigan State University. His research includes educational policy, organizational decision making, leadership, and athletics.

Jennifer Lee Hoffman is an assistant professor at the Center for Leadership in Athletics in the College of Education at the University of Washington. Dr. Hoffman's research examines intercollegiate athletics policy and data in decision making from a critical equity perspective.

David Horton Jr. is an assistant professor in the higher education and student affairs program at Ohio University in Athens, Ohio. Dr. Horton's research centers on the curricular and co-curricular experiences of marginalized groups in community colleges with a special focus on student athletes.

Robin L. Hughes is an associate professor in the Department of Educational leadership and Policy Studies, Higher Education Student Affairs (HESA) at Indiana University, Indianapolis and Bloomington. Her research focuses on sports, issues of race, and how race might impact faculty and students of color who attend institutions of higher education.

Janet H. Lawrence is a professor in the Center for the Study of Higher and Postsecondary Education, School of Education, University of Michigan. In 2007 she conducted the Faculty Perceptions of Intercollegiate Athletics Survey for the Knight Commission on Intercollegiate Athletics.

Nancy Lough is a professor in the higher education graduate program at the University of Nevada, Las Vegas, where she also serves as director of marketing. Dr. Lough guides the Intercollegiate Athletic Administration emphasis and College Sport Leadership Certificate program. Her expertise includes leadership development, gender equity, and sport marketing.

Angela Lumpkin is a professor in the Department of Health, Sport, and Exercise Sciences at the University of Kansas. She previously served as a university dean, department chair, director, and coach. She is the author of 23 books, has published over 50 refereed manuscripts, and delivered nearly 200 professional presentations.

Jacqueline McDowell is an assistant professor in the Department of Recreation, Sport and Tourism at the

University of Illinois at Urbana-Champaign. Dr. Mc-Dowell's research focuses on diversity and inclusion issues in sport and recreation—with a particular focus on identity issues and structural, social, and psychological constraints and facilitators.

Jon L. McNaughtan is a doctoral student in higher education at the University of Michigan. His research interests include well-being, institutional efficiency, and athletics. Prior to doctoral work, Jon worked with executive leadership at Southern Utah University on various institutional challenges and strategic decisions.

Vincent Minjares is the director of academic development at University of California, Berkeley's Athletic Study Center. He recently earned his M.A. in the cultural studies of sport and education program at UC Berkeley. His research interests emphasize student-athlete development and the relationship between learning in sport and learning in school.

Kristina M. Navarro is currently an assistant professor in the College of Education and Professional Studies for the University of Wisconsin system and a faculty affiliate/adjunct professor for the University of Oklahoma Intercollegiate Athletics Administration Graduate program. Dr. Navarro is a former student-athlete and intercollegiate athletics practitioner.

Barbara Osborne, J.D., is an associate professor in exercise and sport science and an adjunct professor in law at the University of North Carolina, Chapel Hill. She is a former student-athlete and college athletics administrator Her research examines legal issues in college athletics, with emphasis on sex discrimination and risk management.

Leticia Oseguera is associate professor in education policy studies and senior research associate in the Center for the Study of Higher Education at Penn State University. Her research focuses on understanding college access and educational opportunities for historically underserved and underrepresented student populations. She is a former Division I student-athlete.

Molly Ott is an assistant professor and the coordinator of the higher education graduate program at Arizona State University. Her research interests pertain to organizational and leadership issues in higher education, especially how structural, climate, and cultural differences among institutions, as well as programs and departments, affect individual stakeholders.

Valyncia Raphael, J.D., is a full-time doctoral student in University of Wisconsin, Madison's School of Education studying higher education leadership and policy analysis. Ms. Raphael's research concentrates on various equity issues in intercollegiate athletics. After earning her Ph.D., Ms. Raphael plans to practice higher education law.

B. David Ridpath is an associate professor and Kahandas Nandola Professor of Sport Management, Department of Sports Administration, and College of Business at Ohio University. Dr. Ridpath has several years of practical experience in the sports industry and teaches classes in marketing, risk management, and intercollegiate athletics governance.

James Satterfield is an associate professor of higher education at Clemson University. His research agenda is the social and political context of intercollegiate athletics. He is the author of several articles related to intercollegiate athletics and the coeditor of the *Journal for the Study of Sports and Athletes in Education*.

John N. Singer is an associate professor of sport management (Department of Health and Kinesiology) at Texas A&M University. Dr. Singer earned his Ph.D. from the Ohio State University and his M.A. and B.A. degrees from Michigan State University. His research focuses primarily on critical race issues in sport contexts.

Earl Smith is professor emeritus of Sociology and Rubin Distinguished Professor of American Ethnic Studies at Wake Forest University. Dr. Smith is the author of numerous books, research articles, and book chapters. Several books are sports related, including *Sociology of Sport and Social Theory* and *Race, Sport and the American Dream*.

Eric M. Snyder is an assistant professor of adult and higher education at the University of Oklahoma. Dr. Snyder's primary interests are located in the field of higher education and include higher education policy and governance, quantitative methodology, and intercollegiate athletics. His research focuses on the development and evaluation of policies that are empirically based and support the complex governing operations within institutions of higher education.

Murray Sperber has been a visiting professor in the cultural studies of sport in education program at University of California, Berkeley since 2008. Previous to that he taught for many years at Indiana University, Bloomington and is a professor emeritus of English and American studies of the school. Sperber authored *Beer & Circus: How Big-Time College Sports is Crippling Undergraduate Education*.

Ellen J. Staurowsky is a full professor in the Department of Sport Management at Drexel University. Dr. Staurowsky is internationally recognized as an expert on social justice issues in sport, which include gender equity and Title IX, the exploitation of athletes, college sport reform, and the misappropriation of American Indian imagery in sport. She is coauthor of the book, *College Athletes for Hire: The Evolution and Legacy of the NCAA Amateur Myth*.

Kyle V. Sweitzer is a data analyst in the Office of Planning and Budgets at Michigan State University. Dr. Sweitzer was an NCAA Division III football and track student-athlete at Juniata College, and earned a Ph.D. in higher education from Penn State University. His research focuses on institutional rankings, reputation, and athletics.

John R. Thelin is a professor of educational policy studies at the University of Kentucky. He was a charter member of the NCAA Research Advisory Board from 2008 through 2010. He is author of *Games Colleges Play* (published by Johns Hopkins University Press). In 2006 he was selected for the Ivy League 50th anniversary gallery of outstanding scholar-athletes.

Derek Van Rheenen directs the Cultural Studies of Sport in Education M.A. Program at the University of California, Berkeley for students studying the intersections of school and sport. He also directs the Athletic Study Center at University of California, Berkeley. Professor Van Rheenen was named a Chancellor's Public Scholar for 2012–2013.

Andrew Zimbalist is the Robert Woods Professor of Economics at Smith College. He has consulted in Latin America and in the sports industry for players' associations, cities, companies, teams, leagues, and universities and has published several dozen articles and 22 books.